COMPUTER NETWORKING WITH INTERNET PROTOCOLS AND TECHNOLOGY

D0169330

AND DATA COMMUNICATIONS TECHNOLOGY

WIRELESS COMMUNICATIONS AND NETWORKS

A comprehensive, state-of-the art survey. Covers fundamental wireless communications topics, including antennas and propagation, signal encoding techniques, spread spectrum, and error correction techniques. Examines satellite, cellular, wireless local loop networks and wireless LANs, including Bluetooth and 802.11. Covers Mobile IP and WAP. ISBN 0-13-040864-6

CRYPTOGRAPHY AND NETWORK SECURITY, THIRD EDITION

A tutorial and survey on network security technology. Each of the basic building blocks of network security, including conventional and public-key cryptography, authentication, and digital signatures, are covered. The book covers important network security tools and applications, including S/MIME IP Security, Kerberos, SSL/TLS, SET, and X509v3. In addition, methods for countering hackers and viruses are explored. **Second edition received the TAA award for the best Computer Science and Engineering Textbook of 1999**. ISBN 0-13-091429-0

BUSINESS DATA COMMUNICATIONS, FOURTH EDITION

A comprehensive presentation of data communications and telecommunications from a business perspective. Covers voice, data, image, and video communications and applications technology and includes a number of case studies. ISBN 0-13-088263-1

LOCAL AND METROPOLITAN AREA NETWORKS, SIXTH EDITION

An in-depth presentation of the technology and architecture of local and metropolitan area networks. Covers topology, transmission media, medium access control, standards, internetworking, and network management. Provides an up-to-date coverage of LAN/MAN systems, including Fast Ethernet, Fibre Channel, and wireless LANs, plus LAN QoS. **Received the 2001 TAA award for long-term excellence in a Computer Science Textbook**. ISBN 0-13-012939-9

ISDN AND BROADBAND ISDN, WITH FRAME RELAY AND ATM: FOURTH EDITION

An in-depth presentation of the technology and architecture of integrated services digital networks (ISDN). Covers the integrated digital network (IDN), xDSL, ISDN services and architecture, signaling system no. 7 (SS7) and provides detailed coverage of the ITU-T protocol standards. Also provides detailed coverage of protocols and congestion control strategies for both frame relay and ATM. ISBN 0-13-973744-8

Prentice Hall   www.prenhall.com/stallings   telephone: 800-526-0485

COMPUTER NETWORKING WITH INTERNET PROTOCOLS AND TECHNOLOGY

William Stallings

PEARSON
Prentice
Hall

Upper Saddle River, New Jersey 07458

Library of Congress Cataloging-in-Publication Data on File

Vice President and Editorial Director, ECS: *Marcia J. Horton*
Publisher: *Alan Apt*
Associate Editor: *Toni D. Holm*
Editorial Assistant: *Patrick Lindner*
Vice President and Director of Production and Manufacturing, ESM: *David W. Riccardi*
Executive Managing Editor: *Vince O'Brien*
Managing Editor: *Camille Trentacoste*
Production Editor: *Rose Kernan*
Director of Creative Services: *Paul Belfanti*
Creative Director: *Carole Anson*
Art Director and Cover Manager: *John Christiana*
Managing Editor, AV Management and Production: *Patricia Burns*
Art Editor: *Xiaohong Zhu*
Manufacturing Manager: *Trudy Pisciotti*
Manufacturing Buyer: *Lisa McDowell*
Marketing Manager: *Pamela Shaffer*
Marketing Assistant: *Barrie Reinhold*
Cover and Interior Designer: *Dina Curro*
Cover Art: *tom white images*

© 2004 Pearson Education, Inc.
Pearson Prentice Hall
Pearson Education, Inc.
Upper Saddle River, NJ 07458

The author and publisher of this book have used their best efforts in preparing this book. These efforts include the development, research, and testing of the theories and programs to determine their effectiveness. The author and publisher make no warranty of any kind, expressed or implied, with regard to these programs or the documentation contained in this book. The author and publisher shall not be liable in any event for incidental or consequential damages in connection with, or arising out of, the furnishing, performance, or use of these programs.

Printed in the United States of America
10 9 8 7 6 5 4 3 2 1
ISBN: 0-13-141098-9

Pearson Education Ltd., *London*
Pearson Education Australia Pty. Ltd., *Sydney*
Pearson Education Singapore, Pte. Ltd.
Pearson Education North Asia Ltd., *Hong Kong*
Pearson Education Canada, Inc., *Toronto*
Pearson Educación de Mexico, S.A. de C.V.
Pearson Education—Japan, *Tokyo*
Pearson Education Malaysia, Pte. Ltd.
Pearson Education, Inc., *Upper Saddle River, New Jersey*

For my loving wife
A

WEB SITE FOR COMPUTER NETWORKING WITH INTERNET PROTOCOLS AND TECHNOLOGY

The Web site at WilliamStallings.com/CNIP/CNIP1e.html provides support for instructors and students using the book. It includes the following elements.

Course Support Materials

The course support materials include

- Copies of figures from the book in PDF format
- Copies of tables from the book in PDF format
- A set of PowerPoint slides for use as lecture aids
- Computer Science Student Support Site: contains a number of links and documents that the student may find useful in his/her ongoing computer science education. The site includes a review of basic, relevant mathematics; advice on research, writing, and doing homework problems; links to computer science research resources, such as report repositories and bibliographies; and other useful links.
- An errata sheet for the book, updated at most monthly

CNIP Courses

The CNIP1e Web site includes links to Web sites for courses taught using the book. These sites can provide useful ideas about scheduling and topic ordering, as well as a number of useful handouts and other materials.

Useful Web Sites

The CNIP1e Web site includes links to relevant Web sites, organized by chapter. The links cover a broad spectrum of topics and will enable students to explore timely issues in greater depth.

Supplemental Documents

The CNIP1e Web site includes a number of documents that expand on the treatment in the book. Topics include standards organizations, Sockets, TCP/IP checksum, URL/URI, BNF, and ASCII.

Internet Mailing List

An Internet mailing list is maintained so that instructors using this book can exchange information, suggestions, and questions with each other and the author. Subscription information is provided at the book's Web site.

Simulation and Modeling Tools

The Web site includes links to the *cnet* Web site and the *modeling tools* Web site. These packages can be used to analyze and experiment with protocol and network design issues. Each site includes downloadable software and background information. The instructor's manual includes more information on loading and using the software and suggested student projects. See Appendix B for more information.

CONTENTS

PREFACE

This book does not pretend to be a comprehensive record; but it aims at helping to disentangle from an immense mass of material the crucial issues and cardinal decisions. Throughout I have set myself to explain faithfully and to the best of my ability.

—*The World Crisis*, Winston Churchill

BACKGROUND

Data network communication and distributed applications rely on underlying communications software that is independent of applications and relieves the application of much of the burden of reliably exchanging data. This communications software is organized into a protocol architecture, the most important incarnation of which is the TCP/IP protocol suite. The TCP/IP protocol suite is now dominant, in terms of products, deployment in data networks, and ongoing computer network research. The most prominent incarnation of this suite is in the Internet and its millions of attached computers.

OBJECTIVES

The objective of this book is to provide an up-to-date survey of developments in the areas of computer networks and Internet-based protocols and algorithms. Central problems that confront the network designer are the need to support multimedia and real-time traffic, the need to control congestion, and the need to provide different levels of quality of service (QoS) to different applications.

The following basic themes serve to unify the discussion:

- **Principles:** Although the scope of this book is broad, there are a number of basic principles that appear repeatedly as themes and that unify this field. Examples are multiplexing, flow control, and error control. The book highlights these principles and contrasts their application in specific areas of technology.

- **Design approaches:** The book examines alternative approaches to meeting specific communication requirements.

- **Standards:** Standards have come to assume an increasingly important, indeed dominant, role in this field. An understanding of the current status and future direction of technology requires a comprehensive discussion of the related standards.

INTENDED AUDIENCE

This book is intended for both a professional and an academic audience. For the professional interested in this field, the book serves as a basic reference volume and is suitable for self study.

As a textbook, it is suitable for an advanced undergraduate or graduate course. The book treats a number of advanced topics and provides a brief survey of the required elementary topics. After Part One, the parts are relatively independent. Fewer parts could be covered for a shorter course, and the parts can be covered in any order.

PLAN OF THE BOOK

The book is divided into seven parts:

- Overview
- Internet Applications
- Transport Protocols
- Quality of Service in IP Networks
- Internet Routing
- Network and Link Layers
- Management Topics

In addition, the book includes an extensive glossary, a list of frequently used acronyms, and a bibliography. Each chapter includes a list of key words, review questions, problems, suggestions for further reading, and pointers to relevant Web sites.

The book is intended for both an academic and a professional audience. For the professional interested in this field, the book serves as a basic reference volume and is suitable for self-study. As a textbook, it can be used for a one-semester or two-semester course. It covers the material in the Communication and Networking core course of the joint ACM/IEEE Computing Curricula 2001. The chapters and parts of the book are sufficiently modular to provide a great deal of flexibility in the design of courses.

TOP-DOWN AND BOTTOM-UP APPROACHES

The book is laid out to present the material in a top-down fashion. This has the advantage of immediately focusing on the most visible part of the material, the applications, and then seeing, progressively, how each layer is supported by the next layer down. This approach makes the most sense for many instructors and students. The application layer is the most visible layer to the student and typically provides the most interest. An understanding of the applications motivates the mechanisms found at the transport layer. The treatment of the application and transport layers enables the student to understand the many design issues at the internet layer, including quality of service and routing issues. Finally, computer networks and data link mechanisms can be treated.

Some readers, and some instructors, are more comfortable with a bottom-up approach. With this approach, each part builds on the material in the previous part, so that it is always clear how a given layer of functionality is supported from below. Accordingly, the book is organized in a modular fashion. After reading Part One, the other parts can be read in a number of possible sequences. See Chapter 0 for a description of each part and for a discussion of the order in which the book can be taught.

INTERNET SERVICES FOR INSTRUCTORS AND STUDENTS

There is a Web site for this book that provides support for students and instructors. The page includes links to relevant sites, transparency masters of figures and tables in the book in PDF (Adobe Acrobat) format, PowerPoint slides, and sign-up information for the book's Internet mailing list. The Web page is at WilliamStallings.com/CNIP/CNIP1e.html; see the section, "Web Site for Computer Networking with Internet Protocols and Technology," following this Preface, for more information. An Internet mailing list has been set up so that instructors using this book can exchange information, suggestions, and questions with each other and with the author. As soon as typos or other errors are discovered, an errata list for this book will be available at WilliamStallings.com. Finally, I maintain the Computer Science Student Resource Site at WilliamStallings.com/StudentSupport.html.

PROJECTS FOR TEACHING COMPUTER NETWORKING

For many instructors, an important component of a computer networks/Internet protocol course is a project or set of projects by which the student gets hands-on experience to reinforce concepts from the text. This book provides an unparalleled degree of support for including a projects component in the course. The instructor's manual not only includes guidance on how to assign and structure the projects, but also includes a set of suggested projects that covers a broad range of topics from the text, including:

- **Sockets programming projects:** The manual includes series of assignments that instruct the student to research a particular topic on the Web or in the literature, and write a report.
- **Simulation projects:** The manual provides support for the use of the *cnet* simulation package: The *cnet* network simulator enables experimentation with various data link layer, network layer, routing and transport layer protocols, and with various network configurations.
- **Performance modeling projects:** An alternative to simulation for assessing the performance of a communications system or networking protocol is analytic modeling. The *tools* package of software serves as the basis for developing such projects.
- **Research projects:** The manual includes series of assignments that instruct the student to research a particular topic on the Web or in the literature, and write a report.
- **Reading/report assignments:** The manual includes a list of papers in the literature, one or more for each chapter, that can be assigned for the student to read and then write a short report.

See Appendix B for details.

ACKNOWLEDGMENTS

This book has benefited from review by a number of people, who gave generously of their time and expertise. The following people reviewed the original manuscript proposal and made numerous detailed suggestions: Paul Tymann (Rochester Institute of Technology), William Perrizo (North Dakota State), and Kenneth Weber (Mount Union College). The following people reviewed portions of the material in the book: Michael J. Donahoo (Baylor University), Gary Harkin (Montana State University), Larry Owens (California State U. Fresno), S. Hossein Hosseini (U. of Wisconsin—Milwaukee), and Dr. Charles Baker (Southern Methodist University).

Thanks also to the many people who provided detailed technical reviews of a single chapter: David Bunde, Dan Li, Ian Sutherland, Wei Zhou, Marc Timme, Brian Borchers, Balbir Singh, Dean Newton, Paul A. Watters, Peter Rabinovitch, Stephen Campbell-Robson, Roger L. Bagula, Diet Ostry, Lars Kristensen, San Skulrattanakulchai, Lieven Marchand, Robert Kolter, Chris Pollett, and Stefan Katzenbeisser.

I would also like to acknowledge Fernando Ariel Gont, who contributed many excellent homework problems.

Finally, I would like to thank the many people responsible for the publication of the book, all of whom did their usual excellent job. This includes the staff at Prentice Hall, particularly my editor Alan Apt, his assistant Patrick Lindner, and production manager Rose Kernan. Also, Jake Warde of Warde Publishers managed the supplements and reviews; and Patricia M. Daly did the copy editing.

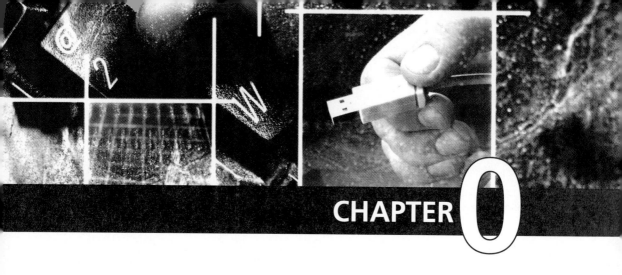

CHAPTER 0

READER'S GUIDE

The combination of space, time, and strength that must be considered as the basic elements of this theory of defense makes this a fairly complicated matter. Consequently, it is not easy to find a fixed point of departure.

—On War,
Carl Von Clausewitz

This book, and the accompanying Web site, cover a lot of material. Here we give the reader some basic background information.

0.1 OUTLINE OF THE BOOK

The book is organized into seven parts:

Part One. Fundamentals: Provides a foundation to the range of topics covered in the book. This part includes a general overview of the Internet, with an emphasis on its history and underlying structure. This is followed by a discussion of protocols, OSI, and the TCP/IP protocol suite. The part also includes a detailed discussion of the Internet Protocol.

Part Two. Applications: Looks at a range of applications that operate over the Internet.

Part Three. Transport Protocols: This part covers the two key transport protocols used by most Internet-based applications: TCP and UDP. This part then discusses end-to-end performance parameters and techniques used by TCP to achieve high throughput and to manage congestion.

Part Four. Quality of Service in IP Networks: Within an IP-based network, techniques are needed to control congestion and to provide the desired QoS to active applications. This part surveys those techniques, beginning with a discussion of integrated and differentiated services. Then, important protocols that relate to QoS are examined, including RSVP, MPLS, and RTP.

Part Five. Internet Routing: Covers the major approaches to routing, including distance-vector, link-state, and path-vector routing, and examines multicast routing.

Part Six. Network and Link Layers: Provides a survey of the underlying network and link protocols and technologies that support Internet traffic.

Part Seven. Management Issues: Deals with two key areas: network security and network management.

A more detailed, chapter-by-chapter summary of each part appears at the beginning of that part.

The book is organized in a modular fashion. After reading Part One, the other parts can be read in a number of possible sequences. Figure 0.1a shows the top-down approach provided by reading the book from front to back. After the background material (Part One), the reader continues at the application level and works down through the layers. This has the advantage of immediately focusing on the most

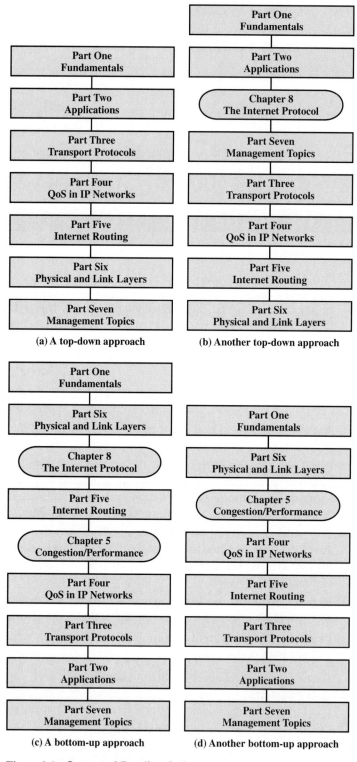

Figure 0.1 Suggested Reading Orders

visible part of the material, the applications, and then seeing, progressively, how each layer is supported by the next layer down. Figure 0.1b is also a top-down approach. In this case, Part Seven, which deals with network security and network management, is covered after Part Two. This is also a reasonable strategy, because much of the material in Part Seven is at the application level. However, because Part Seven covers IP security, Chapter 8 is inserted before Part Seven to provide the necessary background.

Some readers, and some instructors, are more comfortable with a bottom-up approach. With this approach, each part builds on the material in the previous part, so that it is always clear how a given layer of functionality is supported from below. Parts (c) and (d) of Figure 0.1 show two variations on this approach. In both cases, the material in Chapter 5 on congestion and performance is needed before dealing with QoS in IP networks. If Internet routing concepts are covered before QoS, then Chapter 8 needs to be covered before Part Five.

0.2 INTERNET AND WEB RESOURCES FOR THIS BOOK

There are a number of resources available on the Internet and the Web to support this book and to help one keep up with developments in this field.

Web Sites for this Book

A special Web page has been set up for this book at **WilliamStallings.com/Internet/ Internet1e.html**. See the two-page layout at the beginning of this book for a detailed description of that site.

As soon as any typos or other errors are discovered, an errata list for this book will be available at the Web site. Please report any errors that you spot. Errata sheets for my other books, as well as discount ordering information for the books, are at **WilliamStallings.com**.

I also maintain the Computer Science Student Resource Site, at **WilliamStallings.com/StudentSupport.html**. The purpose of this site is to provide documents, information, and links for computer science students. Links are organized into four categories:

- **Math:** Includes a basic math refresher, a queuing analysis primer, a number system primer, and links to numerous math sites
- **How-to:** Advice and guidance for solving homework problems, writing technical reports, and preparing technical presentations
- **Research resources:** Links to important collections of papers, technical reports, and bibliographies
- **Miscellaneous:** A variety of useful documents and links

Other Web Sites

There are numerous Web sites that provide information related to the topics of this book. In subsequent chapters, pointers to specific Web sites can be found in the "Recommended Reading" section. Because the URL for a particular Web site may change, I have not included URLs in the book. For all of the Web sites listed in the book, the appropriate link can be found at this book's Web site.

The following are Web sites of general interest related to the topics in this book:

- **IETF:** Maintains archives that relate to the Internet and IETF activities. Includes keyword-indexed library of RFCs and draft documents as well as many other documents related to the Internet and related protocols.

- **IEEE Communications Society:** Good way to keep up on conferences, publications, and so on.

- **ACM Special Interest Group on Communications (SIGCOMM):** Good way to keep up on conferences, publications, and so on.

- **Network World:** Information and links to resources about data communications and networking.

- **Vendors:** Links to thousands of hardware and software vendors who currently have Web sites, as well as a list of thousands of computer and networking companies in a phone directory.

USENET Newsgroups

A number of USENET newsgroups are devoted to some aspect of data communications, networks, and protocols. As with virtually all USENET groups, there is a high noise-to-signal ratio, but it is worth experimenting to see if any meet your needs. The most relevant are as follows:

- **comp.protocols.tcp-ip:** The TCP/IP protocol suite

- **comp.protocols.dns.std:** Domain Name System standards

- **comp.security.misc:** Computer security and encryption

- **comp.dcom.net-management:** Discussion of network management applications, protocols, and standards

- **comp.protocols.snmp:** Discussion of the SNMP family of protocols

0.3 INTERNET STANDARDS

Many of the protocols that make up the TCP/IP protocol suite have been standardized or are in the process of standardization. By universal agreement, an organization known as the Internet Society is responsible for the development and publication of these standards. The Internet Society is a professional membership organization that oversees a number of boards and task forces involved in Internet development and standardization.

This section provides a brief description of the way in which standards for the TCP/IP protocol suite are developed.

The Internet Organizations and RFC Publication

The Internet Society is the coordinating committee for Internet design, engineering, and management. Areas covered include the operation of the Internet itself and the standardization of protocols used by end systems on the Internet for interoperability. Three organizations under the Internet Society are responsible for the actual work of standards development and publication:

- **Internet Architecture Board (IAB):** Responsible for defining the overall architecture of the Internet, providing guidance and broad direction to the IETF
- **Internet Engineering Task Force (IETF):** The protocol engineering and development arm of the Internet
- **Internet Engineering Steering Group (IESG):** Responsible for technical management of IETF activities and the Internet standards process

Working groups chartered by the IETF carry out the actual development of new standards and protocols for the Internet. Membership in a working group is voluntary; any interested party may participate. During the development of a specification, a working group will make a draft version of the document available as an Internet Draft, which is placed in the IETF's "Internet Drafts" online directory. The document may remain as an Internet Draft for up to six months, and interested parties may review and comment on the draft. During that time, the IESG may approve publication of the draft as an RFC (Request for Comment). If the draft has not progressed to the status of an RFC during the six-month period, it is withdrawn from the directory. The working group may subsequently publish a revised version of the draft.

The IETF is responsible for publishing the RFCs, with approval of the IESG. The RFCs are the working notes of the Internet research and development community. A document in this series may be on essentially any topic related to computer communications and may be anything from a meeting report to the specification of a standard. Appendix A lists all of the RFCs referenced in this book.

The work of the IETF is divided into eight areas, each with an area director and each composed of numerous working groups. Table 0.1 shows the IETF areas and their focus.

The Standardization Process

The decision of which RFCs become Internet standards is made by the IESG, on the recommendation of the IETF. To become a standard, a specification must meet the following criteria:

- Be stable and well understood
- Be technically competent
- Have multiple, independent, and interoperable implementations with substantial operational experience
- Enjoy significant public support
- Be recognizably useful in some or all parts of the Internet

The key difference between these criteria and those used for international standards from ITU is the emphasis here on operational experience.

Table 0.1 IETF Areas

IETF Area	Theme	Example Working Groups
General	IETF processes and procedures	Policy Framework Process for Organization of Internet Standards
Applications	Internet applications	Web-related protocols (HTTP) EDI-Internet integration LDAP
Internet	Internet infrastructure	IPv6 PPP extensions
Operations and management	Standards and definitions for network operations	SNMPv3 Remote Network Monitoring
Routing	Protocols and management for routing information	multicast routing OSPF QoS routing
Security	Security protocols and technologies	Kerberos IPSec X.509 S/MIME TLS
Transport	Transport layer protocols	Differentiated services IP telephony NFS RSVP
Sub-IP	Protocols that monitor, manage, or effect logical circuit technology (e.g., IP over optical), MPLS, protocols that create logical circuits over IP.	Common Control and Measurement Plane General Switch Management Protocol IP over Optical Multiprotocol Label Switching Provider Provisioned Virtual Private Networks Internet Traffic Engineering

The left-hand side of Figure 0.2 shows the series of steps, called the *standards track*, that a specification goes through to become a standard; this process is defined in RFC 2026. The steps involve increasing amounts of scrutiny and testing. At each step, the IETF must make a recommendation for advancement of the protocol, and the IESG must ratify it. The process begins when the IESG approves the publication of an Internet Draft document as an RFC with the status of Proposed Standard.

The white boxes in the diagram represent temporary states, which should be occupied for the minimum practical time. However, a document must remain a Proposed Standard for at least six months and a Draft Standard for at least four months to allow time for review and comment. The gray boxes represent long-term states that may be occupied for years.

For a specification to be advanced to Draft Standard status, there must be at least two independent and interoperable implementations from which adequate operational experience has been obtained.

After significant implementation and operational experience has been obtained, a specification may be elevated to Internet Standard. At this point, the specification is assigned an STD number as well as an RFC number.

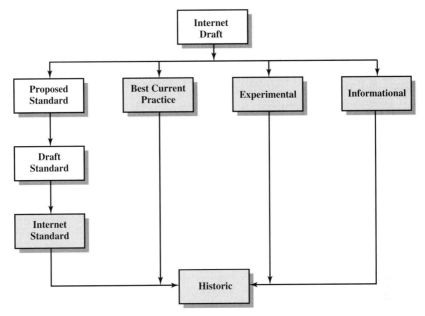

Figure 0.2   Internet RFC Publication Process

Finally, when a protocol becomes obsolete, it is assigned to the Historic state.

Internet Standards Categories

All Internet standards fall into one of two categories:

- **Technical specification (TS):** A TS defines a protocol, service, procedure, convention, or format. The bulk of the Internet standards are TSs.
- **Applicability statement (AS):** An AS specifies how, and under what circumstances, one or more TSs may be applied to support a particular Internet capability. An AS identifies one or more TSs that are relevant to the capability and may specify values or ranges for particular parameters associated with a TS or functional subsets of a TS that are relevant for the capability.

Other RFC Types

There are numerous RFCs that are not destined to become Internet standards. Some RFCs standardize the results of community deliberations about statements of principle or conclusions about what is the best way to perform some operations or IETF process function. Such RFCs are designated as Best Current Practice (BCP). Approval of BCPs follows essentially the same process for approval of Proposed Standards. Unlike standards-track documents, there is not a three-stage process for BCPs; a BCP goes from Internet Draft status to approved BCP in one step.

A protocol or other specification that is not considered ready for standardization may be published as an Experimental RFC. After further work, the specification may be resubmitted. If the specification is generally stable, has resolved known design choices, is believed to be well understood, has received significant community review, and appears to enjoy enough community interest to be considered valuable, then the RFC will be designated a Proposed Standard. Finally, an Informational Specification is published for the general information of the Internet community.

PART ONE

Overview

The purpose of Part One is to provide a background and context for the remainder of this book. Fundamental concepts that are referenced throughout the book are introduced in this part.

ROAD MAP FOR PART ONE

Chapter 1 Data Networks and the Internet

Chapter 1 introduces the Internet, providing a brief history and an overview of its structure. This chapter also surveys the various types of communication networks that are constituent elements of the Internet.

Chapter 2 Protocols and the TCP/IP Protocol Suite

Chapter 2 discusses the concept of a protocol architecture. After a general introduction, the chapter deals with the two most important protocol architectures: the Open Systems Interconnection (OSI) model and TCP/IP. Although the OSI model is often used as the framework for discourse in this area, it is the TCP/IP protocol suite that is the basis for most commercially available interoperable products and that is the focus of this book.

CHAPTER 1

DATA NETWORKS AND THE INTERNET

The whole of this operation is described in minute detail in the official British Naval History, and should be studied with its excellent charts by those who are interested in its technical aspect. So complicated is the full story that the lay reader cannot see the wood for the trees. I have endeavored to render intelligible the broad effects.

—*The World Crisis*,
Winston Churchill

KEY POINTS

- The two traditional technologies for wide area networks (WANs) are circuit switching and packet switching.

- With **circuit switching**, there is a dedicated path through the network between two end stations.

- With **packet switching**, a block of data is broken up into smaller units, called packets, and each packet is routed through the network on the basis of addressing information contained in a packet header.

- The **Internet** is a collection of networks interconnected with routers.

- **Intranet** is a term used to refer to the implementation of Internet technologies within a corporate organization, rather than for external connection to the global Internet.

- A concept similar to that of the intranet is the **extranet**. Like the intranet, the extranet makes use of TCP/IP protocols and applications, especially the Web. The distinguishing feature of the extranet is that it provides access to corporate resources by outside clients, typically suppliers and customers of the organization.

This chapter provides a general overview of data networks and the Internet. The chapter begins with an examination of the underlying network and communications building blocks for the Internet. Next comes a brief history of the Internet, followed by a discussion of its overall structure. Finally, we introduce two related concepts: intranets and extranets.

1.1 DATA NETWORKS

For wide area networks, other than wireless networks, communication is typically achieved by transmitting data from source to destination through a network of intermediate switching nodes. The switching nodes are not concerned with the content of the data; rather their purpose is to provide a switching facility that will move the data from node to node until they reach their destination. Figure 1.1 illustrates a simple network. The end devices that wish to communicate may be referred to as *stations*. The stations may be computers, terminals, telephones, or other communicating devices. We will refer to the switching devices whose purpose is to provide

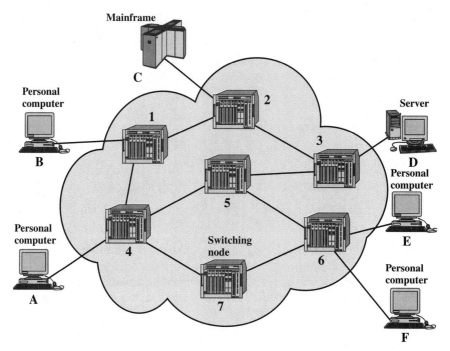

Figure 1.1 Simple Switching Network

communication as *nodes*. The nodes are connected to each other in some topology by transmission links. Each station attaches to a node, and the collection of nodes is referred to as a *communications network*.

In the remainder of this section, we provide a somewhat detailed look at the two traditional approaches to switched networking, circuit and packet switching, and then briefly examine two more recent versions of packet switching: frame relay and asynchronous transfer mode (ATM). We then survey some other types of data networks.

Circuit Switching

Communication via circuit switching implies that there is a dedicated communication path between two stations. That path is a connected sequence of links between nodes. On each physical link, a channel is dedicated to the connection. The most common example of circuit switching is the telephone network.

Communication via circuit switching involves three phases, which can be explained with reference to Figure 1.1.

1. **Circuit establishment.** Before any data can be transmitted, an end-to-end (station-to-station) circuit must be established. For example, station A sends a request to node 4 requesting a connection to station E. Typically, the circuit from A to 4 is a dedicated line, so that part of the connection already exists. Node 4 must find the next leg in a route leading to node 6. Based on routing information and measures of availability and perhaps cost, node 4 selects the

circuit to node 5, allocates a free channel (using time-division multiplexing or frequency-division multiplexing) on that circuit, and sends a message requesting connection to E. So far, a dedicated path has been established from A through 4 to 5. Since a number of stations may attach to 4, it must be able to establish internal paths from multiple stations to multiple nodes. The remainder of the process proceeds similarly. Node 5 dedicates a channel to node 6 and internally ties that channel to the channel from node 4. Node 6 completes the connection to E. In completing the connection, a test is made to determine if E is busy or is prepared to accept the connection.

2. **Data transfer.** Signals can now be transmitted from A through the network to E. The data may be digital (e.g., terminal to host) or analog (e.g., voice). The signaling and transmission may each be either digital or analog. In any case, the path is A-4 circuit, internal switching through 4, 4–5 channel, internal switching through 5, 5–6 channel, internal switching through 6, 6-E circuit. Generally, the connection is full duplex, and data may be transmitted in both directions.

3. **Circuit disconnect.** After some period of data transfer, the connection is terminated, usually by the action of one of the two stations. Signals must be propagated to 4, 5, and 6 to deallocate the dedicated resources.

Note that the connection path is established before data transmission begins. Thus channel capacity must be available and reserved between each pair of nodes in the path, and each node must have internal switching capacity to handle the connection. The switches must have the intelligence to make these allocations and to devise a route through the network.

Circuit switching can be rather inefficient. Channel capacity is dedicated for the duration of a connection, even if no data are being transferred. For a voice connection, utilization may be rather high, but it still does not approach 100%. For a terminal-to-computer connection, the capacity may be idle during most of the time of the connection. In terms of performance, there is a delay prior to data transfer for call establishment. However, once the circuit is established, the network is effectively transparent to the users. Data are transmitted at a fixed data rate with no delay other than the propagation delay through the transmission links. The delay at each node is negligible.

Packet Switching

Around 1970, research began on a new form of architecture for long-distance digital data communications: packet switching. Although the technology of packet switching has evolved substantially since that time, it is remarkable that (1) the basic technology of packet switching is fundamentally the same today as it was in the early-1970s networks, and (2) packet switching remains one of the few effective technologies for long-distance data communications. Two more recent WAN technologies, frame relay and ATM, are essentially variations on the basic packet-switching approach. And much of the technology of packet switching carries directly over to the Internet, with routers and subnetworks in the Internet analogous to packet-switching nodes and links between nodes in a packet-switching network.

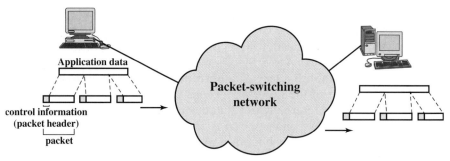

Figure 1.2 The Use of Packets

Many of the advantages of packet switching (flexibility, resource sharing, robustness, responsiveness) come with a cost. The packet-switching network is a distributed collection of packet-switching nodes. Ideally, all packet-switching nodes would always know the state of the entire network. However, because the nodes are distributed, there is always a time delay between a change in status in one portion of the network and the knowledge of that change elsewhere. Furthermore, there is overhead involved in communicating status information. As a result, a packet-switching network can never perform "perfectly," and elaborate algorithms are used to cope with the time delay and overhead penalties of network operation. These algorithms, in the areas of routing and congestion control, carry over into the Internet.

Basic Operation The long-haul circuit-switching telecommunications network was originally designed to handle voice traffic, and the majority of traffic on these networks continues to be voice. A key characteristic of circuit-switching networks is that resources within the network are dedicated to a particular call. For voice connections, the resulting circuit will enjoy a high percentage of utilization because, most of the time, one party or the other is talking. However, as circuit-switching networks began to be used increasingly for data connections, two shortcomings became apparent:

- In a typical terminal-to-host data connection, much of the time the line is idle. Thus, with data connections, a circuit-switching approach is inefficient.
- In a circuit-switching network, the connection provides for transmission at a constant data rate. Thus, each of the two devices that are connected must transmit and receive at the same data rate as the other. This limits the utility of the network in interconnecting a variety of host computers and terminals.

With packet switching, data are transmitted in short blocks, called packets. A typical upper bound on packet length is 1000 octets (bytes). If a source has a longer message to send, the message is broken up into a series of packets (Figure 1.2). Each packet contains a portion (or all for a short message) of the user's data plus some control information. The control information, at a minimum, includes the information that the network requires to be able to route the packet through the network and deliver it to the intended destination. At each node en route, the packet is received, stored briefly, and passed on to the next node.

Figure 1.3 illustrates the basic operation. A transmitting computer or other device sends a message as a sequence of packets (a). Each packet includes control

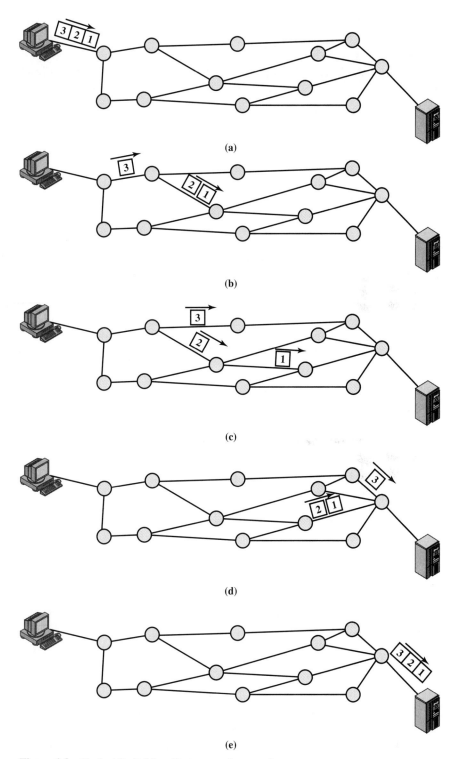

Figure 1.3   Packet Switching: Datagram Approach

information indicating the destination station (computer, terminal, etc.). The packets are initially sent to the node to which the sending station attaches. As each packet arrives, this node stores the packet briefly, determines the next leg of the route, and queues the packet to go out on that link. When the link is available, each packet is transmitted to the next node (b). All of the packets eventually work their way through the network and are delivered to the intended destination.

Now assume that Figure 1.1 depicts a simple packet-switching network. Consider a packet to be sent from station A to station E. The packet will include control information that indicates that the intended destination is E. The packet is sent from A to node 4. Node 4 stores the packet, determines the next leg of the route (say 5), and queues the packet to go out on that link (the 4–5 link). When the link is available, the packet is transmitted to node 5, which will forward the packet to node 6, and finally to E. This approach has a number of advantages over circuit switching:

- Line efficiency is greater, because a single node-to-node link can be dynamically shared by many packets over time. The packets are queued up and transmitted as rapidly as possible over the link. By contrast, with circuit switching, time on a node-to-node link is preallocated using synchronous time division multiplexing. Much of the time, such a link may be idle because a portion of its time is dedicated to a connection that is idle.

- A packet-switching network can carry out data-rate conversion. Two stations of different data rates can exchange packets, because each connects to its node at its proper data rate.

- When traffic becomes heavy on a circuit-switching network, some calls are blocked; that is, the network refuses to accept additional connection requests until the load on the network decreases. On a packet-switching network, packets are still accepted, but delivery delay increases.

- Priorities can be used. Thus, if a node has a number of packets queued for transmission, it can transmit the higher-priority packets first. These packets will therefore experience less delay than lower-priority packets.

Packet switching also has disadvantages relative to circuit switching:

- Each time a packet passes through a packet-switching node, it incurs a delay not present in circuit switching. At a minimum, it incurs a transmission delay equal to the length of the packet in bits divided by the incoming channel rate in bits per second; this is the time it takes to absorb the packet into an internal buffer. In addition, there may be a variable delay due to processing and queuing in the node.

- Because the packets between a given source and destination may vary in length, may take different routes, and may be subject to varying delays in the switches they encounter, the overall packet delay can vary substantially. This phenomenon, called **jitter**, may not be desirable for some applications; for example, in real-time applications including telephone voice and real-time video.

- To route packets through the network, overhead information including the address of the destination and often sequencing information must be added to each packet, which reduces the communication capacity available for carrying user data. This is not needed in circuit switching once the circuit is set up.

- More processing is involved in the transfer of information using packet switching than in circuit switching at each node. In the case of circuit switching, there is virtually no processing at each switch once the circuit is set up.

Switching Technique A station has a message to send through a packet-switching network that is of greater length than the maximum packet size. It therefore breaks the message up into packets and sends these packets, one at a time, to the network. A question arises as to how the network will handle this stream of packets as it attempts to route them through the network and deliver them to the intended destination. Two approaches are used in contemporary networks: datagram and virtual circuit.

In the datagram approach, each packet is treated independently, with no reference to packets that have gone before. This approach is illustrated in Figure 1.3. Each node chooses the next node on a packet's path, taking into account information received from neighboring nodes on traffic, line failures, and so on. So the packets, each with the same destination address, do not all follow the same route (c), and they may arrive out of sequence at the exit point. In this example, the exit node restores the packets to their original order before delivering them to the destination. In some datagram networks, it is up to the destination rather than the exit node to do the reordering. Also, it is possible for a packet to be destroyed in the network. For example, if a packet-switching node crashes momentarily, all of its queued packets may be lost. Again, it is up to either the exit node or the destination to detect the loss of a packet and decide how to recover it. In this technique, each packet, treated independently, is referred to as a **datagram**.

In the virtual circuit approach (Figure 1.4), a preplanned route is established before any packets are sent. Once the route is established, all the packets between a pair of communicating parties follow this same route through the network. Because the route is fixed for the duration of the logical connection, it is somewhat similar to a circuit in a circuit-switching network and is referred to as a **virtual circuit**. Each packet contains a virtual circuit identifier as well as data. Each node on the preestablished route knows where to direct such packets; no routing decisions are required. At any time, each station can have more than one virtual circuit to any other station and can have virtual circuits to more than one station.

So the main characteristic of the virtual circuit technique is that a route between stations is set up prior to data transfer. Note that this does not mean that this is a dedicated path, as in circuit switching. A packet is still buffered at each node and queued for output over a line. The difference from the datagram approach is that, with virtual circuits, the node need not make a routing decision for each packet. It is made only once for all packets using that virtual circuit.

If two stations wish to exchange data over an extended period of time, there are certain advantages to virtual circuits. First, the network may provide services related to the virtual circuit, including sequencing and error control. Sequencing refers to the fact that, because all packets follow the same route, they arrive in the original order. Error control is a service that assures not only that packets arrive in proper sequence, but also that all packets arrive correctly. For example, if a packet

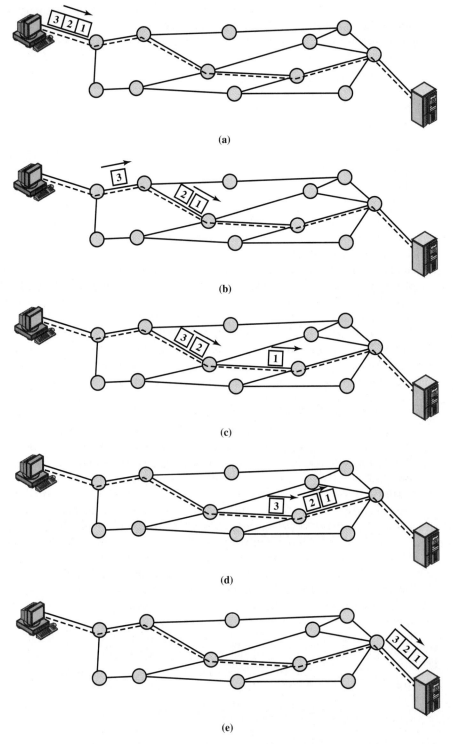

Figure 1.4 Packet Switching: Virtual Circuit Approach

in a sequence from node 4 to node 6 fails to arrive at node 6, or arrives with an error, node 6 can request a retransmission of that packet from node 4 (Figure 1.1). Another advantage is that packets should transit the network more rapidly with a virtual circuit; it is not necessary to make a routing decision for each packet at each node.

One advantage of the datagram approach is that the call setup phase is avoided. Thus, if a station wishes to send only one or a few packets, datagram delivery will be quicker. Another advantage of the datagram service is that it is more flexible. For example, if congestion develops in one part of the network, incoming datagrams can be routed away from the congestion. With the use of virtual circuits, packets follow a predefined route, and thus it is more difficult for the network to adapt to congestion. A third advantage is that datagram delivery is inherently more reliable. With the use of virtual circuits, if a node fails, all virtual circuits that pass through that node are lost. With datagram delivery, if a node fails, subsequent packets may find an alternate route that bypasses that node.

Packet Size There is a significant relationship between packet size and transmission time, as shown in Figure 1.5. In this example, it is assumed that there is a virtual circuit from station X through nodes a and b to station Y. The message to be sent comprises 40 octets, and each packet contains 3 octets of control information, which is placed at the beginning of each packet and is referred to as a header. If the entire message is sent as a single packet of 43 octets (3 octets of header plus 40 octets of data), then the packet is first transmitted from station X to node a (Figure 1.5a). When the entire packet is received, it can then be transmitted from a to b. When the entire packet is received at node b, it is then transferred to station Y. Ignoring switching time, total transmission time is 129 octet-times (43 octets $\times$ 3 packet transmissions).

Suppose now that we break the message up into two packets, each containing 20 octets of the message and, of course, 3 octets each of header, or control information. In this case, node a can begin transmitting the first packet as soon as it has arrived from X, without waiting for the second packet. Because of this overlap in transmission, the total transmission time drops to 92 octet-times. By breaking the message up into five packets, each intermediate node can begin transmission even sooner and the savings in time is greater, with a total of 77 octet-times for transmission. However, this process of using more and smaller packets eventually results in increased, rather than reduced, delay as illustrated in Figure 1.5d. This is because each packet contains a fixed amount of header, and more packets mean more of these headers. Furthermore, the example does not show the processing and queuing delays at each node. These delays are also greater when more packets are handled for a single message. Thus, packet-switched network designers must consider these factors in attempting to find an optimum packet size.

Routing Two related functions, congestion control and routing, are essential to the operation of a packet-switching network. Congestion control is discussed in Chapter 5; here we say a few words about routing.

In virtually all packet-switching networks, some sort of adaptive routing technique is used. That is, the routing decisions that are made change as conditions on the network change. The principal conditions that influence routing decisions are the following:

- **Failure:** When a node or trunk fails, it can no longer be used as part of a route.

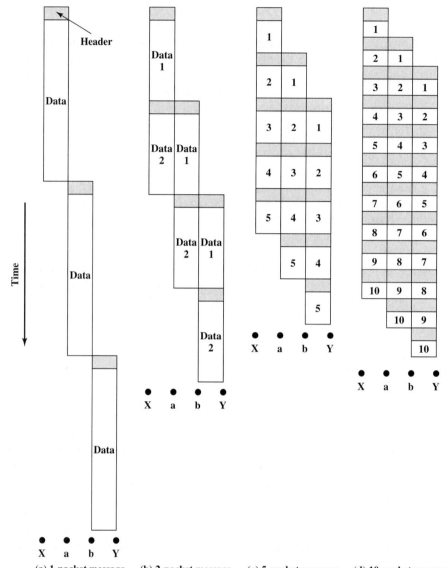

(a) 1-packet message   (b) 2-packet message   (c) 5-packet message   (d) 10-packet message

Figure 1.5   Effect of Packet Size on Transmission Time

- **Congestion:** When a particular portion of the network is heavily congested, it is desirable to route packets around rather than through the area of congestion.

For adaptive routing to be possible, information about the state of the network must be exchanged among the nodes. There is a tradeoff here between the quality of the information and the amount of overhead. The more information that is exchanged, and the more frequently it is exchanged, the better will be the routing decisions that each node makes. On the other hand, this information is itself a load on the network, causing a performance degradation.

Frame Relay

Packet switching was developed at a time when digital long-distance transmission facilities exhibited a relatively high error rate compared to today's facilities. As a result, there is a considerable amount of overhead built into packet-switching schemes to compensate for errors. The overhead includes additional bits added to each packet to introduce redundancy and additional processing at the end stations and the intermediate switching nodes to detect and recover from errors.

With modern high-speed telecommunications systems, this overhead is unnecessary and counterproductive. It is unnecessary because the rate of errors has been dramatically lowered and any remaining errors can easily be caught in the end systems by logic that operates above the level of the packet-switching logic. It is counterproductive because the overhead involved soaks up a significant fraction of the high capacity provided by the network.

Frame relay was developed to take advantage of these high data rates and low error rates. Whereas the original packet-switching networks were designed with a data rate to the end user of about 64 kbps, frame relay networks are designed to operate efficiently at user data rates of up to 2 Mbps. The key to achieving these high data rates is to strip out most of the overhead involved with error control.

ATM

Asynchronous transfer mode (ATM), sometimes referred to as cell relay, is a culmination of developments in circuit switching and packet switching. ATM can be viewed as an evolution from frame relay. The most obvious difference between frame relay and ATM is that frame relay uses variable-length packets, called frames, and ATM uses fixed-length packets, called cells. As with frame relay, ATM provides little overhead for error control, depending on the inherent reliability of the transmission system and on higher layers of logic in the end systems to catch and correct errors. By using a fixed packet length, the processing overhead is reduced even further for ATM compared to frame relay. The result is that ATM is designed to work in the range of 10s and 100s of Mbps, and in the Gbps range.

ATM can also be viewed as an evolution from circuit switching. With circuit switching, only fixed-data-rate circuits are available to the end system. ATM allows the definition of multiple virtual channels with data rates that are dynamically defined at the time the virtual channel is created. By using small, fixed-size cells, ATM is so efficient that it can offer a constant-data-rate channel even though it is using a packet-switching technique. Thus, ATM extends circuit switching to allow multiple channels with the data rate on each channel dynamically set on demand.

Local Area Networks

As with WANs, a local area network (LAN) is a communications network that interconnects a variety of devices and provides a means for information exchange among those devices. There are several key distinctions between LANs and WANs:

1. The scope of the LAN is small, typically a single building or a cluster of buildings. This difference in geographic scope leads to different technical solutions, as we shall see.

2. It is usually the case that the LAN is owned by the same organization that owns the attached devices. For WANs, this is less often the case, or at least a significant fraction of the network assets are not owned. This has two implications. First, care must be taken in the choice of LAN, because there may be a substantial capital investment (compared to dial-up or leased charges for WANs) for both purchase and maintenance. Second, the network management responsibility for a LAN falls solely on the user.

3. The internal data rates of LANs are typically much greater than those of WANs.

LANs come in a number of different configurations. The most common are switched LANs and wireless LANs. The most common switched LAN is a switched Ethernet LAN, which may consist of a single switch with a number of attached devices, or a number of interconnected switches. Two other prominent examples are ATM LANs, which simply use an ATM network in a local area, and Fibre Channel. Wireless LANs use a variety of wireless transmission technologies and organizations.

Wireless Networks

As was just mentioned, wireless LANs are common, being widely used in business environments. Wireless technology is also common for both wide area voice and data networks. Wireless networks provide advantages in the areas of mobility and ease of installation and configuration.

Metropolitan Area Networks

As the name suggests, a MAN occupies a middle ground between LANs and WANs. Interest in MANs has come about as a result of a recognition that the traditional point-to-point and switched network techniques used in WANs may be inadequate for the growing needs of organizations. While frame relay and ATM promise to meet a wide range of high-speed needs, there is a requirement now for both private and public networks that provide high capacity at low costs over a large area. A number of approaches have been implemented, including wireless networks and metropolitan extensions to Ethernet.

The primary market for MANs is the customer that has high capacity needs in a metropolitan area. A MAN is intended to provide the required capacity at lower cost and greater efficiency than obtaining an equivalent service from the local telephone company.

1.2 THE INTERNET

A Brief History of the Internet

The Internet evolved from the ARPANET, which was developed in 1969 by the Advanced Research Projects Agency (ARPA) of the U.S. Department of Defense. It was the first operational packet-switching network. ARPANET began operations in four locations: UCLA, University of Santa Barbara, the University of Utah, and SRI (Stanford Research Institute). Today the number of hosts is in the tens of millions, the number of users in the hundreds of millions, and the number of countries

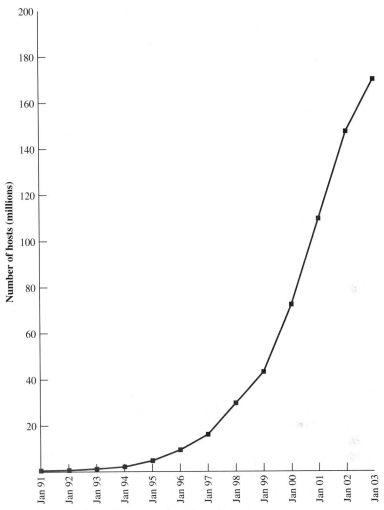

Figure 1.6 Number of Internet Hosts

participating nearing 200. The number of connections to the Internet continues to grow exponentially (Figure 1.6).

ARPANET made use of the new technology of packet switching, which offered advantages over circuit switching, as discussed in the following paragraphs.

When circuit switching is used for data transmission, it is essential that the data rates of the transmitting device and the receiving device be the same. With packet switching this is not necessary. A packet can be sent at the data rate of the transmitting device into the network, travel through the network at a variety of different data rates, usually higher than the transmitter's rate, and then be metered out at the data rate that the receiver was expecting. The packet-switching network and its interfaces can buffer backed-up data to make speed conversion from a higher rate to a lower one possible. It was not just differing data rates that made interconnections difficult at the time of ARPANET's invention; the complete lack of open communication standards made it virtually impossible for a computer made by one manufacturer to communicate electronically with a computer made by another. Of particular interest to its military sponsors, ARPANET also offered adaptive routing. Each packet, individually, was routed to its destination by whatever route seemed fastest at the time of its transmission. Thus, if parts of the network got congested or failed, packets would automatically be routed around the obstacles.

Some of the early applications developed for the ARPANET also offered new functionality. The first two important applications were Telnet and FTP. Telnet provided a *lingua franca* for remote computer terminals. When the ARPANET was introduced, each different computer system needed a different terminal. The Telnet application provided a common denominator terminal. If software was written for each type of computer to support the "Telnet terminal," then one terminal could interact with all computer types. The File Transport Protocol (FTP) offered a similar open functionality. FTP allowed the transparent transfer of files from one computer to the other over the network. This is not as trivial as it may sound because various computers had different word sizes, stored their bits in different orders, and used different word formats. However, the first "killer app" for the ARPANET was electronic mail. Before ARPANET there were electronic mail systems, but they were all single computer systems. In 1972, Ray Tomlinson of Bolt Beranek and Newman (BBN) wrote the first system to provide distributed mail service across a computer network using multiple computers. By 1973, an ARPA study had found that three quarters of all ARPANET traffic was e-mail [HAFN96].

The technology was so successful that ARPA applied the same packet-switching technology to tactical radio communication (packet radio) and to satellite communication (SATNET). Because the three networks operated in very different communication environments, the appropriate values for certain parameters, such as maximum packet size, were different in each case. Faced with the dilemma of integrating these networks, Vint Cerf and Bob Kahn of ARPA started to develop methods and protocols for *internetting*; that is, communicating across arbitrary, multiple, packet-switched networks. They published a very influential paper in May of 1974 [CERF74] outlining their approach to a Transmission Control Protocol. The proposal was refined and details filled in by the ARPANET community, with major contributions from participants from European Networks, such as Cyclades (France), and EIN, eventually leading to the TCP and IP protocols, which, in turn, formed the basis for what eventually became the TCP/IP protocol suite. This provided the foundation for the Internet. In 1982–1983, ARPANET converted from the original NCP protocol to TCP/IP. Many networks then were connected using this technology throughout the world. Nevertheless, use of the ARPANET was generally restricted to ARPA contractors.

National Science Foundation Takes on a Role The NSF extended support to other computer science research groups with CSNET in 1980–1981; in 1986, NSF extended Internet support to all the disciplines of the general research community with the NSFNET backbone. Originally, NSFNET was designed to interconnect six NSF funded supercomputer centers across the country and the centers to supercomputer users nationwide. Eventually, NSF offered interconnection through its backbone to regional packet switched networks across the country. In 1990 the ARPANET was shut down.

Acceptable Use Policies The astonishing growth of the Internet did not go unnoticed by the commercial world. However, in many countries (including the United States up until 1995) national governments subsidized the Internet backbone for their countries. Many of these governments have *acceptable use* policies that limit commercial activities; often, Internet communications over these facilities are limited to research and educational use. Because NSF was subsidizing the Internet backbone in the United States, some felt strongly that the use of the backbone should be restricted to research, education, and government use. This was codified in a voluntary Acceptable Use Policy for the Internet. The "culture" of the Internet also imposed additional informal limitations on commercial uses.

Internet Interconnection Points

In 1991, General Atomics, which operated CERFnet (a California regional network); Performance Systems International operating PSINet (a commercial spin-off from New York's regional network, NYSERnet); and UUNET Technologies, a commercial Internet service provider that owned Alternet, provided nearly all the commercial TCP/IP services in the United States. On their own networks, because they did not use the NSF backbone, they were not subject to NSF's Acceptable Use Policy. However, to communicate between their networks they had been using the NSF backbone, which brought them under the policy. To get around this problem they formed the Commercial Information Interchange (CIX). Originally, it was a mechanism for the networks of the three founders to interchange traffic carried on their networks at a West Coast router so that each network's customers would have access to customers on others' networks at no extra charge. As other providers entered the market, they too found the concept useful and joined the exchange. By 1996, CIX had 147 member networks. One feature of the CIX is that there are no *settlements*, that is, no traffic based fees for use of the interchange. A similar interconnection point was formed in 1994 in England, the London Internet Exchange (LINX); in 1996, it had 24 member networks. Also in 1991, the U.S. government announced that it would no longer subsidize the Internet after 1995. As part of the privatization plan, the government mandated interconnection points called network access points. There are now three, near New York, Chicago, and San Francisco, respectively. There are also metropolitan area exchanges, MAE East and MAE West (Figure 1.7). When the U.S. government privatized the national backbone in 1995, at least the U.S. part of the Internet was opened to virtually unlimited commercial activity. For the last several years the commercial domain, ".com", has been the fastest growing, outstripping the educational domain, ".edu", which previously dominated Internet host registrations.

The World Wide Web

In the spring of 1989, at CERN (the European Laboratory for Particle Physics), Tim Berners-Lee proposed the idea of a distributed hypermedia technology to facilitate the international exchange of research findings using the Internet. Two years later, a

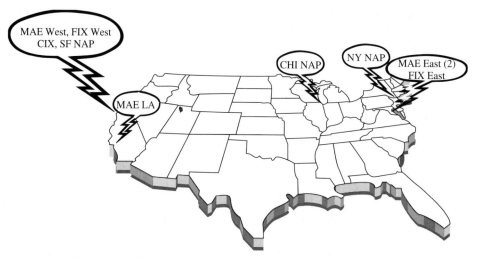

Figure 1.7 U.S. Internet Access Points

prototype World Wide Web (WWW or the Web for short) was developed at CERN using the NeXT computer as a platform. By the end of 1991, CERN released a line-oriented *browser* or reader to a limited population. The explosive growth of the technology came with the development at the first *graphically* oriented browser, *Mosaic*, developed at the NCSA Center at the University of Illinois by Mark Andreasson and others in 1993. Two million copies of Mosaic were delivered over the Internet. Today, the characteristic Web addresses, the URLs (univeral resource locators), are ubiquitous. One cannot read a newspaper or watch TV without seeing the addresses everywhere.

The Web is a system consisting of an internationally distributed collection of *multimedia files* supported by clients (users) and servers (information providers). Each file is addressed in a consistent manner using its URL. The files from the providers are viewed by the clients using *browsers* such as Netscape Navigator or Microsoft's Internet Explorer. Most browsers have graphical display and support multimedia—text, audio, image, video. The user can move from file to file by clicking with a mouse or other pointing device on specially highlighted text or image elements on the browser display; the transfer from one file to the next is called a *hyperlink*. The layout of the browser display is controlled by the *Hypertext Markup Language* (HTML) standard, which defines embedded commands in text files that specify features of the browser display, such as the fonts, colors, images and their placement on the display, and the location of the locations where the user can invoke the hyperlinks and their targets. The last important feature of the Web is the Hypertext Transfer Protocol (HTTP), which is a communications protocol for use in TCP/IP networks for fetching the files from the appropriate servers as specified by the hyperlinks.

What the Internet Looks Like Today

Users now ordinarily connect to the Internet through an Internet service provider (ISP). For home users, the provider is often one of the major online services such as America Online. Today most residential users connect to the ISPs over voice-grade lines using modems at data rates of 56.6 kbps. This is perfectly adequate for e-mail and related services but marginal for graphics-intensive Web surfing. New alternatives have become available in many areas, including ISDN, ADSL, and cable modem.

Users who connect to the Internet through their work often use workstations or PCs connected to their employer-owned LANs, which in turn connect through shared organizational trunks to an ISP. In these cases the shared circuit is T-1 connection, while for very large organizations T-3 connections are sometimes found. Smaller organizations may use 56 kbps or ISDN connections.

The ISPs are connected by "wholesalers," which we can call network service providers. They, in turn, interconnect using Internet connection points, such as CIX, MAE East and West, and the network access points (Figure 1.7). The network service providers use transmission at T-3 rates, with some moving to ATM connections at rates 155 Mbps up to, in the future, 622 Mbps.

The commercial uses of the Internet came in stages. In the early days, limited by the access rules of the ARPANET and, later, by the Acceptable Use Policy, commercial use was limited to (R&D) or other technical units using the Net for research and educational uses, although some informational activities that could be considered marketing were carried on under the name of research and education. When the Internet was privatized in 1995, the first new applications were mainly informational ones for sales and marketing information and public relations. Electronic data interchange (EDI) transactions for intercompany invoices, billing, and the like, which were originally designed for use on dedicated wide area networks and commercial public networks, began to be carried on the Internet. Commercial networks, especially America Online, have long played a customer service role by providing bulletin board type services dealing with technical and usage problems. These activities were gradually extended to the Internet as well. However, the most tempting activity is direct sales to the tens of millions of Internet users throughout the world. The initial infrastructure of the Internet did not support online transactions well. There were three limitations: lack of an easy to use graphical user interface, lack of security, and lack of effective payment systems. The most popular and easy to use interface, the World Wide Web and its browsers, did not become commonly available until 1993 at the earliest. In its early incarnations there was very little support to allow the client browser to submit information (forms) to the server. Moreover, there were not many options for payment for online ordering, and all the options were insecure. One obvious payment method is to use credit card accounts. However, most people are uncomfortable about sending credit card numbers over the Internet, with good reason, because of the lack of security. For example, if the credit card information is not encrypted it is very easy to "listen in" on Internet communications. Moreover, several files of customer's credit card numbers on merchant's computers have been compromised. The ease of collecting and integrating information on customer transactions when they are in electronic form also raises privacy concerns for customers. One of the hottest application areas in financial information systems is "data mining," which often involves collecting large amounts of customer transaction information to improve the targeting of marketing efforts. These limitations are beginning to be ameliorated. The latest browsers support communication with the server by the user filling in forms.

1.3 AN EXAMPLE CONFIGURATION

To give some feel for the scope of concerns of this book, Figure 1.8 illustrates some of the typical communications and network elements in use today. In the upper left-hand portion of the figure, we see an individual residential user connected to an Internet service provider (ISP) through some sort of subscriber connection. Common examples of such a connection are the public telephone network, for which the user requires a dial-up modem (e.g., a 56-kbps modem); a digital subscriber line (DSL),

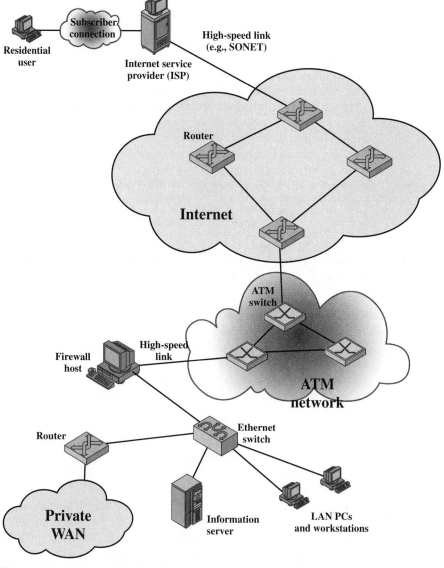

Figure 1.8 A Networking Configuration

which provides a high-speed link over telephone lines and requires a special DSL modem; and a cable TV facility, which requires a cable modem. In each case, there are separate issues concerning signal encoding, error control, and the internal structure of the subscribe network.

Typically, an ISP will consist of a number of interconnected servers (only a single server is shown) connected to the Internet through a high-speed link. One example of such a link is a SONET (synchronous optical network) line. The Internet consists of a number of interconnected routers that span the globe. The routers forward packets of data from source to destination through the Internet.

The lower portion of Figure 1.8 shows a LAN implemented using a single Ethernet switch. This is a common configuration at a small business or other small organization. The LAN is connected to the Internet through a firewall host that provides security services. In this example the firewall connects to the Internet through an ATM network. There is also a router off of the LAN hooked into a private WAN, which might be a private ATM or frame relay network.

A variety of design issues, such as signal encoding and error control, relate to the links between adjacent elements, such as between routers on the Internet or between switches in the ATM network, or between a subscriber and an ISP. The internal structure of the various networks (telephone, ATM, Ethernet) raises additional issues.

1.4 INTRANETS

Intranet is a term used to refer to the implementation of Internet technologies within a corporate organization, rather than for external connection to the global Internet. Increasingly, the intranet approach has been introduced into more traditional corporate networks based on peer LANs and client/server computing. What accounts for the rapid growth of the intranet approach is a long list of attractive features and advantages of an intranet-based approach to corporate computing, including the following:

- Rapid prototyping and deployment of new services (can be measured in hours or days)
- Scales effectively (start small, build as needs, requirements allow)
- Virtually no training required on the part of users and little training required of developers, because the services and user interfaces are familiar from the Internet
- Can be implemented on virtually all platforms with complete interoperability
- Open architecture means large and growing number of add-on applications available across many platforms
- Supports a range of distributed computing architectures (few central servers or many distributed servers)
- Structured to support integration of "legacy" information sources (databases, existing word processing documents, groupware databases)
- Supports a range of media types (audio, video, interactive applications)
- Inexpensive to start, requires little investment either in new software or infrastructure

The enabling technologies for the intranet are the high processing speed and storage capacity of personal computers together with the high data rates of LANs.

Although the term *intranet* refers to the whole range of Internet-based applications, including network news, gopher, and ftp, it is Web technology that is responsible for the almost-instant acceptance of intranets. Thus, the bulk of this section is devoted to a discussion of Web systems. At the close of the section, we briefly mention other intranet applications.

Intranet Web

The Web browser has become the universal information interface. An increasing number of employees have had experience using the Internet Web and are comfortable with the access model it provides. The intranet Web takes advantage of this experience base.

Web Content   An organization can use the intranet Web to enhance management-employee communication and to provide job-related information easily and quickly. Beyond these broad-based Web services, an intranet Web is ideal for providing departmental- and project-level information and services. A group can set up its own Web pages to disseminate information and to maintain project data. With the widespread availability of easy-to-use WYSIWYG page authoring tools, such as Adobe GoLive, it is relatively easy for employees outside the information services group to develop their own Web pages for specific needs.

Web/Database Applications   Although the Web is a powerful and flexible tool for supporting corporate requirements, the HTML used to construct Web pages provides a limited capability for maintaining a large, change base of data. For an intranet to be truly effective, many organizations will want to connect the Web service to a database with its own database management system.

Figure 1.9 illustrates a general strategy for Web/database integration in simple terms. To begin, a client machine (running a Web browser) issues a request for information in the form of a URL reference. This reference triggers a program at the Web server that issues the correct database command to a database server. The output returned to the Web server is converted into an HTML format and returned to the Web browser.

[WHET96] lists the following advantages of a Web/database system compared to a more traditional database approach:

- **Ease of administration:** The only connection to the database server is the Web server. The addition of a new type of database server does not require configuration of all the requisite drivers and interfaces at each type of client machine. Instead, it is only necessary for the Web server to be able to convert between HTML and the database interface.

- **Deployment:** Browsers are already available across almost all platforms, which relieves the developer of the need to implement graphical user interfaces across multiple customer machines and operating systems. In addition, developers can assume that customers already have and will be able to use browsers as soon as the intranet Web server is available, avoiding deployment issues such as installation and synchronized activation.

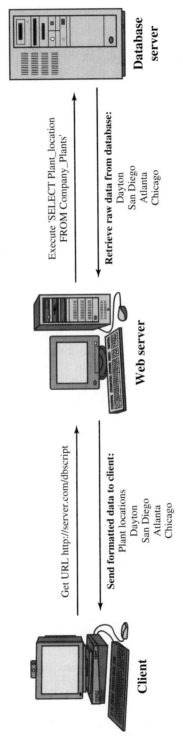

Figure 1.9 Web/Database Connectivity

Database
server

Execute 'SELECT Plant_location
FROM Company_Plants'

Retrieve raw data from database:
Dayton
San Diego
Atlanta
Chicago

Web server

Get URL http://server.com/dbscript

Send formatted data to client:
Plant locations
Dayton
San Diego
Atlanta
Chicago

Client

33

- **Development speed:** Large portions of the normal development cycle, such as deployment and client design, do not apply to Web-based projects. In addition, the text-based tags of HTML allow for rapid modification, making it easy to continually improve the look and feel of the application based on user feedback. By contrast, changing form or content of a typical graphical-based application can be a substantial task.
- **Flexible information presentation:** The hypermedia base of the Web enables the application developer to employ whatever information structure is best for a given application, including the use of hierarchical formats in which progressive levels of detail are available to the user.

These advantages are compelling in the decision to deploy a Web-based database interface. However, managers need to be aware of potential disadvantages, also listed in [WHET96]:

- **Functionality:** Compared to the functionality available with a sophisticated graphical user interface (GUI), a typical Web browser interface is limited. For example, it is difficult with HTML to generate graphical forms with buttons, text fields, and selection menus whose content depend on user input.
- **Stateless operation:** The nature of HTTP is such that each interaction between a browser and a server is a separate transaction, independent of prior or future exchanges. Typically, the Web server keeps no information between transactions to track the state of the user. Such history information can be important. For example, consider an application that allows the user to query a database of parts for cars and trucks. Once the user has indicated that he or she is looking for a specific truck part, subsequent menus should show only parts that pertain to trucks. It is possible to work around this difficulty, but it is awkward.

Other Intranet Technologies

The centerpiece of any intranet strategy is the intranet Web. However, other Internet technologies can also play a key role in the success of an intranet. Perhaps the two most important, after the Web, are electronic mail and network news.

Electronic Mail   Electronic mail is already the most heavily used network application in the corporate world. However, traditional e-mail is generally limited and inflexible. Intranet mail products provide standard, simple methods for attaching documents, sound, images, and other multimedia to mail messages.

In addition to supporting multimedia, intranet mail systems generally make it easy to create and manage an **electronic mailing list**. A mailing list is really nothing more than an alias that has multiple destinations. Mailing lists are usually created to discuss specific topics. Anyone interested in that topic may join that list. Once a user has been added to a list, he or she receives a copy of every message posted to the list. A user can ask a question or respond to someone else's question by sending a message to the list address. The mailing list is thus an effective way of supporting project-level communication.

Network News   Most readers of this book are familiar with **USENET**, otherwise known as network news. USENET is a collection of electronic bulletin boards that work in much the same way as the Internet mailing lists. If you subscribe to a particular news group, you receive all messages posted to that group, and you may post a message that is available to all subscribers. One difference between USENET and Internet mailing lists has to do with the mechanics of the systems. USENET is actually a distributed network of sites that collect and broadcast news group entries. To access a news group, for read or write, one must have access to a USENET node. Another, more significant, difference is the way in which messages are organized. With an electronic mailing list, each subscriber receives messages one at a time, as they are sent. With USENET, the messages are archived at each news site and organized by subject matter. Thus, it is easier to follow the thread of a particular discussion with USENET. This ability to organize and store messages in threads makes USENET ideal for collaborative work.

As with other Internet technologies, USENET is readily adapted to form an intranet news service. The news messages can be stored on a single news servers, or multiple servers within the organization can act as news repositories. New groups are created as needed by departments and projects.

1.5 EXTRANETS

A concept similar to that of the intranet is the **extranet**. Like the intranet, the extranet makes use of TCP/IP protocols and applications, especially the Web. The distinguishing feature of the extranet is that it provides access to corporate resources by outside clients, typically suppliers and customers of the organization. This outside access can be through the Internet or through other data communications networks. An extranet provides more than the simple Web access for the public that virtually all companies now provide. Instead, the extranet provides more extensive access to corporate resources, usually in a fashion that enforces a security policy. As with the intranet, the typical model of operation for the extranet is client/server.

The essential feature of an extranet is that it enables the sharing of information among companies. [PFAF98] lists the following benefits of such sharing:

- **Reduced costs:** Information that must be shared is done in a highly automated fashion, with minimized paperwork and human involvement.
- **More marketable products:** Customers can be directly involved in the design process during the product design cycle, with rapid review of design specifications, automated tools for accepting requirements specifications from customers, and other tools for feedback and review. These capabilities helps firms determine the optimum mix of product features.
- **Increased product quality:** Customer complaints reach suppliers faster and are easier to track, enabling corrections to be made to the product more quickly.
- **Enhanced profits for suppliers:** Up-to-the minute information on what is selling and what is not helps suppliers fine tune their marketplace response.
- **Reduced inventories and reduction of obsolete inventories:** Customer-driven just-in-time manufacturing techniques are enhanced, allowing more refined decision making in procurement.
- **Faster time to market:** Products reach the market more quickly when vendors, designers, marketers, and customers are electronically linked in a new product partnership.

An important consideration with extranets is security. Because corporate Web resources and database resources are made available to outside parties and transactions against these resources are allowed, privacy and authentication concerns must be addressed. Here, we can simply list some of the communications options available for opening up the corporate intranet to outsiders to create an extranet:

- **Long-distance dial-up access:** This enables outsiders to access the Internet directly, using a logon procedure to authenticate the user. This approach may provide the weakest security because of the risk of impersonation, with few tools to counteract such risks.

- **Internet access to intranet with security:** Authentication of users and encryption of communications between user and intranet provide enhanced security. The encryption prevents eavesdropping, and authentication is intended to prevent unauthorized access. However, as with dial-up access, if a hacker is able to defeat the authentication mechanism, then the entire resources of the intranet become vulnerable.

- **Internet access to an external server that duplicates some of a company's intranet data:** This approach reduces the risk of hacker penetration but may also reduce the value of the extranet to external partners.

- **Internet access to an external server that originates database queries to internal servers:** The external server acts as a firewall to enforce the company's security policy. The firewall may employ encryption in communicating to external users, will authenticate external users, and filters the information flow to restrict access on the basis of user. If the firewall is itself secure from hacker attacks, this is a powerful approach.

- **Virtual private network:** The VPN in effect is a generalization of the firewall approach and takes advantage of IP security capabilities to allow secure communications between external users and the company's intranet.

1.6 RECOMMENDED READING AND WEB SITES

The literature on packet switching is enormous. Books with good treatments of this subject include [SPOH97], [BERT92], and [SPRA91].

RFC 1935 is one attempt to answer the question, What is the Internet?

BERT92 Bertsekas, D., and Gallager, R. *Data Networks*. Englewood Cliffs, NJ: Prentice Hall, 1992.

SPOH97 Spohn, D. *Data Network Design*. New York: McGraw-Hill, 1997.

SPRA91 Spragins, J.; Hammond, J.; and Pawlikowski, K. *Telecommunications Protocols and Design*. Reading, MA: Addison-Wesley, 1991.

Recommended Web Site:

- **The Living Internet:** Provides comprehensive and in-depth information about the history of the Internet, plus links to numerous other relevant sites

1.7 KEY TERMS, REVIEW QUESTIONS, AND PROBLEMS

Key Terms

asynchronous transfer mode (ATM) circuit switching data network datagram	extranet frame relay Internet intranet local area network (LAN)	packet switching virtual circuit wide area network (WAN) World Wide Web

Review Questions

1.1 Differentiate between WANs and LANs.

1.2 Why is it useful to have more than one possible path through a network for each pair of stations?

1.3 What is the principal application that has driven the design of circuit-switching networks?

1.4 What shortcomings of circuit switching is packet switching designed to overcome?

1.5 Explain the difference between datagram and virtual circuit operation.

1.6 What is the significance of packet size?

1.7 What conditions influence the routing decision in a packet-switching network?

1.8 Describe the Acceptable Use Policy.

1.9 What is the difference between an intranet and an extranet?

1.10 List some benefits of the information sharing provided by an extranet.

1.11 What are the communications options available for converting an intranet into an extranet?

Problems

1.1 Explain the flaw in the following logic: Packet switching requires control and address bits to be added to each packet. This causes considerable overhead in packet switching. In circuit switching, a transparent circuit is established. No extra bits are needed. Therefore, there is no overhead in circuit switching. Because there is no overhead in circuit switching, line utilization must be more efficient than in packet switching.

1.2 Define the following parameters for a switching network:

N = number of hops between two given end systems
L = message length in bits
B = data rate, in bits per second (bps), on all links
P = fixed packet size, in bits
H = overhead (header) bits per packet
S = call setup time (circuit switching or virtual circuit) in seconds
D = propagation delay per hop in seconds

a. For $N = 4, L = 3200, B = 9600, P = 1024, H = 16, S = 0.2, D = 0.001$, compute the end-to-end delay for circuit switching, virtual circuit packet switching, and datagram packet switching. Assume that there are no acknowledgments. Ignore processing delay at the nodes.

b. Derive general expressions for the three techniques of part (a), taken two at a time (three expressions in all), showing the conditions under which the delays are equal.

1.3 What value of P, as a function of N, L, and H, results in minimum end-to-end delay on a datagram network? Assume that L is much larger than P, and D is zero.

1.4 Assuming no malfunction in any of the stations or nodes of a network, is it possible for a packet to be delivered to the wrong destination?

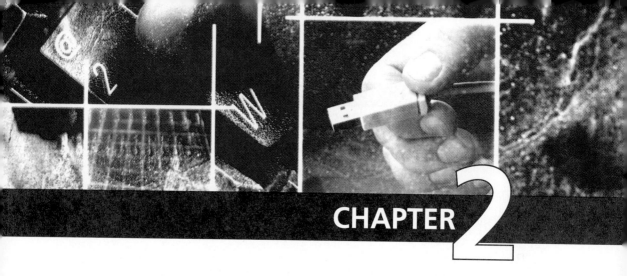

CHAPTER 2

PROTOCOLS AND THE TCP/IP PROTOCOL SUITE

*To destroy communication completely, there must be no rules in common
between transmitter and receiver—neither of alphabet nor of syntax.*

—On Human Communication,
Colin Cherry

KEY POINTS

- A protocol architecture is the layered structure of hardware and software that supports the exchange of data between systems and supports distributed applications, such as electronic mail and file transfer.

- At each layer of a protocol architecture, one or more common protocols are implemented in communicating systems. Each protocol provides a set of rules for the exchange of data between systems.

- The most widely used protocol architecture is the TCP/IP protocol suite, which consists of the following layers: physical, network access, internet, transport, and application.

- Another important protocol architecture is the seven-layer **Open Systems Interconnection** (OSI) model.

This chapter provides a context for the detailed material that follows.

We begin this chapter by introducing the concept of a layered protocol architecture and looking at a simple example. Next, the chapter introduces the Open Systems Interconnection (OSI) reference model. OSI is a standardized architecture that is often used to describe communications functions but that is now rarely implemented. We then examine the most important protocol architecture, the TCP/IP protocol suite. TCP/IP is an Internet-based concept and is the framework for developing a complete range of computer communications standards. Virtually all computer vendors now provide support for this architecture.

2.1 THE NEED FOR A PROTOCOL ARCHITECTURE

When computers, terminals, and/or other data processing devices exchange data, the procedures involved can be quite complex. Consider, for example, the transfer of a file between two computers. There must be a data path between the two computers, either directly or via a communication network. But more is needed. Typical tasks to be performed include the following:

1. The source system must either activate the direct data communication path or inform the communication network of the identity of the desired destination system.
2. The source system must ascertain that the destination system is prepared to receive data.
3. The file transfer application on the source system must ascertain that the file management program on the destination system is prepared to accept and store the file for this particular user.

4. If the file formats used on the two systems are incompatible, one or the other system must perform a format translation function.

It is clear that there must be a high degree of cooperation between the two computer systems. Instead of implementing the logic for this as a single module, the task is broken up into subtasks, each of which is implemented separately. In a protocol architecture, the modules are arranged in a vertical stack. Each layer in the stack performs a related subset of the functions required to communicate with another system. It relies on the next lower layer to perform more primitive functions and to conceal the details of those functions. It provides services to the next higher layer. Ideally, layers should be defined so that changes in one layer do not require changes in other layers.

Of course, it takes two to communicate, so the same set of layered functions must exist in two systems. Communication is achieved by having the corresponding, or **peer**, layers in two systems communicate. The **peer layers** communicate by means of formatted blocks of data that obey a set of rules or conventions known as a **protocol**. The key features of a protocol are as follows:

- **Syntax:** Concerns the format of the data blocks
- **Semantics:** Includes control information for coordination and error handling
- **Timing:** Includes speed matching and sequencing

Appendix 2A provides a specific example of a protocol, the Internet standard Trivial File Transfer Protocol (TFTP).

2.2 A SIMPLE PROTOCOL ARCHITECTURE

Having introduced the concept of a protocol, we can now introduce the concept of a protocol architecture. It is clear that there must be a high degree of cooperation between the two computers. Instead of implementing the logic for this as a single module, the task is broken up into subtasks, each of which is implemented separately. As an example, Figure 2.1 suggests the way in which a file transfer facility

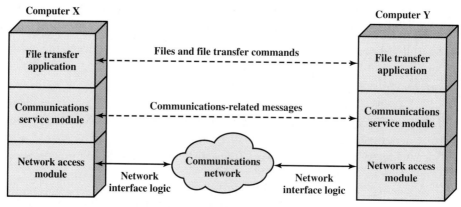

Figure 2.1 A Simplified Architecture for File Transfer

could be implemented. Three modules are used. A file transfer module could perform tasks 3 and 4 in the preceding list. The two modules on the two systems exchange files and commands. However, rather than requiring the file transfer module to deal with the details of actually transferring data and commands, the file transfer modules each rely on a communications service module. This module is responsible for making sure that the file transfer commands and data are reliably exchanged between systems. Among other things, this module would perform task 2. We observe that the nature of the exchange between systems is independent of the nature of the network that interconnects them. Therefore, rather than building details of the network interface into the communications service module, it makes sense to have a third module, a network access module, that performs task 1 by interacting with the network.

To summarize, the file transfer module contains all of the logic that is unique to the file transfer application, such as transmitting passwords, file commands, and file records. There is a need to transmit these files and commands reliably. However, the same sorts of reliability requirements are relevant to a variety of applications (e.g., electronic mail, document transfer). Therefore, a separate communications service module that can be used by a variety of applications meets these requirements. The communications service module is concerned with assuring that the two computer systems are active and ready for data transfer and for keeping track of the data that are being exchanged to assure delivery. However, these tasks are independent of the type of network that is being used. Therefore, the logic for actually dealing with the network is placed in a separate network access module. That way, if the network to be used is changed, only the network access module is affected.

Thus, instead of a single module for performing communications, there is a structured set of modules that implements the communications function. That structure is referred to as a **protocol architecture**. An analogy might be useful at this point. Suppose an executive in office X wishes to send a document to an executive in office Y. The executive in X prepares the document and perhaps attaches a note. This corresponds to the actions of the file transfer application in Figure 2.1. Then the executive in X hands the document to a secretary or administrative assistant (AA). The AA in X puts the document in an envelope and puts Y's address and X's return address on the outside. Perhaps the envelope is also marked "confidential." The AA's actions correspond to the communications service module in Figure 2.1. The AA in X then gives the package to the shipping department. Someone in the shipping department decides how to send the package: mail, United Parcel Service (UPS), or express courier. The shipping department attaches the appropriate postage or shipping documents to the package and ships it out. The shipping department corresponds to the network access module of Figure 2.1. When the package arrives at Y, a similar layered set of actions occurs. The shipping department at Y receives the package and delivers it to the appropriate AA or secretary based on the name on the package. The AA opens the package and hands the enclosed document to the executive to whom it is addressed.

In the remainder of this section, we generalize the preceding example to present a simplified protocol architecture. Following that, we look at more complex, real-world examples: OSI and TCP/IP.

A Three-Layer Model

In very general terms, communications can be said to involve three agents: applications, computers, and networks. Applications execute on computers that typically support multiple simultaneous applications. Computers are connected to networks, and the data to be exchanged are transferred by the network from one computer to another. Thus, the transfer of data from one application to another involves first getting the data to the computer in which the application resides and then getting it to the intended application within the computer.

With these concepts in mind, it appears natural to organize the communication task into three relatively independent layers: network access layer, transport layer, and application layer.

The **network access layer** is concerned with the exchange of data between a computer and the network to which it is attached. The sending computer must provide the network with the address of the destination computer, so that the network may route the data to the appropriate destination. The sending computer may wish to invoke certain services, such as priority, that might be provided by the network. The specific software used at this layer depends on the type of network to be used; different standards have been developed for circuit switching, packet switching, LANs, and others. Thus, it makes sense to separate those functions having to do with network access into a separate layer. By doing this, the remainder of the communications software, above the network access layer, need not be concerned about the specifics of the network to be used. The same higher-layer software should function properly regardless of the particular network to which the computer is attached.

Regardless of the nature of the applications that are exchanging data, there is usually a requirement that data be exchanged reliably. That is, we would like to be assured that all of the data arrive at the destination application and that the data arrive in the same order in which they were sent. As we shall see, the mechanisms for providing reliability are essentially independent of the nature of the applications. Thus, it makes sense to collect those mechanisms in a common layer shared by all applications; this is referred to as the **transport layer**.

Finally, the **application layer** contains the logic needed to support the various user applications. For each different type of application, such as file transfer, a separate module is needed that is peculiar to that application.

Figures 2.2 and 2.3 illustrate this simple architecture. Figure 2.2 shows three computers connected to a network. Each computer contains software at the network access and transport layers and software at the application layer for one or more applications. For successful communication, every entity in the overall system must have a unique address. Actually, two levels of addressing are needed. Each computer on the network must have a unique network address; this allows the network to deliver data to the proper computer. Each application on a computer must have an address that is unique within that computer; this allows the transport layer to support multiple applications at each computer. These latter addresses are known as **service access points** (SAPs), or **ports**, connoting the fact that each application is individually accessing the services of the transport layer.

Figure 2.3 indicates that modules at the same level on different computers communicate with each other by means of a protocol. Let us trace a simple operation.

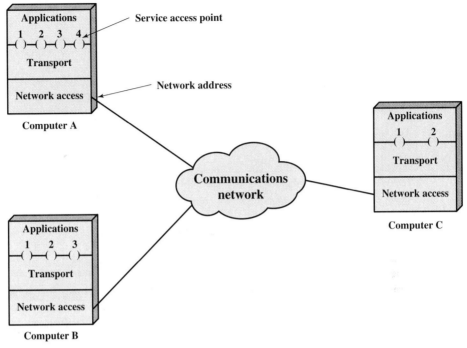

Figure 2.2   Protocol Architectures and Networks

Suppose that an application, associated with SAP 1 at computer X, wishes to send a message to another application, associated with SAP 2 at computer Y. The application at X hands the message over to its transport layer with instructions to send it to SAP 2 on computer Y. The transport layer hands the message over to the network access layer, which instructs the network to send the message to computer Y. Note that the network need not be told the identity of the destination service access point. All that it needs to know is that the data are intended for computer Y.

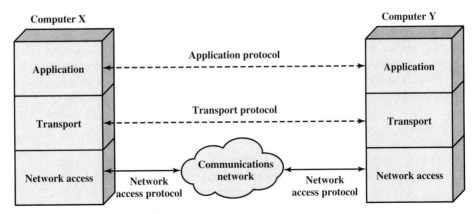

Figure 2.3   Protocols in a Simplified Architecture

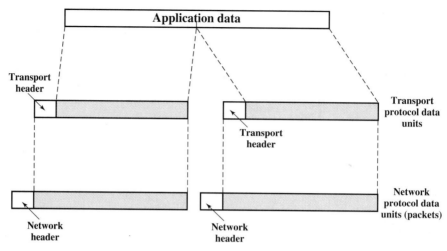

Figure 2.4 Protocol Data Units

To control this operation, control information, as well as user data, must be transmitted, as suggested in Figure 2.4. Let us say that the sending application generates a block of data and passes this to the transport layer. The transport layer may break this block into two smaller pieces to make it more manageable. To each of these pieces the transport layer appends a transport header, containing protocol control information. The combination of data from the next higher layer and control information is known as a **protocol data unit** (PDU); in this case, it is referred to as a **transport PDU**. The header in each transport PDU contains control information to be used by the peer transport protocol at computer B. Examples of items that may be stored in this header include the following:

- **Destination port:** When the destination transport layer receives the transport PDU, it must know to whom the data are to be delivered.

- **Sequence number:** Because the transport protocol is sending a sequence of PDUs, it numbers them sequentially so that if they arrive out of order, the destination transport entity may reorder them.

- **Error-detection code:** The sending transport entity may include a code that is a function of the contents of the remainder of the PDU. The receiving transport protocol performs the same calculation and compares the result with the incoming code. A discrepancy results if there has been some error in transmission. In that case, the receiver can discard the PDU and take corrective action.

The next step is for the transport layer to hand each PDU over to the network layer, with instructions to transmit it to the destination computer. To satisfy this request, the network access protocol must present the data to the network with a request for transmission. As before, this operation requires the use of control information. In this case, the network access protocol appends a network access header to the data it receives from the transport layer, creating a network access PDU, often called a **packet**. Examples of the items that may be stored in the header include the following:

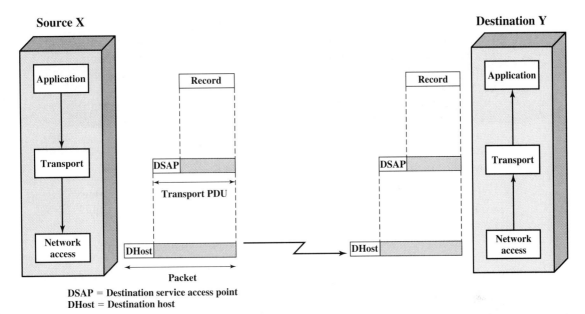

Figure 2.5   Operation of a Protocol Architecture

- **Destination computer address:** The network must know to whom (which computer on the network) the data are to be delivered.
- **Facilities requests:** The network access protocol might want the network to make use of certain facilities, such as priority.

Figure 2.5 puts all of these concepts together, showing the interaction between modules to transfer one block of data. Let us say that the file transfer module in computer X is transferring a file one record at a time to computer Y. Each record is handed over to the transport layer module. We can picture this action as being in the form of a command or procedure call. The arguments of this procedure call include the destination computer address, the destination service access point, and the record. The transport layer appends the destination service access point and other control information to the record to create a transport PDU. This is then handed down to the network access layer by another procedure call. In this case, the arguments for the command are the destination computer address and the transport PDU. The network access layer uses this information to construct a network PDU. The transport PDU is the data field of the network PDU, and the network PDU header includes information concerning the source and destination computer addresses. Note that the transport header is not "visible" at the network access layer; the network access layer is not concerned with the contents of the transport PDU.

The network accepts the network PDU from X and delivers it to Y. The network access module in Y receives the PDU, strips off the header, and transfers the enclosed transport PDU to Y's transport layer module. The transport layer examines the transport PDU header and, on the basis of the SAP field in the header, delivers the enclosed record to the appropriate application, in this case the file transfer module in Y.

Standardized Protocol Architectures

When communication is desired among computers from different vendors, the software development effort can be a nightmare. Different vendors use different data formats and data exchange protocols. Even within one vendor's product line, different model computers may communicate in unique ways.

As the use of computer communications and computer networking proliferates, a one-at-a-time special-purpose approach to communications software development is too costly to be acceptable. The only alternative is for computer vendors to adopt and implement a common set of conventions. For this to happen, standards are needed. Such standards would have two benefits:

- Vendors feel encouraged to implement the standards because of an expectation that, because of wide usage of the standards, their products would be less marketable without them.
- Customers are in a position to require that any vendor wishing to propose equipment to them implement the standards.

Two protocol architectures have served as the basis for the development of interoperable protocol standards: the TCP/IP protocol suite and the OSI reference model. TCP/IP is by far the most widely used interoperable architecture. OSI, though well known, has never lived up to its early promise. There is also a widely used proprietary scheme: IBM's System Network Architecture (SNA). The remainder of this chapter looks at OSI and TCP/IP.

2.3 OSI

Standards are needed to promote interoperability among vendor equipment and to encourage economies of scale. Because of the complexity of the communications task, no single standard will suffice. Rather, the functions should be broken down into more manageable parts and organized as a communications architecture. The architecture would then form the framework for standardization. This line of reasoning led the International Organization for Standardization (ISO) in 1977 to establish a subcommittee to develop such an architecture. The result was the Open Systems Interconnection (OSI) reference model. Although the essential elements of the model were in place quickly, the final ISO standard, ISO 7498, was not published until 1984. A technically compatible version was issued by CCITT (now ITU-T) as X.200.

The Model

A widely accepted structuring technique, and the one chosen by ISO, is layering. The communications functions are partitioned into a hierarchical set of layers. Each layer performs a related subset of the functions required to communicate with another system. It relies on the next lower layer to perform more primitive functions and to conceal the details of those functions. It provides services to the next higher layer. Ideally, the layers should be defined so that changes in one layer do not re-

Table 2.1 Principles Used in Defining the OSI Layers (X.200)

1. Do not create so many layers as to make the system engineering task of describing and integrating the layers more difficult than necessary.

2. Create a boundary at a point where the description of services can be small and the number of interactions across the boundary are minimized.

3. Create separate layers to handle functions that are manifestly different in the process performed or the technology involved.

4. Collect similar functions into the same layer.

5. Select boundaries at a point which past experience has demonstrated to be successful.

6. Create a layer of easily localized functions so that the layer could be totally redesigned and its protocols changed in a major way to take advantage of new advances in architecture, hardware, or software technology without changing the services expected from and provided to the adjacent layers.

7. Create a boundary where it may be useful at some point in time to have the corresponding interface standardized.

8. Create a layer where there is a need for a different level of abstraction in the handling of data, for example morphology, syntax, semantic.

9. Allow changes of functions or protocols to be made within a layer without affecting other layers.

10. Create for each layer boundaries with its upper and lower layer only.

    Similar principles have been applied to sublayering:

11. Create further subgrouping and organization of functions to form sublayers within a layer in cases where distinct communication services need it.

12. Create, where needed, two or more sublayers with a common, and therefore minimal functionality to allow interface operation with adjacent layers.

13. Allow bypassing of sublayers.

quire changes in the other layers. Thus, we have decomposed one problem into a number of more manageable subproblems.

The task of ISO was to define a set of layers and the services performed by each layer. The partitioning should group functions logically and should have enough layers to make each layer manageably small, but should not have so many layers that the processing overhead imposed by the collection of layers is burdensome. The principles that guided the design effort are summarized in Table 2.1. The resulting reference model has seven layers, which are listed with a brief definition in Figure 2.6. Table 2.2 provides ISO's justification for the selection of these layers.

Figure 2.7 illustrates the OSI architecture. Each system contains the seven layers. Communication is between applications in the two computers, labeled application X and application Y in the figure. If application X wishes to send a message to application Y, it invokes the application layer (layer 7). Layer 7 establishes a peer relationship with layer 7 of the target computer, using a layer 7 protocol (application protocol). This protocol requires services from layer 6, so the two layer 6 entities use a protocol of their own, and so on down to the physical layer, which actually transmits bits over a transmission medium.

Note that there is no direct communication between peer layers except at the physical layer. That is, above the physical layer, each protocol entity sends data

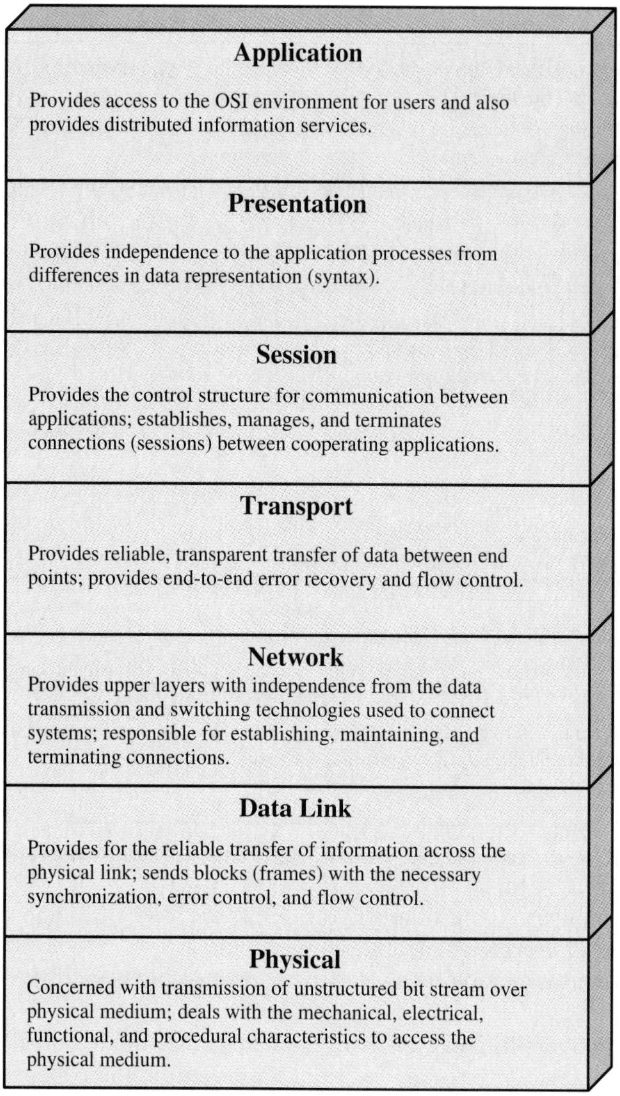

| **Application** |
| Provides access to the OSI environment for users and also provides distributed information services. |

| **Presentation** |
| Provides independence to the application processes from differences in data representation (syntax). |

| **Session** |
| Provides the control structure for communication between applications; establishes, manages, and terminates connections (sessions) between cooperating applications. |

| **Transport** |
| Provides reliable, transparent transfer of data between end points; provides end-to-end error recovery and flow control. |

| **Network** |
| Provides upper layers with independence from the data transmission and switching technologies used to connect systems; responsible for establishing, maintaining, and terminating connections. |

| **Data Link** |
| Provides for the reliable transfer of information across the physical link; sends blocks (frames) with the necessary synchronization, error control, and flow control. |

| **Physical** |
| Concerned with transmission of unstructured bit stream over physical medium; deals with the mechanical, electrical, functional, and procedural characteristics to access the physical medium. |

Figure 2.6   The OSI Layers

down to the next lower layer to get the data across to its peer entity. Even at the physical layer, the OSI model does not stipulate that two systems be directly connected. For example, a packet-switched or circuit-switched network may be used to provide the communication link.

Figure 2.7 also highlights the use of protocol data units (PDUs) within the OSI architecture. First, consider the most common way in which protocols are realized. When application X has a message to send to application Y, it transfers those data to an application entity in the application layer. A header is appended to the data that contains the required information for the peer layer 7 protocol (encapsulation). The

Table 2.2 Justification of the OSI Layers (X.200)

1. It is essential that the architecture permits usage of a realistic variety of physical media for interconnection with different control procedures (for example, V.24, V.25, etc.). Application of principles 3, 5, and 8 (Table 2.1) leads to identification of a **physical layer** as the lowest layer in the architecture.

2. Some physical communication media (for example, telephone line) require specific techniques to be used in order to transmit data between systems despite a relatively high error rate (i.e., an error rate not acceptable for the great majority of applications). These specific techniques are used in data link control procedures, which have been studied and standardized for a number of years. It must also be recognized that new physical communication media (for example, fiber optics) will require different data link control procedures. Application of principles 3, 5, and 8 leads to identification of a **data link layer** on top of the physical layer in the architecture.

3. In the open systems architecture, some open systems will act as the final destination of data. Some open systems may act only as intermediate nodes (forwarding data to other systems). Application of principles 3, 5, and 7 leads to identification of a **network layer** on top of the data link layer. Network oriented protocols such as routing, for example, will be grouped in this layer. Thus, the network layer will provide a connection path (networkconnection) between a pair of transport entities, including the case where intermediate nodes are involved.

4. Control of data transportation from source end open system to destination end open system (which is not performed in intermediate nodes) is the last function to be performed in order to provide the totality of the transport service. Thus, the upper layer in the transport service part of the architecture is the **transport layer**, on top of the network layer. This transport layer relieves higher-layer entities from any concern with the transportation of data between them.

5. There is a need to organize and synchronize dialogue and to manage the exchange of data. Application of principles 3 and 4 leads to the identification of a **session layer** on top of the transport layer.

6. The remaining set of general interest functions are those related to representation and manipulation of structured data for the benefit of application programs. Application of principles 3 and 4 leads to the identification of a **presentation layer** on top of the session layer.

7. Finally, there are applications consisting of application processes that perform information processing. An aspect of these application processes and the protocols by which they communicate comprise the **application layer** as the highest layer of the architecture.

original data plus the header are now passed as a unit to layer 6. The presentation entity treats the whole unit as data and appends its own header (a second encapsulation). This process continues down through layer 2, which generally adds both a header and a trailer. This layer 2 unit, called a frame, is then passed onto the transmission medium by the physical layer. When the frame is received by the target system, the reverse process occurs. As the data ascend, each layer strips off the outermost header, acts on the protocol information contained therein, and passes the remainder up to the next layer.

On the transmission side, any layer may segment the data unit it receives from the next higher layer into several parts, to accommodate its own requirements. These data units must then be reassembled by the corresponding peer layer on the reception side before being passed up.

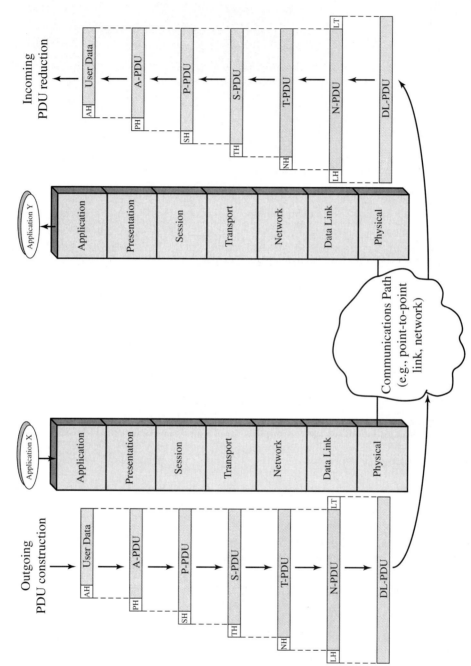

Figure 2.7 The OSI Environment

Standardization within the OSI Framework[1]

The principal motivation for the development of the OSI model was to provide a framework for standardization. Within the model, one or more protocol standards can be developed at each layer. The model defines in general terms the functions to be performed at that layer and facilitates the standards-making process in two ways:

- Because the functions of each layer are well defined, standards can be developed independently and simultaneously for each layer. This speeds up the standards-making process.

- Because the boundaries between layers are well defined, changes in standards in one layer need not affect already existing software in another layer. This makes it easier to introduce new standards.

Figure 2.8 illustrates the use of the OSI model as such a framework. The overall communications function is decomposed into seven distinct layers, using the principles outlined in Table 2.1. These principles essentially amount to using modular design. That is, the overall function is broken up into a number of modules, making the interfaces between modules as simple as possible. In addition, the design principle of

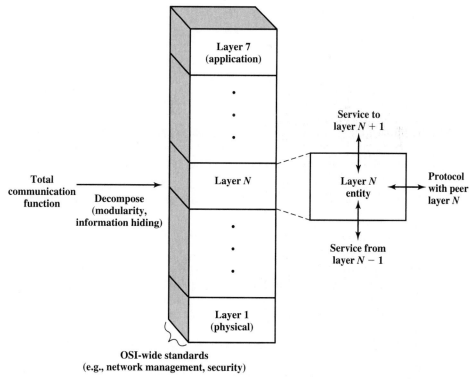

Figure 2.8   The OSI Architecture as a Framework for Standardization

[1]The concepts introduced in this subsection apply as well to the TCP/IP architecture.

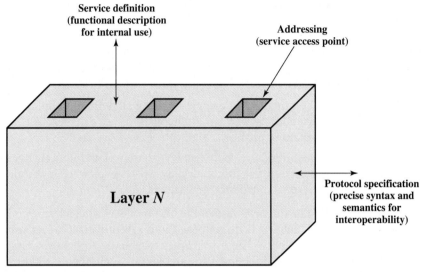

Figure 2.9 Layer-Specific Standards

information hiding is used: Lower layers are concerned with greater levels of detail; upper layers are independent of these details. Each layer provides services to the next higher layer and implements a protocol to the peer layer in other systems.

Figure 2.9 shows more specifically the nature of the standardization required at each layer. Three elements are key:

- **Protocol specification:** Two entities at the same layer in different systems cooperate and interact by means of a protocol. Because two different open systems are involved, the protocol must be specified precisely. This includes the format of the protocol data units exchanged, the semantics of all fields, and the allowable sequence of PDUs.

- **Service definition:** In addition to the protocol or protocols that operate at a given layer, standards are needed for the services that each layer provides to the next higher layer. Typically, the definition of services is equivalent to a functional description that defines what services are provided, but not how the services are to be provided.

- **Addressing:** Each layer provides services to entities at the next higher layer. These entities are referenced by means of a service access point (SAP). Thus, a network service access point (NSAP) indicates a transport entity that is a user of the network service.

The need to provide a precise protocol specification for open systems is self-evident. The other two items listed warrant further comment. With respect to service definitions, the motivation for providing only a functional definition is as follows. First, the interaction between two adjacent layers takes place within the confines of a single open system and is not the concern of any other open system. Thus, as long as peer layers in different systems provide the same services to their next higher layers, the details of how the services are provided may differ from one system to another without loss of interoperability. Second, it will usually be the case that adjacent layers are implemented on the same processor. In that case, we would like to leave the system programmer free to exploit the hardware and operating system to provide an interface that is as efficient as possible.

With respect to addressing, the use of an address mechanism at each layer, implemented as a service access point, allows each layer to multiplex multiple users from the next higher layer. Multiplexing may not occur at each layer, but the model allows for that possibility.

Service Primitives and Parameters

The services between adjacent layers in the OSI architecture are expressed in terms of primitives and parameters. A primitive specifies the function to be performed, and the parameters are used to pass data and control information. The actual form of a primitive is implementation dependent. An example is a procedure call.

Four types of primitives are used in standards to define the interaction between adjacent layers in the architecture (X.210). These are defined in Table 2.3. The layout of Figure 2.10 suggests the time ordering of these events. For example, consider the transfer of data from an (N) entity to a peer (N) entity in another system. The following steps occur:

1. The source (N) entity invokes its $(N-1)$ entity with a *request* primitive. Associated with the primitive are the parameters needed, such as the data to be transmitted and the destination address.
2. The source $(N-1)$ entity prepares an $(N-1)$ PDU to be sent to its peer $(N-1)$ entity.
3. The destination $(N-1)$ entity delivers the data to the appropriate destination (N) entity via an *indication* primitive, which includes the data and source address as parameters.
4. If an acknowledgment is called for, the destination (N) entity issues a *response* primitive to its $(N-1)$ entity.
5. The $(N-1)$ entity conveys the acknowledgment in an $(N-1)$ PDU.
6. The acknowledgment is delivered to the (N) entity as a *confirm* primitive.

Table 2.3 Service Primitive Types

REQUEST	A primitive issued by a service user to invoke some service and to pass the parameters needed to specify fully the requested service
INDICATION	A primitive issued by a service provider either to 1. indicate that a procedure has been invoked by the peer service user on the connection and to provide the associated parameters, or 2. notify the service user of a provider-initiated action
RESPONSE	A primitive issued by a service user to acknowledge or complete some procedure previously invoked by an indication to that user
CONFIRM	A primitive issued by a service provider to acknowledge or complete some procedure previously invoked by a request by the service user

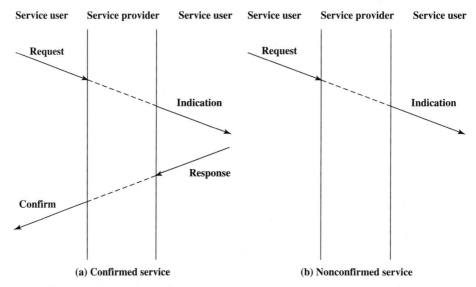

Figure 2.10 Time Sequence Diagrams for Service Primitives

This sequence of events is referred to as a **confirmed service**, as the initiator receives confirmation that the requested service has had the desired effect at the other end. If only request and indication primitives are involved (corresponding to steps 1 through 3), then the service dialogue is a **nonconfirmed service**; the initiator receives no confirmation that the requested action has taken place (Figure 2.10b).

2.4 THE TCP/IP PROTOCOL ARCHITECTURE

The TCP/IP protocol architecture is a result of protocol research and development conducted on the experimental packet-switched network, ARPANET, funded by the Defense Advanced Research Projects Agency (DARPA), and is generally referred to as the TCP/IP protocol suite. This protocol suite consists of a large collection of protocols that have been issued as Internet standards by the Internet Architecture Board (IAB).

The TCP/IP Layers

The TCP/IP model organizes the communication task into five relatively independent layers:

- Physical layer
- Network access layer

- Internet layer
- Host-to-host, or transport layer
- Application layer

The **physical layer** covers the physical interface between a data transmission device (e.g., workstation, computer) and a transmission medium or network. This layer is concerned with specifying the characteristics of the transmission medium, the nature of the signals, the data rate, and related matters.

The **network access layer** is concerned with the exchange of data between an end system (server, workstation, etc.) and the network to which it is attached. The sending computer must provide the network with the address of the destination computer, so that the network may route the data to the appropriate destination. The sending computer may wish to invoke certain services, such as priority, that might be provided by the network. The specific software used at this layer depends on the type of network to be used; different standards have been developed for circuit switching, packet switching (e.g., frame relay), LANs (e.g., Ethernet), and others. Thus it makes sense to separate those functions having to do with network access into a separate layer. By doing this, the remainder of the communications software, above the network access layer, need not be concerned about the specifics of the network to be used. The same higher-layer software should function properly regardless of the particular network to which the computer is attached.

The network access layer is concerned with access to and routing data across a network for two end systems attached to the same network. In those cases where two devices are attached to different networks, procedures are needed to allow data to traverse multiple interconnected networks. This is the function of the **internet layer**. The **Internet Protocol** (IP) is used at this layer to provide the routing function across multiple networks. This protocol is implemented not only in the end systems but also in routers. A router is a processor that connects two networks and whose primary function is to relay data from one network to the other on its route from the source to the destination end system.

Regardless of the nature of the applications that are exchanging data, there is usually a requirement that data be exchanged reliably. That is, we would like to be assured that all of the data arrive at the destination application and that the data arrive in the same order in which they were sent. As we shall see, the mechanisms for providing reliability are essentially independent of the nature of the applications. Thus, it makes sense to collect those mechanisms in a common layer shared by all applications; this is referred to as the **host-to-host layer**, or **transport layer**. The **Transmission Control Protocol** (TCP) is the most commonly used protocol to provide this functionality.

Finally, the **application layer** c§ontains the logic needed to support the various user applications. For each different type of application, such as file transfer, a separate module is needed that is peculiar to that application.

Figure 2.11 illustrates the layers of the TCP/IP and OSI architectures, showing roughly the correspondence in functionality between the two.

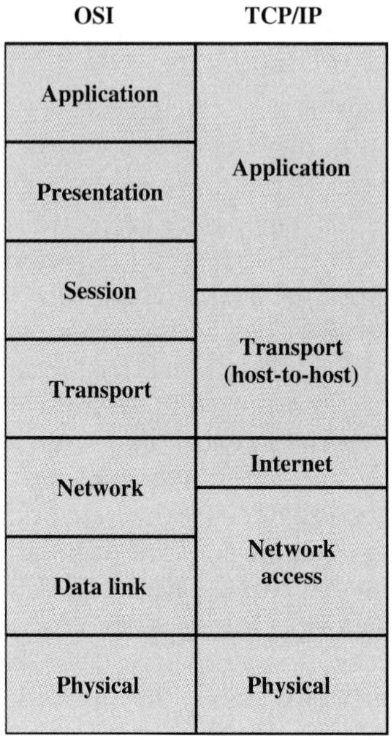

OSI   TCP/IP

OSI	TCP/IP
Application	Application
Presentation	
Session	Transport (host-to-host)
Transport	
Network	Internet
Data link	Network access
Physical	Physical

Figure 2.11 A Comparison of the OSI and TCP/IP Protocol Architectures

TCP and UDP

For most applications running as part of the TCP/IP protocol architecture, the transport layer protocol is TCP. TCP provides a reliable connection for the transfer of data between applications. A connection is simply a temporary logical association between two entities in different systems.

Each TCP PDU, called a **TCP segment**, includes a source port and destination port value in the segment header (Figure 2.12a). These port values identify the respective users (applications) of the two TCP entities. A logical connection refers to a given pair of port values. For the duration of the connection each entity keeps track of TCP segments coming and going to the other entity, in order to regulate the flow of segments and to recover from lost or damaged segments.

The Sequence Number, Acknowledgment Number, and Window fields provide flow control and error control. The 16-bit **Checksum** is used to detect errors in the TCP segment. The significance of these fields is discussed in detail in Part Three.

In addition to TCP, there is one other transport-level protocol that is in common use as part of the TCP/IP protocol suite: the **User Datagram Protocol** (UDP). UDP does not guarantee delivery, preservation of sequence, or protection against duplication. UDP enables a procedure to send messages to other procedures with a minimum of protocol mechanism. Some transaction-oriented applications make use of UDP; one example is SNMP (Simple Network Management Protocol), the standard network management protocol for TCP/IP networks. Because it is connectionless, UDP has very little to do. Essentially, it adds a port addressing capability to IP. This can be seen by examining the UDP header, shown in Figure 2.12b.

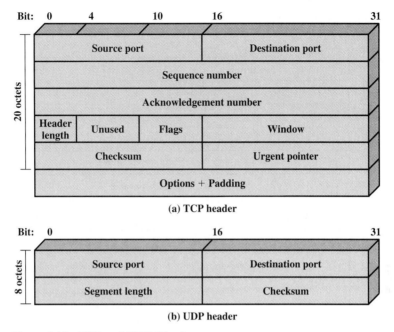

Figure 2.12   TCP and UDP Headers

IP and IPv6

For decades, the keystone of the TCP/IP protocol architecture has been IP. Figure 2.13a shows the IP header format, which is a minimum of 20 octets, or 160 bits. The header includes 32-bit source and destination addresses. The Header Checksum field is used to detect errors in the header to avoid misdelivery. The Protocol field indicates whether TCP, UDP, or some other higher-layer protocol is using IP. The Flags and Fragment Offset fields are used in the fragmentation and reassembly process, in which a single IP datagram is divided into multiple IP datagrams on transmission and then reassembled at the destination.

In 1995, the Internet Engineering Task Force (IETF), which develops protocol standards for the Internet, issued a specification for a next-generation IP, known then as IPng. This specification was turned into a standard in 1996 known as **IPv6**. IPv6 provides a number of functional enhancements over the existing IP, designed to accommodate the higher speeds of today's networks and the mix of data streams, including graphic and video, that are becoming more prevalent. But the driving force behind the development of the new protocol was the need for more addresses. The current IP uses a 32-bit address to specify a source or destination. With the explosive growth of the Internet and of private networks attached to the Internet, this address length became insufficient to accommodate all systems needing addresses. As Figure 2.13b shows, IPv6 includes 128-bit source and destination address fields.

Ultimately, all installations using TCP/IP are expected to migrate from the current IP to IPv6, but this process will take many years, if not decades. The details of IPv4 and IPv6 are discussed in Chapter 8.

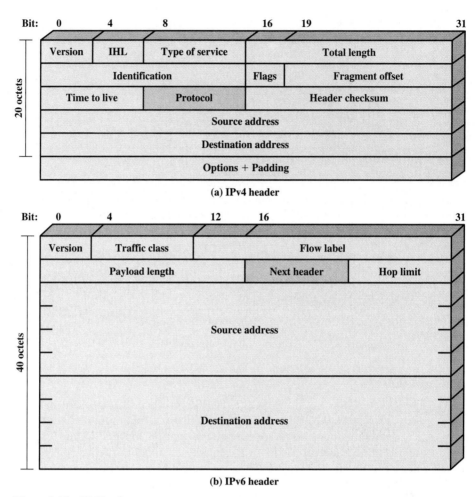

Figure 2.13 IP Headers

Operation of TCP and IP

Figure 2.14 indicates how these protocols are configured for communications. To make clear that the total communications facility may consist of multiple networks, the constituent networks are usually referred to as **subnetworks**. Some sort of network access protocol, such as the Ethernet logic, is used to connect a computer to a subnetwork. This protocol enables the host to send data across the subnetwork to another host or, if the target host is on another subnetwork, to a router that will forward the data. IP is implemented in all of the end systems and the routers. It acts as a relay to move a block of data from one host, through one or more routers, to another host. TCP is implemented only in the end systems; it keeps track of the blocks of data to assure that all are delivered reliably to the appropriate application.

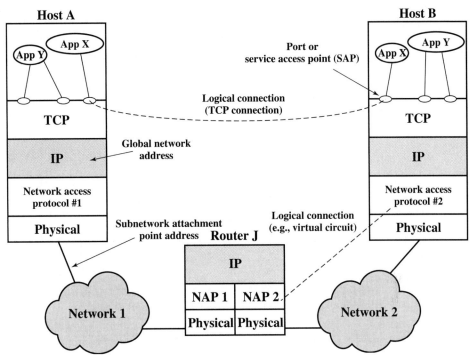

Figure 2.14 TCP/IP Concepts

For successful communication, every entity in the overall system must have a unique address. Actually, two levels of addressing are needed. Each host on a subnetwork must have a unique global internet address; this allows the data to be delivered to the proper host. Each process with a host must have an address that is unique within the host; this allows the host-to-host protocol (TCP) to deliver data to the proper process. These latter addresses are known as ports.

Let us trace a simple operation. Suppose that a process, associated with port 1 at host A, wishes to send a message to another process, associated with port 3 at host B. The process at A hands the message down to TCP with instructions to send it to host B, port 3. TCP hands the message down to IP with instructions to send it to host B. Note that IP need not be told the identity of the destination port. All it needs to know is that the data are intended for host B. Next, IP hands the message down to the network access layer (e.g., Ethernet logic) with instructions to send it to router J (the first hop on the way to B).

To control this operation, control information as well as user data must be transmitted, as suggested in Figure 2.15. Let us say that the sending process generates a block of data and passes this to TCP. TCP may break this block into smaller pieces to make it more manageable. To each of these pieces, TCP appends control information known as the TCP header, forming a **TCP segment**. The control

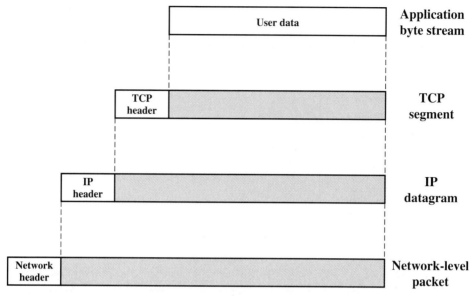

Figure 2.15 Protocol Data Units (PDUs) in the TCP/IP Architecture

information is to be used by the peer TCP protocol entity at host B. Examples of items in this header include the following:

- **Destination port:** When the TCP entity at B receives the segment, it must know to whom the data are to be delivered.
- **Sequence number:** TCP numbers the segments that it sends to a particular destination port sequentially, so that if they arrive out of order, the TCP entity at B can reorder them.
- **Checksum:** The sending TCP includes a code that is a function of the contents of the remainder of the segment. The receiving TCP performs the same calculation and compares the result with the incoming code. A discrepancy results if there has been some error in transmission.

Next, TCP hands each segment over to IP, with instructions to transmit it to B. These segments must be transmitted across one or more subnetworks and relayed through one or more intermediate routers. This operation, too, requires the use of control information. Thus IP appends a header of control information to each segment to form an **IP datagram**. An example of an item stored in the IP header is the destination host address (in this example, B).

Finally, each IP datagram is presented to the network access layer for transmission across the first subnetwork in its journey to the destination. The network access layer appends its own header, creating a packet, or frame. The packet is transmitted across the subnetwork to router J. The packet header contains the information that the subnetwork needs to transfer the data across the subnetwork. Examples of items that may be contained in this header include the following:

- **Destination subnetwork address:** The subnetwork must know to which attached device the packet is to be delivered.
- **Facilities requests:** The network access protocol might request the use of certain subnetwork facilities, such as priority.

At router J, the packet header is stripped off and the IP header examined. On the basis of the destination address information in the IP header, the IP module in the router directs the datagram out across subnetwork 2 to B. To do this, the datagram is again augmented with a network access header.

When the data are received at B, the reverse process occurs. At each layer, the corresponding header is removed, and the remainder is passed on to the next higher layer, until the original user data are delivered to the destination process.

As an aside, the generic name for a block of data exchanged at any protocol level is referred to as a **protocol data unit** (PDU). Thus, a TCP segment is a TCP PDU.

Protocol Interfaces

Each layer in the TCP/IP protocol suite interacts with its immediate adjacent layers. At the source, the application layer makes use of the services of the end-to-end layer and provides data down to that layer. A similar relationship exists at the interface of the end-to-end and internet layers and at the interface of the internet and network access layers. At the destination, each layer delivers data up to the next higher layer.

This use of each individual layer is not required by the architecture. As the figure on the inside back cover suggests, it is possible to develop applications that directly invoke the services of any one of the layers. Most applications require a reliable end-to-end protocol and thus make use of TCP. Some special-purpose applications do not need the services of TCP. Some of these applications, such as the Simple Network Management Protocol (SNMP), use an alternative end-to-end protocol known as the User Datagram Protocol (UDP); others may make use of IP directly. Applications that do not involve internetworking and that do not need TCP have been developed to invoke the network access layer directly.

2.5 INTERNETWORKING

In most cases, a LAN or WAN is not an isolated entity. An organization may have more than one type of LAN at a given site to satisfy a spectrum of needs. An organization may have multiple LANs of the same type at a given site to accommodate performance or security requirements. And an organization may have LANs at various sites and need them to be interconnected via WANs for central control of distributed information exchange.

Table 2.4 lists some commonly used terms relating to the interconnection of networks, or **internetworking**. An interconnected set of networks, from a user's point of view, may appear simply as a larger network. However, if each of the constituent networks retains its identity, and special mechanisms are needed for communicating across multiple networks, then the entire configuration is often referred

Table 2.4 Internetworking Terms

Communication Network

A facility that provides a data transfer service among devices attached to the network.

Internet

A collection of communication networks interconnected by bridges and/or routers.

Intranet

An internet used by a single organization that provides the key Internet applications, especially the World Wide Web. An intranet operates within the organization for internal purposes and can exist as an isolated, self-contained internet, or may have links to the Internet.

Subnetwork

Refers to a constituent network of an internet. This avoids ambiguity because the entire internet, from a user's point of view, is a single network.

End System (ES)

A device attached to one of the networks of an internet that is used to support end-user applications or services.

Intermediate System (IS)

A device used to connect two networks and permit communication between end systems attached to different networks.

Bridge

An IS used to connect two LANs that use similar LAN protocols. The bridge acts as an address filter, picking up packets from one LAN that are intended for a destination on another LAN and passing those packets on. The bridge does not modify the contents of the packets and does not add anything to the packet. The bridge operates at layer 2 of the OSI model.

Router

An IS used to connect two networks that may or may not be similar. The router employs an internet protocol present in each router and each end system of the network. The router operates at layer 3 of the OSI model.

---

to as an **internet**, and each of the constituent networks as a **subnetwork**. The most important example of an internet is referred to simply as the Internet. As the Internet has evolved from its modest beginnings as a research-oriented packet-switching network, it has served as the basis for the development of internetworking technology and as the model for private internets within organizations. These latter are also referred to as **intranets**.

Each constituent subnetwork in an internet supports communication among the devices attached to that subnetwork; these devices are referred to as **end systems** (ESs). In addition, subnetworks are connected by devices referred to in the ISO documents as **intermediate systems** (ISs). ISs provide a communications path and perform the necessary relaying and routing functions so that data can be exchanged between devices attached to different subnetworks in the internet.

Two types of ISs of particular interest are bridges and routers. The differences between them have to do with the types of protocols used for the internetworking logic. In essence, a **bridge** operates at layer 2 of the OSI seven-layer architecture and acts as a relay of frames between like networks. A **router** operates at layer 3 of the OSI architecture and routes packets between potentially different networks. Both the bridge and the router assume that the same upper-layer protocols are in use.

The roles and functions of routers were introduced in the context of IP earlier in this chapter. However, because of the importance of routers in the overall networking scheme, it is worth providing additional comment in this section.

Routers

Internetworking among dissimilar subnetworks is achieved by using routers to interconnect the subnetworks. Essential functions that the router must perform include the following:

1. Provide a link between networks.

2. Provide for the routing and delivery of data between processes on end systems attached to different networks.

3. Provide these functions in such a way as not to require modifications of the networking architecture of any of the attached subnetworks.

The third point implies that the router must accommodate a number of differences among networks, such as the following:

- **Addressing schemes:** The networks may use different schemes for assigning addresses to devices. For example, an IEEE 802 LAN uses 48-bit binary addresses for each attached device; an ATM network typically uses 15-digit decimal addresses (encoded as 4 bits per digit for a 60-bit address). Some form of global network addressing must be provided, as well as a directory service.

- **Maximum packet sizes:** Packets from one network may have to be broken into smaller pieces to be transmitted on another network, a process known as *segmentation,* or *fragmentation.* For example, Ethernet imposes a maximum packet size of 1500 bytes; a maximum packet size of 1600 bytes is common on frame relay networks. A packet that is transmitted on an frame relay network and picked up by a router for retransmission on an Ethernet LAN may have to be fragmented into two smaller ones.

- **Interfaces:** The hardware and software interfaces to various networks differ. The concept of a router must be independent of these differences.

- **Reliability:** Various network services may provide anything from a reliable end-to-end virtual circuit to an unreliable service. The operation of the routers should not depend on an assumption of network reliability.

The preceding requirements are best satisfied by an internetworking protocol, such as IP, that is implemented in all end systems and routers.

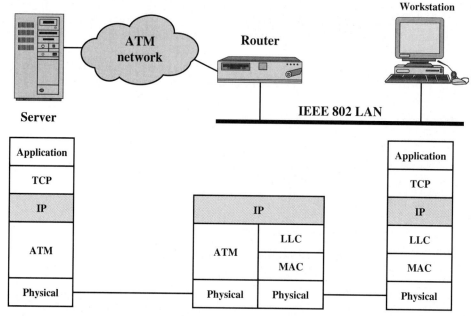

Figure 2.16 Configuration for TCP/IP Example

Internetworking Example

Figure 2.16 depicts a configuration that we will use to illustrate the interactions among protocols for internetworking. In this case, we focus on a server attached to an ATM WAN and a workstation attached to an IEEE 802 LAN, with a router connecting the two networks.[2] The router will provide a link between the server and the workstation that enables these end systems to ignore the details of the intervening networks.

Figures 2.17 through 2.19 outline typical steps in the transfer of a block of data, such as a file or a Web page, from the server, through an internet, and ultimately to an application in the workstation. In this example, the message passes through just one router. Before data can be transmitted, the application and transport layers in the server establish, with the corresponding layer in the workstation, the applicable ground rules for a communication session. These include character code to be used, error-checking method, and the like. The protocol at each layer is used for this purpose and then is used in the transmission of the message.

---

[2]The IEEE 802 protocol architecture consists of a physical layer; a medium access control (MAC) layer concerned with addressing and error control, and a logical link control (LLC) layer, concerned with logical connections and identifying the user of LLC.

1. Preparing the data. The application protocol prepares a block of data for transmission. For example, an e-mail message (SMTP), a file (FTP), or a block of user input (Telnet).

2. Using a common syntax. If necessary, the data are converted to a form expected by the destination. This may include a different character code, the use of encryption, and/or compression.

3. Segmenting the data. TCP may break the data block into a number of segments, keeping track of their sequence. Each TCP segment includes a header containing a sequence number and a frame check sequence to detect errors.

4. Duplicating segments. A copy is made of each TCP segment, in case the loss or damage of a segment necessitates retransmission. When an acknowledgment is received from the other TCP entity, a segment is erased.

5. Fragmenting the segments. IP may break a TCP segment into a number of datagrams to meet size requirements of the intervening networks. Each datagram includes a header containing a destination address, a frame check sequence, and other control information.

6. Framing. An ATM header is added to each IP datagram to form an ATM cell. The header contains a connection identifier and a header error control field.

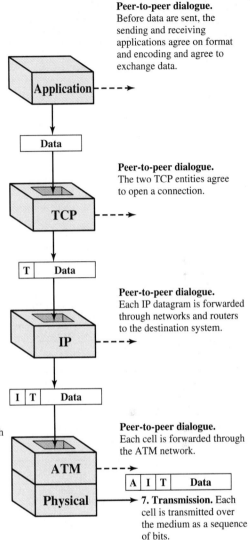

Peer-to-peer dialogue. Before data are sent, the sending and receiving applications agree on format and encoding and agree to exchange data.

Peer-to-peer dialogue. The two TCP entities agree to open a connection.

Peer-to-peer dialogue. Each IP datagram is forwarded through networks and routers to the destination system.

Peer-to-peer dialogue. Each cell is forwarded through the ATM network.

7. Transmission. Each cell is transmitted over the medium as a sequence of bits.

Figure 2.17 Operation of TCP/IP: Action at Sender

2.6 RECOMMENDED READING AND WEB SITES

For the reader interested in greater detail on TCP/IP, there are two three-volume works that are more than adequate. The works by Comer and Stevens have become classics and are considered definitive [COME00, COME99, COME01]. The works by Stevens and Wright are equally worthwhile and more detailed with respect to protocol operation [STEV94, STEV96, WRIG95]. A more compact and very useful reference work is [RODR02], which covers the spectrum of TCP/IP-related protocols in a technically concise but thorough fashion, including coverage of some protocols not found in the other two works.

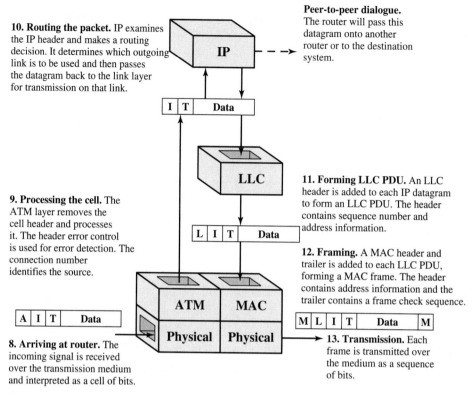

10. Routing the packet. IP examines the IP header and makes a routing decision. It determines which outgoing link is to be used and then passes the datagram back to the link layer for transmission on that link.

Peer-to-peer dialogue. The router will pass this datagram onto another router or to the destination system.

9. Processing the cell. The ATM layer removes the cell header and processes it. The header error control is used for error detection. The connection number identifies the source.

11. Forming LLC PDU. An LLC header is added to each IP datagram to form an LLC PDU. The header contains sequence number and address information.

12. Framing. A MAC header and trailer is added to each LLC PDU, forming a MAC frame. The header contains address information and the trailer contains a frame check sequence.

8. Arriving at router. The incoming signal is received over the transmission medium and interpreted as a cell of bits.

13. Transmission. Each frame is transmitted over the medium as a sequence of bits.

Figure 2.18   Operation of TCP/IP: Action at Router

COME99   Comer, D., and Stevens, D. *Internetworking with TCP/IP, Volume II: Design Implementation, and Internals.* Upper Saddle River, NJ: Prentice Hall, 1999.

COME00   Comer, D. *Internetworking with TCP/IP, Volume I: Principles, Protocols, and Architecture.* Upper Saddle River, NJ: Prentice Hall, 2000.

COME01   Comer, D., and Stevens, D. *Internetworking with TCP/IP, Volume III: Client-Server Programming and Applications.* Upper Saddle River, NJ: Prentice Hall, 2001.

RODR02   Rodriguez, A., et al., *TCP/IP Tutorial and Technical Overview.* Upper Saddle River, NJ: Prentice Hall, 2002.

STEV94   Stevens, W. *TCP/IP Illustrated, Volume 1: The Protocols.* Reading, MA: Addison-Wesley, 1994.

STEV96   Stevens, W. *TCP/IP Illustrated, Volume 3: TCP for Transactions, HTTP, NNTP, and the UNIX(R) Domain Protocol.* Reading, MA: Addison-Wesley, 1996.

WRIG95   Wright, G., and Stevens, W. *TCP/IP Illustrated, Volume 2: The Implementation.* Reading, MA: Addison-Wesley, 1995.

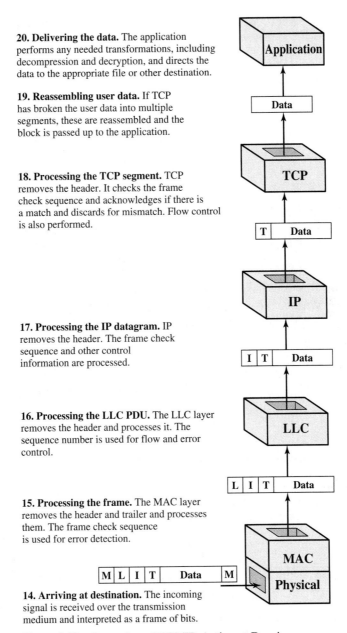

20. Delivering the data. The application performs any needed transformations, including decompression and decryption, and directs the data to the appropriate file or other destination.

19. Reassembling user data. If TCP has broken the user data into multiple segments, these are reassembled and the block is passed up to the application.

18. Processing the TCP segment. TCP removes the header. It checks the frame check sequence and acknowledges if there is a match and discards for mismatch. Flow control is also performed.

17. Processing the IP datagram. IP removes the header. The frame check sequence and other control information are processed.

16. Processing the LLC PDU. The LLC layer removes the header and processes it. The sequence number is used for flow and error control.

15. Processing the frame. The MAC layer removes the header and trailer and processes them. The frame check sequence is used for error detection.

14. Arriving at destination. The incoming signal is received over the transmission medium and interpreted as a frame of bits.

Figure 2.19 Operation of TCP/IP: Action at Receiver

Recommended Web Site:

- **Networking Links:** Excellent collection of links related to TCP/IP

2.7 KEY TERMS, REVIEW QUESTIONS, AND PROBLEMS

Key Terms

application layer	IPv6	protocol data unit (PDU)
bridge	network layer	router
checksum	Open Systems Inter-	service access point (SAP)
data link layer	connection (OSI)	session layer
end system (ES)	peer layer	subnetwork
header	physical layer	Transmission Control Protocol
intermediate system (IS)	port	(TCP)
Internet	presentation layer	transport layer
Internet Protocol (IP)	protocol	User Datagram Protocol
internetworking	protocol architecture	(UDP)

Review Questions

2.1 What is the major function of the network access layer?

2.2 What tasks are performed by the transport layer?

2.3 What is a protocol?

2.4 What is a protocol data unit (PDU)?

2.5 What is a protocol architecture?

2.6 What is TCP/IP?

2.7 What are some advantages to layering as seen in the TCP/IP architecture?

2.8 What is a router?

Problems

2.1 Using the layer models in Figure 2.20, describe the ordering and delivery of a pizza, indicating the interactions at each level.

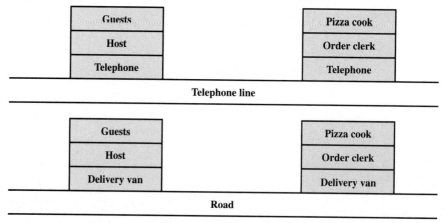

Figure 2.20 Architecture for Problem 2.1

2.2   **a.**   The French and Chinese prime ministers need to come to an agreement by telephone, but neither speaks the other's language. Further, neither has on hand a translator that can translate to the language of the other. However, both prime ministers have English translators on their staffs. Draw a diagram similar to Figure 2.20 to depict the situation, and describe the interaction and each level.

b.   Now suppose that the Chinese prime minister's translator can translate only into Japanese and that the French prime minister has a German translator available. A translator between German and Japanese is available in Germany. Draw a new diagram that reflects this arrangement and describe the hypothetical phone conversation.

2.3   List the major disadvantages with the layered approach to protocols.

2.4   Two blue armies are each poised on opposite hills preparing to attack a single red army in the valley. The red army can defeat either of the blue armies separately but will fail to defeat both blue armies if they attack simultaneously. The blue armies communicate via an unreliable communications system (a foot soldier). The commander with one of the blue armies would like to attack at noon. His problem is this: If he sends a message to the other blue army, ordering the attack, he cannot be sure it will get through. He could ask for acknowledgment, but that might not get through. Is there a protocol that the two blue armies can use to avoid defeat?

2.5   A broadcast network is one in which a transmission from any one attached station is received by all other attached stations over a shared medium. Examples are a bus-topology local area network, such as Ethernet, and a wireless radio network. Discuss the need or lack of need for a network layer (OSI layer 3) in a broadcast network.

2.6   Based on the principles enunciated in Table 2.1,

a.   Design an architecture with eight layers and make a case for it.

b.   Design one with six layers and make a case for that.

2.7   In Figure 2.15, exactly one protocol data unit (PDU) in layer N is encapsulated in a PDU at layer $(N - 1)$. It is also possible to break one N-level PDU into multiple $(N - 1)$-level PDUs (segmentation) or to group multiple N-level PDUs into one $(N - 1)$-level PDU (blocking).

a.   In the case of segmentation, is it necessary that each $(N - 1)$-level segment contain a copy of the N-level header?

b.   In the case of blocking, is it necessary that each N-level PDU retain its own header, or can the data be consolidated into a single N-level PDU with a single N-level header?

2.8   The previous version of the TFTP specification, RFC 783, included the following statement:

> All packets other than those used for termination are acknowledged individually unless a timeout occurs.

The RFC 1350 specification revises this to say

> All packets other than duplicate ACKs and those used for termination are acknowledged unless a timeout occurs.

The change was made to fix a problem referred to as the "Sorcerer's Apprentice." Deduce and explain the problem.

2.9   What is the limiting factor in the time required to transfer a file using TFTP?

APPENDIX 2A THE TRIVIAL FILE TRANSFER PROTOCOL

This appendix provides an overview of the Internet standard Trivial File Transfer Protocol (TFTP), defined in RFC 1350. Our purpose is to give the reader some flavor for the elements of a protocol.

Introduction to TFTP

TFTP is far simpler than the Internet standard FTP (RFC 959). There are no provisions for access control or user identification, so TFTP is only suitable for public access file directories. Because of its simplicity, TFTP is easily and compactly implemented. For example, some diskless devices use TFTP to download their firmware at boot time.

TFTP runs on top of UDP. The TFTP entity that initiates the transfer does so by sending a read or write request in a UDP segment with a destination port of 69 to the target system. This port is recognized by the target UDP module as the identifier of the TFTP module. For the duration of the transfer, each side uses a transfer identifier (TID) as its port number.

TFTP Packets

TFTP entities exchange commands, responses, and file data in the form of packets, each of which is carried in the body of a UDP segment. TFTP supports five types of packets (Figure 2.21); the first two bytes contains an opcode that identifies the packet type:

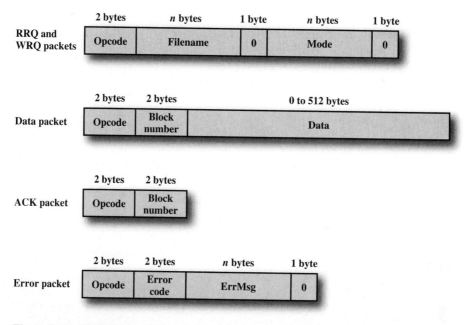

Figure 2.21   TFTP Packet Formats

- **RRQ:** The read request packet requests permission to transfer a file from the other system. The packet includes a file name, which is a sequence of ASCII[3] bytes terminated by a zero byte. The zero byte is the means by which the receiving TFTP entity knows when the file name is terminated. The packet also includes a mode field, which indicates whether the data file is to be interpreted as a string of ASCII bytes or as raw 8-bit bytes of data.

- **WRQ:** The write request packet requests permission to transfer a file to the other system.

- **Data:** The block numbers on data packets begin with one and increase by one for each new block of data. This convention enables the program to use a single number to discriminate between new packets and duplicates. The data field is from zero to 512 bytes long. If it is 512 bytes long, the block is not the last block of data; if it is from zero to 511 bytes long, it signals the end of the transfer.

- **ACK:** This packet is used to acknowledge receipt of a data packet or a WRQ packet. An ACK of a data packet contains the block number of the data packet being acknowledged. An ACK of a WRQ contains a block number of zero.

- **Error:** An error packet can be the acknowledgment of any other type of packet. The error code is an integer indicating the nature of the error (Table 2.5). The error message is intended for human consumption, and should be in ASCII. Like all other strings, it is terminated with a zero byte.

All packets other than duplicate ACKs (explained subsequently) and those used for termination are to be acknowledged. Any packet can be acknowledged by an error packet. If there are no errors, then the following conventions apply. A WRQ or a data packet is acknowledged by an ACK packet. When a RRQ is sent, the other

Table 2.5 TFTP Error Codes

Value	Meaning
0	Not defined, see error message (if any)
1	File not found
2	Access violation
3	Disk full or allocation exceeded
4	Illegal TFTP operation
5	Unknown transfer ID
6	File already exists
7	No such user

---

[3]ASCII is the American Standard Code for Information Interchange, a standard of the American National Standards Institute. It designates a unique 7-bit pattern for each letter, with an eighth bit used for parity. ASCII is equivalent to the International Reference Alphabet (IRA), defined in ITU-T Recommendation T.50. A description and table of the IRA code is contained in a supporting document at this book's Web site.

side responds (in the absence of error) by beginning to transfer the file; thus, the first data block serves as an acknowledgment of the RRQ packet. Unless a file transfer is complete, each ACK packet from one side is followed by a data packet from the other, so that the data packet functions as an acknowledgment. An error packet can be acknowledged by any other kind of packet, depending on the circumstance.

Overview of a Transfer

The example illustrated in Figure 2.22 is of a simple file transfer operation from A to B. No errors occur and the details of the option specification are not explored.

The operation begins when the TFTP module in system A sends a write request (WRQ) to the TFTP module in system B. The WRQ packet is carried as the body of a UDP segment. The write request includes the name of the file (in this case, XXX) and a mode of octet, or raw data. In the UDP header, the destination port number is 69, which alerts the receiving UDP entity that this message is intended for

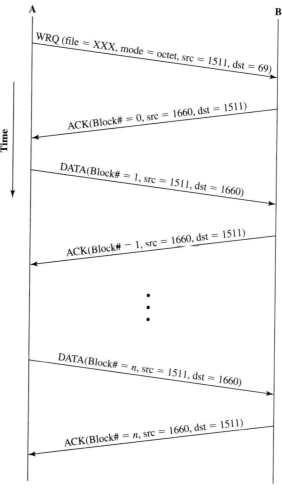

Figure 2.22   Example TFTP Operation

the TFTP application. The source port number is a TID selected by A, in this case 1511. System B is prepared to accept the file and so responds with an ACK with a block number of 0. In the UDP header, the destination port is 1511, which enables the UDP entity at A to route the incoming packet to the TFTP module, which can match this TID with the TID in the WRQ. The source port is a TID selected by B for this file transfer, in this case 1660.

Following this initial exchange, the file transfer proceeds. The transfer consists of one or more data packets from A, each of which is acknowledged by B. The final data packet contains less than 512 bytes of data, which signals the end of the transfer.

Errors and Delays

If TFTP operates over a network or internet (as opposed to a direct data link), it is possible for packets to be lost. Because TFTP operates over UDP, which does not provide a reliable delivery service, there needs to be some mechanism in TFTP to deal with lost packets. TFTP uses the common technique of a timeout mechanism. Suppose that A sends a packet to B that requires an acknowledgment (i.e., any packet other than duplicate ACKs and those used for termination). When A has transmitted the packet, it starts a timer. If the timer expires before the acknowledgment is received from B, A retransmits the same packet. If in fact the original packet was lost, then the retransmission will be the first copy of this packet received by B. If the original packet was not lost but the acknowledgment from B was lost, then B will receive two copies of the same packet from A and simply acknowledges both copies. Because of the use of block numbers, this causes no confusion. The only exception to this rule is for duplicate ACK packets. The second ACK is ignored.

Syntax, Semantics, and Timing

In Section 2.1, it was mentioned that the key features of a protocol can be classified as syntax, semantics, and timing. These categories are easily seen in TFTP. The formats of the various TFTP packets form the **syntax** of the protocol. The **semantics** of the protocol are shown in the definitions of each of the packet types and the error codes. Finally, the sequence in which packets are exchanged, the use of block numbers, and the use of timers are all aspects of the **timing** of TFTP.

PART TWO

Applications

art Two looks at a range of applications that operate over the Internet.

CHAPTER 3

TRADITIONAL APPLICATIONS

A conversation forms a two-way communication link; there is a measure of symmetry between the two parties, and messages pass to and fro. There is a continual stimulus-response, cyclic action; remarks call up other remarks, and the behavior of the two individuals becomes concerted, co-operative, and directed toward some goal. This is true communication.

—On Human Communication,
Colin Cherry

KEY POINTS

- Telnet is a remote logon facility based on the use of a virtual terminal protocol and a network virtual terminal. In essence, both a real terminal's characteristics and a host's representation of a terminal are mapped into a network virtual terminal for data transfer.

- Telnet defines an option negotiation procedure to enable a user and server to agree on enhancements to the default network virtual terminal. Numerous options have been defined in RFCs.

- FTP is a basic file transfer protocol that supports the transfer of files among systems with different characteristics.

- FTP defines a number of data types, file structures, and transfer modes to provide interoperability.

- The most widely used protocol for the transmission of electronic mail is SMTP. SMTP assumes that the content of the message is a simple text block. The MIME standard expands SMTP to support transmission of multimedia information.

This chapter examines three applications that have traditionally been considered mandatory elements of TCP/IP and that were designated as military standards, along with TCP and IP, by the U.S. Department of Defense (DoD): SMTP, FTP, and TELNET.

Refer to the figure on the inside back cover to see the position within the TCP/IP suite of the protocols discussed in this chapter.

3.1 TERMINAL ACCESS—TELNET

The oldest Internet application is Telnet. In its original form, it was the first application demonstrated on the four-node ARPANET deployed in 1969. It took two years to expand the protocol sufficiently to make it truly useful and to work out all the bugs. The first published version of Telnet was RFC 97, "First Cut at a Proposed Telnet Protocol," February 1971. But it wasn't until 1983 that Telnet in its final form was issued as RFC 854 and RFC 855. Telnet is worth studying not only because it is still a useful Internet application, but because it is a pioneering effort in dealing with issues related to application-level protocol design.

Remote Terminal Access and Network Virtual Terminals

An early motivation for data networks like ARPANET was to provide remote access to interactive systems across the network, that is, to allow a terminal user at site A to interact with a process at host B as if it were a local user. The user's local host makes a connection to the remote, target host where the user logs on and is treated like a local user.

Telnet was designed in an era when users interacted with computers by means of so-called dumb terminals. A dumb terminal consists of a keyboard and screen together with primitive communications hardware that enables a stream of character data to be transmitted in each direction. Typically, multiple dumb terminals connect to a host computer, which might be a time-sharing system or a terminal controller that in turn connects to a host computer or a network (Figure 3.1a). The local host computer or terminal controller can establish a connection to a remote host so that the local user can log on to and use the remote host. The challenge in designing Telnet for such an environment is that hosts generally handle only directly connected terminals with a particular set of terminal characteristics, such as the mapping

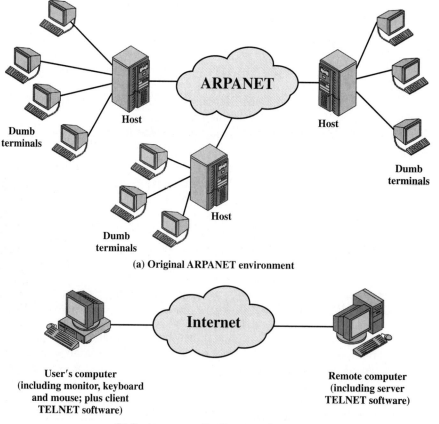

(a) Original ARPANET environment

(b) Contemporary client/server environment

Figure 3.1 Telnet Operational Environment

between special keys and function like Break or Transmit. The early spectrum of host systems and terminals connected to ARPANET varied in many ways. Physically, the terminals had varying keyboards, character sets, display sizes, line lengths, and speeds. Logically, the interaction between terminal and host were governed by the host software, each with its own ways of stopping and starting processes, controlling the flow of output, and so on.

The approach taken by the Telnet designers to deal with this environment was to develop a **virtual terminal protocol (VTP)**. The principal purpose of a VTP is to transform the characteristics of a real terminal into a standardized form, referred to as a **network virtual terminal (NVT)**. An NVT is an imaginary device with a well-defined set of characteristics. Using the VTP, a connection is set up between a terminal user and a remote host. Both sides generate data and control signals in their native language. Each side translates its native data and control signals into those of the NVT and translates incoming NVT traffic into its native data and control signals (Figure 3.2).

For any VTP, there are basically four phases of operation:

- **Connection management:** Includes connection request and termination. For Telnet, TCP is used to set up a connection.

- **Negotiation:** Used to determine a mutually agreeable set of characteristics between the two correspondents. Whereas the NVT has a wide range of capabilities and features, a particular real terminal may be more limited. Furthermore, the NVT has a number of options, such as line length, to be negotiated.

- **Control:** Exchange of control information and commands (e.g., end of line, interrupt process).

- **Data:** Transfer of data between two correspondents.

For Telnet, both control and data characters are conveyed in a single character stream.

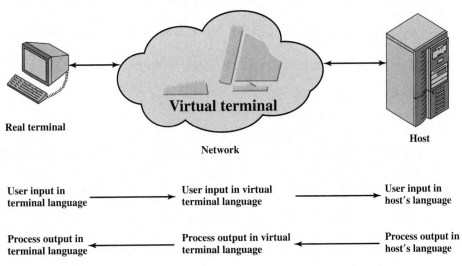

Figure 3.2 Network Virtual Terminal Concept

Although the original environment for which Telnet was designed is of little relevance today, Telnet continues to be used and is included in most implementations of the TCP/IP suite; in particular it is available on PCs for use over the Internet. Such an environment is shown in Figure 3.1b. In this environment, the user's computer includes Telnet software that includes the Telnet protocol and mapping software for translation between the user's keyboard/display and the NVT. Unfortunately, because of the sequential character-oriented nature of Telnet, it cannot support a graphical interface or any two-dimensional capability.

A number of services that provide Telnet access are available on the Internet. Figure 3.3 shows an example session between a personal computer and the United States Library of Congress using Telnet. The address of the Library of Congress server is locis.loc.gov. The user, at his or her PC, opens the Telnet application and then types telnet locis.loc.gov to connect. The server responds with a menu of options, each with a number, and then the prompt, Choice. The user then enters a number for one of the options, the server responds and then prompts again. This is typical of a Telnet session.

Telnet Network Virtual Terminal

The Telnet designers specified a default NVT that is the lowest common denominator of existing systems, so that even simple dumb terminals could use the service. To accommodate systems capable of more sophisticated terminal-type communication, Telnet includes an option negotiation and subnegotiation mechanism, as explained subsequently.

Telnet can be used between two terminals, two processes, or a terminal and a process, using a TCP connection. If the communicating entity is a process, a **server Telnet** module is needed to convert between the NVT representation and the process representation. If the communicating entity is a terminal, a **user Telnet** module is needed to map the characteristics of the terminal into those of the NVT.

The Telnet NVT is a bidirectional character device with a display and keyboard. The display responds to incoming data and the keyboard produces outgoing data, which is sent over the Telnet connection, and if echoes are desired, to the NVT's display as well.

The keyboard can generate representations of all 128 ASCII codes. The user may also instruct the NVT keyboard to generate and send the user control signals listed in Table 3.1.

Telnet Transfer Protocol

Although TCP is capable of full-duplex transmission over a connection (data transmitted in both directions at the same time), Telnet data is sent in half-duplex mode (one direction at a time). In the terminal-to-process direction, the newline character signifies the end of user input. In the process-to-terminal direction, the Telnet Go Ahead command is used for same purpose. When these signals occur in the data stream, the receiver may begin sending data. Because the underlying TCP connection is full duplex, control signals may be sent at any time regardless of the current data transmission direction. This allows the terminal user, for example, to send an Abort Output when the process is sending data to the printer.

```
telnet locis.loc.gov
Trying 140.147.254.3 . . .
Connected to locis.loc.gov.
Escape character is '^]'.
                L O C I S: LIBRARY OF CONGRESS INFORMATION SYSTEM

            To make a choice: type a number, then press ENTER

  1 Copyright Information          - files available and up-to-date

  2 Braille and Audio             - files frozen mid-August 1999

  3 Federal Legislation           - files frozen December 1998

*     *     *     *     *     *     *     *     *     *     *     *     *     *     *

            The LC Catalog Files are available at:
                http://lcweb.loc.gov/catalog/

*     *     *     *     *     *     *     *     *     *     *     *     *     *     *

  8 Searching Hours and Basic Search Commands
  9 Library of Congress General Information
 10 Library of Congress Fast Facts

 12 Comments and Logoff
    Choice:
  9
                  LIBRARY OF CONGRESS GENERAL INFORMATION

LC is a research library serving Congress, the federal government, the library
community world-wide, the US creative community, and any researchers beyond high
school level or age. On-site researchers request materials by filling out request
slips in LC's reading rooms; requesters must present a photo i.d. Staff are avail-
able for assistance in all public reading rooms.

--------------------------------------------------------------------------------

The following phone numbers offer information about hours and other services:

General Research Info:      202-707-6500   Reading Room Hours:        202-707-6400
Exhibits/Tours/Gift Shop:   202-707-8000   Location/Parking:          202-707-4700
Copyright Information:      202-707-3000   Cataloging Products:       202-707-6100
Copyright Forms:            202-707-9100   Cataloging Products fax:   202-707-1334

--------------------------------------------------------------------------------

For information on interlibrary loan, see: http://lcweb.loc.gov/rr/loan/
 12    Return to LOCIS MENU screen
Choice:
```

Figure 3.3   A Telnet Session

Data are sent as a stream of 8-bit bytes. There is no other formatting to the data. Control signals and other nondata information are sent as Telnet commands. These commands occur as strings of bytes embedded in the data byte stream. There are commands corresponding to the user control signals referenced in the preceding subsection. There are also commands used between the Telnet processes as part of the transfer protocol and for option negotiation and subnegotiation. These are shown in Table 3.1.

Table 3.1 Telnet Commands

Command	Code	Explanation
Interpret as Command (IAC)	255	Interpret following byte as command.
User Control Signals		
Are You There (AYT)	246	Requests a visible or audible signal that the remote side is still operating.
Interrupt Process (IP)	244	Interrupts the operation of a remote process. This function is invoked whan a user believes the process is looping, or when an unwanted process has been activated.
Abort Output (AO)	245	Requests that the current user process be allowed to run to completion, but that no more output be sent to the user's terminal. This function also clears any output already produced but not yet printed on the user's terminal.
Erase character (EC)	247	Requests that the previous character be erased from the data stream.
Erase Line (EL)	248	Requests that the previous line (from the current character back to the last newline) be erased from the data stream.
Break (BRK)	243	This code provides a signal outside the ASCII character set to indicate the Break or Attention signal available on many systems.
Process-to-Process Commands		
Go Ahead (GA)	249	The line turnaround signal for half-duplex data transfer.
Data Mark (DM)	242	A stream synchronizing character for use with the Sync signal.
Subnegotiation Begin (SB)	250	Begin subnegotiation command.
Subnegotiation End (SE)	240	End of subnegotiation parameters
WILL, WONT, DO, DONT	251–254	Negotiation messages.

The Interpret as Command (IAC) character (encoded as all 1s, or decimal 255) precedes each Telnet command in the data stream to distinguish it from user or process data. (If a data value of 255 is part of the data stream, it must also be preceded by an IAC.) Thus, simple Telnet commands are 2 bytes long. Option negotiation commands are 3 bytes long. The third byte is the option identifier. Option subnegotiation commands vary in length, but they always begin with the 3-byte sequence (IAC SB option-id) and end with the 2-byte sequence (IAC SE).

The Telnet data transfer protocol minimizes transmission overhead because it does not require extra bytes for message headers. However, processing overhead is high because both User Telnet and Server Telnet must process the transmitted stream one character at a time to perform the data translation (between NVT and native) and to scan for Telnet commands. This is the classic tradeoff between message and stream protocols.

Telnet Synch Mechanism

Before discussing the Telnet Synch mechanism, we need to provide a brief explanation of the TCP urgent data pointer facility. TCP provides a means to communicate to the receiver of data that at some point further along in the data stream than the receiver is currently reading there is urgent data. TCP does not attempt to define what the user specifically does upon being notified of pending urgent data, but the general notion is that the receiving process will take action to process the urgent data quickly. The urgent pointer mechanism exploits the buffering property of TCP. In essence, TCP sends data across a connection in segments. As the destination TCP entity receives the segments, it strips off the TCP header and buffers the data. Ultimately, the buffered data are passed on to the application, but this may not happen immediately or at least may not happen as rapidly as new data arrives. Thus, at any given time, when a TCP segment is received, there may be older data in the buffer awaiting delivery to the destination application. If an incoming segment includes an urgent indication, then TCP should immediately alert the application that there is urgent data waiting. The exact method of alert depends on the operating system and the TCP implementation. In any case, the urgent alert should cause the application to go into an "urgent" mode of operation to clear the buffer as rapidly as possible.

The Telnet synch signal is designed to allow the user to communicate some urgent command to a server process, such as an Interrupt Process (IP) or Abort Output (AO) command. Normally, when a terminal is directly connected to a time-sharing system, the terminal user can press an abort or interrupt key and immediately cause the local process to respond. However, when a terminal is connected to a computer across a network, there is necessarily a time delay, possibly significant, before the interrupt or abort signal reaches the process. The Telnet synch signal partially alleviates this problem.

The Telnet synch signal consists of the Telnet command Data Mark (DM) transmitted in a TCP segment with TCP urgent notification. To send an urgent command, such as AO, or IP, Telnet sends the urgent command followed by the DM sequence (IAC DM) as urgent data. When the destination Telnet receives a TCP urgent notification, it should immediately scan the data stream for Telnet commands as normal, but discard all data. Telnet commands are handled normally. This continues until the DM is found, when processing returns to normal.

Telnet Options

Options enable the two sides of a Telnet connection to use capabilities beyond those provided by the default NVT. Option negotiation allows one side of a Telnet connection to request an option; the other side may either accept or reject that request. If the option is accepted, it is put into effect immediately. Negotiation can take place at any time after the connection is established. In practice, implementations negotiate options as soon as the connection is opened, in order to get the best possible service through the connection.

Telnet options are not part of the Telnet protocol specification, but are generally published in RFCs and assigned identifiers in those RFCs. Some of these are shown in Table 3.2. The options are divided into three major categories. The first category includes options that change, enhance, or refine the characteristics of the NVT.

Table 3.2   Assigned Telnet Options

Option ID	Name	RFC #	Category	Option ID	Name	RFC #	Category
0	Binary transmission	856	2	17	Extended ASCII	698	2
1	Echo	857	1	18	Logout	727	3
2	Reconnection		3	19	Byte macro	732	2
3	Suppress Go Ahead	858	2	20	Data entry terminal	735	1,2
4	Approx Message Size Negotiation	—	2	21	SUPDUP	736, 734	3
5	Status	859	3	22	SUPDUP output	749	3
6	Timing Mark	860	2	23	Send location	779	3
7	Remote controlled trans and echo	726	1	24	Terminal type	930	3
8	Output line width	—	1	25	End of record	885	2
9	Output page size	—	1	26	TACACS user id	927	3
10	Output carriage-return disposition	652	1	27	Output marking	933	3
11	Output horizontal tab stops	653	1	28	Terminal location number	947	3
12	Output horizontal tab disposition	654	1	29	3270 regime	1041	1,2
13	Output formfeed disposition	655	1	30	X.3 PAD	1053	1,2
14	Output vertical tabstops	656	1	31	Negotiate about window size	1073	1
15	Output vertical tab disposition	657	1	32	Send terminal speed information	1079	1
16	Output linefeed disposition	658	1	33	Remote flow control	1080	2

For example, options 8 through 16 allow further definition of the NVT printer char-acteristics. The first category also includes options that define a new virtual terminal to replace the NVT, such as option 20. Options in the second category change the transfer protocol. For example, the Suppress Go Ahead option (3) requests that the GA command not be used. This would make the data transfer protocol full duplex instead of half duplex. Options that define new commands or control features of the transfer protocol are also included in the second category. The End of Record op-tion (25), for example, defines a Telnet command to indicate an end of user input to the process. The third category of options allows other information that is not part of the user data or the transfer protocol to be defined and passed over the connec-tion. This category includes the Status option (5) that requests the remote side to send the status of all options that have been negotiated on the connection.

Most Telnet options can be put into effect on one side of the connection or for one direction of the data transfer without affecting the operation of the other side. For these options, two separate negotiations must take place if the option is desired on both sides of the connection. For example, the End of Record option may be ne-gotiated for the terminal-to-process direction of data transfer. This would enable an EOR Telnet command to indicate the end of user input to the process. It could be separately negotiated in the other direction to define a similar character to signal the end of process data being sent to the printer.

Option Negotiation

Either side may initiate negotiation for an option to be put into effect on either side of the connection. For example, the User Telnet side may initiate negotiation about its own preference for echoing, or Server Telnet may make the request. Negotiation can ask that a new option be enabled for the connection or that a currently enabled option be disabled.

Implementations must obey the following rules to provide correct option negotiation:

1. You may always reject a request to enable an option.
2. You must always accept a request to disable an option.
3. Options are not enabled until the negotiation is complete.
4. Never negotiate (either request or respond) about something that is already true; that is, do not initiate or respond to a request to initiate an option that is already in effect.

There are four option negotiation commands: WILL, WONT, DO, DONT. The interpretation of these commands depends on the context of the negotiation, as il-lustrated in Figure 3.4. The protocol was designed to be unambiguous if both sides make the same request and the messages pass each other on the network. For ex-ample, if side A wishes side B to implement an option, A issues a DO command; if B agrees, it responds with a WILL command. If side B wishes to implement an option on its side, it issues a WILL command; if A agrees, it responds with a DO command. If both A and B make the request for B to implement on option at about the same time, then A issues a DO command and B issues a WILL command; these com-mands cross in the network and both sides receive a response to their command.

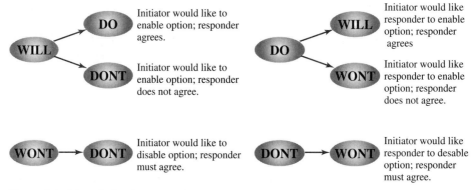

Figure 3.4 Negotiation Messages in Telnet

The actions taken to enable or disable an option depend on the particular option. Some options are defined so that option negotiation determines first if both sides can support the option. Then further negotiation, using Telnet subnegotiation commands, is done to exchange more information. The Terminal Type option works this way. The subnegotiation protocol (i.e., the format, sequencing, and interpretation of the subnegotiation messages) is defined as part of the option specification.

The Longevity of Telnet

Telnet is older than most of its users. [KHAR98a] attributes this remarkable stability to two aspects of its design. First is Telnet's simplicity. RFC 854 is a mere 15 pages, whereas HTTP, described in Chapter 4, is 176 pages. Telnet has a simple mission and fulfills it with a straightforward protocol. But more important is Telnet's evolvability. Option negotiation was a brilliant design feature that did not become common in IETF protocol designs until the late 1980s. The option negotiation feature enables Telnet to evolve to meet new demands without the need for endless new versions of the basic protocol. As of this writing, there are over 100 RFCs that describe Telnet and its options, almost 3% of the entire body of RFCs, with the most recent of these being RFC 2953, Telnet Encryption, dated September 2000. This prolific record indicates Telnet's vitality and continued relevance.

3.2 FILE TRANSFER—FTP

As with Telnet, modern FTP evolved from an era of radically diverse systems. Thus, FTP deals with a variety of commands, transfer modes, and data representations, many of which are now obsolete.

The FTP standard, RFC 959, lists the following objectives:

1. Promote sharing of files (computer programs and/or data).
2. Encourage indirect or implicit (via programs) use of remote computers.
3. Shield a user from variations in file storage systems among hosts.
4. Transfer data reliably and efficiently.

Implicit in these objectives is that FTP deals with file systems, rather than just files. A single file can be viewed as simply a set of bits tagged with a name. This is the view of the Trivial File Transfer Protocol (TFTP, described in Appendix 2A). For TFTP, file transfer is a simple task: Send a request header to read or write a file with some name, then stream the bits across. A mere 11 pages suffice to define the protocol. FTP, on the other hand, considers file systems, and thus deals with metadata such as file pathnames, file organization, access control, and data representation. Accordingly, RFC 959 is 69 pages long.

The FTP Model

As with Telnet, FTP involves a User FTP entity and a Server FTP entity. The host that initiates the transfer is the user. The user chooses the name of the file and the options to be used in the transfer. The server accepts or rejects the transfer request based on its file system protection criteria and on the options requested. If the transfer request is accepted, the server is responsible for establishing and managing the transfer.

FTP operates on two levels (Figure 3.5). To begin operation, an FTP user protocol module establishes a TCP connection with an FTP server protocol module. This connection is used to exchange control information in the form of FTP commands and replies. When a file transfer is agreed, a second TCP connection is established, and the file data is transferred over that connection; this can be considered a data transfer protocol level. Both levels of FTP interact with the TCP/IP software on the local system for setting up TCP connections. Both levels of FTP also interact with the local file management system software to access the local file system and its

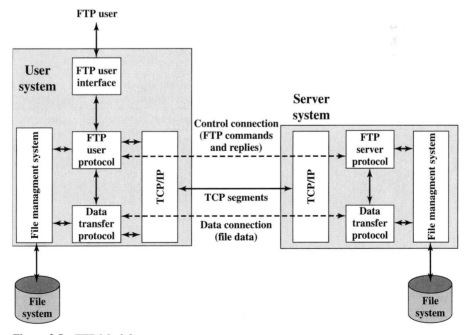

Figure 3.5 FTP Model

files. Finally, there is an FTP user interface that enables either a human user or a program to access User FTP.

The FTP commands specify the parameters for the data connection (data port, transfer mode, representation type, and structure) and the nature of file system operation (store, retrieve, append, delete, etc.). The commands are listed in Table 3.3.

Table 3.3 FTP Commands

Command (parameters)	Description
Access Control	
USER username	Identifies the user to the remote host.
PASS password	Authenticates the user.
ACCT account-information	Identifies the user's account.
REIN	Terminates a user and clears all buffers; ready for new USER command.
Session	
REST marker	Restart. Skips over the file to the specified data marker.
ABOR	Aborts previous FTP service command and associated data transfer.
SITE string	Sends information to the foreign host that is used to provide services specific to that host.
SYST	Used to find out the type of operating system at the server.
STAT [pathname]	Causes a status response to be sent over the control connection.
QUIT	Terminates the user and closes the control connection.
Transfer Parameters	
PORT host-port	Specifies the data port to be used in data connections.
PASV	Requests the server to listen on a data port and wait for a connection, rather than initiate the connection.
TYPE type-code	Specifies the representation type.
STRU structure-code	Specifies the file structure.
MODE mode-code	Specifies the data transfer mode.
Directory Navigation	
CWD pathname	Change working directory.
CDUP	Change to parent directory.
PWD	Print working directory.
MKD pathname	Create directory.
RMD pathname	Remove directory.
SMNT	Mount a different file system data structure.

(continues on next page)

Table 3.3   (continued)

Command (parameters)	Description
FTP Service	
RETR pathname	Retrieve. Transfer file from server to user.
STOR pathname	Store. Transfer file from user to server. If the filename specified in the pathhame already exists it is replaced.
STOU	Store unique. Transfer file from user to server. Server creates uniques filename and returns this to user.
APPE pathname	Append. Transfer data from user to server. If the filename specified in the pathhame already exists, append data to existing file. Otherwise, create new file.
DELE pathname	Delete file.
ALLO integer [R integer]	Allocate. May be required by some servers to reserve sufficient storage. The first argument is the number of bytes. The second, optional, argument is the page or record size.
LIST [pathname]	If pathname specifies a directory, server transfers list of files in directory. If pathname specifies a file, server transfers current information on the file.
NLST [pathname]	Name list. Causes server to transfer a directory listing.
RNFR pathname	Rename from. Specifies old pathname of file to be renamed. Must be followed by RNTO command.
RNTO pathname	Rename to. Specifies the new pathname of a file to be renamed.
HELP [string]	Causes server to send information regarding its implementation status. Optional argument is a command name for which the server returns more specific information.
NOOP	No operation. Server sends an OK reply.

The user data transfer protocol should "listen" on the specified data port, and the server initiates the data connection and data transfer in accordance with the specified parameters.

An interesting point is that FTP uses the Telnet protocol on the control connection. This can be achieved in two ways: First, the FTP user protocol or the FTP server protocol may implement the rules of the Telnet Protocol directly in their own procedures; or, second, the FTP user protocol or the FTP server protocol may make use of the existing Telnet module in the system.

Overview of a Transfer

The following example shows a simple transfer. No errors are encountered and the details of the option specification are not explored. We assume that a user program has invoked User FTP; the user supplies the address of the remote system to which access is desired. In response, the FTP user protocol opens a TCP connection, called the control connection, to the remote host. All commands and responses will pass across this control connection (Figure 3.6a).

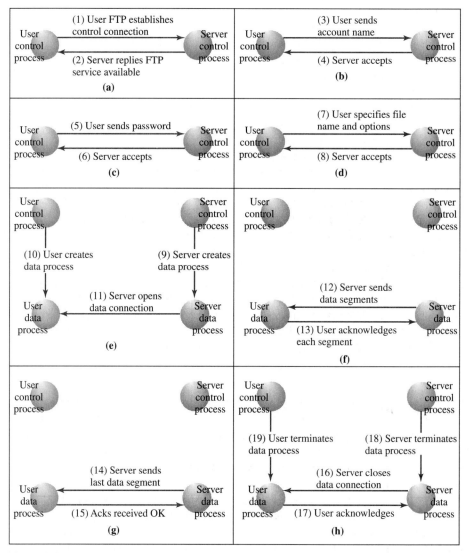

Figure 3.6 Overview of an FTP Transfer

The access control process is shown in Figures 3.6b and 3.6c. The user (or user program) supplies an account name and password to the local system, which in turn forms the FTP commands and sends them to the server. In this case, the account name and password are valid, and are accepted. FTP takes no part in the actual user authorization process. It simply provides a conduit by which the information can be passed to whatever mechanism is used in the server's file management system to control access.

Next, User FTP provides the specific details of the transfer (Figure 3.6d): file name, direction of transfer (get or put), and details of file type and transfer mode. This is done is a sequence of commands (not shown in Figure 3.6d). As with access control, the user might not see all the details of this step. It is the User FTP program that interprets the user's intention and sends a series of FTP commands across the control connection. When all commands are received and acknowledged, the transfer will proceed. Both ends are now in agreement that the file may be transferred in the specified direction, using the data type, file type, and transfer mode given by the FTP user.

Figure 3.6e shows the first step of the data transfer. Logically, each side creates a separate process to manage the data transfer. Server FTP opens a second TCP connection, the data connection, back to User FTP.

Figure 3.6f indicates the manner in which the data transfer proceeds. The file is transferred as a sequence of TCP segments. In this example, the file is transferred from the server to the user. The server and user work together, using the TCP error and flow control mechanisms of the data connection to read data from the source file, encapsulate an appropriate number of bytes in each TCP segment, and write the data in received segments into the destination file at the user host. TCP is responsible for retransmission of segment when it detects an error and for metering the flow out of the source and onto the TCP connection.

When the server has fetched the last day byte for the source file, it sends off the last TCP segment and then initiates a close of the data connection (Figures 3.6g and 3.6h). The user FTP process takes this normal close as a signal that the transfer is completed, and then both user and server terminate the data connection. The control connection remains open and can be used to control another data transfer, over a new data connection, or it may close at this point.

Options

The FTP design assumes that files are objects in a computer's mass storage memory that share a few properties regardless of the machine type. Files have symbolic names that allow them to be uniquely identified with a particular file system or directory. A file has an owner and has protection against unauthorized access or modification by others. A file may be created, read from (copied from), written into, or deleted. Within this fairly simple framework, FTP contrives to support the movement of files among diverse computers over various data networks. To support the needs of specific computers and operating systems, FTP provides a mechanism for negotiating a transfer's options in three dimensions: data type, file type, and transfer mode. It is the job of the system programmer on each system to determine how a particular file on the system can be mapped into one of the standard file types, using one of the standard data types, and transferred using a standard mode, such that it is useful at the destination.

Data Types There are four defined data types: ASCII, EBCDIC, image, and logical byte size. The first two types are most suitable for representing text files. Text files are normally stored as a string of characters, and on most machines, the 8-bit ASCII character code is used. Thus, if the **ASCII** option is used, no character code conversion is required at either end in most cases. The **EBCDIC** option is appropriate when both machines are IBM hosts using the EBCDIC character code.

Files of either ASCII or EBCDIC type may have a further specification of how they are presented to a line or page printer. Because some systems find it convenient to include printer control characters within the text to be printed, three choices are offered:

- **Nonprint:** Suitable for files not destined for a line printer.
- **Telnet formatting:** Embedded control characters (carriage return, line feed, newline, vertical tab, and form feed) are to be extracted from the data stream and used in page formatting.
- **Character control formatting:** This option uses formatting conventions from the FORTRAN programming language.

The **image** type is useful for exchanging arbitrary files between two machines of the same type with the same operating system. An image type transfer is simply a bit-by-bit replication of the file from the source machine on the target machine. The **logical byte size** type is used when there is a data unit size that must be preserved. This type specifies the size of a byte, which need not be 8 bits. This type is most often used to ensure that executable program images compiled on one machine but sent to and stored on a second machine can be correctly interpreted and manipulated on the second machine.

File Types FTP defines three file types: file structure, record structure, and page structure. The purpose of offering several file types is to promote a convenient and efficient interface to the file system of the source and destination computers. Because there are only three defined file types, it is not possible to address the idiosyncrasies of all existing operating systems. But this set of options seems well suited to the majority of machines. The file types are as follows:

- **File structure:** This type assumes that the file is simply a string of bytes (defined by the data type option) that terminates in an end of file marker (Figure 3.7a). Most transfers use this type.
- **Record structure:** This type is used when it is more convenient to treat the file as a sequence of records (Figure 3.7b). A record might be the natural size used by the file system disk interface hardware controller. The record structure type causes transmission of individual records, separated by the standard End of Record marker for the specified data type.
- **Page structure:** This type is used for files that are not stored in a contiguous fashion on the disk and in which this page structure needs to be preserved across the transfer.

Transmission Modes While the data and file types address the needs of the source and destination host operating systems, the transmission mode options are provided to optimize the use of the communications network. Three modes are defined.

The **stream mode** is the simplest and is the default mode. In stream mode, the unmodified, raw data are sent over the data connection. Because there is no specialized processing of the data at either end, this mode imposes the least computational burden on the user and server systems. There is no restriction on the file type used with stream mode. For record-structure files, a 2-byte control code is used to indicate end of record and end of file.

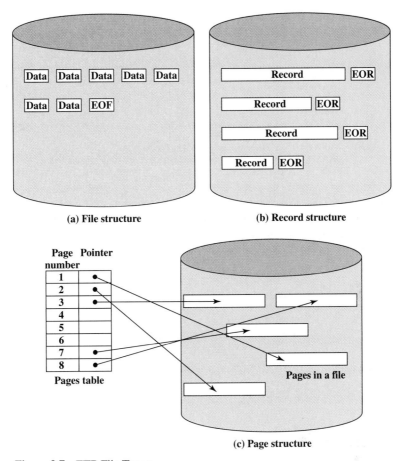

Figure 3.7 FTP File Types

The **block mode** provides for restarting a failed or interrupted transfer. If a fault or interrupt occurs, a transfer can be picked up where it left off, rather then having to retransmit an entire file. When this mode is accepted, the source encapsulates the data for transfer into blocks with the format shown in Figure 3.8a. Each block begins with a header consisting of two fields. The Descriptor field may indicate zero of more of the following:

- **Last block in record:** The record structure is allowed but not required for block mode transmission. Any data type may be used. If the record structure is used, then each record consists of one or more blocks.

- **Last block in file:** Signifies end of file.

- **Suspect data:** The data being transferred may contain errors and is not reliable. This code is not intended for error control within FTP. It is motivated by the desire of sites exchanging certain types of data (e.g., seismic or weather data) to send and receive all the data despite local errors (such as "magnetic tape read errors"), but to indicate in the transmission that certain portions are suspect).

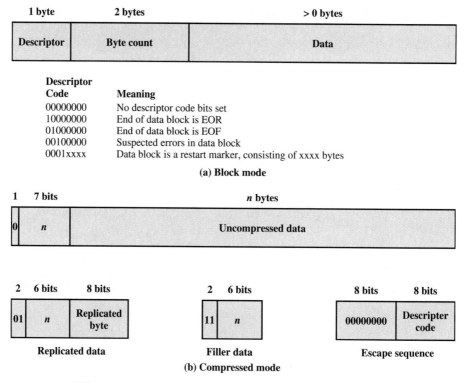

Figure 3.8 FTP Transmission Mode Formats

- **Restart marker:** This block consists of a string of printable characters used by the source to mark a checkpoint in the data stream. The receiver marks the corresponding position in the data stream and returns this information to the sender. The source and destination may, if interrupted, restart the transfer form the last correctly received restart marker. The specification does not establish any specific policy for how checkpointing and restart operations should be conducted.

The Count field in the header indicates the total length of the data block in bytes, thus marking the beginning of the next data block (there are no filler bits).

The **compressed mode** provides a way to improve efficiency of the transfer by allowing the source to squeeze sequences of the same character into a shorter coded sequence. Four different formats are involved in compressed mode (Figure 3.8b). Each format begins with an 8-bit header; the formats are as follows:

- **Uncompressed data:** The header indicates the number of uncompressed bytes to follow; up to 127 bytes can be sent before another header is required.

- **Replicated byte:** When the source file contains a sequence of bytes with the same value, the repeated bytes are extracted and replaced with the replicated byte format. The 2-byte sequence allows repetition of up to 63 of the specified bytes to be defined. The destination FTP entity must replace the replicated byte format with the specified number of the specified character.

- **Filler string:** A further compression is provided for the special character (typically the space character) that appears frequently in text files. The filler string format indicates that up to 63 of these filler characters are to be inserted at the destination.
- **Escape sequence:** The escape sequence consists of a byte of all zeros followed by a descriptor code byte, as defined in the block mode.

3.3 ELECTRONIC MAIL—SMTP AND MIME

The most heavily used application in virtually any distributed system is electronic mail. The Simple Mail Transfer Protocol (SMTP) has always been the workhorse of the TCP/IP suite. However, SMTP has traditionally been limited to the delivery of simple text messages. In recent years, there has been a demand for the capability of delivery mail containing various types of data, including voice, images, and video clips. To satisfy this requirement, a new electronic mail standard, which builds on SMTP, has been defined: the Multi-Purpose Internet Mail Extension (MIME). In this section, we first examine SMTP and then look at MIME.

Simple Mail Transfer Protocol (SMTP)

SMTP is the standard protocol for transferring mail between hosts in the TCP/IP suite; it is defined in RFC 821.

Although messages transferred by SMTP usually follow the format defined in RFC 822, described later, SMTP is not concerned with the format or content of messages themselves, with two exceptions. This concept is often expressed by saying that SMTP uses information written on the *envelope* of the mail (message header) but does not look at the contents (message body) of the envelope. The two exceptions are as follows:

1. SMTP standardizes the message character set as 7-bit ASCII.
2. SMTP adds log information to the start of the delivered message that indicates the path the message took.

Basic Electronic Mail Operation Figure 3.9 illustrates the overall flow of mail in a typical system. Although much of this activity is outside the scope of SMTP, the figure illustrates the context within which SMTP typically operates.

To begin, mail is created by a user agent program in response to user input. Each created message consists of a header that includes the recipient's e-mail address and other information, and a body containing the message to be sent. These messages are then queued in some fashion and provided as input to an SMTP Sender program, which is typically an always-present server program on the host.

Although the structure of the outgoing mail queue will differ depending on the host's operating system, each queued message conceptually has two parts:

1. The message text, consisting of
   - The RFC 822 header: This constitutes the message envelope and includes an indication of the intended recipient or recipients.
   - The body of the message, composed by the user.
2. A list of mail destinations.

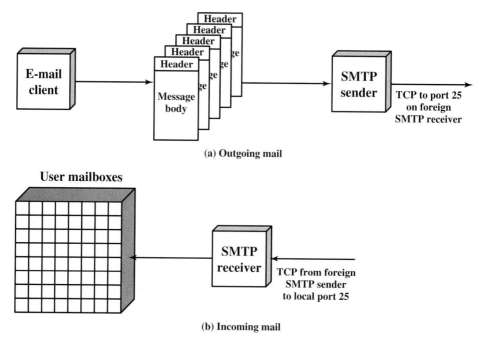

(a) Outgoing mail

(b) Incoming mail

Figure 3.9 SMTP Mail Flow

The list of mail destinations for the message is derived by the user agent from the 822 message header. In some cases, the destination or destinations are literally specified in the message header. In other cases, the user agent may need to expand mailing list names, remove duplicates, and replace mnemonic names with actual mailbox names. If any blind carbon copies (BCCs) are indicated, the user agent needs to prepare messages that conform to this requirement. The basic idea is that the multiple formats and styles preferred by humans in the user interface are re-placed by a standardized list suitable for the SMTP send program.

The **SMTP sender** takes messages from the outgoing mail queue and transmits them to the proper destination host via SMTP transactions over one or more TCP connections to port 25 on the target hosts. A host may have multiple SMTP senders active simultaneously if it has a large volume of outgoing mail, and should also have the capability of creating SMTP receivers on demand so that mail from one host cannot delay mail from another.

Whenever the SMTP sender completes delivery of a particular message to one or more users on a specific host, it deletes the corresponding destinations from that message's destination list. When all destinations for a particular message are processed, the message is deleted from the queue. In processing a queue, the SMTP sender can perform a variety of optimizations. If a particular message is sent to multiple users on a single host, the message text need be sent only once. If multiple messages are ready to send to the same host, the SMTP sender can open a TCP connection, transfer the multiple messages, and then close the connection, rather than opening and closing a connection for each message.

The SMTP sender must deal with a variety of errors. The destination host may be unreachable, out of operation, or the TCP connection may fail while mail is being transferred. The sender can requeue the mail for later delivery but give up after some period rather than keep the message in the queue indefinitely. A common error is a faulty destination address, which can occur due to user input error or because the intended destination user has a new address on a different host. The SMTP sender must either redirect the message if possible or return an error notification to the message's originator.

The **SMTP protocol** is used to transfer a message from the SMTP sender to the SMTP receiver over a TCP connection. SMTP attempts to provide reliable operation but does not guarantee to recover from lost messages. SMTP does not return an end-to-end acknowledgment to a message's originator to indicate that a message is successfully delivered to the message's recipient. Error indications are not guaranteed to be returned either. However, the SMTP-based mail system is generally considered reliable.

The **SMTP receiver** accepts each arriving message and either places it in the appropriate user mailbox or copies it to the local outgoing mail queue if forwarding is required. The SMTP receiver must be able to verify local mail destinations and deal with errors, including transmission errors and lack of storage capacity.

The SMTP sender is responsible for a message up to the point where the SMTP receiver indicates that the transfer is complete; however, this simply means that the message has arrived at the SMTP receiver, not that the message has been delivered to and retrieved by the intended final recipient. The SMTP receiver's error-handling responsibilities are generally limited to giving up on TCP connections that fail or are inactive for very long periods. Thus, the sender has most of the error recovery responsibility. Errors during completion indication may cause duplicate, but not lost, messages.

In most cases, messages go directly from the mail originator's machine to the destination machine over a single TCP connection. However, mail will occasionally go through intermediate machines via an SMTP forwarding capability, in which case the message must traverse a series of TCP connections between source and destination. One way for this to happen is for the sender to specify a route to the destination in the form of a sequence of servers. A more common event is forwarding required because a user has moved.

It is important to note that the SMTP protocol is limited to the conversation that takes place between the SMTP sender and the SMTP receiver. SMTP's main function is the transfer of messages, although there are some ancillary functions dealing with mail destination verification and handling. The rest of the mail-handling apparatus depicted in Figure 3.9 is beyond the scope of SMTP and may differ from one system to another.

We now turn to a discussion of the main elements of SMTP.

SMTP Overview The operation of SMTP consists of a series of commands and responses exchanged between the SMTP sender and receiver. The initiative is with the SMTP sender, who establishes the TCP connection. Once the connection is established, the SMTP sender sends commands over the connection to the receiver. Each command generates exactly one reply from the SMTP receiver.

Table 3.4 SMTP Commands

Name	Command Form	Description
HELO	HELO\<SP>\<domain>\<CRLF>	Send identification
MAIL	MAIL\<SP>FROM: \<reverse-path>\<CRLF>	Identifies originator of mail
RCPT	RCPT\<SP>TO:\<forward-path>\<CRLF>	Identifies recipient of mail
DATA	DATA\<CRLF>	Transfer message text
RSET	RSET\<CRLF>	Abort current mail transaction
NOOP	NOOP\<CRLF>	No operation
QUIT	QUIT\<CRLF>	Close TCP connection
SEND	SEND\<SP>FROM: \<reverse-path> \<CRLF>	Send mail to terminal
SOML	SOML\<SP>FROM: \<reverse-path> \<CRLF>	Send mail to terminal if possible; otherwise to mailbox
SAML	SAML\<SP>FROM: \<reverse-path> \<CRLF>	Send mail to terminal and mailbox
VRFY	VRFY\<SP>\<string> \<CRLF>	Confirm user name
EXPN	EXPN\<SP>\<string> \<CRLF>	Return membership of mailing list
HELP	HELP[\<SP>\<string>]\<CRLF>	Send system-specific documentation
TURN	TURN\<CRLF>	Reverse role of sender and receiver

\<CRLF>=carriage return, line feed
\<SP>=space
Square brackets denote optional elements.
Shaded commands are optional in a conformant SMTP implementation.

Table 3.4 lists the **SMTP commands**. Each command consists of a single line of text, beginning with a four-letter command code followed in some cases by an argument field. Most replies are a single-line, although multiple-line replies are possible. The table indicates those commands that all receivers must be able to recognize. The other commands are optional and may be ignored by the receiver.

SMTP replies are listed in Table 3.5. Each reply begins with a three-digit code and may be followed by additional information. The leading digit indicates the category of the reply:

- **Positive Completion reply:** The requested action has been successfully completed. A new request may be initiated.
- **Positive Intermediate reply:** The command has been accepted, but the requested action is being held in abeyance, pending receipt of further information. The sender-SMTP should send another command specifying this information. This reply is used in command sequence groups.
- **Transient Negative Completion reply:** The command was not accepted and the requested action did not occur. However, the error condition is temporary and the action may be requested again.
- **Permanent Negative Completion reply:** The command was not accepted and the requested action did not occur.

Table 3.5   SMTP Replies

Code	Description
Positive Completion Reply	
211	System status, or system help reply
214	Help message (Information on how to use the receiver or the meaning of a particular non-standard command; this reply is useful only to the human user)
220	<domain> Service ready
221	<domain> Service closing transmission channel
250	Requested mail action okay, completed
251	User not local; will forward to <forward-path>
Positive Intermediate Reply	
354	Start mail input; end with <CRLF>.<CRLF>
Transient Negative Completion Reply	
421	<domain> Service not available, losing transmission channel (This may be a reply to any command if the service knows it must shut down)
450	Requested mail action not taken: mailbox unavailable (e.g., mailbox busy)
451	Requested action aborted: local error in processing
452	Requested action not taken: insufficient system storage
Permanent Negative Completion Reply	
500	Syntax error, command unrecognized (This may include errors such as command line too long)
501	Syntax error in parameters or arguments
502	Command not implemented
503	Bad sequence of commands
504	Command parameter not implemented
550	Requested action not taken: mailbox unavailable (e.g., mailbox not found, no access)
551	User not local; please try <forward-path>
552	Requested mail action aborted: exceeded storage allocation
553	Requested action not taken: mailbox name not allowed (e.g., mailbox syntax incorrect)
554	Transaction failed

Basic SMTP operation occurs in three phases: connection setup, exchange of one or more command-response pairs, and connection termination. We examine each phase in turn.

Connection Setup An SMTP sender will attempt to set up a TCP connection with a target host when it has one or more mail messages to deliver to that host. The sequence is quite simple:

1. The sender opens a TCP connection with the receiver.
2. Once the connection is established, the receiver identifies itself with "220 Service Ready".
3. The sender identifies itself with the HELO command.
4. The receiver accepts the sender's identification with "250 OK".

If the mail service on the destination is unavailable, the destination host returns a "421 Service Not Available" reply in step 2 and the process is terminated.

Mail Transfer Once a connection has been established, the SMTP sender may send one or more messages to the SMTP receiver. There are three logical phases to the transfer of a message:

1. A MAIL command identifies the originator of the message.
2. One or more RCPT commands identify the recipients for this message.
3. A DATA command transfers the message text.

The **MAIL command** gives the reverse path, which can be used to report errors. If the receiver is prepared to accept messages from this originator, it returns a "250 OK" reply. Otherwise the receiver returns a reply indicating failure to execute the command (codes 451, 452, 552) or an error in the command (codes 421, 500, 501).

The **RCPT command** identifies an individual recipient of the mail data; multiple recipients are specified by multiple use of this command. A separate reply is returned for each RCPT command, with one of the following possibilities:

1. The receiver accepts the destination with a 250 reply; this indicates that the designated mailbox is on the receiver's system.
2. The destination will require forwarding and the receiver will forward (251).
3. The destination requires forwarding but the receiver will not forward; the sender must resend to the forwarding address (551).
4. A mailbox does not exist for this recipient at this host (550).
5. The destination is rejected due to some other failure to execute (codes 450, 451, 452, 552, 553) or an error in the command (codes 421, 500, 501, 503).

The advantage of using a separate RCPT phase is that the sender will not send the message until it is assured that the receiver is prepared to receive the message for at least one recipient, thereby avoiding the overhead of sending an entire message only to learn that the destination is unknown. Once the SMTP receiver has agreed to receive the mail message for at least one recipient, the SMTP sender uses the **DATA command** to initiate the transfer of the message. If the SMTP receiver is still prepared to receive the message, it returns a 354 message; otherwise the receiver returns a reply indicating failure to execute the command (codes 451, 554) or an error in the command (codes 421, 500, 501, 503). If the 354 reply is returned, the SMTP sender proceeds to send the message over the TCP connection as a sequence of ASCII lines. The end of the message is indicated by a line containing only a period. The SMTP receiver responds with a 250 OK reply if the message is accepted or with the appropriate error code (451, 452, 552, 554).

An example, taken from RFC 821, illustrates the process:

```
S: MAIL FROM:<Smith@Alpha.ARPA>
R: 250 OK

S: RCPT TO:<Jones@Beta.ARPA>
R: 250 OK

S: RCPT TO:<Green@Beta.ARPA>
R: 550 No such user here

S: RCPT TO:<Brown@Beta.ARPA>
R: 250 OK

S: DATA
R: 354 Start mail input; end with <CRLF>.<CRLF>
S: Blah blah blah...
S: ...etc. etc. etc.
S: <CRLF>.<CRLF>
R: 250 OK
```

The SMTP sender is transmitting mail that originates with the user Smith@Alpha.ARPA. The message is addressed to three users on machine Beta.ARPA, namely, Jones, Green, and Brown. The SMTP receiver indicates that it has mailboxes for Jones and Brown but does not have information on Green. Because at least one of the intended recipients has been verified, the sender proceeds to send the text message.

Connection Closing The SMTP sender closes the connection in two steps. First, the sender sends a QUIT command and waits for a reply. The second step is to initiate a TCP close operation for the TCP connection. The receiver initiates its TCP close after sending its reply to the QUIT command.

RFC 822 RFC 822 defines a format for text messages that are sent using electronic mail. The SMTP standard adopts RFC 822 as the format for use in constructing messages for transmission via SMTP. In the RFC 822 context, messages are viewed as having an envelope and contents. The envelope contains whatever information is needed to accomplish transmission and delivery. The contents comprise the object to be delivered to the recipient. The RFC 822 standard applies only to the contents. However, the content standard includes a set of header fields that may be used by the mail system to create the envelope, and the standard is intended to facilitate the acquisition of such information by programs.

An RFC 822 message consists of a sequence of lines of text and uses a general "memo" framework. That is, a message consists of some number of header lines, which follow a rigid format, followed by a body portion consisting of arbitrary text.

A header line usually consists of a keyword, followed by a colon, followed by the keyword's arguments; the format allows a long line to be broken up into several lines. The most frequently used keywords are From, To, Subject, and Date. Here is an example message:

```
Date: Tue, 16 Jan 1996 10:37:17 (EST)
From: "William Stallings" <ws@host.com>
Subject: The Syntax in RFC 822
To: Smith@Other-host.com
Cc: Jones@Yet-Another-Host.com

Hello. This section begins the actual message body, which is delimited
from the message heading by a blank line.
```

Another field that is commonly found in RFC 822 headers is Message-ID. This field contains a unique identifier associated with this message.

Multipurpose Internet Mail Extensions (MIME)

MIME is an extension to the RFC 822 framework that is intended to address some of the problems and limitations of the use of SMTP and RFC 822 for electronic mail. [RODR02] lists the following limitations of the SMTP/822 scheme:

1. SMTP cannot transmit executable files or other binary objects. A number of schemes are in use for converting binary files into a text form that can be used by SMTP mail systems, including the popular UNIX UUencode/UUdecode scheme. However, none of these is a standard or even a de facto standard.
2. SMTP cannot transmit text data that includes national language characters because these are represented by 8-bit codes with values of 128 decimal or higher, and SMTP is limited to 7-bit ASCII.
3. SMTP servers may reject mail messages over a certain size.
4. SMTP gateways that translate between the character codes ASCII and EBCDIC do not use a consistent set of mappings, resulting in translation problems.
5. SMTP gateways to X.400 electronic mail networks cannot handle nontextual data included in X.400 messages.
6. Some SMTP implementations do not adhere completely to the SMTP standards defined in RFC 821. Common problems include the following:
   - Deletion, addition, or reordering of carriage return and linefeed
   - Truncating or wrapping lines longer than 76 characters
   - Removal of trailing white space (tab and space characters)
   - Padding of lines in a message to the same length
   - Conversion of tab characters into multiple space characters

MIME is intended to resolve these problems in a manner that is compatible with existing RFC 822 implementations. The specification is provided in RFCs 2045 through 2049.

Overview The MIME specification includes the following elements:

1. Five new message header fields are defined, which may be included in an RFC 822 header. These fields provide information about the body of the message.
2. A number of content formats are defined, thus standardizing representations that support multimedia electronic mail.
3. Transfer encodings are defined that enable the conversion of any content format into a form that is protected from alteration by the mail system.

In this subsection, we introduce the five message header fields. The next two subsections deal with content formats and transfer encodings.

The five header fields defined in MIME are as follows:

- **MIME-Version:** Must have the parameter value 1.0. This field indicates that the message conforms to the RFCs.
- **Content-Type:** Describes the data contained in the body with sufficient detail that the receiving user agent can pick an appropriate agent or mechanism to present the data to the user or otherwise deal with the data in an appropriate manner.
- **Content-Transfer-Encoding:** Indicates the type of transformation that has been used to represent the body of the message in a way that is acceptable for mail transport.
- **Content-ID:** Used to uniquely identify MIME entities in multiple contexts.
- **Content-Description:** A plain text description of the object with the body; this is useful when the object is not displayable (e.g., audio data).

Any or all of these fields may appear in a normal RFC 822 header. A compliant implementation must support the MIME-Version, Content-Type, and Content-Transfer-Encoding fields; the Content-ID and Content-Description fields are optional and may be ignored by the recipient implementation.

MIME Content Types The bulk of the MIME specification is concerned with the definition of a variety of content types. This reflects the need to provide standardized ways of dealing with a wide variety of information representations in a multimedia environment.

Table 3.6 lists the MIME content types. There are seven different major types of content and a total of 14 subtypes. In general, a content type declares the general type of data, and the subtype specifies a particular format for that type of data.

For the **text type** of body, no special software is required to get the full meaning of the text, aside from support of the indicated character set. The only defined subtype is plain text, which is simply a string of ASCII characters or ISO 8859 characters. An earlier version of the MIME specification included a *richtext* subtype, which allows greater formatting flexibility. It is expected that this subtype will reappear in a later RFC.

The **multipart type** indicates that the body contains multiple, independent parts. The Content-Type header field includes a parameter, called boundary, that defines the delimiter between body parts. This boundary should not appear in any parts of the message. Each boundary starts on a newline and consists of two hyphens followed by the boundary value. The final boundary, which indicates the end of the

Table 3.6 MIME Content Types

Type	Subtype	Description
Text	Plain	Unformatted text; may be ASCII or ISO 8859.
Multipart	Mixed	The different parts are independent but are to be transmitted together. They should be presented to the receiver in the order that they appear in the mail message.
	Parallel	Differs from Mixed only in that no order is defined for delivering the parts to the receiver.
	Alternative	The different parts are alternative versions of the same information. They are ordered in increasing faithfulness to the original and the recipient's mail system should display the "best" version to the user.
	Digest	Similar to Mixed, but the default type/subtype of each part is message/rfc822.
Message	rfc822	The body is itself an encapsulated message that conforms to RFC 822.
	Partial	Used to allow fragmentation of large mail items, in a way that is transparent to the recipient.
	External-body	Contains a pointer to an object that exists elsewhere.
Image	jpeg	The image is in JPEG format, JFIF encoding.
	gif	The image is in GIF format.
Video	mpeg	MPEG format.
Audio	Basic	Single-channel 8-bit ISDN mu-law encoding at a sample rate of 8 kHz.
Application	PostScript	Adobe Postscript.
	octet-stream	General binary data consisting of 8-bit bytes.

last part, also has a suffix of two hyphens. Within each part, there may be an optional ordinary MIME header.

Here is a simple example of a multipart message, containing two parts both consisting of simple text:

```
From: John Smith <js@company.com>
To:  Ned Jones <ned@soft.com>
Subject: Sample message
MIME-Version: 1.0
Content-type: multipart/mixed; boundary="simple boundary"

This is the preamble.  It is to be ignored, though it is a handy place
for mail composers to include an explanatory note to non-MIME confor-
mant readers.
—simple boundary

This is implicitly typed plain ASCII text. It does NOT end with a
linebreak.
—simple boundary
Content-type: text/plain; charset=us-ascii

This is explicitly typed plain ASCII text. It DOES end with a linebreak.

—simple boundary—
This is the epilogue.  It is also to be ignored.
```

There are four subtypes of the multipart type, all of which have the same over-all syntax. The **multipart/mixed subtype** is used when there are multiple independent body parts that need to be bundled in a particular order. For the **multipart/parallel subtype**, the order of the parts is not significant. If the recipient's system is appropriate, the multiple parts can be presented in parallel. For example, a picture or text part could be accompanied by a voice commentary that is played while the picture or text is displayed.

For the **multipart/alternative subtype**, the various parts are different representations of the same information. The following is an example:

```
From: John Smith <js@company.com>
To:  Ned Jones <ned@soft.com>
Subject: Formatted text mail
MIME-Version: 1.0
Content-Type: multipart/alternative; boundary="boundary42"

—boundary42
Content-Type: text/plain; charset=us-ascii

   ...plain text version of message goes here....
—boundary42
Content-Type: text/richtext

   .... RFC 1341 richtext version of same message goes here ...
—boundary42—
```

In this subtype, the body parts are ordered in terms of increasing preference. For this example, if the recipient system is capable of displaying the message in the richtext format, this is done; otherwise, the plain text format is used.

The **multipart/digest subtype** is used when each of the body parts is interpreted as an RFC 822 message with headers. This subtype enables the construction of a message whose parts are individual messages. For example, the moderator of a group might collect e-mail messages from participants, bundle these messages, and send them out in one encapsulating MIME message.

The **message type** provides a number of important capabilities in MIME. The **message/rfc822 subtype** indicates that the body is an entire message, including header and body. Despite the name of this subtype, the encapsulated message may be not only a simple RFC 822 message, but also any MIME message.

The **message/partial subtype** enables fragmentation of a large message into a number of parts, which must be reassembled at the destination. For this subtype, three parameters are specified in the Content-Type: Message/Partial field:

- **id:** A value that is common to each fragment of the same message, so that the fragments can be identified at the recipient for reassembly, but unique across different messages.

- **number:** A sequence number that indicates the position of this fragment in the original message. The first fragment is numbered 1, the second 2, and so on.

- **total:** The total number of parts. The last fragment is identified by having the same value for the *number* and *total* parameters.

The **message/external-body subtype** indicates that the actual data to be conveyed in this message are not contained in the body. Instead, the body contains the information needed to access the data. As with the other message types, the message/external-body subtype has an outer header and an encapsulated message with its own header. The only necessary field in the outer header is the Content-type field, which identifies this as a message/external-body subtype. The inner header is the message header for the encapsulated message.

The Content-type field in the outer header must include an access-type parameter, which has one of the following values:

- **FTP:** The message body is accessible as a file using the File Transfer Protocol (FTP). For this access type, the following additional parameters are mandatory: name, the name of the file; and site, the domain name of the host where the file resides. Optional parameters are: directory, the directory in which the file is located; and mode, which indicates how FTP should retrieve the file (e.g., ASCII, image). Before the file transfer can take place, the user will need to provide a user id and password. These are not transmitted with the message for security reasons.

- **TFTP:** The message body is accessible as a file using the Trivial File Transfer Protocol (TFTP). The same parameters as for FTP are used, and the user id and password must also be supplied.

- **Anon-FTP:** Identical to FTP, except that the user is not asked to supply a user ID and password. The parameter name supplies the name of the file.

- **local-file:** The message body is accessible as a file on the recipient's machine.

- **AFS:** The message body is accessible as a file via the global AFS (Andrew File System). The parameter name supplies the name of the file.

- **mail-server:** The message body is accessible by sending an e-mail message to a mail server. A *server* parameter must be included that gives the e-mail address of the server. The body of the original message, known as the phantom body, should contain the exact command to be sent to the mail server.

The **image type** indicates that the body contains a displayable image. The subtype, jpeg or gif, specifies the image format. In future, more subtypes will be added to this list.

The **video type** indicates that the body contains a time-varying picture image, possibly with color and coordinated sound. The only subtype so far specified is mpeg.

The **audio type** indicates that the body contains audio data. The only subtype, basic, conforms to an ISDN service known as "64-kbps, 8-kHz Structured, Usable for Speech Information," with a digitized speech algorithm referred to as μ-law PCM (pulse code modulation). This general type is the typical way of transmitting speech signals over a digital network. The term μ-*law* refers to the specific encoding technique; it is the standard technique used in North America and Japan. A competing system, known as A-law, is standard in Europe.

The **application type** refers to other kinds of data, typically either uninterpreted binary data or information to be processed by a mail-based application. The **application/octet-stream subtype** indicates general binary data in a sequence of

Table 3.7   MIME Transfer Encodings

7bit	The data are all represented by short lines of ASCII characters.
8bit	The lines are short, but there may be non-ASCII characters (octets with the high-order bit set).
binary	Not only may non-ASCII characters be present but the lines are not necessarily short enough for SMTP transport.
quoted-printable	Encodes the data in such a way that if the data being encoded are mostly ASCII text, the encoded form of the data remains largely recognizable by humans.
base64	Encodes data by mapping 6-bit blocks of input to 8-bit blocks of output, all of which are printable ASCII characters.
x-token	A named nonstandard encoding.

octets. RFC 2045 recommends that the receiving implementation should offer to put the data in a file or use the data as input to a program.

The **application/Postscript subtype** indicates the use of Adobe Postscript.

MIME Transfer Encodings The other major component of the MIME specification, in addition to content type specification, is a definition of transfer encodings for message bodies. The objective is to provide reliable delivery across the largest range of environments.

The MIME standard defines two methods of encoding data. The Content-Transfer-Encoding field can actually take on six values, as listed in Table 3.7. However, three of these values (7bit, 8bit, and binary) indicate that no encoding has been done but provide some information about the nature of the data. For SMTP transfer, it is safe to use the 7bit form. The 8bit and binary forms may be usable in other mail transport contexts. Another Content-Transfer-Encoding value is x-token, which indicates that some other encoding scheme is used, for which a name is to be supplied. This could be a vendor-specific or application-specific scheme. The two actual encoding schemes defined are quoted-printable and base64. Two schemes are defined to provide a choice between a transfer technique that is essentially human readable, and one that is safe for all types of data in a way that is reasonably compact.

The **quoted-printable** transfer encoding is useful when the data consist largely of octets that correspond to printable ASCII characters. In essence, it represents nonsafe characters by the hexadecimal representation of their code and introduces reversible (soft) line breaks to limit message lines to 76 characters. The encoding rules are as follows:

1. General 8-bit representation: This rule is to be used when none of the other rules apply. Any character is represented by an equal sign followed by a two-digit hexadecimal representation of the octet's value. For example, the ASCII form feed, which has an 8-bit value of decimal 12, is represented by "=0C"

2. Literal representation: Any character in the range decimal 33 ("!") through decimal 126 ("~"), except decimal 61 ("=") is represented as that ASCII character.

3. White space: Octets with the values 9 and 32 may be represented as ASCII tab and space characters, respectively, except at the end of a line. Any white space

(tab or blank) at the end of a line must be represented by rule 1. On decoding, any trailing white space on a line is deleted. This eliminates any white space added by intermediate transport agents.

4. Line breaks: Any line break, regardless of its initial representation, is represented by the RFC 822 line break, which is a carriage-return/line-feed combination.

5. Soft line breaks: If an encoded line would be longer than 76 characters (excluding (<CRLF>), a soft line break must be inserted at or before character position 75. A soft line break consists of the hexadecimal sequence 3D0D0A, which is the ASCII code for an equal sign followed by carriage return, line feed.

The **base64 transfer encoding**, also known as radix-64 encoding, is a common one for encoding arbitrary binary data in such a way as to be invulnerable to the processing by mail transport programs. This technique maps arbitrary binary input into printable character output. The form of encoding has the following relevant characteristics:

1. The range of the function is a character set that is universally representable at all sites, not a specific binary encoding of that character set. Thus, the characters themselves can be encoded into whatever form is needed by a specific system. For example, the character "E" is represented in an ASCII-based system as hexadecimal 45 and in an EBCDIC-based system as hexadecimal C5.

2. The character set consists of 65 printable characters, one of which is used for padding. With $2^6 = 64$ available characters, each character can be used to represent 6 bits of input.

3. No control characters are included in the set. Thus, a message encoded in radix 64 can traverse mail-handling systems that scan the data stream for control characters.

4. The hyphen character ("-") is not used. This character has significance in the RFC 822 format and should therefore be avoided.

Table 3.8 shows the mapping of 6-bit input values to characters. The character set consists of the alphanumeric characters plus "+" and "/". The "=" character is used as the padding character.

Figure 3.10 illustrates the simple mapping scheme. Binary input is processed in blocks of 3 octets, or 24 bits. Each set of 6 bits in the 24-bit block is mapped into a character. In the figure, the characters are shown encoded as 8-bit quantities. In this typical case, each 24-bit input is expanded to 32 bits of output.

For example, consider the 24-bit raw text sequence 00100011 01011100 10010001, which can be expressed in hexadecimal as 235C91. We arrange this input in blocks of 6 bits:

001000 110101 110010 010001

The extracted 6-bit decimal values are 8, 53, 50, and 17. Looking these up in Table 3.8 yields the radix-64 encoding as the following characters: I1yR. If these characters are stored in 8-bit ASCII format with parity bit set to zero, we have

01001001 00110001 01111001 01010010

Table 3.8   Radix-64 Encoding

6-bit value	Character encoding	6-bit value	Character encoding	6-bit value	Character encoding	6-bit value	Character encoding
0	A	16	Q	32	g	48	w
1	B	17	R	33	h	49	x
2	C	18	S	34	i	50	y
3	D	19	T	35	j	51	z
4	E	20	U	36	k	52	0
5	F	21	V	37	l	53	1
6	G	22	W	38	m	54	2
7	H	23	X	39	n	55	3
8	I	24	Y	40	o	56	4
9	J	25	Z	41	p	57	5
10	K	26	a	42	q	58	6
11	L	27	b	43	r	59	7
12	M	28	c	44	s	60	8
13	N	29	d	45	t	61	9
14	O	30	e	46	u	62	+
15	P	31	f	47	v	63	/
						(pad)	=

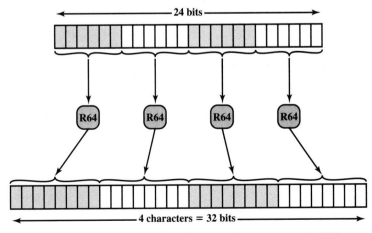

Figure 3.10   Printable Encoding of Binary Data into Radix-64 Format

In hexadecimal, this is 49317952. To summarize,

Input Data	
Binary representation	00100011 01011100 10010001
Hexadecimal representation	235C91

Radix-64 Encoding of Input Data	
Character representation	I1yR
ASCII code (8 bit, zero parity)	01001001 00110001 01111001 01010010
Hexadecimal representation	49317952

3.4 RECOMMENDED READING AND WEB SITES

Three papers by Khare provide good overviews of Telnet, FTP, and SMTP [KHAR98a, KHAR98b, KHAR98c].

[HOFF00] is a good overview of SMTP and related email standards. [KANE98] is a comprehensive look at SMTP and related mail standards, plus a comparison with proprietary schemes. [ROSE98] provides a book-length treatment of electronic mail, including some coverage of SMTP and MIME.

HOFF00 Hoffman, P. "Overview of Internet Mail Standards." *The Internet Protocol Journal*, June 2000 (www.cisco.com/warp/public/759)

KANE98 Kanel, J.; Givler, J.; Leiba, B.; and Segmuller, W. "Internet Messaging Frameworks." *IBM Systems Journal*, No. 1, 1998.

KHAR98a Khare, R. "Telnet: The Mother of All (Application) Protocols." *IEEE Internet Computing*, May/June 1998.

KHAR98b Khare, R. "I Want My FTP: Bits on Demand." *IEEE Internet Computing*, July/August 1998.

KHAR98c Khare, R. "The Spec's in the Mail." *IEEE Internet Computing*, September/October 1998.

ROSE98 Rose, M., and Strom, D. *Internet Messaging: From the Desktop to the Enterprise.* Upper Saddle River, NJ: Prentice Hall, 1998.

Recommended Web Site:

- **Telnet.org:** Lots of stuff related to Telnet

3.5 KEY TERMS, REVIEW QUESTIONS, AND PROBLEMS

Key Terms

dumb terminal	radix 64	Telnet
File Transfer Protocol (FTP)	remote terminal access	user Telnet
Multipurpose Internet Mail	server Telnet	virtual terminal protocol (VTP)
Extensions (MIME)	Simple Mail Transfer Protocol	
network virtual terminal (NVT)	(SMTP)	

Review Questions

3.1 What is a network virtual terminal?

3.2 What are the four phases of operation of a typical virtual terminal protocol?

3.3 What is the distinction between User Telnet and Server Telnet?

3.4 Briefly summarize the Telnet synch mechanism.

3.5 List and briefly define the categories of Telnet options.

3.6 Explain the use of the terms WILL, WONT, DO, DONT in Telnet.

3.7 What is the distinction between User FTP and Server FTP?

3.8 What data types are supported by FTP?

3.9 What file types are supported by FTP?

3.10 What transmission modes are supported by FTP?

3.11 How is the restart marker used in FTP?

3.12 What is the difference between the RFC 821 and RFC 822?

3.13 What are the SMTP and MIME standards?

3.14 What is the difference between a MIME content type and a MIME transfer encoding?

3.15 Briefly explain radix-64 encoding.

Problems

Note: For some of the problems in this Chapter, you will need to consult the relevant RFCs.

3.1 When a Telnet implementation issues a WILL command, RFC 854 states that it must wait until receiving a DO command before enabling the option and that if a DONT command is received, the option remains disabled. Thus, the side issuing the WILL command must remember that it has issued that command and wait for a reply. A similar requirement applies to the DO command. However, RFC 854 does not explicitly state that a Telnet implementation must remember beginning a DONT or WONT negotiation. At first glance, it seems reasonable to simply issue the DONT or WONT and disable the option immediately and ignore the WONT/DONT response from the other side. This is so because the other side has no choice but to agree to disable the option. However, this strategy is incorrect because it could lead to an endless loop. Demonstrate the problem by showing a sequence of commands that lead to an endless loop if Telnet implementations do not remember beginning a DONT or WONT negotiation. *Hint:* Suppose one side decides to disable an option and then decides to reenable that option.

3.2 It is unclear from RFC 854 whether or not a TELNET implementation may allow new requests about an option that is currently under negotiation; it certainly seems limiting to prohibit "option typeahead." Suppose an option is disabled, and we decide in quick succession to enable it, disable it, and reenable it. We send WILL WONT WILL and at the end remember that we are negotiating. Might this create a problem?

3.3 Electronic mail systems differ in the manner in which multiple recipients are handled. In some systems, the originating user agent or mail sender makes all the necessary copies and these are sent out independently. An alternative approach is to determine the route for each destination first. Then a single message is sent out on a common portion of the route and copies are only made when the routes diverge; this process is referred to as mail bagging. Discuss the relative advantages and disadvantages of the two methods.

3.4 Excluding the connection establishment and termination, what is the minimum number of network round trips to send a small email message using SMTP?

3.5 Although TCP is a full-duplex protocol, SMTP uses TCP in a half-duplex fashion. The client sends a command and then stops and waits for the reply. How can this half-duplex operation fool the TCP slow start mechanism when the network is running near capacity?

3.6 Classify a Mail Transfer Agent (MTA) as either client, server or both.

3.7 Give some reasons for using a relay system instead of having the local MTA deliver mail to the final recipients and accept mail directly from any host on the Internet.

3.8 Explain the differences between the intended use for the quoted-printable and Base64 encodings

3.9 Suppose you need to send one message to three different users: user1@example.com, user2@example.com and user3@example.com. Is there any difference between sending one separate message per user and sending only one message with multiple (three) recipients? If so, which one?

3.10 If a MTA has accepted the task of relaying a mail message and later finds that the mail cannot be delivered to any of the recipients, it must construct an error notification message, and send it to the originator of the mail message (as indicated by the reverse-path). In order to prevent mail loops, MTAs should not send notification messages about problems with notification messages. How do you think MTAs prevent loops in error reporting?

3.11 We've seen that the character sequence "<CR><LF>.<CR><LF>" indicates the end of mail data to a SMTP-server. What happens if the mail data itself contains that character sequence?

3.12 Users are free to define and use additional header fields other than the ones defined in RFC 822. Such header fields must begin with the string "X-". Why?

3.13 Suppose you find some technical problems with the mail account user@example.com. Who should you try to contact in order to solve them?

3.14 Explain why servers generally call bind() to specify a port number, while clients usually don't.

CHAPTER 4

MODERN APPLICATIONS

Investigators have published numerous reports of birds taking turns vocalizing; the bird spoken to gave its full attention to the speaker and never vocalized at the same time, as if the two were holding a conversation.

Researchers and scholars who have studied the data on avian communication carefully write that (a) the communication code of birds such as crows has not been broken by any means; (b) probably all birds have wider vocabularies than anyone realizes; and (c) greater complexity and depth are recognized in avian communication as research progresses.

—The Human Nature of Birds,
Theodore Barber

KEY POINTS

- The rapid growth in the use of the Web is due to the standardization of all the elements that support Web applications. A key element is HTTP, which is the protocol for the exchange of Web-based information between Web browsers and Web servers.

- Three types of intermediate devices can be used in HTTP networks: proxies, gateways, and tunnels.

- HTTP uses a request/response style of communication.

- The Domain Name System (DNS) is a directory lookup service that provides a mapping between the name of a host on the Internet and its numerical address.

- DNS makes use of a distributed, hierarchical database to maintain a mapping from names to addresses and to provide related information about hosts on the Internet.

- The Session Initiation Protocol (SIP) is an application-level control protocol for setting up, modifying, and terminating real-time sessions between participants over an IP data network.

- SIP uses the Session Description Protocol (SDP) to describe the media content to be used during a session.

- The Sockets application programming interface (API) provides a convenient, standardized way to write application programs that use TCP or IP for communication across the Internet.

This chapter looks at some of the most widely used and more advanced Internet application protocols. These should give the reader a feel for the range and diversity of applications supported by a communications architecture. The chapter begins with HTTP, which is the support protocol on which the World Wide Web (WWW) operates. Then we look at DNS, which is an essential name/address directory lookup service for the Internet. The third protocol that we examine, SIP, is more recent than the other two and is used to support Voice over IP (VoIP) and a variety of other multimedia data services. Finally, the chapter examines the Sockets interface used to develop Internet applications.

Refer to the figure on the inside back cover to see the position within the TCP/IP suite of the protocols discussed in this chapter.

4.1 WEB ACCESS—HTTP

The Hypertext Transfer Protocol (HTTP) is the foundation protocol of the World Wide Web (WWW) and can be used in any client/server application involving hypertext. The name is somewhat misleading in that HTTP is not a protocol for transferring hypertext; rather it is a protocol for transmitting information with the efficiency necessary for making hypertext jumps. The data transferred by the protocol can be plaintext, hypertext, audio, images, or any Internet-accessible information.

We begin with an overview of HTTP concepts and operation and then look at some of the details, basing our discussion on the most recent version to be put on the Internet standards track, HTTP 1.1 (RFC 2616). A number of important terms defined in the HTTP specification are summarized in Table 4.1; these will be introduced as the discussion proceeds.

Table 4.1   Key Terms Related to HTTP

Cache A program's local store of response messages and the subsystem that controls its message storage, retrieval, and deletion. A cache stores cacheable responses in order to reduce the response time and network bandwidth consumption on future, equivalent requests. Any client or server may include a cache, though a cache cannot be used by a server while it is acting as a tunnel.	**Origin Server** The server on which a given resource resides or is to be created. **Proxy** An intermediary program that acts as both a server and a client for the purpose of making requests on behalf of other clients. Requests are serviced internally or by passing them, with possible translation, on to other servers. A proxy must interpret and, if necessary, rewrite a request message before forwarding it. Proxies are often used as client-side portals through network firewalls and as helper applications for handling requests via protocols not implemented by the user agent.
Client An application program that establishes connections for the purpose of sending requests.	
Connection A transport layer virtual circuit established between two application programs for the purposes of communication.	
Entity A particular representation or rendition of a data resource, or reply from a service resource, that may be enclosed within a request or response message. An entity consists of entity headers and an entity body.	**Resource** A network data object or service which can be identified by a URI. **Server** An application program that accepts connections in order to service requests by sending back responses.
Gateway A server that acts as an intermediary for some other server. Unlike a proxy, a gateway receives requests as if it were the original server for the requested resource; the requesting client may not be aware that it is communicating with a gateway. Gateways are often used as server-side portals through network firewalls and as protocol translators for access to resources stored on non-HTTP systems.	**Tunnel** An intermediary program that is acting as a blind relay between two connections. Once active, a tunnel is not considered a party to the HTTP communication, though the tunnel may have been initiated by an HTTP request. A tunnel ceases to exist when both ends of the relayed connections are closed. Tunnels are used when a portal is necessary and the intermediary cannot, or should not, interpret the relayed communication.
Message The basic unit of HTTP communication, consisting of a structured sequence of octets transmitted via the connection.	**User Agent** The client that initiates a request. These are often browsers, editors, spiders, or other end-user tools.

HTTP Overview

HTTP is a transaction-oriented client/server protocol. The most typical use of HTTP is between a Web browser and a Web server. To provide reliability, HTTP makes use of TCP. Nevertheless, HTTP is a "stateless" protocol: Each transaction is treated independently. Accordingly, a typical implementation will create a new TCP connection between client and server for each transaction and then terminate the connection as soon as the transaction completes, although the specification does not dictate this one-to-one relationship between transaction and connection lifetimes.

The stateless nature of HTTP is well suited to its typical application. A normal session of a user with a Web browser involves retrieving a sequence of Web pages and documents. The sequence is, ideally, performed rapidly, and the locations of the various pages and documents may be a number of widely distributed servers.

Another important feature of HTTP is that it is flexible in the formats that it can handle. When a client issues a request to a server, it may include a prioritized list of formats that it can handle, and the server replies with the appropriate format. For example, a lynx browser cannot handle images, so a Web server need not transmit any images on Web pages. This arrangement prevents the transmission of unnecessary information and provides the basis for extending the set of formats with new standardized and proprietary specifications.

Figure 4.1 illustrates three examples of HTTP operation. The simplest case is one in which a user agent establishes a direct connection with an origin server. The *user agent* is the client that initiates the request, such as a Web browser being run on behalf of an end user. The *origin server* is the server on which a resource of interest resides; an example is a Web server at which a desired Web home page resides. For this case, the client opens a TCP connection that is end-to-end between the client and the server. The client then issues an HTTP request. The request consists of a specific command, referred to as a method, an address [referred to as a Uniform Resource Locator[1] (URL)], and a MIME-like message containing request parameters, information about the client, and perhaps some additional content information.

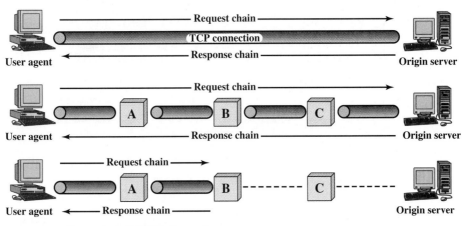

Figure 4.1   Examples of HTTP Operation

When the server receives the request, it attempts to perform the requested action and then returns an HTTP response. The response includes status information, a success/error code, and a MIME-like message containing information about the server, information about the response itself, and possible body content. The TCP connection is then closed.

The middle part of Figure 4.1 shows a case in which there is not an end-to-end TCP connection between the user agent and the origin server. Instead, there are one or more intermediate systems with TCP connections between logically adjacent systems. Each intermediate system acts as a relay, so that a request initiated by the client is relayed through the intermediate systems to the server, and the response from the server is relayed back to the client.

Three forms of intermediate system are defined in the HTTP specification: proxy, gateway, and tunnel, all of which are illustrated in Figure 4.2.

Proxy A proxy acts on behalf of other clients and presents requests from other clients to a server. The proxy acts as a server in interacting with a client and as a client in interacting with a server. There are two scenarios that call for the use of a proxy:

- **Security intermediary:** The client and server may be separated by a security intermediary such as a firewall, with the proxy on the client side of the firewall. Typically, the client is part of a network secured by a firewall and the server is external to the secured network. In this case, the server must authenticate itself to the firewall to set up a connection with the proxy. The proxy accepts responses after they have passed through the firewall.

- **Different versions of HTTP:** If the client and server are running different versions of HTTP, then the proxy can implement both versions and perform the required mapping.

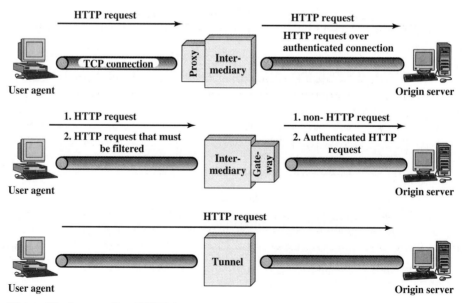

Figure 4.2 Intermediate HTTP Systems

In summary, a proxy is a forwarding agent, receiving a request for a URL object, modifying the request, and forwarding the request toward the server identified in the URL.

Gateway A gateway is a server that appears to the client as if it were an origin server. It acts on behalf of other servers that may not be able to communicate directly with a client. There are two scenarios in which gateways can be used:

- **Security intermediary:** The client and server may be separated by a security intermediary such as a firewall, with the gateway on the server side of the firewall. Typically, the server is connected to a network protected by a firewall, with the client external to the network. In this case the client must authenticate itself to the gateway, which can then pass the request on to the server.
- **Non-HTTP server:** Web browsers have built into them the capability to contact servers for protocols other than HTTP, such as FTP and Gopher servers. This capability can also be provided by a gateway. The client makes an HTTP request to a gateway server. The gateway server then contacts the relevant FTP or Gopher server to obtain the desired result. This result is then converted into a form suitable for HTTP and transmitted back to the client.

Tunnel Unlike the proxy and the gateway, the tunnel performs no operations on HTTP requests and responses. Instead, a tunnel is simply a relay point between two TCP connections, and the HTTP messages are passed unchanged as if there were a single HTTP connection between user agent and origin server. Tunnels are used when there must be an intermediary system between client and server but it is not necessary for that system to understand the contents of messages. An example is a firewall in which a client or server external to a protected network can establish an authenticated connection and then maintain that connection for purposes of HTTP transactions.

Cache Returning to Figure 4.1, the lowest portion of the figure shows an example of a cache. A cache is a facility that may store previous requests and responses for handling new requests. If a new request arrives that is the same as a stored request, then the cache can supply the stored response rather than accessing the resource indicated in the URL. The cache can operate on a client or server or on an intermediate system other than a tunnel. In the figure, intermediary B has cached a request/response transaction, so that a corresponding new request from the client need not travel the entire chain to the origin server, but is handled by B.

Not all transactions can be cached, and a client or server can dictate that a certain transaction may be cached only for a given time limit.

Messages

The best way to describe the functionality of HTTP is to describe the individual elements of the HTTP message. HTTP consists of two types of messages: requests from clients to servers, and responses from servers to clients. The general structure of such messages is shown in Figure 4.3. More formally, using enhanced BNF (Backus-Naur Form) notation[2] (Table 4.2), we have

---

[2]A description of BNF is contained in a supporting document at this book's Web site.

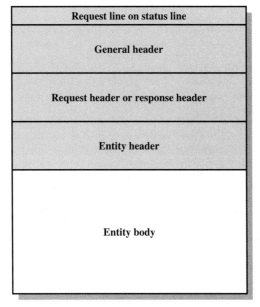

Figure 4.3   General Structure of HTTP Messages

Table 4.2   Augmented BNF Notation Used in URL and HTTP Specifications

- Words in lowercase represent variables or names of rules.
- A rule has the form

```
name = definition
```

- DIGIT is any decimal digit; CRLF is carriage return, line feed; SP is one or more spaces.
- Quotation marks enclose literal text.
- Angle brackets, "<" ">", may be used within a definition to enclose a rule name when their presence will facilitate clarity.
- Elements separated by bar ("|") are alternatives.
- Ordinary parentheses are used simply for grouping.
- The character "*" preceding an element indicates repetition. The full form is

```
<I>*<J>element
```

indicating at least I and at most J occurrences of element. *element allows any number, including 0; 1*element requires at least one element; and 1*2element allows 1 or 2 elements; <N>element means exactly N elements.
- Square brackets, "[" "]", enclose optional elements.
- The construct "#" is used to define, with the following form:

```
<I>#<J>element
```

indicating at least I and at most J elements, each separated by a comma and optional linear white space.
- A semicolon at the right of a rule starts a comment that continues to the end of the line.

```
HTTP-Message = Simple-Request | Simple-Response | Full-Request | Full-Response
Full-Request =  Request-Line
  *( General-Header |  Request-Header |  Entity-Header )
  CRLF
  [ Entity-Body ]
Full-Response = Status-Line
  *( General-Header |  Response-Header |  Entity-Header )
  CRLF
  [ Entity-Body ]
Simple-Request  = "GET" SP Request-URL CRLF
Simple-Response = [ Entity-Body ]
```

The Simple-Request and Simple-Response messages were defined in HTTP/0.9. The request is a simple GET command with the requested URL; the response is simply a block containing the information identified in the URL. In HTTP/1.1, the use of these simple forms is discouraged because it prevents the client from using content negotiation and the server from identifying the media type of the returned entity.

With full requests and responses, the following fields are used:

- **Request-Line:** Identifies the message type and the requested resource
- **Status-Line:** Provides status information about this response
- **General-Header:** Contains fields that are applicable to both request and response messages but that do not apply to the entity being transferred
- **Request-Header:** Contains information about the request and the client
- **Response-Header:** Contains information about the response
- **Entity-Header:** Contains information about the resource identified by the request and information about the entity body
- **Entity-Body:** The body of the message

All of the HTTP headers consist of a sequence of fields, following the same generic format as RFC 822 (described in Chapter 3). Each field begins on a new line and consists of the field name followed by a colon and the field value.

Although the basic transaction mechanism is simple, there is a large number of fields and parameters defined in HTTP; these are listed in Table 4.3. In the remainder of this section, we look at the general header fields. The following sections describe request headers, response headers, and entities.

General Header Fields General header fields can be used in both request and response messages. These fields are applicable in both types of messages and contain information that does not directly apply to the entity being transferred. The fields are as follows:

- **Cache-Control:** Specifies directives that must be obeyed by any caching mechanisms along the request/response chain. The purpose is to prevent a cache from adversely interfering with this particular request or response.
- **Connection:** Contains a list of keywords and header field names that only apply to this TCP connection between the sender and the nearest nontunnel recipient.
- **Date:** Date and time at which the message originated.

Table 4.3 HTTP Elements

ALL MESSAGES			
General Header Fields		**Entity Header Fields**	
Cache-Control	Keep-Alive	Allow	Derived-From
Connection	MIME-Version	Content-Encoding	Expires
Date	Pragma	Content-Language	Last-Modified
Forwarded	Upgrade	Content-Length	Link
		Content-MD5	Title
		Content-Range	Transfer-Encoding
		Content-Type	URI-Header
		Content-Version	extension-header
REQUEST MESSAGES			
Request Methods		**Request Header Fields**	
OPTIONS	MOVE	Accept	If-Modified-Since
GET	DELETE	Accept-Charset	Proxy-Authorization
HEAD	LINK	Accept-Encoding	Range
POST	UNLINK	Accept-Language	Referrer
PUT	TRACE	Authorization	Unless
PATCH	WRAPPED	From	User-Agent
COPY	extension-method	Host	
RESPONSE MESSAGES			
Response Status Codes			**Response Header Fields**
Continue	Moved Temporarily	Request Timeout	Location
Switching Protocols	See Other	Conflict	Proxy-Authenticate
OK	Not Modified	Gone	Public
Created	Use Proxy	Length Required	Retry-After
Accepted	Bad Request	Unless True	Server
Non-Authoritative	Unauthorized	Internal Server Error	WWW-Authenticate
Information	Payment Required	Not Implemented	
No Content	Forbidden	Bad Gateway	
Reset Content	Not Found	Service Unavailable	
Partial Content	Method Not Allowed	Gateway Timeout	
Multiple Choices	None Acceptable	extension code	
Moved Permanently	Proxy Authentication Required		

- **Forwarded:** Used by gateways and proxies to indicate intermediate steps along a request or response chain. Each gateway or proxy that handles a message may attach a Forwarded field that gives its URL.

- **Keep-Alive:** May be present if the keep-alive keyword is present in an incoming Connection field, to provide information to the requester of the persistent connection. This field may indicate a maximum time that the sender will keep the connection open waiting for the next request or the maximum number of additional requests that will be allowed on the current persistent connection.

- **MIME-Version:** Indicates that the message complies with the indicated version of MIME.
- **Pragma:** Contains implementation-specific directives that may apply to any recipient along the request/response chain.
- **Upgrade:** Used in a request to specify what additional protocols the client supports and would like to use; used in a response to indicate which protocol will be used.

Request Messages

A full request message consists of a status line followed by one or more general, request, and entity headers, followed by an optional entity body.

Request Methods A full request message always begins with a Request-Line, which has the following format:

```
Request-Line = Method SP Request-URL SP HTTP-Version CRLF
```

The Method parameter indicates the actual request command, called a method in HTTP. Request-URL is the URL of the requested resource, and HTTP-Version is the version number of HTTP used by the sender.

The following request methods are defined in HTTP/1.1:

- **OPTIONS:** A request for information about the options available for the request/response chain identified by this URL.
- **GET:** A request to retrieve the information identified in the URL and return it in a entity body. A GET is conditional if the If-Modified-Since header field is included and is partial if a Range header field is included.
- **HEAD:** This request is identical to a GET, except that the server's response must not include an entity body; all of the header fields in the response are the same as if the entity body were present. This enables a client to get information about a resource without transferring the entity body.
- **POST:** A request to accept the attached entity as a new subordinate to the identified URL. The posted entity is subordinate to that URL in the same way that a file is subordinate to a directory containing it, a news article is subordinate to a newsgroup to which it is posted, or a record is subordinate to a database.
- **PUT:** A request to accept the attached entity and store it under the supplied URL. This may be a new resource with a new URL or a replacement of the contents of an existing resource with an existing URL.
- **PATCH:** Similar to a PUT, except that the entity contains a list of differences from the content of the original resource identified in the URL.
- **COPY:** Requests that a copy of the resource identified by the URL in the Request-Line be copied to the location(s) given in the URL-Header field in the Entity-Header of this message.

- **MOVE:** Requests that the resource identified by the URL in the Request-Line be moved to the location(s) given in the URL-Header field in the Entity-Header of this message. Equivalent to a COPY followed by a DELETE.
- **DELETE:** Requests that the origin server delete the resource identified by the URL in the Request-Line.
- **LINK:** Establishes one or more link relationships from the resource identified in the Request-Line. The links are defined in the Link field in the Entity-Header.
- **UNLINK:** Removes one or more link relationships from the resource identified in the Request-Line. The links are defined in the Link field in the Entity-Header.
- **TRACE:** Requests that the server return whatever is received as the entity body of the response. This can be used for testing and diagnostic purposes.
- **WRAPPED:** Allows a client to send one or more encapsulated requests. The requests may be encrypted or otherwise processed. The server must unwrap the requests and process accordingly.
- **Extension-method:** Allows additional methods to be defined without changing the protocol, but these methods cannot be assumed to be recognizable by the recipient.

Request Header Fields Request header fields function as request modifiers, providing additional information and parameters related to the request. The following fields are defined in HTTP/1.1:

- **Accept:** A list of media types and ranges that are acceptable as a response to this request.
- **Accept-Charset:** A list of character sets acceptable for the response.
- **Accept-Encoding:** List of acceptable content encodings for the entity body. Content encodings are primarily used to allow a document to be compressed or encrypted. Typically, the resource is stored in this encoding and only decoded before actual use.
- **Accept-Language:** Restricts the set of natural languages that are preferred for the response.
- **Authorization:** Contains a field value, referred to as *credentials*, used by the client to authenticate itself to the server.
- **From:** The Internet e-mail address for the human user who controls the requesting user agent.
- **Host:** Specifies the Internet host of the resource being requested.
- **If-Modified-Since:** Used with the GET method. This header includes a date/time parameter; the resource is to be transferred only if it has been modified since the date/time specified. This feature allows for efficient cache update. A caching mechanism can periodically issue GET messages to an origin server, and will receive only a small response message unless an update is needed.
- **Proxy-Authorization:** Allows the client to identify itself to a proxy that requires authentication.
- **Range:** For future study. The intent is that, in a GET message, a client can request only a portion of the identified resource.

- **Referrer:** The URL of the resource from which the Request-URL was obtained. This enables a server to generate lists of back-links.
- **Unless:** Similar in function to the If-Modified-Since field, with two differences: (1) it is not restricted to the GET method, and (2) comparison is based on any Entity-Header field value rather than a date/time value.
- **User-Agent:** Contains information about the user agent originating this request. This is used for statistical purposes, the tracing of protocol violations, and automated recognition of user agents for the sake of tailoring responses to avoid particular user agent limitations.

Response Messages

A full response message consists of a status line followed by one or more general, response, and entity headers, followed by an optional entity body.

Status Codes A full response message always begins with a Status-Line, which has the following format:

```
Status-Line = HTTP-Version SP Status-Code SP Reason-Phrase CRLF
```

The HTTP-Version value is the version number of HTTP used by the sender. The Status-Code is a three-digit integer that indicates the response to a received request, and the Reason-Phrase provides a short textual explanation of the status code.

HTTP/1.1 includes a rather large number of status codes; these are listed in Table 4.4, together with a brief definition. The codes are organized into the following categories:

- **Informational:** The request has been received and processing continues. No entity body accompanies this response.
- **Successful:** The request was successfully received, understood, and accepted. The information returned in the response message depends on the request method, as follows:
  - —GET: The contents of the entity-body correspond to the requested resource.
  - —HEAD: No entity body is returned.
  - —POST: The entity describes or contains the result of the action.
  - —TRACE: The entity contains the request message.
  - —Other methods: The entity describes the result of the action.
- **Redirection:** Further action is required to complete the request.
- **Client Error:** The request contains a syntax error or the request cannot be fulfilled.
- **Server Error:** The server failed to fulfill an apparently valid request.

Response Header Fields Response header fields provide additional information related to the response that cannot be placed in the Status-Line. The following fields are defined in HTTP/1.1:

- **Location:** Defines the exact location of the resource identified by the Request-URL.

Table 4.4 HTTP Status Codes

Informational	
Continue	Initial part of request received; client may continue with request.
Switching Protocols	Server will switch to requested new application protocol.

Successful	
OK	Request has succeeded and the appropriate response information is included.
Created	Request fulfilled and a new resource has been created; the URI(s) are included.
Accepted	Request accepted but processing not completed. The request may or may not eventually be acted upon.
Non-authoritative Information	Returned contents of entity header is not the definitive set available from origin server, but is gathered from a local or third-party copy.
No Content	Server has fulfilled request but there is no information to send back.
Reset Content	Request has succeeded and the user agent should reset the document view that caused the request to be generated.
Partial Content	Server has fulfilled the partial GET request and the corresponding information is included.

Redirection	
Multiple Choices	Requested resource is available at multiple locations and a preferred location could not be determined.
Moved Permanently	Requested resource has been assigned a new permanent URI; future reference should use this URI
Moved Temporarily	Requested resource resides temporarily under a different URI.
See Other	Response to the request can be found under a different URI and should be retrieved using a GET on that resource.
Not Modified	The client has performed a conditional GET, access is allowed, and the document has not been modified since the date/time specified in the request.
Use Proxy	Requested resource must be accessed through the proxy indicated in the Location field.

Client Error	
Bad Request	Malformed syntax in request.
Unauthorized	Request requires user authentication.
Payment Required	Reserved for future use.
Forbidden	Server refuses to fulfill request; used when server does not wish to reveal why the request was refused.
Not Found	Requested URI not found.
Method Not Allowed	Method (command) not allowed for the requested resource.
None Acceptable	Resource found that matches requested URI, but does not satisfy conditions specified in the request.
Proxy Authentication Required	Client must first authenticate itself with the proxy.
Request Timeout	Client did not produce a request within the time that the server was prepared to wait.
Conflict	Request could not be completed due to a conflict with the current state of the resource.
Gone	Requested resource no longer available at the server and no forwarding address is known.
Length Required	Server refuses to accept request without a defined content length.
Unless True	Condition given in the Unless field was true when tested on server.

Server Error	
Internal Server Error	Server encountered an unexpected condition that prevented it from fulfilling the request.
Not Implemented	Server does not support the functionality required to fulfill the request.
Bad Gateway	Server, while acting as a gateway or proxy, received an invalid response from the upstream server it accessed to fulfill the request.
Service Unavailable	Server unable to handle request due to temporary overloading or maintenance of the server.
Gateway Timeout	Server, while acting as a gateway or proxy, did not receive a timely response from the upstream server it accessed to fulfill the request.

- **Proxy-Authenticate:** Included with a response that has a status code of Proxy Authentication Required. This field contains a "challenge" that indicates the authentication scheme and parameters required.
- **Public:** Lists the nonstandard methods supported by this server.
- **Retry-After:** Included with a response that has a status code of Service Unavailable, and indicates how long the service is expected to be unavailable.
- **Server:** Identifies the software product used by the origin server to handle the request.
- **WWW-Authenticate:** Included with a response that has a status code of Unauthorized. This field contains a "challenge" that indicates the authentication scheme and parameters required.

Entities

An entity consists of an entity header and an entity body in a request or response message. An entity may represent a data resource, or it may constitute other information supplied with a request or response.

Entity Header Fields Entity header fields provide optional information about the entity body or, if no body is present, about the resource identified by the request. The following fields are defined in HTTP/1.1:

- **Allow:** Lists methods supported by the resource identified in the Request-URL. This field must be included with a response that has a status code of Method Not Allowed and may be included in other responses.
- **Content-Encoding:** Indicates what content encodings have been applied to the resource. The only encoding currently defined is zip compression.
- **Content-Language:** Identifies the natural language(s) of the intended audience of the enclosed entity.
- **Content-Length:** The size of the entity body in octets.
- **Content-MD5:** For future study. MD5 refers to the MD5 hash code function, described in Chapter 21.
- **Content-Range:** For future study. The intent is that this will indicate a portion of the identified resource that is included in this response.
- **Content-Type:** Indicates the media type of the entity body.
- **Content-Version:** A version tag associated with an evolving entity.
- **Derived-From:** Indicates the version tag of the resource from which this entity was derived before modifications were made by the sender. This field and the Content-Version field can be used to manage multiple updates by a group of users.
- **Expires:** Date/time after which the entity should be considered stale.
- **Last-Modified:** Date/time that the sender believes the resource was last modified.
- **Link:** Defines links to other resources.
- **Title:** A textual title for the entity.
- **Transfer-Encoding:** Indicates what type of transformation has been applied to the message body to transfer it safely between the sender and the recipient.

The only encoding defined in the standard is *chunked*. The chunked option defines a procedure for breaking an entity body into labeled chunks that are transmitted separately.

- **URL-Header:** Informs the recipient of other URLs by which the resource can be identified.

- **Extension-Header:** Allows additional fields to be defined without changing the protocol, but these fields cannot be assumed to be recognizable by the recipient.

Entity Body An entity body consists of an arbitrary sequence of octets. HTTP is designed to be able to transfer any type of content, including text, binary data, audio, images, and video. When an entity body is present in a message, the interpretation of the octets in the body is determined by the entity header fields Content-Encoding, Content-Type, and Transfer-Encoding. These define a three-layer, ordered encoding model:

```
entity-body := Transfer-Encoding( Content-Encoding( Content-Type( data ) ) )
```

The data are the content of a resource identified by a URL. The Content-Type field determines the way in which the data are interpreted. A Content-Encoding may be applied to the data and stored at the URL instead of the data. Finally, on transfer, a Transfer-Encoding may be applied to form the entity body of the message.

4.2 INTERNET DIRECTORY SERVICE—DNS

The Domain Name System (DNS) is a directory lookup service that provides a mapping between the name of a host on the Internet and its numerical address. DNS is essential to the functioning of the Internet. It is defined in RFCs 1034 and 1035.

Four elements comprise the DNS:

- **Domain name space:** DNS uses a tree-structured name space to identify resources on the Internet.

- **DNS database:** Conceptually, each node and leaf in the name space tree structure names a set of information (e.g., IP address, type of resource) that is contained in a resource record (RR). The collection of all RRs is organized into a distributed database.

- **Name servers:** These are server programs that hold information about a portion of the domain name tree structure and the associated RRs.

- **Resolvers:** These are programs that extract information from name servers in response to client requests. A typical client request is for an IP address corresponding to a given domain name.

In the next two sections, we examine domain names and the DNS database, respectively. We then describe the operation of DNS, which includes a discussion of name servers and resolvers.

Domain Names

The 32-bit IP address provides a way of uniquely identifying devices attached to the Internet. This address is interpreted as having two components: a network number, which identifies a network on the Internet, and a host address, which identifies a unique host on that network. The practical use of IP addresses presents two problems:

1. Routers devise a path through the Internet on the basis of the network number. If each router needed to keep a master table that listed every network and the preferred path to that network, the management of the tables would be cumbersome and time consuming. It would be better to group the networks in such a way as to simplify the routing function.

2. The 32-bit address is usually written as four decimal numbers, corresponding to the four octets of the address. This number scheme is effective for computer processing but is not convenient for users, who can more easily remember names than numerical addresses.

These problems are addressed by the concept of **domain**. In general terms, a domain refers to a group of hosts that are under the administrative control of a single entity, such as a company or government agency. Domains are organized hierarchically, so that a given domain may consist of a number of subordinate domains. Names are assigned to domains and reflect this hierarchical organization.

Figure 4.4 shows a portion of the domain naming tree. At the very top level are a small number of domains that encompass the entire Internet. Table 4.5 lists the currently-defined top-level domains. Each subordinate level is named by prefixing a subordinate name to the name at the next highest level. For example,

- edu is the domain of college-level U.S. educational institutions.
- mit.edu is the domain for M.I.T.
- lcs.mit.edu is the domain for the Laboratory for Computer Science at M.I.T.

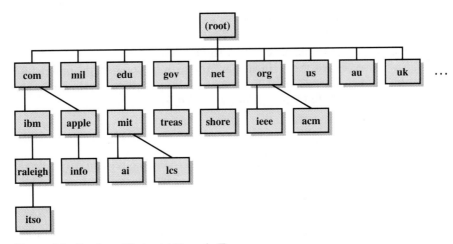

Figure 4.4 Portion of Internet Domain Tree

Table 4.5 Top-Level Internet Domains

Domain	Contents
com	Commercial organizations
edu	Educational institutions
gov	U.S. federal government agencies
mil	U.S. military
net	Network support centers, Internet service providers, and other network-related organizations
org	Nonprofit organizations
us	U.S. state and local government agencies, schools, libraries, and museums
country code	ISO standard 2-letter identifier for country-specific domains (e.g., au, ca, uk)
biz	Dedicated exclusively for private businesses
info	Unrestricted use
name	Individuals, for email addresses and personalized domain names.
museum	restricted to museums, museum organizations, and individual members of the museum profession
coop	Member-owned cooperative organizations, such as credit unions
aero	Aviation community
pro	Medical, legal, and accounting professions
arpa	Temporary ARPA domain (still used)
int	International organizations

As you move down the naming tree, you eventually get to leaf nodes that identify specific hosts on the Internet. These hosts are assigned Internet addresses. An Internet-wide organization is responsible for assigning domain names so that every domain name is unique. The actual assignment of addresses is delegated down the hierarchy. Thus, the mil domain is assigned a large group of addresses. The U.S. Department of Defense (DoD) then allocates portions of this address space to various DoD organizations for eventual assignment to hosts.

For example, the main host at MIT, with a domain name of mit.edu, has four IP addresses: 18.7.21.77, 18.7.21.69, 18.7.21.70, and 18.7.21.110. The subordinate domain lcs.mit.edu has the IP address 18.26.0.36.[3]

The DNS Database

DNS is based on a hierarchical database containing **resource records (RRs)** that include the name, IP address, and other information about hosts. The key features of the database are as follows:

---

[3]You should be able to demonstrate the name/address function by connecting your Web browser to your local ISP. The ISP should provide a ping or nslookup tool that allows you to enter a domain name and retrieve an IP address.

- **Variable-depth hierarchy for names:** DNS allows essentially unlimited levels and uses the period (.) as the level delimiter in printed names, as described earlier.

- **Distributed database:** The database resides in DNS servers scattered throughout the Internet and private intranets.

- **Distribution controlled by the database:** The DNS database is divided into thousands of separately managed zones, which are managed by separate administrators. Distribution and update of records is controlled by the database software.

Using this database, DNS servers provide a name-to-address directory service for network applications that need to locate specific servers. For example, every time an e-mail message is sent or a Web page is accessed, there must be a DNS name lookup to determine the IP address of the e-mail server or Web server.

Figure 4.5 shows the structure of a RR. It consists of the following elements:

- **Domain name:** Although the syntax of domain names in messages, described subsequently, is precisely defined, the form of the domain name in a RR is described in general terms. In essence, the domain name in a RR must correspond to the human readable form, which consists of a series of labels of alphanumeric characters or hyphens, with each pair of labels separated by a period.

- **Type:** Identifies the type of resource in this RR. The various types are listed in Table 4.6.[4]

- **Class:** Identifies the protocol family. The only commonly used value is IN, for the Internet.

- **Time to live:** Typically, when a RR is retrieved from a name server, the retriever will cache the RR so that it need not query the name server repeatedly. This field specifies the time interval that the resource record may be cached before the source of the information should again be consulted. A zero value is interpreted to mean that the RR can only be used for the transaction in progress, and should not be cached.

- **Rdata field length:** Length of the Rdata field in octets.

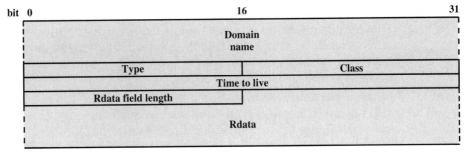

Figure 4.5 DNS Resource Record Format

---

[4]Note: The SRV RR type is defined in RFC 2782.

Table 4.6 Resource Record Types

Type	Description
A	A host address. This RR type maps the name of a system to its IP address. Some systems (e.g., routers) have multiple addresses, and there is a separate RR for each.
CNAME	Canonical name. Specifies an alias name for a host and maps this to the canonical (true) name.
HINFO	Host information. Designates the processor and operating system used by the host.
MINFO	Mailbox or mail list information. Maps a mailbox or mail list name to a host name.
MX	Mail exchange. Identifies the systems that relay mail into the organization.
NS	Authoritative name server for this domain.
PTR	Domain name pointer. Points to another part of the domain name space.
SOA	Start of a zone of authority (which part of naming hierarchy is implemented). Includes parameters related to this zone.
SRV	For a given service provides name of server or servers in domain that provide that service.
TXT	Arbitrary text. Provides a way to add text comments to the database.
WKS	Well-known services. May list the application services available at this host.

- **Rdata:** A variable length string of octets that describes the resource. The format of this information varies according to the type of the RR. For example, for the A type, the Rdata is a 32-bit IP address, and for the CNAME type, the Rdata is a domain name.

DNS Operation

DNS operation typically includes the following steps (Figure 4.6):

1. A user program requests an IP address for a domain name.
2. A resolver module in the local host or local ISP formulates a query for a local name server in the same domain as the resolver.
3. The local name server checks to see if the name is in its local database or cache, and, if so, returns the IP address to the requestor. Otherwise, the name server queries other available name servers, starting down from the root of the DNS tree or as high up the tree as possible.
4. When a response is received at the local name server, it stores the name/address mapping in its local cache and may maintain this entry for the amount of time specified in the time to live field of the retrieved RR.
5. The user program is given the IP address or an error message.

The results of these behind-the-scenes activities are seen by the user in a way illustrated in Figure 3.3. Here, a user issues a Telnet connection request to locis.loc.gov. This is resolved by DNS to the IP address of 140.147.254.3.

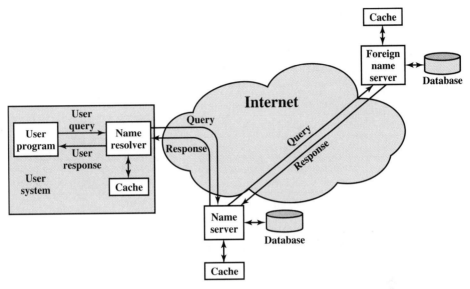

Figure 4.6 DNS Name Resolution

The distributed DNS database that supports the DNS functionality must be updated frequently because of the rapid and continued growth of the Internet. Accordingly, dynamic updating functions for DNS have been defined. In essence, DNS name servers automatically send out updates to other relevant name servers as conditions warrant.

The Server Hierarchy The DNS database is distributed hierarchically, residing in DNS name servers scattered throughout the Internet. Name servers can be operated by any organization that owns a domain; that is, any organization that has responsibility for a subtree of the hierarchical domain name space. Each name server is configured with a subset of the domain name space, known as a **zone**, which is a collection of one or more (or all) subdomains within a domain, along with the associated RRs. This set of data is called authoritative, because this name server is responsible for maintaining an accurate set or RRs for this portion of the domain name hierarchy. The hierarchical structure can extend to any depth. Thus, a portion of the name space assigned to an authoritative name server can be delegated to a subordinate name server in a way that corresponds to the structure of the domain name tree. For example, a name server corresponds to the domain ibm.com. A portion of that domain is defined by the name watson.ibm.com, which corresponds to the node watson.ibm.com and all of the branches and leaf nodes underneath the node watson.ibm.com.

At the top of the server hierarchy are 13 **root name servers** that share responsibility for the top level zones (Table 4.7). This replication is to prevent the root server from becoming a bottleneck. Even so, each individual root server is quite busy. For example, the Internet Software Consortium reports that its server (F) answers almost 300 million DNS requests daily (www.isc.org/services/public/F-root-server.html).

Consider a query by a program on a user host for watson.ibm.com. This query is sent to the local server and the following steps occur:

Table 4.7 Internet Root Servers

Server	Operator	Cities	IP Addr
A	VeriSign Global Registry Services	Herndon VA, US	198.41.0.4
B	Information Sciences Institute	Marina Del Rey CA, US	128.9.0.107
C	Cogent Communications	Herndon VA, US	192.33.4.12
D	University of Maryland	College Park MD, US	128.8.10.90
E	NASA Ames Research Center	Mountain View CA, US	192.203.230.10
F	Internet Software Consortium	Palo Alto CA, US; San Francisco CA, US	IPv4: 192.5.5.241 IPv6: 2001:500::1035
G	U.S. DOD Network Information Center	Vienna VA, US	192.112.36.4
H	U.S. Army Research Lab	Aberdeen MD, US	128.63.2.53
I	Autonomica	Stockholm, SE	192.36.148.17
J	VeriSign Global Registry Services	Herndon VA, US	192.58.128.30
K	Reseaux IP Europeens—Network Coordination Centre	London, UK	193.0.14.129
L	Internet Corporation for Assigned Names and Numbers	Los Angeles CA, US	198.32.64.12
M	WIDE Project	Tokyo, JP	202.12.27.33

1. If the local server already has the IP address for watson.ibm.com in its local cache, it returns the IP address.

2. If the name is not in the local name server's cache, it sends the query to a root server. The root server in turn forwards the request to a server with an NS record for ibm.com. If this server has the information for watson.ibm.com, it returns the IP address.

3. If there is a delegated name server just for watson.ibm.com, then the ibm.com name server forwards the request to the watson.ibm.com name server, which returns the IP address.

Typically, single queries are carried over UDP. Queries for a group of names are carried over TCP.

Name Resolution As Figure 4.6 indicates, each query begins at a name resolver located in the user host system (e.g., gethostbyname in UNIX). Each resolver is configured to know the name and address of a local DNS name server. If the resolver does not have the requested name in its cache, it sends a DNS query to the local DNS server, which either returns an address immediately, or does so after querying one or more other servers. Again, resolvers use UDP for single queries and TCP for group queries.

There are two methods by which queries are forwarded and results returned. Suppose a name server (A) forwards a DNS request to another name server (B). If

B has the name/address in its local cache or local database, it can return the IP address to A. If not, then B can do either of the following:

1. Query another name server for the desired result and then send the result back to A. This is known as a **recursive** technique.

2. Return to A the address of the next server (C) to whom the request should be sent. A then sends out a new DNS request to C. This is known as the **iterative** technique.

In exchanges between name servers, either the iterative or recursive technique may be used. For requests sent by a name resolver, the recursive technique is used.

DNS Messages DNS messages use a single format, shown in Figure 4.7. There are five possible sections to a DNS message: header, question, answer, authority, and additional records.

The **header section** is always present and consists of the following fields:

- **Identifier:** Assigned by the program that generates any kind of query. The same identifier is used in any response, enabling the sender to match queries and responses.
- **Query Response:** Indicates whether this message is a query or response.
- **Opcode:** Indicates whether this is a standard query, an inverse query (address to name), or a server status request. This value is set by the originator and copied into the response.
- **Authoritative Answer:** Valid in a response, and indicates whether the responding name server is an authority for the domain name in question.
- **Truncated:** Indicates whether the response message was truncated due to length greater than permitted on the transmission channel. If so, the requestor will use a TCP connection to resend the query.
- **Recursion Desired:** If set, directs the server to pursue the query recursively.
- **Recursion Available:** Set or cleared in a response to denote whether recursive query support is available in the name server.
- **Response Code:** Possible values are: no error, format error (server unable to interpret query), server failure, name error (domain name does not exist), not implemented (this kind of query not supported), and refused (for policy reasons).
- **QDcount:** Number of entries in question section (zero or more).
- **ANcount:** Number of RRs in answer section (zero or more).
- **NScount:** Number of RRs in authority section (zero or more).
- **ARcount:** Number of RRs in additional records section (zero or more).

The **question section** contains the queries for the name server. If present, it typically contains only one entry. Each entry contains the following fields:

- **Domain Name:** A domain name represented as a sequence of labels, where each label consists of a length octet followed by that number of octets. The domain name terminates with the zero length octet for the null label of the root.

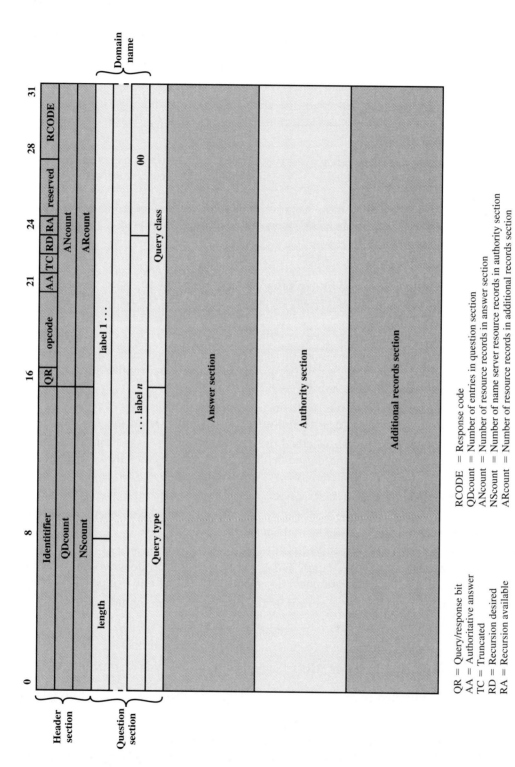

QR = Query/response bit
AA = Authoritative answer
TC = Truncated
RD = Recursion desired
RA = Recursion available

RCODE = Response code
QDcount = Number of entries in question section
ANcount = Number of resource records in answer section
NScount = Number of name server resource records in authority section
ARcount = Number of resource records in additional records section

Figure 4.7 DNS Message Format

- **Query Type:** Indicates type of query. The values for this field include all values valid for the Type field in the RR format (Figure 4.5), together with some more general codes that match more than one type of RR.
- **Query Class:** Specifies the class of query, typically Internet.

The **answer section** contains RRs that answer the question; the **authority section** contains RRs that point toward an authoritative name server; the **additional records section** contains RRs that relate to the query but are not strictly answers for the question.

4.3 VOICE OVER IP AND MULTIMEDIA SUPPORT—SIP

The Session Initiation Protocol (SIP), defined in RFC 3261, is an application-level control protocol for setting up, modifying, and terminating real-time sessions between participants over an IP data network. The key driving force behind SIP is to enable Internet telephony, also referred to as voice over IP (VoIP). SIP can support any type of single media or multimedia session, including teleconferencing.

SIP supports five facets of establishing and terminating multimedia communications:

- **User location:** Users can move to other locations and access their telephony or other application features from remote locations.
- **User availability:** Determination of the willingness of the called party to engage in communications.
- **User capabilities:** Determination of the media and media parameters to be used.
- **Session setup:** Setup up point-to-point and multiparty calls, with agreed session parameters.
- **Session management:** Including transfer and termination of sessions, modifying session parameters, and invoking services.

SIP employs design elements developed for earlier protocols. SIP is based on an HTTP-like request/response transaction model. Each transaction consists of a client request that invokes a particular method, or function, on the server and at least one response. SIP uses most of the header fields, encoding rules, and status codes of HTTP. This provides a readable text-based format for displaying information. SIP also uses concepts similar to the recursive and iterative searches of DNS. SIP incorporates the use of a Session Description Protocol (SDP), which defines session content using a set of types similar to those used in MIME.

SIP Components and Protocols

An SIP network can be viewed of consisting of components defined on two dimensions: client/server and individual network elements. RFC 3261 defines **client** and **server** as follows:

- **Client:** A client is any network element that sends SIP requests and receives SIP responses. Clients may or may not interact directly with a human user. User agent clients and proxies are clients.

- **Server:** A server is a network element that receives requests in order to service them and sends back responses to those requests. Examples of servers are proxies, user agent servers, redirect servers, and registrars.

The individual elements of a standard SIP network are as follows:

- **User Agent:** Resides in every SIP end station. It acts in two roles:
  - **—User agent client (UAC):** Issues SIP requests
  - **—User agent server (UAS):** Receives SIP requests and generates a response that accepts, rejects, or redirects the request
- **Redirect Server:** Used during session initiation to determine the address of the called device. The redirect server returns this information to the calling device, directing the UAC to contact an alternate URI. This is analogous to iterative searches in DNS.
- **Proxy Server:** An intermediary entity that acts as both a server and a client for the purpose of making requests on behalf of other clients. A proxy server primarily plays the role of routing, which means its job is to ensure that a request is sent to another entity closer to the targeted user. Proxies are also useful for enforcing policy (for example, making sure a user is allowed to make a call). A proxy interprets, and, if necessary, rewrites specific parts of a request message before forwarding it. This is analogous to recursive searches in DNS.
- **Registrar:** A server that accepts REGISTER requests and places the information it receives (the SIP address and associated IP address of the registering device) in those requests into the location service for the domain it handles.
- **Location Service:** A location service is used by a SIP redirect or proxy server to obtain information about a callee's possible location(s). For this purpose, the location service maintains a database of SIP-address/IP-address mappings.

The various servers are defined in RFC 3261 as logical devices. They may be implemented as separate servers configured on the Internet or they may be combined into a single application that resides in a physical server.

Figure 4.8 shows how some of the SIP components relate to one another and the protocols that are employed. A user agent acting as a client (in this case UAC alice) uses SIP to set up a session with a user agent that will act as a server (in this case UAS bob). The session initiation dialogue uses SIP and involves one or more proxy servers to forward requests and responses between the two user agents. The user agents also make use of the Session Description Protocol (SDP), which is used to describe the media session.

The proxy servers may also act as redirect servers as needed. If redirection is done, a proxy server will need to consult the location service database, which may be colocated with a proxy server or not. The communication between the proxy server and the location service is beyond the scope of the SIP standard. DNS is also an important part of SIP operation. Typically, a UAC will make a request using the domain name of the UAS, rather than an IP address. A proxy server will need to consult a DNS server to find a proxy server for the target domain.

SIP typically runs on top of UDP for performance reasons, and provides its own reliability mechanisms, but may also use TCP. If a secure, encrypted transport

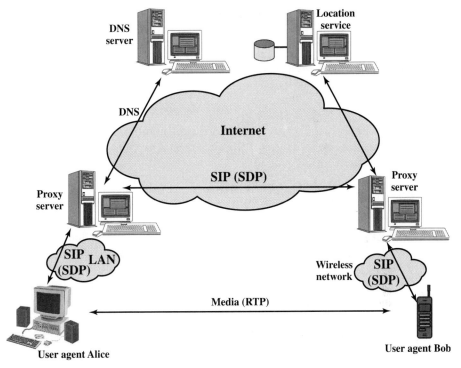

Figure 4.8   SIP Components and Protocols

mechanism is desired, SIP messages may alternatively be carried over the Transport Layer Security (TLS) protocol, described in Chapter 15.

Associated with SIP is the Session Description Protocol (SDP), defined in RFC 2327. SIP is used to invite one or more participants to a session, while the SDP-encoded body of the SIP message contains information about what media encodings (e.g., voice, video) the parties can and will use. Once this information is exchanged and acknowledged, all participants are aware of the participants' IP addresses, available transmission capacity, and media type. Then data transmission begins, using an appropriate transport protocol. Typically, the Real-Time Transport Protocol (RTP), described in Chapter 10, is used. Throughout the session, participants can make changes to session parameters, such as new media types or new parties to the session, using SIP messages.

SIP Uniform Resource Identifier

A resource within a SIP network is identified by a Uniform Resource Identifier (URI).[5] Examples of communications resources include the following:

- A user of an online service
- An appearance on a multiline phone

---

[5]A URI is a generic identifier used to name any resource on the Internet. The URL, used for Web addresses, is a type of URI. See RFC 2396 or the supporting document at this book's Web site for more detail.

- A mailbox on a messaging system
- A telephone number at a gateway service
- A group (such as "sales" or "helpdesk") in an organization

SIP URIs have a format based on e-mail address formats, namely user@domain. There are two common schemes. An ordinary SIP URI is of the form

`sip:bob@biloxi.com`

The URI may also include a password, port number, and related parameters. If secure transmission is required, "sip:" is replaced by "sips:". In the latter case, SIP messages are transported over TLS.

Examples of Operation

The SIP specification is quite complex; the main document, RFC 3261, is 269 pages long. To give some feel for its operation, we present a few examples.

Figure 4.9 shows an unsuccessful attempt by user Alice to establish a session with user Bob, whose URI is bob@biloxi.com.[6] Alice's UAC is configured to com-

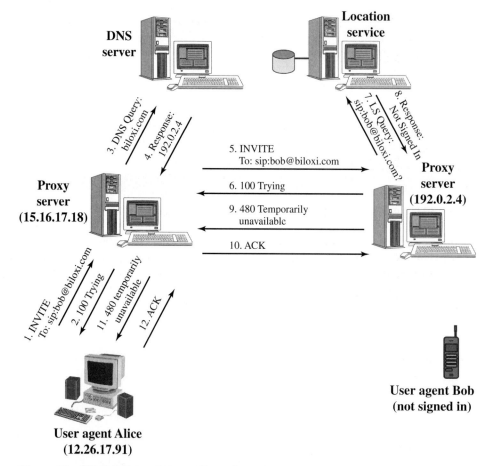

Figure 4.9 SIP Call Setup Attempt Scenario

municate with a proxy server (the outbound server) in its domain and begins by sending an INVITE message to the proxy server that indicates its desire to invite Bob's UAS into a session (1); the server acknowledges the request (2). Although Bob's UAS is identified by its URI, the outbound proxy server needs to take into account the possibility that Bob is not currently available or that Bob has moved. Accordingly, the outbound proxy server should forward the INVITE request to the proxy server that is responsible for the domain biloxi.com. The outbound proxy thus consults a local DNS server to obtain the IP address of the biloxi.com proxy server (3), by asking for the SRV resource record (Table 4.6) that contains information on the proxy server for biloxi.com.

The DNS server responds (4) with the IP address of the biloxi.com proxy server (the inbound server). Alice's proxy server can now forward the INVITE message to the inbound proxy server (5), which acknowledges the message (6). The inbound proxy server now consults a location server to determine the location of Bob (7), and the location server responds that Bob is not signed in, and therefore not available for SIP messages (8). This information is communicated back to the outbound proxy server (9, 10) and then to Alice (11, 12).

The next example (Figure 4.10) makes use of two message types that are not yet part of the SIP standard but that are documented in RFC 2848 and are likely to be incorporated in a later revision of SIP. These message types support telephony applications. At the end of the preceding example, Alice was informed that Bob was not available. Alice's UAC then issues a SUBSCRIBE message (1), indicating that it wants to be informed when Bob is available. This request is forwarded through the two proxies in our example to a PINT (PSTN-Internet Networking)[7] server (2, 3). A PINT server acts as a gateway between an IP network from which comes a request to place a telephone call and a telephone network that executes the call by connecting to the destination telephone. In this example, we assume that the PINT server logic is colocated with the location service. It could also be the case that Bob is attached to the Internet rather than a PSTN, in which case, the equivalent of PINT logic is needed to handle SUBSCRIBE requests. In this example, we assume that latter and assume that the PINT functionality is implemented in the location service. In any case, the location service authorizes subscription by returning an OK message (4), which is passed back to Alice (5, 6). The location service then immediately sends a NOTIFY message with Bob's current status of not signed in (7, 8, 9), which Alice's UAC acknowledges (10, 11, 12).

Figure 4.11 continues the example of Figure 4.10. Bob signs on by sending a REGISTER message to the proxy in its domain (1). The proxy updates the database at the location service to reflect registration (2). The update is confirmed to the proxy (3), which confirms the registration to Bob (4). The PINT functionality learns of Bob's new status from the location server (here we assume that they are

---

[6]Figures 4.9 through 4.12 are adapted from ones developed by Professor H. Charles Baker of Southern Methodist University.
[7]PSTN is the public switched telephone network.

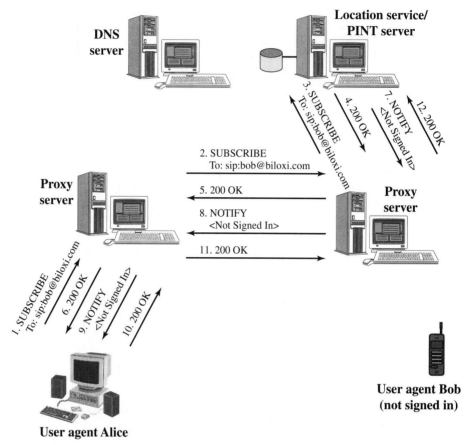

Figure 4.10 SIP Presence Example

colocated) and sends a NOTIFY message containing the new status of Bob (5), which is forwarded to Alice (6, 7). Alice's UAC acknowledges receipt of the notification (8, 9, 10).

Now that Bob is registered, Alice can try again to establish a session, as shown in Figure 4.12. This figure shows the same flow as Figure 4.9, with a few differences. We assume that Alice's proxy server has cached the IP address of the proxy server for domain biloxi.com, and therefore need not consult the DNS server. A ringing response is sent from Bob back to A (8, 9, 10) while the UAS at Bob is alerting the local media application (e.g., telephony). When the media application accepts the call, Bob's UAS sends back an OK response to Alice (11, 12, 13).

Finally, Alice's UAC sends an acknowledgement message to Bob's UAS to confirm the reception of the final response (14). In this example, the ACK is sent directly from Alice to Bob, bypassing the two proxies. This occurs because the endpoints have learned each other's address from the INVITE/200 (OK) exchange, which was not known when the initial INVITE was sent. The media session has now begun, and Alice and Bob can exchange data over an RTP connection.

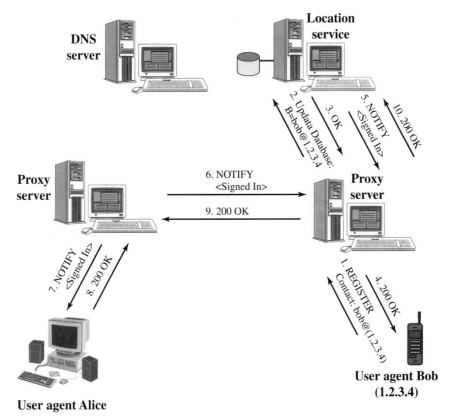

Figure 4.11 SIP Registration and Notification Example

SIP Messages

As was mentioned, SIP is a text-based protocol with a syntax similar to that of HTTP. There are two different types of SIP messages, requests and responses. The format difference between the two types of messages is seen in the first line. The first line of a request has a method, defining the nature of the request and a Request-URI, indicating where the request should be sent. The first line of a response has a **response code**. All messages include a header, consisting of a number of lines, each line beginning with a header label. A message can also contain a body, such as an SDP media description.

SIP Requests RFC 3261 defines the following methods:

- **REGISTER:** Used by a user agent to notify a SIP network of its current IP address and the URLs for which it would like to receive calls
- **INVITE:** Used to establish a media session between user agents
- **ACK:** Confirms reliable message exchanges
- **CANCEL:** Terminates a pending request, but does not undo a completed call
- **BYE:** Terminates a session between two users in a conference
- **OPTIONS:** Solicits information about the capabilities of the callee, but does not set up a call

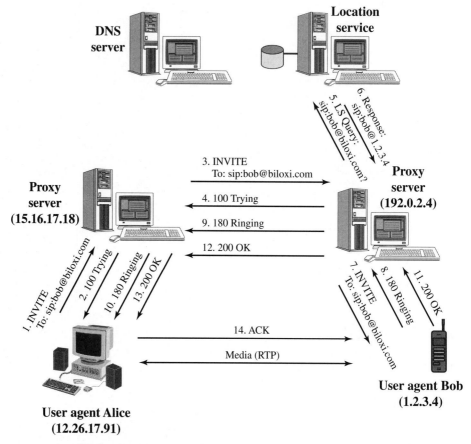

Figure 4.12   SIP Successful Call Setup

Table 4.8 shows the header fields that are defined for SIP. For example, the header of message (1) in Figure 4.12 might look like this:

```
INVITE sip:bob@biloxi.com SIP/2.0
Via: SIP/2.0/UDP 12.26.17.91:5060
Max-Forwards: 70
To: Bob <sip:bob@biloxi.com>
From: Alice <sip:alice@atlanta.com>;tag=1928301774
Call-ID: a84b4c76e66710@12.26.17.91
CSeq: 314159 INVITE
Contact: <sip:alice@atlanta.com>
Content-Type: application/sdp
Content-Length: 142
```

The boldface type used for header labels is not typical but is used here for clarity. The first line contains the method name (**INVITE**), a SIP URI, and the version number of SIP that is used. The lines that follow are a list of header fields. This example contains the minimum required set.

Table 4.8 SIP Header Fields

Accept	Indicates acceptable media types	Version of MIME used
Accept-Encoding	Acceptable content encodings	Minimum refresh interval
Accept-Language	Acceptable languages	Organization of originator of this message
Alert-Info	Alternative ring or ringback tone	Priority set by UAC
Allow		Authentication challenge
Authentication-Info		Authentication credentials of UA for proxy use
Authorization	Authentication credentials of UA	Features proxy must support
Call-ID	Uniquely identifies an invitation	Inserted by proxy to force future requests to be routed through this proxy
Call-Info		URI that may be different from From field
Contact	Provides a URI	Options UAS must support
Content-Disposition	How message body is to be interpreted	How long service may be unavailable
Content-Encoding	Additional encodings applied to message body	Route that must be followed
Content-Language	Language of message body	Information about UAS
Content-Length	Size of message body	Subject of session
Content-Type	Media type of message body	Options supported
Cseq	Sequence number incremented for each new request	Time when request sent
Date	Current date and time	Recipient of request
Error-Info	Additional information about error status response	Features not supported by UAS
Expires	Time after which message expires	Information about UAC originating request
From	Initiator of request	Path taken by request so far
In-Reply-To	Call-ID that his call references or returns	Additional information about response status
Max-Forwards	Maximum number of proxies that can forward request	Authenticate challenge.

MIME-Version		
Min-Expires		
Organization		
Priority		
Proxy-Authenticate		
Proxy-Authorization		
Proxy-Require		
Record-Route		
Reply-To		
Require		
Retry-After		
Route		
Server		
Subject		
Supported		
Timestamp		
To		
Unsupported		
User-Agent		
Via		
Warning		
WWW-Authenticate		

The **Via** headers show the path the request has taken in the SIP network (source and intervening proxies) and are used to route responses back along the same path. In message (1), there is only one Via header, inserted by Alice. The Via line contains the IP address (12.26.17.91), port number (5060), and transport protocol (UDP) that Alice wants Bob to use in his response. Subsequent proxies add additional Via headers.

Max-Forwards serves to limit the number of hops a request can make on the way to its destination. It consists of an integer that is decremented by one by each proxy that forwards the request. If the Max-Forwards value reaches 0 before the request reaches its destination, it will be rejected with a 483 (Too Many Hops) error response.

To contains a display name (Bob) and a SIP or SIPS URI (sip:bob@biloxi.com) toward which the request was originally directed. **From** also contains a display name (Alice) and a SIP or SIPS URI (sip:alice@atlanta.com) that indicate the originator of the request. This header field also has a tag parameter containing a random string (1928301774) that was added to the URI by the UAC. It is used to identify the session.

Call-ID contains a globally unique identifier for this call, generated by the combination of a random string and the host name or IP address. The combination of the To tag, From tag, and Call-ID completely defines a peer-to-peer SIP relationship between Alice and Bob and is referred to as a dialog.

CSeq or Command Sequence contains an integer and a method name. The CSeq number is initialized at the start of a call (314159 in this example), incremented for each new request within a dialog, and is a traditional sequence number. The CSeq is used to distinguish a retransmission from a new request.

The **Contact** header contains a SIP URI for direct communication between UAs. While the Via header field tells other elements where to send the response, the Contact header field tells other elements where to send future requests for this dialog.

The **Content-Type** indicates the type of the message body. **Content-Length** gives the length in octets of the message body.

SIP Responses Table 4.9 lists the response types defined in RFC 3261 (compare Table 4.4). These are in the following categories:

- **Provisional (1xx):** Request received and being processed.
- **Success (2xx):** The action was successfully received, understood, and accepted.
- **Redirection (3xx):** Further action needs to be taken in order to complete the request.
- **Client Error (4xx):** The request contains bad syntax or cannot be fulfilled at this server.
- **Server Error (5xx):** The server failed to fulfill an apparently valid request.
- **Global Failure (6xx):** The request cannot be fulfilled at any server.

For example, the header of message (11) in Figure 4.12 might look like this:

```
SIP/2.0 200 OK
Via: SIP/2.0/UDP server10.biloxi.com
Via: SIP/2.0/UDP bigbox3.site3.atlanta.com
Via: SIP/2.0/UDP 12.26.17.91:5060
```

Table 4.9 SIP Response Codes

Provisional	Client Error
100 Trying	400 Bad Request
180 Ringing	401 Unauthorized
181 Call Is Being Forwarded	402 Payment Required
182 Queued	403 Forbidden
183 Session Progress	404 Not Found
Success	405 Method Not Allowed
200 OK	406 Not Acceptable
Redirection	407 Proxy Authentication Required
300 Multiple Choices	408 Request Timeout
301 Moved Permanently	410 Gone
302 Moved Temporarily	413 Request Entity Too Large
305 Use Proxy	414 Request-URI Too Long
380 Alternative Service	415 Unsupported Media Type
Server Error	416 Unsupported URI Scheme
500 Server Internal Error	420 Bad Extension
501 Not Implemented	421 Extension Required
502 Bad Gateway	423 Interval Too Brief
503 Service Unavailable	480 Temporarily Unavailable
504 Server Timeout	481 Call/Transaction Does Not Exist
505 Version Not Supported	482 Loop Detected
513 Message Too Large	483 Too Many Hops
Global Failure	484 Address Incomplete
600 Busy Everywhere	485 Ambiguous
603 Decline	486 Busy Here
604 Does Not Exist Anywhere	487 Request Terminated
606 Not Acceptable	488 Not Acceptable Here
	491 Request Pending
	493 Undecipherable

```
To: Bob <sip:bob@biloxi.com>;tag=a6c85cf
From: Alice <sip:alice@atlanta.com>;tag=1928301774
Call-ID: a84b4c76e66710@12.26.17.91
CSeq: 314159 INVITE
Contact: <sip:bob@biloxi.com>
Content-Type: application/sdp
Content-Length: 131
```

The first line contains the version number of SIP that is used and the response code and name. The lines that follow are a list of header fields. The Via, To, From, Call-ID, and CSeq header fields are copied from the INVITE request. (There are three Via header field values—one added by Alice's SIP UAC, one added by the atlanta.com proxy, and one added by the biloxi.com proxy.) Bob's SIP phone has added a tag parameter to the To header field. This tag will be incorporated by both endpoints into the dialog and will be included in all future requests and responses in this call.

Session Description Protocol

The Session Description Protocol (SDP), defined in RFC 2327, describes the content of sessions, including telephony, Internet radio, and multimedia applications. SDP includes information about the following [SCHU99]:

- **Media streams:** A session can include multiple streams of differing content. SDP currently defines audio, video, data, control, and application as stream types, similar to the MIME types used for Internet mail (Table 3.6).
- **Addresses:** Indicates the destination addresses, which may be a multicast address, for a media stream.
- **Ports:** For each stream, the UDP port numbers for sending and receiving are specified.
- **Payload types:** For each media stream type in use (e.g., telephony), the payload type indicates the media formats that can be used during the session.
- **Start and stop times:** These apply to broadcast sessions, like a television or radio program. The start, stop, and repeat times of the session are indicated.
- **Originator:** For broadcast sessions, the originator is specified, with contact information. This may be useful if a receiver encounters technical difficulties.

4.4 SOCKETS

The concept of sockets and sockets programming was developed in the 1980s in the UNIX environment as the Berkeley Sockets Interface. In essence, a socket enables communication between a client and server process and may be either connection-oriented or connectionless. A socket can be considered an endpoint in a communication. A client socket in one computer uses an address to call a server socket on another computer. Once the appropriate sockets are engaged, the two computers can exchange data.

Typically, computers with server sockets keep a TCP or UDP port open, ready for unscheduled incoming calls. The client typically determines the socket identification of the desired server by finding it in a Domain Name System (DNS) database. Once a connection is made, the server switches the dialogue to a different port number to free up the main port number for additional incoming calls.

Internet applications, such as TELNET and remote login (rlogin) make use of sockets, with the details hidden from the user. However, sockets can be constructed from within a program (in a language such as C or Java), enabling the programmer to easily support networking functions and applications. The sockets programming mechanism includes sufficient semantics to permit unrelated processes on different hosts to communicate.

The Berkeley Sockets Interface is the de facto standard application programming interface (API) for developing networking applications, spanning a wide range of operating systems. Windows Sockets (WinSock) is based on the Berkeley specification. The sockets API provides generic access to interprocess communications services. Thus, the sockets capability is ideally suited for students to learn the principles of protocols and distributed applications by hands-on program development.

The Socket

Recall from Chapter 2 that each TCP and UDP header includes source port and destination port fields (Figure 2.12). These **port** values identify the respective users (applications) of the two TCP entities. Also, each IPv4 and IPv6 header includes source address and destination address fields (Figure 2.13); these **IP addresses** identify the respective host systems. The concatenation of a port value and an IP address forms a **socket**, which is unique throughout the Internet. Thus, in Figure 2.14, the combination of the IP address for host B and the port number for application X uniquely identifies the socket location of application X. As the figure indicates, an application may have multiple socket addresses, one for each port in the application.

The socket is used to define an **application programming interface** (API), which is a generic communication interface for writing programs that use TCP or UDP. In practice, when used as an API, a socket is identified by the triple (protocol, local-address, local-process). The local-address is an IP address and the local-process is a port number. Because port numbers are unique within a system, the port number implies the protocol (TCP or UDP). However, for clarity and ease of implementation, sockets used for an API include the protocol as well as the IP address and port number in defining a unique socket.

Corresponding to the two protocols, the Sockets API recognizes two types of sockets: stream sockets and datagram sockets. **Stream sockets** make use of TCP, which provides a connection-oriented reliable data transfer. Therefore, with stream sockets, all blocks of data sent between a pair of sockets are guaranteed for delivery and arrive in the order that they were sent. **Datagram sockets** make use of UDP, which does not provide the connection-oriented features of TCP. Therefore, with datagram sockets, delivery is not guaranteed, nor is order necessarily preserved.

There is a third type of socket provided by the Sockets API: raw sockets. **Raw sockets** allow direct access to lower layer protocols, such as IP and ICMP.

Socket Interface Calls

Table 4.10 lists the most important of the socket interface calls.

Socket Setup The first step in using Sockets is to create a new socket using the socket() command. This command includes three parameters, the protocol family is always PF_INET, for the TCP/IP protocol suite. *Type* specifies whether this is a stream or datagram socket, and *protocol* specifies either TCP or UDP. The reason that both *type* and *protocol* need to be specified is to allow additional transport-level

Table 4.10   Socket Functions

Function	Description
Socket Setup	
int sockfd = socket (int protocolFamily, int type, int protocol)	Creates a TCP or UDP socket; returns descriptor of socket if no error, otherwise −1.
int bind (int sockfd, struct sockaddr *localAddress, int addrlen)	Assigns the local IP address and port for a socket. Returns 0 for success and −1 for error.
Socket Connection	
int listen (int sockfd, int backlog)	Indicates given socket is ready to accept incoming connection, where backlog indicates the number of connection requests that can be queued while the local process has not yet issued the accept call.
int sockfd = accept (int sockfd, struct sockaddr *clientAddress, int *addrlen)	Accept first call waiting on listen queue; if queue empty, block process waiting for incoming call.
int connect (int sockfd, struct sockaddr *foreignAddress, int addrlen)	Establishes a connection between the given socket and the remote socket associated with sockaddr.
int getpeername (int sockfd, struct sockaddr *foreignAddress, int *addrlen)	Returns the remote information (on the other end of the connectionm) for a socket in a sockaddr structure.
Socket Communication	
int send (int sockfd, const void *msg, int len, int flags)	Send the bytes contained in buffer pointed to by *msg over the given socket.
int recv(int sockfd, void *buf, int len, unsigned int flags)	Copies up to a specified number of bytes, received on the socket, into a specified location.
close(sockfd)	Terminates connection on a socket. No further sends or receives are allowed.
int shutdown(int sockfd, int how)	Terminates connection on a socket. The second parameter indicates whether sends, receives, or both are disallowed.
int sendto(int sockfd, const void *msg, int len, unsigned int flags, const struct destAddr *to, int destAddrLen)	Sends bytes in datagram style between specified sockets.
int recvfrom(int sockfd, void *buf, int len, unsigned int flags, struct sockaddr *fromAddr, int *fromAddrLen)	Receives bytes in datagram style.

(continues on next page)

Table 410 (continued)

Socket Control	
int getsockopt (int sockfd, in level, int optName, void *optVal, unsigned int optLen)	Retrieves a socket option.
int setsockopt (int sockfd, in level, int optName, void *optVal, unsigned int optLen)	Sets the options on a socket.
Host and Service Information	
int gethostname(char *hostname, unsigned int length)	Returns local host name.
struct hostent *gethostbyname (const char *hostname)	Returns a hosent structure containing a description of the named host, including its address.
struct hostent *gethostbyaddr (const *address, int addrlen, int addressFamily)	Given an IP address, returns a hosent struction containing a description of the host with that address.
struct servent *getservbyname(const char *serviceName, const char *protocol	Given the name of a service (e.g., echo) and the protocol supporting that service, returns a servent structure for that host.
struct servent *getservbyport (int port, const char *protocol)	Given a port and the name of the service protocol, returns a servent structure for that service.

protocols to be included in a future implementation. Thus, there might be more than one datagram-style transport protocol or more than one connection-oriented transport protocol. The socket() command returns an integer result that identifies this socket; it is similar to a Unix file descriptor. The exact socket data structure depends on the implementation. It includes the source port and IP address and, if a connection is open or pending, the destination port and IP address and various options and parameters associated with the connection.

After a socket is created, it must have an address to listen to. The bind() function binds a socket to a socket address. The address has the following structure:

```
struct sockaddr_in {
    short int sin_family;            // Address family (TCP/IP)
    unsigned short int sin_port;     // Port number
    struct in_addr sin_addr;         // Internet address
    unsigned char sin_zero[8];       // Same size as struct sockaddr
};
```

Socket Connection For a stream socket, once the socket is created, a connection must be set up to a remote socket. One side functions as a client, and requests a connection to the other side, which acts as a server.

The server side of a connection setup requires two steps. First, a server application issues a listen(), indicating that the given socket is ready to accept incoming connections. The parameter *backlog* is the number of connections allowed on the incoming queue. Each incoming connection is placed in this queue until a matching accept() is issued by the server side. Next, the accept() call is used to remove one request from the queue. If the queue is empty, the accept() blocks the process until a connection request arrives. If there is a waiting call, then accept() returns a new file descriptor for the connection. This creates a new socket, which has the IP address and port number of the remote party, the IP address of this system, and a new port number. The reason that a new socket with a new port number is assigned is that this enables the local application to continue to listen for more requests. As a result, an application may have multiple connections active at any time, each with a different local port number. This new port number is returned across the TCP connection to the requesting system.

A client application issues a connect() that specifies a local socket and the address of a remote socket. If the connection attempt is unsuccessful connect() returns the value −1. If the attempt is successful, connect() returns a 0 and fills in the file descriptor parameter to include the IP address and port number of the local and foreign sockets. Recall that the remote port number may differ from that specified in the *foreignAddress* parameter because the port number is changed on the remote host.

Once a connection is set up, getpeername() can be used to find out who is on the other end of the connected stream socket. The function returns a value in the *sockfd* parameter.

Socket Communication For **stream communication**, the functions send() and recv() are used to send or receive data over the connection identified by the sockfd parameter. In the send() call, the *msg* parameter points to the block of data to be sent and the *len* parameter specifies the number of bytes to be sent. The *flags* parameter contains control flags, typically set to 0. The send() call returns the number of bytes sent, which may be less than the number specified in the len parameter. In the recv() call, the *buf* parameter points to the buffer for storing incoming data, with an upper limit on the number of bytes set by the *len* parameter.

At any time, either side can close the connection with the close() call, which prevents further sends and receives. The shutdown() call allows the caller to terminate sending or receiving or both.

Figure 4.13 shows the interaction of the clients and server sides in setting up, using, and terminating a connection.

For **datagram communication**, the functions sendto() and recvfrom() are used. The sendto() call includes all the parameters of the send() call plus a specification of

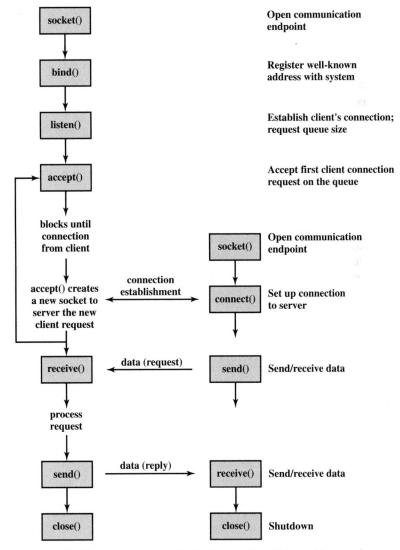

Figure 4.13 Socket Systems Calls for Connection-Oriented Protocol

the destination address (IP address and port). Similarly, the recvfrom() call includes an address parameter, which is filled in when data are received.

Other System Calls Table 4.10 also includes some other useful system calls. The getsockopt() and setsockopt() calls enable the user to read and alter options related to a socket.

The remaining calls listed in Table 4.10 deal with obtaining name or address information. The two most important are gethostbyname() and gethostname(). To set up a connection to a remote host, or to send a datagram block to a remote host, the IP address and port number of the remote socket must be known. Typically, an application will only have the domain name of the remote host. The gethostname() call is used to return the address of the remote host. In addition, the local address must be known. Unless this information is configured into the application, the local Sockets implementation can obtain this information in two steps. First, the application issues a gethostname() call, which returns the name of this system, and then a gethostbyname() call using the local name to get the local address.

Examples

To get a feel for the use of Sockets, we look at some basic examples in this section.[8]

Socket Establishment The following function shows how to use the socket(), bind(), and listen() functions to establish a socket which can accept calls:

```
int establish(unsigned short portnum)
{ char    myname[MAXHOSTNAME+1];
  int     s;
  struct sockaddr_in sa;
  struct hostent *hp;

  memset(&sa, 0, sizeof(struct sockaddr_in));      /* clear our address */
  gethostname(myname, MAXHOSTNAME);                      /* who are we? */
  hp= gethostbyname(myname);                       /* get our address info */
  if (hp == NULL)                                    /* we don't exist !? */
    return(-1);
  sa.sin_family= hp->h_addrtype;              /* this is our host address */
  sa.sin_port= htons(portnum);                /* this is our port number */
  if ((s= socket(AF_INET, SOCK_STREAM, 0)) < 0)       /* create socket */
    return(-1);
  if (bind(s,(struct sockaddr *)&sa,sizeof(struct sockaddr_in)) < 0) {
    close(s);
    return(-1);                               /* bind address to socket */
  }
  listen(s, 3);                             /* max # of queued connects */
  return(s);
}
```

Once a socket is established, a simple server program then waits for incoming calls. This code forks off incoming calls as new jobs so that multiple connections can be handled simultaneously.

---

[8]These examples are taken, with permission, from *BSD Sockets: A Quick and Dirty Primer*, by Jim Frost, 1996 (world.std.com/~jimf/papers/sockets/sockets.html).

```
#include <errno.h>                          /* obligatory includes */
#include <signal.h>
#include <stdio.h>
#include <unistd.h>
#include <sys/types.h>
#include <sys/socket.h>
#include <sys/wait.h>
#include <netinet/in.h>
#include <netdb.h>

#define PORTNUM 50000           /* random port number, we need something */

void fireman(void);
void do_something(int);

main()
{ int s, t;

  if ((s= establish(PORTNUM)) < 0) {            /* establish connection */
    perror("establish");
    exit(1);
  }

  signal(SIGCHLD, fireman);                 /* this eliminates zombies */

  for (;;) {                                    /* loop for requests */
    if ((t= get_connection(s)) < 0) {              /* get a connection */
      if (errno == EINTR)           /* EINTR might happen on accept(), */
        continue;                                      /* try again */
      perror("accept");                                     /* bad */
      exit(1);
    }
    switch(fork()) {                      /* try to handle connection */
    case -1 :                             /* bad news.  scream and die */
      perror("fork");
      close(s);
      close(t);
      exit(1);
    case 0 :                           /* we're the child, do something */
      close(s);
      do_something(t);
      exit(0);
    default :                             /* we're the parent so look for */
      close(t);                                /* another connection */
      continue;
    }
  }
}

        /* as children die we should get catch their returns or else we get
         * zombies, A Bad Thing.  fireman() catches falling children.
                                                                        */
void fireman(void)
{
  while (waitpid(-1, NULL, WNOHANG) > 0)
    ;
}
```

```
                        /* this is the function that plays with the socket.  it will be called

                                                  * after getting a connection.

                                                                             */
void do_something(int s)
{

                                           /* do your thing with the socket here
    :
    :

                                                                             */
}
```

On the client side, code is needed for calling to a remote socket. Here is an example, which returns a connected socket through which data can flow.

```
int call_socket(char *hostname, unsigned short portnum)
{ struct sockaddr_in sa;
  struct hostent      *hp;
  int a, s;

  if ((hp= gethostbyname(hostname)) == NULL) {   /* do we know the host's */
    errno= ECONNREFUSED;                                        /* address? */
    return(-1);                                                      /* no */
  }

  memset(&sa,0,sizeof(sa));
  memcpy((char *)&sa.sin_addr,hp->h_addr,hp->h_length);    /* set address */
  sa.sin_family= hp->h_addrtype;
  sa.sin_port= htons((u_short)portnum);

  if ((s= socket(hp->h_addrtype,SOCK_STREAM,0)) < 0)          /* get socket */
    return(-1);
  if (connect(s,(struct sockaddr *)&sa,sizeof sa) < 0) {       /* connect */
    close(s);
    return(-1);
  }
  return(s);
}
```

Finally, here is an example of a function to read a number of characters into a buffer. Keep in mind that the recv function does not necessarily return the number of bytes asked for, so that a loop is needed to get all of the bytes.

```
int read_data(int s,                            /* connected socket */
              char *buf,                      /* pointer to the buffer */
              int n                    /* number of characters (bytes) we want */
              )
{ int bcount;                                   /* counts bytes read */
  int br;                                     /* bytes read this pass */

  bcount= 0;
  br= 0;
  while (bcount < n) {                            /* loop until full buffer */
```

```
    if ((br= recv(s,buf,n-bcount)) > 0) {
      bcount += br;                               /* increment byte counter */
      buf += br;                             /* move buffer ptr for next read */
    }
    else if (br < 0)                         /* signal an error to the caller */
      return(-1);
  }
  return(bcount);
}
```

4.5 RECOMMENDED READING AND WEB SITES

[GOUR02] provides comprehensive coverage of HTTP. Another good treatment is [KRIS01]. [SCHU98] is a good overview of SIP. [GOOD02] and [SCHU99] discuss SIP in the context of VoIP. [DIAN02] looks at SIP in the context of the support of multimedia services over the Internet. An excellent concise introduction to using Sockets is [DONA01]; another good overview is [HALL01]. [MCKU96] and [WRIG95] provide details of Sockets implementation.

DIAN02 Dianda, J.; Gurbani, V.; and Jones, M. "Session Initiation Protocol Services Architecture." *Bell Labs Technical Journal*, Volume 7, Number 1, 2002.

DONA01 Donahoo, M., and Clavert, K. *The Pocket Guide to TCP/IP Sockets.* San Francisco, CA: Morgan Kaufmann, 2001.

GOOD02 Goode, B. "Voice Over Internet Protocol (VoIP)." *Proceedings of the IEEE*, September 2002.

GOUR02 Gourley, D., et al. *HTTP: The Definitive Guide.* Sebastopol, CA: O'Reilly, 2002.

HALL01 Hall, B. *Beej's Guide to Network Programming Using Internet Sockets.* 2001. http://www.ecst.csuchico.edu/~beej/guide/net/html/.

KRIS01 Krishnamurthy, B., and Rexford, J. *Web Protocols and Practice: HTTP/1.1, Networking Protocols, Caching, and Traffic Measurement.* Upper Saddle River, NJ: Prentice Hall, 2001.

MCKU96 McKusick, M.; Bostic, K.; Karels, M.; and Quartermain, J. *The Design and Implementation of the 4.4BSD UNIX Operating System.* Reading, MA: Addison-Wesley, 1996.

SCHU98 Schulzrinne, H., and Rosenberg, J. "The Session Initiation Protocol: Providing Advanced Telephony Access Across the Internet." *Bell Labs Technical Journal*, October-December 1998.

SCHU99 Schulzrinne, H., and Rosenberg, J. "The IETF Internet Telephony Architecture and Protocols." *IEEE Network*, May/June 1999.

WRIG95 Wright, G., and Stevens, W. *TCP/IP Illustrated, Volume 2: The Implementation.* Reading, MA: Addison-Wesley, 1995.

Recommended Web Sites:

- **WWW consortium:** Contains up-to-date information on HTTP and related topics.
- **DNS extensions working group:** Chartered by IETF to develop standards related to DNS. The Web site includes all relevant RFCs and Internet drafts.

- **SIP Forum:** Nonprofit organization to promote SIP. Site contains product information, white papers, and other useful information and links.
- **SIP working group:** Chartered by IETF to develop standards related to SIP. The Web site includes all relevant RFCs and Internet drafts.

4.6 KEY TERMS, REVIEW QUESTIONS, AND PROBLEMS

Key Terms

application programming interface (API)	iterative technique	SIP method
	name server	SIP proxy server
Backus-Naur Form (BNF)	origin server	SIP redirect server
datagram sockets	raw sockets	SIP registrar
domain	recursive technique	socket
domain name	resolver	Sockets
Domain Name Service (DNS)	resource record (RR)	stream sockets
HTTP gateway	root name server	Uniform Resource Identifier (URI)
HTTP method	Session Description Protocol (SDP)	
HTTP proxy		Uniform Resource Locator (URL)
HTTP tunnel	Session Initiation Protocol (SIP)	
Hypertext Transfer Protocol (HTTP)		voice over IP (VoIP)
	SIP location service	zone

Review Questions

4.1 What is meant by saying that HTTP is a stateless protocol?

4.2 Explain the differences among HTTP proxy, gateway, and tunnel.

4.3 What is the function of the cache in HTTP?

4.4 What is DNS?

4.5 What is the difference between a name server and a resolver in DNS?

4.6 What is a DNS resource record?

4.7 Give a brief description of DNS operation.

4.8 What is the difference between a domain and a zone?

4.9 Explain the difference between the recursive technique and the iterative technique in DNS.

4.10 What are the five key services provided by SIP?

4.11 List and briefly define the major components in an SIP network.

4.12 What is the session description protocol?

4.13 What is the purpose of the Sockets interface?

4.14 What is a socket?

4.15 Explain the difference between stream sockets and datagram sockets.

Problems

Note: For some of the problems in this chapter, you will need to consult the relevant RFCs.

4.1 Prior to persistent connections, one separate TCP connection was used to fetch each URL. Analyze the advantages of persistent connections over the old HTTP paradigm of one connection per data transfer.

4.2 Classify a DNS resolver and a DNS name server as either client, server, or both.

4.3 A DNS resolver typically issues a query using UDP but may also use TCP. Is there a problem using TCP for this purpose? If so, what do you suggest is the solution? *Hint: consider Figure 2.12.*

4.4 What's the main difference between a primary and a secondary name server?

4.5 Name servers can be accessed on UDP port 53 as well as on TCP port 53. When is each protocol used, and why?

4.6 We query an authoritative name server for the 'example.com' zone, in order to get the IP address of www.example.com, the web site of a large company. We get eight A records in response to our query. We repeat this query several times, and note that we continue getting the same eight A records, but in a different order each time. Suggest a reason why.

4.7 The dig tool is available for UNIX and Windows operating systems. It can also be used from the Web. Here are three sites that, at the time of this writing, provided free access to dig:

http://www.webmaster-toolkit.com/dig.shtml
http://www.webhostselect.com/whs/dig-tool.jsp
http://www.gont.com.ar/tools/dig

Use the 'dig' tool to get the list of root servers.

4.8 Discuss the advantages of using a several 'stub resolvers' along with a caching-only name server, instead of a several 'full resolvers'.

4.9 Choose a root server, and use the 'dig' tool to send it a query for the IP address of www.example.com, with the RD (Recursion Desired) bit set. Does it support recursive lookups? Why or why not?

4.10 Type 'dig www.example.com A' in order to get the IP address of www.example.com. What's the TTL of the A record returned in the response? Wait a while, and repeat the query. Why has the TTL changed?

4.11 With the widespread use of x-DSL and cable-modem technologies, many home users now host web sites on their own desktop computers. As their IP addresses are dynamically assigned by their Internet Service Providers (ISPs), users must update their DNS records every time their IP addresses change (it's usually done by some computer software on the user machine that automatically contacts the name server to update the corresponding data whenever the assigned IP address changes). This service is usually called 'Dynamic DNS'. However, in order for these updates to work as expected, there's one field of each resource record that must be set to a quite different value from the typical ones. Which one, and why?

4.12 Secondary name servers periodically query the primary to check whether the zone data has been updated. Regardless of how many resource records the zone data contains, the secondary name servers need to query only primary one resource record to detect any changes on the zone data. Which resource record will they query? How will they use the requested information to detect changes?

4.13 A user on the host 170.210.17.145 is using a web browser to visit www.example.com. In order to resolve the 'www.example.com' domain to an IP address, a query is sent to an authoritative name server for the 'example.com' domain. In response, the name server returns a list of four IP addresses, in the following order {192.168.0.1, 128.0.0.1, 200.47.57.1, 170.210.10.130}. Even though it is the last IP address in the list returned by the name server, the web browser creates a connection to 170.210.17.130. Why?

4.14 Before the deployment of the Domain Name System, a simple text file ('HOSTS.TXT') centrally maintained at the SRI Network Information Center was used to enable mapping between host names and addresses. Each host connected to the Internet had to have an updated local copy of it to be able to use host names instead of having to cope directly with their IP addresses. Discuss the main advantages of the DNS over the old centralized HOSTS.TXT system.

PART THREE

Transport Protocols

Part Three looks at protocol design and performance issues at the transport protocol level.

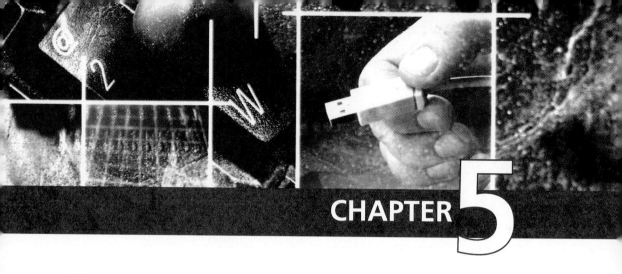

CHAPTER 5

CONGESTION AND PERFORMANCE ISSUES

At St. Paul's a great throng crammed the platform. She saw a sea of faces, each stamped with a kind of purposeful, hungry urgency, a determination to get into this train. As before, when she was on the Northern Line, she thought there must be some rule, some operating law, that would stop more than a limited, controlled number getting in. Authority would appear and stop it.

—*King Solomon's Carpet,*
Barbara Vine (Ruth Rendell)

The thoughts in which Swedenborg lived were, the universality of each law in nature; the Platonic doctrine of the scale or degrees; the version or conversion of each into the other, and so the correspondence of all the parts; the fine secret that little explains large, and large, little. This theory dates from the oldest philosophers, and derives perhaps its best illustration from the newest. It is this; that nature iterates her means perpetually on successive planes. In the old aphorism, nature is always self-similar.

—*Representative Men,*
Ralph Waldo Emerson

KEY POINTS

- The increasing data rate (capacity) requirements of applications have spurred the development of higher speeds in data networks and the Internet. The higher available capacity has in turn encouraged ever more data-intensive applications.

163

- Two critical performance requirements for applications are response time and throughput.

- Two critical performance metrics for data networks and the Internet are delay and throughput. Delay elements include transmission delay, propagation delay, processing delay, and queuing delay.

- With increasing data rates, particularly with the use of gigabit speeds, the delay × throughput product becomes a critical parameter limiting performance.

- Congestion occurs when the number of packets being transmitted through a network begins to approach the packet-handling capacity of the network.

- The objective of congestion control is to maintain the number of packets within the network below the level at which performance falls off dramatically.

A key design issue that must be confronted both with data networks, such as packet-switching, frame relay, and ATM networks, and also with internets, is that of congestion control. The phenomenon of congestion is a complex one, as is the subject of congestion control. In very general terms, congestion occurs when the number of packets[1] being transmitted through a network begins to approach the packet-handling capacity of the network. The objective of congestion control is to maintain the number of packets within the network below the level at which performance falls off dramatically.

This chapter focuses on the issues of congestion and congestion control. We begin with a discussion of the performance requirements from an application point of view and performance metrics from the point of view of the transmission of packets over networks and internets. The chapter then discusses the effects of congestion and approaches to managing these effects. Finally, the concept of self-similar traffic is introduced, to show that performance problems in congested networks may be more severe than previously understood.

5.1 THE NEED FOR SPEED AND QUALITY OF SERVICE

Momentous changes in the way corporations do business and process information have been driven by changes in networking technology and at the same time have driven those changes. It is hard to separate chicken and egg in this field. Similarly, the use of the Internet by both businesses and individuals reflects this cyclic dependency: The availability of new image-based services on the Internet (i.e., the Web) has resulted in an increase in the total number of users and the traffic volume

---

[1]In this chapter we use the term *packet* in a broad sense, to include packets in a packet-switching network, frames in a frame relay network, cells in an ATM network, or IP datagrams in an internet.

generated by each user. This, in turn, has resulted in a need to increase the speed and efficiency of the Internet. On the other hand, it is only such increased speed that makes the use of Web-based applications palatable to the end user.

In this section, we survey some of the end-user factors that fit into this equation. We begin with the need for high-speed LANs in the business environment, because this need has appeared first and has forced the pace of networking development. Then we look at business WAN requirements. Then we offer a few words about the effect of changes in commercial electronics on network requirements. Finally, we relate the requirements for quality of service (QoS) to the Internet.

The Emergence of High-Speed LANs

Personal computers and microcomputer workstations began to achieve widespread acceptance in business computing in the early 1980s and have now achieved virtually the status of the telephone: an essential tool for office workers. Until relatively recently, office LANs provided basic connectivity services—connecting personal computers and terminals to mainframes and midrange systems that ran corporate applications, and providing workgroup connectivity at the departmental or divisional level. In both cases, traffic patterns were relatively light, with an emphasis on file transfer and electronic mail. The LANs that were available for this type of workload, primarily Ethernet and token ring, are well suited to this environment.

In the 1990s, two significant trends altered the role of the personal computer and therefore the requirements on the LAN:

1. The speed and computing power of personal computers continued to enjoy explosive growth. These more powerful platforms support graphics-intensive applications and ever more elaborate graphical user interfaces to the operating system.

2. MIS (management information systems) organizations have recognized the LAN as a viable and essential computing platform, resulting in the focus on network computing. This trend began with client/server computing, which has become a dominant architecture in the business environment, and the more recent Web-focused intranet trend. Both of these approaches involve the frequent transfer of potentially large volumes of data in a transaction-oriented environment.

The effect of these trends has been to increase the volume of data to be handled over LANs and, because applications are more interactive, to reduce the acceptable delay on data transfers. The earlier generation of 10-Mbps Ethernets and 16-Mbps token rings is simply not up to the job of supporting these requirements.

The following are examples of requirements that call for higher-speed LANs:

*   **Centralized server farms:** In many applications, there is a need for user, or client, systems to be able to draw huge amounts of data from multiple centralized servers, called server farms. An example is a color publishing operation, in which servers typically contain tens of gigabytes of image data that must be downloaded to imaging workstations. As the performance of the servers themselves has increased, the bottleneck has shifted to the network.

*   **Power workgroups:** These groups typically consist of a small number of cooperating users who need to draw massive data files across the network.

Examples are a software development group that runs tests on a new software version, or a computer-aided design (CAD) company that regularly runs simulations of new designs. In such cases, large amounts of data are distributed to several workstations, processed, and updated at very high speed for multiple iterations.

- **High-speed local backbone:** As processing demand grows, LANs proliferate at a site, and high-speed interconnection is necessary.

Corporate Wide Area Networking Needs

As recently as the early 1990s, there was an emphasis in many organizations on a centralized data processing model. In a typical environment, there might be significant computing facilities at a few regional offices, consisting of mainframes or well-equipped midrange systems. These centralized facilities could handle most corporate applications, including basic finance, accounting, and personnel programs, as well as many of the business-specific applications. Smaller, outlying offices (e.g., a bank branch) could be equipped with terminals or basic personal computers linked to one of the regional centers in a transaction-oriented environment.

This model began to change in the early 1990s, and the change accelerated through the mid-1990s. Many organizations have dispersed their employees into multiple smaller offices. There is a growing use of telecommuting. Most significant, the nature of the application structure has changed. First client/server computing and, more recently, intranet computing have fundamentally restructured the organizational data processing environment. There is now much more reliance on personal computers, workstations, and servers and much less use of centralized mainframe and midrange systems. Furthermore, the virtually universal deployment of graphical user interfaces to the desktop enables the end user to exploit graphic applications, multimedia, and other data-intensive applications. In addition, most organizations require access to the Internet. When a few clicks of the mouse can trigger huge volumes of data, traffic patterns have become more unpredictable while the average load has risen.

All of these trends means that more data must be transported off premises and into the wide area. It has long been accepted that in the typical business environment, about 80% of the traffic remains local and about 20% traverses wide area links. But this rule no longer applies to most companies, with a greater percentage of the traffic going into the WAN environment [COHE96]. This traffic flow shift places a greater burden on LAN backbones and, of course, on the WAN facilities used by a corporation. Thus, just as in the local area, changes in corporate data traffic patterns are driving the creation of high-speed WANs.

Digital Electronics

The rapid conversion of consumer electronics to digital technology is having an impact on both the Internet and corporate intranets. As these new gadgets come into view and proliferate, they dramatically increase the amount of image and video traffic carried by networks.

Two noteworthy examples of this trend are digital versatile disks and digital still cameras.

Digital Versatile Disk (DVD) With the capacious DVD, the electronics industry has at last found an acceptable replacement for the analog VHS videotape. The DVD will replace the videotape used in videocassette recorders (VCRs) and, more important for this discussion, replace the CD-ROM in personal computers and servers. The DVD takes video into the digital age. It delivers movies with picture quality that outshines laser disks, and it can be randomly accessed like audio CDs, which DVD machines can also play. Vast volumes of data can be crammed onto the disk, currently seven times as much as a CD-ROM. With DVD's huge storage capacity and vivid quality, PC games have become more realistic and educational software incorporates more video. Following in the wake of these developments is a new crest of traffic over the Internet and corporate intranets, as this material is incorporated into Web sites.

A related product development is the digital camcorder. This product will make it easier for individuals and companies to make digital video files to be placed on corporate and Internet Web sites, again adding to the traffic burden.

Digital Still Camera Although the digital still camera has been around for about many years, it is only recently beginning to take off because prices have dropped to reasonable levels. As yet, quality does not approach that of film, but the convenience for use in networks is unsurpassed. An individual can take a picture of a loved one or pet and transfer it to a Web page. Companies can quickly develop online product catalogs with full-color pictures of every product. Thus, there has been a dramatic growth in the amount of online image and video traffic in recent years.

QoS on the Internet

The Internet and the Internet Protocol (IP) were designed to provide a **best-effort**, fair delivery service. Under a best-effort scheme, the Internet (or a private intranet) treats all packets equally. As the level of traffic on the network grows, and congestion occurs, all packet delivery is slowed down. If congestion becomes severe, packets are dropped more or less at random to ease the congestion. No distinction is made in terms of the relative importance of any traffic or of the timeliness requirements of any of the traffic.

But the needs of users have changed. With the tremendous increase in traffic volume and the introduction of new real-time, multimedia, and multicasting applications, the traditional Internet protocols and services are woefully inadequate. A company may have spent millions of dollars installing an IP-based internet designed to transport data among LANs but now finds that new real-time, multimedia, and multicasting applications are not well supported by such a configuration. The only networking scheme designed from day one to support both traditional TCP and User Datagram Protocol (UDP) traffic and real-time traffic is ATM. However, reliance on ATM means either constructing a second networking infrastructure for real-time traffic or replacing the existing IP-based configuration with ATM, both of which are costly alternatives.

Traffic on a network or internet can be divided into two broad categories: elastic and inelastic. A consideration of their differing requirements clarifies the need for an enhanced internet architecture.

Elastic traffic can adjust, over wide ranges, to changes in delay and throughput across an internet and still meet the needs of its applications. This is the traditional type of traffic supported on TCP/IP-based internets and is the type of traffic for which internets were designed. With TCP, traffic on individual connections adjusts to congestion by reducing the rate at which data are presented to the network.

Elastic applications include common Internet-based applications, such as file transfer, electronic mail, remote logon, network management, and Web access. But there are differences among the requirements of these applications. For example,

- E-mail is generally quite insensitive to changes in delay.
- When file transfer is done online, as it frequently is, the user expects the delay to be proportional to the file size and so is sensitive to changes in throughput.
- With network management, delay is generally not a serious concern. However, if failures in an internet are the cause of congestion, then the need for network management messages to get through with minimum delay increases with increased congestion.
- Interactive applications, such as remote logon and Web access, are quite sensitive to delay.

So, even if we confine our attention to elastic traffic, a QoS-based internet service could be of benefit. Without such a service, routers are dealing evenhandedly with arriving IP packets, with no concern for the type of application and whether this packet is part of a large transfer or a small one. Under such circumstances, and if congestion develops, it is unlikely that resources will be allocated in such a way as to meet the needs of all applications fairly. When inelastic traffic is added to the mix, matters are even more unsatisfactory.

Inelastic traffic does not easily adapt, if at all, to changes in delay and throughput across an internet. The prime example is real-time traffic, such as voice and video. The requirements for inelastic traffic may include the following:

- **Throughput:** A minimum throughput value may be required. Unlike most elastic traffic, which can continue to deliver data with perhaps degraded service, many inelastic applications require a firm minimum throughput.
- **Delay:** An example of a delay-sensitive application is stock trading; someone who consistently receives later service will consistently act later, and with greater disadvantage.
- **Delay variation:** The larger the allowable delay, the longer the real delay in delivering the data and the greater the size of the delay buffer required at receivers. Real-time interactive applications, such as teleconferencing, may require a reasonable upper bound on delay variation.
- **Packet loss:** Real-time applications vary in the amount of packet loss, if any, that they can sustain.

These requirements are difficult to meet in an environment with variable queuing delays and congestion losses. Accordingly, inelastic traffic introduces two new requirements into the internet architecture. First, some means is needed to give preferential treatment to applications with more demanding requirements. Applications need to be able to state their requirements, either ahead of time in some sort of service request function, or on the fly, by means of fields in the IP packet header.

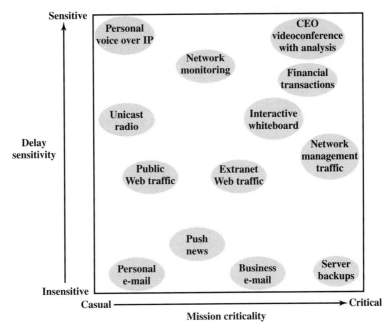

Figure 5.1 A Comparison of Application Delay Sensitivity and Criticality in an Enterprise [CROL00]

A second requirement in supporting inelastic traffic in an internet architecture is that elastic traffic must still be supported. Inelastic applications typically do not back off and reduce demand in the face of congestion, in contrast to TCP-based applications. Therefore, in times of congestion, inelastic traffic will continue to supply a high load, and elastic traffic will be crowded off the internet. A reservation protocol can help control this situation by denying service requests that would leave too few resources available to handle current elastic traffic.

Another way to look at the traffic requirements of an organization is shown in Figure 5.1. Applications can be characterized by two broad categories. The requirement of delay sensitivity can be satisfied by a QoS that emphasizes timely delivery and/or provides a high data rate. The requirement of criticality can be satisfied by a QoS that emphasizes reliability.

5.2 PERFORMANCE REQUIREMENTS

This section considers performance requirements from the point of view of applications. Two key parameters are response time and throughput.

Response Time

Response time is the time it takes a system to react to a given input. In an interactive transaction, it may be defined as the time between the last keystroke by the user and the beginning of the display of a result by the computer. For different types of applications, a slightly different definition is needed. In general, it is the time it takes for the system to respond to a request to perform a particular task.

Ideally, one would like the response time for any application to be short. However, it is almost invariably the case that shorter response time imposes greater cost. This cost comes from two sources:

- **Computer processing power:** The faster the computer, the shorter the response time. Of course, increased processing power means increased cost.

- **Competing requirements:** Providing rapid response time to some processes may penalize other processes.

Thus the value of a given level of response time must be assessed versus the cost of achieving that response time.

Table 5.1, based on [MART88], lists six general ranges of response times. Design difficulties are faced when a response time of less than 1 second is required.

That rapid response time is the key to productivity in interactive applications has been confirmed in a number of studies [SHNE84; THAD81; GUYN88]. These

Table 5.1 Response Time Ranges

Greater than 15 Seconds This rules out conversational interaction. For certain types of applications, certain types of users may be content to sit at a terminal for more than 15 seconds waiting for the answer to a single simple inquiry. However, for a busy person, captivity for more than 15 seconds seems intolerable. If such delays will occur, the system should be designed so that the user can turn to other activities and request the response at some later time.
Greater than 4 Seconds These are generally too long for a conversation requiring the operator to retain information in short-term memory (the operator's memory, not the computer's). Such delays would be very inhibiting in problem-solving activity and frustrating in data entry activity. However, after a major closure, delays from 4 to 15 seconds can be tolerated.
2 to 4 Seconds A delay longer than 2 seconds can be inhibiting to terminal operations demanding a high level of concentration. A wait of 2 to 4 seconds at a terminal can seem surprisingly long when the user is absorbed and emotionally committed to complete what he or she is doing. Again, a delay in this range may be acceptable after a minor closure has occurred.
Less than 2 Seconds When the terminal user has to remember information throughout several responses, the response time must be short. The more detailed the information remembered, the greater the need for responses of less than 2 seconds. For elaborate terminal activities, 2 seconds represents an important response-time limit.
Subsecond Response Time Certain types of thought-intensive work, especially with graphics applications, require very short response times to maintain the user's interest and attention for long periods of time.
Decisecond Response Time A response to pressing a key and seeing the character displayed on the screen or clicking a screen object with a mouse needs to be almost instantaneous—less than 0.1 second after the action. Interaction with a mouse requires extremely fast interaction if the designer is to avoid the use of alien syntax (one with commands, mnemonics, punctuation, etc.).

studies show that when a computer and a user interact at a pace that ensures that neither has to wait for the other, productivity increases significantly, the cost of the work done on the computer therefore drops, and quality tends to improve. It used to be widely accepted that a relatively slow response, up to 2 seconds, was acceptable for most interactive applications because the person was thinking about the next task. However, it now appears that productivity increases as rapid response times are achieved.

The results reported on response time are based on an analysis of online transactions. A transaction consists of a user command from a terminal and the system's reply. It is the fundamental unit of work for online system users. It can be divided into two time sequences:

- **User response time:** The time span between the moment a user receives a complete reply to one command and enters the next command. People often refer to this as think time.

- **System response time:** The time span between the moment the user enters a command and the moment a complete response is displayed on the terminal.

As an example of the effect of reduced system response time, Figure 5.2 shows the results of a study carried out on engineers using a computer-aided design graphics program for the design of integrated circuit chips and boards [SMIT88]. Each transaction consists of a command by the engineer that alters in some way the graphic image being displayed on the screen. The results show that the rate of transactions increases as system response time falls and rises dramatically once system response time falls below 1 second. What is happening is that as the system response time falls, so does the user response time. This has to do with the effects of short-term memory and human attention span.

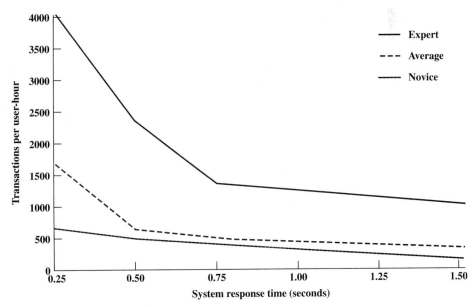

Figure 5.2   Response Time Results for High-Function Graphics

In terms of the types of computer-based information systems that we have been discussing, rapid response time is most critical for transaction processing systems. The output of management information systems and decision support systems is generally a report or the results of some modeling exercise. In these cases, rapid turnaround is not essential. For office automation applications, the need for rapid response time occurs when documents are being prepared or modified, but there is less urgency for things such as electronic mail and computer teleconferencing. The implication in terms of communications is this: If there is a communications facility between an interactive user and the application and a rapid response time is required, then the communications system must be designed so that its contribution to delay is compatible with that requirement. Thus, if a transaction processing application requires a response time of 1 second and the average time it takes the computer application to generate a response is 0.75 second, then the delay due to the communications facility must be no more than 0.25 second.

Another area where response time has become critical is the use of the World Wide Web, either over the Internet or over a corporate intranet. The time it takes for a typical Web page to come up on the user's screen varies greatly. Response times can be gauged based on the level of user involvement in the session; in particular, systems with vary fast response times tend to command more user attention.

As Figure 5.3 indicates, Web systems with a 3-second or better response time maintain a high level of user attention. With a response time of between 3 and 10 seconds, some user concentration is lost, and response times above 10 seconds discourage the user, who may simply abort the session. For an organization that maintains an Internet Web site, much of the response time is determined by forces beyond the organization's control, such as the Internet throughput and the end user's access speed. In such circumstances, the organization may consider keeping the image content of each page low and relying heavily on text, to promote rapid

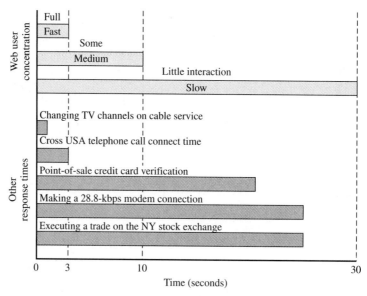

Figure 5.3   Response Time Requirements [SEVC96]

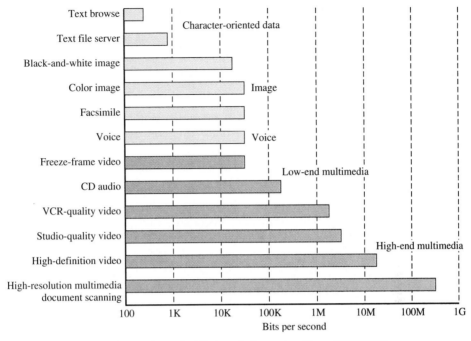

Figure 5.4   Required Data Rates for Various Information Types [TEGE95]

response time. For intranets, the organization has more control over delivery data rates and can afford more elaborate Web pages.

Throughput

The trend toward higher and higher transmission speed makes possible increased support for different services (e.g., Integrated Services Digital Network [ISDN] and broadband-based multimedia services) that once seemed too demanding for digital communication. To make effective use of these new capabilities, it is essential to have a sense of the demands each service puts on the storage and communications of integrated information systems. Services can be grouped into data, audio, image, and video, whose demands on information systems vary widely. Figure 5.4 gives an indication of the data rates required for various information types.[2]

5.3 PERFORMANCE METRICS

From a user's point of view, the two most important measures of the performance of a communication link or network are throughput and delay. This section clarifies these concepts.

---

[2]Note the use of a log scale for the *x*-axis. A basic review of log scales is in the math refresher document at the Computer Science Student Resource Site at WilliamStallings.com/StudentSupport.html.

Throughput

Throughput, or capacity, is generally expressed as a data rate in bits per second (bps).[3] Consider two systems connected by a single point-to-point communications link. The capacity potentially available for an application is equal to the data rate on the link. However, only some fraction of this capacity is actually available to the application (Figure 5.5). One factor that reduces the available capacity is whether the line is multiplexed. For example, if there are multiple TCP connections using the link, supporting multiple applications, then on average only a certain specific fraction of the link's capacity is available for any given application. In addition, the effective capacity available for a given application is reduced by the amount of protocol overhead. This overhead has two components:

- **Header bits:** Each layer of processing in the protocol architecture makes use a header to encapsulate a protocol data unit (Figure 2.15). For example, the TCP and IPv4 headers together contribute at least 40 bytes of overhead.
- **Control overhead:** A certain amount of time is consumed in control functions, such as sending acknowledgements, limiting the amount of data that can flow at any given time, and so forth.

Delay

Sometimes, we are interested in the average time it takes for a block of data to go from an application on one system to another system. At other times, we are interested in a round-trip delay, which consists of the delay in getting data from one system to another plus the delay in receiving an acknowledgement back from the remote system. In either case, there are four types of delay that contribute to overall delay:

- **Transmission delay:** Time for the transmitter to send out all of the bits of the packet. For example, with a line speed of 1 Mbps, a packet of 100 octets would take 800 μs to transmit.
- **Propagation delay:** The time for one bit to transit from source to destination.
- **Processing delay:** The time required to process the packet at the source prior to sending, at any intermediate router or switch, and at the destination prior to delivering to an application.

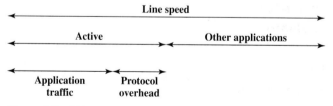

Figure 5.5   Effective Throughput

---

[3]The term *bandwidth* is often used in the literature to refer to transmission capacity, expressed in bps. The correct definition of bandwidth is the difference between the limiting (upper and lower) frequencies of a continuous frequency spectrum. Although higher bandwidth generally means higher transmission capacity, it is not correct to talk of a bandwidth in units of bps.

- **Queuing delay:** The time spend waiting in a queue at any point along the route.

The interaction between delay and throughput is of critical importance, and we discuss this topic next. The concept of queuing delay is then discussed.

The Delay × Throughput Product

Suppose that a user at a PC at one end of the United States sends a 1-megabit file to a remote server on the other end over a data link operating at 64 kbps. Ignore any processing or queuing delays. Assume that we are using a fiber optic link with a propagation rate of the speed of light (approximately 3×10^8 m/s) and that the distance is 4800 km. Then the time it takes for the first bit to arrive at the server (propagation delay) is $(4800 \times 10^3)/(3 \times 10^8) = 0.016$ s. During that time, the host has transmitted $(64 \times 10^3)(0.016) = 1024$ bits. The total amount of time to transmit the entire file is the time it takes to pump the entire file out onto the channel plus the time it takes for the last bit that is transmitted to make it across the channel to the destination. This quantity is just the transmission delay plus the propagation delay. In this case, the transmission delay is $(10^6)/(64 \times 10^3) = 15.625$ s, and the total delay is 15.641 s. Clearly, the transmission delay dominates the propagation delay, and a higher-speed channel would reduce the time required to transmit the file.

Now suppose that we have a 1-Gbps data link. The propagation delay is still the same. But now the transmission delay is 0.001 s, for a total time to transmit the file of 0.017 s. In this case, the propagation delay dominates the transmission delay. It is clear that increasing the data rate of the channel will not noticeably speed up the delivery of the file. This has profound implications for performance and for protocol design, as we now show.

The preceding analysis depends on the data rate of the link, the distance, the velocity of propagation of the signal, and the size of the packet. These parameters can be combined into a single critical system parameter, commonly denoted as a, defined as

$$a = \frac{\text{propagation delay}}{\text{transmission delay}} = \frac{d/v}{L/R} = \frac{R \times D}{L} \tag{5.1}$$

where

R = data rate, or capacity, of the link

L = number of bits in a packet

d = distance between source and destination

v = velocity of propagation of the signal

D = propagation delay

Looking at the final fraction in Equation (5.1), we see that a can also be expressed as

$$a = \frac{\text{length of the transmission channel in bits}}{\text{length of the packet in bits}}$$

Thus, for a fixed packet length, the parameter a is dependent on the $R \times D$ product. In our example, for the 64-kbps link, $a = 1.024 \times 10^{-3}$; and for the 1-Gbps link, $a = 16$.

To see the impact of the parameter a, let us consider two examples, one in which a is much less than 1, and one in which a is much greater than 1. Suppose that we send a sequence of packets from source to destination and wait for an acknowledgment to each packet before sending the next one; this is known as a **stop-and-wait protocol**. For convenience, transmission time is normalized to 1 and hence the propagation time, by Equation (5.1), is a. For the case of $a > 1$, the link's bit length is greater than that of the packet; this is shown in Figure 5.6a; we assume that the ACK packet is small enough that we can ignore its transmission time. Station A begins transmitting a packet at time 0. At $t = 1$, A completes transmission. At $t = a$, the leading edge of the packet reaches the receiving station B. At $t = 1 + a$, B has received the entire packet and immediately transmits a small acknowledgment packet. This acknowledgment arrives back at A at $t = 1 + 2a$. Total elapsed time is $1 + 2a$. Hence, the normalized rate at which packets can be transmitted is $1/(1 + 2a)$. The same result is achieved with $a < 1$, as illustrated in Figure 5.6b.

Figure 5.7 shows normalized throughput as a function of a. For values of a greater than one, the stop-and-wait protocol is clearly inefficient. For gigabit wide area networks, even for large packets (e.g., 1 Mb), the communications channel is seriously underutilized.

How might performance on a gigabit link be improved? If a large number of users each use a small portion of the capacity, then for each user, the effective capacity is considerably smaller, reducing a. Each user, however, is making do with a smaller data rate; for video, graphics-intensive, and multimedia applications, the smaller data rate may be inadequate. If an application uses a communications channel with high a, then performance can be improved by allowing the application to treat the channel as a pipeline, and fill it with a continuous flow of packets, not waiting for an acknowledgment to any individual packet. This creates difficulties in three areas. Suppose that system A is sending a stream of packets to system B. Consider the following issues:

- **Flow control:** B may need to temporarily restrict the flow of packets from A because a buffer is filling up or an application is temporarily busy. But by the

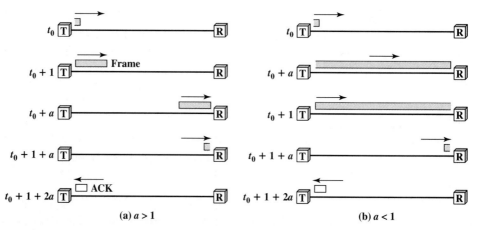

(a) $a > 1$ (b) $a < 1$

Figure 5.6 Effect of a on Link Utilization

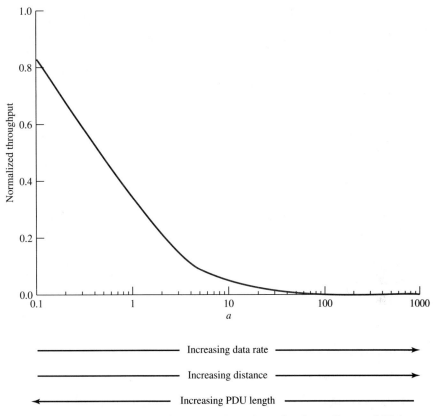

Figure 5.7 Normalized Throughput as a Function of *a* for a Stop-and-Wait Protocol

time a signal from B arrives back at A, many additional packets will have been transmitted and be in the pipeline. If B cannot absorb these packets, they must be discarded.

- **Error control:** If B detects an error in an incoming packet, it may send a request back to A for retransmission of that packet. But if B is unable to store incoming packets out of order, then A must retransmit not only the packet in error but also all subsequent packets that were put in the pipeline after the error was discovered but before B's request arrived at A.

- **Congestion control:** As is discussed subsequently, there are various methods by which A can learn that there is congestion in the network and that A should reduce the flow of packets. However, with a large value of *a*, there may be many packets placed in the pipeline between the onset of congestion and the time that A learns about it.

All of these are difficulties for the protocol designer. We explore a number of design approaches in this and later chapters.

Queuing Delays

In many cases, queuing delays in a communication or networking system are the dominant performance concern. The reason for this is that queuing delay can grow dramatically as a system approaches capacity. It is important to have a basic feel for queuing effects because the behavior of most systems under a changing load is not what one would intuitively expect. If there is an environment in which there is a shared facility (e.g., a network, a transmission line, a time-sharing system), then the performance of that system typically responds in an exponential way to increases in demand.

Figure 5.8 is a representative example. The upper line shows what typically happens to user response time on a shared facility as the load on that facility increases. The load is expressed as a fraction of capacity. Thus, if we are dealing with a router that is capable of processing and forwarding 1000 packets per second, then a load of 0.5 represents an arrival rate of 500 packets per second, and the response time is the amount of time it takes to retransmit any incoming packet. The lower line is a simple projection[4] based on a knowledge of the behavior of the system up to a load of 0.5. Note that while things appear rosy when the simple projection is made, performance on the system will in fact collapse beyond a load of about 0.8 to 0.9.

Appendix 5A contains a discussion of queuing delay performance considerations.

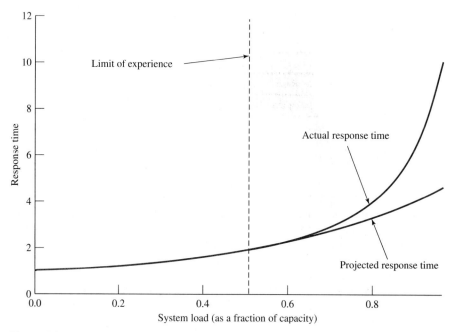

Figure 5.8 Projected versus Actual Response Time

---

[4]The lower line is based on fitting a third-order polynomial to the data available up to a load of 0.5.

5.4 THE EFFECTS OF CONGESTION

A key design issue that must be confronted both with data networks, such as packet-switching, frame relay, and ATM networks, and also with internets, is that of congestion control. The phenomenon of congestion is a complex one, as is the subject of congestion control. In very general terms, congestion occurs when the number of packets being transmitted through a network begins to approach the packet-handling capacity of the network. The objective of congestion control is to maintain the number of packets within the network below the level at which performance falls off dramatically.

To understand the issues involved in congestion control, we need to look at some results from queuing theory. In essence, a data network or internet is a network of queues. At each node (data network switch, internet router), there is a queue of packets for each outgoing channel. If the rate at which packets arrive and queue up exceeds the rate at which packets can be transmitted, the queue size grows without bound and the delay experienced by a packet goes to infinity. Even if the packet arrival rate is less than the packet transmission rate, queue length will grow dramatically as the arrival rate approaches the transmission rate. As a rule of thumb, when the line for which packets are queuing becomes more than 80% utilized, the queue length grows at an alarming rate. This growth in queue length means that the delay experienced by a packet at each node increases. Further, since the size of any queue is finite, as queue length grows, eventually the queue must overflow.

Consider the queuing situation at a single packet switch or router, such as is illustrated in Figure 5.9. Any given node has a number of I/O ports[5] attached to it: one or more to other nodes, and zero or more to end systems. On each port, packets arrive and depart. We can consider that there are two buffers, or queues, at each port, one to accept arriving packets, and one to hold packets that are waiting to depart. In practice, there might be two fixed-size buffers associated with each port, or there might be a pool of memory available for all buffering activities. In the latter case, we can think of each port having two variable-size buffers associated with it, subject to the constraint that the sum of all buffer sizes is a constant.

In any case, as packets arrive, they are stored in the input buffer of the corresponding port. The node examines each incoming packet, makes a routing decision, and then moves the packet to the appropriate output buffer. Packets queued for output are transmitted as rapidly as possible; this is, in effect, statistical time division multiplexing. If packets arrive too fast for the node to process them (make routing decisions) or faster than packets can be cleared from the outgoing buffers, then eventually packets will arrive for which no memory is available.

When such a saturation point is reached, one of two general strategies can be adopted. The first such strategy is to discard any incoming packet for which there is no available buffer space. The alternative is for the node that is experiencing these problems to exercise some sort of flow control over its neighbors so that the traffic flow remains manageable. But, as Figure 5.10 illustrates, each of a node's neighbors is also managing a number of queues. If node 6 restrains the flow of packets from

---

[5]In the case of a switch of a packet-switching, frame relay, or ATM network, each I/O port connects to a transmission link that connects to another node or end system. In the case of a router of an internet, each I/O port connects to either a direct link to another node or to a subnetwork.

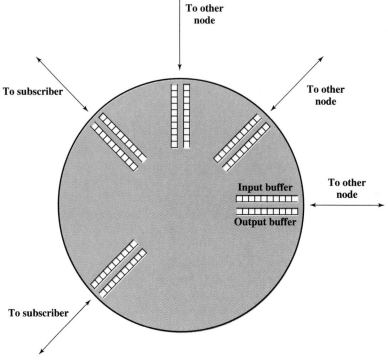

Figure 5.9 Input and Output Queues at Node

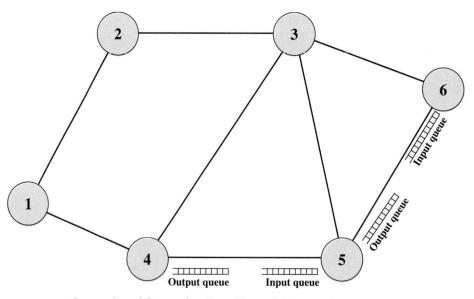

Figure 5.10 Interaction of Queues in a Data Network

node 5, this causes the output buffer in node 5 for the port to node 6 to fill up. Thus, congestion at one point in the network can quickly propagate throughout a region or the entire network. While flow control is indeed a powerful tool, we need to use it in such a way as to manage the traffic on the entire network.

Ideal Performance

Figure 5.11 suggests the ideal goal for network utilization. The top graph plots the steady-state total throughput (number of packets delivered to destination end systems) through the network as a function of the offered load (number of packets

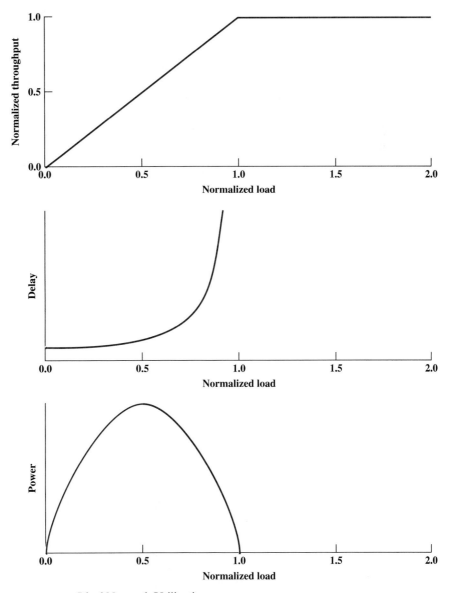

Figure 5.11   Ideal Network Utilization

transmitted by source end systems), both normalized to the maximum theoretical throughput of the network. For example, if a network consists of a single node with two full-duplex 1-Mbps links, then the theoretical capacity of the network is 2 Mbps, consisting of a 1-Mbps flow in each direction. In the ideal case, the throughput of the network increases to accommodate load up to an offered load equal to the full capacity of the network; then normalized throughput remains at 1.0 at higher input loads. Note, however, what happens to the end-to-end delay experienced by the average packet even with this assumption of ideal performance. At a negligible load, there is some small constant amount of delay that consists of the propagation delay through the network from source to destination plus processing delay at each node. As the load on the network increases, queuing delays at each node are added to this fixed amount of delay. When the load exceeds the network capacity, delays increase without bound.

Here is a simple intuitive explanation of why delay must go to infinity. Suppose that each node in the network is equipped with buffers of infinite size and suppose that the input load exceeds network capacity. Under ideal conditions, the network will continue to sustain a normalized throughput of 1.0. Therefore, the rate of packets leaving the network is 1.0. Because the rate of packets entering the network is greater than 1.0, internal queue sizes grow. In the steady state, with input greater than output, these queue sizes grow without bound and therefore queuing delays grow without bound.

It is important to grasp the meaning of Figure 5.11 before looking at real-world conditions. This figure represents the ideal, but unattainable, goal of all traffic and congestion control schemes. No scheme can exceed the performance depicted in Figure 5.11.

You will sometimes see the term *power* used in network performance literature. *Power* is defined as the ratio of throughput to delay, and this is depicted for the ideal case in the bottom graph of Figure 5.11. It has been shown that, typically, a network configuration and congestion control scheme that results in higher throughput also results in higher delay [JAIN91], and that power is a concise metric that can be used to compare different schemes.

Practical Performance

The ideal case reflected in Figure 5.11 assumes infinite buffers and no overhead related to packet transmission or congestion control. In practice, buffers are finite, leading to buffer overflow, and attempts to control congestion consume network capacity in the exchange of control signals.

Let us consider what happens in a network with finite buffers if no attempt is made to control congestion or to restrain input from end systems. The details will, of course, differ depending on network configuration and on the statistics of the presented traffic. However, the graphs in Figure 5.12 depict the devastating outcome in general terms.

At light loads, throughput and hence network utilization increases as the offered load increases. As the load continues to increase, a point is reached (point A in the plot) beyond which the throughput of the network increases at a rate slower than the rate at which offered load is increased. This is due to network entry into a

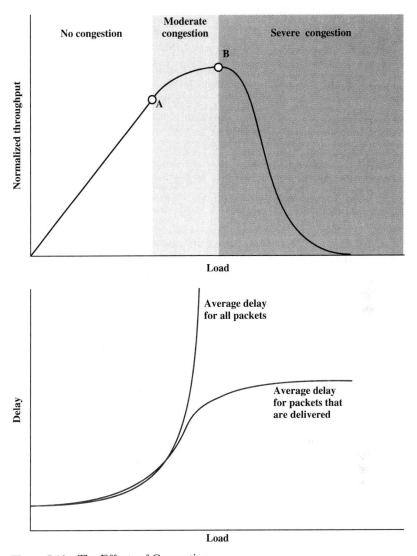

Figure 5.12   The Effects of Congestion

moderate congestion state. In this region, the network continues to cope with the load, although with increased delays. The departure of throughput from the ideal is accounted for by a number of factors. For one thing, the load is unlikely to be spread uniformly throughout the network. Therefore, while some nodes may experience moderate congestion, others may be experiencing severe congestion and may need to discard traffic. In addition, as the load increases, the network will attempt to balance the load by routing packets through areas of lower congestion. For the routing function to work, an increased number of routing messages must be exchanged between nodes to alert each other to areas of congestion; this overhead reduces the capacity available for data packets.

As the load on the network continues to increase, the queue lengths of the various nodes continue to grow. Eventually, a point is reached (point B in the plot) beyond which throughput actually drops with increased offered load. The reason for this is that the buffers at each node are of finite size. When the buffers at a node become full, the node must discard packets. Thus, the sources must retransmit the discarded packets in addition to new packets. This only exacerbates the situation: As more and more packets are retransmitted, the load on the system grows, and more buffers become saturated. While the system is trying desperately to clear the backlog, users are pumping old and new packets into the system. Even successfully delivered packets may be retransmitted because it takes too long, at a higher layer (e.g., transport layer), to acknowledge them: The sender assumes the packet did not get through and retransmits. Under these circumstances, the effective capacity of the system declines to zero.

The lower graph in Figure 5.12 reflects the effects on delay. The graph shows the average delay for packets that are delivered, as well as the average delay for all packets. The delay for packets that are delivered reaches some maximum value proportional to the amount of time a packet can spend in a finite queue. However, at the steady state, most packets are not being delivered. Furthermore, if packets are acknowledged and timeouts occur, as mentioned in the preceding paragraph, those packets that do get through will be retransmitted, so that in some sense, those packets also have infinite delay.

5.5 CONGESTION CONTROL

In this book, we discuss various techniques for controlling congestion in packet-switching, frame relay, and ATM networks, and in IP-based internets. To give context to this discussion, Figure 5.13 provides a general depiction of important congestion control techniques.

Backpressure

We have already made reference to backpressure as a technique for congestion control. This technique produces an effect similar to backpressure in fluids flowing down a pipe. When the end of a pipe is closed (or restricted), the fluid pressure backs up the pipe to the point of origin, where the flow is stopped (or slowed).

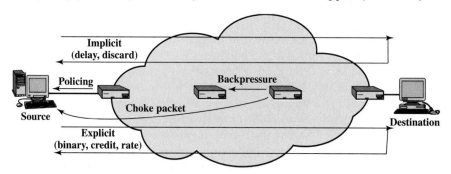

Figure 5.13   Mechanisms for Congestion Control

Backpressure can be exerted on the basis of links or logical connections (e.g., virtual circuits). Referring again to Figure 5.10, if node 6 becomes congested (buffers fill up), then node 6 can slow down or halt the flow of all packets from node 5 (or node 3, or both nodes 5 and 3). If this restriction persists, node 5 will need to slow down or halt traffic on its incoming links. This flow restriction propagates backward (against the flow of data traffic) to sources, which are restricted in the flow of new packets into the network.

Backpressure can be selectively applied to logical connections, so that the flow from one node to the next is only restricted or halted on some connections, generally the ones with the most traffic. In this case, the restriction propagates back along the connection to the source.

Backpressure is of limited utility. It can be used in a connection-oriented network that allows hop-by-hop (from one node to the next) flow control. X.25-based packet-switching networks typically provide this feature. However, neither frame relay nor ATM has any capability for restricting flow on a hop-by-hop basis. In the case of IP-based internets, there have traditionally been no built-in facilities for regulating the flow of data from one router to the next along a path through the internet. Recently, some flow-based schemes have been developed; this topic is introduced in Part Four.

Choke Packet

A choke packet is a control packet generated at a congested node and transmitted back to a source node to restrict traffic flow. An example of a choke packet is the ICMP (Internet Control Message Protocol) Source Quench packet. Either a router or a destination end system may send this message to a source end system, requesting that it reduce the rate at which it is sending traffic to the internet destination. On receipt of a source quench message, the source host should cut back the rate at which it is sending traffic to the specified destination until it no longer receives source quench messages. The source quench message can be used by a router or host that must discard IP packets because of a full buffer. In that case, the router or host will issue a source quench message for every packet that it discards. In addition, a system may anticipate congestion and issue source quench messages when its buffers approach capacity. In that case, the packet referred to in the source quench message may well be delivered. Thus, receipt of a source quench message does not imply delivery or nondelivery of the corresponding packet.

The choke package is a relatively crude technique for controlling congestion. More sophisticated forms of explicit congestion signaling are discussed subsequently.

Implicit Congestion Signaling

When network congestion occurs, two things may happen: (1) The transmission delay for an individual packet from source to destination increases, so that it is noticeably longer than the fixed propagation delay; and (2) packets are discarded. If a source is able to detect increased delays and packet discards, then it has implicit evidence of network congestion. If all sources can detect congestion and, in response, reduce flow on the basis of congestion, then the network congestion will be relieved.

Thus, congestion control on the basis of implicit signaling is the responsibility of end systems and does not require action on the part of network nodes.

Implicit signaling is an effective congestion control technique in connectionless configurations, such as datagram packet-switching networks and IP-based internets. In such cases, there are no logical connections through the internet on which flow can be regulated. However, between the two end systems, logical connections can be established at the TCP level. TCP includes mechanisms for acknowledging receipt of TCP segments and for regulating the flow of data between source and destination on a TCP connection. TCP congestion control techniques based on the ability to detect increased delay and segment loss are discussed in Chapter 7.

Implicit signaling can also be used in connection-oriented networks. For example, in frame relay networks, the LAPF data link control protocol, which is end to end, includes facilities similar to those of TCP for flow and error control. LAPF control is capable of detecting lost frames and adjusting the flow of data accordingly.

Explicit Congestion Signaling

It is desirable to use as much of the available capacity in a network as possible but still react to congestion in a controlled and fair manner. This is the purpose of explicit congestion avoidance techniques. In general terms, for explicit congestion avoidance, the network alerts end systems to growing congestion within the network and the end systems take steps to reduce the offered load to the network.

Typically, explicit congestion control techniques operate over connection-oriented networks and control the flow of packets over individual connections. Explicit congestion signaling approaches can work in one of two directions:

- **Backward:** Notifies the source that congestion avoidance procedures should be initiated where applicable for traffic in the opposite direction of the received notification. It indicates that the packets that the user transmits on this logical connection may encounter congested resources. Backward information is transmitted either by altering bits in a header of a data packet headed for the source to be controlled or by transmitting separate control packets to the source.

- **Forward:** Notifies the user that congestion avoidance procedures should be initiated where applicable for traffic in the same direction as the received notification. It indicates that this packet, on this logical connection, has encountered congested resources. Again, this information may be transmitted either as altered bits in data packets or in separate control packets. In some schemes, when a forward signal is received by an end system, it echoes the signal back along the logical connection to the source. In other schemes, the end system is expected to exercise flow control upon the source end system at a higher layer (e.g., TCP).

We can divide explicit congestion signaling approaches into three general categories:

- **Binary:** A bit is set in a data packet as it is forwarded by the congested node. When a source receives a binary indication of congestion on a logical connection, it may reduce its traffic flow.

- **Credit based:** These schemes are based on providing an explicit credit to a source over a logical connection. The credit indicates how many octets or how many packets the source may transmit. When the credit is exhausted, the source must await additional credit before sending additional data. Credit-based schemes are common for end-to-end flow control, in which a destination system uses credit to prevent the source from overflowing the destination buffers, but credit-based schemes have also been considered for congestion control.
- **Rate based:** These schemes are based on providing an explicit data rate limit to the source over a logical connection. The source may transmit data at a rate up to the set limit. To control congestion, any node along the path of the connection can reduce the data rate limit in a control message to the source.

5.6 TRAFFIC MANAGEMENT

There are a number of issues related to congestion control that might be included under the general category of traffic management. In its simplest form, congestion control is concerned with efficient use of a network at high load. The various mechanisms discussed in the previous section can be applied as the situation arises, without regard to the particular source or destination affected. When a node is saturated and must discard packets, it can apply some simple rule, such as discard the most recent arrival. However, other considerations can be used to refine the application of congestion control techniques and discard policy. We briefly introduce several of those areas here.

Fairness

As congestion develops, flows of packets between sources and destinations will experience increased delays and, with high congestion, packet losses. In the absence of other requirements, we would like to assure that the various flows suffer from congestion equally. Simply to discard on a last-in-first-discarded basis may not be fair. As an example of a technique that might promote fairness, a node can maintain a separate queue for each logical connection or for each source-destination pair. If all of the queue buffers are of equal length, then the queues with the highest traffic load will suffer discards more often, allowing lower-traffic connections a fair share of the capacity.

Quality of Service

We might wish to treat different traffic flows differently. For example, as [JAIN92] points out, some applications, such as voice and video, are delay sensitive but loss insensitive. Others, such as file transfer and electronic mail, are delay insensitive but loss sensitive. Still others, such as interactive graphics or interactive computing applications, are delay sensitive and loss sensitive. Also, different traffic flows have different priorities; for example, network management traffic, particularly during times of congestion or failure, is more important than application traffic.

It is particularly important during periods of congestion that traffic flows with different requirements be treated differently and provided a different quality of service (QoS). For example, a node might transmit higher-priority packets ahead of lower-priority packets in the same queue. Or a node might maintain different queues for different QoS levels and give preferential treatment to the higher levels.

Reservations

One way to avoid congestion and also to provide assured service to applications is to use a reservation scheme. Such a scheme is an integral part of ATM networks. When a logical connection is established, the network and the user enter into a traffic contract, which specifies a data rate and other characteristics of the traffic flow. The network agrees to give a defined QoS so long as the traffic flow is within contract parameters; excess traffic is either discarded or handled on a best-effort basis, subject to discard. If the current outstanding reservations are such that the network resources are inadequate to meet the new reservation, then the new reservation is denied. A similar type of scheme has now been developed for IP-based internets (RSVP, which is discussed in Chapter 10).

One aspect of a reservation scheme is traffic policing (Figure 5.13). A node in the network, typically the node to which the end system attaches, monitors the traffic flow and compares it to the traffic contract. Excess traffic is either discarded or marked to indicate that it is liable to discard or delay.

5.7 THE NEED FOR FLOW AND ERROR CONTROL

Flow Control

Flow control is a protocol mechanism that enables a destination entity to regulate the flow of packets sent by a source entity. Flow control limits the amount or rate of data that is sent. The destination system may need to limit the flow for one of several reasons, including the following:

1. As each packet arrives, the destination must do a certain amount of processing of the packet header. The source may attempt to send packets faster than the destination can process them.

2. The destination protocol entity may buffer the incoming data for delivery to a higher-level protocol user. If that user is slow in retrieving the data, the buffer may fill up and the destination may need to limit or temporarily halt the flow from the source.

3. The destination may buffer the incoming data for retransmission on another I/O port (e.g., in the case of a bridge or router, or a packet-switching node) and may need to limit the incoming flow to match the outgoing flow.

The first two reasons come into play between end systems, either at the link level (two end systems connected by a direct link) or across a network. The final case deals with the forwarding of packets across a switched network (e.g., via packet-switched nodes) or across an internetwork (e.g., via bridges or routers).

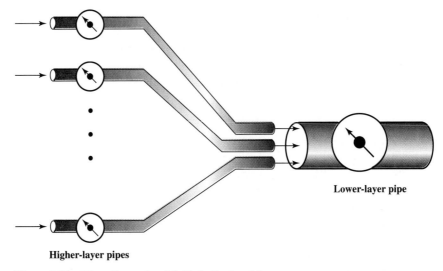

Figure 5.14 Flow Control at Multiple Protocol Layers

Flow control can be exercised at a number of protocol levels, The effect is indicated in Figure 5.14. One example of this would be the case of a number of X.25 virtual circuits (OSI level 3) multiplexed over a data link using LAPB (the X.25 data link control protocol). Another example would be the multiplexing of multiple TCP connections over an HDLC (high-level data link control) link. Flow control is exercised along each logical connection at the higher level independently of the flow control on the other connections. The total traffic on all of the connections is subjected to further flow control at the lower level.

Further complicating the study of flow control is that fact that it can be employed in various contexts, as suggested in Figure 5.15. The figure indicates two end

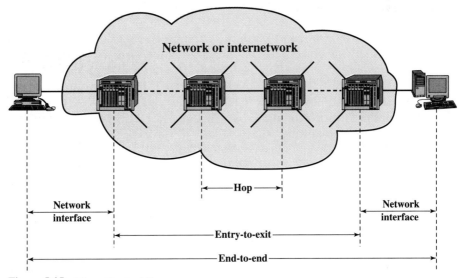

Figure 5.15 Flow Control Scope

systems connected through a network or internetwork. In the case of a network, the intermediate systems are individual network nodes, such as packet, frame relay, or ATM switches. In the case of an internetwork, the intermediate systems are typically routers. We now briefly consider the relationship between the protocol level of flow control and the scope across which flow control is exercised.

Hop Scope Between intermediate systems that are directly connected, flow control can be exercised at the link level. For example, in the case of adjacent packet-switching nodes, a data link control protocol called LAPB (link access protocol, balanced; similar to HDLC) is used. Each packet-switching node buffers incoming packets and routes them on the appropriate outgoing link. To assure that its buffers do not overflow, it can use LAPB flow control to limit the volume of incoming traffic. Link-level flow control can also be used between directly connected routers in an internetwork. Again, a router may use a link-level protocol such as HDLC to limit the volume of incoming datagrams to avoid buffer overflow.

Network Interface A link-level protocol is also often used across the interface link between an end system and a network or internetwork. Again, in the case of an X.25 packet-switching network, LAPB enables the network to limit the total flow of packets from an end system into the network. In other networks, such as frame relay and ATM network, no flow control is exercised at the link level.

Flow control can also occur at a network protocol layer across the network interface. In this case, flow control is exercised for individual logical connections. A common example of this is X.25, in which flow control can be exercised between the end system and the network on each individual virtual circuit.

Entry-to-Exit Some networks provide a form of flow control between entry and exit nodes for logical connections, such as virtual circuits. The objective in this context is to regulate input traffic so as to avoid the overflow of buffers at the exit point. The details of this mechanism are transparent to end users but may affect the flow of data across the network interface.

End-to-End Flow control can be exercised on logical connections between end systems. Here the objective is for the receiving end system to regulate incoming flow so as to avoid buffer overflow and to satisfy application requirements. TCP provides such end-to-end flow control over individual TCP connections between end systems. End-to-end flow control can also be exercised on an X.25 virtual circuit basis. End-to-end flow control at the data link layer is also frequently employed. Examples include the following:

- In a circuit-switched or ATM network, if a link control protocol such as HDLC is implemented in the end systems, then it operates end to end.

- Logical link control (LLC) operating across a LAN is exercised between end systems. In this case, the flow control operates over logical connections between end systems.

- The LAPF (Link Access Procedure for Frame Mode Bearer Services) control protocol enables the use of flow control mechanisms over logical connections between end systems across a frame relay network.

Error Control

Error control techniques are used to recover from the loss or damage of packets in transit between source and destination. Typically, error control involves error detection, based on a frame check sequence (FCS), and packet retransmission. Error control and flow control are implemented together in a single mechanism that regulates the flow of packets and determines when one or more packets need to be retransmitted. Thus, error control, as with flow control, is a function that is performed at various protocol levels.

5.8   SELF-SIMILAR TRAFFIC

The queuing analysis referred to in Section 5.3 and Appendix 5A has been tremendously useful to network designers and systems analysts in doing capacity planning and performance prediction. However, in many real-world cases, it has been found that the predicted results from a queuing analysis differ substantially from the actual observed performance. The validity of queuing analysis depends on the Poisson nature of the data traffic. In recent years, a number of studies have demonstrated that for some environments, the traffic pattern is **self-similar** rather than Poisson.[6]

In the early 1990s, a seminal event in the field of network performance modeling occurred, with the publication of a paper by a group of BellCore and Boston University researchers on the self-similar nature of Ethernet traffic [LELA94]. Although a number of researchers had observed over the years that network traffic did not always obey the Poisson assumptions used in queuing analysis, this paper for the first time provided an explanation and a systematic approach to modeling realistic data traffic patterns.

Simply put, network traffic is burstier and exhibits greater variance than previously suspected. The authors of the aforementioned paper reported the results of a massive study of Ethernet traffic and demonstrated that it has a self-similar, or fractal, characteristic. That means that the traffic has similar statistical properties at a range of time scales: milliseconds, seconds, minutes, hours, even days and weeks. This has several important consequences. One is that you cannot expect that the traffic will "smooth out" over an extended period of time; instead, not only does the data cluster, but the clusters cluster. Another consequence is that the merging of traffic streams, such as is done by a statistical multiplexer or an ATM switch, does not result in a smoothing of traffic. Again, bursty data streams that are multiplexed tend to produce a bursty aggregate stream.

One practical effect of self-similarity is that the buffers needed at switches and multiplexers must be bigger than those predicted by traditional queuing analysis and simulations. Further, these larger buffers create greater delays in individual streams than originally anticipated.

---

[6]In literature, you will often see reference to traffic that exhibits **long-range dependence**. There are processes that are long-range dependent but not self-similar, and processes that are self-similar but not long-range dependent. However, for the cases of interest in this book, self-similarity implies long-range dependence and vice versa.

Self-similarity is not confined to Ethernet traffic or indeed to LAN traffic in general. This first paper sparked a surge of research in the United States, Europe, Australia, and elsewhere. The results are in: Self-similarity appears in ATM traffic, compressed digital video streams, SS7 control traffic on ISDN-based networks, Web traffic between browsers and servers, and more.

The discovery of the fractal nature of data traffic should not be surprising. Such self-similarity is quite common in both natural and human-made phenomena; it is seen in natural landscapes, in the distribution of earthquakes, in ocean waves, in turbulent flow, in the fluctuations in the stock market, as well as in the pattern of errors and data traffic on communication channels.

The implications of this new view of data traffic are startling and reveal the importance of this topic. For example, the whole area of buffer design and management requires rethinking. In traditional network engineering, it is assumed that linear increases in buffer sizes will produce nearly exponential decreases in packet loss and that an increase in buffer size will result in a proportional increase in the effective use of transmission capacity. With self-similar traffic, these assumptions are false. The decrease in loss with buffer size is far less than expected, and a modest increase in utilization requires a significant increase in buffer size.

Other aspects of network design are also affected. With self-similar traffic, a slight increase in the number of active connections through a switch can result in a large increase in packet loss. In general, the parameters of a network design are more sensitive to the actual traffic pattern than expected. To cope with this sensitivity, designs need to be more conservative. Priority scheduling schemes need to be reexamined. For example, if a switch manages multiple priority classes and does not enforce a bandwidth limitation on the highest-priority class, then a prolonged burst of traffic from the highest priority could starve other classes for an extended period of time.

The explanation for these strange results is that surges in traffic tend to be concentrated in waves. There may be a long period with low-level traffic followed by a period in which traffic peaks tend to cluster so that it is difficult for a switch or network to clear the backlog from one peak before the next peak arrives. Therefore, a static congestion control strategy must assume that such waves of multiple peak periods will occur. A dynamic congestion control strategy is difficult to implement. Such a strategy is based on measurement of recent traffic and can fail utterly to adapt to rapidly changing conditions.

Congestion prevention by appropriate sizing of switches and networks is difficult because data network traffic does not exhibit a predictable level of busy period traffic; patterns can change over a period of days, weeks, or months. Congestion avoidance by monitoring traffic levels and adapting flow control and traffic routing policies is difficult because congestion can occur unexpectedly and with dramatic intensity. Finally, congestion recovery is complicated by the need to make sure that critical network control messages are not lost in the repeated waves of traffic hitting the network.

The reason that this fundamental nature of data traffic has been missed up until recently is that it requires the processing of a massive amount of data over a long observation period to detect and confirm this behavior. And yet the practical effects are all too obvious. ATM switch vendors, among others, have found that their products did not perform as advertised once in the field because of inadequate buffering and the failure to take into account the delays caused by burstiness.

5.9 RECOMMENDED READING AND WEB SITES

[KLEI92] provides an informative discussion of the delay/bandwidth tradeoff. [YANG95] is a comprehensive survey of congestion control techniques. [JAIN90] and [JAIN92] provide excellent discussions of the requirements for congestion control, the various approaches that can be taken, and performance considerations. An excellent discussion of data network performance issues is provided by [KLEI93]. While somewhat dated, the definitive reference on flow control is [GERL80].

A good practical reference on queuing analysis is [TANN95]; it provides detailed guidance for the application of queuing analysis plus a number of worked-out examples. The book also contains a disk with an extensive library of subroutines in Pascal for calculating the characteristics of many queuing situations. Another excellent practical reference is [GUNT00].

[STAL02] contains a detailed discussion of self-similar data traffic. [LELA94] is one of the most important networking papers of the decade and launched this new examination of data traffic performance. [PAXS95] provides a solid analysis of TCP-based self-similar traffic and includes a number of useful appendices on underlying mathematical concepts of general interest in self-similar traffic modeling.

GERL80   Gerla, M., and Kleinrock, L. "Flow Control: A Comparative Survey." *IEEE Transactions on Communications*, April 1980.

GUNT00   Gunther, N. *The Practical Performance Analyst.* New York: Authors Choice Press, 2000.

JAIN90   Jain, R. "Congestion Control in Computer Networks: Issues and Trends." *IEEE Network Magazine*, May 1990.

JAIN92   Jain, R. "Myths About Congestion Management in High-Speed Networks." *Internetworking: Research and Experience*, Volume 3, 1992.

KLEI92   Kleinrock, L. "The Latency/Bandwidth Tradeoff in Gigabit Networks." *IEEE Communications Magazine*, April 1992.

KLEI93   Kleinrock, L. "On the Modeling and Analysis of Computer Networks." *Proceedings of the IEEE*, August 1993.

LELA94   Leland, W.; Taqqu, M.; Willinger, W.; and Wilson, D. "On the Self-Similar Nature of Ethernet Traffic (Extended Version)." *IEEE/ACM Transactions on Networking*, February 1994.

PAXS95   Paxson, V., and Floyd, S. "Wide Area Traffic: The Failure of Poisson Modeling." *IEEE/ACM Transactions on Networking*, June 1995.

STAL02   Stallings, W. *High-Speed Networks and Internets: Performance and Quality of Service, 2nd Ed.* Upper Saddle River, NJ: Prentice Hall, 2002.

TANN95   Tanner, M. *Practical Queueing Analysis.* New York: McGraw-Hill, 1995.

YANG95   Yang, C., and Reddy, A. "A Taxonomy for Congestion Control Algorithms in Packet Switching Networks." *IEEE Network*, July/August 1995.

Recommended Web Site:

- **Myron Hlynka's Queueing Theory Page:** Includes FAQ, examples, links to other queuing sites, even queuing theory employment opportunities.

5.10 KEY TERMS, REVIEW QUESTIONS, AND PROBLEMS

Key Terms

arrival rate	flow control	service time
backpressure	implicit congestion signaling	stop-and-wait protocol
cell delay variation	processing delay	system response time
choke packet	propagation delay	throughput
congestion	quality of service (QoS)	traffic management
congestion control	queuing delay	transmission delay
delay	residence time	user response time
delay variation	reservations	utilization
error control	response time	waiting line
explicit congestion signaling	self-similar	waiting time

Review Questions

5.1 When a node experiences saturation with respect to incoming packets, what general strategies may be used?

5.2 Why is it that when the load exceeds the network capacity, delay tends to infinity?

5.3 Give a brief explanation of each of the congestion control techniques illustrated in Figure 5.5.

5.4 What is the difference between backward and forward explicit congestion signaling?

5.5 Briefly explain the three general approaches to explicit congestion signaling.

5.6 List some reasons for using flow control.

5.7 What is self-similar data traffic?

Problems

5.1 Consider a communications link using a stop-and-wait scheme, in which a series of messages is sent, with each message segmented into a number of packets. Ignore errors and frame overhead.

  a. What is the effect on line utilization of increasing the message size so that fewer messages will be required? Other factors remain constant.

  b. What is the effect on line utilization of increasing the number of packets for a constant message size?

  c. What is the effect on line utilization of increasing packet size?

5.2 A channel has a data rate of 4 kbps and a propagation delay of 20 ms. For what range of packet sizes does stop-and-wait give an efficiency of at least 50%?

5.3 A proposed congestion control technique is known as isarithmic control. In this method, the total number of frames in transit is fixed by inserting a fixed number of permits into the network. These permits circulate at random through the frame relay network. Whenever a frame handler wants to relay a frame just given to it by an attached user, it must first capture and destroy a permit. When the frame is delivered to the destination user by the frame handler to which it attaches, that frame handler reissues the permit. List three potential problems with this technique.

5.4 In IPv4, each router that handles a datagram decrements the time-to-live (TTL) field in the header (Figure 2.13a) by the number of seconds that the datagram remains at the router, or by 1 if the time is less than one second. When a router receives a datagram whose TTL is 1, it may not forward the datagram but must discard it; if a destination end system receives such a datagram, it may deliver it to the IP user. If a datagram remains at a router for a longer period of time than the incoming TTL, it must be discarded.

Now consider a router with an infinite buffer in steady-state overload: The packet arrival rate exceeds the rate at which packets can be transmitted. The router employs no congestion control techniques other than discard. What can you say about the number or proportion of packets flowing through this router that will successfully reach their destination?

5.5 Appendix 5A provides an intuitive argument to justify Little's formula. Develop a similar argument to justify the relationship $r = \lambda T_r$.

5.6 The owner of a shop observes that on average 18 customers per hour arrive and there are typically 8 customers in the shop. What is the average length of time each customer spends in the shop?

5.7 A simulation program of a multiprocessor system starts running with no jobs in the queue and ends with no jobs in the queue. The simulation program reports the average number of jobs in the system over the simulation run as 12.356, the average arrival rate as 25.6 jobs per minute, and the average delay for a job of 8.34 minutes. Was the simulation correct?

5.8 If an M/M/1 queue has arrivals at a rate of 2 per minute and serves at a rate of 4 per minute, how many customers are found in the system on average? How many customers are found in service on average?

5.9 What is the utilization of an M/M/1 queue that has four people waiting on average?

5.10 Messages arrive at random to be sent across a communications link with a data rate of 9600 bps. The link is 70% utilized, and the average message length is 1000 octets. Determine the average waiting time for constant-length messages and for exponentially distributed length messages.

5.11 Messages arrive at a switching center for a particular outgoing communications line in a Poisson manner with a mean arrival rate of 180 messages per hour. Message length is distributed exponentially with a mean length of 14,400 characters. Line speed is 9600 bps.
a. What is the mean waiting time in the switching center?
b. How many messages will be waiting in the switching center for transmission on the average?

5.12 Often inputs to a queuing system are not independent and random but occur in clusters. Mean waiting delays are greater for this type of arrival pattern than for Poisson arrivals. This problem demonstrates the effect with a simple example. Assume items arrive at a queue in fixed-size batches of M items. The batches have a Poisson arrival distribution with mean rate λ/M, yielding a customer arrival rate of λ. For each item, the service time is T_s, and the standard deviation of service time of σ_{T_s}.
a. If we treat the batches as large-size items, what is the mean and variance of batch service time? What is the mean batch waiting time?
b. What is the mean waiting time for service for an item once its batch begins service? Assume that an item may be in any of the M positions in a batch with equal probability. What is the total mean waiting time for an item?
c. Verify the results of (b) by showing that for $M = 1$, the results reduce to the M/G/1 case. How do the results vary for values of $M > 1$?

APPENDIX 5A QUEUING EFFECTS

In this appendix, we provide an overview of queuing analysis. For a more detailed discussion, see the Queuing Analysis document at the Computer Science Student Resource Site at WilliamStallings.com/StudentSupport.html.

Queuing Models

The simplest queuing system is depicted in Figure 5.16. The central element of the system is a server, which provides some service to items. Items from some population of items arrive at the system to be served. If the server is idle, an item is served immediately. Otherwise, an arriving item joins a waiting line.[7] When the server has completed serving an item, the item departs. If there are items waiting in the queue, one is immediately dispatched to the server.

Queue Parameters Figure 5.16 also illustrates some important parameters associated with a queuing model. Items arrive at the facility at some average rate (items arriving per second) λ. Examples of items arriving include packets arriving at a router and calls arriving at a telephone exchange. At any given time, a certain number of items will be waiting in the waiting line (zero or more); the average number waiting is w, and the mean time that an item must wait is T_w. T_w is averaged over all incoming items, including those that do not wait at all. The server handles incoming items with an average service time T_s; this is the time interval between the dispatching of an item to the server and the departure of that item from the server. Utilization, ρ, is the fraction of time that the server is busy, measured over some interval of time. Finally, two parameters apply to the system as a whole. The average number of items resident in the system, including the item being served (if any) and the items waiting (if any), is r; and the average time that an item spends in the system, waiting and being served, is T_r; we refer to this as the *mean residence time*.[8]

If we assume that the capacity of the queue is infinite, then no items are ever lost from the system; they are just delayed until they can be served. As the arrival rate increases, the utilization increases and with it, congestion. The queue becomes longer, increasing waiting time. At $\rho = 1$, the server becomes saturated, working 100% of the time. So long as utilization is less than 100%, the server can keep up with arrivals, so that the average departure rate equals the average arrival rate. Once the server is saturated, working 100% of the time, the departure rate remains constant, no matter how great the arrival rate becomes. Thus, the theoretical maximum input rate that can be handled by the system is

$$\lambda_{\max} = \frac{1}{T_s}$$

However, queues become very large near system saturation, growing without bound when $\rho = 1$. Practical considerations, such as response time requirements or buffer sizes, usually limit the input rate for a single server to 70 to 90% of the theoretical maximum.

Model Characteristics Before deriving any analytic equations for the queuing model, certain key characteristics of the model must be chosen. The following are the typical choices, usually reasonable in a data communications context:

---

[7]The waiting line is referred to as a queue in some treatments in the literature; it is also common to refer to the entire system as a queue. Unless otherwise noted, we use the term *queue* to mean waiting line.

[8]Again, in some of the literature, this is referred to as the mean queuing time, while other treatments use mean queuing time to mean the average time spent waiting in the waiting line (before being served).

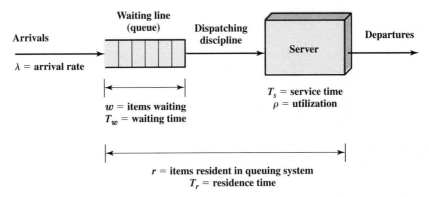

Figure 5.16   Queuing System Structure and Parameters for Single-Server Queue

- **Item population:** We assume that items arrive from a source population so large that it can be viewed as infinite. The effect of this assumption is that the arrival rate is not altered as items enter the system. If the population is finite, then the population available for arrival is reduced by the number of items currently in the system; this would typically reduce the arrival rate proportionally. Networking and server problems can usually be handled with an infinite-population assumption.

- **Queue size:** We assume an infinite queue size. Thus, the queue can grow without bound. With a finite queue, items can be lost from the system; that is, if the queue is full and additional items arrive, some items must be discarded. In practice, any queue is finite, but in many cases, this makes no substantive difference to the analysis.

- **Dispatching discipline:** When the server becomes free, and if there is more than one item waiting, a decision must be made as to which item to dispatch next. The simplest approach is first-in, first-out (FIFO), also known as first-come, first-served (FCFS); this discipline is what is normally implied when the term *queue* is used. Another possibility is last-in, first-out (LIFO). A common approach is a dispatching discipline based on relative priority. For example, a router may use QoS (quality of service) information to give preferential treatment to some packets.

Table 5.2 summarizes the notation that is used in Figure 5.16 and introduces some other useful parameters. In particular, we are often interested in the variability of various parameters, and this is neatly captured in the standard deviation.

Queuing Results

Basic Queuing Relationships To proceed much further, we are going to have to make some simplifying assumptions. These assumptions risk making the models less valid for various real-world situations. Fortunately, in many cases, the results will be sufficiently accurate for planning and design purposes.

Table 5.2   Some Queuing Parameters

λ = arrival rate; mean number of arrivals per second
T_s = mean service time for each arrival; amount of time being served, not counting time waiting in the queue
σ_{T_s} = standard deviation of service time
ρ = utilization; fraction of time facility (server or servers) is busy
r = mean number of items in system, waiting and being served
R = number of items in system, waiting and being served
T_r = mean time an item spends in system (residence time)
T_R = time an item spends in system (residence time)
σ_r = standard deviation of r
σ_{T_r} = standard deviation of T_r
w = mean number of items waiting to be served
σ_w = standard deviation of w
T_w = mean waiting time (including items that have to wait and items with waiting time = 0)
T_d = mean waiting time for items that have to wait
N = number of servers

There are, however, some relationships that are true in the general case, and these are illustrated in Table 5.3. By themselves, these relationships are not particularly helpful, although they can be used to answer a few basic questions. For example, consider a spy from Burger King trying to figure out how many people are inside the McDonald's across the way. He can't sit inside the McDonald's all day, so he has to determine an answer just based on observing the traffic in and out of the building. Over the course of the day, he observes that on average 32 customers per hour go into the restaurant. He notes certain people and finds that on average a customer stays inside 12 minutes. Using Little's formula, the spy deduces that there are on average 6.4 customers in McDonald's at any given time (6.4 = 32 customers/hour × 0.2 hours/customer).

It would be useful at this point to gain an intuitive grasp of the equations in Table 5.3. For the equation $\rho = \lambda T_s$, consider that for an arrival rate of λ the average time between arrivals is $1/\lambda = T$. If T is greater than T_s, then during a time interval T, the server is only busy for a time T_s for a utilization of $T_s/T = \lambda T_s$.

Table 5.3   Some Basic Queuing Relationships

$\rho = \lambda T_s$	
$r = \lambda T_r$	Little's formula
$w = \lambda T_w$	Little's formula
$T_r = T_w + T_s$	
$r = w + \rho$	

To understand Little's formula, consider the following argument, which focuses on the experience of a single item. When the item arrives, it will find on average w items waiting ahead of it. When the item leaves the queue behind it to be serviced, it will leave behind on average the same number of items in the queue, namely w. To see this, note that while the item is waiting, the line in front of it shrinks until the item is at the front of the line; meanwhile, additional items arrive and get in line behind this item. When the item leaves the queue to be serviced, the number of items behind it, on average, is w, because w is defined as the average number of items waiting. Further, the average time that the item was waiting for service is T_w. Since items arrive at a rate of λ, we can reason that in the time T_w, a total of λT_w items must have arrived. Thus $w = \lambda T_w$. Similar reasoning can be applied to the relationship $r = \lambda T_r$.

Turning to the next equation in Table 5.3, it is easy to observe that the time that an item spends in the system is the sum of the time waiting for service plus the time being served. Thus, on average, $T_r = T_w + T_s$. The last equation is easily justified. At any time, the number of items in the system is the sum of the number of items waiting for service plus the number of items being served. For a single server, the average number of items being served is ρ. Therefore, $r = w + \rho$ for a single server.

Assumptions The fundamental task of a queuing analysis is as follows: Given the following information as input,

- Arrival rate
- Service time
- Number of servers

   provide as output information concerning

- Items waiting
- Waiting time
- Items waiting and being served
- Residence time

What specifically would we like to know about these outputs? Certainly we would like to know their average values (w, T_w, r, T_r). In addition, it would be useful to know something about their variability. Thus, the standard deviation of each would be useful $(\sigma_r, \sigma_{T_r}, \sigma_w, \sigma_{T_w})$. Other measures may also be useful. For example, to design a buffer associated with a router or multiplexer, it might be useful to know for what buffer size the probability of overflow is less than 0.001. That is, what is the value of N such that $\Pr[\text{items waiting} < N] = 0.999$?

To answer such questions in general requires complete knowledge of the probability distribution of the interarrival times (time between successive arrivals) and service time. Furthermore, even with that knowledge, the resulting formulas are exceedingly complex. Thus, to make the problem tractable, we need to make some simplifying assumptions.

The most important of these assumptions concerns the arrival rate. We assume that the interarrival times are exponential, which is equivalent to saying that the number of arrivals in a period t obeys the Poisson distribution, which is equivalent to saying that the arrivals occur randomly and independent of one another. This assumption is almost invariably made. Without it, most queuing analysis is impractical, or at least quite difficult. With this assumption, it turns out that many useful results can be obtained if only the mean and standard deviation of the arrival rate and service time are known. Matters can be made even simpler and more detailed results can be obtained if it is assumed that the service time is exponential or constant.

A convenient notation, called **Kendall's notation**, has been developed for summarizing the principal assumptions that are made in developing a queuing model. The notation is X/Y/N, where X refers to the distribution of the interarrival times, Y refers to the distribution of service times, and N refers to the number of servers. The most common distributions are denoted as follows:

G = general distribution of interarrival times or service times

GI = general distribution of interarrival times with the restriction that interarrival times are independent

M = negative exponential distribution

D = deterministic arrivals or fixed-length service.

Thus, M/M/1 refers to a single-server queuing model with Poisson arrivals (exponential interarrival times) and exponential service times.

Single-Server Queues Table 5.4a provides some equations for single-server queues that follow the M/G/1 model. That is, the arrival rate is Poisson and the service time is general. Making use of a scaling factor, A, the equations for some of the key output variables are straightforward. Note that the key factor in the scaling

Table 5.4 Formulas for Single-Server Queues

Assumptions:	**1.** Poisson arrival rate.
	2. Dispatching discipline does not give preference to items based on service times.
	3. Formulas for standard deviation assume first-in, first-out dispatching.
	4. No items are discarded from the queue.

(a) General Service Times (M/G/1)	**(b) Exponential Service Times (M/M/1)**	**(c) Constant Service Times (M/D/1)**
$A = \dfrac{1}{2}\left[1 + \left(\dfrac{\sigma_{T_s}}{T_s}\right)^2\right]$	$r = \dfrac{\rho}{1-\rho} \qquad w = \dfrac{\rho^2}{1-\rho}$	$r = \dfrac{\rho^2}{2(1-\rho)} + \rho$
$r = \rho + \dfrac{\rho^2 A}{1-\rho}$	$T_r = \dfrac{T_s}{1-\rho} \qquad T_w = \dfrac{\rho T_s}{1-\rho}$	$w = \dfrac{\rho^2}{2(1-\rho)}$
$w = \dfrac{\rho^2 A}{1-\rho}$	$\sigma_r = \dfrac{\sqrt{\rho}}{1-\rho} \qquad \sigma_{T_r} = \dfrac{T_s}{1-\rho}$	$T_r = \dfrac{T_s(2-\rho)}{2(1-\rho)}$
$T_r = T_s + \dfrac{\rho T_s A}{1-\rho}$		$T_w = \dfrac{\rho T_s}{2(1-\rho)}$
$T_w = \dfrac{\rho T_s A}{1-\rho}$		$\sigma_r = \dfrac{1}{1-\rho}\sqrt{\rho - \dfrac{3\rho^2}{2} + \dfrac{5\rho^3}{6} - \dfrac{\rho^4}{12}}$
		$\sigma_{T_r} = \dfrac{T_s}{1-\rho}\sqrt{\dfrac{\rho}{3} - \dfrac{\rho^2}{12}}$

parameter is the ratio of the standard deviation of service time to the mean (σ_{T_s}/T_s), known as the **coefficient of variation**; this gives a normalized measure of variability. No other information about the service time is needed. Two special cases are of some interest. When the standard deviation is equal to the mean, the service time distribution is exponential (M/M/1). This is the simplest case, and the easiest one for calculating results. Table 5.4b shows the simplified versions of equations for the standard deviation of r and T_r, plus some other parameters of interest. The other interesting case is a standard deviation of service time equal to zero, that is, a constant service time (M/D/1). The corresponding equations are shown in Table 5.4c.

The poorest performance is exhibited by the exponential service time, and the best by a constant service time. In many cases, we can consider the exponential service time to be a worst case, so that an analysis based on this assumption will give conservative results. This is nice, because tables are available for the M/M/1 case and values can be looked up quickly.

What value of σ_{T_s}/T_s are we likely to encounter? We can consider four regions:

- **Zero:** This is the case of constant service time (M/D/1). For example, if all transmitted packets are of the same length, they would fit this category.

- **Ratio less than 1:** Because this ratio is better than the exponential case, using M/M/1 tables will give queue sizes and times that are slightly larger than they should be. Using the M/M/1 model would give answers on the safe side. An example of this category might be a data entry application for a particular form.

- **Ratio close to 1:** This is a common occurrence and corresponds to exponential service time (M/M/1). That is, service times are essentially random. Consider message lengths to a computer terminal: A full screen might be 1920 characters, with message sizes varying over the full range. Airline reservations, file lookups on inquiries, shared LAN, and packet-switching networks are examples of systems that often fit this category.

- **Ratio greater than 1:** If you observe this, you need to use the M/G/1 model and not rely on the M/M/1 model. A common occurrence of this is a bimodal distribution, with a wide spread between the peaks. An example is a system that experiences many short messages, many long messages, and few in between.

The same consideration applies to the arrival rate. For a Poisson arrival rate, the interarrival times are exponential, and the ratio of standard deviation to mean is 1. If the observed ratio is much less than one, then arrivals tend to be evenly spaced (not much variability), and the Poisson assumption will overestimate queue sizes and delays. On the other hand, if the ratio is greater than 1, then arrivals tend to cluster and congestion becomes more acute; this latter is an example of self-similar traffic.

CHAPTER 6

TRANSPORT PROTOCOLS

"I tell you," went on Syme with passion, "that every time a train comes in I feel that it has broken past batteries of besiegers, and that man has won a battle against chaos. You say contemptuously that when one has left Sloane Square one must come to Victoria. I say that one might do a thousand things instead, and that whenever I really come there I have the sense of hairbreadth escape. And when I hear the guard shout out the word 'Victoria', it is not an unmeaning word. It is to me the cry of a herald announcing conquest. It is to me indeed 'Victoria'; it is the victory of Adam."

—*The Man Who Was Thursday*,
G. K. Chesterton

KEY POINTS

- The transport protocol provides an end-to-end data transfer service that shields upper-layer protocols from the details of the intervening network or networks. A transport protocol can be either connection oriented, such as TCP, or connectionless, such as UDP.

- If the underlying network or internetwork service is unreliable, such as with the use of IP, then a reliable connection-oriented transport protocol becomes quite complex. The basic cause of this complexity is the need to deal with the relatively large and variable delays experienced between end systems. These large, variable delays complicate the flow control and error control techniques.

- TCP provides services in the following general areas: connection management, data transport, special capabilities, and error reporting.

- TCP uses a credit-based flow control technique that separates acknowledgments from the management of the size of the sliding window.

In a protocol architecture, the transport protocol sits above a network or internetwork layer, which provides network-related services, and just below application and other upper-layer protocols. The transport protocol provides services to transport service (TS) users, such as FTP, SMTP, and TELNET. The local transport entity communicates with some remote transport entity, using the services of some lower layer, such as the Internet Protocol. The general service provided by a transport protocol is the end-to-end transport of data in a way that shields the TS user from the details of the underlying communications systems.

We begin this chapter by examining the protocol mechanisms required to provide these services. We find that most of the complexity relates to reliable connection-oriented services. As might be expected, the less the network service provides, the more the transport protocol must do. The remainder of the chapter looks at two widely used transport protocols: Transmission Control Protocol (TCP) and User Datagram Protocol (UDP).

Refer to the figure on the inside back cover to see the position within the TCP/IP suite of the protocols discussed in this chapter.

6.1 CONNECTION-ORIENTED TRANSPORT PROTOCOL MECHANISMS

Two basic types of transport service are possible: connection oriented and connectionless or datagram service. A connection-oriented service provides for the establishment, maintenance, and termination of a logical connection between TS users. This has, so far, been the most common type of protocol service available and has a wide variety of applications. The connection-oriented service generally implies that the service is reliable. This section looks at the transport protocol mechanisms needed to support the connection-oriented service.

A full-feature connection-oriented transport protocol, such as TCP, is very complex. For purposes of clarity we present the transport protocol mechanisms in an evolutionary fashion. We begin with a network service that makes life easy for the transport protocol, by guaranteeing the delivery of all transport data units in order and defining the required mechanisms. Then we look at the transport protocol mechanisms required to cope with an unreliable network service. All of this discussion applies in general to transport-level protocols. In Sections 6.2 and 6.3, we apply the concepts developed in this section to describe TCP.

Reliable Sequencing Network Service

Let us assume that the network service accepts messages of arbitrary length and, with virtually 100% reliability, delivers them in sequence to the destination. Examples of such networks include the following:

- A highly reliable packet-switching network with an X.25 interface
- A frame relay network using the LAPF control protocol
- An IEEE 802.3 LAN using the connection-oriented LLC service

In all of these cases, the transport protocol is used as an end-to-end protocol between two systems attached to the same network, rather than across an internet.

The assumption of a reliable sequencing networking services allows the use of a quite simple transport protocol. Four issues need to be addressed:

- Addressing
- Multiplexing
- Flow control
- Connection establishment/termination

Addressing The issue concerned with addressing is simply this: A user of a given transport entity wishes either to establish a connection with or make a data transfer to a user of some other transport entity using the same transport protocol. The target user needs to be specified by all of the following:

- User identification
- Transport entity identification
- Host address
- Network number

The transport protocol must be able to derive the information listed above from the TS user address. Typically, the user address is specified as (Host, Port). The *Port* variable represents a particular TS user at the specified host. Generally, there will be a single transport entity at each host, so a transport entity identification is not needed. If more than one transport entity is present, there is usually only one of each type. In this latter case, the address should include a designation of the type of transport protocol (e.g., TCP, UDP). In the case of a single network, *Host* identifies an attached network device. In the case of an internet, *Host* is a global internet address. In TCP, the combination of port and host is referred to as a **socket**.

Because routing is not a concern of the transport layer, it simply passes the *Host* portion of the address down to the network service. *Port* is included in a transport header, to be used at the destination by the destination transport protocol entity.

One question remains to be addressed: How does the initiating TS user know the address of the destination TS user? Two static and two dynamic strategies suggest themselves:

1. The TS user knows the address it wishes to use ahead of time. This is basically a system configuration function. For example, a process may be running that is only of concern to a limited number of TS users, such as a process that collects statistics on performance. From time to time, a central network management routine connects to the process to obtain the statistics. These processes generally are not, and should not be, well known and accessible to all.

2. Some commonly used services are assigned "well-known addresses." Examples include the server side of FTP, SMTP, and some other standard protocols. Table 6.1 shows the port numbers of some common applications. A current list is maintained at www.iana.org.

3. A name server is provided. The TS user requests a service by some generic or global name. The request is sent to the name server, which does a directory

Table 6.1 Some Assigned Port Numbers

20	FTP (default data)
21	FTP (control)
23	Telnet
25	SMTP
53	DNS
69	TFTP
80	HTTP
161	SNMP agent
162	SNMP management
179	BGP
5060	SIP over TCP or UDP
5061	SIP using TLS over TCP; SIPS over TCP

lookup and returns an address. The transport entity then proceeds with the connection. This service is useful for commonly used applications that change location from time to time. For example, a data entry process may be moved from one host to another on a local network to balance load.

4. In some cases, the target user is to be a process that is spawned at request time. The initiating user can send a process request to a well-known address. The user at that address is a privileged system process that will spawn the new process and return an address. For example, a programmer has developed a private application (e.g., a simulation program) that will execute on a remote server but be invoked from a local workstation. A request can be issued to a remote job-management process that spawns the simulation process.

Multiplexing With respect to the interface between the transport protocol and higher-level protocols, the transport protocol performs a multiplexing/demultiplexing function. That is, multiple users employ the same transport protocol and are distinguished by port numbers or service access points.

Flow Control Whereas flow control is a relatively simple mechanism at the link layer, it is a rather complex mechanism at the transport layer, for two main reasons:

- The transmission delay between transport entities can be long compared to actual transmission time, as discussed in Chapter 5. This means that there is a considerable delay in the communication of flow control information.

- Because the transport layer operates over a network or internet, the amount of the transmission delay may be highly variable. This makes it difficult to effectively use a timeout mechanism for retransmission of lost data.

In general, there are two reasons why one transport entity would want to restrain the rate of segment[1] transmission over a connection from another transport entity:

- The user of the receiving transport entity cannot keep up with the flow of data.

- The receiving transport entity itself cannot keep up with the flow of segments.

How do such problems manifest themselves? Presumably a transport entity has a certain amount of buffer space. Incoming segments are added to the buffer. Each buffered segment is processed (i.e., the transport header is examined) and the data are sent to the TS user. Either of the two problems just mentioned will cause the buffer to fill up. Thus, the transport entity needs to take steps to stop or slow the flow of segments to prevent buffer overflow. This requirement is difficult to fulfill because of the annoying time gap between sender and receiver. We return to this point subsequently. First, we present four ways of coping with the flow control requirement. The receiving transport entity can:

1. Do nothing.
2. Refuse to accept further segments from the network service.
3. Use a credit scheme.

---

[1]Recall from Chapter 2 that the blocks of data (protocol data units) exchanged by TCP entities are referred to as TCP segments.

Alternative 1 means that the segments that overflow the buffer are discarded. The sending transport entity, failing to get an acknowledgment, will retransmit. This is a shame, because the advantage of a reliable network is that one never has to retransmit. Furthermore, the effect of this maneuver is to exacerbate the problem. The sender has increased its output to include new segments plus retransmitted old segments.

The second alternative is a backpressure mechanism that relies on the network service to do the work. When a buffer of a transport entity is full, it refuses additional data from the network service. This triggers flow control procedures within the network that throttle the network service at the sending end. This service, in turn, refuses additional segments from its transport entity. It should be clear that this mechanism is clumsy and coarse grained. For example, if multiple transport connections are multiplexed on a single network connection (virtual circuit), flow control is exercised only on the aggregate of all transport connections.

The third alternative, a credit scheme, involves the use of sequence numbers on segments, an allowable window of transmission, and the use of acknowledgments to adjust the window size. This is the approach used in TCP.

The motivation for the credit scheme is to overcome the inefficiencies associated with the stop-and-wait technique described in Section 5.3. With the stop-and-wait technique, the essence of the problem is that only one PDU at a time can be in transit between source and destination. In situations where the bit length of the link is greater than the PDU length ($a > 1$), serious inefficiencies result. Efficiency can be greatly improved by allowing multiple PDUs to be in transit at the same time. The general strategy for allowing for multiple PDUs to be in transit is as follows:

1. The receiver allocates a buffer space sufficient to hold a number of PDUs.

2. The sender is allowed to send a number of PDUs without waiting for an acknowledgement, because it knows that the receiver has room to accept multiple PDUs.

3. To keep track of which PDUs have been acknowledged, sequence numbers are used.

For the credit scheme, each individual octet of data that is transmitted is considered to have a unique sequence number. In addition to data, each transmitted segment includes in its header three fields related to flow control: sequence number (SN), acknowledgment number (AN), and window (W). When a transport entity sends a segment, it includes the sequence number of the first octet in the segment data field. A transport entity acknowledges an incoming segment with a return segment that includes ($AN = i, W = j$), with the following interpretation:

- All octets through sequence number $SN = i - 1$ are acknowledged; the next expected octet has sequence number i.

- Permission is granted to send an additional window of $W = j$ octets of data; that is, the j octets corresponding to sequence numbers i through $i + j - 1$.

Figure 6.1 illustrates the mechanism. For simplicity, we show data flow in one direction only and assume that 200 octets of data are sent in each segment. Initially, through the connection establishment process, the sending and receiving sequence

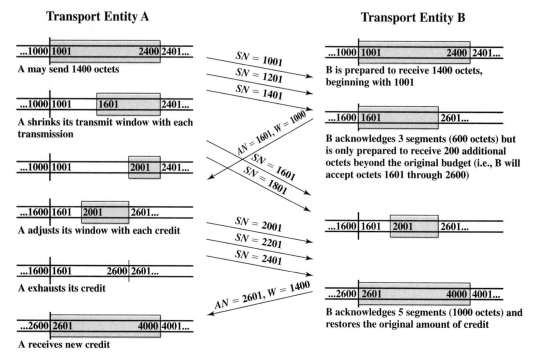

Figure 6.1 Example of TCP Credit Allocation Mechanism

numbers are synchronized and A is granted an initial credit allocation of 1400 octets, beginning with octet number 1001. After sending 600 octets in three segments, A has shrunk its window to a size of 800 octets (numbers 1601 through 2400). After B receives these three segments, 600 octets out of its original 1400 octets of credit are accounted for, and 800 octets of credit are outstanding. Now suppose that, at this point, B is capable of absorbing 1000 octets of incoming data on this connection. Accordingly, B acknowledges receipt of all octets through 1600 and issues a credit of 1000 octets. This means that A can send octets 1601 through 2600 (5 segments). However, by the time that B's message has arrived at A, A has already sent two segments, containing octets 1601 through 2000 (which was permissible under the initial allocation). Thus, A's remaining credit upon receipt of B's credit allocation is only 600 octets (3 segments). As the exchange proceeds, A advances the trailing edge of its window each time that it transmits and advances the leading edge only when it is granted credit.

Figure 6.2 shows the view of this mechanism from the sending and receiving sides. Typically, both sides take both views because data may be exchanged in both directions. Note that the receiver is not required to immediately acknowledge incoming segments but may wait and issue a cumulative acknowledgment for a number of segments.

The receiver needs to adopt some policy concerning the amount of data it permits the sender to transmit. The conservative approach is to only allow new segments

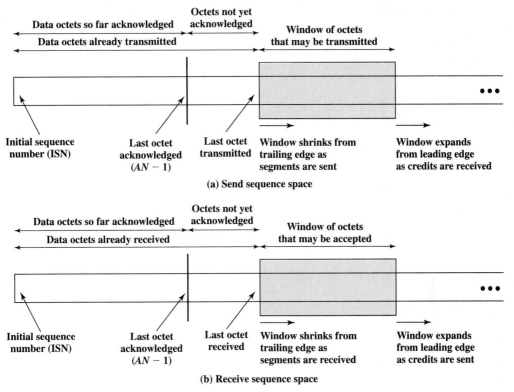

Figure 6.2 Sending and Receiving Flow Control Perspectives

up to the limit of available buffer space. If this policy were in effect in Figure 6.1, the first credit message implies that B has 1000 available octets in its buffer, and the second message that B has 1400 available octets.

A conservative flow control scheme may limit the throughput of the transport connection in long-delay situations. The receiver could potentially increase throughput by optimistically granting credit for space it does not have. For example, if a receiver's buffer is full but it anticipates that it can release space for 1000 octets within a round-trip propagation time, it could immediately send a credit of 1000. If the receiver can keep up with the sender, this scheme may increase throughput and can do no harm. If the sender is faster than the receiver, however, some segments may be discarded, necessitating a retransmission. Because retransmissions are not otherwise necessary with a reliable network service (in the absence of internet congestion), an optimistic flow control scheme will complicate the protocol.

Connection Establishment and Termination Even with a reliable network service, there is a need for connection establishment and termination procedures to support connection-oriented service. Connection establishment serves three main purposes:

- It allows each end to assure that the other exists.

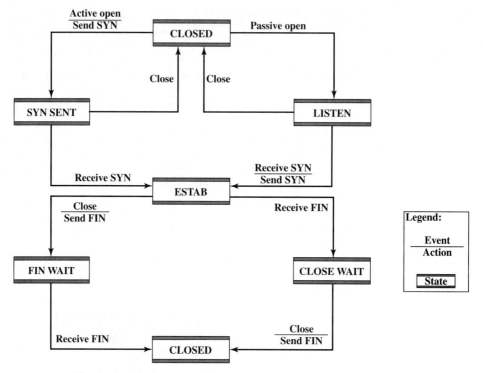

Figure 6.3   Simple Connection State Diagram

- It allows exchange or negotiation of optional parameters (e.g., maximum segment size, maximum window size, quality of service).

- It triggers allocation of transport entity resources (e.g., buffer space, entry in connection table).

Connection establishment is by mutual agreement and can be accomplished by a simple set of user commands and control segments, as shown in the state diagram of Figure 6.3. To begin, a TS user is in a CLOSED state (i.e., it has no open transport connection). The TS user can signal to the local TCP entity that it will passively wait for a request with a Passive Open command. A server program, such as time-sharing or a file transfer application, might do this. After the Passive Open command is issued, the transport entity creates a connection object of some sort (i.e., a table entry) that is in the LISTEN state. The TS user may change its mind by sending a Close command.

From the CLOSED state, a TS user may open a connection by issuing an Active Open command, which instructs the transport entity to attempt connection establishment with a designated remote TS user, which triggers the transport entity to send a SYN (for synchronize) segment. This segment is carried to the receiving transport entity and interpreted as a request for connection to a particular port. If

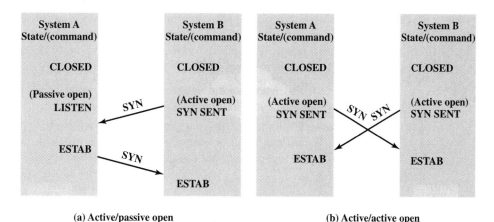

(a) Active/passive open   (b) Active/active open

Figure 6.4 Connection Establishment Scenarios

the destination transport entity is in the LISTEN state for that port, then a connection is established by the following actions by the receiving transport entity:

- Signal the local TS user that a connection is open.
- Send a SYN as confirmation to the remote transport entity.
- Put the connection object in an ESTAB (established) state.

When the responding SYN is received by the initiating transport entity, it too can move the connection to an ESTAB state. The connection is prematurely aborted if either TS user issues a Close command.

Figure 6.4 shows the robustness of this protocol. Either side can initiate a connection. Further, if both sides initiate the connection at about the same time, it is established without confusion. This is because the SYN segment functions both as a connection request and a connection acknowledgment.

The reader may ask what happens if a SYN comes in while the requested TS user is idle (not listening). Three courses may be followed:

- The transport entity can reject the request by sending a RST (reset) segment back to the other transport entity.
- The request can be queued until the local TS user issues a matching Open.
- The transport entity can interrupt or otherwise signal the local TS user to notify it of a pending request.

Note that if the third mechanism is used, a Passive Open command is not strictly necessary but may be replaced by an Accept command, which is a signal from the user to the transport entity that it accepts the request for connection.

Connection termination is handled similarly. Either side, or both sides, may initiate a close. The connection is closed by mutual agreement. This strategy allows for either abrupt or graceful termination. With abrupt termination, data in transit may be lost; a graceful termination prevents either side from closing the connection until all data have been delivered. To achieve the latter, a connection in the FIN WAIT state must continue to accept data segments until a FIN (finish) segment is received.

Figure 6.3 illustrates the procedure for graceful termination. First, consider the side that initiates the termination procedure:

1. In response to a TS user's Close primitive, a transport entity sends a FIN segment to the other side of the connection, requesting termination.

2. Having sent the FIN, the transport entity places the connection in the FIN WAIT state. In this state, the transport entity must continue to accept data from the other side and deliver that data to its user.

3. When a FIN is received in response, the transport entity informs its user and closes the connection.

From the point of view of the side that does not initiate a termination:

1. When a FIN segment is received, the transport entity informs its user of the termination request and places the connection in the CLOSE WAIT state. In this state, the transport entity must continue to accept data from its user and transmit it in data segments to the other side.

2. When the user issues a Close primitive, the transport entity sends a responding FIN segment to the other side and closes the connection.

This procedure ensures that both sides have received all outstanding data and that both sides agree to connection termination before actual termination.

Unreliable Network Service

A more difficult case for a transport protocol is that of an unreliable network service. Examples of such networks are as follows:

- An internetwork using IP
- A frame relay network using only the LAPF core protocol
- An IEEE 802.3 LAN using the unacknowledged connectionless LLC service

The problem is not just that segments are occasionally lost, but that segments may arrive out of sequence due to variable transit delays. As we shall see, elaborate machinery is required to cope with these two interrelated network deficiencies. We shall also see that a discouraging pattern emerges. The combination of unreliability and nonsequencing creates problems with every mechanism we have discussed so far. Generally, the solution to each problem raises new problems. Although there are problems to be overcome for protocols at all levels, it seems that there are more difficulties with a reliable connection-oriented transport protocol than any other sort of protocol.

In the remainder of this section, unless otherwise noted, the mechanisms discussed are those used by TCP. Seven issues need to be addressed:

- Ordered delivery
- Retransmission strategy
- Duplicate detection

- Flow control
- Connection establishment
- Connection termination
- Failure recovery

Ordered Delivery With an unreliable network service, it is possible that segments, even if they are all delivered, may arrive out of order. The required solution to this problem is to number segments sequentially. The approach used by TCP is that each data octet that is transmitted is implicitly numbered. Thus, the first segment may have a sequence number of 1. If that segment has 200 octets of data, then the second segment would have the sequence number 201, and so on. For simplicity in the discussions of this section, we will continue to assume that each successive segment's sequence number is 200 more than that of the previous segment; that is, each segment contains exactly 200 octets of data.

Retransmission Strategy Two events necessitate the retransmission of a segment. First, a segment may be damaged in transit but nevertheless arrive at its destination. If a checksum is included with the segment, the receiving transport entity can detect the error and discard the segment. The second contingency is that a segment fails to arrive. In either case, the sending transport entity does not know that the segment transmission was unsuccessful. To cover this contingency, a positive acknowledgment scheme is used: The receiver must acknowledge each successfully received segment by returning a segment containing an acknowledgment number. For efficiency, we do not require one acknowledgment per segment. Rather, a cumulative acknowledgment can be used. Thus, the receiver may receive segments numbered 1, 201, and 401, but only send $AN = 601$ back. The sender must interpret $AN = 601$ to mean that the segment with $SN = 401$ and all previous segments have been successfully received.

If a segment does not arrive successfully, no acknowledgment will be issued and a retransmission is in order. To cope with this situation, there must be a timer associated with each segment as it is sent. If the timer expires before the segment is acknowledged, the sender must retransmit.

Incidentally, the retransmission timer is only one of a number of timers needed for proper functioning of a transport protocol. These are listed in Table 6.2, together with a brief explanation.

Table 6.2 Transport Protocol Timers

Retransmission timer	Retransmit an unacknowledged segment
Reconnection timer	Minimum time between closing one connection and opening another with the same destination address
Window timer	Maximum time between ACK/CREDIT segments
Retransmit-SYN timer	Time between attempts to open a connection
Persistence timer	Abort connection when no segments are acknowledged
Inactivity timer	Abort connection when no segments are received

Duplicate Detection If a segment is lost and then retransmitted, no confusion will result. If, however, one or more segments in sequence are successfully delivered, but the corresponding ACK is lost, then the sending transport entity will time out and one or more segments will be retransmitted. If these retransmitted segments arrive successfully, they will be duplicates of previously received segments. Thus, the receiver must be able to recognize duplicates. The fact that each segment carries a sequence number helps; nevertheless, duplicate detection and handling is no easy matter. There are two cases:

- A duplicate is received prior to the close of the connection.
- A duplicate is received after the close of the connection.

The second case is discussed in the subsection on connection establishment. We deal with the first case here.

Notice that we say "a" duplicate rather than "the" duplicate. From the sender's point of view, the retransmitted segment is the duplicate. However, the retransmitted segment may arrive before the original segment, in which case the receiver views the original segment as the duplicate. In any case, two tactics are needed to cope with a duplicate received prior to the close of a connection:

- The receiver must assume that its acknowledgment was lost and therefore must acknowledge the duplicate. Consequently, the sender must not get confused if it receives multiple acknowledgments to the same segment.
- The sequence number space must be long enough so as not to "cycle" in less than the maximum possible segment lifetime (time it takes segment to transit network).

Figure 6.5 illustrates the reason for the latter requirement. In this example, the sequence space is of length 1600; that is, after $SN = 1600$, the sequence numbers cycle back and begin with $SN = 1$. For simplicity, we assume the receiving transport entity maintains a credit window size of 600. Suppose that A has transmitted data segments with $SN = 1, 201$, and 401. B has received the two segments with $SN = 201$ and $SN = 401$, but the segment with $SN = 1$ is delayed in transit. Thus, B does not send any acknowledgments. Eventually, A times out and retransmits segment $SN = 1$. When the duplicate segment $SN = 1$ arrives, B acknowledges 1, 201, and 401 with $AN = 601$. Meanwhile, A has timed out again and retransmits $SN = 201$, which B acknowledges with another $AN = 601$. Things now seem to have sorted themselves out and data transfer continues. When the sequence space is exhausted, A cycles back to $SN = 1$ and continues. Alas, the old segment $SN = 1$ makes a belated appearance and is accepted by B before the new segment $SN = 1$ arrives. When the new segment $SN = 1$ does arrive, it is treated as a duplicate and discarded.

It should be clear that the untimely emergence of the old segment would have caused no difficulty if the sequence numbers had not yet wrapped around. The problem is as follows: How big must the sequence space be? This depends on, among other things, whether the network enforces a maximum packet lifetime, and the rate at which segments are being transmitted. Fortunately, each addition of a single bit to the sequence number field doubles the sequence space, so it is rather easy to select a safe size.

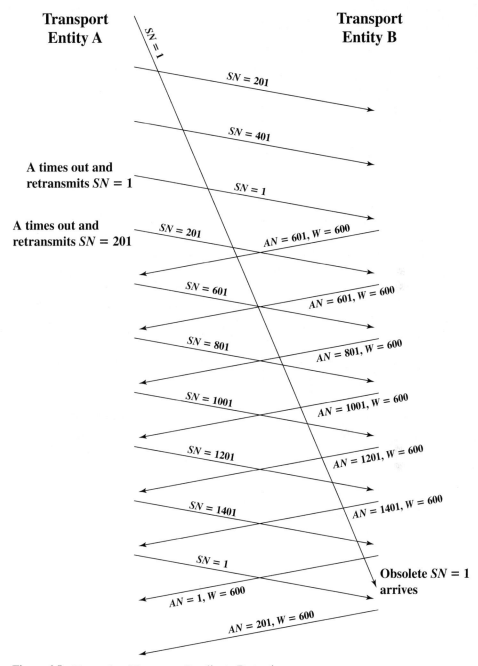

Figure 6.5 Example of Incorrect Duplicate Detection

Flow Control The credit allocation flow control mechanism described earlier is quite robust in the face of an unreliable network service and requires little enhancement. As was mentioned, a segment containing $(AN = i, W = j)$ acknowledges all octets through number $i - 1$ and grants credit for an additional j octets beginning with octet i. The credit allocation mechanism is quite flexible. For example, suppose that the last octet of data received by B was octet number $i - 1$ and that the last segment issued by B was $(AN = i, W = j)$. Then

- To increase credit to an amount $k(k > j)$ when no additional data have arrived, B issues $(AN = i, W = k)$.
- To acknowledge an incoming segment containing m octets of data $(m < j)$ without granting additional credit, B issues $(AN = i + m, W = j - m)$.

If an ACK/CREDIT segment is lost, little harm is done. Future acknowledgments will resynchronize the protocol. Further, if no new acknowledgments are forthcoming, the sender times out and retransmits a data segment, which triggers a new acknowledgment. However, it is still possible for deadlock to occur. Consider a situation in which B sends $(AN = i, W = 0)$, temporarily closing the window. Subsequently, B sends $(AN = i, W = j)$, but this segment is lost. A is awaiting the opportunity to send data and B thinks that it has granted that opportunity. To overcome this problem, a window timer can be used. This timer is reset with each outgoing segment (all segments contain the AN and W fields). If the timer ever expires, the protocol entity is required to send a segment, even if it duplicates a previous one. This breaks the deadlock and also assures the other end that the protocol entity is still alive.

Connection Establishment As with other protocol mechanisms, connection establishment must take into account the unreliability of a network service. Recall that a connection establishment calls for the exchange of SYNs, a procedure sometimes referred to as a two-way handshake. Suppose that A issues a SYN to B. It expects to get a SYN back, confirming the connection. Two things can go wrong: A's SYN can be lost or B's answering SYN can be lost. Both cases can be handled by use of a retransmit-SYN timer (Table 6.2). After A issues a SYN, it will reissue the SYN when the timer expires.

This gives rise, potentially, to duplicate SYNs. If A's initial SYN was lost, there are no duplicates. If B's response was lost, then B may receive two SYNs from A. Further, if B's response was not lost, but simply delayed, A may get two responding SYNs. All of this means that A and B must simply ignore duplicate SYNs once a connection is established.

There are other problems to contend with. Just as a delayed SYN or lost response can give rise to a duplicate SYN, a delayed data segment or lost acknowledgment can give rise to duplicate data segments, as we have seen in Figure 6.5. Such a delayed or duplicated data segment can interfere with data transfer, as illustrated in Figure 6.6. Assume that with each new connection, each transport protocol entity begins numbering its data segments with sequence number 1. In the figure, a duplicate copy of segment $SN = 401$ from an old connection arrives during the lifetime of a new connection and is delivered to B before delivery of the legitimate data segment $SN = 401$. One way of attacking this problem is to start each new connection with a different sequence number that is far removed from the last sequence number of the most recent connection. For this purpose, the connection request is of the form SYN i, where $i + 1$ is the sequence number of the first data segment that will be sent on this connection.

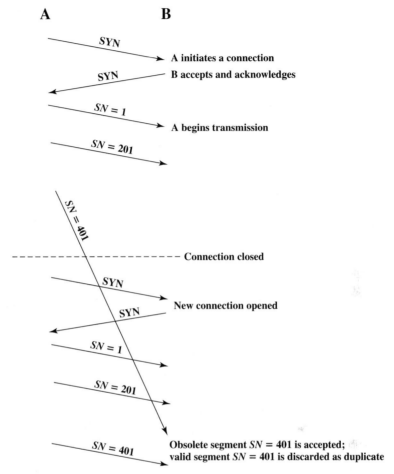

Figure 6.6 The Two-Way Handshake: Problem with Obsolete Data Segment

Now consider that a duplicate SYN i may survive past the termination of the connection. Figure 6.7 depicts the problem that may arise. An old SYN i arrives at B after the connection is terminated. B assumes that this is a fresh request and responds with SYN j, meaning that B accepts the connection request and will begin transmitting with $SN = j + 1$. Meanwhile, A has decided to open a new connection with B and sends SYN k. B discards this as a duplicate. Now both sides have transmitted and subsequently received a SYN segment, and therefore think that a valid connection exists. However, when A initiates data transfer with a segment numbered $k + 1$, B rejects the segment as being out of sequence.

The way out of this problem is for each side to acknowledge explicitly the other's SYN and sequence number. The procedure is known as a three-way handshake. The revised connection state diagram, which is the one employed by TCP, is shown in the upper part of Figure 6.8. A new state (SYN RECEIVED) is added. In this state, the transport entity hesitates during connection opening to

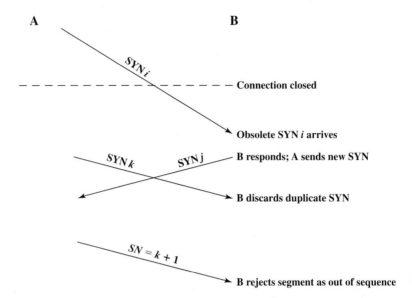

A   B

SYN i

Connection closed

Obsolete SYN *i* arrives

SYN k   *SYN j*   B responds; A sends new SYN

B discards duplicate SYN

SN = k + 1

B rejects segment as out of sequence

Figure 6.7   Two-Way Handshake: Problem with Obsolete SYN Segments

assure that the SYN segments sent by the two sides have both been acknowl-edged before the connection is declared established. In addition to the new state, there is a control segment (RST) to reset the other side when a duplicate SYN is detected.

Figure 6.9 illustrates typical three-way handshake operations. In Figure 6.9a, transport entity A initiates the connection, with a SYN including the sending se-quence number, i. The value i is referred to as the initial sequence number (ISN) and is associated with the SYN; the first data octet to be transmitted will have sequence number $i + 1$. The responding SYN acknowledges the ISN with $(AN = i + 1)$ and includes its ISN. A acknowledges B's SYN/ACK in its first data segment, which be-gins with sequence number $i + 1$. Figure 6.9b shows a situation in which an old SYN i arrives at B after the close of the relevant connection. B assumes that this is a fresh request and responds with SYN j, $AN = i + 1$. When A receives this message, it realizes that it has not requested a connection and therefore sends an RST, $AN = j$. Note that the $AN = j$ portion of the RST message is essential so that an old dupli-cate RST does not abort a legitimate connection establishment. Figure 6.9c shows a case in which an old SYN/ACK arrives in the middle of a new connection establish-ment. Because of the use of sequence numbers in the acknowledgments, this event causes no mischief.

For simplicity, the upper part of Figure 6.8 does not include transitions in which RST is sent. The basic rule is as follows: Send an RST if the connection state is not yet OPEN and an invalid ACK (one that does not reference something that was sent) is received. The reader should try various combinations of events to see that this connection establishment procedure works in spite of any combination of old and lost segments.

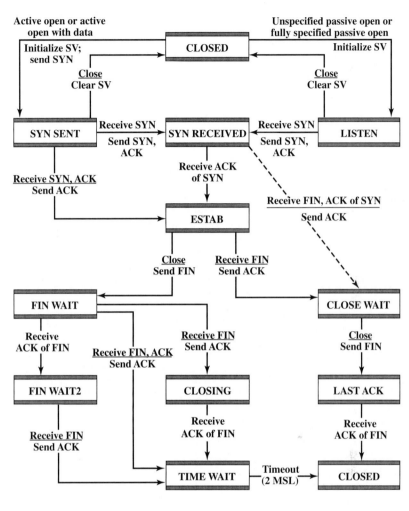

Figure 6.8 TCP Entity State Diagram

Connection Termination The state diagram of Figure 6.3 defines the use of a simple two-way handshake for connection establishment, which was found to be unsatisfactory in the face of an unreliable network service. Similarly, the two-way handshake defined in that diagram for connection termination is inadequate for an unreliable network service. Misordering of segments could cause the following scenario. A transport entity in the CLOSE WAIT state sends its last data segment, followed by a FIN segment, but the FIN segment arrives at the other side before the last data segment. The receiving transport entity will accept that FIN, close the connection, and lose the last segment of data. To avoid this problem, a sequence number can be associated with the FIN, which can be assigned the next sequence number

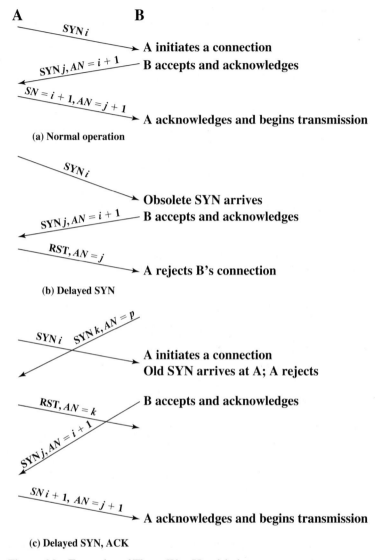

Figure 6.9   Examples of Three-Way Handshake

after the last octet of transmitted data. With this refinement, the receiving transport entity, upon receiving a FIN, will wait if necessary for the late-arriving data before closing the connection.

A more serious problem is the potential loss of segments and the potential presence of obsolete segments. Figure 6.8 shows that the termination procedure adopts a similar solution to that used for connection establishment. Each side must explicitly acknowledge the FIN of the other, using an ACK with the sequence number of the FIN to be acknowledged. For a graceful close, a transport entity requires the following:

• It must send a FIN i and receive $AN = i + 1$.

- It must receive a FIN j and send $AN = j + 1$.
- It must wait an interval equal to twice the maximum expected segment lifetime.

Failure Recovery When the system upon which a transport entity is running fails and subsequently restarts, the state information of all active connections is lost. The affected connections become *half open* because the side that did not fail does not yet realize the problem. The still active side of a half-open connection can close the connection using a persistence timer. This timer measures the time the transport machine will continue to await an acknowledgment (or other appropriate reply) of a transmitted segment after the segment has been retransmitted the maximum number of times. When the timer expires, the transport entity assumes that the other transport entity or the intervening network has failed, closes the connection, and signals an abnormal close to the TS user.

In the event that a transport entity fails and quickly restarts, half-open connections can be terminated more quickly by the use of the RST segment. The failed side returns an RST i to every segment i that it receives. When the RST i reaches the other side, it must be checked for validity based on the sequence number i, because the RST could be in response to an old segment. If the reset is valid, the transport entity performs an abnormal termination.

These measures clean up the situation at the transport level. The decision as to whether to reopen the connection is up to the TS users. The problem is one of synchronization. At the time of failure, there may have been one or more outstanding segments in either direction. The TS user on the side that did not fail knows how much data it has received, but the other user may not, if state information were lost. Thus, there is the danger that some user data will be lost or duplicated.

6.2 TCP SERVICES

In this section and the next we look at TCP (RFC 793), first at the service it provides to the TS user and then at the internal protocol details.

Service Categories

In general, the service provided by TCP is the reliable end-to-end transport of data between host processes. More specifically, the standard calls out the following categories of service: multiplexing, connection management, data transport, special capabilities, and error reporting (Table 6.3).

Multiplexing A TCP entity within a host can simultaneously provide service to multiple processes. A process with a host using TCP services is identified with a port. As was described in Section 4.4, the concatenation of a port number with an Internet address forms a socket, which is unique throughout the Internet. TCP provides service by means of a logical connection between a pair of sockets.

As an example, Figure 6.10 shows three hosts attached to the Internet. Each host has a unique Internet address, and the TCP entity within each host supports multiple ports, with one or more port per application. In this example, there are two TCP connections active between application Y on host A and application Y on host

Table 6.3 Summary of TCP Services

Multiplexing	Supports multiple users by means of ports.
Connection Management	
Connection establishment	Establishes connection between unconnected pair of sockets with specified security and precedence.
Connection maintenance	Maintains connection for transport of data.
Connection termination	Provides graceful close and abort.
Data Transport	
Full duplex	Delivers simultaneous bidirectional data flow between the two sockets of the connection.
Timely	Delivers within user-specified timeout or notifies user and terminates connection.
Ordered	Delivers data in the same sequence that it was provided by source user.
Labeled	Security and precedence level of the connection associated with each data transfer.
Flow controlled	Flow of data across the connection is regulated.
Error controlled	Data are delivered free of error.
Special Capabilities	
Data stream push	Pushes data through connection and delivers it to user.
Urgent data signaling	Expedites transfer and delivery of data.
Error Reporting	Reports service failure.

B (e.g., FTP connections). There is also a TCP connection between application Z on host A and application Z on host C. Thus TCP can support multiple connections to the application layer simultaneously and can support multiple connections to the same application in the application layer simultaneously. These are both instances of multiplexing.

Connection Management Connection management in TCP consists of three services: connection establishment, connection maintenance, and connection termination. **Connection management** enables two TCP users to set up a logical connection between their respective sockets. A logical connection has certain properties that endure for the lifetime of the connection, such as timer values and precedence; these are specified by the two TCP users at the time of connection establishment. A connection between two sockets may be set up if

- No connection between the two sockets currently exists. From a given socket, it is possible to maintain more than one connection simultaneously, but only one connection to any specific remote socket at a time is permitted.
- Internal TCP resources (e.g., buffer space) are sufficient.
- Both users have agreed to the connection.

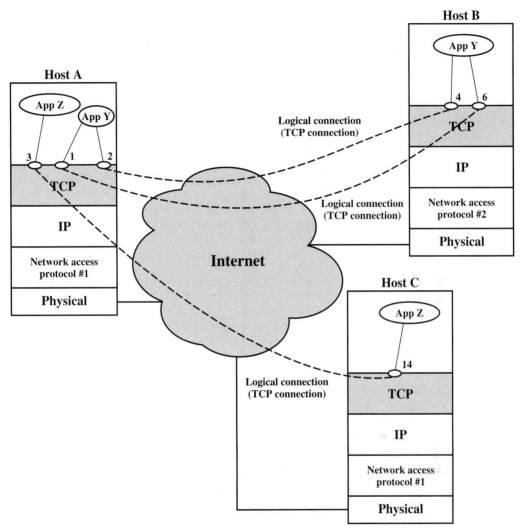

Figure 6.10 Multiplexing Example

Connection maintenance provides for the exchange of data between the two sockets and supports the data transport and special capability services described next. **Connection termination** may be either abrupt or graceful. With an abrupt termination, data in transit may be lost. A graceful termination prevents either side from shutting down until all outstanding data have been delivered.

Data Transport The data transport service consists of six subservices:

- **Full duplex:** Both users may transmit at any time that the connection is maintained; there is no need to take turns.

- **Timely:** The user may request timely delivery of data by associating a timeout with data submitted for transmission. If TCP fails to deliver the data within the specified timeout, it notifies the user of service failure and abruptly terminates the connection.

- **Ordered:** TCP users exchange streams of octets, transmitted in segments. TCP guarantees that the stream of data presented by one user to TCP will be delivered in the same order to the remote user.

- **Labeled:** TCP establishes a connection only if the security designations provided by both users requesting the connection match. If the precedence levels do not match, the higher level is associated with the connection.

- **Flow controlled:** TCP regulates the flow of data to prevent internal TCP congestion that could lead to service degradation and failure, and in response to the buffer allocation provided by the user.

- **Error controlled:** TCP makes use of a simple checksum and delivers data that is free of errors within the probabilities supported by the checksum.

Special Capabilities TCP provides two useful facilities for labeling data, push and urgent:

- **Data stream push:** Ordinarily, TCP decides when sufficient data have accumulated to form a segment for transmission. The TCP user can require TCP to transmit all outstanding data up to and including that labeled with a push flag. On the receiving end, TCP will deliver these data to the user in the same manner. A user might request this if it has come to a logical break in the data.

- **Urgent data signaling:** This provides a means of informing the destination TCP user that significant or "urgent" data is in the upcoming data stream. It is up to the destination user to determine appropriate action.

We will return to the topic of push and urgent signaling subsequently.

Error Reporting TCP will report service failure resulting from catastrophic conditions in the internetwork environment for which TCP cannot compensate.

TCP Service Primitives

The services provided by TCP are defined in terms of primitives and parameters. A primitive specifies the function to be performed, and the parameters are used to pass data and control information. The actual form of a primitive is implementation dependent. Table 6.4 lists TCP service request primitives, which are issued by a TCP

Table 6.4 TCP Service Request Primitives

Primitive	Parameters	Description
Unspecified Passive Open	source-port, [timeout], [timeout-action], [precedence], [security-range]	Listen for connection attempt at specified security and precedence from any remote destination.
Fully Specified Passive Open	source-port, destination-port, destination-address, [timeout], [timeout-action], [precedence], [security-range]	Listen for connection attempt at specified security and precedence from specified destination.
Active Open	source-port, destination-port, destination-address, [timeout], [timeout-action], [precedence], [security]	Request connection at a particular security and precedence to a specified destination.
Active Open with Data	source-port, destination-port, destination-address, [timeout], [timeout-action], [precedence], [security], data, data-length, PUSH-flag, URGENT-flag	Request connection at a particular security and precedence to a specified destination and transmit data with the request.
Send	local-connection-name, data, data-length, PUSH-flag, URGENT-flag, [timeout], [timeout-action]	Transfer data across named connection.
Allocate	local-connection-name, data-length	Issue incremental allocation for receive data to TCP.
Close	local-connection-name	Close connection gracefully.
Abort	local-connection-name	Close connection abruptly.
Status	local-connection-name	Query connection status.

Note: Square brackets indicate optional parameters.

user to TCP, and Table 6.5 lists TCP service response primitives, which are issued by TCP to a local TCP user. Table 6.6 provides a brief definition of the parameters involved. The two passive open commands signal the TCP user's willingness to accept a connection request. The active open with data allows the user to begin transmitting data with the opening of the connection.

Figure 6.11 shows the context for use of the TCP service primitives and parameters. Users of TCP, at the application level, exchange request and response primitives with TCP. Many of these TCP service primitives trigger the transmission of one or more TCP segments to the remote socket. These segments are submitted to IP in an IP Send primitive and delivered by IP to TCP in an IP Deliver primitive.

Table 6.5 TCP Service Response Primitives

Primitive	Parameters	Description
Open ID	local-connection-name, source-port, destination-port*, destination-address*	Informs TCP user of connection name assigned to pending connection requested in an Open primitive.
Open Failure	local-connection-name	Reports failure of an Active Open request.
Open Success	local-connection-name	Reports completion of pending Open request.
Deliver	local-connection-name, data, data-length, URGENT-flag	Reports arrival of data.
Closing	local-connection-name	Reports that remote TCP user has issued a Close and that all data sent by remote user has been delivered.
Terminate	local-connection-name, description	Reports that the connection has been terminated; a description of the reason for termination is provided.
Status Response	local-connection-name, source-port, source-address, destination-port, destination-address, connection-state, receive-window, send-window, amount-awaiting-ACK, amount-awaiting-receipt, urgent-state, precedence, security, timeout	Reports current status of connection.
Error	local-connection-name, description	Reports service-request or internal error.

* = Not used for Unspecified Passive Open.

6.3 TRANSMISSION CONTROL PROTOCOL

Basic Operation

TCP provides a means for two users to exchange as streams of octets. The data streams are transmitted in segments, with each segment consisting of a TCP header and a portion of the user data. Some segments carry no data but consist solely of the header; these are used for connection management.

Figure 6.12 illustrates the basic operation of TCP. Data are passed to TCP by a user in a sequence of TCP Send primitives. These data are buffered in a **send buffer**. From time to time, TCP assembles data from the send buffer into a segment and transmits the segment. Each segment is transmitted by the IP service and delivered to the destination TCP entity, which strips off the segment header and places the data in a **receive buffer**. From time to time, the receiving TCP entity notifies its user, by means of the TCP Deliver primitive, that data are available for delivery.

Table 6.6   TCP Service Parameters

Source Port	Local TCP user.
Timeout	Longest delay allowed for data delivery before automatic connection termination or error report; user specified.
Timeout-action	Indicates whether the connection is terminated or an error is reported to the TCP user in the event of a timeout.
Precedence	Precedence level for a connection. Takes on values zero (lowest) through seven (highest); same parameter as defined for IP.
Security-range	Allowed ranges in compartment, handling restrictions, transmission control codes, and security levels.
Destination Port	Remote TCP user.
Destination Address	Internet address of remote host.
Security	Security information for a connection, including security level, compartment, handling restrictions, and transmission control code; same parameter as defined for IP.
Data	Block of data sent by TCP user or delivered to a TCP user.
Data Length	Length of block of data sent or delivered.
PUSH flag	If set, indicates that the associated data are to be provided with the data stream push service.
URGENT flag	If set, indicates that the associated data are to be provided with the urgent data signaling service.
Local Connection Name	Identifier of a connection defined by a (local socket, remote socket) pair; provided by TCP.
Description	Supplementary information in a Terminate or Error primitive.
Source Address	Internet address of the local host.
Connection State	State of referenced connection (CLOSED, ACTIVE OPEN, PASSIVE OPEN, ESTABLISHED, CLOSING).
Receive Window	Amount of data in octets the local TCP entity is willing to receive.
Send Window	Amount of data in octets permitted to be sent to remote TCP entity.
Amount Awaiting ACK	Amount of previously transmitted data awaiting acknowledgment.
Amount Awaiting Receipt	Amount of data in octets buffered at local TCP entity pending receipt by local TCP user.
Urgent State	Indicates to the receiving TCP user whether there are urgent data available or whether all urgent data, if any, have been delivered to the user.

One difficulty that TCP faces is that segments may arrive out of order. To compensate, TCP numbers each transmitted segment sequentially, placing the sequence number in the TCP header. Thus, there is no ambiguity about the intended order, and the data can be reordered appropriately by the destination TCP entity before delivery to the destination user.

A second difficulty is that TCP segments may be lost. The use of sequence numbers and acknowledgments deals with this problem, enabling a TCP entity to retransmit a lost segment. To be able to retransmit segments, TCP must save a copy of each transmitted segment in a **segment buffer** until that segment is acknowledged.

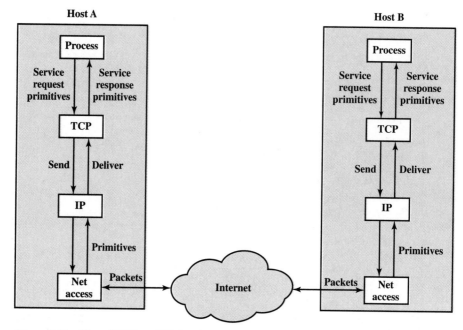

Figure 6.11 Use of TCP and IP Service Primitives

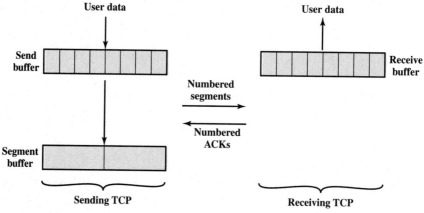

Figure 6.12 Basic TCP Operation

TCP Header Format

TCP uses only a single type of protocol data unit, called a TCP segment. The header is shown in Figure 6.13. Because one header must serve to perform all protocol mechanisms, it is rather large, with a minimum length of 20 octets. The fields are as follows:

- **Source Port (16 bits):** Source TCP user.
- **Destination Port (16 bits):** Destination TCP user.

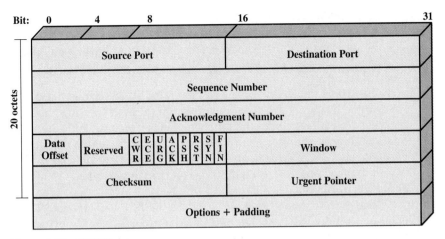

Figure 6.13 TCP Header

- **Sequence Number (32 bits):** Sequence number of the first data octet in this segment except when the SYN flag is set. If SYN is set, this field contains the initial sequence number (ISN) and the first data octet in this segment has sequence number ISN + 1.

- **Acknowledgment Number (32 bits):** Contains the sequence number of the next data octet that the TCP entity expects to receive.

- **Data Offset (4 bits):** Number of 32-bit words in the header.

- **Reserved (4 bits):** Reserved for future use.

- **Flags (6 bits):** For each flag, if set to 1, the meaning is as follows:

  CWR: congestion window reduced.

  ECE: ECN-Echo; the CWR and ECE bits, defined in RFC 3168, are used for the explicit congestion notification function, which is described in Chapter 7.

  URG: urgent pointer field significant.

  ACK: acknowledgment field significant.

  PSH: push function.

  RST: reset the connection.

  SYN: synchronize the sequence numbers.

  FIN: no more data from sender.

- **Window (16 bits):** Flow control credit allocation, in octets. Contains the number of data octets, beginning with the sequence number indicated in the acknowledgment field that the sender is willing to accept.

- **Checksum (16 bits):** The ones complement of the ones complement sum of all the 16-bit words in the segment plus a pseudoheader, described subsequently.[2]

---

[2] A discussion of this checksum is contained in a supporting document at this book's Web site.

- **Urgent Pointer (16 bits):** This value, when added to the segment sequence number, contains the sequence number of the last octet in a sequence of urgent data. This allows the receiver to know how much urgent data are coming.
- **Options (Variable):** Zero or more options may be included.

The **checksum** field applies to the entire segment plus a pseudoheader prefixed to the header at the time of calculation (at both transmission and reception). The pseudoheader includes the following fields from the IP header: source and destination internet address and protocol, plus a segment length field. By including the pseudoheader, TCP protects itself from misdelivery by IP. That is, if IP delivers a packet to the wrong host, even if the packet contains no bit errors, the receiving TCP entity will detect the delivery error.

The **push function** (PSH flag) enables the TCP user to control TCP's management of its buffers. In general, buffering improves efficiency by enabling the TCP sender to send fewer large segments rather than many small segments. This cuts down on processing at the sender, possibly in transit, and at the receiver. At the receiver, buffering minimizes the number of times an application is signaled or interrupted to take delivery. But the tradeoff is that buffering increases delay. The push function allows applications to bypass buffering, which reduces delay. The push function can also be used at the end of a logical block of data to speed up completion of delivery.

The **urgent function** (URG flag and Urgent Pointer) is a means of signaling the destination application that urgent data have arrived. The urgent signal is given to the application in advance of delivery of the data to the application. One example of the use of urgent signaling is the Telnet synch mechanism, described in Section 3.1.

The following options are defined for TCP:

- **Maximum segment size:** Included in a SYN segment to indicate the maximum incoming segment size allowable.
- **Window scale:** Included in a SYN segment. Ordinarily, the Window field in the TCP header gives a credit allocation in octets. When the Window Scale option is in use, the value in the Window field is multiplied by a 2^F, where F is the value of the window scale option. This option is defined in RFC 1323.
- **Sack-permitted:** Indicates that selective acknowledgement is allowed.
- **Sack:** Allows the receiver to inform the sender of all the segments that are received successfully. The sender will only retransmit segments that have not been received. The Sack and Sack-permitted options are defined in RFC 2018.
- **Timestamps:** Allows the sending of a timestamp in a data segment and the return of an echo of that timestamp in a return ACK segment. This option is defined in RFC 1323.

By comparing the TCP header to the TCP user interface defined in Tables 6.3 and 6.4, the reader may feel that some items are missing from the TCP header; that is indeed the case. TCP is designed specifically to work with IP. Hence, some TCP user parameters are passed down by TCP to IP for inclusion in the IP header. The relevant ones are as follows:

- Precedence: a 3-bit field
- Normal-delay/low-delay
- Normal-throughput/high-throughput
- Normal-reliability/high-reliability
- Security: an 11-bit field

It is worth observing that this TCP/IP linkage means that the required minimum overhead for every data unit is 40 octets.

TCP Mechanisms

We can group TCP mechanisms into the categories of connection establishment, data transfer, and connection termination.

Connection Establishment Connection establishment in TCP always uses a three-way handshake. When the SYN flag is set, the segment is essentially a request for connection and functions as explained in Section 6.1. To initiate a connection, an entity sends a SYN, $SN = X$, where X is the initial sequence number. The receiver responds with SYN, $SN = Y$, $AN = X + 1$ by setting both the SYN and ACK flags. Note that the acknowledgment indicates that the receiver is now expecting to receive a segment beginning with data octet $X + 1$, acknowledging the SYN, which occupies $SN = X$. Finally, the initiator responds with $AN = Y + 1$. If the two sides issue crossing SYNs, no problem results: Both sides respond with SYN/ACKs (Figure 6.8).

A connection is uniquely determined by the source and destination sockets (host, port). Thus, at any one time, there can only be a single TCP connection between a unique pair of ports. However, a given port can support multiple connections, each with a different partner port.

Data Transfer Although data are transferred in segments over a transport connection, data transfer is viewed logically as consisting of a stream of octets. Hence every octet is numbered, modulo 2^{32}. Each segment contains the sequence number of the first octet in the data field. Flow control is exercised using a credit allocation scheme in which the credit is a number of octets rather than a number of segments, as explained in Section 6.1.

If, during data exchange, a segment arrives that is apparently not meant for the current connection, the RST flag is set on an outgoing segment. Examples of this situation are delayed duplicate SYNs and an acknowledgment of data not yet sent.

Connection Termination The normal means of terminating a connection is a graceful close. Each TCP user must issue a CLOSE primitive. The transport entity sets the FIN bit on the last segment that it sends out, which also contains the last of the data to be sent on this connection.

An abrupt termination occurs if the user issues an ABORT primitive. In this case, the entity abandons all attempts to send or receive data and discards data in its transmission and reception buffers. An RST segment is sent to the other side.

TCP Implementation Policy Options

The TCP standard provides a precise specification of the protocol to be used between TCP entities. However, certain aspects of the protocol admit several possible implementation options. Although two implementations that choose alternative options will be interoperable, there may be performance implications. The design areas for which options are specified are the following:

- Send policy
- Deliver policy
- Accept policy
- Retransmit policy
- Acknowledge policy

Send Policy In the absence of both pushed data and a closed transmission window (see Figure 6.2a), a sending TCP entity is free to transmit data at its own convenience, within its current credit allocation. As data are issued by the user, they are buffered in the transmit buffer. TCP may construct a segment for each batch of data provided by its user or it may wait until a certain amount of data accumulates before constructing and sending a segment. The actual policy will depend on performance considerations. If transmissions are infrequent and large, there is low overhead in terms of segment generation and processing. On the other hand, if transmissions are frequent and small, the system is providing quick response.

Deliver Policy In the absence of a Push, a receiving TCP entity is free to deliver data to the user at its own convenience. It may deliver data as each in-order segment is received, or it may buffer data from a number of segments in the receive buffer before delivery. The actual policy will depend on performance considerations. If deliveries are infrequent and large, the user is not receiving data as promptly as may be desirable. On the other hand, if deliveries are frequent and small, there may be unnecessary processing both in TCP and in the user software, as well as an unnecessary number of operating system interrupts.

Accept Policy When all data segments arrive in order over a TCP connection, TCP places the data in a receive buffer for delivery to the user. It is possible, however, for segments to arrive out of order. In this case, the receiving TCP entity has two options:

- **In-order:** Accept only segments that arrive in order; any segment that arrives out of order is discarded.
- **In-window:** Accept all segments that are within the receive window (see Figure 6.2b).

The in-order policy makes for a simple implementation but places a burden on the networking facility, as the sending TCP must time out and retransmit segments that were successfully received but discarded because of misordering. Furthermore, if a single segment is lost in transit, then all subsequent segments must be retransmitted once the sending TCP times out on the lost segment.

The in-window policy may reduce transmissions but requires a more complex acceptance test and a more sophisticated data storage scheme to buffer and keep track of data accepted out of order.

Retransmit Policy TCP maintains a queue of segments that have been sent but not yet acknowledged. The TCP specification states that TCP will retransmit a segment if it fails to receive an acknowledgment within a given time. A TCP implementation may employ one of three retransmission strategies:

- **First-only:** Maintain one retransmission timer for the entire queue. If an acknowledgment is received, remove the appropriate segment or segments from the queue and reset the timer. If the timer expires, retransmit the segment at the front of the queue and reset the timer.

- **Batch:** Maintain one retransmission timer for the entire queue. If an acknowledgment is received, remove the appropriate segment or segments from the queue and reset the timer. If the timer expires, retransmit all segments in the queue and reset the timer.

- **Individual:** Maintain one timer for each segment in the queue. If an acknowledgment is received, remove the appropriate segment or segments from the queue and destroy the corresponding timer or timers. If any timer expires, retransmit the corresponding segment individually and reset its timer.

The first-only policy is efficient in terms of traffic generated, because only lost segments (or segments whose ACK was lost) are retransmitted. Because the timer for the second segment in the queue is not set until the first segment is acknowledged, however, there can be considerable delays. The individual policy solves this problem at the expense of a more complex implementation. The batch policy also reduces the likelihood of long delays but may result in unnecessary retransmissions.

The actual effectiveness of the retransmit policy depends in part on the accept policy of the receiver. If the receiver is using an in-order accept policy, then it will discard segments received after a lost segment. This fits best with batch retransmission. If the receiver is using an in-window accept policy, then a first-only or individual retransmission policy is best. Of course, in a mixed network of computers, both accept policies may be in use.

Acknowledge Policy When a data segment arrives that is in sequence, the receiving TCP entity has two options concerning the timing of acknowledgment:

- **Immediate:** When data are accepted, immediately transmit an empty (no data) segment containing the appropriate acknowledgment number.

- **Cumulative:** When data are accepted, record the need for acknowledgment, but wait for an outbound segment with data on which to piggyback the acknowledgment. To avoid long delay, set a window timer (Table 6.2); if the timer expires before an acknowledgment is sent, transmit an empty segment containing the appropriate acknowledgment number.

The immediate policy is simple and keeps the remote TCP entity fully informed, which limits unnecessary retransmissions. However, this policy results in extra segment transmissions, namely, empty segments used only to ACK. Furthermore, the policy can cause a further load on the network. Consider that a TCP entity receives a segment and immediately sends an ACK. Then the data in the segment are released to the application, which expands the receive window, triggering another empty TCP segment to provide additional credit to the sending TCP entity.

Because of the potential overhead of the immediate policy, the cumulative policy is typically used. Recognize, however, that the use of this policy requires more processing at the receiving end and complicates the task of estimating round-trip time by the sending TCP entity.

6.4 UDP

In addition to TCP, there is one other transport-level protocol that is in common use as part of the TCP/IP protocol suite: the User Datagram Protocol (UDP), specified in RFC 768. UDP provides a connectionless service for application-level procedures. Thus, UDP is basically an unreliable service; delivery and duplicate protection are not guaranteed. However, this does reduce the overhead of the protocol and may be adequate in many cases. An example of the use of UDP is in the context of network management, as described in Chapter 16.

The strengths of the connection-oriented approach are clear. It allows connection-related features such as flow control, error control, and sequenced delivery. Connectionless service, however, is more appropriate in some contexts. At lower layers (internet, network), a connectionless, or datagram, service is more robust (e.g., see discussion in Section 1.1). In addition, it represents a "least common denominator" of service to be expected at higher layers. Further, even at transport and above there is justification for a connectionless service. There are instances in which the overhead of connection establishment and termination is unjustified or even counterproductive. Some examples are as follows:

- **Inward data collection:** Involves the periodic active or passive sampling of data sources, such as sensors, and automatic self-test reports from security equipment or network components. In a real-time monitoring situation, the loss of an occasional data unit would not cause distress, because the next report should arrive shortly.
- **Outward data dissemination:** Includes broadcast messages to network users, the announcement of a new node or the change of address of a service, and the distribution of real-time clock values.
- **Request-response:** Applications in which a transaction service is provided by a common server to a number of distributed TS users, and for which a single request-response sequence is typical. Use of the service is regulated at the application level, and lower-level connections are often unnecessary and cumbersome.
- **Real-time applications:** Such as voice and telemetry, involving a degree of redundancy and/or a real-time transmission requirement. These must not have connection-oriented functions such as retransmission.

Thus, there is a place at the transport level for both a connection-oriented and a connectionless type of service.

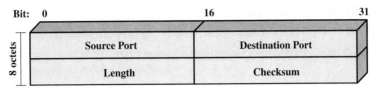

Figure 6.14   UDP Header

UDP sits on top of IP. Because it is connectionless, UDP has very little to do. Essentially, it adds a port addressing capability to IP. This is best seen by examining the UDP header, shown in Figure 6.14. The header includes a source port and destination port. The length field contains the length of the entire UDP segment, including header and data. The checksum is the same algorithm used for TCP and IP. For UDP, the checksum applies to the entire UDP segment plus a pseudoheader prefixed to the UDP header at the time of calculation and which is the same pseudoheader used for TCP. If an error is detected, the segment is discarded and no further action is taken.

The checksum field in UDP is optional. If it is not used, it is set to zero. However, it should be pointed out that the IP checksum applies only to the IP header and not to the data field, which in this case consists of the UDP header and the user data. Thus, if no checksum calculation is performed by UDP, then no check is made on the user data.

6.5 RECOMMENDED READING AND WEB SITES

[IREN99] is a comprehensive survey of transport protocol services and protocol mechanisms, with a brief discussion of a number of different transport protocols.

> **IREN99**   Iren, S.; Amer, P.; and Conrad, P. "The Transport Layer: Tutorial and Survey." *ACM Computing Surveys*, December 1999.

Recommended Web Site:

- **TCP/IP Resources List:** A useful collection of FAQs, tutorials, guides, Web sites, and books about TCP/IP

6.6 KEY TERMS, REVIEW QUESTIONS, AND PROBLEMS

Key Terms

checksum	port	Transmission Control Protocol
credit	sequence number	(TCP)
data stream push	socket	transport protocol
duplicate detection	TCP implementation policy	urgent data signaling
flow control	options	User Datagram Protocol
multiplexing		(UDP)

Review Questions

6.1 What addressing elements are needed to specify a target transport service (TS) user?

6.2 Describe four strategies by which a sending TS user can learn the address of a receiving TS user.

6.3 Explain the use of multiplexing in the context of a transport protocol.

6.4 Briefly describe the credit scheme used by TCP for flow control.

6.5 Explain the two-way and three-way handshake mechanisms.

6.6 What is the benefit of the three-way handshake mechanism?

6.7 Define the urgent and push features of TCP.

6.8 What is a TCP implementation policy option?

6.9 What does UDP provide that is not provided by IP?

Problems

6.1 It is common practice in most transport protocols (indeed, most protocols at all levels) for control and data to be multiplexed over the same logical channel on a per-user-connection basis. An alternative is to establish a single control transport connection between each pair of communicating transport entities. This connection would be used to carry control signals relating to all user transport connections between the two entities. Discuss the implications of this strategy.

6.2 The discussion of flow control with a reliable network service referred to a backpressure mechanism utilizing a lower-level flow control protocol. Discuss the disadvantages of this strategy.

6.3 Two transport entities communicate across a reliable network. Let the normalized time to transmit a segment equal 1. Assume that the end-to-end propagation delay is 3, and that it takes a time 2 to deliver data from a received segment to the transport user. The sender initially granted a credit of seven segments. The receiver uses a conservative flow control policy, and updates its credit allocation at every opportunity. What is the maximum achievable throughput?

6.4 Someone posting to comp.protocols.tcp-ip complained about a throughput of 120 kbps on a 256 kbps link with a 128-ms round-trip delay between the United States and Japan, and a throughput of 33 kbps when the link was routed over a satellite.
   a. What is the utilization over the two links? Assume a 500-ms round-trip delay for the satellite link.
   b. What does the window size appear to be for the two cases?
   c. How big should the window size be for the satellite link?

6.5 Draw diagrams similar to Figure 6.4 for the following (assume a reliable sequenced network service):
   a. Connection termination: active/passive
   b. Connection termination: active/active
   c. Connection rejection
   d. Connection abortion: User issues an OPEN to a listening user, and then issues a CLOSE before any data are exchanged

6.6 With a reliable sequencing network service, are segment sequence numbers strictly necessary? What, if any, capability is lost without them?

6.7 Consider a connection-oriented network service that suffers a reset. How could this be dealt with by a transport protocol that assumes that the network service is reliable except for resets?

6.8   The discussion of retransmission strategy made reference to three problems associated with dynamic timer calculation. What modifications to the strategy would help to alleviate those problems?

6.9   In a network that has a maximum packet size of 128 bytes, a maximum packet lifetime of 30 s, and an 8-bit packet sequence number, what is the maximum data rate per connection?

6.10   Is a deadlock possible using only a two-way handshake instead of a three-way handshake? Give an example or prove otherwise.

6.11   Listed are four strategies that can be used to provide a transport user with the address of the destination transport user. For each one, describe an analogy with the Postal Service user.
   a.   Know the address ahead of time.
   b.   Make use of a "well-known address."
   c.   Use a name server.
   d.   Addressee is spawned at request time.

6.12   In a credit flow control scheme such as that of TCP, what provision could be made for credit allocations that are lost or misordered in transit?

6.13   What happens in Figure 6.3 if a SYN comes in while the requested user is in CLOSED? Is there any way to get the attention of the user when it is not listening?

6.14   In discussing connection termination with reference to Figure 6.8, it was stated that in addition to receiving an acknowledgement of its FIN and sending an acknowledgement of the incoming FIN, a TCP entity must wait an interval equal to twice the maximum expected segment lifetime (the TIME WAIT state). Receiving an ACK to its FIN assures that all of the segments it sent have been received by the other side. Sending an ACK to the other side's FIN assures the other side that all its segments have been received. Give a reason why it is still necessary to wait before closing the connection.

6.15   The Window Scale option limited to a factor of 2^{14}. Suggest a reason for this limit.

6.16   A poor implementation of TCP's sliding-window scheme can lead to extremely poor performance. There is a phenomenon known as the Silly Window Syndrome (SWS), which can easily cause degradation in performance by several factors of 10. As an example of SWS, consider an application that is engaged in a lengthy file transfer, and that TCP is transferring this file in 200-octet segments. The receiver initially provides a credit of 1000. The sender uses up this window with 5 segments of 200 octets. Now suppose that the receiver returns an acknowledgment to each segment and provides an additional credit of 200 octets for every received segment. From the receiver's point of view, this opens the window back up to 1000 octets. However, from the sender's point of view, if the first acknowledgment arrives after five segments have been sent, a window of only 200 octets becomes available. Assume that at some point, the receiver calculates a window of 200 octets but has only 50 octets to send until it reaches a "push" point. It therefore sends 50 octets in one segment, followed by 150 octets in the next segment, and then resumes transmission of 200-octet segments. What might now happen to cause a performance problem? State the SWS in more general terms.

6.17   TCP mandates that both the receiver and the sender should incorporate mechanisms to cope with SWS.
   a.   Suggest a strategy for the receiver. *Hint:* Let the receiver "lie" about how much buffer space is available under certain circumstances. State a reasonable rule of thumb for this.
   b.   Suggest a strategy for the sender. *Hint:* Consider the relationship between the maximum possible send window and what is currently available to send.

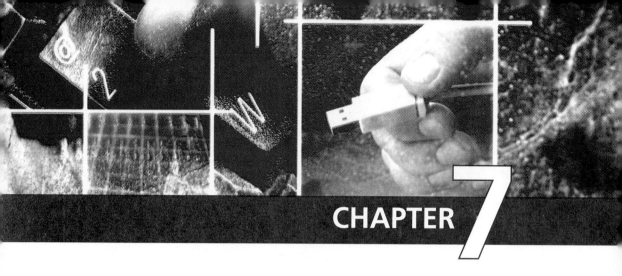

CHAPTER 7

TCP TRAFFIC CONTROL

The foregoing observations should make us reconsider the widely held view that birds live only in the present. In fact, birds are aware of more than immediately present stimuli; they remember the past and anticipate the future.

—*The Minds of Birds*,
Alexander Skutch

KEY POINTS

- TCP uses a sliding-window flow control mechanism that allows multiple segments to be in transit at a time.

- The throughput on a TCP connection depends on the window size, propagation delay, and data rate.

- Although the TCP credit-based mechanism was designed for end-to-end flow control, it is also used to assist in internetwork congestion control. When a TCP entity detects the presence of congestion in the Internet, it reduces the flow of data onto the Internet until it detects an easing in congestion.

- A key element in TCP congestion control is the value of the retransmission timer. A variety of algorithms and strategies have been introduced to make the most effective use of the timer.

- Another important factor in TCP congestion control is the management of the window for segment transmission. Again, a variety of strategies are used to optimize performance.

- The most recent TCP congestion control technique, explicit congestion notification, involves explicit signals to the TCP endpoints from routers in the Internet indicating the onset of congestion.

To achieve good performance for end systems and for the connecting networks as a whole, the design and implementation of the transport protocol is a vital ingredient. The transport protocol provides an interface between applications and the networking facility that enables the applications to request a desired quality of service. Connection-oriented transport protocols, such as TCP, divide the total flow of application data into disjoint logical streams and may allocate resources differentially among those streams. Finally, the transport protocol's policies for transmission and retransmission of data units have a profound impact on the level of congestion in the networking facility.

This chapter examines performance implications of TCP. We begin with a discussion of performance aspects of the TCP flow control mechanism. Then we examine the complex issue of TCP congestion control.

7.1 TCP FLOW CONTROL AND ERROR CONTROL

In this section, we look at the way in which TCP traditionally managed flow and error control, and the performance implications.

Effect of Window Size on Performance

In Chapter 5, we showed that the throughput on a link that used a stop-and-wait protocol depended on the propagation delay (D) and the data rate (R), and more specifically the $R \times D$ product. For TCP, which allows multiple segments to be in transit at one time, throughput depends on the window size, propagation delay, and data rate.

We use the following notation:

W = TCP window size (octets)

R = Data rate (bps) at TCP source available to a given TCP connection

D = Propagation delay (seconds) between TCP source and destination over a given TCP connection

For simplicity, let us ignore the overhead bits in a TCP segment. Suppose that a source TCP entity A begins to transmit a sequence of octets over a connection to a destination B. Figure 7.1 illustrates the operation. A begins to emit a sequence of frames at time $t = 0$. The leading edge of the first segment arrives at B at $t = D$.

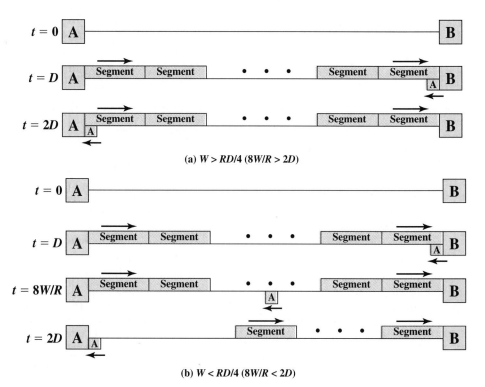

(a) $W > RD/4$ ($8W/R > 2D$)

(b) $W < RD/4$ ($8W/R < 2D$)

Figure 7.1   Timing of TCP Flow Control

Assume that the time to absorb the first segment and the processing time at B is negligible. Then B can immediately acknowledge the first segment at $t = D$, granting additional credit. It will take an addition D seconds for the acknowledgment to reach A, at $t = 2D$. During that time, the source, if not limited, could transmit a total of $2RD$ bits, or $RD/4$ octets. In fact, the source is limited to window size of W octets until an acknowledgment is received. Accordingly, if $W > RD/4$, the maximum possible utilization can be achieved over this connection (Figure 7.1a). If $W < RD/4$, then A will send a total of W octets before it receives the ACK to the first segment and must wait until the ACK arrives before it can resume transmission (Figure 7.1b). In this case, the maximum achievable normalized throughput is just the ratio of W to $RD/4$. Thus, the normalized throughput S can be expressed as

$$S = \begin{cases} 1 & W > RD/4 \\ \dfrac{4W}{RD} & W < RD/4 \end{cases} \qquad (7.1)$$

Figure 7.2 shows the maximum throughput achievable as a function of the RD product. The maximum window size is $2^{16} - 1 = 65{,}535$ octets. This should suffice for most applications. For example, the figure shows that the RD product for a 1-Gbps Ethernet with an extent of 100 m is less than 10^3 bits. Even in the case of a T-1 (1.544 Mbps) satellite link, the maximum window size provides good performance. However, one can imagine network connections for which the default window size is inadequate. One example, shown in the figure, is an optical SDH (synchronous digital hierarchy) link operating at 155 Mbps between two distant

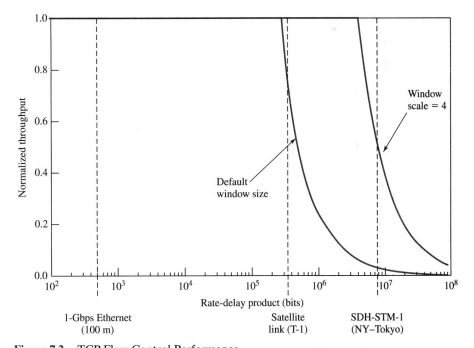

Figure 7.2   TCP Flow Control Performance

points. For such cases, the window scale factor can be used to improve potential throughput. The figure also shows the use of a window scale factor of 4, which increases the window size to $2^{20} - 1 \approx 10^6$ octets.

Figure 7.2 gives some feel for the performance potential of a TCP connection. However, there are many complicating factors to take into account, including the following:

1. In most cases, a number of TCP connections are multiplexed over the same network interface, so each connection is only allocated a fraction of the available capacity. This reduces R and therefore reduces inefficiency.

2. On the other hand, many TCP connections will involve a hop across multiple networks. In that case, D is the sum of the delays across each network plus the delays at each router along the path. The router delays will often be the biggest contributor to D, especially in times of congestion.

3. The value of R referred to in Equation (7.1) refers to the data rate available to the connection at the source TCP entity. If this data rate is greater than the data rate encountered on one of the hops from source to destination, then an attempt to transmit at the higher data rate will create a bottleneck en route, increasing D.

4. If any segments are lost and must be retransmitted, throughput is reduced. The magnitude of the impact of lost segments on performance will depend on the retransmission policy, discussed in the following subsection.

In modern internets, few segments will be lost due to transmission line errors.[1] Rather most segment losses are due to the dropping of packets by congested routers or by congested network switches (e.g., packet switches, frame relay switches). Congestion control is an issue that involves the network or Internet as a whole. However, there are measures that can be taken by individual TCP entities to avoid or relieve congestion, and these are discussed in Section 7.2.

Retransmission Strategy

A key design issue in TCP is the value of the retransmission timer. If the value is too small, there will be many unnecessary retransmissions, wasting network capacity. If the value is too large, the protocol will be sluggish in responding to a lost segment. The timer should be set at a value somewhat longer than the round-trip delay (send segment, receive ACK). Of course, this delay is variable even under constant network load. Worse, the statistics of the delay will vary with changing Internet conditions.

Two strategies suggest themselves. A fixed timer value could be used, based on an understanding of the internet's typical behavior. This strategy suffers from an inability to respond to changing network conditions. If the value is set too high, the service will always be sluggish. If it is set too low, there will be unnecessary retransmissions. Thus, a positive feedback condition can develop, in which Internet congestion leads to more retransmissions, which increases congestion.

---

[1]As wireless links become increasingly prevalent in the Internet, this statement may become less true. However, most wireless links make use of powerful error-correcting codes at the link level.

An adaptive scheme has its own problems. Suppose that the TCP entity keeps track of the time taken to acknowledge data segments and sets its retransmission timer based on the average of the observed delays. This value cannot be trusted for three reasons:

- The peer TCP entity may not acknowledge a segment immediately. Recall that we gave it the privilege of cumulative acknowledgments.
- If a segment has been retransmitted, the sender cannot know whether the received ACK is a response to the initial transmission or to the retransmission.
- Internet conditions may change suddenly.

The problem admits of no complete solution. There will always be some uncertainty concerning the best value for the retransmission timer. In the next subsection, we look at the time calculation specified in RFC 793. Section 7.2 examines more elaborate strategies for timeout selection.

Adaptive Retransmission Timer

As network or Internet conditions change, a static retransmission timer is likely to be either too long or too short. Accordingly, virtually all TCP implementations attempt to estimate the current round-trip delay by observing the pattern of delay for recent segments and then set the timer to a value somewhat greater than the estimated round-trip delay.

Simple Average One approach would be simply to take the average of observed round-trip times over a number of segments. If the average accurately predicts future round-trip delays, then the resulting retransmission timer will yield good performance. The simple averaging method can be expressed as follows:

$$\text{ARTT}(K + 1) = \frac{1}{K + 1} \sum_{i=1}^{K+1} \text{RTT}(i) \qquad (7.2)$$

where $\text{RTT}(i)$ is the round-trip time observed for the ith transmitted segment, and $\text{ARTT}(K)$ is the average round-trip time for the first K segments.

This expression can be rewritten as follows:

$$\text{ARTT}(K + 1) = \frac{K}{K + 1} \text{ARTT}(K) + \frac{1}{K + 1} \text{RTT}(K + 1) \qquad (7.3)$$

With this formulation, it is not necessary to recalculate the entire summation each time.

Exponential Average Note that each term in the summation is given equal weight; that is, each term is multiplied by the same constant $1/(K + 1)$. Typically, we would like to give greater weight to more recent instances because they are more likely to reflect future behavior. A common technique for predicting the next value on the basis of a time series of past values, and the one specified in RFC 793, is exponential averaging:

$$\text{SRTT}(K + 1) = \alpha \times \text{SRTT}(K) + (1 - \alpha) \times \text{RTT}(K + 1) \qquad (7.4)$$

where $\text{SRTT}(K)$ is called the smoothed round-trip time estimate. Compare this with Equation (7.3). By using a constant value of $\alpha(0 < \alpha < 1)$, independent of the number of past observations (independent of K), we have a circumstance in which all past values are considered, but the more distant ones have less weight. To see this more clearly, consider the following expansion of Equation (7.4):

$$SRTT(K + 1) = (1 - \alpha)RTT(K + 1) + \alpha(1 - \alpha)RTT(K) + \alpha^2(1 - \alpha)$$
$$RTT(K - 1) + \ldots + \alpha^K(1 - \alpha)RTT(1)$$

Since both α and $(1 - \alpha)$ are less than one, each successive term in the preceding equation is smaller. For example, for $\alpha = 0.8$, the expansion is

$$SRTT(K + 1) = 0.2\,RTT(K + 1) + 0.16\,RTT(K) + 0.128\,RTT(K - 1) + \ldots$$

The older the observation, the less it is counted in the average.

The size of the coefficient as a function of its position in the expansion is shown in Figure 7.3. The smaller the value of α, the greater the weight given to the more recent observations. For $\alpha = 0.5$, virtually all of the weight is given to the four or five most recent observations, whereas for $\alpha = 0.875$, the averaging is effectively spread out over the ten or so most recent observations. The advantage of using a small value of α is that the average will quickly reflect a rapid change in the

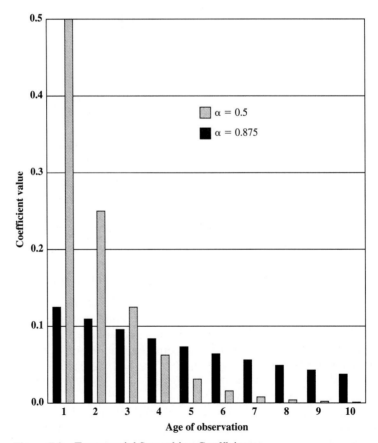

Figure 7.3 Exponential Smoothing Coefficients

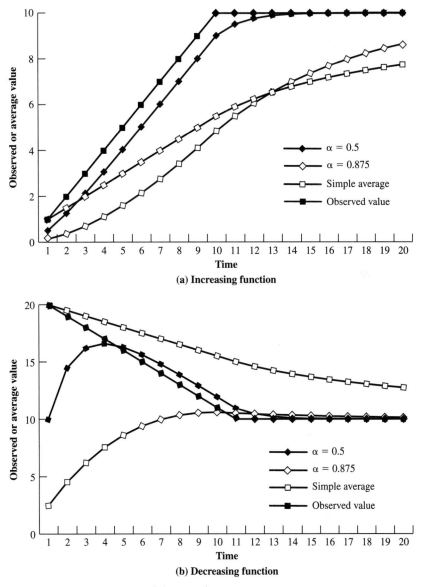

Figure 7.4   Use of Exponential Averaging

observed quantity. The disadvantage is that if there is a brief surge in the value of the observed quantity and it then settles back to some average value, the use of a small value of α will result in jerky changes in the average.

Figure 7.4 compares simple averaging with exponential averaging (for two different values of α). In part (a) of the figure, the observed value begins at 1, grows gradually to a value of 10, and then stays there. In part (b) of the figure, the observed value begins at 20, declines gradually to 10, and then stays there. In both cases, we start out with an estimate of $SRTT(0) = 0$. Note that exponential averaging tracks changes in RTT faster than does simple averaging and that the smaller value of α results in a more rapid reaction to the change in the observed value.

Equation (7.4) is used in RFC 793 to estimate the current round-trip time. As was mentioned, the retransmission timer should be set at a value somewhat greater than the estimated round-trip time. One possibility is to use a constant value:

$$RTO(K + 1) = SRTT(K + 1) + \Delta$$

where RTO is the retransmission timer (also called the retransmission timeout) and Δ is a constant. The disadvantage of this is that Δ is not proportional to SRTT. For large values of SRTT, Δ is relatively small and fluctuations in the actual RTT will result in unnecessary retransmissions. For small values of SRTT, Δ is relatively large and causes unnecessary delays in retransmitting lost segments. Accordingly, RFC 793 specifies the use of a timer whose value is proportional to SRTT, within limits:

$$RTO(K + 1) = MIN(UBOUND, MAX(LBOUND, \beta \times SRTT(K + 1))) \quad (7.5)$$

where UBOUND and LBOUND are prechosen fixed upper and lower bounds on the timer value and β is a constant. RFC 793 does not recommend specific values but does list as "example values" the following: α between 0.8 and 0.9 and β between 1.3 and 2.0.

7.2 TCP CONGESTION CONTROL

Congestion in a network or Internet creates obvious problems for the end systems: reduced availability and throughput, and lengthened response times. Within a switched network, such as a packet-switching or frame relay network, dynamic routing can be used to help alleviate congestion by spreading the load more evenly among the switches and links. Similarly, Internet routing algorithms can spread the load among the routers and networks to relieve congestion. However, these measures are only effective for dealing with unbalanced loads and brief surges in traffic. Ultimately, congestion can only be controlled by limiting the total amount of data entering the Internet to the amount that the Internet can carry. This is the underlying objective of all congestion control mechanisms.

Congestion control in a TCP/IP-based Internet is a complex and difficult undertaking, whose study has generated numerous research efforts, implementation experiments, and papers over a period of decades. The task is a difficult one because of the following factors:

1. IP is a connectionless, stateless protocol that includes no provision for detecting, much less controlling congestion.

2. TCP provides only end-to-end flow control and can only deduce the presence of congestion within the intervening Internet by indirect means.[2] Further, because delays in a network or Internet are variable and may be long (relative to segment size), a TCP entity's knowledge of conditions is unreliable.

[2]Unless explicit congestion notification (ECN) is used. See Section 7.3.

3. There is no cooperative, distributed algorithm to bind together the various TCP entities. Therefore, the TCP entities cannot cooperate to maintain a certain total level of flow and, indeed, are more likely to compete selfishly for available resources.

With regard to the connectionless IP environment, the ICMP Source Quench message provides a blunt and crude instrument for restraining source flow but is not an effective means, by itself, for congestion control. RSVP (Resource Reservation Protocol), described in Chapter 10, may in future help to control congestion, but its widespread implementation is a long way off.

The only tool in TCP that relates to network congestion is the sliding-window flow and error control mechanism. This mechanism is designed for the management of end-to-end traffic. However, a number of clever techniques have been developed that enable the use of this mechanism for congestion detection, avoidance, and recovery. This section surveys some of the most important and widely implemented mechanisms. We begin first with a discussion of the relationship between TCP flow and congestion control.

TCP Flow and Congestion Control

The rate at which a TCP entity can send data is determined by the rate of incoming ACKs with new credit. The rate of ACK arrival is determined by the bottleneck in the round-trip path between source and destination, and that bottleneck may be either the destination or the Internet.

Figure 7.5a, based on a figure in [JACO88], illustrates a case in which the bottleneck is somewhere in the Internet. The configuration is abstracted as a pipe connecting source and destination. The thickness (height) of the pipe is proportional to the data rate. The source and destination are on high-capacity networks, and each can operate at that high capacity. The thinner central portion of the pipe represents a lower-speed link somewhere in the Internet or a router that creates the bottleneck. Each segment is represented by a rectangle whose area is proportional to the number of bits. So when a segment is squeezed into a narrower pipe, it spreads out in time. The time Pb is the minimum segment spacing on the slowest link. As segments arrive at the destination, this spacing is preserved even though the data rate increases, because the interarrival time does not change. Accordingly, the segment spacing at the receiver, Pr, equals Pb. If the destination acknowledges segments as they come in, then the spacing of ACK segments as they leave the receiver is determined by the segment arrival spacing, so that Ar = Pr. Finally, since the time slot Pb is big enough for a data segment, it is big enough for an ACK segment, so Ab = Ar and As = Ar.

The returning ACKs function as pacing signals. In the steady state, after an initial burst, the sender's segment rate will match the arrival rate of the ACKs. Thus, the sender's segment rate is equal to that of the slowest link on the path. In this way, TCP automatically senses the network bottleneck and regulates its flow accordingly. This has been referred to as TCP's *self-clocking* behavior.

This self-clocking behavior works equally well if the bottleneck is at the receiver. Suppose that the receiver can only absorb segments on a given connection slowly, either because of its native processing load or because of the press of incoming segments on other connections. Figure 7.5b represents this case. Here, we assume

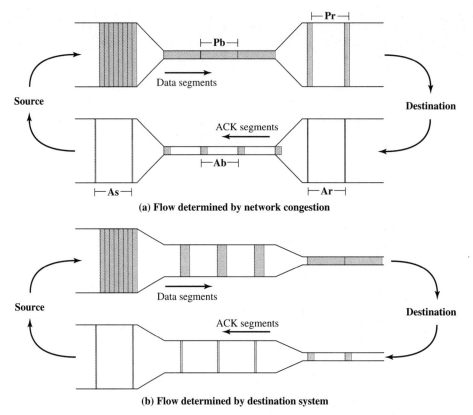

(a) Flow determined by network congestion

(b) Flow determined by destination system

Figure 7.5   TCP Segment Pacing

that the slowest link in the network is relatively wide, about half the data rate of the source, but that the pipe at the destination is narrow. In that case, ACKs will be emitted at a rate equal to the absorption capacity of the destination, and the resulting ACK stream paces the source so that segments arrive only as fast as can be handled.

Figure 7.5 illustrates an important point: The source has no way of knowing whether the pacing rate at which it receives ACKs reflects the status of the Internet (congestion control) or the status of the destination (flow control). If ACKs arrive relatively slowly due to network congestion, it might be advisable for the source to transmit segments even more slowly than the ACK pace, to help relieve Internet congestion. On the other hand, if the slow pace is due to flow control from the destination, then this pace should dictate the TCP send policy.

The bottleneck along a round-trip path between source and destination can occur in a variety of places and be either logical or physical. Figure 7.6 illustrates the possibilities. In this example, if the sender dedicates its entire LAN capacity to a single TCP connection, then it has a potential throughput of 10 Mbps. In that case the 1.5-Mbps links between each router and the intervening Internet become bottlenecks. This is a physical bottleneck, and once a steady state is reached, TCP can efficiently use the available capacity. However, more often the bottleneck will be logical and due to queuing effects at a router, network switch, or the destination. Such

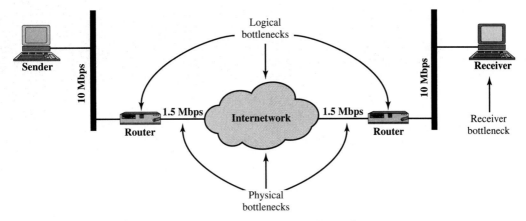

Figure 7.6   Context for TCP Flow and Congestion Control

queuing delays fluctuate with the overall load, making it difficult to achieve a steady-state flow.

The fluctuations in delays that are inherent in an IP-based Internet present a challenge in designing flow policies for TCP sources. If TCP flows are too slow, then the Internet is underutilized and throughputs are unnecessarily low. If one or a few TCP sources use excessive capacity, then other TCP flows will be crowded out. If many TCP sources use excessive capacity, then segments will be lost in transit, forcing retransmission, or ACKs will be excessively delayed, triggering unnecessary retransmissions as sources time out. Furthermore, such retransmission can have a positive feedback effect: As more segments are retransmitted, congestion grows, which increases delays and the number of dropped segments. These effects result in even more retransmissions, which make the problem even worse.

It can be seen, then, that although the TCP sliding-window mechanism is designed for end-to-end flow control, it must be used in a way that takes into account the need for congestion control. Since the publication of RFC 793, a number of techniques have been implemented that are intended to improve TCP congestion control characteristics. Table 7.1 lists some of the most popular of these techniques.

Table 7.1   Implementation of TCP Congestion Control Measures

Measure	RFC 1122	TCP Tahoe	TCP Reno
RTT Variance Estimation	✓	✓	✓
Exponential RTO Backoff	✓	✓	✓
Karn's Algorithm	✓	✓	✓
Slow Start	✓	✓	✓
Dynamic Window Sizing on Congestion	✓	✓	✓
Fast Retransmit		✓	✓
Fast Recovery			✓

None of these techniques extend or violate the original TCP standard; rather they represent implementation policies that are within the scope of the TCP specification. The table indicates which of these techniques are mandated in RFC 1122 and also shows which have been implemented in the popular Berkeley version of UNIX. Two successive releases of the Berkeley TCP code, referred to as Tahoe and Reno, are often referenced in the literature on the effects of various TCP congestion control techniques.

The techniques listed in Table 7.1 fall into two categories: retransmission timer management and window management. We examine each of these in turn.

Retransmission Timer Management

The first three techniques that we examine deal with the calculation of the retransmission timer (RTO). The value of this timer can have a critical effect on TCP's reaction to congestion. The techniques are as follows:

- RTT variance estimation
- Exponential RTO backoff
- Karn's algorithm

RTT Variance Estimation (Jacobson's Algorithm) The technique specified in the TCP standard, and described in Equations (7.4) and (7.5), enables a TCP entity to adapt to changes in round-trip time. However, it does not cope well with a situation in which the round-trip time exhibits a relatively high variance. [ZHAN86] points out three sources of high variance:

1. If the data rate on the TCP connection is relatively low, then the transmission delay will be relatively large compared to propagation time and the variance in delay due to variance in IP datagram size will be significant. Thus, the SRTT estimator is heavily influenced by characteristics that are a property of the data and not of the network.

2. Internet traffic load and conditions may change abruptly due to traffic from other sources, causing abrupt changes in RTT.

3. The peer TCP entity may not acknowledge each segment immediately because of its own processing delays and because it exercises its privilege to use cumulative acknowledgments.

The original TCP specification tries to account for this variability by multiplying the RTT estimator by a constant factor:

$$\text{RTO}(K + 1) = \beta \times \text{SRTT}(K + 1)$$

where typically a value of $\beta = 2$ is used. In a stable environment, with low variance of RTT, this formulation results in an unnecessarily high value of RTO, and in an unstable environment a value of 2 may be inadequate to protect against unnecessary retransmissions.

A more effective approach is to estimate the variability in RTT values and to use that as input into the calculation of an RTO. One possibility would be to calculate the sample standard deviation. However, this involves a square and a square root calculation. A variation measure that is easier to estimate is the mean deviation, defined as[3]

$$\text{MDEV}(X) = \text{E}[|X - \text{E}[X]|]$$

where $\text{E}[X]$ is the expected value of X.

As with the estimate of RTT, a simple average could be used to estimate MDEV:

$$\text{AERR}(K + 1) = \text{RTT}(K + 1) - \text{ARTT}(K)$$

$$\text{ADEV}(K + 1) = \frac{1}{K + 1} \sum_{i=1}^{K+1} |\text{AERR}(i)|$$

$$= \frac{K}{K + 1}\text{ADEV}(K) + \frac{1}{K + 1}|\text{AERR}(K + 1)|$$

where $\text{ARTT}(K)$ is the simple average defined in Equation (7.2) and $\text{AERR}(K)$ is the sample mean deviation measured at time K.

As with the definition of ARRT, each term in the summation of ADEV is given equal weight; that is, each term is multiplied by the same constant $1/(K + 1)$. Again, we would like to give greater weight to more recent instances because they are more likely to reflect future behavior. Jacobson, who proposed the use of a dynamic estimate of variability in estimating RTT [JACO88], suggests using the same exponential smoothing technique as is used for the calculation of SRTT. The complete algorithm proposed by Jacobson can be expressed as follows:

$$\text{SRTT}(K + 1) = (1 - g) \times \text{SRTT}(K) + g \times \text{RTT}(K + 1)$$
$$\text{SERR}(K + 1) = \text{RTT}(K + 1) - \text{SRTT}(K)$$
$$\text{SDEV}(K + 1) = (1 - h) \times \text{SDEV}(K) + h \times |\text{SERR}(K + 1)| \tag{7.6}$$
$$\text{RTO}(K + 1) = \text{SRTT}(K + 1) + f \times \text{SDEV}(K + 1)$$

As in the RFC 793 definition [Equation (7.4)], SRTT is an exponentially smoothed estimate of RTT, with $(1 - g)$ equivalent to α. Now, however, instead of multiplying the estimate SRTT by a constant [Equation (7.5)], a multiple of the estimated mean deviation is added to SRTT to form the retransmission timer. Based on his timing experiments, Jacobson proposed the following values for the constants in his original paper [JACO88]:

$$g = 1/8 = 0.125$$
$$h = 1/4 = 0.25$$
$$f = 2$$

After further research [JACO90a], he recommended using $f = 4$, and this is the value used in most current implementations. The most recent official specification of the retransmission timer estimation algorithm, RFC 2988, adds a refinement to the calculation of the retransmission timer:

$$\text{RTO}(K + 1) = \text{SRTT}(K + 1) + \text{MAX}[G, f \times \text{SDEV}(K + 1)]$$

---

[3]In [JACO88], Jacobson says that the mean deviation is a more conservative estimate because it is larger than the standard deviation. This is not true in general; however, the mean deviation is a perfectly respectable measure of dispersion.

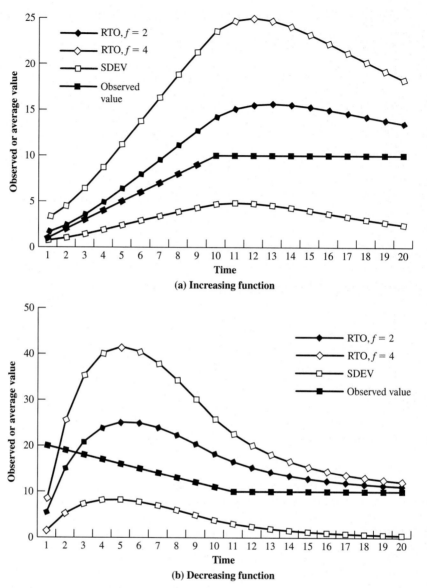

Figure 7.7   Jacobson's RTO Calculation

where $f = 4$ and G is the granularity of the clock used by the algorithm. Thus, a zero or small value of the variance term is rounded to G.

Figure 7.7 illustrates the use of Equation (7.6) on the same data set used in Figure 7.4. Once the arrival times stabilize, the variation estimate SDEV declines. The values of RTO for both $f = 2$ and $f = 4$ are quite conservative as long as RTT is changing, but then begin to converge to RTT when it stabilizes.

Experience has shown that Jacobson's algorithm can significantly improve TCP performance. However, it does not stand by itself. Two other factors must be considered:

1. What RTO value should be used on a retransmitted segment? The exponential RTO backoff algorithm is used for this purpose.

2. Which round-trip samples should be used as input to Jacobson's algorithm? Karn's algorithm determines which samples to use.

Exponential RTO Backoff When a TCP sender times out on a segment, it must retransmit that segment. RFC 793 assumes that the same RTO value will be used for this retransmitted segment. However, because the timeout is probably due to network congestion, manifested as a dropped packet or a long delay in round-trip time, maintaining the same RTO value is ill advised.

Consider the following scenario. There are a number of active TCP connections from various sources sending traffic into an Internet. A region of congestion develops such that segments on many of these connections are lost or delayed past the RTO time of the connections. Therefore, at roughly the same time, many segments will be retransmitted into the internet, maintaining or even increasing the congestion. All of the sources then wait a local (to each connection) RTO time and retransmit yet again. This pattern of behavior could cause a sustained condition of congestion.

A more sensible policy dictates that a TCP source increase its RTO each time a segment is retransmitted; this is referred to as a *backoff* process. In the scenario of the preceding paragraph, after the first retransmission of a segment on each affected connection, the TCP sources will all wait a longer time before performing a second retransmission. This may give the Internet time to clear the current congestion. If a second retransmission is required, each TCP source will then wait an even longer time before timing out for a third retransmission, giving the Internet an even longer period to recover.

A simple technique for implementing RTO backoff is to multiply the RTO for a segment by a constant value for each retransmission:

$$\text{RTO} = q \times \text{RTO} \tag{7.7}$$

Equation (7.7) causes RTO to grow exponentially with each retransmission. The most commonly used value of q is 2. With this value, the technique is referred to as *binary exponential backoff*. This is the same technique used in the Ethernet CSMA/CD protocol.

Karn's Algorithm If no segments are retransmitted, the sampling process for Jacobson's algorithm is straightforward. The RTT for each segment can be included in the calculation. Suppose, however, that a segment times out and must be retransmitted. If an acknowledgment is subsequently received, there are two possibilities:

1. This is the ACK to the first transmission of the segment. In this case, the RTT is simply longer than expected but is an accurate reflection of network conditions.

2. This is the ACK to the second transmission.

The sending TCP entity cannot distinguish between these two cases. If the second case is true and the TCP entity simply measures the RTT from the first transmission until receipt of the ACK, the measured time will be much too long. The measured RTT will be on the order of the actual RTT plus the RTO. Feeding this false RTT into Jacobson's algorithm will produce an unnecessarily high value of SRTT and therefore

RTO. Furthermore, this effect propagates forward a number of iterations, since the SRTT value of one iteration is an input value in the next iteration.

An even worse approach would be to measure the RTT from the *second* transmission to the receipt of the ACK. If this is in fact the ACK to the first transmission, then the measured RTT will be much too small, producing a too low value of SRTT and RTO. This is likely to have a positive feedback effect, causing additional retransmissions and additional false measurements.

Karn's algorithm [KARN91] solves this problem with the following rules:

1. Do not use the measured RTT for a retransmitted segment to update SRTT and SDEV [Equation (7.6)].
2. Calculate the backoff RTO using Equation (7.7) when a retransmission occurs.
3. Use the backoff RTO value for succeeding segments until an acknowledgment arrives for a segment that has not been retransmitted.

When an acknowledgment is received to an unretransmitted segment, Jacobson's algorithm is again activated to compute future RTO values.

Window Management

In addition to techniques for improving the effectiveness of the retransmission timer, a number of approaches to managing the send window have been examined. The size of TCP's send window can have a critical effect on whether TCP can be used efficiently without causing congestion. We discuss five important techniques:

- Slow start
- Dynamic window sizing on congestion
- Fast retransmit
- Fast recovery
- Limited transmit

The first four on the preceding list are found in virtually all modern implementations of TCP and are documented in RFC 2581. Limited transmit is a more recently defined technique (RFC 3042) that is beginning to show up in TCP implementations.

Slow Start The larger the send window used in TCP, the more segments that a TCP source can send before it must wait for an acknowledgment. In the ordinary course of events, the self-clocking nature of TCP (see Figure 7.5) paces TCP appropriately. However, when a connection is first initialized, it has no such pacing to guide it.

One strategy that could be followed is for the TCP sender to begin sending from some relatively large but not maximum window, hoping to approximate the window size that would ultimately be provided by the connection. This is risky because the sender might flood the Internet with many segments before it realized from timeouts that the flow was excessive. Instead, some means of gradually expanding the window until pacing takes over is needed.

Jacobson [JACO88] recommends a procedure known as slow start. We define a congestion window, measured in segments rather than octets. At any time, TCP transmission is constrained by the following relationship:

$$awnd = \text{MIN}[credit, cwnd] \tag{7.8}$$

where

  awnd = allowed window, in segments. This is the number of segments that
         TCP is currently allowed to send without receiving further acknowl-
         edgments.

  cwnd = congestion window, in segments. A window used by TCP during start-
         up and to reduce flow during periods of congestion.

  credit = the amount of unused credit granted in the most recent acknowledg-
         ment, in segments. When an acknowledgment is received, this value is
         calculated as *window/segment_size*, where *window* is a field in the
         incoming TCP segment (the amount of data the peer TCP entity is
         willing to accept).

When a new connection is opened, the TCP entity initializes *cwnd* = 1. That is,
TCP is only allowed to send 1 segment and then must wait for an acknowledgment
before transmitting a second segment. Each time an acknowledgment is received,
the value of *cwnd* is increased by 1, up to some maximum value.

In effect, the slow-start mechanism probes the Internet to make sure that the
TCP entity is not sending too many segments into an already congested environment. As acknowledgments arrive, TCP is able to open up its window until the flow
is controlled by the incoming ACKs rather than by *cwnd*.

The term *slow start* is a bit of a misnomer, because *cwnd* actually grows exponentially. When the first ACK arrives, TCP opens *cwnd* to 2 and can send two segments. When these two segments are ACKed, TCP can slide the window 1 segment
for each incoming ACK and can increase *cwnd* by 1 for each incoming ACK. Therefore, at this point TCP can send four segments. When these four are ACKed, TCP
will be able to send eight segments. Figure 7.8 illustrates this phenomenon. In this
example, A is sending 100-octet segments, and after approximately four round-trip
times, A is able to fill the pipe with a continuous flow of segments.

Dynamic Window Sizing on Congestion The slow-start algorithm has
been found to work effectively for initializing a connection. It enables the TCP
sender to determine quickly a reasonable window size for the connection. Might not
the same technique be useful when there is a surge in congestion? In particular, suppose a TCP entity initiates a connection and goes through the slow-start procedure.
At some point, either before or after *cwnd* reaches the size of the credit allocated by
the other side, a segment is lost (timeout). This is a signal that congestion is occurring. It is not clear how serious the congestion is. Therefore, a prudent procedure
would be to reset *cwnd* = 1 and begin the slow-start process all over.

This seems like a reasonable, conservative procedure, but in fact it is not conservative enough. Jacobson [JACO88] points out that "it is easy to drive a network
into saturation but hard for the net to recover." In other words, once congestion occurs, it may take a long time for the congestion to clear.[4] Thus, the exponential
growth of *cwnd* under slow start may be too aggressive and may worsen the
congestion. Instead, Jacobson proposed the use of slow start to begin with, followed
by a linear growth in *cwnd*. The rules are as follows. When a timeout occurs,

---

[4]Kleinrock refers to this phenomenon as the long-tail effect during a rush-hour period. See Sections 2.7
and 2.10 of [KLEI76] for a detailed discussion. This effect results from ordinary Poisson traffic. If the traffic exhibits long-range dependence (self-similar), the effect is even more pronounced.

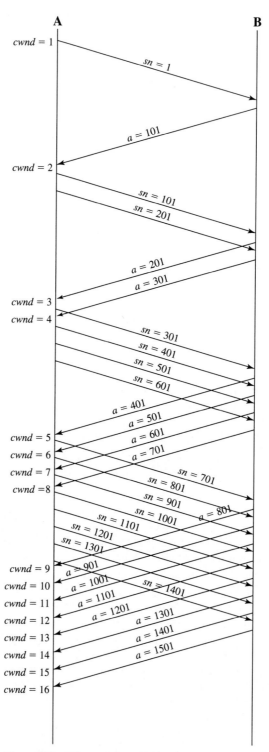

Figure 7.8 Effect of Slow Start

1. Set a slow-start threshold equal to half the current congestion window; that is, set *ssthresh* = *cwnd*/2.
2. Set *cwnd* = 1 and perform the slow-start process until *cwnd* = *ssthresh*. In this phase, *cwnd* is increased by 1 for every ACK received.
3. For *cwnd* ≥ *ssthresh*, increase *cwnd* by one for each round-trip time.

Figure 7.9 illustrates the use of slow start. The left half of the figure shows a connection starting up and repeats Figure 7.8. Added to this figure is one final segment

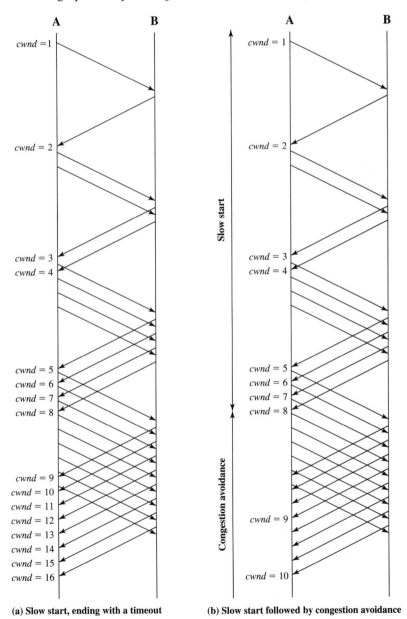

(a) Slow start, ending with a timeout   (b) Slow start followed by congestion avoidance

Figure 7.9   Slow Start and Congestion Avoidance

that will time out. The behavior after timeout is shown in Figure 7.9b. The value of *ssthresh* is set to 8. Until this threshold is reached, TCP uses the exponential slow-start procedure to expand the congestion window. Afterward, *cwnd* is increased linearly. This behavior is easily seen in Figure 7.10. Note that it takes 11 round-trip times to recover to the *cwnd* level that initially took 4 round-trip times to achieve.

Fast Retransmit The retransmission timer (RTO) that is used by a sending TCP entity to determine when to retransmit a segment will generally be noticeably longer than the actual round-trip time (RTT) that the ACK for that segment will take to reach the sender. Both the original RFC 793 algorithm and the Jacobson algorithm set the value of RTO at somewhat greater than the estimated round-trip time SRTT. Several factors make this margin desirable:

1. RTO is calculated on the basis of a prediction of the next RTT, estimated from past values of RTT. If delays in the network fluctuate, then the estimated RTT may be smaller than the actual RTT.
2. Similarly, if delays at the destination fluctuate, the estimated RTT becomes unreliable.
3. The destination system may not ACK each segment but cumulatively ACK multiple segments, while at the same time sending ACKs when it has any data to send. This behavior contributes to fluctuations in RTT.

A consequence of these factors is that if a segment is lost, TCP may be slow to retransmit. If the destination TCP is using an in-order accept policy (see Section 6.3), then many segments may be lost. Even in the more likely case that the destination TCP is using an in-window accept policy, a slow retransmission can cause problems. To see this, suppose that A transmits a sequence of segments, the first of which is lost. So long as its send window is not empty and RTO does not expire, A can continue to

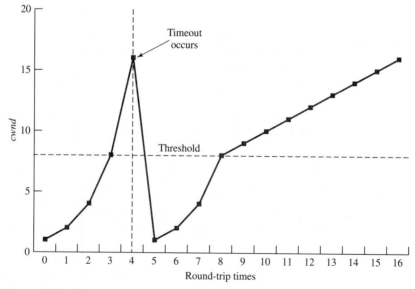

Figure 7.10 Illustration of Slow Start and Congestion Avoidance

transmit without receiving an acknowledgment. B receives all of these segments except the first. But B must buffer all of these incoming segments until the missing one is retransmitted; it cannot clear its buffer by sending the data to an application until the missing segment arrives. If retransmission of the missing segment is delayed too long, B will have to begin discarding incoming segments.

Jacobson [JACO90b] proposed two procedures, called fast retransmit and fast recovery, that under some circumstances improve on the performance provided by RTO. Fast retransmit takes advantage of the following rule in TCP. If a TCP entity receives a segment out of order, it must immediately issue an ACK for the last in-order segment that was received. TCP will continue to repeat this ACK with each incoming segment until the missing segment arrives to "plug the hole" in its buffer. When the hole is plugged, TCP sends a cumulative ACK for all of the in-order segments received so far.

When a source TCP receives a duplicate ACK, it means that either (1) the segment following the ACKed segment was delayed so that it ultimately arrived out of order, or (2) that segment was lost. In case (1), the segment does ultimately arrive and therefore TCP should not retransmit. But in case (2) the arrival of a duplicate ACK can function as an early warning system to tell the source TCP that a segment has been lost and must be retransmitted. To make sure that we have case (2) rather than case (1), Jacobson recommends that a TCP sender wait until it receives three duplicate ACKs to the same segment (that is, a total of four ACKs to the same segment). Under these circumstances, it is highly likely that the following segment has been lost and should be retransmitted immediately, rather than waiting for a timeout.

Figure 7.11 illustrates the fast retransmit process. A sends a sequence of segments with 200 octets of data in each. Segment 1201 is lost, but A will not normally react to this until a time RTO has elapsed, and will continue to send segments until its window closes. B receives segment 1001 (octets 1001 through 1200) and acknowledges it with an ACK 1201. It then receives segment 1401 (octets 1401 through 1600). Because this segment is out of order, B repeats the ACK 1201 and will continue to repeat it with each incoming segment until segment 1201 arrives. By the time A receives four ACKs to segment 1001, it has sent seven segments beyond segment 1201. A immediately retransmits segment 1201 and then picks up where it left off.

Note that A can assume that segments subsequent to 1201 have been getting through. Otherwise, B would not be receiving the additional segments that trigger the duplicate ACKs.

Fast Recovery When a TCP entity retransmits a segment using fast retransmit, it knows (or rather assumes) that a segment was lost, even though it has not yet timed out on that segment. Accordingly, the TCP entity should take congestion avoidance measures. One obvious strategy is the slow-start/congestion avoidance procedure used when a timeout occurs. That is, the entity could set *ssthresh* to *cwnd*/2, set *cwnd* = 1 and begin the exponential slow-start process until *cwnd* = *ssthresh*, and then increase *cwnd* linearly. Jacobson [JACO90b] argues that this approach is unnecessarily conservative. As was just pointed out, the very fact that multiple ACKs have returned indicates that data segments are getting through fairly regularly to the other side. So Jacobson proposes a fast recovery technique: Retransmit the lost segment, cut *cwnd* in half, and then proceed with the linear increase of *cwnd*. This technique avoids the initial exponential slow-start process.

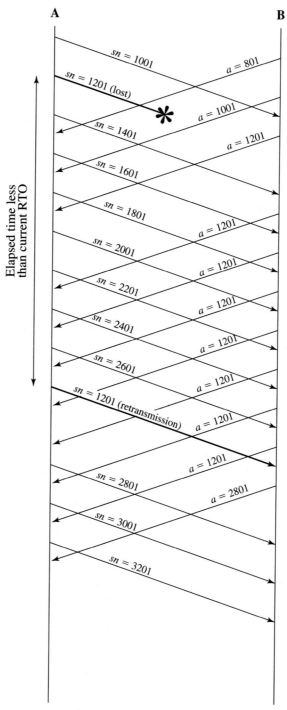

Figure 7.11 Fast Retransmit

More precisely, the fast recovery technique can be stated as follows:

1. When the third duplicate ACK arrives,
   a. Set *ssthresh* = *cwnd*/2.
   b. Retransmit the missing segment.
   c. Set *cwnd* = *ssthresh* + 3.
   The reason for adding 3 to *ssthresh* is that this accounts for the number of segments that have left the network and that the other end has cached.

2. Each time an additional duplicate ACK (for the same segment) arrives, increment *cwnd* by 1 and transmit a segment if possible. This accounts for the additional segment that has left the network and that triggered the duplicate ACK.

3. When the next ACK arrives that acknowledges new data (i.e., a cumulative acknowledgment of the missing segment plus other later segments), set *cwnd* = *ssthresh*.

An example,[5] from [HOE96], illustrates the operation (Figure 7.12). The y-axis in the upper figure represents segment numbers.[6] In the upper figure, each small diamond shape represents a segment transmitted at that time, with the height proportional to the size of the segment. These segments are bounded by two lines: The lower line indicates the last acknowledged sequence number (SND.UNA) and the upper line represents that sequence number plus the send window (SND.UNA + SND.WND).[7] Small tick marks on the bottom bounding line indicate duplicate ACKs. The lower figure shows the value of *cwnd* over the same time frame.

In the early part of this time period, a stable flow is maintained, with a stable window size and a full pipe; during this period *cwnd* remains at a maximum value equal to the receiver's stable credit allocation (10 segments). Just before time 5.43 (circled region), duplicate ACKs for segment 579 begin to arrive. When the third duplicate arrives, segment 580 is retransmitted, and *cwnd* is reduced by half plus three segments. We then enter a region in which the source can transmit one additional segment for each duplicate ACK received. Note that in this region the values of SND.UNA and SND.WND remain constant. In this example, the source is unable to transmit any segments until *cwnd* regains its former value. At this point, the source transmits one segment for each incoming duplicate ACK. As *cwnd* continues to grow, we get an inflated *cwnd* that accounts for cached segments at the destination side. Finally, at just before 5.6 seconds, a cumulative ACK is received for a large number of segments. This ACK arrives in a time RTT from the retransmission of segment 580. This ACK causes *cwnd* to be retracted to *ssthresh*, and the sender then enters the linear congestion avoidance mode.

Limited Transmit As we have seen, TCP implementations are equipped with two mechanisms for detecting a segment loss: the adaptive retransmission timer and fast retransmit. The fast retransmit timer is designed to overcome a tendency for the

---

[5]In this example, *cwnd* is expressed in octets rather than segments. To translate to segments, divide *cwnd* by the maximum segment size, which is assumed to be 1024 octets.

[6]To simplify, the segment number of a segment is the closest integer to the highest sequence number in the segment divided by 1024 octets.

[7]See Figure 6.2

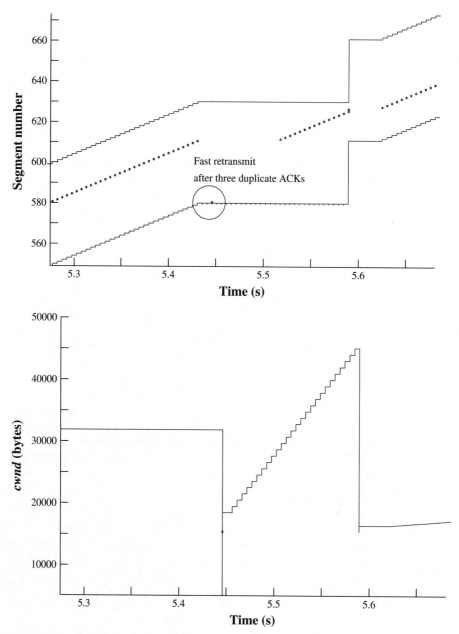

Figure 7.12 Fast Recovery Example

retransmission timeout mechanism to be slow to react in some situations. However, even the fast retransmit timer has shortcomings. In particular, if the congestion window (*cwnd*) at the TCP sender is small, the fast retransmit mechanism may not be triggered. For example, suppose the sender has *cwnd* = 3. If one segment is dropped by the network, then at most two duplicate ACKs will arrive at the sender.

Because three duplicate ACKs are required to trigger fast retransmit, the sender will wait for the retransmission timer to expire before retransmitting. Several questions arise:

1. Under what circumstances will the sender have a small congestion window?
2. Is the problem common; that is, is it common for the TCP sender to have to rely on retransmission timeout rather than fast retransmit?
3. If the problem is common, why not address it by reducing the number of duplicate ACKS required to trigger fast retransmit?

As to the first question, a number of studies cite three circumstances the result in a small congestion window [MORR97, BALA98, LIN98]:

- There is only a limited amount of data to send.
- The receiver imposes a small limit on its advertised receive window (the credit that it grants).
- End-to-end congestion control over a connection with a small RD product [see discussion around Equation (7.1)] results in a small congestion window.

With respect to the second question, [BALA98] reports on a study of a busy Web server, which found that 56% of retransmissions were due to an RTO expiration, with only 44% handled by fast retransmit.

Finally, with respect to the third question, reducing the number of duplicate ACKs is likely to lead to unnecessary retransmissions. The reason for this is that duplicate ACKs can well result from packet reordering. [BENN99] shows that segment reordering over the Internet is not a rare event.

Thus, simply retransmitting after one or two duplicate ACKs is not a good solution. Instead, RFC 3042 defines a mechanism for transmitting new segments, even when this is not dictated by the current congestion conditions. Specifically, the limited transmit algorithm calls for a TCP sender to transmit a new segment when the following three conditions are met:

1. Two consecutive duplicate ACKs are received. That is, a total of three ACKs to a transmitted segment are received.
2. The destination TCP entity's advertised window allows the transmission of the segment. That is, sufficient credit remains available to the source TCP entity to be able to send a new segment.
3. The amount of outstanding data, after sending the new segment, would remain less than or equal to $cwnd + 2$. That is, the sender may only send two segments beyond the congestion window.

Thus, limited transmit allows a modest transmission of data beyond what would normally be permitted by the TCP congestion control mechanism.

7.3 EXPLICIT CONGESTION NOTIFICATION

One of the most recent mechanisms introduced to provide TCP congestion control is **explicit congestion notification** ECN, which is defined in RFC 3168. In general terms, with ECN, routers in the Internet alert end systems to growing congestion within the Internet and the end systems take steps to reduce the offered load to the Internet. This approach differs from the **implicit congestion notification** that characterizes all of the methods discussed in Section 7.2. With implicit congestion notification, TCP deduces the presence and extent of congestion by noting increasing delays or dropped segments. ECN has several benefits over implicit congestion notification:

1. The use of ECN prevents unnecessary lost segments. The Internet can alert end systems of growing congestion before it reaches the point where packets must be dropped. Thus, retransmissions, which only add to the traffic load, are avoided.

2. With ECN, sources can be informed of congestion quickly and unambiguously, without the sources having to wait for either a retransmit timeout or three duplicate ACKs to infer a dropped packet.

The disadvantage of ECN is that it requires changes to both the TCP header and the IP header, plus new information must be communicated between TCP and IP, necessitating new parameters in IP service primitives.

The following changes are required for the operation of TCP:

1. Two new bits are added to the TCP header. The TCP entity on hosts (end systems) must be able to recognize and set these bits.

2. TCP entities must be able to exchange ECN information with the adjacent IP layer.

3. TCP entities must be able to enable the use of ECN by means of negotiation at connection establishment time.

4. TCP entities must be able to respond to the receipt of ECN information.

5. Two new bits are added to the IP header. The IP entity on hosts and routers must be able to recognize and set these bits.

6. IP entities in hosts must be able to exchange ECN information with the adjacent TCP layer.

7. IP entities in routers must be able to set ECN bits on the basis of congestion.

In this section we describe ECN and encompass the first six tasks just enumerated. Task 7 is a router issue and is discussed in Chapter 9. We begin by looking at the changes to the TCP and IP headers, and then describe the operation of ECN.

IP Header

Prior to the introduction of the differentiated services (DS) capability, discussed in Chapter 9, the IPv4 header included an 8-bit Type of Service field and the IPv6 header included an 8-bit traffic class field. With the introduction of DS, these fields were reallocated, so that the leftmost 6 bits were dedicated to a DS field, with the rightmost 2 bits designated as currently unused (CU). RFC 3260 now specifies that the CU bits be renamed as the ECN field (Figure 2.13).

The ECN field has the following interpretations:

Value	Label	Meaning
00	Not-ECT	Packet is not using ECN.
01	ECT (1)	ECN-capable transport. Set by the data sender to indicate that the TCP endpoints are ECN capable.
10	ECT (0)	ECN-capable transport. Set by the data sender to indicate that the TCP endpoints are ECN capable.
11	CE	Congestion experienced. Set by router to indicate congestion to an end node.

A bit pattern of 10 or 01 is set by a sending IP entity to indicate that the TCP connection for this IP packet is ECN capable. That is, the TCP and IP entities in the sending system support ECN for this TCP connection and for this flow of IP packets. Routers treat the values 10 and 01 as equivalent, and senders are free to use either 10 or 01 to indicate ECT, on a packet-by-packet basis. The primary motivation for duplicate values is the desire to allow mechanisms for the data sender to verify that network elements are not erasing the CE value, and that data receivers are properly reporting to the sender the receipt of packets with the CE value set, as required by the transport protocol. The procedure followed is one suggested in [SAVA99]: The sending system uses either ECT(0) or ECT(1) in the IP packet or packets needed to carry a TCP segment. The receiving system then echoes the same ECT value in returning packet that carries an ACK segment.

A pattern of 00 indicates a packet that is not using ECN. A pattern of 11 is set by a router to indicate congestion to the end nodes.

TCP Header

To support ECN, two new flag bits are added to the TCP header (Figure 6.13):

- **ECN-Echo (ECE) flag:** Used by the data receiver to inform the data sender when a CE packet has been received (an IP packet with ECN field value of 11).
- **Congestion Window Reduced (CWR) flag:** Used by the data sender to inform the data receiver that the sender's congestion window has been reduced.

TCP Initialization

The two TCP header bits just defined are used in the connection establishment phase to enable the TCP end points to agree to use ECN. Assume that host A initiates the establishment of a TCP connection with host B and desires the use of ECN. Initialization proceeds as follows:

1. A sends a SYN segment to B with both the ECE and CWR flags set. This indicates that A is ECN-capable and is prepared to participate in ECN as both a sender and receiver.
2. If B is prepared to participate in ECN, it returns a SYN-ACK segment with the ECE flag set but the CWR flag not set.
3. If B is not prepared to participate in ECN, it should return a SYN-ACK segment with both the ECE and CWR flags not set (equal to zero).

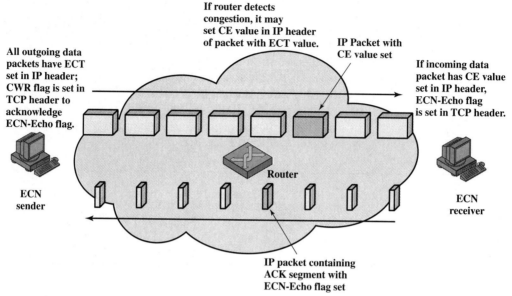

Figure 7.13 Basic ECN Operation

Basic Operation

Figure 7.13, based on a figure in [HUST00], illustrates the basic operation of ECN. A TCP host sending data segments sets the ECT code (10 or 01) in the IP header of every data segment sent. If the sender receives a TCP segment with the ECE flag set in the TCP header, the sender adjusts its congestion window as if it had undergone fast recovery from a single lost segment. The next data segment that the host sends will have the TCP CWR flag set, to indicate to the receiver that it has reacted to the congestion.

Inside the Internet, if a router begins to experience congestion, the router may set the CE code (11) in the header of any packet with the ECT code set in the IP header. This requires that the router be able to recognize the onset of congestion prior to the point at which the router must begin to discard packets. We discuss techniques for this in Chapter 9.

At the destination, when the receiver receives a packet with the ECT code set in the IP header, it begins to set the ECE flag on all outgoing segments that are acknowledgments (with or without data). The receiver continues to set the ECE flag on outgoing segments until it receives a segment with the CWR flag set.

7.4 RECOMMENDED READING AND WEB SITES

Perhaps the best coverage of the various TCP strategies for flow and congestion control is to be found in [STEV94]. An essential paper for understanding the issues involved is the classic [JACO88]. [FLOY01] surveys recently developed TCP congestion control mechanisms, many of which are appearing in TCP implementations. Another useful survey is [HUST00]. [ALLM99] discusses methods for assessing performance of TCP implementations. [TIER01] describes, and provides links to, practical TCP performance analysis tools. [FLOY94] provides a rationale and performance results for TCP explicit congestion notification.

ALLM99 Allman, M., and Falk, A. "On the Effective Evaluation of TCP." *Computer Communication Review*, October 1999.

FLOY94 Floyd, S. "TCP and Explicit Congestion Notification." *ACM Computer Communications Review*, October 1994.

FLOY01 Floyd, S. "A Report on Some Recent Developments in TCP Congestion Control." *IEEE Communications Magazine*, April 2001.

HUST00 Huston, G. "TCP Performance." *The Internet Protocol Journal*, June 2000. http://www.cisco.com/warp/public/759.

JACO88 Jacobson, V. "Congestion Avoidance and Control." *Proceedings, SIGCOMM '88, Computer Communication Review*, August 1988; reprinted in *Computer Communication Review*, January 1995; a slightly revised version is available at ftp.ee.lbl.gov/papers/congavoid.ps.Z.

STEV94 Stevens, W. *TCP/IP Illustrated, Volume 1: The Protocols.* Reading, MA: Addison-Wesley, 1994.

TIER01 Tierney, B. "TCP Tuning Guide for Distributed Applications on Wide Area Networks." *;login:*, February 2001. http://www-didc.lbl.gov/TCP-tuning.

Recommended Web Sites:

- **Center for Internet Research:** One of the most active groups in the areas covered in this chapter. The site contains many papers and useful pointers.
- **TCP-Friendly Website:** Summarizes some of the recent work on adaptive congestion control algorithms for non-TCP–based applications, with a specific focus on schemes that share bandwidth fairly with TCP connections.
- **Raj Jain's home page:** This site contains many of his papers on the areas covered in this chapter plus useful pointers.

7.5 KEY TERMS, REVIEW QUESTIONS, AND PROBLEMS

Key Terms

adaptive retransmission timer	fast recovery	limited transmit
error control	fast retransmit	retransmission strategy
explicit congestion notification (ECN)	flow control	retransmission timer (RTO)
exponential average	implicit congestion notification	round-trip time (RTT)
exponential backoff	Jacobson's algorithm	slow start
	Karn's algorithm	

Review Questions

7.1 What parameters determine the effective utilization of a TCP connection?

7.2 Why is the observed average round-trip time on a TCP connection untrustworthy?

7.3 What is the difference between a simple average and an exponential average?

7.4 In general terms, how can TCP be used to deal with network or internet congestion?

7.5 What factors make the task of TCP congestion control difficult?

7.6   Briefly describe Jacobson's algorithm.
7.7   Briefly describe exponential RTO backoff.
7.8   Briefly describe Karn's algorithm.
7.9   Briefly describe slow start.
7.10 Briefly describe dynamic window sizing on congestion.
7.11 Briefly describe fast retransmit.
7.12 Briefly describe fast recovery.
7.13 Briefly describe limited transmit.
7.14 What is the difference between explicit and implicit congestion notification?
7.15 What are some of the advantages and disadvantages of explicit congestion notification compared to implicit congestion notification?
7.16 What changes to TCP need to be made to support explicit congestion notification?
7.17 What changes to TCP need to be made to support implicit congestion notification?

Problems

7.1   Derive Equation (7.3) from Equation (7.2).

7.2   Figure 7.5 shows TCP neatly self-clocking. The ACKs arrive at the sender with the spacing they were given by the receiver.

    a.   What conditions would cause the stream of ACKs to arrive in a nonuniform manner? That is, under what conditions would we find the returning ACKs clumping together so that they arrive in bursts, with larger gaps in between?

    b.   What effect would this ACK clumping have on performance?

7.3   One difficulty with the original TCP SRTT estimator is the choice of an initial value. In the absence of any special knowledge of network conditions, the typical approach is to pick an arbitrary value, such as 3 seconds, and hope that this will converge quickly to an accurate value. If this estimate is too small, TCP will perform unnecessary retransmissions. If it is too large, TCP will wait a long time before retransmitting if the first segment is lost. Also, the convergence may be slow, as this problem indicates.

    a.   Choose $\alpha = 0.85$ and $SRTT(0) = 3$ seconds, and assume all measured RTT values $= 1$ second and no packet loss. What is $SRTT(19)$? *Hint:* Equation (7.4) can be rewritten to simplify the calculation, using the expression $(1 - \alpha^n)/(1 - \alpha)$.

    b.   Now let $SRTT(0) = 1$ second and assume measured RTT values $= 3$ seconds and no packet loss. What is $SRTT(19)$?

7.4   A poor implementation of TCP's sliding-window scheme can lead to extremely poor performance. There is a phenomenon known as the Silly Window Syndrome (SWS), which can easily cause degradation in performance by several factors of ten. As an example of SWS, consider an application that is engaged in a lengthy file transfer, and TCP is transferring this file in 200-octet segments. The receiver initially provides a credit of 1000. The sender uses up this window with 5 segments of 200 octets. Now suppose that the receiver returns an acknowledgment to each segment and provides an additional credit of 200 octets for every received segment. From the receiver's point of view, this opens the window back up to 1000 octets. However, from the sender's point of view, if the first acknowledgment arrives after five segments have been sent, a window of only 200 octets becomes available. Assume that at some point, the receiver calculates a window of 200 octets but has only 50 octets to send until it reaches a "push" point. It therefore sends 50 octets in one segment, followed by 150 octets in the next segment, and then resumes transmission of 200-octet segments. What might now happen to cause a performance problem? State the SWS in more general terms.

7.5   TCP mandates that both the receiver and the sender should incorporate mechanisms to cope with SWS.

    a.   Suggest a strategy for the receiver. *Hint:* Let the receiver "lie" about how much buffer space is available under certain circumstances. State a reasonable rule of thumb for this.

b. Suggest a strategy for the sender. *Hint:* Consider the relationship between the maximum possible send window and what is currently available to send.

7.6 Calculate the standard deviation and the mean deviation of the following random variables:
    a. X takes on the values $1, 0, 0, 0$ for four equally likely outcomes.
    b. Y takes on the values 1 with probability 0.7 and 0 with probability 0.3.

7.7 In Equation (7.6), rewrite the definition of $SRTT(K + 1)$ so that it is a function of $SERR(K + 1)$. Interpret the result.

7.8 A TCP entity opens a connection and uses slow start. Approximately how many round-trip times are required before TCP can send N segments?

7.9 Although slow start with congestion avoidance is an effective technique for coping with congestion, it can result in long recovery times in high-speed networks, as this problem demonstrates.
    a. Assume a round-trip delay of 60 ms (about what might occur across a continent) and a link with an available bandwidth of 1 Gbps and a segment size of 576 octets. Determine the window size needed to keep the pipe full and the time it will take to reach that window size after a timeout using Jacobson's approach.
    b. Repeat (a) for a segment size of 16 kbytes.

7.10 In the discussion of fast retransmit, it is stated that the destination may have to discard some out-of-order segments because its buffer overflows. But doesn't the flow credit issued by the destination control the source's window so that overflow cannot occur?

7.11 Prior to the introduction of ECN for TCP and the Internet, two forms of explicit congestion notification had been developed for data networks:
    • **Backward explicit congestion notification (BECN):** Notifies the user that congestion avoidance procedures should be initiated where applicable for traffic in the opposite direction of the received packet. It indicates that the packets that the user transmits on this logical connection may encounter congested resources.
    • **Forward explicit congestion notification (FECN):** Notifies the user that congestion avoidance procedures should be initiated where applicable for traffic in the same direction as the received packet. It indicates that this packet, on this logical connection, has encountered congested resources.
    a. Which form of ECN is defined for TCP/IP?
    b. What is the advantage of the form of ECN used by TCP/IP over the alternative?

7.12 It was stated in Section 7.2 that the primary motivation for the use of two ECT codes is the desire to allow mechanisms for the data sender to verify that network elements are not erasing the CE value, and that data receivers are properly reporting to the sender the receipt of packets with the CE value set, as required by the transport protocol. Explain exactly how this would work.

7.13 Initially, the possibility of using a single bit in the IP header for the ECN function was considered. The final design uses two ECN bits.
    a. The two-bit alternative conveys two pieces of information to intermediate routers and to destination IP entities: whether the TCP connection for this IP packet is ECN capable and whether congestion has been experienced. How can we manage to convey all this information in a single bit? *Hint:* The TCP entities know from their own negotiation whether this is an ECN capable connection or not.
    b. What are some drawbacks to a one-bit design that satisfies the requirements just stated; that is a one-bit design that manages the convey both pieces of information?

PART FOUR

Quality of Service in IP Networks

The demands on IP-based internets are rising both in terms of volume and types of service. IP-based internets were designed for applications that are relatively delay insensitive, can tolerate variations in throughput, and can tolerate packet loss, and they were initially deployed using relatively low-capacity links and supporting a modest demand. Today, IP-based internets are being asked to support high volumes of traffic over high-capacity links, and the traffic mix includes real-time or near-real-time applications that are sensitive to delay and throughput variations and to packet loss. Key design requirements for IP-based internets include:

- **Control congestion:** The enemy of any switching network is congestion. It is congestion that prevents the network from satisfying its traffic demands in an efficient and responsive manner. If congestion is not controlled, switch or router buffers fill up and packets must be discarded. For applications that can tolerate packet loss, discarding means the packets must be re-transmitted, increasing congestion. For applications that are intolerant of packet loss, discarding means reduction in quality of service (QoS).

- **Provide low delay:** Delay is minimized when congestion is absent and queue lengths are very short. However, to support many applications, network utilization must be relatively high. This suggests at least a degree of congestion and therefore some excess delay.

- **Provide high throughput:** High throughput can be achieved by dedicating capacity. However, to utilize the network efficiently, some amount of statistical multiplexing must be done, which to some extent conflicts with the provision of high throughput.

- **Support QoS:** The provision of different levels of QoS to different traffic flows requires intelligent treatment of packets as they flow through the network.

- **Provide fair service:** Another desirable goal is fairness. In general terms, fairness refers to the provision of an approximately equal amount of capacity to all competing traffic flows with the same QoS.

Chapter 8 Internet Protocols

Before embarking on a discussion of IP-based QoS, we need a more detailed description of IP and IPv6. Chapter 8 begins with an examination of the requirements for an internetworking facility and the various design approaches that can be taken to satisfy those requirements. The remainder of the chapter deals with the Internet Protocol (IP) and the more recent IPv6.

Chapter 9 Integrated and Differentiated Services

Until relatively recently, traffic management by IP routers consisted of dropping packets when buffers became full and letting end-system software, especially TCP, cope with the results. To respond to the new demands on IP-based networks, an elaborate set of mechanisms and protocols is being developed. Two complementary efforts have been pursued: integrated services and differentiated services. Chapter 9 provides an overview of these architectures, discussing its motivation and functionality. Two important traffic control mechanisms are also discussed: queuing discipline and packet discard strategy.

Chapter 10 Protocols for QoS Support

Chapter 10 examines three important approaches to supporting the provision of QoS in internets. The chapter begins with RSVP (Resource ReserVation Protocol), which is designed to support the IS architecture by enabling the reservation of resources in a datagram environment. Next covered is MPLS (multiprotocol label switching), which is a framework for labeling traffic and routing based on traffic flows. The chapter ends with a discussion of RTP (Real-Time Transport Protocol), which provides transport-level support for real-time application.

CHAPTER 8

INTERNET PROTOCOLS

She occupied herself with studying a map on the opposite wall because she knew she would have to change trains at some point. Tottenham Court Road must be that point, an interchange from the black line to the red. This train would take her there, was bearing her there rapidly now, and at the station she would follow the signs, for signs there must be, to the Central Line going westward.

—King Solomon's Carpet,
Barbara Vine (Ruth Rendell)

KEY POINTS

- An internet consists of multiple separate networks that are interconnected by routers. Data are transmitted in packets from a source system to a destination across a path involving multiple networks and routers. Typically, a connectionless or datagram operation is used. A router accepts datagrams and relays them on toward their destination and is responsible for determining the route, much the same way as packet-switching nodes operate.

- The most widely used protocol for internetworking is the Internet Protocol (IP). IP attaches a header to upper-layer (e.g., TCP) data to form an IP datagram. The header includes source and destination addresses, information used for fragmentation and reassembly, a time to live field, a type-of-service field, and a checksum.

- A next-generation IP, known as IPv6, has been defined. IPv6 provides longer address fields and more functionality than the current IP.

The purpose of this chapter is to examine the Internet Protocol, which is the foundation on which all of the internet-based protocols and on which internetworking is based. We begin with a discussion of internetworking. The remainder of the chapter is devoted to the two standard internet protocols: IPv4 and IPv6.

Refer to the figure on the inside back cover to see the position within the TCP/IP suite of the protocols discussed in this chapter.

8.1 PRINCIPLES OF INTERNETWORKING

In this section, we examine the essential functions of an internetwork protocol. For convenience, we refer specifically to the Internet Standard IP, but it should be understood that the narrative in this section applies to any connectionless Internet Protocol, such as IPv6.

Basic Operation

IP provides a connectionless, or datagram, service between end systems. There are a number of advantages to this approach:

- A connectionless internet facility is flexible. It can deal with a variety of networks, some of which are themselves connectionless. In essence, IP requires very little from the constituent networks.

- A connectionless internet service can be made highly robust. This is basically the same argument made for a datagram network service versus a virtual circuit service.

- A connectionless internet service is best for connectionless transport protocols, because it does not impose unnecessary overhead.

Figure 8.1 depicts a typical example using IP, in which two LANs are interconnected by a frame relay WAN.[1] The figure depicts the operation of the Internet Protocol for data exchange between host A on one LAN (network 1) and host B on another LAN (network 2) through the WAN. The figure shows the protocol architecture and format of the data unit at each stage. The end systems and routers must all share a common Internet Protocol. In addition, the end systems must share the same protocols above IP. The intermediate routers need only implement up through IP.

The IP at A receives blocks of data to be sent to B from the higher layers of software in A. IP attaches a header (at time t_1) specifying, among other things, the global internet address of B. That address is logically in two parts: network identifier and end system identifier. The combination of IP header and upper-level data is called an Internet Protocol data unit (PDU), or simply a datagram (see Figure 2.15). The datagram is then encapsulated with the LAN protocol (LLC header at t_2; MAC header and trailer at t_3) and sent to the router, which strips off the LAN fields to read the IP header (t_6). The router then encapsulates the datagram with the frame relay protocol fields (t_8) and transmits it across the WAN to another router. This router strips off the frame relay fields and recovers the datagram, which it then wraps in LAN fields appropriate to LAN 2 and sends it to B.

Let us now look at this example in more detail. End system A has a datagram to transmit to end system B; the datagram includes the internet address of B. The IP module in A recognizes that the destination (B) is on another network. So the first step is to send the data to a router, in this case router X. To do this, IP passes the datagram down to the next lower layer (in this case LLC) with instructions to send it to router X. LLC in turn passes this information down to the MAC layer, which inserts the MAC-level address of router X into the MAC header. Thus, the block of data transmitted onto LAN 1 includes data from a layer or layers above TCP, plus a TCP header, an IP header, an LLC header, and a MAC header and trailer (time t_3 in Figure 8.1).

Next, the packet travels through network 1 to router X. The router removes MAC and LLC fields and analyzes the IP header to determine the ultimate destination of the data, in this case B. The router must now make a routing decision. There are three possibilities:

1. The destination station B is connected directly to one of the networks to which the router is attached. If so, the router sends the datagram directly to the destination.

[1]The IEEE 802 protocol architecture consists of a physical layer; a medium access control (MAC) layer concerned with addressing and error control, and a logical link control (LLC) layer, concerned with logical connections and identifying the user of LLC.

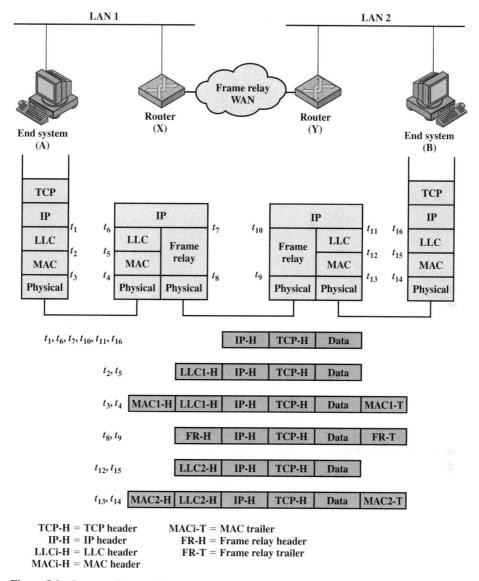

Figure 8.1   Internet Protocol Operation

2. To reach the destination, one or more additional routers must be traversed. If so, a routing decision must be made: To which router should the datagram be sent? In both cases 1 and 2, the IP module in the router sends the datagram down to the next lower layer with the destination network address. Please note that we are speaking here of a lower-layer address that refers to this network.

3. The router does not know the destination address. In this case, the router returns an error message to the source of the datagram.

In this example, the data must pass through router Y before reaching the destination. So router X constructs a new frame by appending a frame relay header and trailer to the IP data unit. The frame relay header indicates a logical connection to router Y. When this frame arrives at router Y, the frame header and trailer are stripped off. The router determines that this IP data unit is destined for B, which is connected directly to a network to which this router is attached. The router therefore creates a frame with a layer-2 destination address of B and sends it out onto LAN 2. The data finally arrive at B, where the LAN and IP headers can be stripped off.

At each router, before the data can be forwarded, the router may need to fragment the data unit to accommodate a smaller maximum packet size limitation on the outgoing network. The data unit is split into two or more fragments, each of which becomes an independent IP data unit. Each new data unit is wrapped in a lower-layer packet and queued for transmission. The router may also limit the length of its queue for each network to which it attaches so as to avoid having a slow network penalize a faster one. Once the queue limit is reached, additional data units are simply dropped.

The process just described continues through as many routers as it takes for the data unit to reach its destination. As with a router, the destination end system recovers the IP data unit from its network wrapping. If fragmentation has occurred, the IP module in the destination end system buffers the incoming data until the entire original data field can be reassembled. This block of data is then passed to a higher layer in the end system.

This service offered by IP is an unreliable one. That is, IP does not guarantee that all data will be delivered or that the data that are delivered will arrive in the proper order. It is the responsibility of the next higher layer (e.g., TCP) to recover from any errors that occur. This approach provides for a great deal of flexibility.

With the Internet Protocol approach, each unit of data is passed from router to router in an attempt to get from source to destination. Because delivery is not guaranteed, there is no particular reliability requirement on any of the networks. Thus, the protocol will work with any combination of network types. Because the sequence of delivery is not guaranteed, successive data units can follow different paths through the internet. This allows the protocol to react to both congestion and failure in the internet by changing routes.

Design Issues

With that brief sketch of the operation of an IP-controlled internet, we can now go back and examine some design issues in greater detail:

- Routing
- Datagram lifetime
- Fragmentation and reassembly
- Error control
- Flow control
- Addressing

Routing For the purpose of routing, each end system and router maintains a routing table that lists, for each possible destination network, the next router to which the internet datagram should be sent.

The routing table may be static or dynamic. A static table, however, could contain alternate routes if a particular router is unavailable. A dynamic table is more flexible in responding to both error and congestion conditions. In the Internet, for example, when a router goes down, all of its neighbors will send out a status report, allowing other routers and stations to update their routing tables. A similar scheme can be used to control congestion. Congestion control is particularly important because of the mismatch in capacity between local and wide area networks. Part Five discusses routing protocols.

Routing tables may also be used to support other internetworking services, such as security and priority. For example, individual networks might be classified to handle data up to a given security classification. The routing mechanism must assure that data of a given security level are not allowed to pass through networks not cleared to handle such data.

Another routing technique is source routing. The source station specifies the route by including a sequential list of routers in the datagram. This, again, could be useful for security or priority requirements.

Finally, we mention a service related to routing: route recording. To record a route, each router appends its internet address to a list of addresses in the datagram. This feature is useful for testing and debugging purposes.

Datagram Lifetime If dynamic or alternate routing is used, the potential exists for a datagram to loop indefinitely through the internet. This is undesirable for two reasons. First, an endlessly circulating datagram consumes resources. Second, we saw in Chapter 6 that a transport protocol may depend on the existence of an upper bound on datagram lifetime. To avoid these problems, each datagram can be marked with a lifetime. Once the lifetime expires, the datagram is discarded.

A simple way to implement lifetime is to use a hop count. Each time that a datagram passes through a router, the count is decremented. Alternatively, the lifetime could be a true measure of time. This requires that the routers must somehow know how long it has been since the datagram or fragment last crossed a router, to know by how much to decrement the lifetime field. This would seem to require some global clocking mechanism. The advantage of using a true time measure is that it can be used in the reassembly algorithm, described next.

Fragmentation and Reassembly Individual networks within an internet may specify different maximum packet sizes. It would be inefficient and unwieldy to try to dictate uniform packet size across networks. Thus, routers may need to fragment incoming datagrams into smaller pieces, called segments or fragments, before transmitting on to the next network.

If datagrams can be fragmented (perhaps more than once) in the course of their travels, the question arises as to where they should be reassembled. The easiest solution is to have reassembly performed at the destination only. The principal disadvantage of this approach is that fragments can only get smaller as data move through the internet. This may impair the efficiency of some networks. However, if intermediate router reassembly is allowed, the following disadvantages result:

1. Large buffers are required at routers, and there is the risk that all of the buffer space will be used up storing partial datagrams.

2. All fragments of a datagram must pass through the same router. This inhibits the use of dynamic routing.

In IP, datagram fragments are reassembled at the destination end system. The IP fragmentation technique uses the following information in the IP header:

- Data Unit Identifier (ID)
- Data Length
- Offset
- More Flag

The *ID* is a means of uniquely identifying an end-system-originated datagram. In IP, it consists of the source and destination addresses, a number that corresponds to the protocol layer that generated the data (e.g., TCP), and an identification supplied by that protocol layer. The *Data Length* is the length of the user data field in octets, and the *Offset* is the position of a fragment of user data in the data field of the original datagram, in multiples of 64 bits.

The source end system creates a datagram with a *Data Length* equal to the entire length of the data field, with *Offset* = 0, and a *More Flag* set to 0 (false). To fragment a long datagram into two pieces, an IP module in a router performs the following tasks:

1. Create two new datagrams and copy the header fields of the incoming datagram into both.
2. Divide the incoming user data field into two approximately equal portions along a 64-bit boundary, placing one portion in each new datagram. The first portion must be a multiple of 64 bits (8 octets).
3. Set the *Data Length* of the first new datagram to the length of the inserted data, and set *More Flag* to 1 (true). The *Offset* field is unchanged.
4. Set the *Data Length* of the second new datagram to the length of the inserted data, and add the length of the first data portion divided by 8 to the *Offset* field. The *More Flag* remains the same.

Figure 8.2 gives an example. The procedure is easily generalized to an *n*-way split.

To reassemble a datagram, there must be sufficient buffer space at the reassembly point. As fragments with the same ID arrive, their data fields are inserted in the proper position in the buffer until the entire data field is reassembled, which is achieved when a contiguous set of data exists starting with an *Offset* of zero and ending with data from a fragment with a false *More Flag*.

One eventuality that must be dealt with is that one or more of the fragments may not get through: The IP service does not guarantee delivery. Some method is needed to decide when to abandon a reassembly effort to free up buffer space. Two approaches are commonly used. First, assign a reassembly lifetime to the first fragment to arrive. This is a local, real-time clock assigned by the reassembly function and decremented while the fragments of the original datagram are being buffered. If the time expires prior to complete reassembly, the received fragments are discarded. A second approach is to make use of the datagram lifetime, which is part of the header of each incoming fragment. The lifetime field continues to be decremented

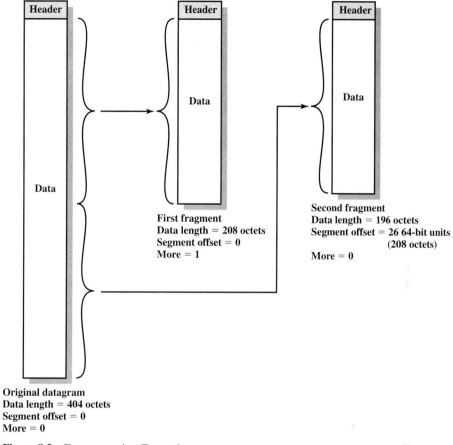

Figure 8.2 Fragmentation Example

by the reassembly function; as with the first approach, if the lifetime expires prior to complete reassembly, the received fragments are discarded.

Error Control The internetwork facility does not guarantee successful delivery of every datagram. When a router discards a datagram, the router should attempt to return some information to the source, if possible. The source Internet Protocol entity may use this information to modify its transmission strategy and may notify higher layers. To report that a specific datagram has been discarded, some means of datagram identification is needed.

Datagrams may be discarded for a number of reasons, including lifetime expiration, congestion, and checksum error. In the latter case, notification is not possible because the source address field may have been damaged.

Flow Control Internet flow control allows routers and/or receiving stations to limit the rate at which they receive data. For the connectionless type of service we are describing, flow control mechanisms are limited. The best approach would seem to be to send flow control packets, requesting reduced data flow, to other routers and source stations. We will see one example of this with ICMP, discussed subsequently.

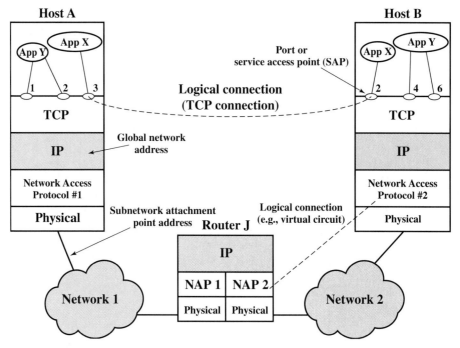

Figure 8.3 TCP/IP Concepts

Addressing The concept of addressing in a communications architecture is a complex one and covers a number of issues, including

- Addressing level
- Addressing scope
- Addressing mode

During the discussion, we illustrate the concepts using Figure 8.3, which repeats Figure 2.14, and which shows a configuration using the TCP/IP architecture.

Addressing level refers to the level in the communications architecture at which an entity is named. Typically, a unique address is associated with each end system (e.g., workstation or server) and each intermediate system (e.g., router) in a configuration. In the case of the TCP/IP architecture, this is referred to as an IP address, or simply an internet address. The IP address is used to route a PDU through a network or networks to a system indicated by an IP address in the PDU. A lower level of addressing is needed for any individual network that has multiple attached systems, such as a frame relay or ATM network. In this case, a unique address is assigned to each device attached to the network. In Figure 8.3, such addresses are referred to as subnetwork attachment point addresses; more simply, they are network addresses.

Once data arrive at a destination system, they must be routed to some process or application in the system. Typically, a system will support multiple applications and an application may support multiple users. Each application and, perhaps, each

Table 8.1 Addressing Modes

Destination	Network Address	Internet Address	Port Address
Unicast	Individual	Individual	Individual
Multicast	Individual	Individual	Group
	Individual	All	Group
	All	All	Group
Broadcast	Individual	Individual	All
	Individual	All	All
	All	All	All

concurrent user of an application, is assigned a unique identifier, referred to as a port in the TCP/IP architecture and as a service access point (SAP) in the OSI architecture.

Another issue that relates to the address of an end system or intermediate system is **addressing scope**. The internet address is a global address. The key characteristics of a global address are as follows:

- **Global nonambiguity:** A global address identifies a unique system. Synonyms are permitted. That is, a system may have more than one global address.
- **Global applicability:** It is possible at any system to identify any other system, by means of the global address of the other system.

Because a global address is unique and globally applicable, it enables an internet to route data from any system attached to any network to any other system attached to any other network.

Another addressing concept is that of **addressing mode**. Most commonly, an address refers to a single system or port; in this case it is referred to as an individual or **unicast** address. It is also possible for an address to refer to more than one entity or port. Such an address identifies multiple simultaneous recipients for data. For example, a user might wish to send a memo to a number of individuals. The network control center may wish to notify all users that the network is going down. An address for multiple recipients may be **broadcast**, intended for all entities within a domain, or **multicast**, intended for a specific subset of entities. Table 8.1 illustrates some of the possibilities.

8.2 INTERNET PROTOCOL

In this section, we look at version 4 of IP, officially defined in RFC 791. Although it is intended that IPv4 will ultimately be replaced by IPv6, it is currently the standard IP used in TCP/IP networks.

The Internet Protocol (IP) is part of the TCP/IP suite and is the most widely used internetworking protocol. As with any protocol standard, IP is specified in two parts:

- The interface with a higher layer (e.g., TCP), specifying the services that IP provides
- The actual protocol format and mechanisms

In this section, we examine first IP services and then the protocol. This is followed by a discussion of IP address formats. Finally, the Internet Control Message Protocol (ICMP), which is an integral part of IP, is described.

IP Services

The services to be provided across adjacent protocol layers (e.g., between IP and TCP) are expressed in terms of primitives and parameters. A primitive specifies the function to be performed, and the parameters are used to pass data and control information. The actual form of a primitive is implementation dependent. An example is a subroutine call.

IP provides two service primitives at the interface to the next higher layer. The Send primitive is used to request transmission of a data unit. The Deliver primitive is used by IP to notify a user of the arrival of a data unit. The parameters associated with the two primitives are as follows:

- **Source address:** Internetwork address of sending IP entity.
- **Destination address:** Internetwork address of destination IP entity.
- **Protocol:** Recipient protocol entity (an IP user, such as TCP).
- **Type of service indicators:** Used to specify the treatment of the data unit in its transmission through component networks.
- **Identification:** Used in combination with the source and destination addresses and user protocol to identify the data unit uniquely. This parameter is needed for reassembly and error reporting.
- **Don't fragment identifier:** Indicates whether IP can fragment data to accomplish delivery.
- **Time to live:** Measured in seconds.
- **Data length:** Length of data being transmitted.
- **Option data:** Options requested by the IP user.
- **Data:** User data to be transmitted.

The *identification, don't fragment identifier*, and *time to live* parameters are present in the Send primitive but not in the Deliver primitive. These three parameters provide instructions to IP that are not of concern to the recipient IP user.

The options parameter allows for future extensibility and for inclusion of parameters that are usually not invoked. The currently defined options are as follows:

- **Security:** Allows a security label to be attached to a datagram.
- **Source routing:** A sequenced list of router addresses that specifies the route to be followed. Routing may be strict (only identified routers may be visited) or loose (other intermediate routers may be visited).
- **Route recording:** A field is allocated to record the sequence of routers visited by the datagram.
- **Stream identification:** Names reserved resources used for stream service. This service provides special handling for volatile periodic traffic (e.g., voice).
- **Timestamping:** The source IP entity and some or all intermediate routers add a timestamp (precision to milliseconds) to the data unit as it goes by.

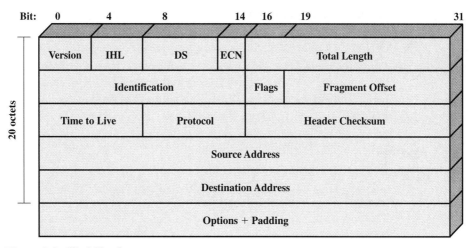

Figure 8.4 IPv4 Header

Internet Protocol

The protocol between IP entities is best described with reference to the IP datagram format, shown in Figure 8.4. The fields are as follows:

- **Version (4 bits):** Indicates version number, to allow evolution of the protocol; the value is 4.

- **Internet Header Length (IHL) (4 bits):** Length of header in 32-bit words. The minimum value is five, for a minimum header length of 20 octets.

- **DS/ECN (8 bits):** Prior to the introduction of differentiated services, this field was referred to as the **Type of Service** field and specified reliability, precedence, delay, and throughput parameters. This interpretation has now been superseded. The first 6 bits of the TOS field are now referred to as the DS (differentiated services) field, discussed in Chapter 9. The remaining 2 bits are reserved for an ECN (explicit congestion notification) field, discussed in Chapters 7 and 9.

- **Total Length (16 bits):** Total datagram length, including header plus data, in octets.

- **Identification (16 bits):** A sequence number that, together with the source address, destination address, and user protocol, is intended to identify a datagram uniquely. Thus, this number should be unique for the datagram's source address, destination address, and user protocol for the time during which the datagram will remain in the internet.

- **Flags (3 bits):** Only two of the bits are currently defined. The More bit is used for fragmentation and reassembly, as previously explained. The Don't Fragment bit prohibits fragmentation when set. This bit may be useful if it is known that the destination does not have the capability to reassemble fragments. However, if this bit is set, the datagram will be discarded if it exceeds the maximum size of an en route network. Therefore, if the bit is set, it may be advisable to use source routing to avoid networks with small maximum packet size.

- **Fragment Offset (13 bits):** Indicates where in the original datagram this fragment belongs, measured in 64-bit units. This implies that fragments other than the last fragment must contain a data field that is a multiple of 64 bits in length.
- **Time to Live (8 bits):** Specifies how long, in seconds, a datagram is allowed to remain in the internet. Every router that processes a datagram must decrease the TTL by at least one, so the TTL is somewhat similar to a hop count.
- **Protocol (8 bits):** Indicates the next-higher-level protocol that is to receive the data field at the destination; thus, this field identifies the type of the next header in the packet after the IP header.
- **Header Checksum (16 bits):** An error-detecting code applied to the header only. Because some header fields may change during transit (e.g., time to live, fragmentation-related fields), this is reverified and recomputed at each router. The checksum is formed by taking the ones complement of the 16-bit ones complement addition of all 16-bit words in the header. For purposes of computation, the checksum field is itself initialized to a value of zero.[2]
- **Source Address (32 bits):** Coded to allow a variable allocation of bits to specify the network and the end system attached to the specified network, as discussed subsequently.
- **Destination Address (32 bits):** Same characteristics as source address.
- **Options (variable):** Encodes the options requested by the sending user.
- **Padding (variable):** Used to ensure that the datagram header is a multiple of 32 bits in length.
- **Data (variable):** The data field must be an integer multiple of 8 bits in length. The maximum length of the datagram (data field plus header) is 65,535 octets.

It should be clear how the IP services specified in the Send and Deliver primitives map into the fields of the IP datagram.

IP Addresses

The source and destination address fields in the IP header each contain a 32-bit global internet address, generally consisting of a network identifier and a host identifier.

Network Classes The address is coded to allow a variable allocation of bits to specify network and host, as depicted in Figure 8.5. This encoding provides flexibility in assigning addresses to hosts and allows a mix of network sizes on an internet. The three principal network classes are best suited to the following conditions:

- **Class A:** Few networks, each with many hosts
- **Class B:** Medium number of networks, each with a medium number of hosts
- **Class C:** Many networks, each with a few hosts

In a particular environment, it may be best to use addresses all from one class. For example, a corporate internetwork that consist of a large number of departmental local area networks may need to use Class C addresses exclusively. However, the

---

[2]A discussion of this checksum is contained in a supporting document at this book's Web site.

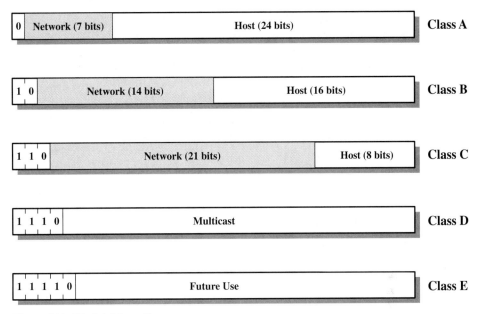

Figure 8.5 IPv4 Address Formats

format of the addresses is such that it is possible to mix all three classes of addresses on the same internetwork; this is what is done in the case of the Internet itself. A mixture of classes is appropriate for an internetwork consisting of a few large networks, many small networks, plus some medium-sized networks.

IP addresses are usually written in what is called *dotted decimal notation*, with a decimal number representing each of the octets of the 32-bit address. For example, the IP address 11000000 11100100 00010001 00111001 is written as 192.228.17.57.

Note that all Class A network addresses begin with a binary 0. Network addresses with a first octet of 0 (binary 00000000) and 127 (binary 01111111) are reserved, so there are 126 potential Class A network numbers, which have a first dotted decimal number in the range 1 to 126. Class B network addresses begin with a binary 10, so that the range of the first decimal number in a Class B address is 128 to 191(binary 10000000 to 10111111). The second octet is also part of the Class B network address, so that there are $2^{14} = 16{,}384$ Class B network addresses. For Class C addresses, the first decimal number ranges from 192 to 223 (11000000 to 11011111). The total number of Class C network addresses is $2^{21} = 2{,}097{,}152$.

Subnets and Subnet Masks The concept of subnet was introduced to address the following requirement. Consider an internet that includes one or more WANs and a number of sites, each of which has a number of LANs. We would like to allow arbitrary complexity of interconnected LAN structures within an organization while insulating the overall internet against explosive growth in network numbers and routing complexity. One approach to this problem is to assign a single network number to all of the LANs at a site. From the point of view of the rest of the internet, there is a single network at that site, which simplifies addressing and routing.

To allow the routers within the site to function properly, each LAN is assigned a subnet number. The *host* portion of the internet address is partitioned into a subnet number and a host number to accommodate this new level of addressing.

Within the subnetted network, the local routers must route on the basis of an extended network number consisting of the *network* portion of the IP address and the subnet number. The bit positions containing this extended network number are indicated by the address mask. The use of the address mask allows the host to determine whether an outgoing datagram is destined for a host on the same LAN (send directly) or another LAN (send datagram to router). It is assumed that some other means (e.g., manual configuration) are used to create address masks and make them known to the local routers.

Table 8.2a shows the calculations involved in the use of a subnet mask. Note that the effect of the subnet mask is to erase the portion of the host field that refers to an actual host on a subnet. What remains is the network number and the subnet number. Figure 8.6 shows an example of the use of subnetting. The figure shows a local complex consisting of three LANs and two routers. To the rest of the internet, this complex is a single network with a Class C address of the form 192.228.17.*x*, where the leftmost three octets are the network number and the rightmost octet contains a host number *x*. Both routers R1 and R2 are configured with a subnet mask with the value 255.255.255.224 (see Table 8.2a). For example, if a datagram with the destination address 192.228.17.57 arrives at R1 from either the rest of the internet or from LAN Y,

Table 8.2   IP Addresses and Subnet Masks [STEI95]

(a) Dotted decimal and binary representations of IP address and subnet masks

	Binary Representation	Dotted Decimal
IP address	11000000.11100100.00010001.00111001	192.228.17.57
Subnet mask	11111111.11111111.11111111.11100000	255.255.255.224
Bitwise AND of address and mask (resultant network/subnet number)	11000000.11100100.00010001.00100000	192.228.17.32
Subnet number	11000000.11100100.00010001.001	1
Host number	00000000.00000000.00000000.00011001	25

(b) Default subnet masks

	Binary Representation	Dotted Decimal
Class A default mask	11111111.00000000.00000000.00000000	255.0.0.0
Example Class A mask	11111111.11000000.00000000.00000000	255.192.0.0
Class B default mask	11111111.11111111.00000000.00000000	255.255.0.0
Example Class B mask	11111111.11111111.11111000.00000000	255.255.248.0
Class C default mask	11111111.11111111.11111111.00000000	255.255.255.0
Example Class C mask	11111111.11111111.11111111.11111100	255.255.255.252

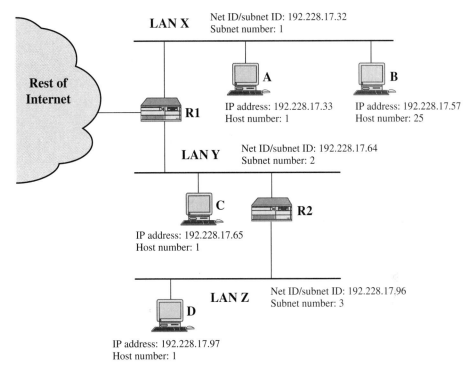

LAN X Net ID/subnet ID: 192.228.17.32
Subnet number: 1

Rest of Internet

R1

A
IP address: 192.228.17.33
Host number: 1

B
IP address: 192.228.17.57
Host number: 25

LAN Y Net ID/subnet ID: 192.228.17.64
Subnet number: 2

C
IP address: 192.228.17.65
Host number: 1

R2

D **LAN Z** Net ID/subnet ID: 192.228.17.96
Subnet number: 3

IP address: 192.228.17.97
Host number: 1

Figure 8.6 Example of Subnetworking

R1 applies the subnet mask to determine that this address refers to subnet 1, which is LAN X, and so forwards the datagram to LAN X. Similarly, if a datagram with that destination address arrives at R2 from LAN Z, R2 applies the mask and then determines from its forwarding database that datagrams destined for subnet 1 should be forwarded to R1. Hosts must also employ a subnet mask to make routing decisions.

The default subnet mask for a given class of addresses is a null mask (Table 8.2b), which yields the same network and host number as the non-subnetted address.

Internet Control Message Protocol (ICMP)

The IP standard specifies that a compliant implementation must also implement ICMP (RFC 792). ICMP provides a means for transferring messages from routers and other hosts to a host. In essence, ICMP provides feedback about problems in the communication environment. Examples of its use are when a datagram cannot reach its destination, when the router does not have the buffering capacity to forward a datagram, and when the router can direct the station to send traffic on a shorter route. In most cases, an ICMP message is sent in response to a datagram, either by a router along the datagram's path or by the intended destination host.

Although ICMP is, in effect, at the same level as IP in the TCP/IP architecture, it is a user of IP. An ICMP message is constructed and then passed down to IP, which encapsulates the message with an IP header and then transmits the resulting datagram in the usual fashion. Because ICMP messages are transmitted in IP datagrams, their delivery is not guaranteed and their use cannot be considered reliable.

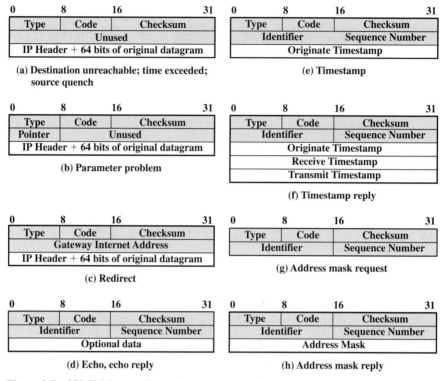

Figure 8.7 ICMP Message Formats

Figure 8.7 shows the format of the various ICMP message types. An ICMP message starts with a 64-bit header consisting of the following:

- **Type (8 bits):** Specifies the type of ICMP message.
- **Code (8 bits):** Used to specify parameters of the message that can be encoded in one or a few bits.
- **Checksum (16 bits):** Checksum of the entire ICMP message. This is the same checksum algorithm used for IP.
- **Parameters (32 bits):** Used to specify more lengthy parameters.

These fields are generally followed by additional information fields that further specify the content of the message.

In those cases in which the ICMP message refers to a prior datagram, the information field includes the entire IP header plus the first 64 bits of the data field of the original datagram. This enables the source host to match the incoming ICMP message with the prior datagram. The reason for including the first 64 bits of the data field is that this will enable the IP module in the host to determine which upper-level protocol or protocols were involved. In particular, the first 64 bits would include a portion of the TCP header or other transport-level header.

The **destination unreachable** message covers a number of contingencies. A router may return this message if it does not know how to reach the destination network. In some networks, an attached router may be able to determine if a particular host is unreachable, and return the message. The destination host itself may return this message if the user protocol or some higher-level service access point is unreachable. This could happen if the corresponding field in the IP header was set incorrectly. If the datagram specifies a source route that is unusable, a message is returned. Finally, if a router must fragment a datagram but the Don't Fragment flag is set, the datagram is discarded and a message is returned.

A router will return a **time exceeded** message if the lifetime of the datagram expires. A host will send this message if it cannot complete reassembly within a time limit.

A syntactic or semantic error in an IP header will cause a **parameter problem** message to be returned by a router or host. For example, an incorrect argument may be provided with an option. The parameter field contains a pointer to the octet in the original header where the error was detected.

The **source quench** message provides a rudimentary form of flow control. Either a router or a destination host may send this message to a source host, requesting that it reduce the rate at which it is sending traffic to the internet destination. On receipt of a source quench message, the source host should cut back the rate at which it is sending traffic to the specified destination until it no longer receives source quench messages. The source quench message can be used by a router or host that must discard datagrams because of a full buffer. In that case, the router or host will issue a source quench message for every datagram that it discards. In addition, a system may anticipate congestion and issue source quench messages when its buffers approach capacity. In that case, the datagram referred to in the source quench message may well be delivered. Thus, receipt of a source quench message does not imply delivery or nondelivery of the corresponding datagram.

A router sends a **redirect** message to a host on a directly connected router to advise the host of a better route to a particular destination. The following is an example, using Figure 8.6. Router R1 receives a datagram from host C on network Y, to which R1 is attached. R1 checks its routing table and obtains the address for the next router, R2, on the route to the datagram's internet destination network, Z. Because R2 and the host identified by the internet source address of the datagram are on the same network, R1 sends a redirect message to C. The redirect message advises the host to send its traffic for network Z directly to router R2, because this is a shorter path to the destination. The router forwards the original datagram to its internet destination (via R2). The address of R2 is contained in the parameter field of the redirect message.

The **echo** and **echo reply** messages provide a mechanism for testing that communication is possible between entities. The recipient of an echo message is obligated to return the message in an echo reply message. An identifier and sequence number are associated with the echo message to be matched in the echo reply message. The identifier might be used like a service access point to identify a particular session, and the sequence number might be incremented on each echo request sent.

The **timestamp** and **timestamp reply** messages provide a mechanism for sampling the delay characteristics of the internet. The sender of a timestamp message may include an identifier and sequence number in the parameters field and include the time that the message is sent (originate timestamp). The receiver records the time it received the message and the time that it transmits the reply message in the timestamp reply message. If the timestamp message is sent using strict source routing, then the delay characteristics of a particular route can be measured.

The **address mask request** and **address mask reply** messages are useful in an environment that includes subnets. The address mask request and reply messages allow a host to learn the address mask for the LAN to which it connects. The host broadcasts an address mask request message on the LAN. The router on the LAN responds with an address mask reply message that contains the address mask.

8.3 IPV6

The Internet Protocol (IP) has been the foundation of the Internet and virtually all multivendor private internetworks. This protocol is reaching the end of its useful life and a new protocol, known as IPv6 (IP version 6), has been defined to ultimately replace IP.[3]

We first look at the motivation for developing a new version of IP and then examine some of its details.

IP Next Generation

The driving motivation for the adoption of a new version of IP was the limitation imposed by the 32-bit address field in IPv4. With a 32-bit address field, it is possible in principle to assign 2^{32} different addresses, which is over 4 billion possible addresses. One might think that this number of addresses was more than adequate to meet addressing needs on the Internet. However, in the late 1980s it was perceived that there would be a problem, and this problem began to manifest itself in the early 1990s. Reasons for the inadequacy of 32-bit addresses include the following:

- The two-level structure of the IP address (network number, host number) is convenient but wasteful of the address space. Once a network number is assigned to a network, all of the host-number addresses for that network number are assigned to that network. The address space for that network may be sparsely used, but as far as the effective IP address space is concerned, if a network number is used, then all addresses within the network are used.

- The IP addressing model generally requires that a unique network number be assigned to each IP network whether or not it is actually connected to the Internet.

- Networks are proliferating rapidly. Most organizations boast multiple LANs, not just a single LAN system. Wireless networks have rapidly assumed a major role. The Internet itself has grown explosively for years.

- Growth of TCP/IP usage into new areas will result in a rapid growth in the demand for unique IP addresses. Examples include using TCP/IP to interconnect electronic point-of-sale terminals and for cable television receivers.

---

[3]You may think this narrative has skipped a few versions. The currently deployed version of IP is IP version 4; previous versions of IP (1 through 3) were successively defined and replaced to reach IPv4. Version 5 is the number assigned to the Stream Protocol, a connection-oriented internet-layer protocol; hence the use of the label version 6.

- Typically, a single IP address is assigned to each host. A more flexible arrangement is to allow multiple IP addresses per host. This of course increases the demand for IP addresses.

So the need for an increased address space dictated that a new version of IP was needed. In addition, IP is a very old protocol, and new requirements in the areas of address configuration, routing flexibility, and traffic support had been defined.

In response to these needs, the Internet Engineering Task Force (IETF) issued a call for proposals for a next generation IP (IPng) in July of 1992. A number of proposals were received, and by 1994 the final design for IPng emerged. A major milestone was reached with the publication of RFC 1752, "The Recommendation for the IP Next Generation Protocol," issued in January 1995. RFC 1752 outlines the requirements for IPng, specifies the PDU formats, and highlights the IPng approach in the areas of addressing, routing, and security. A number of other Internet documents defined details of the protocol, now officially called IPv6; these include an overall specification of IPv6 (RFC 2460), an RFC dealing with addressing structure of IPv6 (RFC 2373), and numerous others.

IPv6 includes the following enhancements over IPv4:

- **Expanded address space:** IPv6 uses 128-bit addresses instead of the 32-bit addresses of IPv4. This is an increase of address space by a factor of 2^{96}. It has been pointed out [HIND95] that this allows on the order of 6×10^{23} unique addresses per square meter of the surface of the earth. Even if addresses are very inefficiently allocated, this address space seems secure.

- **Improved option mechanism:** IPv6 options are placed in separate optional headers that are located between the IPv6 header and the transport-layer header. Most of these optional headers are not examined or processed by any router on the packet's path. This simplifies and speeds up router processing of IPv6 packets compared to IPv4 datagrams.[4] It also makes it easier to add additional options.

- **Address autoconfiguration:** This capability provides for dynamic assignment of IPv6 addresses.

- **Increased addressing flexibility:** IPv6 includes the concept of an anycast address, for which a packet is delivered to just one of a set of nodes. The scalability of multicast routing is improved by adding a scope field to multicast addresses.

- **Support for resource allocation:** IPv6 enables the labeling of packets for a particular traffic flow for which the sender requests special handling. This aids in the support of specialized traffic such as real-time video.

All of these features are explored in the remainder of this section, except for the security features, which are discussed in Chapter 16.

---

[4]The protocol data unit for IPv6 is referred to as a packet rather than a datagram, which is the term used for IPv4 PDUs.

IPv6 Structure

An IPv6 packet has the following general form:

```
←40 octets→←————————————0 or more————————————→
```

| IPv6 header | Extension header | • • • | Extension header | Transport-level PDU |

The only header that is required is referred to simply as the IPv6 header. This is of fixed size with a length of 40 octets, compared to 20 octets for the mandatory portion of the IPv4 header (Figure 8.4). The following extension headers have been defined:

- **Hop-by-Hop Options header:** Defines special options that require hop-by-hop processing
- **Routing header:** Provides extended routing, similar to IPv4 source routing
- **Fragment header:** Contains fragmentation and reassembly information
- **Authentication header:** Provides packet integrity and authentication
- **Encapsulating Security Payload header:** Provides privacy
- **Destination Options header:** Contains optional information to be examined by the destination node

The IPv6 standard recommends that, when multiple extension headers are used, the IPv6 headers appear in the following order:

1. IPv6 header: Mandatory, must always appear first
2. Hop-by-Hop Options header
3. Destination Options header: For options to be processed by the first destination that appears in the IPv6 Destination Address field plus subsequent destinations listed in the Routing header
4. Routing header
5. Fragment header
6. Authentication header
7. Encapsulating Security Payload header
8. Destination Options header: For options to be processed only by the final destination of the packet

Figure 8.8 shows an example of an IPv6 packet that includes an instance of each header, except those related to security. Note that the IPv6 header and each extension header include a Next Header field. This field identifies the type of the immediately following header. If the next header is an extension header, then this field contains the type identifier of that header. Otherwise, this field contains the protocol identifier of the upper-layer protocol using IPv6 (typically a transport-level protocol), using the same values as the IPv4 Protocol field. In Figure 8.8, the upper-layer protocol is TCP, so that the upper-layer data carried by the IPv6 packet consist of a TCP header followed by a block of application data.

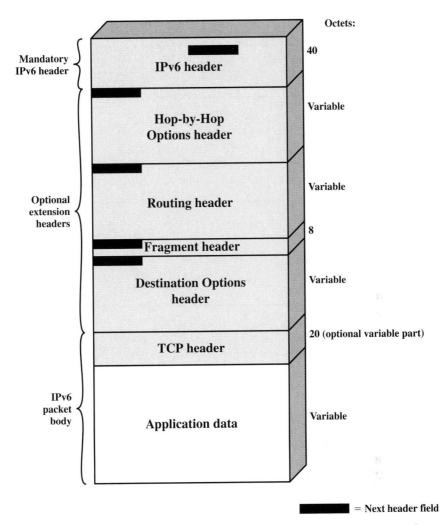

Figure 8.8 IPv6 Packet with Extension Headers (Containing a TCP Segment)

We first look at the main IPv6 header and then examine each of the extensions in turn.

IPv6 Header

The IPv6 header has a fixed length of 40 octets, consisting of the following fields (Figure 8.9):

- **Version (4 bits):** Internet protocol version number; the value is 6.
- **DS/ECN (8 bits):** Prior to the introduction of differentiated services, this field was referred to as the **Traffic Class** field and was reserved for use by originating nodes and/or forwarding routers to identify and distinguish between different classes or priorities of IPv6 packets. The first six bits of the Traffic Class

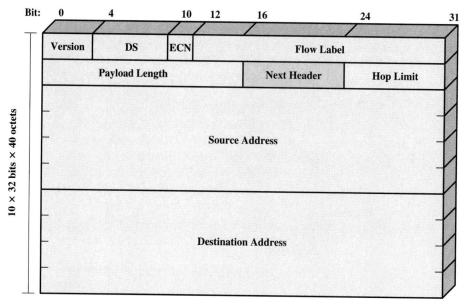

Figure 8.9   IPv6 Header

field are now referred to as the DS (differentiated services) field, discussed in Chapter 9. The remaining 2 bits are reserved for an ECN (explicit congestion notification) field, discussed in Chapters 7 and 9.

- **Flow Label (20 bits):** May be used by a host to label those packets for which it is requesting special handling by routers within a network; discussed subsequently.

- **Payload Length (16 bits):** Length of the remainder of the IPv6 packet following the header, in octets. In other words, this is the total length of all of the extension headers plus the transport-level PDU.

- **Next Header (8 bits):** Identifies the type of header immediately following the IPv6 header; this will either be an IPv6 extension header or a higher-layer header, such as TCP or UDP.

- **Hop Limit (8 bits):** The remaining number of allowable hops for this packet. The hop limit is set to some desired maximum value by the source and decremented by 1 by each node that forwards the packet. The packet is discarded if Hop Limit is decremented to zero. This is a simplification over the processing required for the time-to-live field of IPv4. The consensus was that the extra effort in accounting for time intervals in IPv4 added no significant value to the protocol. In fact, IPv4 routers, as a general rule, treat the time-to-live field as a hop limit field.

- **Source Address (128 bits):** The address of the originator of the packet.

- **Destination Address (128 bits):** The address of the intended recipient of the packet. This may not in fact be the intended ultimate destination if a Routing header is present, as explained subsequently.

Although the IPv6 header is longer than the mandatory portion of the IPv4 header (40 octets versus 20 octets), it contains fewer fields (8 versus 12). Thus, routers have less processing to do per header, which should speed up routing.

Flow Label The IPv6 standard defines a flow as a sequence of packets sent from a particular source to a particular (unicast or multicast) destination for which the source desires special handling by the intervening routers. A flow is uniquely identified by the combination of a source address, destination address, and a nonzero 20-bit flow label. Thus, all packets that are to be part of the same flow are assigned the same flow label by the source.

From the source's point of view, a flow typically will be a sequence of packets that are generated from a single application instance at the source and that have the same transfer service requirements. A flow may comprise a single TCP connection or even multiple TCP connections; an example of the latter is a file transfer application, which could have one control connection and multiple data connections. A single application may generate a single flow or multiple flows. An example of the latter is multimedia conferencing, which might have one flow for audio and one for graphic windows, each with different transfer requirements in terms of data rate, delay, and delay variation.

From the router's point of view, a flow is a sequence of packets that share attributes that affect how these packets are handled by the router. These include path, resource allocation, discard requirements, accounting, and security attributes. The router may treat packets from different flows differently in a number of ways, including allocating different buffer sizes, giving different precedence in terms of forwarding, and requesting different quality of service from networks.

There is no special significance to any particular flow label. Instead the special handling to be provided for a packet flow must be declared in some other way. For example, a source might negotiate or request special handling ahead of time from routers by means of a control protocol, or at transmission time by information in one of the extension headers in the packet, such as the Hop-by-Hop Options header. Examples of special handling that might be requested include some sort of non-default quality of service and some form of real-time service.

In principle, all of a user's requirements for a particular flow could be defined in an extension header and included with each packet. If we wish to leave the concept of flow open to include a wide variety of requirements, this design approach could result in very large packet headers. The alternative, adopted for IPv6, is the flow label, in which the flow requirements are defined prior to flow commencement and a unique flow label is assigned to the flow. In this case, the router must save flow requirement information about each flow.

The following rules apply to the flow label:

1. Hosts or routers that do not support the Flow Label field must set the field to zero when originating a packet, pass the field unchanged when forwarding a packet, and ignore the field when receiving a packet.

2. All packets originating from a given source with the same nonzero Flow Label must have the same Destination Address, Source Address, Hop-by-Hop

Options header contents (if this header is present), and Routing header contents (if this header is present). The intent is that a router can decide how to route and process the packet by simply looking up the flow label in a table and without examining the rest of the header.

3. The source assigns a flow label to a flow. New flow labels must be chosen (pseudo-) randomly and uniformly in the range 1 to $2^{20} - 1$, subject to the restriction that a source must not reuse a flow label for a new flow within the lifetime of the existing flow. The zero flow label is reserved to indicate that no flow label is being used.

This last point requires some elaboration. The router must maintain information about the characteristics of each active flow that may pass through it, presumably in some sort of table. To forward packets efficiently and rapidly, table lookup must be efficient. One alternative is to have a table with 2^{20} (about one million) entries, one for each possible flow label; this imposes an unnecessary memory burden on the router. Another alternative is to have one entry in the table per active flow, include the flow label with each entry, and require the router to search the entire table each time a packet is encountered. This imposes an unnecessary processing burden on the router. Instead, most router designs are likely to use some sort of hash table approach. With this approach a moderate-sized table is used, and each flow entry is mapped into the table using a hashing function on the flow label. The hashing function might simply be the low-order few bits (say 8 or 10) of the flow label or some simple calculation on the 20 bits of the flow label. In any case, the efficiency of the hash approach typically depends on the flow labels being uniformly distributed over their possible range. Hence requirement number 3 in the preceding list.

IPv6 Addresses

IPv6 addresses are 128 bits in length. Addresses are assigned to individual interfaces on nodes, not to the nodes themselves.[5] A single interface may have multiple unique unicast addresses. Any of the unicast addresses associated with a node's interface may be used to uniquely identify that node.

The combination of long addresses and multiple addresses per interface enables improved routing efficiency over IPv4. In IPv4, addresses generally do not have a structure that assists routing, and therefore a router may need to maintain a huge table of routing paths. Longer internet addresses allow for aggregating addresses by hierarchies of network, access provider, geography, corporation, and so on. Such aggregation should make for smaller routing tables and faster table lookups. The allowance for multiple addresses per interface would allow a subscriber that uses multiple access providers across the same interface to have separate addresses aggregated under each provider's address space.

---

[5]In IPv6, a *node* is any device that implements IPv6; this includes hosts and routers.

IPv6 allows three types of addresses:

- **Unicast:** An identifier for a single interface. A packet sent to a unicast address is delivered to the interface identified by that address.
- **Anycast:** An identifier for a set of interfaces (typically belonging to different nodes). A packet sent to an anycast address is delivered to one of the interfaces identified by that address (the "nearest" one, according to the routing protocols' measure of distance).
- **Multicast:** An identifier for a set of interfaces (typically belonging to different nodes). A packet sent to a multicast address is delivered to all interfaces identified by that address.

Hop-by-Hop Options Header

The Hop-by-Hop Options header carries optional information that, if present, must be examined by every router along the path. This header consists of (Figure 8.10a):

- **Next Header (8 bits):** Identifies the type of header immediately following this header.

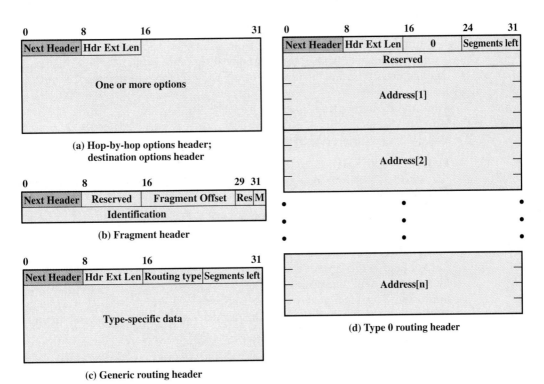

(a) Hop-by-hop options header;
destination options header

(b) Fragment header

(c) Generic routing header

(d) Type 0 routing header

Figure 8.10   IPv6 Extension Headers

- **Header Extension Length (8 bits):** Length of this header in 64-bit units, not including the first 64 bits.

- **Options:** A variable-length field consisting of one or more option definitions. Each definition is in the form of three subfields: Option Type (8 bits), which identifies the option; Length (8 bits), which specifies the length of the Option Data field in octets; and Option Data, which is a variable-length specification of the option.

It is actually the lowest-order five bits of the Option Type field that are used to specify a particular option. The high-order two bits indicate that action to be taken by a node that does not recognize this option type, as follows:

- 00—Skip over this option and continue processing the header.

- 01—Discard the packet.

- 10—Discard the packet and send an ICMP Parameter Problem message to the packet's Source Address, pointing to the unrecognized Option Type.

- 11—Discard the packet and, only if the packet's Destination Address is not a multicast address, send an ICMP Parameter Problem message to the packet's Source Address, pointing to the unrecognized Option Type.

The third highest-order bit specifies whether the Option Data field does not change (0) or may change (1) en route from source to destination. Data that may change must be excluded from authentication calculations, as discussed in Chapter 16.

These conventions for the Option Type field also apply to the Destination Options header.

Four hop-by-hop options have been specified so far:

- **Pad1:** Used to insert one byte of padding into the Options area of the header.

- **PadN:** Used to insert N bytes ($N \geq 2$) of padding into the Options area of the header. The two padding options ensure that the header is a multiple of 8 bytes in length.

- **Jumbo payload:** Used to send IPv6 packets with payloads longer than 65,535 octets. The Option Data field of this option is 32 bits long and gives the length of the packet in octets, excluding the IPv6 header. For such packets, the Payload Length field in the IPv6 header must be set to zero, and there must be no Fragment header. With this option, IPv6 supports packet sizes up to more than 4 billion octets. This facilitates the transmission of large video packets and enables IPv6 to make the best use of available capacity over any transmission medium.

- **Router alert:** Informs the router that the contents of this packet is of interest to the router and to handle any control data accordingly. The absence of this option in an IPv6 datagram informs the router that the packet does not contain information needed by the router and hence can be safely routed without further packet parsing. Hosts originating IPv6 packets are required to include this option in certain circumstances. The purpose of this option is to provide efficient support for protocols such as RSVP (Chapter 10) that generate packets that need to be examined by intermediate routers for purposes of traffic control. Rather than requiring the intermediate routers to look in detail at the extension headers of a packet, this option alerts the router when such attention is required.

Fragment Header

In IPv6, fragmentation may only be performed by source nodes, not by routers along a packet's delivery path. To take full advantage of the internetworking environment, a node must perform a path discovery algorithm that enables it to learn the smallest maximum transmission unit (MTU) supported by any network on the path. With this knowledge, the source node will fragment, as required, for each given destination address. Otherwise the source must limit all packets to 1280 octets, which is the minimum MTU that must be supported by each network.

The fragment header consists of the following (Figure 8.10b):

- **Next Header (8 bits):** Identifies the type of header immediately following this header.

- **Reserved (8 bits):** For future use.

- **Fragment Offset (13 bits):** Indicates where in the original packet the payload of this fragment belongs. It is measured in 64-bit units. This implies that fragments (other than the last fragment) must contain a data field that is a multiple of 64 bits long.

- **Res (2 bits):** Reserved for future use.

- **M Flag (1 bit):** 1 = more fragments; 0 = last fragment.

- **Identification (32 bits):** Intended to uniquely identify the original packet. The identifier must be unique for the packet's source address and destination address for the time during which the packet will remain in the internet. All fragments with the same identifier, source address, and destination address are reassembled to form the original packet.

The fragmentation algorithm is the same as that described in Section 8.3.

Routing Header

The Routing header contains a list of one or more intermediate nodes to be visited on the way to a packet's destination. All routing headers start with a 32-bit block consisting of four 8-bit fields, followed by routing data specific to a given routing type (Figure 8.10c). The four 8-bit fields are as follows:

- **Next Header:** Identifies the type of header immediately following this header.

- **Header Extension Length:** Length of this header in 64-bit units, not including the first 64 bits.
- **Routing Type:** Identifies a particular Routing header variant. If a router does not recognize the Routing Type value, it must discard the packet.
- **Segments Left:** Number of route segments remaining; that is, the number of explicitly listed intermediate nodes still to be visited before reaching the final destination.

The only specific routing header format defined in RFC 2460 is the Type 0 Routing header (Figure 8.10d). When using the Type 0 Routing header, the source node does not place the ultimate destination address in the IPv6 header. Instead, that address is the last address listed in the Routing header (Address[n] in Figure 8.10d), and the IPv6 header contains the destination address of the first desired router on the path. The Routing header will not be examined until the packet reaches the node identified in the IPv6 header. At that point, the IPv6 and Routing header contents are updated and the packet is forwarded. The update consists of placing the next address to be visited in the IPv6 header and decrementing the Segments Left field in the Routing header.

Destination Options Header

The Destination Options header carries optional information that, if present, is examined only by the packet's destination node. The format of this header is the same as that of the Hop-by-Hop Options header (Figure 8.10a).

8.4 RECOMMENDED READING AND WEB SITES

[RODR02] provides clear coverage of all of the topics in this chapter. Good coverage of internetworking and IPv4 can be found in [COME01] and [STEV94]. [HUIT98] is a straightforward technical description of the various RFCs that together make up the IPv6 specification; the book provides a discussion of the purpose of various features and of the operation of the protocol. [KESH98] provides an instructive look at present and future router functionality. [METZ02] describes the IPv6 anycast feature.

COME01   Comer, D. *Internetworking with TCP/IP, Volume I: Principles, Protocols, and Architecture.* Upper Saddle River, NJ: Prentice Hall, 2001.

HUIT98   Huitema, C. *IPv6: The New Internet Protocol.* Upper Saddle River, NJ: Prentice Hall, 1998.

KESH98   Keshav, S., and Sharma, R. "Issues and Trends in Router Design." *IEEE Communications Magazine*, May 1998.

METZ02   Metz, C. "IP Anycast." *IEEE Internet Computing*, March 2002.

RODR02   Rodriguez, A., et al., *TCP/IP Tutorial and Technical Overview.* Upper Saddle River, NJ: Prentice Hall, 2002.

STEV94   Stevens, W. *TCP/IP Illustrated, Volume 1: The Protocols.* Reading, MA: Addison-Wesley, 1994.

Recommended Web Sites:

- **IPv6:** Information about IPv6 and related topics.
- **IPv6 Information Page:** Includes introductory material, news on recent IPv6 product developments, and related links.
- **IPv6 Forum:** An industry consortium that promotes IPv6-related products. Includes a number of white papers and articles.

8.5 KEY TERMS, REVIEW QUESTIONS, AND PROBLEMS

Key Terms

broadcast	Internet Protocol (IP)	segmentation
datagram lifetime	internetworking	subnet
end system	intranet	subnet mask
fragmentation	IPv4	subnetwork
intermediate system	IPv6	traffic class
Internet	multicast	unicast
Internet Control Message	reassembly	
Protocol (ICMP)	router	

Review Questions

8.1 Give some reasons for using fragmentation and reassembly.

8.2 List the requirements for an internetworking facility.

8.3 What are the pros and cons of limiting reassembly to the endpoint as compared to allowing en route reassembly.

8.4 Explain the function of the three flags in the IPv4 header.

8.5 How is the IPv4 header checksum calculated?

8.6 What is the difference between the traffic class and flow label fields in the IPv6 header?

8.7 Briefly explain the three types of IPv6 addresses.

8.8 What is the purpose of each of the IPv6 header types?

Problems

8.1 In the discussion of IP, it was mentioned that the *identifier, don't fragment identifier*, and *time to live* parameters are present in the Send primitive but not in the Deliver primitive because they are only of concern to IP. For each of these parameters indicate whether it is of concern to the IP entity in the source, the IP entities in any intermediate routers, and the IP entity in the destination end systems. Justify your answer.

8.2 What is the header overhead in the IP protocol?

8.3 Describe some circumstances where it might be desirable to use source routing rather than let the routers make the routing decision.

8.4 Because of fragmentation, an IP datagram can arrive in several pieces, not necessarily in the correct order. The IP entity at the receiving end system must accumulate these fragments until the original datagram is reconstituted.

    a. Consider that the IP entity creates a buffer for assembling the data field in the original datagram. As assembly proceeds, the buffer will contain blocks of data and "holes" between the data blocks. Describe an algorithm for reassembly based on this concept.

    b. For the algorithm in part (a), it is necessary to keep track of the holes. Describe a simple mechanism for doing this.

8.5 A 4480-octet datagram is to be transmitted and needs to be fragmented because it will pass through an Ethernet with a maximum payload of 1500 octets. Show the Total Length, More Flag, and Fragment Offset values in each of the resulting fragments.

8.6 The IP checksum needs to be recalculated at routers because of changes to the IP header, such as the lifetime field. It is possible to recalculate the checksum from scratch. Suggest a procedure that involves less calculation. *Hint:* Suppose that the value in octet k is changed by $Z = \text{new\_value} - \text{old\_value}$; consider the effect of this change on the checksum.

8.7 An IP datagram is to be fragmented. Which options in the option field need to be copied into the header of each fragment, and which need only be retained in the first fragment? Justify the handling of each option.

8.8 A transport layer message consisting of 1500 bits of data and 160 bits of header is sent to an internet layer, which appends another 160 bits of header. This is then transmitted through two networks, each of which uses a 24-bit packet header. The destination network has a maximum packet size of 800 bits. How many bits, including headers, are delivered to the network-layer protocol at the destination?

8.9 The architecture suggested by Figure 8.3 is to be used. What functions could be added to the routers to alleviate some of the problems caused by the mismatched local and long-haul networks?

8.10 Should internetworking be concerned with a network's internal routing? Why or why not?

8.11 Compare the individual fields of the IPv4 header with the IPv6 header. Account for the functionality provided by each IPv4 field by showing how the same functionality is provided in IPv6.

8.12 Justify the recommended order in which IPv6 extension headers appear (i.e., why is the Hop-by-Hop Options header first, why is the Routing header before the Fragment header, and so on).

8.13 For Type 0 IPv6 routing, specify the algorithm for updating the IPv6 and Routing headers by intermediate nodes.

CHAPTER 9

INTEGRATED AND DIFFERENTIATED SERVICES

Real-Time Traffic Characteristics
Requirements for Real-Time Communication
Hard versus Soft Real-Time Applications

The organization for the control and guidance of the trade should therefore be of so complete a character that the trade may be either dispersed about the ocean or concentrated along particular routes; or in some places dispersed and in others concentrated; and that changes from one policy to the other can be made when necessary at any time.
—*The World Crisis,*
Winston Churchill

KEY POINTS

- The integrated services architecture is a response to the growing variety and volume of traffic experienced in the Internet and intranets. It provides a framework for the development of protocols such as RSVP to handle multimedia/multicast traffic and provides guidance to router vendors on the development of efficient techniques for handling a varied load.

- An important component of an ISA implementation is the queuing discipline used at the routers. The use of multiple queues with different dispatching disciplines can improve service.

- Another approach to congestion management in internets is proactive packet discard. In this technique, a router discards one or more incoming packets before the output buffer is completely full, in order to improve the performance of the network. The most important example of proactive packet discard is known as random early detection (RED).

- The differentiated services architecture is designed to provide a simple, easy-to-implement, low-overhead tool to support a range of network services that are differentiated on the basis of performance. Differentiated services are provided on the basis of a 6-bit label in the IP header, which classifies traffic in terms of the type of service to be given by routers for that traffic.

- As part of the DS standardization effort, specific types of per-hop behavior (PHB) need to be defined, which can be associated with specific differentiated services. The PHB indicates how various traffic flows are to be handled.

As the Internet and private internets grow in scale, a host of new demands march steadily into view. Low-volume TELNET conversations are leapfrogged by high-volume client/server applications. To this has more recently been added the tremendous volume of Web traffic, which is increasingly graphics intensive. Now real-time voice and video applications add to the burden.

To cope with these demands, it is not enough to increase internet capacity. Sensible and effective methods for managing the traffic and controlling congestion are needed. This is the focus of this chapter. In recent years, two different, complementary traffic management frameworks have emerged from the IETF standards process: integrated services (IS) and differentiated services (DS).

In essence, an IS framework is concerned with providing an integrated, or collective, service to the set of traffic demands placed on a given domain (e.g., a portion of the Internet that implements a particular instance of the integrated services architecture). We can think of the IS provider as consisting of the network elements within the domain. The IS provider views the totality of the current traffic demand and (1) limits the demand that is satisfied to that which can be handled by the current capacity of the network and (2) reserves resources within the domain to provide a particular QoS (quality of service) to particular portions of the satisfied demand.

In contrast, a DS framework does not attempt to view the total traffic demand in any overall or integrated sense, nor does it attempt to reserve network capacity in advance. Rather, in the DS framework, traffic is classified into a number of traffic groups. Each group is labeled appropriately, and the service provided by network elements depends on group membership, with packets belonging to different groups being handled differently.

The chapter begins with a look at the Integrated Services Architecture (ISA). ISA is the specific framework within which IS are offered. The chapter then covers important resource allocation and congestion control mechanisms in the areas of queuing discipline and packet discard policy that can be incorporated into an IS framework. Finally, we look at DS.

9.1 INTEGRATED SERVICES ARCHITECTURE (ISA)

Historically, IP-based internets have been able to provide a simple best-effort delivery service to all applications they carry. Although the IPv4 header is equipped with fields that can specify precedence and type of service, this information has generally been ignored by routers, both in the selection of routes and the treatment of individual packets.

But the needs of users have changed. A company may have spent millions of dollars installing an IP-based internet designed to transport data among LANs but now finds that new real-time, multimedia, and multicasting applications are not well supported by such a configuration. The only networking scheme designed from day one to support both traditional TCP and UDP traffic and real-time traffic is ATM. However, reliance on ATM means either constructing a second networking infrastructure for real-time traffic or replacing the existing IP-based configuration with ATM, both of which are costly alternatives.

Thus, there is a strong need to be able to support a variety of traffic, with a variety of QoS requirements, within the TCP/IP architecture. However, the fundamental requirement is to add new functionality to routers and a means for requesting QoS-based service from internets. To meet this requirement, the IETF is developing a suite of standards under the general umbrella of the Integrated Services Architecture (ISA). ISA, intended to provide QoS transport over IP-based internets, is defined in overall terms in RFC 1633, while other documents fill in the details. A number of vendors have implemented portions of the ISA in routers and end-system software.

This section provides an overview of ISA.

Internet Traffic

Traffic on a network or internet can be divided into two broad categories: elastic and inelastic. A consideration of their differing requirements clarifies the need for an enhanced internet architecture.

Elastic Traffic Elastic traffic is that which can adjust, over wide ranges, to changes in delay and throughput across an internet and still meet the needs of its applications. This is the traditional type of traffic supported on TCP/IP-based internets and is the type of traffic for which internets were designed. Applications that generate such traffic typically use TCP or UDP as a transport protocol. In the case of UDP, the application will use as much capacity as is available up to the rate that the application generates data. In the case of TCP, the application will use as much capacity as is available up to the maximum rate that the end-to-end receiver can accept data. Also with TCP, traffic on individual connections adjusts to congestion by reducing the rate at which data are presented to the network; this involves the RTT (round-trip time) backoff and slow-start mechanisms described in Section 7.2.

Applications that can be classified as elastic include the common applications that operate over TCP or UDP, such as file transfer (FTP), electronic mail (SMTP), remote logon (TELNET), network management (SNMP), and Web access (HTTP). There are differences among the requirements of these applications. For example,

- E-mail is generally quite insensitive to changes in delay.
- When file transfer is done online, as it frequently is, the user expects the delay to be proportional to the file size and so is sensitive to changes in throughput.
- With network management, delay is generally not a serious concern. However, if failures in an internet are the cause of congestion, then the need for SNMP messages to get through with minimum delay increases with increased congestion.
- Interactive applications, such as remote logon and Web access, are quite sensitive to delay.

It is important to realize that it is not per-packet delay that is the quantity of interest. As noted in [CLAR95], observation of real delays across the Internet suggest that wide variations in delay do not occur. Because of the congestion control mechanisms in TCP, when congestion develops, delays only increase modestly before the arrival rate from the various TCP connections slow down. Instead, the QoS perceived by the user relates to the total elapsed time to transfer an element of the current application. For an interactive TELNET-based application, the element may be a single keystroke or single line. For a Web access, the element is a Web page, which could be as little as a few kilobytes or could be substantially larger for an image-rich page. For a scientific application, the element could be many megabytes of data.

For very small elements, the total elapsed time is dominated by the delay time across the internet. However, for larger elements, the total elapsed time is dictated by the sliding-window performance of TCP and is therefore dominated by the throughput achieved over the TCP connection. Thus, for large transfers, the transfer time is proportional to the size of the file and the degree to which the source slows due to congestion.

It should be clear that even if we confine our attention to elastic traffic, a QoS-based internet service could be of benefit. Without such a service, routers are dealing evenhandedly with arriving IP packets, with no concern for the type of application and whether this packet is part of a large transfer element or a small one. Under such circumstances, and if congestion develops, it is unlikely that resources will be allocated in such a way as to meet the needs of all applications fairly. When inelastic traffic is added to the mix, matters are even more unsatisfactory.

Inelastic Traffic Inelastic traffic does not easily adapt, if at all, to changes in delay and throughput across an internet. The prime example is real-time traffic, which is discussed in Appendix 9A. The requirements for inelastic traffic may include the following:

- **Throughput:** A minimum throughput value may be required. Unlike most elastic traffic, which can continue to deliver data with perhaps degraded service, many inelastic applications absolutely require a given minimum throughput.
- **Delay:** An example of a delay-sensitive application is stock trading; someone who consistently receives later service will consistently act later, and with greater disadvantage.
- **Jitter:** As explained in Appendix 9A, the magnitude of delay variation is a critical factor in real-time applications. The larger the allowable delay variation, the longer the real delay in delivering the data and the greater the size of the delay buffer required at receivers. Real-time interactive applications, such as teleconferencing, may require a reasonable upper bound on jitter.
- **Packet loss:** Real-time applications vary in the amount of packet loss, if any, that they can sustain.

These requirements are difficult to meet in an environment with variable queuing delays and congestion losses. Accordingly, inelastic traffic introduces two new requirements into the internet architecture. First, some means are needed to give preferential treatment to applications with more demanding requirements. Applications need to be able to state their requirements, either ahead of time in some sort of service request function or on the fly, by means of fields in the IP packet header. The former approach provides more flexibility in stating requirements, and it enables the network to anticipate demands and deny new requests if the required resources are unavailable. This approach implies the use of some sort of resource reservation protocol.

A second requirement in supporting inelastic traffic in an internet architecture is that elastic traffic must still be supported. Inelastic applications typically do not back off and reduce demand in the face of congestion, in contrast to TCP-based applications. Therefore, in times of congestion, inelastic traffic will continue to supply a high load, and elastic traffic will be crowded off the internet. A reservation protocol can help control this situation by denying service requests that would leave too few resources available to handle current elastic traffic.

ISA Approach

The purpose of ISA is to enable the provision of QoS support over IP-based internets. The central design issue for ISA is how to share the available capacity in times of congestion.

For an IP-based internet that provides only a best-effort service, the tools for controlling congestion and providing service are limited. In essence, routers have two mechanisms to work with:

- **Routing algorithm:** Most routing protocols in use in internets allow routes to be selected to minimize delay. Routers exchange information to get a picture of the delays throughout the internet. Minimum-delay routing helps to balance loads, thus decreasing local congestion, and helps to reduce delays seen by individual TCP connections.

- **Packet discard:** When a router's buffer overflows, it discards packets. Typically, the most recent packet is discarded. The effect of lost packets on a TCP connection is that the sending TCP entity backs off and reduces its load, thus helping to alleviate internet congestion.

These tools have worked reasonably well, especially with the refinements in TCP congestion control techniques described in Section 7.2. However, as the discussion in the preceding subsection shows, such techniques are inadequate for the variety of traffic now coming to internets.

ISA is an overall architecture within which a number of enhancements to the traditional best-effort mechanisms are being developed. In ISA, each IP packet can be associated with a flow. RFC 1633 defines a flow as a distinguishable stream of related IP packets that results from a single user activity and requires the same QoS. For example, a flow might consist of one transport connection or one video stream distinguishable by the ISA. A flow differs from a TCP connection in two respects: A flow is unidirectional, and there can be more than one recipient of a flow (multicast). Typically, an IP packet is identified as a member of a flow on the basis of source and destination IP addresses and port numbers, and protocol type. The flow identifier in the IPv6 header is not necessarily equivalent to an ISA flow, but in the future the IPv6 flow identifier could be used in ISA.

ISA makes use of the following functions to manage congestion and provide QoS transport:

- **Admission control:** For QoS transport (other than default best-effort transport), ISA requires that a reservation be made for a new flow. If the routers collectively determine that there are insufficient resources to guarantee the requested QoS, then the flow is not admitted. The protocol RSVP, discussed in Chapter 10, is used to make reservations.

- **Routing algorithm:** The routing decision may be based on a variety of QoS parameters, not just minimum delay. For example, the routing protocol OSPF (Chapter 11) can select routes based on QoS.

- **Queuing discipline:** A vital element of the ISA is an effective queuing policy that takes into account the differing requirements of different flows. Queuing policies are discussed in Section 9.2.

- **Discard policy:** A queuing policy determines which packet to transmit next if a number of packets are queued for the same output port. A separate issue is the choice and timing of packet discards. A discard policy can be an important element in managing congestion and meeting QoS guarantees. Discard policies are discussed in Section 9.3.

ISA Components

Figure 9.1 is a general depiction of the implementation architecture for ISA within a router. Below the thick horizontal line are the forwarding functions of the router; these are executed for each packet and therefore must be highly optimized. The remaining functions, above the line, are background functions that create data structures used by the forwarding functions.

The principal background functions are as follows:

- **Reservation protocol:** This protocol is used among routers and between routers and end systems to reserve resources for a new flow at a given level of QoS. The reservation protocol is responsible for maintaining flow-specific state information at the end systems and at the routers along the path of the flow. The RSVP protocol described in Chapter 10 is used for this purpose. The reservation protocol updates the traffic control database used by the packet scheduler to determine the service provided for packets of each flow.

- **Admission control:** When a new flow is requested, the reservation protocol invokes the admission control function. This function determines if sufficient resources are available for this flow at the requested QoS. This determination

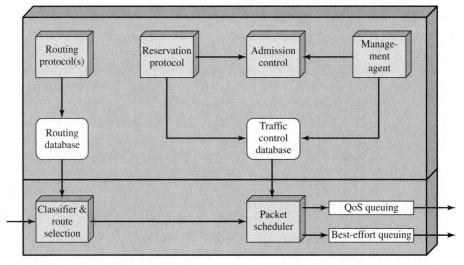

Figure 9.1   Integrated Services Architecture Implemented in Router

is based on the current level of commitment to other reservations and/or on the current load on the network.

- **Management agent:** A network management agent is able to modify the traffic control database and to direct the admission control module in order to set admission control policies.

- **Routing protocol:** The routing protocol is responsible for maintaining a routing database that gives the next hop to be taken for each destination address and each flow.

These background functions support the main task of the router, which is the forwarding of packets. The two principal functional areas that accomplish forwarding are as follows:

- **Classifier and route selection:** For the purposes of forwarding and traffic control, incoming packets must be mapped into classes. A class may correspond to a single flow or to a set of flows with the same QoS requirements. For example, the packets of all video flows or the packets of all flows attributable to a particular organization may be treated identically for purposes of resource allocation and queuing discipline. The selection of class is based on fields in the IP header. Based on the packet's class and its destination IP address, this function determines the next-hop address for this packet.

- **Packet scheduler:** This function manages one or more queues for each output port. It determines the order in which queued packets are transmitted and the selection of packets for discard, if necessary. Decisions are made based on a packet's class, the contents of the traffic control database, and current and past activity on this outgoing port. Part of the packet scheduler's task is that of policing, which is the function of determining whether the packet traffic in a given flow exceeds the requested capacity and, if so, deciding how to treat the excess packets.

ISA Services

ISA service for a flow of packets is defined on two levels. First, a number of general categories of service are provided, each of which provides a certain general type of service guarantees. Second, within each category, the service for a particular flow is specified by the values of certain parameters; together, these values are referred to as a traffic specification (TSpec). Currently, three categories of service are defined:

- Guaranteed
- Controlled Load
- Best effort

An application can request a reservation for a flow for a guaranteed or controlled load QoS, with a TSpec that define the exact amount of service required. If the reservation is accepted, then the TSpec is part of the contract between the data flow and the service. The service agrees to provide the requested QoS as long as the flow's data traffic continues to be described accurately by the TSpec. Packets that are not part of a reserved flow are by default given a best-effort delivery service.

Before looking at the ISA service categories, one general concept should be defined: the token bucket traffic specification. This is a way of characterizing traffic that has three advantages in the context of ISA:

1. Many traffic sources can be defined easily and accurately by a token bucket scheme.

2. The token bucket scheme provides a concise description of the load to be imposed by a flow, enabling the service to determine easily the resource requirement.

3. The token bucket scheme provides the input parameters to a policing function.

A token bucket traffic specification consists of two parameters: a token replenishment rate R and a bucket size B. The token rate R specifies the continually sustainable data rate; that is, over a relatively long period of time, the average data rate to be supported for this flow is R. The bucket size B specifies the amount by which the data rate can exceed R for short periods of time. The exact condition is as follows: during any time period T, the amount of data sent cannot exceed $RT + B$.

Figure 9.2 illustrates this scheme and explains the use of the term *bucket*. The bucket represents a counter that indicates the allowable number of octets of IP data that can be sent at any time. The bucket fills with *octet tokens* at the rate of R (i.e., the counter is incremented R times per second), up to the bucket capacity (up to the maximum counter value). IP packets arrive and are queued for processing. An IP

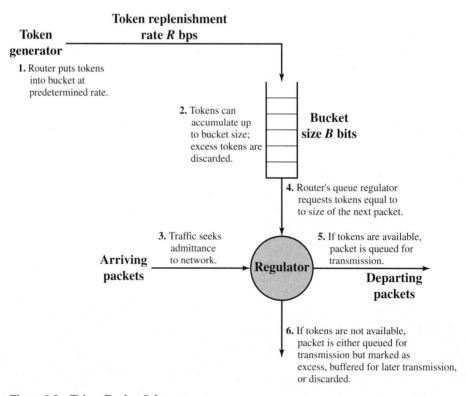

Figure 9.2 Token Bucket Scheme

packet may be processed if there are sufficient octet tokens to match the IP data size. If so, the packet is processed and the bucket is drained of the corresponding number of tokens. If a packet arrives and there are insufficient tokens available, then the packet exceeds the TSpec for this flow. The treatment for such packets is not specified in the ISA documents; common actions are relegating the packet to best-effort service, discarding the packet, or marking the packet in such a way that it may be discarded in future.

Over the long run, the rate of IP data allowed by the token bucket is R. However, if there is an idle or relatively slow period, the bucket capacity builds up, so that at most an additional B octets above the stated rate can be accepted. Thus, B is a measure of the degree of burstiness of the data flow that is allowed.

Guaranteed Service The key elements of the guaranteed service are as follows:

1. The service provides assured capacity level, or data rate.
2. There is a specified upper bound on the queuing delay through the network. This must be added to the propagation delay, or latency, to arrive at the bound on total delay through the network.
3. There are no queuing losses. That is, no packets are lost due to buffer overflow; packets may be lost due to failures in the network or changes in routing paths.

With this service, an application provides a characterization of its expected traffic profile, and the service determines the end-to-end delay that it can guarantee.

One category of applications for this service is those that need an upper bound on delay so that a delay buffer can be used for real-time playback of incoming data and that do not tolerate packet losses because of the degradation in the quality of the output. Another example is applications with hard real-time deadlines.

The guaranteed service is the most demanding service provided by ISA. Because the delay bound is firm, the delay has to be set at a large value to cover rare cases of long queuing delays.

Controlled Load The key elements of the controlled load service are as follows:

1. The service tightly approximates the behavior visible to applications receiving best-effort service under unloaded conditions.
2. There is no specified upper bound on the queuing delay through the network. However, the service ensures that a very high percentage of the packets do not experience delays that greatly exceed the minimum transit delay (i.e., the delay due to propagation time plus router processing time with no queuing delays).
3. A very high percentage of transmitted packets will be successfully delivered (i.e., almost no queuing loss).

As was mentioned, the risk in an internet that provides QoS for real-time applications is that best-effort traffic is crowded out. This is because best-effort types of applications employ TCP, which will back off in the face of congestion and delays. The controlled load service guarantees that the network will set aside sufficient resources so that an application that receives this service will see a network that responds as if these real-time applications were not present and competing for resources.

The controlled service is useful for applications that have been referred to as adaptive real-time applications [CLAR92]. Such applications do not require an a priori upper bound on the delay through the network. Rather, the receiver measures the jitter experienced by incoming packets and sets the playback point to the minimum delay that still produces a sufficiently low loss rate. For example, video can be adaptive by dropping a frame or delaying the output stream slightly; voice can be adaptive by adjusting silent periods (e.g., see [RAMJ94]).

9.2 QUEUING DISCIPLINE[1]

An important component of an ISA implementation is the queuing discipline used at the routers. Routers traditionally have used a first-in, first-out (FIFO) queuing discipline, also known as first-come, first-served (FCFS), at each output port. A single queue is maintained at each output port. When a new packet arrives and is routed to an output port, it is placed at the end of the queue. As long as the queue is not empty, the router transmits packets from the queue, taking the oldest remaining packet next.

There are several drawbacks to the FIFO queuing discipline:

1. No special treatment is given to packets from flows that are of higher priority or are more delay sensitive. If a number of packets from different flows are ready to forward, they are handled strictly in FIFO order.

2. If a number of smaller packets are queued behind a long packet, then FIFO queuing results in a larger average delay per packet than if the shorter packets were transmitted before the longer packet. In general, flows of larger packets get better service.

3. A greedy TCP connection can crowd out more altruistic connections. If congestion occurs and one TCP connection fails to back off, other connections along the same path segment must back off more than they would otherwise have to do.

Fair Queuing (FQ)

To overcome some of the drawbacks of FIFO queuing, Nagle proposed a scheme called fair queuing [NAGL87]. In this scheme, a router maintains multiple queues at each output port. Nagle suggested maintaining one queue for each source (Figure 9.3); it would also be possible to maintain one queue for each flow.

With fair queuing, each incoming packet is placed in the appropriate queue. The queues are serviced in round-robin fashion, taking one packet from each nonempty queue in turn. Empty queues are skipped over.

This scheme is fair in that each busy flow gets to send exactly one packet per cycle. Further, this is a form of load balancing among the various flows. Also note that there is no advantage in being greedy. A greedy flow finds that its queues become long, increasing its delays, whereas other flows are unaffected by this behavior.

---

[1]This section is more difficult than the remainder of the chapter and may be skipped on a first reading.

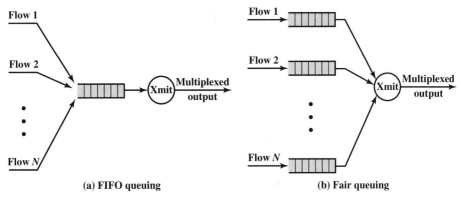

(a) FIFO queuing   (b) Fair queuing

Figure 9.3   FIFO and Fair Queuing

Processor Sharing (PS)

A serious drawback to the fair queuing scheme is that short packets are penalized: More capacity goes to flows with longer average packet size compared to flows with shorter average packet size. The reason for this is that each queue transmits one packet per cycle.

This disadvantage is overcome with bit-round fair queuing (BRFQ), which uses packet length as well as flow identification to schedule packets; this technique is described in [DEME90].

To understand BRFQ, let us first consider an ideal policy that is not practical to implement. Set up the multiple queues, as in FQ, but now transmit only one bit from each queue on each round. In this way, longer packets no longer receive an advantage, and each busy source receives exactly the same amount of capacity. In particular, if there are N queues and each of the queues always has a packet to send, then each queue receives exactly $1/N$ of the available capacity.

This bit-by-bit approach is known as processor sharing (PS). To understand what follows, it will be useful to define some terms:

$R(t)$ = number of rounds in the PS service discipline that have occurred up to time t, normalized to the output data rate

$N(t)$ = number of nonempty queues at time t

P_i^α = transmission time for packet i in queue α, normalized to the output data rate

τ_i^α = arrival time for packet i in queue α

S_i^α = value of $R(t)$ when packet i in queue α begins transmission

F_i^α = value of $R(t)$ when packet i in queue α ends transmission

We can think of $R(t)$ as a virtual time, which records the rate of service seen by the packet at the head of a queue. An equivalent definition is as follows:

$$R'(t) = \frac{d}{dt}R(t) = \frac{1}{\max[1, N(t)]}$$

As an example, consider three queues with a traffic pattern characterized by the following table:

| | Queue α | | Queue β | | Queue γ |
	Packet 1	Packet 2	Packet 1	Packet 2	Packet 1
Real arrival time τ_i	0	2	1	2	3
Transmission time P_i	3	1	1	4	3
Virtual start time S_i	0	3	1	2	2
Virtual finish time F_i	3	4	2	6	5

The values of τ_i and P_i are given; the values of S_i and F_i are determined by the PS queuing policy. The thin black solid lines in Figure 9.4 show the service provided to the three queues. The first packet to arrive at queue α receives one unit of service in the real interval $[0, 1]$, with the virtual time $R(1) = 1$ at the end of that interval.

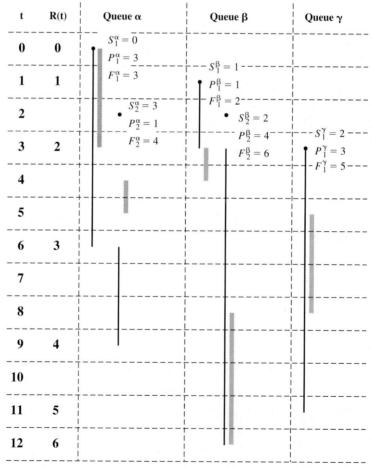

Figure 9.4 Example of PS and BRFQ (Based on [GREE92])

In the real interval $[1, 3]$, bits are being transmitted from two queues, so each receives a service rate of $R' = 1/2$ and accumulates one unit of service in this interval, so that $R(3) = R(1) + 1/2 \times (3 - 1) = 2$. Similarly, in the interval $[3, 9]$, all three queues are active, so each receives service at rate $R' = 1/3$ and accumulates two units of service in this interval. This is enough service for two packets to be completely transmitted from α and one packet from β; an additional packet from β, and one packet from γ are in progress at $t = 9$.

The following recurrence relationships summarize how the PS system evolves in virtual time:

$$\begin{aligned} F_i^\alpha &= S_i^\alpha + P_i^\alpha \\ S_i^\alpha &= \max[F_{i-1}^\alpha, R(\tau_i^\alpha)] \end{aligned} \tag{9.1}$$

Note that from these equations, we can compute a packet's virtual finishing time the moment it arrives. However, we cannot compute the packet's real finishing time on its arrival because the real finishing time depends on future arrivals.

Bit-Round Fair Queuing (BRFQ)

We wish to transmit entire packets rather than individual bits. BRFQ is designed to emulate a bit-by-bit round-robin discipline. BRFQ is implemented by computing virtual starting and finishing times on the fly as if PS were running. The BRFQ rule is simply this: Whenever a packet finishes transmission, the next packet sent is the one with the smallest value of F_i^α.

PS and BRFQ are compared in Figure 9.4. The solid lines represent the transmission times under PS, and the gray bars represent BRFQ transmission. Note that the order of transmission of packets, based on either real start time or real finish time, is not exactly the same for BRFQ and PS. Nevertheless, BRFQ gives a good approximation to the performance of PS. In fact, it is demonstrated in [GREE92] that the throughput and average delay experienced by each flow under BRFQ converge to that under PS as time increases.

Figure 9.5a shows timing diagrams of three flows at a router output port. In the first three rows, vertical arrows denote the arrival times of packets, with length proportional to packet size. The packets arriving on flow 1 are twice as long as those on the other flows. The next three rows show the packet transmission times under various queuing disciplines.[2] The shading is provided simply to clarify the relationship between the arrival timing diagrams and the transmission timing diagrams. In this case, both FIFO and FQ yield the same output pattern. BRFQ provides the same amount of service to all flows as do the other disciplines, but when multiple packets arrive at the same time, preference is given to short packets. Accordingly, flows 2 and 3 experience lower average delay than under FIFO or FQ.

In Figure 9.5b, an additional flow is added, so that the router cannot keep up with the demand. Delays will increase as the queue lengths grow. If all of the sources are well-behaved TCP entities, then the flows will back off and congestion eases. Meanwhile, differences are apparent among the different policies. Under FIFO, the

---

[2]We will use the convention that ties are resolved in favor of the flow with the smallest flow number.

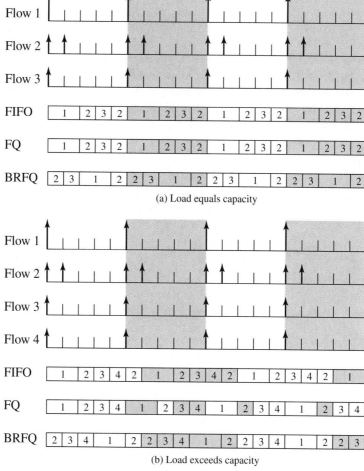

Figure 9.5 Comparison of FIFO and Fair Queuing

delays experienced by all flows uniformly grow at a rate of one time unit every five time units. With fair queuing, only flow 2 is penalized; all other flows experience no increase in delay. Consequently, the queue for flow 2 is the only one that grows. Eventually, flow 2 will detect the growing delay and back off. In one sense, this is fair, because each flow is allowed to send one packet per cycle. But the demand from flow 1 and flow 2 is in fact identical, and flow 1 gains an advantage because it uses larger packets. BRFQ instead is fair on the basis of amount of data transmitted rather than number of packets transmitted. Like FIFO, BRFQ causes all delays to increase, but in the case of BRFQ, smaller packets are given preference.

Generalized Processor Sharing (GPS)

BRFQ is an improvement over FQ or FIFO in that it fairly allocates the available capacity among all active flows through a node. However, it is not able to provide different amounts of the capacity to different flows. To support QoS transport, this differential allocation capability is needed. The approach that has received the widest acceptance is an enhancement of BRFQ known as weighted fair queuing (WFQ).[3] Again, it will clarify the description if we first look at a bit-by-bit round-robin version.

To take into account the differing demands of different sources, we can generalize the PS discipline to allow for arbitrary capacity allocations. With GPS, each flow α is assigned a weight ϕ_α that determines how many bits are transmitted from that queue during each round. Thus, if the weight for a given flow is 5, then during each round that the queue is nonempty, 5 bits will be transmitted. Some thought should convince you that we can model this process by modifying Equation (9.1) as follows:

$$F_i^\alpha = S_i^\alpha + \frac{P_i^\alpha}{\phi_\alpha}$$

$$S_i^\alpha = \max[F_{i-1}^\alpha, R(\tau_i^\alpha)] \tag{9.2}$$

In effect, we set the effective packet length to $1/\phi_\alpha$ times the true packet length. It is easy to see that, at any given time, the service rate g_i for a nonempty flow i is

$$g_i = \frac{\phi_i}{\displaystyle\sum_j \phi_j} C \tag{9.3}$$

where the sum is taken over all active queues and C is the outgoing link data rate.

GPS is attractive because it provides a means of responding to different service requests. If a source requests a given service rate g_i for a flow, then the node can grant the request if sufficient capacity is available and can assign the proper weight to guarantee the service. Equally important, GPS provides a way of guaranteeing that delays for a well-behaved flow do not exceed some bound. Consider a set of flows that are defined by, and limited to, the token bucket specification described in Section 9.1, where B_i and R_i are the bucket size and token rate, respectively, for flow i. Now let the weight assigned to each flow equal the token rate; that is, $\phi_i = R_i$. Then the maximum delay experienced by flow i, D_i, is bounded by

$$D_i \leq \frac{B_i}{R_i} \tag{9.4}$$

The proof of this is given in [PARE94]; here we give an intuitive argument. Assume a situation in which all of the flows have been low or idle for some time and that all of the buckets are full. Then all of the flows begin to transmit at the maximum rate. The network is configured, by reservation, to handle the maximum rate R_i from each flow. At this rate, tokens are added to the bucket as fast as they are drained. If the node keeps up with the flow, then the queue length at the node will not exceed the bucket size. So the delay experienced by the flow through the node will not exceed the bucket size divided by the token rate, which is Equation (9.4).

---

[3]The concept of WFQ was first introduced in [DEME90]; it is briefly mentioned in that paper, with no analysis, and the term *WFQ* is not used. The first rigorous analysis of WFQ is reported in [PARE93] and [PARE94], where it is referred to as *packet-by-packet generalized processor sharing* (PGPS).

Weighted Fair Queuing (WFQ)

Again, we wish to transmit entire packets rather than individual bits. Just as BRFQ emulates the bit-by-bit PS, WFQ emulates the bit-by-bit GPS. The strategy is the same: whenever a packet finishes transmission, the next packet sent is the one with the smallest value of F_i^α. In this case, Equation (9.2) governs the calculation of F_i^α.

Figure 9.6, based on examples in [ZHAN95], illustrates the action of WFQ and compares it to FIFO. All packets have the same size of 1 and the link speed is 1. The guaranteed rate for connection 1 is 0.5 and the guaranteed rate for the other 10 connections is 0.05. In the upper example, flow 1 sends 11 back-to-back packets starting at time 0 and the other flows send a single packet at time 0. Under FIFO, one packet from each flow is transmitted and then the remaining 10 packets of flow 1.[4] Under WFQ, because the first ten packets of flow 1 all have PS finish times smaller than packets on other connections, the node will transmit these packets first. In both cases, each flow receives the guaranteed flow rate over the interval of 20 time units, but the relative delays suffered are changed to favor flow 1 in WFQ. The lower part

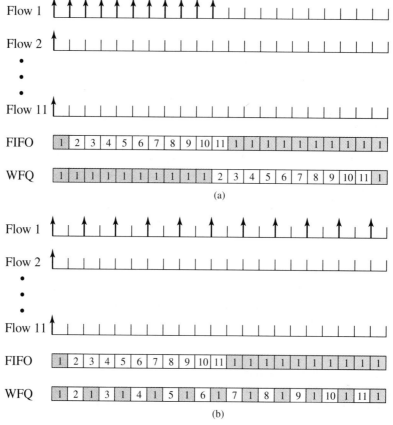

Figure 9.6 Comparison of FIFO and WFQ

---

[4]Note that the same result is achieved with FQ. This is also true in part (b) of the figure.

of the example is more revealing. Here, the packets from flow 1 arrive uniformly at the desired rate. Under FIFO, all but the first packet are substantially delayed because of other traffic that should be getting a smaller portion of capacity. WFQ closely approximates giving a uniform and appropriate amount of service to each flow.

It was pointed out that GPS is attractive because it enables a router to assign the appropriate weight to each flow to guarantee service and because it is possible to guarantee an upper bound on delay. These qualities carry over to the WFQ approximation to GPS. In this case, Equation (9.4) must be modified as follows:

$$D_i \leq \frac{B_i}{R_i} + \frac{(K_i - 1)L_i}{R_i} + \sum_{m=1}^{K_i} \frac{L_{\max}}{C_m} \qquad (9.5)$$

where

D_i = maximum delay experienced by flow i

B_i = token bucket size for flow i

R_i = token rate for flow i

K_i = number of nodes in the path flow i through the internet

L_i = maximum packet size for flow i

$L_{\max}$ = maximum packet length for all flows through all nodes on the path of flow i

C_m = outgoing link capacity at node m

The first term carries over from the GPS case and accounts for delay due to bucket size, which is the same as delay due to burstiness. The second term is proportional to the delay experienced at each node for each packet by this flow. The final term reflects the consequence of packet-by-packet rather than bit-by-bit transmission. Again, we give an intuitive explanation. In both BRFQ and WFQ, a packet may leave some time later than it would have under bit-by-bit processing (PS or GPS). The reason is that the node can only choose for transmission among all the packets that have already arrived. If the next packet chosen is relatively large and a small packet arrives during this transmission, it may be that under GPS, this small packet has the earliest finish time and therefore should have been transmitted first under WFQ. Because it did not arrive, it was not transmitted and has to be delayed up to at most the full length of the longest packet that moves through this node.

Equation (9.5) is important in the design of an ISA. It says that there is an easy way to set parameters in a router to guarantee a given rate of service. Further, at this rate, an upper bound on delay can be granted to the user. Finally, [PARE94] shows that the maximum queue size needed at each node is proportional to the maximum delay defined in Equation (9.5); in particular, it approaches $g_i D_i$. Thus, the node can easily determine the resources required to grant a particular reservation.

9.3 RANDOM EARLY DETECTION

Another approach to congestion management in internets is proactive packet discard. In this technique, a router discards one or more incoming packets before the output buffer is completely full, in order to improve the performance of the network. This technique is designed for use on a single FIFO queue and so can be used in any internet architecture. In the context of ISA, proactive packet discard can be exercised on one or more queues for elastic traffic at each router to improve the performance provided to the elastic traffic.

The most important example of proactive packet discard is known as random early detection (RED), introduced in [FLOY93]. RED has already been implemented by a number of vendors. In this section, we look first at the motivation and objectives for RED and then examine its design.

Motivation

When there is a surge of congestion on a network, router buffers fill up and routers begin to drop packets. For TCP traffic, this is a signal to enter the slow start phase, which reduces the load on the network and relieves the congestion. There are two difficulties with this scenario. First, lost packets must be retransmitted, adding to the load on the network and imposing significant delays on the TCP flows. More serious is the phenomenon termed *global synchronization*. With a traffic burst, queues fill up and a number of packets are dropped. The likely result is that many TCP connections are affected and enter slow start. This causes a dramatic drop in network traffic, so that for a time the network is unnecessarily underutilized. Because many TCP connections entered slow start at about the same time, they will come out of slow start at about the same time, causing another big burst and another cycle of feast and famine.

One solution is to use bigger buffers at each router to reduce the probability of dropping packets. This is a bad solution for two reasons. First, as these big buffers fill up, the delays suffered by all connections increase dramatically. Worse, if the traffic is self-similar, which it very well might be, in essence you cannot build buffers big enough: Big bursts arrive one after another so that congestion is sustained and the buffer requirements grow.

A better solution would be to anticipate the onset of congestion and tell one TCP connection at a time to slow down. Then measure the effect of that one slowdown before, if necessary, slowing down another connection. In this fashion, as congestion begins, the brakes are gradually applied to reduce traffic load gently, with minimal impact on TCP connections and without global synchronization. RED provides this solution.

RED Design Goals

[FLOY93] lists the following design goals for RED:

- **Congestion avoidance:** RED is designed to avoid congestion rather than react to it. Thus, RED must detect the onset of congestion to maintain the network in a region of low delay and high throughput.

- **Global synchronization avoidance:** When the onset of congestion is recognized, the router must decide which connection or connections to notify to back off. In current implementations, this notification is implicit and provided by dropping packets. By detecting congestion early and notifying only as many connections as necessary, global synchronization is avoided.

- **Avoidance of bias against bursty traffic:** The onset of congestion is likely to occur with the arrival of a burst of traffic from one or a few sources. This burst adds to the burden already supported at the router. If only arriving packets are selected for dropping, then it is likely that the discard algorithm will be biased against burst sources as compared to smooth sources with the same average traffic.

- **Bound on average queue length:** RED should be able to control the average queue size and therefore control the average delay.

RED Algorithm

In general terms, the RED algorithm performs the following steps for each packet arrival:

```
calculate the average queue size avg
    if   avg < THmin
            queue packet
    else if THmin ≤ avg < THmax
            calculate probability Pa
            with probability Pa
                    discard packet
            else with probability 1 - Pa
                    queue packet
    else if  avg ≥ THmax
            discard packet
```

The algorithm performs two functions each time a new packet arrives at a FIFO output queue. The first step is to compute the average queue length, avg. This average queue length is compared to two thresholds (Figure 9.7). If avg is less than a lower threshold TH_{min}, congestion is assumed to be minimal or nonexistent, and the packet is placed in the queue. If avg is greater than or equal to an upper threshold TH_{max}, congestion is assumed to be serious, and the packet is discarded. If avg is between the two thresholds, then we are in an area that might indicate the onset of congestion. In this region, a probability P_a is calculated that depends on the exact value of avg and that increases the closer avg gets to the upper threshold. When the queue is in this region, the packet is discarded with probability P_a and queued with probability $1 - P_a$.

In essence, the first part of the algorithm (calculate queue size) determines the degree of burstiness to be allowed, and the second part of the algorithm (determine packet discard) determines the frequency of dropped packets given the current level of congestion.

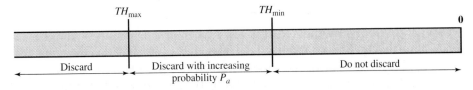

Figure 9.7 RED Buffer

```
Initialization:
    avg ← 0
    count ← -1
For each packet arrival
    CALCULATE AVERAGE QUEUE SIZE
        if the queue is not empty (i.e., q > 0)
            avg ← (1 - w_q)avg + w_q q
        else
            m ← f(time - q_time)
            avg ← (1 - w_q)^m avg
    DETERMINE PACKET DISCARD
        if avg < TH_min
            queue packet
            count ← -1
        else if TH_min ≤ avg ≤ TH_max
            increment count
            Pb ← P_max(avg - TH_min)/(TH_max - TH_min)
            Pa ← Pb/(1 - count × Pb)
            with probability P_a
                discard packet
                count ← 0
            else with probability 1 - P_a
                queue packet
        else if avg > TH_max
            discard packet
            count ← 0
When queue becomes empty
    q_time ← time
```

Saved Variables:

$avg:$ average queue size
$q\_time:$ start of queue idle time
$count:$ packets since last discarded packet

Fixed Parameters:

w_q: queue weight
$TH_{min}:$ Minimum threshold for queue
$TH_{max}:$ Maximum threshold for queue
$P_{max}:$ Maximum value for Pb

Other:

P_a: current packet-marking probability
P_b: temporary probability used in calculation
$q:$ current queue size
$time:$ current time
$f(t):$ a linear function of time t

Figure 9.8   RED Algorithm

Using Figure 9.8, we now examine the RED algorithm in more detail.

Calculating Average Queue Size The average queue size is calculated using an exponentially weighted average of previous queue lengths. The **else** clause takes into account periods when the queue is empty by estimating the number m of small packets that could have been transmitted by the router during the idle period.

One might ask why an average queue size is used when it would be simpler to use the actual queue size. The purpose of using an average queue size is to filter out transient congestion at the router. The weight, w_q, determines how rapidly *avg* changes in response to changes in actual queue size. [FLOY93] recommends a quite small value of 0.002. As a result, *avg* lags considerably behind changes in actual queue size. The use of this small weight prevents the algorithm from reacting to short bursts of congestion.

Determining Packet Discard If *avg* is less than TH_{min}, the incoming packet is queued, and if *avg* is greater than or equal to TH_{max}, the incoming packet is automatically discarded. The critical region is for a value of *avg* between the two thresholds. In this region, RED assigns a probability of discard to an incoming packet that depends on two factors:

- The closer *avg* is to TH_{max}, the higher the probability of discard.
- As long as *avg* is in the critical range, we keep a *count* of how many consecutive packets escape discard; the higher the value of *count*, the higher the probability of discard.

The steps in the calculation shown in Figure 9.8 make it difficult to figure out exactly what is going on, so a brief discussion is in order. First, a temporary probability value, P_b, is calculated. This is a value that increases linearly from 0 at $avg = TH_{min}$ to some maximum value P_{max} at $avg = TH_{max}$. This is seen more easily if we define the quantity F:

$$F = \frac{avg - TH_{min}}{TH_{max} - TH_{min}}$$

which is the fraction of the critical region less than *avg*. Then we have

$$P_b = F \times P_{max} \qquad 0 \le F \le 1$$

Probabilistic phenomena behave in ways that produce clusters. For example, if we flip a fair coin many times, we cannot expect to see a uniform alternating series of heads and tails. Instead, there will be many clusters of all heads, clusters of all tails, clusters of mostly heads, and so on, with a long-term average of 50-50. For the RED algorithm, we would like to space the discards relatively evenly so that a bursty source is not penalized. So, rather than use P_b directly, it is used in the calculation of a second probability P_a, which is the probability used to determine discard. Substituting F into the equation from Figure 9.8, we get the following definition:

$$P_a = \frac{F \times P_{max}}{1 - count \times F \times P_{max}} = \frac{1}{\dfrac{1}{F \times P_{max}} - count}$$

$$= \frac{P_b}{1 - count \times P_b} = \frac{1}{\dfrac{1}{P_b} - count}$$

Figure 9.9 gives some insight into this function. For a given value of *count*, P_a increases gradually from $P_a = 0$ at $avg = TH_{min}$ to the maximum value shown at $avg = TH_{max}$. This is a reasonable design: There is a smooth increase of P_a as the value of avg approaches TH_{max}. But the true nature of the function is revealed if we

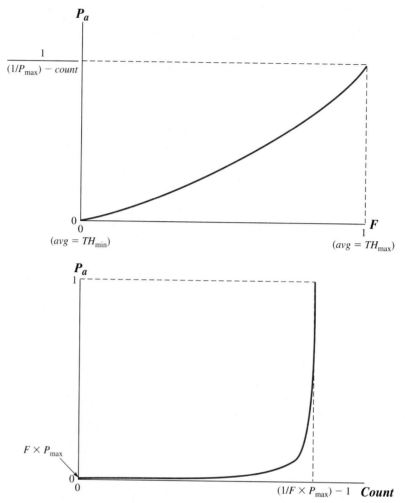

Figure 9.9 RED Probability Parameter

hold F constant and plot P_a as a function of count. The value of P_a increases slowly and then rises dramatically until it reaches $P_a = 1$ at count $= (1/F \times P_{max}) - 1$. Thus, for most values of *count*, the probability of discard is extremely low, and it becomes very near to 1 when *count* becomes very near to its maximum value. The effect of this is to force a more or less uniform spacing of discards. In fact, it can be shown that if we let P_a be the discard probability and X be the number of packets that arrive after a discarded packet until the next packet is discarded, then X is a uniformly distributed random variable from $\{1, 2, \ldots, 1/P_b\}$:

$$\Pr[X = n] = \begin{cases} F \times P_{max} & 1 \leq n \leq \dfrac{1}{F \times P_{max}} \\[2ex] 0 & n > \dfrac{1}{F \times P_{max}} \end{cases}$$

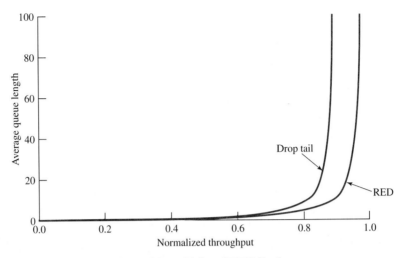

Figure 9.10   Comparison of Drop Tail and RED Performance

$$E[X] = \frac{1}{2 \times F \times P_{max}} + \frac{1}{2}$$

As an example, [FLOY93] recommends a value $P_{max} = 0.02$. When the average queue size is halfway between TH_{min} and TH_{max} ($F = 0.5$), roughly one out of 50 (one out of $1/P_{max}$) arriving packets is discarded.

Figure 9.10 shows the results of a simulation [FLOY93] comparing RED to a *drop-tail* policy, which simply drops an arriving packet if the queue is full. At high levels of congestion, RED is superior to drop tail in providing high throughput.

Explicit Congestion Notification

The RED mechanism can also be used to provide explicit congestion notification (ECN). Instead of dropping a packet at the onset of congestion, the RED algorithm can set the congestion experienced (CE) code value in the packet's IP header (see Chapter 7). This value is then communicated to the end systems, which can reduce the flow of traffic into the Internet, thus reducing congestion.

9.4 DIFFERENTIATED SERVICES

The Integrated Services Architecture (ISA) and RSVP are intended to support QoS offering in the Internet and in private internets. Although ISA in general and RSVP in particular are useful tools in this regard, these features are relatively complex to deploy. Further, they may not scale well to handle large volumes of traffic because of the amount of control signaling required to coordinate integrated QoS offerings and because of the maintenance of state information required at routers.

As the burden on the Internet grows, and as the variety of applications grow, there is an immediate need to provide differing levels of QoS to different traffic flows. The differentiated services (DS) architecture (RFC 2475) is designed to provide a simple, easy-to-implement, low-overhead tool to support a range of network services that are differentiated on the basis of performance.

Several key characteristics of DS contribute to its efficiency and ease of deployment:

- IP packets are labeled for differing QoS treatment using the existing IPv4 Type of Service field (Figure 2.13a) or IPv6 Traffic Class field (Figure 2.13b). Thus, no change is required to IP.
- A service level agreement (SLA) is established between the service provider (internet domain) and the customer prior to the use of DS. This avoids the need to incorporate DS mechanisms in applications. Thus, existing applications need not be modified to use DS.
- DS provides a built-in aggregation mechanism. All traffic with the same DS field is treated the same by the network service. For example, multiple voice connections are not handled individually but in the aggregate. This provides for good scaling to larger networks and traffic loads.
- DS is implemented in individual routers by queuing and forwarding packets based on the DS field. Routers deal with each packet individually and do not have to save state information on packet flows.

Today, DS is the most widely accepted QoS mechanism in enterprise networks.

Although DS is intended to provide a simple service based on relatively simple mechanisms, the set of RFCs related to DS is relatively complex. Table 9.1 summarizes some of the key terms from these specifications.

Services

The DS type of service is provided within a DS domain, which is defined as a contiguous portion of the Internet over which a consistent set of DS policies are administered. Typically, a DS domain would be under the control of one administrative entity. The services provided across a DS domain are defined in a service level agreement (SLA), which is a service contract between a customer and the service provider that specifies the forwarding service that the customer should receive for various classes of packets. A customer may be a user organization or another DS domain. Once the SLA is established, the customer submits packets with the DS field marked to indicate the packet class. The service provider must assure that the customer gets at least the agreed QoS for each packet class. To provide that QoS, the service provider must configure the appropriate forwarding policies at each router (based on DS field value) and must measure the performance being provided each class on an ongoing basis.

If a customer submits packets intended for destinations within the DS domain, then the DS domain is expected to provide the agreed service. If the destination is beyond the customer's DS domain, then the DS domain will attempt to forward the packets through other domains, requesting the most appropriate service to match the requested service.

A draft DS framework document lists the following detailed performance parameters that might be included in an SLA:

Table 9.1   Terminology for Differentiated Services

Behavior Aggregate	A set of packets with the same DS codepoint crossing a link in a particular direction.
Classifier	Selects packets based on the DS field (BA classifier) or on multiple fields within the packet header (MF classifier).
DS Boundary Node	A DS node that connects one DS domain to a node in another domain.
DS Codepoint	A specified value of the 6-bit DSCP portion of the 8-bit DS field in the IP header.
DS Domain	A contiguous (connected) set of nodes, capable of implementing differentiated services, that operate with a common set of service provisioning policies and per-hop behavior definitions.
DS Interior Node	A DS node that is not a DS boundary node.
DS Node	A node that supports differentiated services. Typically, a DS node is a router. A host system that provides differentiated services for applications in the host is also a DS node.
Dropping	The process of discarding packets based on specified rules; also called **policing**.
Marking	The process of setting the DS codepoint in a packet. Packets may be marked on initiation and may be re-marked by an en route DS node.
Metering	The process of measuring the temporal properties (e.g., rate) of a packet stream selected by a classifier. The instantaneous state of that process may affect marking, shaping, and dropping functions.
Per-Hop Behavior (PHB)	The externally observable forwarding behavior applied at a node to a behavior aggregate.
Service Level Agreement (SLA)	A service contract between a customer and a service provider that specifies the forwarding service a customer should receive.
Shaping	The process of delaying packets within a packet stream to cause it to conform to some defined traffic profile.
Traffic Conditioning	Control functions performed to enforce rules specified in a TCA, including metering, marking, shaping, and dropping.
Traffic Conditioning Agreement (TCA)	An agreement specifying classifying rules and traffic conditioning rules that are to apply to packets selected by the classifier.

- Detailed service performance parameters such as expected throughput, drop probability, latency
- Constraints on the ingress and egress points at which the service is provided, indicating the scope of the service
- Traffic profiles that must be adhered to for the requested service to be provided, such as token bucket parameters
- Disposition of traffic submitted in excess of the specified profile

The framework document also gives some examples of services that might be provided:

1. Traffic offered at service level A will be delivered with low latency.
2. Traffic offered at service level B will be delivered with low loss.
3. Ninety percent of in-profile traffic delivered at service level C will experience no more than 50 ms latency.

4. Ninety-five percent of in-profile traffic delivered at service level D will be delivered.

5. Traffic offered at service level E will be allotted twice the bandwidth of traffic delivered at service level F.

6. Traffic with drop precedence X has a higher probability of delivery than traffic with drop precedence Y.

The first two examples are qualitative and are valid only in comparison to other traffic, such as default traffic that gets a best-effort service. The next two examples are quantitative and provide a specific guarantee that can be verified by measurement on the actual service without comparison to any other services offered at the same time. The final two examples are a mixture of quantitative and qualitative.

DS Field

Packets are labeled for service handling by means of the 6-bit DS field in the IPv4 header or the IPv6 header (Figure 2.13). The value of the DS field, referred to as the **DS codepoint**, is the label used to classify packets for differentiated services. Figure 9.11a shows the DS field.

With a 6-bit codepoint, there are in principle 64 different classes of traffic that could be defined. These 64 codepoints are allocated across three pools of codepoints, as follows:

- Codepoints of the form xxxxx0, where x is either 0 or 1, are reserved for assignment as standards.

- Codepoints of the form xxxx11 are reserved for experimental or local use.

- Codepoints of the form xxxx01 are also reserved for experimental or local use but may be allocated for future standards action as needed.

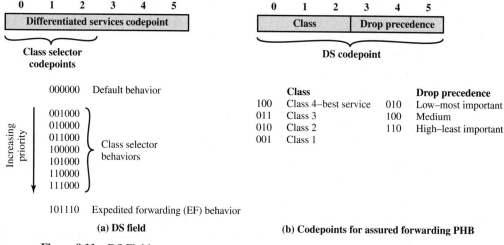

(a) DS field

(b) Codepoints for assured forwarding PHB

Figure 9.11   DS Field

Within the first pool, several assignments are made in RFC 2474. The code-point 000000 is the default packet class. The default class is the best-effort forwarding behavior in existing routers. Such packets are forwarded in the order that they are received as soon as link capacity becomes available. If other higher-priority packets in other DS classes are available for transmission, these are given preference over best-effort default packets.

Codepoints of the form xxx000 are reserved to provide backward compatibility with the IPv4 precedence service. To explain this requirement, we need to digress to an explanation of the IPv4 precedence service. The IPv4 type of service (TOS) field includes two subfields: a 3-bit precedence subfield and a 4-bit TOS subfield. These subfields serve complementary functions. The TOS subfield provides guidance to the IP entity (in the source or router) on selecting the next hop for this datagram, and the precedence subfield provides guidance about the relative allocation of router resources for this datagram.

The precedence field is set to indicate the degree of urgency or priority to be associated with a datagram. If a router supports the precedence subfield, there are three approaches to responding:

- **Route selection:** A particular route may be selected if the router has a smaller queue for that route or if the next hop on that route supports network precedence or priority (e.g., a token ring network supports priority).
- **Network service:** If the network on the next hop supports precedence, then that service is invoked.
- **Queuing discipline:** A router may use precedence to affect how queues are handled. For example, a router may give preferential treatment in queues to datagrams with higher precedence.

RFC 1812, Requirements for IP Version 4 Routers, provides recommendations for queuing discipline that fall into two categories:

- **Queue service**

  a. Routers SHOULD implement precedence-ordered queue service. Precedence-ordered queue service means that when a packet is selected for output on a (logical) link, the packet of highest precedence that has been queued for that link is sent.

  b. Any router MAY implement other policy-based throughput management procedures that result in other than strict precedence ordering, but it MUST be configurable to suppress them (i.e., use strict ordering).

- **Congestion control.** When a router receives a packet beyond its storage capacity, it must discard it or some other packet or packets.

  a. A router MAY discard the packet it has just received; this is the simplest but not the best policy.

  b. Ideally, the router should select a packet from one of the sessions most heavily abusing the link, given that the applicable QoS policy permits this. A recommended policy in datagram environments using FIFO queues is to discard a packet randomly selected from the queue. An equivalent algorithm in routers using fair queues is to discard from the longest queue. A router MAY use these algorithms to determine which packet to discard.

c. If precedence-ordered queue service is implemented and enabled, the router MUST NOT discard a packet whose IP precedence is higher than that of a packet that is not discarded.

d. A router MAY protect packets whose IP headers request the maximum reliability TOS, except where doing so would be in violation of the previous rule.

e. A router MAY protect fragmented IP packets, on the theory that dropping a fragment of a datagram may increase congestion by causing all fragments of the datagram to be retransmitted by the source.

f. To help prevent routing perturbations or disruption of management functions, the router MAY protect packets used for routing control, link control, or network management from being discarded. Dedicated routers (i.e., routers that are not also general purpose hosts, terminal servers, etc.) can achieve an approximation of this rule by protecting packets whose source or destination is the router itself.

The DS codepoints of the form xxx000 should provide a service that at minimum is equivalent to that of the IPv4 precedence functionality.

DS Configuration and Operation

Figure 9.12 illustrates the type of configuration envisioned in the DS documents. A DS domain consists of a set of contiguous routers; that is, it is possible to get from any router in the domain to any other router in the domain by a path that does not include routers outside the domain. Within a domain, the interpretation of DS codepoints is uniform, so that a uniform, consistent service is provided.

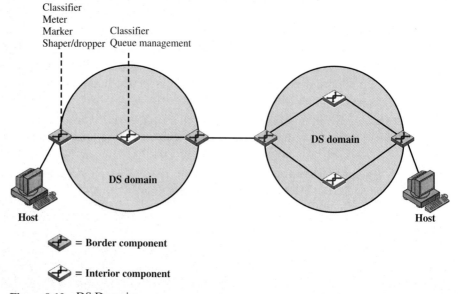

Figure 9.12 DS Domains

Routers in a DS domain are either boundary nodes or interior nodes. Typically, the interior nodes implement simple mechanisms for handling packets based on their DS codepoint values. This includes queuing discipline to give preferential treatment depending on codepoint value, and packet dropping rules to dictate which packets should be dropped first in the event of buffer saturation. The DS specifications refer to the forwarding treatment provided at a router as per-hop behavior (PHB). This PHB must be available at all routers, and typically PHB is the only part of DS implemented in interior routers.

The boundary nodes include PHB mechanisms but also more sophisticated traffic conditioning mechanisms required to provide the desired service. Thus, interior routers have minimal functionality and minimal overhead in providing the DS service, while most of the complexity is in the boundary nodes. The boundary node function can also be provided by a host system attached to the domain, on behalf of the applications at that host system.

The traffic conditioning function consists of five elements:

- **Classifier:** Separates submitted packets into different classes. This is the foundation of providing differentiated services. A classifier may separate traffic only on the basis of the DS codepoint (behavior aggregate classifier) or based on multiple fields within the packet header or even the packet payload (multifield classifier).

- **Meter:** Measures submitted traffic for conformance to a profile. The meter determines whether a given packet stream class is within or exceeds the service level guaranteed for that class.

- **Marker:** Re-marks packets with a different codepoint as needed. This may be done for packets that exceed the profile; for example, if a given throughput is guaranteed for a particular service class, any packets in that class that exceed the throughput in some defined time interval may be re-marked for best effort handling. Also, re-marking may be required at the boundary between two DS domains. For example, if a given traffic class is to receive the highest supported priority, and this is a value of 3 in one domain and 7 in the next domain, then packets with a priority 3 value traversing the first domain are remarked as priority 7 when entering the second domain.

- **Shaper:** Delays packets as necessary so that the packet stream in a given class does not exceed the traffic rate specified in the profile for that class.

- **Dropper:** Drops packets when the rate of packets of a given class exceeds that specified in the profile for that class.

Figure 9.13 illustrates the relationship between the elements of traffic conditioning. After a flow is classified, its resource consumption must be measured. The metering function measures the volume of packets over a particular time interval to determine a flow's compliance with the traffic agreement. If the host is bursty, a simple data rate or packet rate may not be sufficient to capture the desired traffic characteristics. A token bucket scheme, such as that illustrated in Figure 9.2, is an example of a way to define a traffic profile to take into account both packet rate and burstiness.

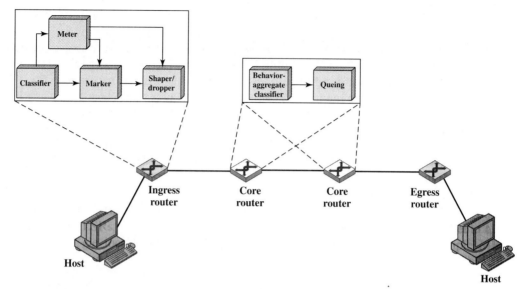

Figure 9.13 DS Functions

If a traffic flow exceeds some profile, several approaches can be taken. Individual packets in excess of the profile may be re-marked for lower-quality handling and allowed to pass into the DS domain. A traffic shaper may absorb a burst of packets in a buffer and pace the packets over a longer period of time. A dropper may drop packets if the buffer used for pacing becomes saturated.

Per-Hop Behavior

As part of the DS standardization effort, specific types of PHB need to be defined, which can be associated with specific differentiated services. Currently, two standards-track PHBs have been issued: expedited forwarding PHB (RFCs 3246 and 3247) and assured forwarding PHB (RFC 2597).

Expedited Forwarding PHB RFC 3246 defines the expedited forwarding (EF) PHB as a building block for low-loss, low-delay, and low-jitter end-to-end services through DS domains. In essence, such a service should appear to the endpoints as providing close to the performance of a point-to-point connection or leased line.

In an internet or packet-switching network, a low-loss, low-delay, and low-jitter service is difficult to achieve. By its nature, an internet involves queues at each node, or router, where packets are buffered waiting to use a shared output link. It is the queuing behavior at each node that results in loss, delays, and jitter. Thus, unless the internet is grossly oversized to eliminate all queuing effects, care must be taken in handling traffic for EF PHB to assure that queuing effects do not result in loss, delay, or jitter above a given threshold. RFC 3246 declares that the intent of the EF PHB is to provide a PHB in which suitably marked packets usually encounter short or empty queues. The relative absence of queues minimizes delay and jitter.

Furthermore, if queues remain short relative to the buffer space available, packet loss is also kept to a minimum.

The EF PHB is designed to configuring nodes so that the traffic aggregate[5] has a well-defined minimum departure rate. (*Well-defined* means "independent of the dynamic state of the node." In particular, independent of the intensity of other traffic at the node.) The general concept outlined in RFC 3246 is this: The border nodes control the traffic aggregate to limit its characteristics (rate, burstiness) to some predefined level. Interior nodes must treat the incoming traffic in such a way that queuing effects do not appear. In general terms, the requirement on interior nodes is that the aggregate's maximum arrival rate must be less than the aggregate's minimum departure rate.

RFC 3246 does not mandate a specific queuing policy at the interior nodes to achieve the EF PHB. The RFC notes that a simple priority scheme could achieve the desired effect, with the EF traffic given absolute priority over other traffic. So long as the EF traffic itself did not overwhelm an interior node, this scheme would result in acceptable queuing delays for the EF PHB. However, the risk of a simple priority scheme is that packet flows for other PHB traffic would be disrupted. Thus, some more sophisticated queuing policy might be warranted.

Assured Forwarding PHB The assured forwarding (AF) PHB is designed to provide a service superior to best-effort but one that does not require the reservation of resources within an internet and does not require the use of detailed discrimination among flows from different users. The concept behind the AF PHB was first introduced in [CLAR98] and is referred to as explicit allocation. The AF PHB is more complex than explicit allocation, but it is useful to first highlight the key elements of the explicit allocation scheme:

1. Users are offered the choice of a number of classes of service for their traffic. Each class describes a different traffic profile in terms of an aggregate data rate and burstiness.

2. Traffic from a user within a given class is monitored at a boundary node. Each packet in a traffic flow is marked *in* or *out* based on whether it does or does not exceed the traffic profile.

3. Inside the network, there is no separation of traffic from different users or even traffic from different classes. Instead, all traffic is treated as a single pool of packets, with the only distinction being whether each packet has been marked *in* or *out*.

4. When congestion occurs, the interior nodes implement a dropping scheme in which *out* packets are dropped before *in* packets.

5. Different users will see different levels of service because they will have different quantities of *in* packets in the service queues.

---

[5]The term *traffic aggregate* refers to the flow of packets associated with a particular service for a particular user.

The advantage of this approach is its simplicity. Very little work is required by the internal nodes. Marking of the traffic at the boundary nodes based on traffic profiles provides different levels of service to different classes.

The AF PHB defined in RFC 2597 expands on the preceding approach in the following ways:

1. Four AF classes are defined, allowing the definition of four distinct traffic profiles. A user may select one or more of these classes to satisfy requirements.

2. Within each class, packets are marked by the customer or by the service provider with one of three drop precedence values. In case of congestion, the drop precedence of a packet determines the relative importance of the packet within the AF class. A congested DS node tries to protect packets with a lower drop precedence value from being lost by preferably discarding packets with a higher drop precedence value.

This approach is still simpler to implement than any sort of resource reservation scheme but provides considerable flexibility. Within an interior DS node, traffic from the four classes can be treated separately, with different amounts of resources (buffer space, data rate) assigned to the four classes. Within each class, packets are handled based on drop precedence. Thus, as RFC 2597 points out, the level of forwarding assurance of an IP packet depends on

- How much forwarding resources have been allocated to the AF class that the packet belongs to
- The current load of the AF class, and, in case of congestion within the class
- The drop precedence of the packet

RFC 2597 does not mandate any mechanisms at the interior nodes to manage the AF traffic. It does reference the RED algorithm as a possible way of managing congestion.

Figure 9.11b shows the recommended codepoints for AF PHB in the DS field.

9.5 RECOMMENDED READING AND WEB SITES

Perhaps the clearest and most comprehensive book-length treatment of the topics of this chapter is [ARMI00]. [SHEN95] is a masterful analysis of the rationale for a QoS-based internet architecture. [XIAO99] provides an overview and overall framework for Internet QoS as well as integrated and differentiated services. A quite readable overview of the many issues relating to the provision of QoS over the Internet is provided in [ECON01].

RFC 1633 is the defining document for the Integrated Services Architecture and provides an excellent overview. [CLAR92] and [CLAR95] provide valuable surveys of the issues involved in internet service allocation for real-time and elastic applications, respectively. [WHIT97] is a broad survey of ISA. [ZHAN95] is a broad survey of queuing disciplines that can be used in an ISA, including an analysis of FQ and WFQ. [CLAR92] provides an analysis of WFQ and some alternative disciplines. [FLOY97] considers the congestion impacts from an increasing deployment of non-congestion-controlled best-effort traffic (traffic without the TCP congestion control mechanism) and measures that can be taken by routers, including the queuing and packet discard strategies discussed in this chapter.

[CARP02] and [WEIS98] are instructive surveys of differentiated services, while [KUMA98] looks at DS and supporting router mechanisms that go beyond the current RFCs. For a thorough treatment of DS, see [KILK99].

Two papers that compare IS and DS in terms of services and performance are [BERN00] and [HARJ00].

ARMI00   Armitage, G. *Quality of Service in IP Networks.* Indianapolis, IN: Macmillan Technical Publishing, 2000.

BERN00   Bernet, Y. "The Complementary Roles of RSVP and Differentiated Services in the Full-Service QoS Network." *IEEE Communications Magazine*, February 2000.

CARP02   Carpenter, B., and Nichols, K. "Differentiated Services in the Internet." *Proceedings of the IEEE*, September 2002.

CLAR92   Clark, D.; Shenker, S.; and Zhang, L. "Supporting Real-Time Applications in an Integrated Services Packet Network: Architecture and Mechanism" *Proceedings, SIGCOMM '92*, August 1992.

CLAR95   Clark, D. *Adding Service Discrimination to the Internet.* MIT Laboratory for Computer Science Technical Report, September 1995. Available at http://ana-www.lcs.mit.edu/anaWeb/papers.html.

ECON01   *The Economist.* "Upgrading the Internet." March 24, 2001.

FLOY97   Floyd, S., and Fall, K. "Router Mechanisms to Support End-to-End Congestion Control." *Proceedings, SIGCOMM'97*, 1997.

HARJ00   Harju, J., and Kivimaki, P. "Cooperation and Comparison of DiffServ and IntServ: Performance Measurements." *Proceedings, 23rd Annual IEEE Conference on Local Computer Networks*, November 2000.

KILK99   Kilkki, K. *Differentiated Services for the Internet.* Indianapolis, IN: Macmillan Technical Publishing, 1999.

KUMA98   Kumar, V.; Lakshman, T.; and Stiliadis, D. "Beyond Best Effort: Router Architectures for the Differentiated Services of Tomorrow's Internet." *IEEE Communications Magazine*, May 1998.

SHEN95   Shenker, S. "Fundamental Design Issues for the Future Internet." *IEEE Journal on Selected Areas in Communications*, September 1995.

WEIS98   Weiss, W. "QoS with Differentiated Services." *Bell Labs Technical Journal*, October–December 1998.

WHIT97   White, P., and Crowcroft, J. "The Integrated Services in the Internet: State of the Art." *Proceedings of the IEEE*, December 1997.

XIAO99   Xiao, X., and Ni, L. "Internet QoS: A Big Picture." *IEEE Network*, March/April 1999.

ZHAN95   Zhang, H. "Service Disciplines for Guaranteed Performance Service in Packet-Switching Networks." *Proceedings of the IEEE*, October 1995.

Recommended Web Site:

- **Integrated services working group:** Chartered by IETF to develop standards related to integrated services. The Web site includes all relevant RFCs and Internet drafts.

9.6 KEY TERMS, REVIEW QUESTIONS, AND PROBLEMS

Key Terms

assured forwarding PHB
   controlled load
differentiated services (DS)
elastic traffic
expedited forwarding PHB
	fair queuing
	guaranteed service
	integrated services
	   architecture (ISA)
	per-hop behavior (PHB)
		random early detection (RED)
		real-time traffic
		weighted fair queuing (WFQ)

Review Questions

9.1 What is the Integrated Services Architecture?

9.2 What is the difference between elastic and inelastic traffic?

9.3 What are the major functions that are part of an ISA?

9.4 List and briefly describe the three categories of service offered by ISA.

9.5 What is the difference between FIFO queuing and WFQ queuing?

9.6 Briefly describe random early detection.

9.7 What characteristics of DS contribute to its efficiency and ease of deployment?

9.8 What is the purpose of a DS codepoint?

9.9 List and briefly explain the five main functions of DS traffic conditioning.

9.10 What is meant by per-hop behavior?

9.11 What are some desirable properties for real-time communications?

9.12 What is the difference between hard and soft real-time applications?

Problems

9.1 The IPv6 standard states that if a packet with a nonzero flow label arrives at a router and the router has no information for that flow label, the router should ignore the flow label and forward the packet.

   a. What are the disadvantages of treating this event as an error, discarding the packet, and sending an ICMP message?

   b. Are there situations in which routing the packet as if its flow label were zero will cause the wrong result? Explain.

9.2 The IPv6 flow mechanism assumes that the state associated with a given flow label is stored in routers, so the routers know how to handle packets that carry that flow label. A design requirement is to flush flow labels that are no longer being used (stale flow label) from routers.

   a. Assume that a source always sends a control message to all affected routers deleting a flow label when the source finishes with that flow. In that case, how could a stale flow label persist?

   b. Suggest router and source mechanisms to overcome the problem of stale flow labels.

9.3 The question arises as to which packets generated by a source should carry nonzero IPv6 flow labels. For some applications, the answer is obvious. Small exchanges of data should have a zero flow label because it is not worth creating a flow for a few packets. Real-time flows should have a flow label; such flows are a primary reason flow labels were created. A more difficult issue is what to do with peers sending large amounts of best-effort traffic (e.g., TCP connections). Make a case for assigning a unique flow label to each long-term TCP connection. Make a case for not doing this.

9.4 The original IPv6 specifications combined the Priority and Flow Label fields into a single 28-bit Flow Label field. This allowed flows to redefine the interpretation of different values of priority. Suggest reasons, other than the introduction of DS and ECN, why the final specification includes the Priority field as a distinct field.

9.5 The token bucket scheme places a limit on the length of time at which traffic can depart at the maximum data rate. Let the token bucket be defined by a bucket size b octets and a token arrival rate of r octets/second, and let the maximum output data rate be M octets/second.

    a. Derive a formula for S, which is the length of the maximum-rate burst. That is, for how long can a flow transmit at the maximum output rate when governed by a token bucket?

    b. What is the value of S for $b = 250$ KB, $r = 2$ MB/s, and $M = 25$ MB/s?
    Hint: The formula for S is not so simple as it might appear, because more tokens arrive while the burst is being output.

9.6 The GPS queuing discipline described in Section 9.2 can be defined as follows. Let $S_i(\tau, t)$ be the amount of flow i traffic transmitted in an interval $[\tau, t]$. Then a GPS server is defined as one for which

$$\frac{S_i(\tau, t)}{S_j(\tau, t)} \geq \frac{\phi_i}{\phi_j}, \quad j = 1, 2, \ldots, N$$

Validate this definition by showing that Equation (9.3) can be derived from it.

9.7 In the RED algorithm, there are a number of parameters to be set. Let us consider some of the design issues involved.

    a. What is the relationship between the value chosen for TH_{min} and the degree of burstiness of the traffic?

    b. What is the relationship between the value $(TH_{max} - TH_{min})$ and the typical RTT seen by TCP?

9.8 One way to quantify the EF PHB performance requirement is with the following set of equations relating to packets leaving a node through some interface I to an external communications link:

$$d_j \leq f_j + E_a \quad j > 0$$
$$f_0 = d_0 = 0$$
$$f_j = \text{MAX}[a_j, \text{MIN}(d_{j-1}, f_{j-1})] + (L_j/R)$$

where

d_j = departure time of the jth EF packet to depart from I; measured at the time the last bit leaves the node

f_j = target departure time for the jth EF packet to depart from I; the ideal time at or before which the last bit of that packet leaves the node

a_j = arrival time at this node of the last bit of the jth EF packet destined to depart from I

E_a = error term for the treatment of individual EF packets; it represents the worst case deviation between actual departure time of an EF packet and the ideal departure time of the same packet

L_j = length in bits of the jth EF packet destined to depart from I

R = EF configured rate at I in bps; this is not the actual data rate on the line but rather the desired data rate for this EF PHB

This definition assumes that EF packets should ideally be served at a rate R or faster. It must take into account cases: (1) An EF packet arrives when all previous EF packets have already departed; (2) an EF packet arrives at a device that still contains waiting EF packets. With these facts in mind, explain the equations. *Hint:* For the second case, there are two subcases.

9.9 Now consider an alternative set of equations for EF PHB:

$$D_j \leq F_j + E_p \qquad j > 0$$

$$F_0 = D_0 = 0$$

$$F_j = \text{MAX}[A_j, \text{MIN}(D_{j-1}, F_{j-1})] + (L_j/R)$$

where

D_j = departure time of the jth EF packet to arrive at this node and destined to depart from I; measured at the time the last bit leaves the node

F_j = target departure time for the jth EF packet to arrive at this node and destined to depart from I; the ideal time at or before which the last bit of that packet leaves the node

E_p = error term for the treatment of individual EF packets; it represents the worst case deviation between actual departure time of an EF packet and the ideal departure time of the same packet

A_j = arrival time at this node of the last bit of the jth EF packet to arrive at this node and destined to depart from I

L_j = length in bits of the jth EF packet to arrive at this node and destined to depart from I

R = EF configured rate at I in bps; this is not the actual data rate on the line but rather the desired data rate for this EF PHB

Explain the difference between this definition and that of Problem 9.9.

9.10 A single video source transmits 30 frames per second, each containing 2 Mbits of data. The data experiences a delay jitter of 1 s. What size of delay buffer is required at the destination to eliminate the jitter?

APPENDIX 9A REAL-TIME TRAFFIC

The widespread deployment of high-speed LANs and WANs and the increase in the line capacity on the Internet and other internets has opened up the possibility of using IP-based networks for the transport of real-time traffic. However, it is important to recognize that the requirements of real-time traffic differ from those of high-speed but non-real-time traffic.

With traditional internet applications, such as file transfer, electronic mail, and client/server applications including the Web, the performance metrics of interest are generally throughput and delay. There is also a concern with reliability, and mechanisms are used to make sure that no data are lost, corrupted, or misordered during transit. By contrast, real-time applications are more concerned with timing issues. In most cases, there is a requirement that data be delivered at a constant rate equal to the sending rate. In other cases, a deadline is associated with each block of data, such that the data are not usable after the deadline has expired.

Real-Time Traffic Characteristics

Figure 9.14 illustrates a typical real-time environment. Here, a server is generating audio to be transmitted at 64 kbps. The digitized audio is transmitted in packets containing 160 octets of data, so that one packet is issued every 20 ms. These packets are passed through an internet and delivered to a multimedia PC, which plays the audio in real time as it arrives. However, because of the variable delay imposed by the Internet, the interarrival times between packets are not maintained at a fixed 20 ms at the destination. To compensate for this, the incoming packets are buffered, delayed slightly, and then released at a constant rate to the software that generates the audio.

The compensation provided by the delay buffer is limited. To understand this, we need to define the concept of *delay jitter*, which is the maximum variation

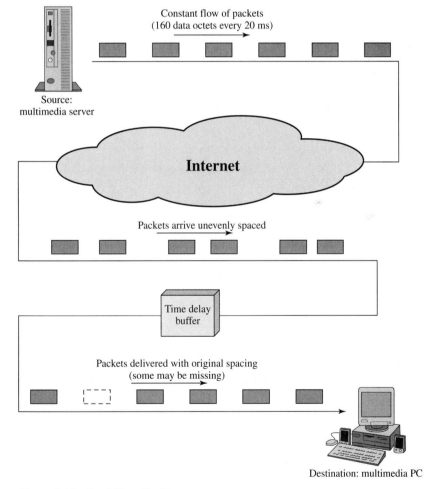

Figure 9.14   Real-Time Traffic

in delay experienced by packets in a single session. For example, if the minimum end-to-end delay seen by any packet is 1 ms and the maximum is 6 ms, then the delay jitter is 5 ms. As long as the time delay buffer delays incoming packets by at least 5 ms, then the output of the buffer will include all incoming packets. However, if the buffer delayed packets only by 4 ms, then any incoming packets that had experienced a relative delay of more than 4 ms (an absolute delay of more than 5 ms) would have to be discarded so as not to be played back out of order.

The description of real-time traffic so far implies a series of equal-size packets generated at a constant rate. This is not always the profile of the traffic. Figure 9.15 illustrates some of the common possibilities:

- **Continuous data source:** Fixed-size packets are generated at fixed intervals. This characterizes applications that are constantly generating data, have few redundancies, and that are too important to compress in a lossy way. Examples are air traffic control radar and real-time simulations.

- **On/off source:** The source alternates between periods when fixed-size packets are generated at fixed intervals and periods of inactivity. A voice source, such as in telephony or audio conferencing, fits this profile.

- **Variable packet size:** The source generates variable-length packets at uniform intervals. An example is digitized video in which different frames may experience different compression ratios for the same output quality level.

Requirements for Real-Time Communication

[ARAS94] lists the following as desirable properties for real-time communication:

- Low jitter
- Low latency
- Ability to easily integrate non-real-time and real-time services

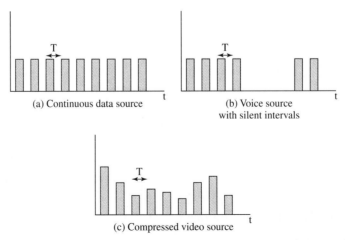

(a) Continuous data source

(b) Voice source with silent intervals

(c) Compressed video source

Figure 9.15 Real-Time Packet Transmission (Based on [ARAS94])

- Adaptable to dynamically changing network and traffic conditions
- Good performance for large networks and large numbers of connections
- Modest buffer requirements within the network
- High effective capacity utilization
- Low overhead in header bits per packet
- Low processing overhead per packet within the network and at the end system

These requirements are difficult to meet in a wide area IP-based network or internet. Neither TCP nor UDP by itself is appropriate. We will see that RTP provides a reasonable foundation for addressing these issues.

Hard versus Soft Real-Time Applications

A distinction needs to be made between hard and soft real-time communication applications. Soft real-time applications can tolerate the loss of some portion of the communicated data, while hard real-time applications have zero loss tolerance. In general, soft real-time applications impose fewer requirements on the network, and it is therefore permissible to focus on maximizing network utilization, even at the cost of some lost or misordered packets. In hard real-time applications, a deterministic upper bound on jitter and high reliability take precedence over network utilization considerations.

CHAPTER 10

PROTOCOLS FOR QoS SUPPORT

One thing to be thankful for was that no more could get in. She had to revise this at Angel and again at Old Street. Perhaps a point was never reached where no more could get in, but they would be pushed and crushed until they died or the sides of the car burst with the pressure of them.

—King Solomon's Carpet,
Barbara Vine
(Ruth Rendell)

KEY POINTS

- The RSVP (Resource ReSerVation Protocol) is designed to support the Integrated Services Architecture by enabling end systems to reserve Internet resources for a connection-oriented transfer with a specified QoS.

- Thus, the use of resource reservation can enable routers to decide ahead of time if they can meet the requirement to deliver a unicast or multicast transmission to all designated receivers and to reserve the appropriate resources if possible.

- Multiprotocol Label Switching (MPLS) is a protocol designed to address a number of issues, including traffic engineering, QoS, virtual private networks, and IP/ATM integration.

- An MPLS network or internet consists of a set of nodes, called **label switched routers** (LSRs), capable of switching and routing packets on the basis of which a label has been appended to each packet.

- The Real-Time Transport Protocol (RTP) is a transport-level alternative to TCP or UDP for supporting real-time traffic.

As this book has stressed, the demands on data networks continue their relentless rise. Traditional data-oriented applications, such as file transfer, electronic mail, USENET news, and client/server systems, place an increasing load on LANs, the Internet, and private internets. This increasing load is due not just to the number of users and the increased amount of time of their use but also to increasing reliance on image as well as text and numerical data. At the same time, there is increasing use of video and audio. One option for multimedia applications is to use a combination of dedicated circuits and ATM technology. But the timing of the demand has outrun any hope of installing a desktop-to-desktop ATM infrastructure. On the Internet and corporate intranets, there is an explosive growth in the use of audio and video on Web pages. In addition, these networks are being used for audio/video teleconferencing and other multicast "radio" and video applications.

Thus, the burden of meeting these new demands falls on the TCP/IP architecture over a packet-based network infrastructure. The central issues that must be addressed are capacity and burstiness. Audio and video applications generate huge numbers of bits per second, and the traffic has to be streamed, or transmitted in a smooth continuous flow rather than in bursts. This contrasts with conventional types of data as text, files, and graphics, for which the uneven flow typical of packet transmission is acceptable.

In the absence of a universal ATM service, designers have looked for ways to accommodate both bursty and stream traffic within the TCP/IP architecture. The problem has been attacked with a number of complementary techniques:

1. To increased capacity, corporate LANs and WANs, as well as the Internet backbone structure and corporate internets, have been upgraded to higher data rates, with high-performance switches and routers. However, it is uneconomical and, indeed, given the self-similar nature of much of the traffic (see Section 5.8), virtually impossible to size the network infrastructure to handle the peak busy period traffic. Accordingly, intelligent routing policies (Part Five) coupled with end-to-end flow control techniques (Chapter 7) are vital in dealing with the high volume such networks support.

2. Multimedia applications inevitably imply multicast transmission. Efficient techniques for multicasting over an internet are needed. This topic is covered in Chapter 12.

3. Users need to be able to intelligently allocate network capacity and assign priorities to various traffic types. In essence, the Internet needs to supply a QoS (quality of service) capability.

4. A transport protocol appropriate for the streaming requirements of video and other real-time data is needed.

The first two items have been addressed in other chapters. This chapter looks at some key protocols that support the provision of QoS on the Internet. We begin with an examination of RSVP (Resource ReSerVation Protocol), which is designed to be an integral component of an Integrated Services Architecture (ISA). We then look at MPLS (Multiprotocol Label Switching). Finally, we examine RTP (Real-Time Transport Protocol).

10.1 RESOURCE RESERVATION: RSVP

A key task, perhaps the key task, of an internet is to deliver data from a source to one or more destinations with the desired QoS (throughput, delay, delay variance, etc.). This task becomes increasingly difficult on any internet with increasing number of users, data rate of applications, and use of multicasting. One tool for coping with a high demand is dynamic routing. A dynamic routing scheme, supported by protocols such as OSPF and BGP (Part Five), can respond quickly to failures in the internet by routing around points of failure. More important, a dynamic routing scheme can, to some extent, cope with congestion, first by load balancing to smooth out the load across the internet, and second by routing around areas of developing congestion using least-cost routing. In the case of multicasting, dynamic routing schemes have been supplemented with multicast routing capabilities that take advantage of shared paths from a source to multicast destinations to minimize the number of packet duplications.

Another tool available to routers is the ability to process packets on the basis of a QoS (quality of service) label. We have seen that routers can (1) use a queue discipline that gives preference to packets on the basis of QoS; (2) select among alternate routes on the basis of QoS characteristics of each path; and (3) when possible, invoke QoS treatment in the subnetwork of the next hop.

All of these techniques are means of coping with the traffic presented to the internet but are not preventive in any way. Based only on the use of dynamic routing and QoS, a router is unable to anticipate congestion and prevent applications from causing an overload. Instead, the router can simply supply a best-effort delivery service, in which some packets may be lost and others delivered with less than the requested QoS.

As the demands on internets grow, it appears that prevention as well as reaction to congestion is needed. As this section shows, a means to implement a prevention strategy is resource reservation.

Preventive measures can be useful in both unicast and multicast transmission. For unicast, two applications agree on a specific QoS for a session and expect the internet to support that QoS. If the internet is heavily loaded, it may not provide the desired QoS and instead deliver packets at a reduced QoS. In that case, the applications may have preferred to wait before initiating the session or at least to have been alerted to the potential for reduced QoS. A way of dealing with this situation is to have the unicast applications reserve resources in order to meet a given QoS. Routers along an intended path could then preallocate resources (queue space, outgoing capacity) to assure the desired QoS. If a router could not meet the resource reservation because of prior outstanding reservations, then the applications could be informed. The applications may then decide to try again at a reduced QoS reservation or may decide to try later.

Multicast transmission presents a much more compelling case for implementing resource reservation. A multicast transmission can generate a tremendous amount of internet traffic if either the application is high volume (e.g., video) or the group of multicast destinations is large and scattered, or both. What makes the case for multicast resource reservation is that much of the potential load generated by a multicast source may easily be prevented. This is so for two reasons:

1. Some members of an existing multicast group may not require delivery from a particular source over some given period of time. For example, there may be two "channels" (two multicast sources) broadcasting to a particular multicast group at the same time. A multicast destination may wish to "tune in" to only one channel at a time.

2. Some members of a group may only be able to handle a portion of the source transmission. For example, a video source may transmit a video stream that consists of two components: a basic component that provides a reduced picture quality, and an enhanced component. Some receivers may not have the processing power to handle the enhanced component, or may be connected to the internet through a subnetwork or link that does not have the capacity for the full signal.

Thus, the use of resource reservation can enable routers to decide ahead of time if they can meet the requirement to deliver a multicast transmission to all designated multicast receivers and to reserve the appropriate resources if possible.

Internet resource reservation differs from the type of resource reservation that may be implemented in a connection-oriented network, such as ATM or frame relay. An internet resource reservation scheme must interact with a dynamic routing strategy that allows the route followed by packets of a given transmission to change. When the route changes, the resource reservations must be changed. To deal with this dynamic situation, the concept of *soft state* is used. A soft state is simply a set of state information at a router that expires unless regularly refreshed from the entity that requested the state. If a route for a given transmission changes, then some soft states will expire and new resource reservations will invoke the appropriate soft states on the new routers along the route. Thus, the end systems requesting resources must periodically renew their requests during the course of an application transmission.

We now turn to the protocol that has been developed for performing resource reservation in an internet environment: RSVP, defined in RFC 2205.

RSVP Goals and Characteristics

Perhaps the best way to introduce RSVP is to list the design goals and characteristics. In [ZHAN93], the developers of RSVP list the following design goals:

1. Provide the ability of heterogeneous receivers to make reservations specifically tailored to their own needs. As was mentioned, some members of a multicast group may be able to handle or may want to handle only a portion of a multicast transmission, such as a low-resolution component of a video signal. Differing resource reservations among members of the same multicast group should be allowed.

2. Deal gracefully with changes in multicast group membership. Membership in a group can be dynamic. Thus, reservations must be dynamic, and again, this suggests that separate dynamic reservations are needed for each multicast group member.

3. Specify resource requirements in such a way that the aggregate resources reserved for a multicast group reflect the resources actually needed. Multicast routing takes place over a tree such that packet splitting is minimized. Therefore, when resources are reserved for individual multicast group members, these reservations must be aggregated to take into account the common path segments shared by the routes to different group members.

4. Enable receivers to select one source from among multiple sources transmitting to a multicast group. This is the channel-changing capability described earlier.

5. Deal gracefully with changes in routes, automatically reestablishing the resource reservation along the new paths as long as adequate resources are available. Because routes may change during the course of an application's transmission, the resource reservations must also change so that the routers actually on the current path receive the reservations.

6. Control protocol overhead. Just as resource reservations are aggregated to take advantage of common path segments among multiple multicast receivers, so the actual RSVP reservation request messages should be aggregated to minimize the amount of RSVP traffic in the internet.

7. Be independent of routing protocol. RSVP is not a routing protocol; its task is to establish and maintain resource reservations over a path or distribution tree, independent of how the path or tree was created.

Based on these design goals, RFC 2205 lists the following characteristics of RSVP:

- **Unicast and multicast:** RSVP makes reservations for both unicast and multicast transmissions, adapting dynamically to changing group membership as well as to changing routes, and reserving resources based on the individual requirements of multicast members.
- **Simplex:** RSVP makes reservations for unidirectional data flow. Data exchanges between two end systems require separate reservations in the two directions.
- **Receiver-initiated reservation:** The receiver of a data flow initiates and maintains the resource reservation for that flow.
- **Maintaining soft state in the internet:** RSVP maintains a soft state at intermediate routers and leaves the responsibility for maintaining these reservation states to end users.
- **Providing different reservation styles:** These allow RSVP users to specify how reservations for the same multicast group should be aggregated at the intermediate switches. This feature enables a more efficient use of internet resources.
- **Transparent operation through non-RSVP routers:** Because reservations and RSVP are independent of routing protocol, there is no fundamental conflict in a mixed environment in which some routers do not employ RSVP. These routers will simply use a best-effort delivery technique.

It is worth elaborating on two of these design characteristics: receiver-initiated reservations, and soft state.

Receiver-Initiated Reservation In previous attempts at resource reservation, including the approach taken in frame relay and ATM networks, the source of a data flow requests a given set of resources. In a strictly unicast environment, this approach is reasonable. A transmitting application is able to transmit data at a certain rate and has a given QoS designed into the transmission scheme. However, this approach is inadequate for multicasting. As was mentioned, different members of the same multicast group may have different resource requirements. If the source transmission flow can be divided into component subflows, then some multicast members may only require a single subflow. If there are multiple sources transmitting to a multicast group, then a particular multicast receiver may want to select only one or a subset of all sources to receive. Finally, the QoS requirements of different receivers may differ depending on the output equipment, processing power, and link speed of the receiver.

It therefore makes sense for receivers rather than senders to make resource reservations. A sender needs to provide the routers with the traffic characteristics of the transmission (data rate, variability), but it is the receivers that must specify the desired QoS. Routers can then aggregate multicast resource reservations to take advantage of shared path segments along the distribution tree.

Soft State RSVP makes use of the concept of a soft state. This concept was first introduced by David Clark in [CLAR88], and it is worth quoting his description:

> While the datagram has served very well in solving the most important goals of the Internet, the goals of resource management and accountability have proved difficult to achieve. Most datagrams are part of some sequence of packets from source to destination, rather than isolated units at the application level. However, the gateway[1] cannot directly see the existence of this sequence, because it is forced to deal with each packet in isolation. Therefore, resource management decisions or accounting must be done on each packet separately.
>
> This suggests that there may be a better building block than the datagram for the next generation of architecture. The general characteristic of this building block is that it would identify a sequence of packets traveling from source to destination. I have used the term *flow* to characterize this building block. It would be necessary for the gateways to have flow state in order to remember the nature of the flows which are passing through them, but the state information would not be critical in maintaining the described type of service associated with the flow. Instead, that type of service would be enforced by the end points, which would periodically send messages to ensure that the proper type of service was being associated with the flow. In this way, the state information associated with the flow could be lost in a crash without permanent disruption of the service features being used. I call this concept *soft state*.

In essence, a connection-oriented scheme takes a hard-state approach, in which the nature of the connection along a fixed route is defined by the state information in the intermediate switching nodes. RSVP takes a soft-state, or connectionless, approach, in which the reservation state is cached information in the routers that is installed and periodically refreshed by end systems. If a state is not refreshed within a required time limit, the router discards the state. If a new route becomes preferred for a given flow, the end systems provide the reservation to the new routers on the route.

Data Flows

Three concepts relating to data flows form the basis of RSVP operation: session, flow specification, and filter specification.

A session is a data flow identified by its destination. The reason for using the term *session* rather than simply *destination* is that it reflects the soft-state nature of RSVP operation. Once a reservation is made at a router by a particular destination, the router considers this as a session and allocates resources for the life of that session. In particular, a session is defined by the following:

Session:	Destination IP address
	IP protocol identifier
	Destination port

---

[1] *Gateway* is the term used for *router* in most of the earlier RFCs and TCP/IP literature; it is still occasionally used today (e.g., Border Gateway Protocol).

The destination IP address may be unicast or multicast. The protocol identifier indicates the user of IP (e.g., TCP or UDP), and the destination port is the TCP or UDP port for the user of this transport-layer protocol. If the address is multicast, the destination port may not be necessary, because there is typically a different multicast address for different applications.

A reservation request issued by a destination end system is called a *flow descriptor* and consists of a *flowspec* and a *filter spec*. The flowspec specifies a desired QoS and is used to set parameters in a node's packet scheduler. That is, the router will transmit packets with a given set of preferences based on the current flowspecs. The filter spec defines the set of packets for which a reservation is requested. Thus, the filter spec together with the session define the set of packets, or flow, that are to receive the desired QoS. Any other packets addressed to the same destination are handled as best-effort traffic.

The content of the flowspec is beyond the scope of RSVP, which is merely a carrier of the request. In general, a flowspec contains the following elements:

> **Flowspec:** Service class
> Rspec
> Tspec

The service class is an identifier of a type of service being requested; it includes information used by the router to merge requests. The other two parameters are sets of numeric values. The Rspec (R for reserve) parameter defines the desired QoS, and the Tspec (T for traffic) parameter describes the data flow. The contents of Rspec and Tspec are opaque to RSVP.

In principle, the filter spec may designate an arbitrary subset of the packets of one session (i.e., the packets arriving with the destination specified by this session). For example, a filter spec could specify only specific sources, or specific source protocols, or in general only packets that have a match on certain fields in any of the protocol headers in the packet. The current RSVP version uses a restricted filter spec consisting of the following elements:

> **Filter spec:** Source address
> UDP/TCP source port

Figure 10.1 indicates the relationship among session, flowspec, and filter spec. Each incoming packet is part of at most one session and is treated according to the logical flow indicated in the figure for that session. If a packet belongs to no session, it is given a best-effort delivery service.

RSVP Operation

Much of the complexity of RSVP has to do with dealing with multicast transmission. Unicast transmission is treated as a special case. In what follows, we examine the general operation of RSVP for multicast resource reservation. The internet configuration shown in Figure 10.2a is used in the discussion. This configuration consist of four routers connected as shown. The link between two routers, indicated by a

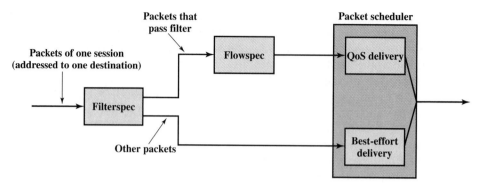

Figure 10.1 Treatment of Packets of One Session at One Router

line, could be a point-to-point link or a subnetwork. Three hosts, G1, G2, and G3, are members of a multicast group and can receive datagrams with the corresponding destination multicast address. Two hosts, S1 and S2, transmit data to this multicast address. The heavy black lines indicate the routing tree for source S1 and this multicast group, and the heavy gray lines indicate the routing tree for source S2 and this multicast group. The arrowed lines indicate packet transmission from S1 (black) and S2 (gray).

We can see that all four routers need to be aware of the resource reservations of each multicast destination. Thus, resource requests from the destinations must propagate backward through the routing trees toward each potential host.

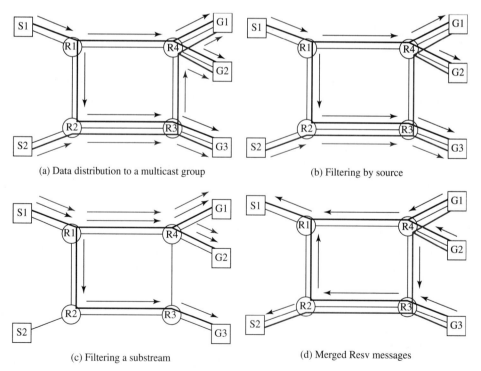

(a) Data distribution to a multicast group

(b) Filtering by source

(c) Filtering a substream

(d) Merged Resv messages

Figure 10.2 RSVP Operation (Based on Figure in [BRAD94])

Filtering Figure 10.2b shows the case that G3 has set up a resource reservation with a filter spec that includes both S1 and S2, whereas G1 and G2 have requested transmissions from S1 only. R3 continues to deliver packets from S2 for this multicast address to G3 but does not forward such packets to R4 for delivery to G1 and G2. The reservation activity that produces this result is as follows. Both G1 and G2 send an RSVP request with a filter spec that excludes S2. Because G1 and G2 are the only members of the multicast group reachable from R4, R4 no longer needs to forward packets for this session. Therefore, it can merge the two filter spec requests and send these in an RSVP message to R3. Having received this message, R3 will no longer forward packets for this session to R4. However, it still needs to forward such packets to G3. Accordingly, R3 stores this reservation but does not propagate it back up to R2.

Data packets that are addressed to a particular session but do not match any of the filter specs are treated as best-effort traffic .

A more fine-grained example of filtering is illustrated in Figure 10.2c. Here we only consider transmissions from S1, for clarity. Suppose that two types of packets are transmitted to the same multicast address representing two substreams (e.g., two parts of a video signal). These are illustrated by black and gray arrowed lines. G1 and G2 have sent reservations with no restriction on the source, whereas G3 has used a filter spec that eliminates one of the two substreams. This request propagates from R3 to R2 to R1. R1 then blocks transmission of part of the stream to G3. This saves resources on the links from R1 to R2, R2 to R3, and R3 to G3, as well as resources in R2, R3, and G3.

Reservation Styles The manner in which resource requirements from multiple receivers in the same multicast group are aggregated is determined by the reservation style. These styles are, in turn, characterized by two different options in the reservation request:

- **Reservation attribute:** A receiver may specify a resource reservation that is to be shared among a number of senders (shared) or may specify a resource reservation that is to be allocated to each sender (distinct). In the former case, the receiver is characterizing the entire data flow that it is to receive on this multicast address from the combined transmission of all sources in the filter spec. In the latter case, the receiver is saying that it is simultaneously capable of receiving a given data flow from each sender characterized in its filter spec.
- **Sender selection:** A receiver may either provide a list of sources (explicit) or implicitly select all sources by providing no filter spec (wild card).

Based on these two options, three reservation styles are defined in RSVP, as shown in Table 10.1. The **wildcard-filter (WF) style** specifies a single resource reservation to be shared by all senders to this address. If all of the receivers use this style, then we can think of this style as a shared pipe whose capacity (or quality) is the largest of the resource requests from all receivers downstream from any point on the distribution tree. The size is independent of the number of senders using it. This type of reservation is propagated upstream to all senders. Symbolically, this style is represented in the form WF(*{Q}), where the asterisk represents wildcard sender selection and Q is the flowspec.

Table 10.1 Reservation Attributes and Styles

Sender Selection	Reservation Attribute	
	Distinct	**Shared**
Explicit	Fixed-filter (FF) style	Shared-explicit (SE) style
Wildcard	—	Wildcard-filter (WF) style

To see the effects of the WF style, we use the router configuration of Figure 10.3a, taken from the RSVP specification. This is a router along the distribution tree that forwards packets on port y for receiver R1 and on port z for receivers R2 and R3. Transmissions for this group arrive on port w from S1 and on port x from S2 and S3. Transmissions from all sources are forwarded to all destinations through this router.

Figure 10.3b shows the way in which the router handles WF requests. For simplicity, the flowspec is a one-dimensional quantity in multiples of some unit resource B. The *Receive* column shows the requests that arrive from the receivers. The *Reserve* column shows the resulting reservation state for each outgoing port. The *Send* column indicates the requests that are sent upstream to the previous-hop nodes. Note that the router must reserve a pipe of capacity 4B for port y and of capacity 3B for port z. In the latter case, the router has merged the requests from R2 and R3 to support the maximum requirement for that port. However, in passing requests upstream the router must merge all outgoing requests and send a request for 4B upstream on both ports w and x.

Now suppose that the distribution tree is such that this router forwards packets from S1 on both ports y and z but forwards packets from S2 and S3 only on port z, because the internet topology provides a shorter path from S2 and S3 to R1. Figure 10.3c indicates the way in which resource requests are merged in this case. The only change is that the request sent upstream on port x is for 3B. This is because packets arriving from this port are only to be forwarded on port z, which has a maximum flowspec request of 3B.

A good example of the use of the WF style is for an audio teleconference with multiple sites. Typically, only one person at a time speaks, so a shared capacity can be used by all senders.

The **fixed-filter (FF) style** specifies a distinct reservation for each sender and provides an explicit list of senders. Symbolically, this style is represented in the form FF(S1{Q1}, S2{Q2}, ...), where Si is a requested sender and Qi is the resource request for that sender. The total reservation on a link for a given session is the sum of the Qi for all requested senders.

Figure 10.3d illustrates the operation of the FF style. In the Reserve column, each box represents one reserved pipe on the outgoing link. All of the incoming requests for S1 are merged to send a request for 4B out on port w. The flow descriptors for senders S2 and S3 are packed (not merged) into the request sent of port x; for this request, the maximum requested flowspec amount for each source is used.

A good example of the use of the FF style is for video distribution. To receive video signals simultaneously from different sources requires a separate pipe for each of the streams. The merging and packing operations at the routers assure that

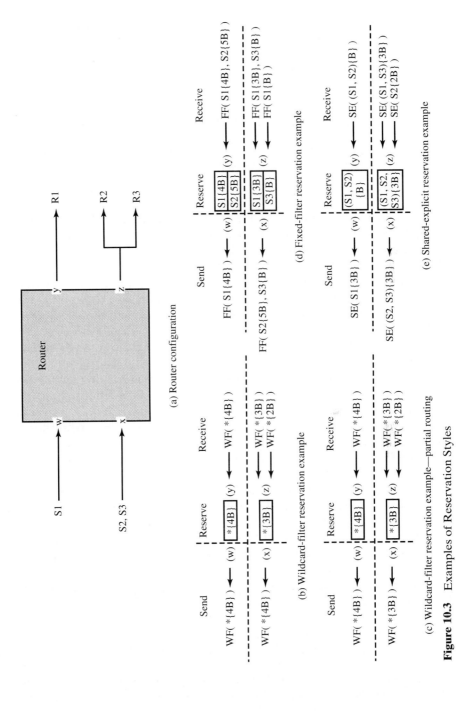

Figure 10.3 Examples of Reservation Styles

adequate resources are available. For example, in Figure 10.2a, R3 must reserve resources for two distinct video streams going to G3, but it needs only a single pipe on the stream going to R4 even though that stream is feeding two destinations (G1 and G2). Thus, with FF style, it may be possible to share resources among multiple receivers but it is never possible to share resources among multiple senders.

The **shared-explicit (SE) style** specifies a single resource reservation to be shared among an explicit list of senders. Symbolically, this style is represented in the form SE(S1, S2, ... {Q}). Figure 10.3e illustrates the operation of this style. When SE-style reservations are merged, the resulting filter spec is the union of the original filter specs, and the resulting flowspec is the largest flowspec.

As with the WF style, the SE style is appropriate for multicast applications in which there are multiple data sources but they are unlikely to transmit simultaneously.

RSVP Protocol Mechanisms

RSVP uses two basic message types: Resv and Path. Resv messages originate at multicast group receivers and propagate upstream through the distribution tree, being merged and packed when appropriate at each node along the way. These messages create soft states within the routers of the distribution tree that define the resources reserved for this session (this multicast address). Ultimately, the merged Resv messages reach the sending hosts, enabling the hosts to set up appropriate traffic control parameters for the first hop. Figure 10.3d indicates the flow of Resv messages. Note that messages are merged so that only a single message flows upstream along any branch of the combined distribution trees. However, these messages must be repeated periodically to maintain the soft states.

The Path message is used to provide upstream routing information. In all of the multicast routing protocols currently in use, only a downstream route, in the form of a distribution tree, is maintained. However, the Resv messages must propagate upstream through all intermediate routers and to all sending hosts. In the absence of reverse routing information from the routing protocol, RSVP provides this with the Path message. Each host that wishes to participate as a sender in a multicast group issues a Path message that is transmitted throughout the distribution tree to all multicast destinations. Along the way, each router and each destination host creates a path state that indicates the reverse hop to be used for this source. Figure 10.2a indicates the paths taken by these messages, which is the same as the paths taken by data packets. Figure 10.4 illustrates the operation of the protocol from the host perspective. The following events occur:

a. A receiver joins a multicast group by sending an IGMP (Internet Group Message Protocol) join message to a neighboring router.
b. A potential sender issues a Path message to the multicast group address.
c. A receiver receives a Path message identifying a sender.
d. Now that the receiver has reverse path information, it may begin sending Resv messages, specifying the desired flow descriptors.
e. The Resv message propagates through the internet and is delivered to the sender.
f. The sender starts sending data packets.
g. The receiver starts receiving data packets.

Events a and b may happen in either order.

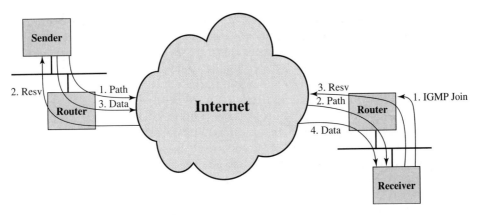

Figure 10.4   RSVP Host Model

10.2 MULTIPROTOCOL LABEL SWITCHING

In Parts Four and Five, we look at a number of IP-based mechanisms designed to improve the performance of IP-based networks and to provide different levels of QoS to different service users. Although the routing protocols discussed in Part Five have as their fundamental purpose dynamically finding a route through an internet between any source and any destination, they also provide support for performance goals in two ways:

1. Because these protocols are distributed and dynamic, they can react to congestion by altering routes to avoid pockets of heavy traffic. This tends to smooth out and balance the load on the internet, improving overall performance.

2. Routes can be based on various metrics, such as hop count and delay. Thus a routing algorithm develops information that can be used in determining how to handle packets with different service needs.

More directly, the topics covered so far in Part Four (IS, DS, RSVP) provide enhancements to an IP-based internet that explicitly provide support for QoS. However, none of the mechanisms or protocols so far discussed in Part Four directly addresses the performance issue: how to improve the overall throughput and delay characteristics of an internet. MPLS is a promising effort to provide the kind of traffic management and connection-oriented QoS support found in ATM networks, to speed up the IP packet forwarding process, and to retain the flexibility of an IP-based networking approach.

Background

The roots of MPLS go back to a number of efforts in the mid-1990s to marry IP and ATM technologies. The first such effort to reach the marketplace was IP switching, developed by Ipsilon. To compete with this offering, numerous other companies announced their own products, notably Cisco Systems (tag switching), IBM (aggregate route-based IP switching), and Cascade (IP navigator). The goal of all these products was to improve the throughput and delay performance of IP, and all took the same basic approach: Use a standard routing protocol such as OSPF to define paths between endpoints; assign packets to these paths as they enter the network; and use ATM switches to move packets along the paths. When these products came out, ATM switches were much faster than IP routers, and the intent was to improve performance by pushing as much of the traffic as possible down to the ATM level and using ATM switching hardware.

In response to these proprietary initiatives, the IETF set up the MPLS working group in 1997 to develop a common, standardized approach. The working group issued its first set of Proposed Standards in 2001. The key specification is RFC 3031. Meanwhile, however, the market did not stand still. The late 1990s saw the introduction of a number of routers that are as fast as ATM switches, eliminating the need to provide both ATM and IP technology in the same network. Nevertheless, MPLS has a strong role to play. MPLS reduces the amount of per-packet processing required at each router in an IP-based network, enhancing router performance even more. More significantly, MPLS provides significant new capabilities in four areas that have ensured its popularity: QoS support, traffic engineering, virtual private networks, and multiprotocol support. Before turning to the details of MPLS, we briefly examine each of these.

Connection–Oriented QoS Support Network managers and users require increasingly sophisticated QoS support for a number of reasons. [SIKE00] lists the following key requirements:

- Guarantee a fixed amount of capacity for specific applications, such as audio/video conference.
- Control latency and jitter and ensure capacity for voice.
- Provide very specific, guaranteed, and quantifiable service level agreements, or traffic contracts.
- Configure varying degrees of QoS for multiple network customers.

A connectionless network, such as in IP-based internet, cannot provide truly firm QoS commitments. A differentiated service (DS) framework works in only a general way and upon aggregates of traffic from a number of sources. An IS framework, using RSVP, has some of the flavor of a connection-oriented approach but is nevertheless limited in terms of its flexibility and scalability. For services such as voice and video that require a network with high predictability, the DS and IS approaches, by themselves, may prove inadequate on a heavily loaded network. By contrast, a connection-oriented network, as we have seen, has powerful traffic management and QoS capabilities. MPLS imposes a connection-oriented framework on an IP-based internet and thus provides the foundation for sophisticated and reliable QoS traffic contracts.

Traffic Engineering MPLS makes it easy to commit network resources in such a way as to balance the load in the face of a given demand and to commit to differential levels of support to meet various user traffic requirements. The ability to define routes dynamically, plan resource commitments on the basis of known demand, and optimize network utilization is referred to as *traffic engineering*.

With the basic IP mechanism, there is a primitive form of automated traffic engineering. Specifically, routing protocols such as OSPF enable routers to dynamically change the route to a given destination on a packet-by-packet basis to try to balance load. But such dynamic routing reacts in a very simple manner to congestion and does not provide a way to support QoS. All traffic between two endpoints follows the same route, which may be changed when congestion occurs. MPLS, on the other hand, is aware of not just individual packets but flows of packets in which each flow has certain QoS requirements and a predictable traffic demand. With MPLS, it is possible to set up routes on the basis of these individual flows, with two different flows between the same endpoints perhaps following different routers. Further, when congestion threatens, MPLS paths can be rerouted intelligently. That is, instead of simply changing the route on a packet-by-packet basis, with MPLS, the routes are changed on a flow-by-flow basis, taking advantage of the known traffic demands of each flow. Effective use of traffic engineering can substantially increase usable network capacity.

Virtual Private Network (VPN) Support MPLS provides an efficient mechanism for supporting VPNs. With a VPN, the traffic of a given enterprise or group passes transparently through an internet in a way that effectively segregates that traffic from other packets on the internet, proving performance guarantees and security.

Multiprotocol Support MPLS can be used on a number of networking technologies. Our focus in Part Four is on IP-based internets, and this is likely to be the principal area of use. MPLS is an enhancement to the way a connectionless IP-based internet is operated, requiring an upgrade to IP routers to support the MPLS features. MPLS-enabled routers can coexist with ordinary IP routers, facilitating the introduction of evolution to MPLS schemes. MPLS is also designed to work in ATM and frame relay networks. Again, MPLS-enabled ATM switches and MPLS-enabled frame relay switches can be configured to coexist with ordinary switches. Furthermore, MPLS can be used in a pure IP-based internet, a pure ATM network, a pure frame relay network, or an internet that includes two or even all three technologies. This universal nature of MPLS should appeal to users who currently have mixed network technologies and seek ways to optimize resources and expand QoS support.

For the remainder of this discussion, we focus on the use of MPLS in IP-based internets, with brief comments about formatting issues for ATM and frame relay networks. Table 10.2 defines key MPLS terms used in our discussion.

MPLS Operation

An MPLS network or internet[2] consists of a set of nodes, called **label switched routers** (LSRs) capable of switching and routing packets on the basis of which a label has been appended to each packet. Labels define a flow of packets between two endpoints or, in the case of multicast, between a source endpoint and a multicast group of destination endpoints. For each distinct flow, called a **forwarding equivalence class** (FEC), a specific path through the network of LSRs is defined. Thus, MPLS is a connection-oriented technology. Associated with each FEC is a traffic characterization that defines the QoS requirements for that flow. The LSRs need not

---

[2]For simplicity, we will use the term *network* for the remainder of this section. In the case of an IP-based internet, we are referring to the Internet, where the IP routers function as MPLS nodes.

Table 10.2 MPLS Terminology

Forwarding Equivalence Class (FEC) A group of IP packets that are forwarded in the same manner (e.g., over the same path, with the same forwarding treatment).	**Label Stack** An ordered set of labels.
	Merge Point A node at which label merging is done.
Frame Merge Label merging, when it is applied to operation over frame based media, so that the potential problem of cell interleave is not an issue.	**MPLS Domain** A contiguous set of nodes that operate MPLS routing and forwarding and that are also in one Routing or Administrative Domain.
Label A short fixed-length physically contiguous identifier that is used to identify a FEC, usually of local significance.	**MPLS Edge Node** An MPLS node that connects an MPLS domain with a node that is outside of the domain, either because it does not run MPLS, and/or because it is in a different domain. Note that if an LSR has a neighboring host that is not running MPLS, then that LSR is an MPLS edge node.
Label Merging The replacement of multiple incoming labels for a particular FEC with a single outgoing label.	
Label Swap The basic forwarding operation consisting of looking up an incoming label to determine the outgoing label, encapsulation, port, and other data handling information.	**MPLS Egress Node** An MPLS edge node in its role in handling traffic as it leaves an MPLS domain.
Label Swapping A forwarding paradigm allowing streamlined forwarding of data by using labels to identify classes of data packets that are treated indistinguishably when forwarding.	**MPLS Ingress Node** An MPLS edge node in its role in handling traffic as it enters an MPLS domain.
	MPLS Label A short, fixed-length physically contiguous identifier that is used to identify a FEC, usually of local significance. A label is carried in a packet header.
Label Switched Hop The hop between two MPLS nodes, on which forwarding is done using labels.	
Label Switched Path The path through one or more LSRs at one level of the hierarchy followed by a packets in a particular FEC.	**MPLS Node** A node that is running MPLS. An MPLS node will be aware of MPLS control protocols, will operate one or more L3 routing protocols, and will be capable of forwarding packets based on labels. An MPLS node may optionally be also capable of forwarding native L3 packets.
Label Switching Router (LSR) An MPLS node that is capable of forwarding native L3 packets.	

examine or process the IP header but rather simply forward each packet based on its label value. Thus, the forwarding process is simpler than with an IP router.

Figure 10.5, based on one in [REDF00], depicts the operation of MPLS within a domain of MPLS-enabled routers. The following are key elements of the operation:

1. Prior to the routing and delivery of packets in a given FEC, a path through the network, known as a **label switched path** (LSP), must be defined and the QoS parameters along that path must be established. The QoS parameters determine (1) how much resources to commit to the path, and (2) what queuing and discarding policy to establish at each LSR for packets in this FEC. To accomplish these tasks, two protocols are used to exchange the necessary information among routers:

   a. An interior routing protocol, such as OSPF, is used to exchange reachability and routing information.

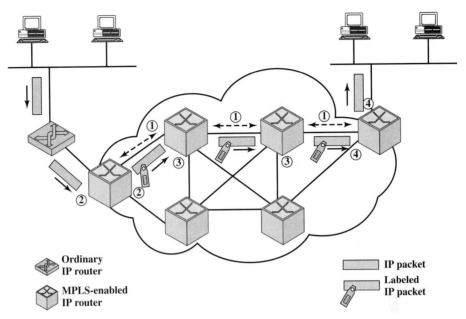

Figure 10.5 MPLS Operation

    b. Labels must be assigned to the packets for a particular FEC. Because the use of globally unique labels would impose a management burden and limit the number of usable labels, labels have local significance only, as discussed subsequently. A network operator can specify explicit routes manually and assign the appropriate label values. Alternatively, a protocol is used to determine the route and establish label values between adjacent LSRs. Either of two protocols can be used for this purpose: the Label Distribution Protocol (LDP) or an enhanced version of RSVP.

2. A packet enters an MPLS domain through an ingress edge LSR, where it is processed to determine which network-layer services it requires, defining its QoS. The LSR assigns this packet to a particular FEC, and therefore a particular LSP; appends the appropriate label to the packet; and forwards the packet. If no LSP yet exists for this FEC, the edge LSR must cooperate with the other LSRs in defining a new LSP.

3. Within the MPLS domain, as each LSR receives a labeled packet, it

    a. Removes the incoming label and attaches the appropriate outgoing label to the packet

    b. Forwards the packet to the next LSR along the LSP

4. The egress edge LSR strips the label, reads the IP packet header, and forwards the packet to its final destination.

    Several key features of MLSP operation can be noted at this point:

1. An MPLS domain consists of a contiguous, or connected, set of MPLS-enabled routers. Traffic can enter or exit the domain from an endpoint on a directly connected network, as shown in the upper-right corner of Figure 10.5. Traffic may also arrive from an ordinary router that connects to a portion of the internet not using MPLS, as shown in the upper-left corner of Figure 10.5.

2. The FEC for a packet can be determined by one or more of a number of parameters, as specified by the network manager. Among the possible parameters are the following:

—Source and/or destination IP addresses or IP network addresses

—Source and/or destination port numbers

—IP protocol ID

—Differentiated services codepoint

—IPv6 flow label

3. Forwarding is achieved by doing a simple lookup in a predefined table that maps label values to next hop addresses. There is no need to examine or process the IP header or to make a routing decision based on destination IP address.

4. A particular per-hop behavior (PHB) can be defined at an LSR for a given FEC. The PHB defines the queuing priority of the packets for this FEC and the discard policy.

5. Packets sent between the same endpoints may belong to different FECs. Thus, they will be labeled differently, will experience different PHB at each LSR, and may follow different paths through the network.

Figure 10.6 shows the label-handling and forwarding operation in more detail. Each LSR maintains a forwarding table for each LSP passing through the LSR. When a labeled packet arrives, the LSR indexes the forwarding table to determine the next

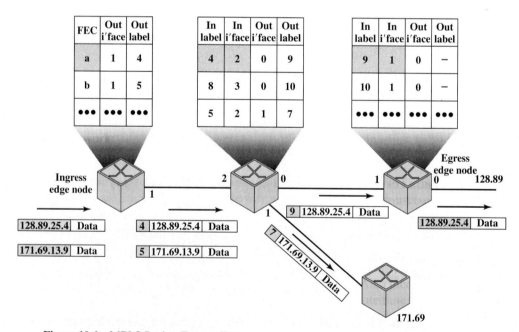

Figure 10.6   MPLS Packet Forwarding

hop. For scalability, as was mentioned, labels have local significance only. Thus, the LSR removes the incoming label from the packet and attaches the matching outgoing label before forwarding the packet. The ingress edge LSR determines the FEC for each incoming unlabeled packet and, on the basis of the FEC, assigns the packet to a particular LSP, attaches the corresponding label, and forwards the packet.

Label Stacking

One of the most powerful features of MPLS is label stacking. A labeled packet may carry a number of labels, organized as a last-in-first-out stack. Processing is always based on the top label. At any LSR, a label may be added to the stack (push operation) or removed from the stack (pop operation). Label stacking allows the aggregation of LSPs into a single LSP for a portion of the route through a network, creating a tunnel. At the beginning of the tunnel, an LSR assigns the same label to packets from a number of LSPs by pushing the label onto each packet's stack. At the end of the tunnel, another LSR pops the top element from the label stack, revealing the inner label. This is similar to ATM, which has one level of stacking (virtual channels inside virtual paths) but MPLS supports unlimited stacking.

Label stacking provides considerable flexibility. An enterprise could establish MPLS-enabled networks at various sites and establish a number of LSPs at each site. The enterprise could then use label stacking to aggregate multiple flows of its own traffic before handing it to an access provider. The access provider could aggregate traffic from multiple enterprises before handing it to a larger service provider. Service providers could aggregate many LSPs into a relatively small number of tunnels between points of presence. Fewer tunnels means smaller tables, making it easier for a provider to scale the network core.

Label Format and Placement

An MPLS label is a 32-bit field consisting of the following elements (Figure 10.7), defined in RFC 3032:

- **Label value:** Locally significant 20-bit label
- **Exp:** 3 bits reserved for experimental use. For example, these bits could communicate DS information or PHB guidance.
- **S:** Set to one for the oldest entry in the stack, and zero for all other entries.
- **Time to live (TTL):** 8 bits used to encode a hop count, or time to live, value.

Bits: 20   3   1   8

| Label value | Exp | S | Time to live |

Exp = experimental
S = bottom of stack bit

Figure 10.7   MPLS Label Format

Time to Live Processing A key field in the IP packet header is the TTL field (IPv4, Figure 2.13a), or hop limit (IPv6, Figure 2.13b). In an ordinary IP-based internet, this field is decremented at each router and the packet is dropped if the count falls to zero. This is done to avoid looping or having the packet remain too long in the Internet due to faulty routing. Because an LSR does not examine the IP header, the TTL field is included in the label so that the TTL function is still supported. The rules for processing the TTL field in the label are as follows:

1. When an IP packet arrives at an ingress edge LSR of an MPLS domain, a single label stack entry is added to the packet. The TTL value of this label stack entry is set to the value of the IP TTL value. If the IP TTL field needs to be decremented, as part of the IP processing, it is assumed that this has already been done.

2. When an MPLS packet arrives at an internal LSR of an MPLS domain, the TTL value in the top label stack entry is decremented. Then

   a. If this value is zero, the MPLS packet is not forwarded. Depending on the label value in the label stack entry, the packet may be simply discarded, or it may be passed to the appropriate "ordinary" network layer for error processing (e.g., for the generation of an ICMP error message).

   b. If this value is positive, it is placed in the TTL field of the top label stack entry for the outgoing MPLS packet, and the packet is forwarded. The outgoing TTL value is a function solely of the incoming TTL value and is independent of whether any labels are pushed or popped before forwarding. There is no significance to the value of the TTL field in any label stack entry which is not at the top of the stack.

3. When an MPLS packet arrives at an egress edge LSR of an MPLS domain, the TTL value in the single label stack entry is decremented and the label is popped, resulting in an empty label stack. Then

   a. If this value is zero, the IP packet is not forwarded. Depending on the label value in the label stack entry, the packet may be simply discarded, or it may be passed to the appropriate "ordinary" network layer for error processing.

   b. If this value is positive, it is placed in the TTL field of the IP header, and the IP packet is forwarded using ordinary IP routing. Note that the IP header checksum must be modified prior to forwarding

Label Stack The label stack entries appear after the data link layer headers, but before any network layer headers. The top of the label stack appears earliest in the packet (closest to the data link header), and the bottom appears latest (closest to the network layer header). The network layer packet immediately follows the label stack entry that has the S bit set. In data link frame, such as for PPP (point-to-point protocol), the label stack appears between the IP header and the data link header (Figure 10.8a). For an IEEE 802 frame, the label stack appears between the IP header and the LLC (logical link control) header (Figure 10.8b).

If MPLS is used over a connection-oriented network service, a slightly different approach may be taken, as shown in Figures 10.8c and d. For ATM cells, the label value in the topmost label is placed in the VPI/VCI field in the ATM cell header. The entire top label remains at the top of the label stack, which is inserted between the cell header and the IP header. Placing the label value in the ATM cell header

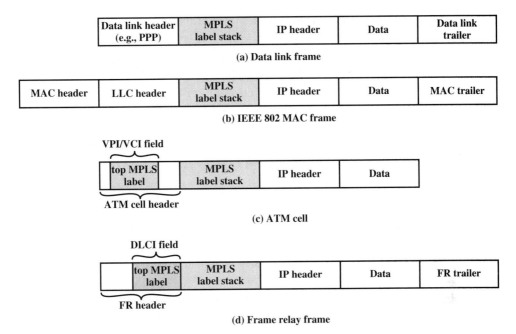

Figure 10.8   Position of MPLS Label

facilitates switching by an ATM switch, which would, as usual, only need to look at the cell header. Similarly, the topmost label value can be placed in the DLCI (data link connection identifier) field of a frame relay header. Note that in both these cases, the Time to Live field is not visible to the switch and so is not decremented. The reader should consult the MPLS specifications for the details of the way this situation is handled.

FECs, LSPs, and Labels

To understand MPLS, it is necessary to understand the operational relationship among FECs, LSPs, and labels. The specifications covering all of the ramifications of this relationship are lengthy. In the remainder of this section, we provide a summary.

The essence of MPLS functionality is that traffic is grouped into FECs. The traffic in an FEC transits an MPLS domain along an LSP. Individual packets in an FEC are uniquely identified as being part of a given FEC by means of a locally significant label. At each LSR, each labeled packet is forwarded on the basis of its label value, with the LSR replacing the incoming label value with an outgoing label value.

The overall scheme described in the previous paragraph imposes a number of requirements. Specifically,

1. Each traffic flow must be assigned to a particular FEC.
2. A routing protocol is needed to determine the topology and current conditions in the domain so that a particular LSP can be assigned to an FEC. The routing protocol must be able to gather and use information to support the QoS requirements of the FEC.

3. Individual LSRs must become aware of the LSP for a given FEC, must assign an incoming label to the LSP, and must communicate that label to any other LSR that may send it packets for this FEC.

The first requirement is outside the scope of the MPLS specifications. The assignment needs to be done either by manual configuration, or by means of some signaling protocol, or by an analysis of incoming packets at ingress LSRs. Before looking at the other two requirements, let us consider topology of LSPs. We can classify these in the following manner:

- **Unique ingress and egress LSR:** In this case a single path through the MPLS domain is needed.

- **Unique egress LSR, multiple ingress LSRs:** If traffic assigned to a single FEC can arise from different sources that enter the network at different ingress LSRs, then this situation occurs. An example is an enterprise intranet at a single location but with access to an MPLS domain through multiple MPLS ingress LSRs. This situation would call for multiple paths through the MPLS domain, probably sharing a final few hops.

- **Multiple egress LSRs for unicast traffic:** RFC 3031 states that most commonly, a packet is assigned to an FEC based (completely or partially) on its network layer destination address. If not, then it is possible that the FEC would require paths to multiple distinct egress LSRs. However, more likely, there would be a cluster of destination networks all of which are reached via the same MPLS egress LSR.

- **Multicast:** RFC 3031 lists multicast as a subject for further study.

Route Selection Route selection refers to the selection of an LSP for a particular FEC. The MPLS architecture supports two options: hop-by-hop routing and explicit routing.

With **hop-by-hop routing**, each LSR independently chooses the next hop for each FEC. RFC 3031 implies that this option makes use of an ordinary routing protocol, such as OSPF. This option provides some of the advantages of MPLS, including rapid switching by labels, the ability to use label stacking, and differential treatment of packets from different FECs following the same route. However, because of the limited use of performance metrics in typical routing protocols, hop-by-hop routing does not readily support traffic engineering or policy routing (defining routes based on some policy related to QoS, security, or some other consideration).

With **explicit routing**, a single LSR, usually the ingress or egress LSR, specifies some or all of the LSRs in the LSP for a given FEC. For strict explicit routing, an LSR specifies all of the LSRs on an LSP. For loose explicit routing, only some of the LSRs are specified. Explicit routing provides all of the benefits of MPLS, including the ability to do traffic engineering and policy routing.

Explicit routes can be selected by configuration, that is, set up ahead of time, or dynamically. Dynamic explicit routing would provide the best scope for traffic engineering. For dynamic explicit routing, the LSR setting up the LSP would need information about the topology of the MPLS domain as well as QoS-related information about that domain. An MPLS traffic engineering specification (RFC 2702) suggests that the QoS-related information falls into two categories:

- A set of attributes associated with an FEC or a collection of similar FECs that collectively specify their behavioral characteristics.
- A set of attributes associated with resources (nodes, links) that constrain the placement of LSPs through them.

A routing algorithm that takes into account the traffic requirements of various flows and that takes into account the resources available along various hops and through various nodes is referred to as a **constraint-based routing algorithm**. In essence, a network that uses a constraint-based routing algorithm is aware of current utilization, existing capacity, and committed services at all times. Traditional routing algorithms, such as OSPF and BGP, do not employ a sufficient array of cost metrics in their algorithms to qualify as constraint based. Furthermore, for any given route calculation, only a single cost metric (e.g., number of hops, delay) can be used. For MPLS, it is necessary either to augment an existing routing protocol or to deploy a new one. For example, an enhanced version of OSPF has been defined (RFC 2676) that provides at least some of the support required for MPLS. Examples of metrics that would be useful to constraint based routing are

- Maximum link data rate
- Current capacity reservation
- Packet loss ratio
- Link propagation delay

Label Distribution Route selection consists of defining an LSP for an FEC. A separate function is the actual setting up of the LSP. For this purpose, each LSR on the LSP must

1. Assign a label to the LSP to be used to recognize incoming packets that belong to the corresponding FEC.
2. Inform all potential upstream nodes (nodes that will send packets for this FEC to this LSR) of the label assigned by this LSR to this FEC, so that these nodes can properly label packets to be sent to this LSR.
3. Learn the next hop for this LSP and learn the label that the downstream node (LSR that is the next hop) has assigned to this FEC. This will enable this LSR to map an incoming label to an outgoing label.

The first item in the preceding list is a local function. Items 2 and 3 must either be done by manual configuration or require the use of some sort of label distribution protocol. Thus, the essence of a label distribution protocol is that it enables one LSR to inform others of the label/FEC bindings it has made. In addition, a label distribution protocol enables two LSRs to learn each other's MPLS capabilities. The MPLS architecture does not assume a single label distribution protocol but allows for multiple such protocols. Specifically, RFC 3031 refers to a new label distribution protocol and to enhancements to existing protocols, such as RSVP and BGP, to serve the purpose.

The relationship between label distribution and route selection is complex. It is best to look at in the context of the two types of route selection.

With hop-by-hop route selection, no specific attention is paid to traffic engineering or policy routing concerns, as we have seen. In such a case, an ordinary routing protocol such as OSPF is used to determine the next hop by each LSR. A relatively straightforward label distribution protocol can operate using the routing protocol to design routes.

With explicit route selection, a more sophisticated routing algorithm must be implemented, one that does not employ a single metric to design a route. In this case, a label distribution protocol could make use of a separate route selection protocol, such as an enhanced OSPF, or incorporate a routing algorithm into a more complex label distribution protocol.

10.3 REAL-TIME TRANSPORT PROTOCOL (RTP)

The most widely used transport-level protocol is TCP. Although TCP has proven its value in supporting a wide range of distributed applications, it is not suited for use with real-time distributed applications. By a real-time distributed application, we mean one in which a source is generating a stream of data at a constant rate, and one or more destinations must deliver that data to an application at the same constant rate. Examples of such applications include audio and video conferencing, live video distribution (not for storage but for immediate play), shared workspaces, remote medical diagnosis, telephony, command and control systems, distributed interactive simulations, games, and real-time monitoring. A number of features of TCP disqualify it for use as the transport protocol for such applications:

1. TCP is a point-to-point protocol that sets up a connection between two end points. Therefore, it is not suitable for multicast distribution.

2. TCP includes mechanisms for retransmission of lost segments, which then arrive out of order. Such segments are not usable in most real-time applications.

3. TCP contains no convenient mechanism for associating timing information with segments, which is another real-time requirement.

The other widely used transport protocol, UDP, does not exhibit the first two characteristics listed but, like TCP, does not provide timing information. By itself, UDP does not provide any general-purpose tools useful for real-time applications.

Although each real-time application could include its own mechanisms for supporting real-time transport, there are a number of common features that warrant the definition of a common protocol. A protocol designed for this purpose is the Real-Time Transport Protocol (RTP), defined in RFC 1889. RTP is best suited to soft real-time communication. It lacks the necessary mechanisms to support hard real-time traffic.

This section provides an overview of RTP. We begin with a discussion of real-time transport requirements. Next, we examine the philosophical approach of RTP. The remainder of the section is devoted to the two protocols that make up RTP: The first is simply called RTP and is a data transfer protocol; the other is a control protocol known as RTCP (RTP Control Protocol).

RTP Protocol Architecture

In RTP, there is close coupling between the RTP functionality and the application-layer functionality. Indeed, RTP is best viewed as a framework that applications can use directly to implement a single protocol. Without the application-specific information, RTP is not a full protocol. On the other hand, RTP imposes a structure and defines common functions so that individual real-time applications are relieved of part of their burden.

RTP follows the principles of protocol architecture design outlined in a paper by Clark and Tennenhouse [CLAR90]. The two key concepts presented in that paper are application-level framing and integrated layer processing.

Application–Level Framing   In a traditional transport protocol, such as TCP, the responsibility for recovering from lost portions of data is performed transparently at the transport layer. [CLAR90] lists two scenarios in which it might be more appropriate for recovery from lost data to be performed by the application:

1. The application, within limits, may accept less than perfect delivery and continue unchecked. This is the case for real-time audio and video. For such applications, it may be necessary to inform the source in more general terms about the quality of the delivery rather than to ask for retransmission. If too much data are being lost, the source might perhaps move to a lower-quality transmission that places lower demands on the network, increasing the probability of delivery.

2. It may be preferable to have the application rather than the transport protocol provide data for retransmission. This is useful in the following contexts:
    a. The sending application may recompute lost data values rather than storing them.
    b. The sending application can provide revised values rather than simply retransmitting lost values, or send new data that "fix" the consequences of the original loss.

To enable the application to have control over the retransmission function, Clark and Tennenhouse propose that lower layers, such as presentation and transport, deal with data in units that the application specifies. The application should break the flow of data into application-level data units (ADUs), and the lower layers must preserve these ADU boundaries as they process the data. The application-level frame is the unit of error recovery. Thus, if a portion of an ADU is lost in transmission, the application will typically be unable to make use of the remaining portions. In such a case, the application layer will discard all arriving portions and arrange for retransmission of the entire ADU, if necessary.

Integrated Layer Processing   In a typical layered protocol architecture, such as TCP/IP or OSI, each layer of the architecture contains a subset of the functions to be performed for communications, and each layer must logically be structured as a separate module in end systems. Thus, on transmission, a block of data flows down through and is sequentially processed by each layer of the architecture. This structure restricts the implementer from invoking certain functions in parallel or out of the layered order to achieve greater efficiency. Integrated layer processing, as proposed in [CLAR90], captures the idea that adjacent layers may be tightly coupled and that the implementer should be free to implement the functions in those layers in a tightly coupled manner.

The idea that a strict protocol layering may lead to inefficiencies has been propounded by a number of researchers. For example, [CROW92] examined the inefficiencies of running a remote procedure call (RPC) on top of TCP and suggested a tighter coupling of the two layers. The researchers argued that the integrated layer processing approach is preferable for efficient data transfer.

Figure 10.9 illustrates the manner in which RTP realizes the principle of integrated layer processing. RTP is designed to run on top of a connectionless transport protocol such as UDP. UDP provides the basic port addressing functionality of the transport layer. RTP contains further transport-level functions, such as sequencing. However, RTP by itself is not complete. It is completed by modifications and/or additions to the RTP headers to include application-layer functionality. The figure indicates that several different standards for encoding video data can be used in conjunction with RTP for video transmission.

RTP Data Transfer Protocol

We first look at the basic concepts of the RTP data transfer protocol and then examine the protocol header format. Throughout this section, the term *RTP* will refer to the RTP data transfer protocol.

RTP Concepts RTP supports the transfer of real-time data among a number of participants in a session. A session is simply a logical association among two or more RTP entities that is maintained for the duration of the data transfer. A session is defined by the following:

- **RTP port number:** The destination port address is used by all participants for RTP transfers. If UDP is the lower layer, this port number appears in the Destination Port field (see Figure 6.14) of the UDP header.

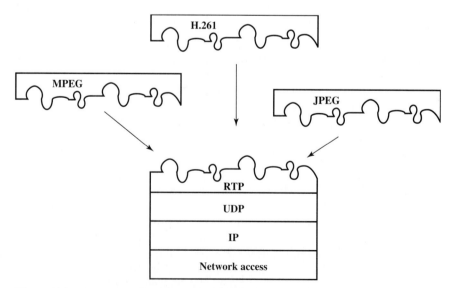

Figure 10.9 RTP Protocol Architecture [THOM96]

- **RTCP port number:** The destination port address is used by all participants for RTCP transfers.
- **Participant IP addresses:** This can either be a multicast IP address, so that the multicast group defines the participants, or a set of unicast IP addresses.

The process of setting up a session is beyond the scope of RTP and RTCP.

Although RTP can be used for unicast real-time transmission, its strength lies in its ability to support multicast transmission. For this purpose, each RTP data unit includes a source identifier that identifies which member of the group generated the data. It also includes a timestamp so that the proper timing can be re-created on the receiving end using a delay buffer. RTP also identifies the payload format of the data being transmitted.

RTP allows the use of two kinds of RTP relays: translators and mixers. First we need to define the concept of relay. A relay operating at a given protocol layer is an intermediate system that acts as both a destination and a source in a data transfer. For example, suppose that system A wishes to send data to system B but cannot do so directly. Possible reasons are that B may be behind a firewall or B may not be able to use the format transmitted by A. In such a case, A may be able to send the data to an intermediate relay R. R accepts the data unit, makes any necessary changes or performs any necessary processing, and then transmits the data to B.

A **mixer** is an RTP relay that receives streams of RTP packets from one or more sources, combines these streams, and forwards a new RTP packet stream to one or more destinations. The mixer may change the data format or simply perform the mixing function. Because the timing among the multiple inputs is not typically synchronized, the mixer provides the timing information in the combined packet stream and identifies itself as the source of synchronization.

An example of the use of a mixer is to combine a number of on/off sources such as audio. Suppose that a number of systems are members of an audio session and each generates its own RTP stream. Most of the time only one source is active, although occasionally more than one source will be "speaking" at the same time. A new system may wish to join the session, but its link to the network may not be of sufficient capacity to carry all of the RTP streams. Instead, a mixer could receive all of the RTP streams, combine them into a single stream, and retransmit that stream to the new session member. If more than one incoming stream is active at one time, the mixer would simply sum their PCM values. The RTP header generated by the mixer includes the identifier(s) of the source(s) that contributed to the data in each packet.

The **translator** is a simpler device that produces one or more outgoing RTP packets for each incoming RTP packet. The translator may change the format of the data in the packet or use a different lower-level protocol suite to transfer from one domain to another. Examples of translator use include the following:

- A potential recipient may not be able to handle a high-speed video signal used by the other participants. The translator converts the video to a lower-quality format requiring a lower data rate.
- An application-level firewall may prevent the forwarding of IP packets. Two translators are used, one on each side of the firewall, with the outside one funneling all multicast packets received through a secure connection to the translator inside the firewall. The inside translator then sends out RTP packets to a multicast group protected by the firewall.

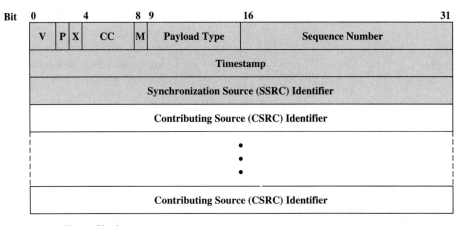

V   = Version
P   = Padding
X   = Extension
CC = CSRC count
M = Marker

Figure 10.10   RTP Header

- A translator can replicate an incoming multicast RTP packet and send it to a number of unicast destinations.

RTP Fixed Header   Each RTP packet includes a fixed header and may also include additional application-specific header fields. Figure 10.10 shows the fixed header. The first twelve octets (shaded portion) are always present and consist of the following fields:

- **Version (2 bits):** Current version is 2.
- **Padding (1 bit):** Indicates whether padding octets appear at the end of the payload. If so, the last octet of the payload contains a count of the number of padding octets. Padding is used if the application requires that the payload be an integer multiple of some length, such as 32 bits.
- **Extension (1 bit):** If set, the fixed header is followed by exactly one extension header, which is used for experimental extensions to RTP.
- **CSRC Count (4 bits):** The number of CSRC (contributing source) identifiers that follow the fixed header.
- **Marker (1 bit):** The interpretation of the marker bit depends on the payload type; it is typically used to indicate a boundary in the data stream. For video, it is set to mark the end of a frame. For audio, it is set to mark the beginning of a talk spurt.
- **Payload Type (7 bits):** Identifies the format of the RTP payload, which follows the RTP header.
- **Sequence Number (16 bits):** Each source starts with a random sequence number, which is incremented by one for each RTP data packet sent. This allows for loss detection and packet sequencing within a series of packets with the same timestamp. A number of consecutive packets may have the same time-

stamp if they are logically generated at the same time; an example is several packets belonging to the same video frame.

- **Timestamp (32 bits):** Corresponds to the instant of generation of the first octet of data in the payload. The time units of this field depend on the payload type. The values must be generated from a local clock at the source.

- **Synchronization Source Identifier:** A randomly generated value that uniquely identifies the source within a session.

Following the fixed header, there may be one or more of the following field:

- **Contributing Source Identifier:** Identifies a contributing source for the payload. These identifiers are supplied by a mixer.

The Payload Type field identifies the media type of the payload and the format of the data, including the use of compression or encryption. In a steady state, a source should only use one payload type during a session but may change the payload type in response to changing conditions, as discovered by RTCP. Table 10.3 summarizes the payload types defined in RFC 1890.

RTP Control Protocol (RTCP)

The RTP data transfer protocol is used only for the transmission of user data, typically in multicast fashion among all participants in a session. A separate control protocol (RTCP) also operates in a multicast fashion to provide feedback to RTP data sources as well as all session participants. RTCP uses the same underlying transport service as RTP (usually UDP) and a separate port number. Each participant periodically issues an RTCP packet to all other session members. RFC 1889 outlines four functions performed by RTCP:

- **Quality of Service (QoS) and congestion control:** RTCP provides feedback on the quality of data distribution. Because RTCP packets are multicast, all session members can assess how well other members are performing and receiving. Sender reports enable receivers to estimate data rates and the quality of the transmission. Receiver reports indicate any problems encountered by receivers, including missing packets and excessive jitter. For example, an audio-video application might decide to reduce the rate of transmission over low-speed links if the traffic quality over the links is not high enough to support the current rate. The feedback from receivers is also important in diagnosing distribution faults. By monitoring reports from all session recipients, a network manager can tell whether a problem is specific to a single user or more widespread.

- **Identification:** RTCP packets carry a persistent textual description of the RTCP source. This provides more information about the source of data packets than the random SSRC identifier and enables a user to associate multiple streams from different sessions. For example, separate sessions for audio and video may be in progress.

- **Session size estimation and scaling:** To perform the first two functions, all participants send periodic RTCP packets. The rate of transmission of such packets must be scaled down as the number of participants increases. In a session with

Table 10.3 Payload Types for Standard Audio and Video Encodings (RFC 1890)

0	PCMU audio	16–23	unassigned audio
1	1016 audio	24	unassigned video
2	G721 audio	25	CelB video
3	GSM audio	26	JPEG video
4	unassigned audio	27	unassigned
5	DV14 audio (8 kHz)	28	nv video
6	DV14 audio (16 kHz)	29–30	unassigned video
7	LPC audio	31	H261 video
8	PCMA audio	32	MPV video
9	G722 audio	33	MP2T video
10	L16 audio (stereo)	34–71	unassigned
11	L16 audio (mono)	72–76	reserved
12–13	unassigned audio	77–95	unassigned
14	MPA audio	96–127	dynamic
15	G728 audio		

few participants, RTCP packets are sent at the maximum rate of one every five seconds. RFC 1889 includes a relatively complex algorithm by which each participant limits its RTCP rate on the basis of the total session population. The objective is to limit RTCP traffic to less than 5% of total session traffic.

- **Session control:** RTCP optionally provides minimal session control information. An example is a participant identification to be displayed in the user interface.

An RTCP transmission consists of a number of separate RTCP packets bundled in a single UDP datagram (or other lower-level data unit). The following packet types are defined in RFC 1889:

- Sender Report (SR)
- Receiver Report (RR)
- Source Description (SDES)
- Goodbye (BYE)
- Application Specific

Figure 10.11 depicts the formats of these packet types. Each type begins with a 32-bit word containing the following fields:

- **Version (2 bits):** Current version is 2.
- **Padding (1 bit):** If set, indicates that this packet contains padding octets at the end of the control information. If so, the last octet of the padding contains a count of the number of padding octets.
- **Count (5 bits):** The number of reception report blocks contained in an SR or RR packet (RC), or the number of source items contained in an SDES or BYE packet.
- **Packet Type (8 bits):** Identifies RTCP packet type.
- **Length (16 bits):** Length of this packet in 32 bit words, minus one.

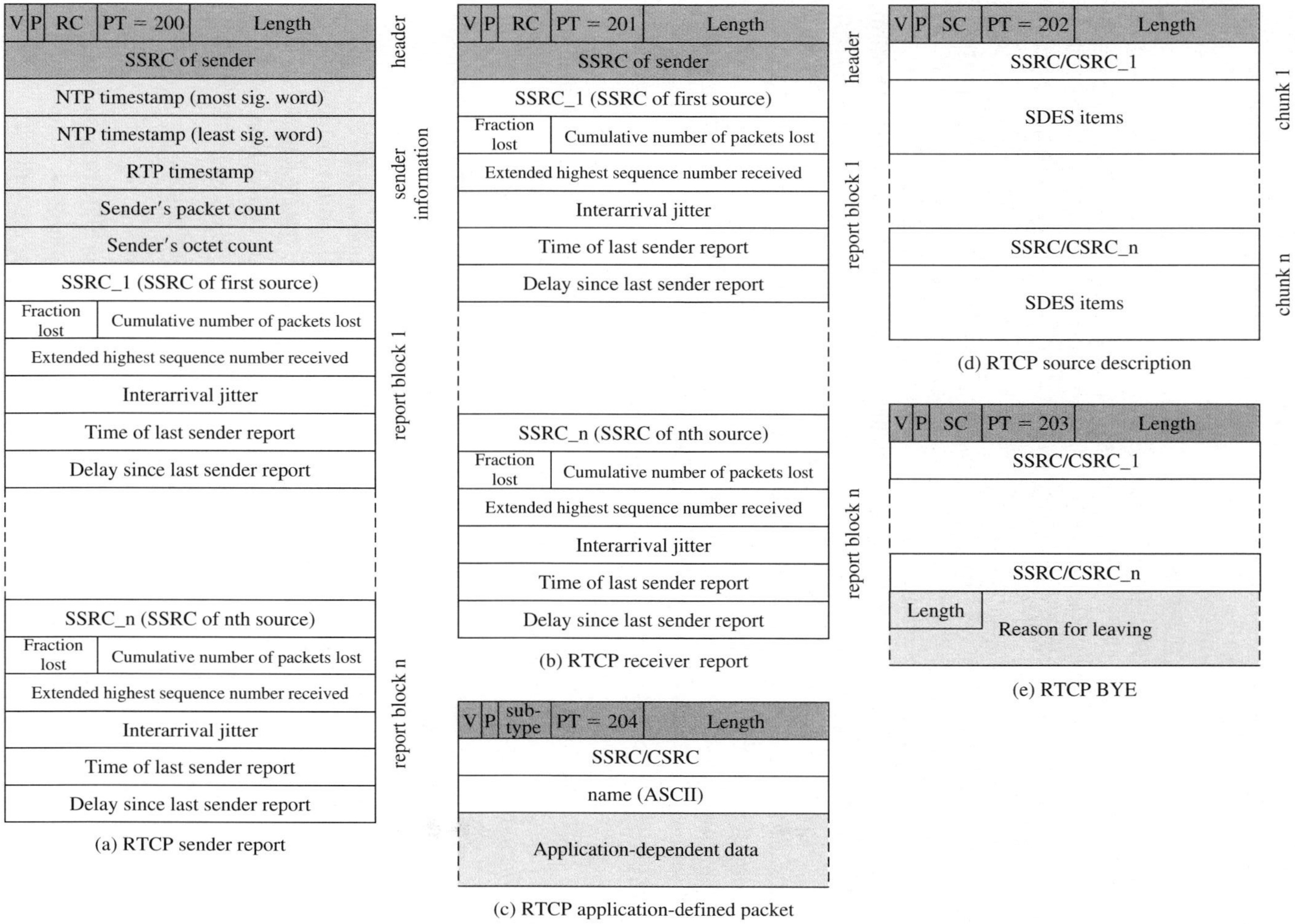

(a) RTCP sender report

V	P	RC	PT = 200	Length

SSRC of sender — header

NTP timestamp (most sig. word)
NTP timestamp (least sig. word)
RTP timestamp
Sender's packet count
Sender's octet count — sender information

SSRC_1 (SSRC of first source)

| Fraction lost | Cumulative number of packets lost |

Extended highest sequence number received
Interarrival jitter
Time of last sender report
Delay since last sender report — report block 1

SSRC_n (SSRC of nth source)

| Fraction lost | Cumulative number of packets lost |

Extended highest sequence number received
Interarrival jitter
Time of last sender report
Delay since last sender report — report block n

(b) RTCP receiver report

V	P	RC	PT = 201	Length

SSRC of sender — header

SSRC_1 (SSRC of first source)

| Fraction lost | Cumulative number of packets lost |

Extended highest sequence number received
Interarrival jitter
Time of last sender report
Delay since last sender report — report block 1

SSRC_n (SSRC of nth source)

| Fraction lost | Cumulative number of packets lost |

Extended highest sequence number received
Interarrival jitter
Time of last sender report
Delay since last sender report — report block n

(c) RTCP application-defined packet

V	P	sub-type	PT = 204	Length

SSRC/CSRC
name (ASCII)
Application-dependent data

(d) RTCP source description

V	P	SC	PT = 202	Length

SSRC/CSRC_1
SDES items — chunk 1

SSRC/CSRC_n
SDES items — chunk n

(e) RTCP BYE

V	P	SC	PT = 203	Length

SSRC/CSRC_1

SSRC/CSRC_n

| Length | Reason for leaving |

Figure 10.11 RTCP Formats

375

In addition, the Sender Report and Receiver Report packets contain the following field:

- **Synchronization Source Identifier:** Identifies the source of this RTCP packet.

We now turn to a description of each packet type.

Sender Report (SR) RTCP receivers provide reception quality feedback using a Sender Report or a Receiver Report, depending on whether the receiver is also a sender during this session. Figure 10.11a shows the format of a Sender Report. The Sender Report consists of a header, already described; a sender information block; and zero or more reception report blocks. The sender information block includes the following fields:

- **NTP Timestamp (64 bits):** The absolute wallclock time when this report was sent; this is an unsigned fixed-point number with the integer part in the first 32 bits and the fractional part in the last 32 bits. This may be used by the sender in combination with timestamps returned in receiver reports to measure round-trip time to those receivers.

- **RTP Timestamp (32 bits):** This is the relative time used to create timestamps in RTP data packets. This lets recipients place this report in the appropriate time sequence with RTP data packets from this source.

- **Sender's Packet Count (32 bits):** Total number of RTP data packets transmitted by this sender so far in this session.

- **Sender's Octet Count (32 bits):** Total number of RTP payload octets transmitted by this sender so far in this session.

Following the sender information block are zero or more reception report blocks. One reception block is included for each source from which this participant has received data during this session. Each block includes the following fields:

- **SSRC_n (32 bits):** Identifies the source referred to by this report block.

- **Fraction lost (8 bits):** The fraction of RTP data packets from SSRC_n lost since the previous SR or RR packet was sent.

- **Cumulative number of packets lost (24 bits):** Total number of RTP data packets from SSRC_n lost during this session.

- **Extended highest sequence number received (32 bits):** The least significant 16 bits record the highest RTP data sequence number received from SSRC_n. The most significant 16 bits record the number of times the sequence number has wrapped back to zero.

- **Interarrival jitter (32 bits):** An estimate of the jitter experienced on RTP data packets from SSRC_n, explained later.

- **Last SR timestamp (32 bits):** The middle 32 bits of the NTP timestamp in the last SR packet received from SSRC_n. This captures the least significant half of the integer and the most significant half of the fractional part of the timestamp and should be adequate.

- **Delay since last SR (32 bits):** The delay, expressed in units of 2^{-16} seconds, between receipt of the last SR packet from SSRC_n and the transmission of this report block. These last two fields can be used by a source to estimate round-trip time to a particular receiver.

Recall that delay jitter was defined as the maximum variation in delay experienced by packets in a single session. There is no simple way to measure this quantity at the receiver, but it is possible to estimate the average jitter in the following way. At a particular receiver, define the following parameters for a given source:

$S(I)$ = Timestamp from RTP data packet I

$R(I)$ = Time of arrival for RTP data packet I, expressed in RTP timestamp units. The receiver must use the same clock frequency (increment interval) as the source but need not synchronize time values with the source

$D(I)$ = The difference between the interarrival time at the receiver and the spacing between adjacent RTP data packets leaving the source

$J(I)$ = Estimated average interarrival jitter up to the receipt of RTP data packet I

The value of $D(I)$ is calculated as

$$D(I) = (R(I) - R(I - 1)) - (S(I) - S(I - 1))$$

Thus, $D(I)$ measures how much the spacing between arriving packets differs from the spacing between transmitted packets. In the absence of jitter, the spacings will be the same and $D(I)$ will have a value of 0. The interarrival jitter is calculated continuously as each data packet I is received, according to the following formula:

$$J(I) = \frac{15}{16}J(I - 1) + \frac{1}{16}|D(I)|$$

$J(I)$ is calculated as an exponential average[3] of observed values of $D(I)$. Only a small weight is given to the most recent observation, so that temporary fluctuations do not invalidate the estimate.

The values in the Sender Report enable senders, receivers, and network managers to monitor conditions on the network as they relate to a particular session. For example, packet loss values give an indication of persistent congestion, while the jitter measures transient congestion. The jitter measure may provide a warning of increasing congestion before it leads to packet loss.

Receiver Report (RR) The format for the Receiver Report (Figure 10.11b) is the same as that for a Sender Report, except that the Packet Type field has a different value and there is no sender information block.

Source Description (SDES) The Source Description packet (Figure 10.11d) is used by a source to provide more information about itself. The packet consists of a 32-bit header followed by zero or more chunks, each of which contains information describing this source. Each chunk begins with an identifier for this source or for a contributing source. This is followed by a list of descriptive items. Table 10.4 lists the types of descriptive items defined in RFC 1889.

---

[3]For comparison, see Equation (7.3).

Table 10.4 SDES Types (RFC 1889)

Value	Name	Description
0	END	End of SDES list
1	CNAME	Canonical name: unique among all participants within one RTP session
2	NAME	Real user name of the source
3	EMAIL	E-mail address
4	PHONE	Telephone number
5	LOC	Geographic location
6	TOOL	Name of application generating the stream
7	NOTE	Transient message describing the current state of the source
8	PRIV	Private experimental or application-specific extensions

Goodbye (BYE) The BYE packet indicates that one or more sources are no longer active. This confirms to receivers that a prolonged silence is due to departure rather than network failure. If a BYE packet is received by a mixer, it is forwarded with the list of sources unchanged. The format of the BYE packet consists of a 32-bit header followed by one or more source identifiers. Optionally, the packet may include a textual description of the reason for leaving.

Application-Defined Packet This packet is intended for experimental use for functions and features that are application specific. Ultimately, an experimental packet type that proves generally useful may be assigned a packet type number and become part of the standardized RTCP.

10.4 RECOMMENDED READING AND WEB SITES

[ZHAN93] is a good overview of the philosophy and functionality of RSVP, written by its developers. [HARN02] provides a thorough treatment of MPLS. [WANG01] covers not only MPLS but IS and DS; it also has an excellent chapter on MPLS traffic engineering. [VISW98] includes a concise overview of the MPLS architecture and describes the various proprietary efforts that preceded MPLS. [LAWR01] looks at the design of MPLS switches.

HARN02 Harnedy, S. *The MPLS Primer: An Introduction to Multiprotocol Label Switching.* Upper Saddle River, NJ: Prentice Hall, 2002.

LAWR01 Lawrence, J. "Designing Multiprotocol Label Switching Networks." *IEEE Communications Magazine,* July 2001.

VISW98 Viswanathan, A., et al. "Evolution of Multiprotocol Label Switching." *IEEE Communications Magazine,* May 1998.

WANG01 Wang, Z. *Internet QoS: Architectures and Mechanisms for Quality of Service.* San Francisco, CA: Morgan Kaufmann, 2001.

ZHAN93 Zhang, L.; Deering, S.; Estrin, D.; Shenker, S.; and Zappala, D. "RSVP: A New Resource ReSerVation Protocol." *IEEE Network,* September 1993.

Recommended Web Sites:

- **RSVP Project:** Home page for RSVP development.
- **RSVP Working Group:** Chartered by IETF to develop standards related to differentiated services. The Web site includes all relevant RFCs and Internet drafts.
- **MPLS Forum:** An industry forum to promote MPLS.
- **MPLS Resource Center:** Clearinghouse for information on MPLS.
- **MPLS Working Group:** Chartered by IETF to develop standards related to MPLS. The Web site includes all relevant RFCs and Internet drafts.
- **Audio/Video Transport Working Group:** Chartered by IETF to develop standards related to RTP. The Web site includes all relevant RFCs and Internet drafts.
- **About RTP:** Web site devoted to RTP developments, including technical and industry developments.

10.5 KEY TERMS, REVIEW QUESTIONS, AND PROBLEMS

Key Terms

data flow
label stacking
Multiprotocol Label
    Switching (MPLS)
	Real-Time Transport Protocol
	    (RTP)
	receiver-initiated reservation
	Resource ReSerVation
	    Protocol (RSVP)
		RTP Control Protocol
		    (RTCP)
		soft state
		traffic engineering

Review Questions

10.1 What are the primary motivations for multicast resource reservation?

10.2 List the design goals for RSVP.

10.3 What are the key characteristics of RSVP?

10.4 What is meant by receiver-initiated reservation?

10.5 Explain the concept of a soft state.

10.6 What is the difference between a flowspec and a filter spec in RSVP?

10.7 What is traffic engineering?

10.8 What is an MPLS forwarding equivalence class?

10.9 What is an MPLS label switched path?

10.10 Explain label stacking.

10.11 What is meant by a constraint-based routing algorithm?

10.12 What is the purpose of RTP?

10.13 What is the difference between RTP and RTCP?

Problems

10.1   In RSVP, because the UDP/TCP port numbers are used for packet classification, each router must be able to examine these fields. This requirement raises problems in the following areas:

   a. IPv4 fragmentation

   b. IPv6 header processing

   c. IP-level security

   Indicate the nature of the problem in each area, and suggest a solution.

10.2   Consider Figure 10.3a. This diagram appears to be a simplification, because each (source, destination) pair in a multicast routing scheme has a separate routing tree. Therefore, the output ports of the diagram should be labeled not just on the basis of destination but on the basis of (source, destination) pairs. Justify your agreement or disagreement.

10.3   The MPLS specification allows a LSR to use a technique known as *penultimate hop popping*. With this technique, the next-to-last LSR in a LSP is allowed to remove the label from a packet and send it without the label to the last LSR in that LSP.

   a. Explain why this action is possible; that is, why it results in correct behavior.

   b. What is the advantage of penultimate hop popping?

10.4   In the TCP/IP protocol suite, it is standard practice for the header corresponding to a given protocol layer to contain information that identifies the protocol used in the next higher layer. This information is needed so that the recipient of the PDU, when stripping off a given header, knows how to interpret the remaining bits so as to identify and process the header portion. For example, the IPv4 and IPv6 headers have a Protocol and Next Header field, respectively (Figure 2.13); TCP and UDP both have a Port field (Figure 2.12), which can be used to identify the protocol on top of TCP or UDP. However, each MPLS node processes a packet whose top element is the MPLS label field, which contains no explicit information about the protocol that is encapsulated. Typically, that protocol is IPv4, but it could be some other network-layer protocol.

   a. Along an LSP, which MPLS nodes would need to identify the packet's network layer protocol?

   b. What conditions must we impose on the MPLS label in order for proper processing to occur?

   c. Are such restrictions needed on all of the labels in an MPLS label stack or, if not, which ones?

10.5   Argue the effectiveness, or lack thereof, of using RTP as a means of alleviating network congestion for multicast traffic.

10.6   Illustrate how the last two fields in an RTCP SR or RR receiver report block can be used to calculate round-trip propagation time.

PART FIVE

Internet Routing

The architecture of today's Internet is built on a collection of a small number (a dozen or so at the time of writing) core backbone providers called network service providers (NSPs). Each backbone consists of a packet-switching network running over high-speed lines and a boundary of high-performance routers. The NSPs share traffic at exchange points. Local and regional Internet service providers (ISPs) maintain their own communications facilities of routers and lines and contract with backbone providers to carry their traffic for the long haul.

Private networks owned and operated by businesses typically consist of a number of Ethernet-type LANs interconnected by leased lines or by public or private packet-switching networks. These networks, in turn, have one or more access points into the Internet.

The traffic that the Internet and these private internetworks must carry continues to grow and change. The demand generated by traditional data-based applications, such as electronic mail, USENET news, file transfer, and remote logon, is sufficient to challenge these systems. But the driving factors are the heavy use of the World Wide Web, which demands real-time response, and the increasing use of voice, image, and even video over internetwork architectures.

These internetwork schemes are essentially datagram packet-switching technology with routers functioning as the switches. This technology was not designed to handle voice and video and is straining to meet the demands placed on it. While some foresee the replacement of this conglomeration of Ethernet-based LANs, packet-based WANs, and IP-datagram-based routers with a seamless ATM transport service from desktop to backbone, that day is far off. Meanwhile, the internetworking and routing functions of these networks must be engineered to meet the load.

The performance problems in an internetwork environment are most readily seen on the Internet itself. During at least one period in 1996, some NSPs posted packet loss rates of 30% to 50%, while throughout the year some NSPs experienced losses approaching 30% with some regularity [BRUN96]. A 10% loss is noticeable in service performance, while a 50% loss almost renders the service unusable. More recent studies continue to show these performance degradations [BORT01]. Much of the problem can be traced not just to the sheer volume of traffic but also to the poor performance of the routers in maintaining routing tables and in selecting the best routes for a given class of traffic. These problems also show up in private internetworks, particularly when intranet services such as the Web are provided and when Ethernets and packet-switching WANs are used to carry voice and video.

The type of congestion control and traffic policing strategies that have proved effective in ATM networks do not directly carry over to a connectionless, packet-based internetwork architecture. The latter architecture does not rely on end-to-end virtual channels that can be managed in terms of capacity and variability of bit rate. Instead, the key to effective performance management in a packet-based internetwork environment is the router. The router must

1. Have the processing capacity to move IP datagrams through the router at extremely high rates.

2. Have sufficient knowledge of the networked configuration to pick a route that is appropriate to a given class of traffic and to compensate for congestion and failure in the internetwork.

3. Employ a scheme for exchanging routing information with other routers that is effective and does not excessively contribute to the traffic burden.

The first point is addressed in the domain of processor and operating system design and does not concern us here. The remaining points hinge on the routing function and the routing protocol that supports that function. This is the focus of Part Five.

ROAD MAP FOR PART FIVE

Chapter 11 Interior Routing Protocols

The central task of a router is to forward IP datagrams along a route that is preferred under some criterion. For this purpose, a routing metric, or cost function, is assigned to each router-to-router hop through the Internet for a given type of service. The router must choose a route that minimizes the path cost for a datagram. Chapter 11 presents the algorithms that are typically used to compute this minimum path.

To determine a minimum-cost route, a router must have some information about the cost of alternative paths through the internetwork of which it is a part. Chapters 11 and 12 look at important protocols that are used for the acquisition of such routing information. Chapter 11 focuses on interior routing protocols, which are used among routers within an autonomous system (AS). In essence, an AS is a connected set of routers and networks managed by a single organization and using a common routing protocol. Chapter 11 examines the two most important interior routing protocols: RIP and OSPF.

Chapter 12 Exterior Routing Protocols and Multicast

Routers within a single AS, using an interior routing protocol, must exchange detailed information about the topology and traffic conditions within the AS. In contrast, exterior routing protocols, used between ASs, generally exchange less information concerning general routes between networks in different ASs. Chapter 12 examines two exterior routing protocols: BGP and IDRP. The chapter also examines the concept of multicasting and the use of multicast routing protocols.

CHAPTER 11

INTERIOR ROUTING PROTOCOLS

The map of the London Underground, which can be seen inside every train, has been called a model of its kind, a work of art. It presents the underground network as a geometric grid. The tube lines do not, of course, lie at right angles to one another like the streets of Manhattan. Nor do they branch off at acute angles or form perfect oblongs.

—King Solomon's Carpet,
    Barbara Vine
    (Ruth Rendell)

KEY POINTS

- Routing protocols in an internet function in a similar fashion to those used in packet-switching networks. An internet routing protocol is used to exchange information about reachability and traffic delays, allowing each router to construct a next-hop routing table for paths through the internet. Typically, relatively simple routing protocols are used between autonomous systems within a larger internet and more complex routing protocols are used within each autonomous system.

- The routing function attempts to find the least-cost route through a network or an internet, with cost based on number of hops, expected delay, or other metrics. Adaptive routing algorithms typically rely on the exchange of information about traffic conditions among nodes.

- A relatively simple interior routing protocol is the Routing Information Protocol (RIP). Despite its simplicity, it is suitable for smaller internets and is one of the most widely used routing protocols.

- The Open Shortest Path First protocol (OSPF) is now considered the preferred interior routing protocol for TCP/IP-based internets.

Routing protocols are an essential ingredient to the operation of an internet. Internets operate on the basis of routers that forward IP datagrams from router to router on a path from the source host to the destination host. For a router to perform its function, it must have some idea of the topology of the internet and the best route to follow. It is the purpose of the routing protocol to provide the needed information.

We begin this chapter with a discussion of the basic principles of internet routing, including a consideration of routing in high-speed internets. Next, we discuss the fundamental concept of a routing algorithm. Then we look at two important routing protocols, RIP and OSPF, that typify two distinct approaches to gathering routing information.

11.1 INTERNET ROUTING PRINCIPLES

One of the most complex and critical aspects of internet design is routing. This section begins with a discussion of the routing mechanism. Then we look at the general architecture of internet routing.

The Routing Function

The routers in an internet perform much the same function as packet-switching nodes (PSNs) in a packet-switching network. Just as the PSN is responsible for receiving and forwarding packets through a packet-switching network, the router is responsible for receiving and forwarding IP datagrams through an internet. For this purpose, the routers of an internet need to make routing decisions based on knowledge of the topology and conditions of the internet.

As is discussed in the Section 11.2, the routing decision is based on some form of least-cost criterion. If the criterion is to minimize the number of hops, each hop (edge) has a value of 1. More typically, a cost is associated with each hop. The cost may be inversely proportional to the link capacity, proportional to the current load on the link, or some combination. Or the cost may include other criteria, such as the monetary cost of using the hop. In any case, these hop costs are used as input to a least-cost routing algorithm, such as those described in Section 11.2.

Fixed Routing In a simple configuration, a fixed routing scheme is possible, in which a single, permanent route is configured for each source-destination pair of nodes in the network. The routes are fixed, or at most only change when there is a change in the topology of the network. Thus, the link costs used in designing routes cannot be based on any dynamic variable such as traffic. They could, however, be based on estimated traffic volumes between various source-destination pairs or the capacity of each link.

Consider the configuration of Figure 11.1, consisting of five networks and eight routers. A link cost is associated with the output side of each router for each network. In a fixed routing scheme, this cost might reflect the expected traffic load between a given router and a given attached network. Figure 11.2 suggests how fixed routing might be implemented. Each router maintains a table that has an entry for each network in the configuration. It is not necessary to have an entry for each possible destination host; for purposes of routing, only the network portion is of interest. Once an IP datagram has reached a router attached to the destination network, that router can deliver the datagram to the appropriate destination host on that network. Fortunately, an IP address typically consists of a host portion and a network portion (Figure 8.5), so that destination network is easily extracted from the IP datagram.

Each entry in the routing table indicates a destination network and the next router to take for that destination. It is not necessary for a router to store the complete route for each possible destination. Rather, it is sufficient to know, for each destination, the identity of the next node on the route. To see this, suppose that the least-cost route from X to Y begins with the X-A link. Call the remainder of the route R_1; this is the part from A to Y. Define R_2 as the least-cost route from A to Y. If the cost of R_1 is greater than that of R_2, then the X-Y route can be improved by using R_2 instead. If the cost of R_1 is less than R_2, then R_2 is not the least-cost route from A to Y. Therefore, $R_1 = R_2$. Thus, at each point along a route, it is only necessary to know the identity of the next hop, not the entire route. In our example, the route from router F to network 2 begins by going through router H. The route from router H to network 2 goes through router G. Finally, router G is directly attached to network 2. Thus, the complete route from router F to network 2 is F-H-G.

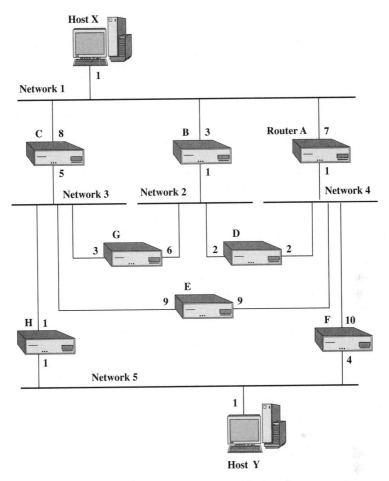

Figure 11.1   A Configuration of Routers and Networks

Such a routing table is required in each router. In addition, it may be desirable to configure routing tables in hosts. If a host is attached to a single network and that network has only one attached router, then a routing table is not needed for that host: All off-network traffic must be directed to the single router. However, if there are multiple routers attached to the network, then the host should have a table that indicates which router to use for each off-network destination. The alternative is to designate a default router, but this is not an optimal solution. Figure 11.2 shows the routing table for host X.

Adaptive Routing   In virtually all internet configurations, the routers employ some sort of adaptive routing technique. With adaptive routing, as conditions in the internet change, the routes used for forwarding datagrams may change. The principal conditions that influence routing decisions are as follows:

- **Failure:** When a network or router fails, it can no longer be used as part of a route.

Router A Table	
Network	Router
1	D
2	D
3	D
4	—
5	F

Router D Table	
Network	Router
1	B
2	—
3	G
4	—
5	F

Router G Table	
Network	Router
1	B
2	—
3	—
4	D
5	H

Router B Table	
Network	Router
1	—
2	—
3	G
4	D
5	G

Router E Table	
Network	Router
1	D
2	D
3	—
4	—
5	H

Router H Table	
Network	Router
1	C
2	G
3	—
4	G
5	—

Router C Table	
Network	Router
1	—
2	B
3	—
4	A
5	H

Router F Table	
Network	Router
1	H
2	H
3	H
4	—
5	—

Host X Table	
Network	Router
1	—
2	B
3	B
4	A
5	A

Figure 11.2 Routing Tables for Figure 11.1

- **Congestion:** When a particular portion of the internet is heavily congested, it is desirable to route datagrams around rather than through the area of congestion. Thus, the routing strategy can help to avoid, or at least avoid exacerbating, congestion; this is critical in high-speed internets.

There are several drawbacks associated with the use of adaptive routing:

- The routing decision is more complex; therefore, the processing burden on routers increases.

- In most cases, adaptive strategies depend on status information that is collected at one place but used at another. There is a tradeoff here between the quality of the information and the amount of overhead. The more information that is exchanged, and the more frequently it is exchanged, the better will be the routing decisions that each node makes. On the other hand, this information is itself a load on the constituent networks, causing a performance degradation.

- An adaptive strategy may react too quickly, causing congestion-producing oscillation, or too slowly, being irrelevant.

- An adaptive strategy can produce pathologies, such as fluttering and looping.

It is worth elaborating on these last two points. If an adaptive strategy reacts very quickly, minor fluctuations in load in the internet may cause a number of routers to shift traffic to a temporarily less loaded region. This quick reaction, in turn, causes a surge of traffic in the new region, which may result in some of the traffic being rerouted back in the direction it came from. If an adaptive strategy reacts very slowly to changes in load, by the time that routing decisions are made, the load distribution may have changed so markedly that the new routing decisions are inappropriate.

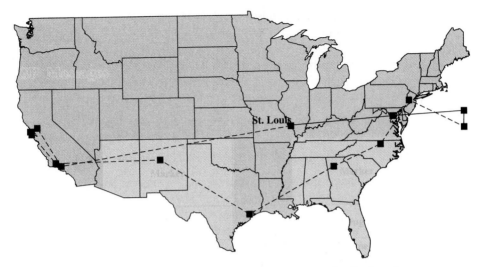

Figure 11.3 Example of Fluttering: Routes Taken by Alternating Packets from wust1 (St. Louis, Missouri) to umann (Mannheim, Germany)

Fluttering refers to rapid oscillations in routing. This can be caused by the router's attempt to do load splitting, or balancing. RFC 1812 describes load splitting in the following way: "At the end of the Next-Hop selection process, multiple routes may still remain. The router may retain more than one route and employ a load-splitting mechanism to divide traffic among them." Such load splitting can lead to aberrant behavior. An example reported in [PAXS97] is illustrated in Figure 11.3. In this instance, a router in St. Louis split its load for the umann destination between a next hop to Washington, D.C. (solid; 17 hops to umann) and Anaheim (dotted line; 29 hops). The result was that successive packets bound for umann travel via a radically different route. The [PAXS97] study consisted of observation of Internet traffic at selected locations over several days; a number of instances of fluttering were observed.

While fluttering does provide a load-balancing effect, it can cause a number of problems, including the following:

- If fluttering occurs in only one direction, the route characteristics in the two directions, including timing and error characteristics, differ. This can confuse management and troubleshooting applications that try to measure route characteristics.

- With two distinct routes between source and destination, estimating round-trip times and available capacity becomes difficult.

- When the two routes have different propagation times, TCP packets will arrive out of order, which can lead to spurious fast retransmission by generating duplicate acknowledgments, wasting capacity.

A more serious pathology is **looping**, in which packets forwarded by a router eventually return to the router. Routing algorithms are designed to prevent looping, but looping may occur when the internet experiences a change in connectivity and that change is not immediately propagated to all of the other routers. In their observations over three days, [PAXS97] observed 60 instances of looping, some of these lasting several hours and a few lasting more than half a day. Such extremely persistent loops will clearly disrupt traffic for some sources.

Despite their problems, adaptive routing strategies are by far more prevalent than fixed routing, for two reasons:

- An adaptive routing strategy can improve performance, as seen by the network user.
- An adaptive routing strategy can aid in congestion control.

These benefits may or may not be realized, depending on the soundness of the design and the nature of the load. By and large, adaptive routing is an extraordinarily complex task to perform properly. This accounts for the fact that routing protocols have undergone a continual evolution over the years.

A convenient way to classify adaptive routing strategies is on the basis of information source: local, adjacent nodes, all nodes. An example of an adaptive routing strategy that relies only on local information is one in which a router routes each datagram to the outgoing network for which it has the shortest queue length Q. This would have the effect of balancing the load on outgoing networks. However, some outgoing networks may not be headed in the correct general direction. We can improve matters by also taking into account preferred direction. In this case, each network attached to the router would have a bias B_i, for each destination network i. For each incoming datagram headed for network i, the router would choose the outgoing link that minimizes $Q + B_i$. Thus a router would tend to send datagrams in the right direction, with a concession made to current traffic delays.

Adaptive schemes based only on local information are rarely used; such schemes do not exploit information from adjacent routers or more distant routers, which would improve the quality of the routing decisions. Strategies based on information from adjacent routers or all routers are commonly found. Both take advantage of information that each router has about delays and outages that it experiences. Strategies based on information from adjacent routers are called distance-vector algorithms, and strategies based on information from all routers are called link-state algorithms; these are discussed subsequently. In either case, a routing protocol is needed for the exchange of information.

A final point: The actual routing mechanism is independent of the type of routing protocol and is independent of whether there is a routing protocol or a fixed routing strategy. Consider Figures 11.1 and 11.2, which were used to illustrate fixed routing. The link costs illustrated in Figure 11.1 can be dynamic costs, which reflect current delays at the corresponding interfaces. The routing tables in Figure 11.2 could be constructed from information provided by a routing protocol rather than configured ahead of time.

Autonomous Systems

To proceed in our discussion of routing protocols, we need to introduce the concept of an autonomous system. An autonomous system (AS) exhibits the following characteristics:

1. An AS is a set of routers and networks managed by a single organization.

2. An AS consists of a group of routers exchanging information via a common routing protocol.

3. Except in times of failure, an AS is connected (in a graph-theoretic sense); that is, there is a path between any pair of nodes.

A common routing protocol, which we shall refer to as an **interior routing protocol** (IRP), passes routing information between routers within an AS. The protocol used within the AS does not need to be implemented outside of the system. This flexibility allows IRPs to be custom tailored to specific applications and requirements.

It may happen, however, that an internet will be constructed of more than one AS. For example, all of the LANs at a site, such as an office complex or campus, could be linked by routers to form an AS. This system might be linked through a wide area network to other ASs. The situation is illustrated in Figure 11.4. In this case, the routing algorithms and information in routing tables used by routers in different ASs may differ. Nevertheless, the routers in one AS need at least a minimal level of information concerning networks outside the system that can be reached. We refer to the protocol used to pass routing information between routers in different ASs is referred to as an **exterior routing protocol** (ERP).[1]

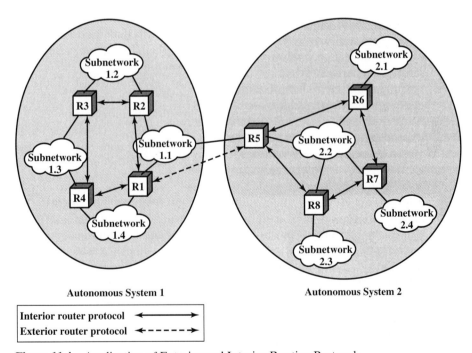

Figure 11.4 Application of Exterior and Interior Routing Protocols

---

[1]In the literature, the terms *interior gateway protocol* (IGP) and *exterior gateway protocol* (EGP) are often used for what are referred to here as IRP and ERP. However, because the terms *IGP* and *EGP* also refer to specific protocols, we avoid their use to define the general concepts.

We can expect that an ERP will need to pass less information than an IRP, for the following reason: If a datagram is to be transferred from a host in one AS to a host in another AS, a router in the first system need only determine the target AS and devise a route to get into that target system. Once the datagram enters the target AS, the routers within that system can cooperate to deliver the datagram; the ERP is not concerned with, and does not know about, the details of the route followed within the target AS.

In the remainder of this chapter, we look at what are perhaps the most important examples of interior routing protocols: RIP and OSPF. Chapter 12 examines two important exterior routing protocols: BGP and IDRP.

Approaches to Routing

Internet routing protocols employ one of three approaches to gathering and using routing information: distance-vector routing, link-state routing, and path-vector routing.

Distance-vector routing requires that each node (router or host that implements the routing protocol) exchange information with its neighboring nodes. Two nodes are said to be neighbors if they are both directly connected to the same network. For this purpose, each node maintains a vector of link costs for each directly attached network and distance and next-hop vectors for each destination. The relatively simple Routing Information Protocol (RIP), described in Section 11.3, uses this approach.

Distance-vector routing requires the transmission of a considerable amount of information by each router. Each router must send a distance vector to all of its neighbors, and that vector contains the estimated path cost to all networks in the configuration. Furthermore, when there is a significant change in a link cost or when a link is unavailable, it may take a considerable amount of time for this information to propagate through the internet.

Link-state routing is designed to overcome the drawbacks of distance-vector routing. When a router is initialized, it determines the link cost on each of its network interfaces. The router then advertises this set of link costs to all other routers in the internet topology, not just neighboring routers. From then on, the router monitors its link costs. Whenever there is a significant change (a link cost increases or decreases substantially, a new link is created, an existing link becomes unavailable), the router again advertises its set of link costs to all other routers in the configuration. The Open Shortest Path First (OSPF) protocol, described in Section 11.4, is an example of a routing protocol that uses link-state routing.

Both link-state and distance-vector approaches have been used for interior router protocols. Neither approach is effective for an exterior router protocol.

In a distance-vector routing protocol, each router advertises to its neighbors a vector listing each network it can reach, together with a distance metric associated with the path to that network. Each router builds up a routing database on the basis of these neighbor updates but does not know the identity of intermediate routers and networks on any particular path. There are two problems with this approach for an exterior router protocol:

1. This distance-vector protocol assumes that all routers share a common distance metric with which to judge router preferences. This may not be the case among different ASs. If different routers attach different meanings to a given metric, it may not be possible to create stable, loop-free routes.

2. A given AS may have different priorities from other ASs and may have restrictions that prohibit the use of certain other ASs. A distance-vector algorithm gives no information about the ASs that will be visited along a route.

In a link-state routing protocol, each router advertises its link metrics to all other routers. Each router builds up a picture of the complete topology of the configuration and then performs a routing calculation. This approach also has problems if used in an exterior router protocol:

1. Again, different ASs may use different metrics and have different restrictions. Although the link-state protocol does allow a router to build up a picture of the entire topology, the metrics used may vary from one AS to another, making it impossible to perform a consistent routing algorithm.

2. The flooding of link-state information to all routers implementing an exterior router protocol across multiple ASs may be unmanageable.

An alternative, known as **path-vector routing**, is to dispense with routing metrics and simply provide information about which networks can be reached by a given router and the ASs that must be crossed to get there. The approach differs from a distance-vector algorithm in two respects: First, the path-vector approach does not include a distance or cost estimate. Second, each block of routing information lists all of the ASs visited in order to reach the destination network by this route.

Because a path vector lists the ASs that a datagram must traverse if it follows this route, the path information enables a router to perform policy routing. That is, a router may decide to avoid a particular path in order to avoid transiting a particular AS. For example, information that is confidential may be limited to certain kinds of ASs. Or a router may have information about the performance or quality of the portion of the internet that is included in an AS that leads the router to avoid that AS. Examples of performance or quality metrics include link speed, capacity, tendency to become congested, and overall quality of operation. Another criterion that could be used is minimizing the number of transit ASs.

Chapter 12 discusses two examples of path-vector routing.

11.2 LEAST-COST ALGORITHMS

Virtually all packet-switching networks and all internets base their routing decision on some form of least-cost criterion. If the criterion is to minimize the number of hops, each link has a value of 1. More typically, the link value is inversely proportional to the link capacity, proportional to the current load on the link, or some combination. In any case, these link or hop costs are used as input to a least-cost routing algorithm, which can be simply stated as follows:

Given a network of nodes connected by bidirectional links, where each link has a cost associated with it in each direction, define the cost of a path between two nodes as the sum of the costs of the links traversed. For each pair of nodes, find a path with the least cost.

Note that the cost of a link may differ in its two directions. This would be true, for example, if the cost of a link equaled the length of the queue of packets awaiting transmission from each of the two nodes on the link.

Most least-cost routing algorithms in use in packet-switching networks and internets are variations of one of two common algorithms, known as Dijkstra's algorithm and the Bellman-Ford algorithm. This section provides a summary of these two algorithms.

Dijkstra's Algorithm

Dijkstra's algorithm [DIJK59] can be stated as follows: Find the shortest paths from a given source node to all other nodes, by developing the paths in order of increasing path length. The algorithm proceeds in stages. By the kth stage, the shortest paths to the k nodes closest to (least cost away from) the source node have been determined; these nodes are in a set T. At stage $(k + 1)$, the node not in T that has the shortest path from the source node is added to T. As each node is added to T, its path from the source is defined. The algorithm can be formally described as follows. Define:

N = set of nodes in the network

s = source node

T = set of nodes so far incorporated by the algorithm

$w(i, j)$ = link cost from node i to node j; $w(i, i) = 0$; $w(i, j) = \infty$ if the two nodes are not directly connected; $w(i, j) \geq 0$ if the two nodes are directly connected

$L(n)$ = cost of the least-cost path from node s to node n that is currently known to the algorithm; at termination, this is the cost of the least-cost path in the graph from s to n

The algorithm has three steps; steps 2 and 3 are repeated until $T = N$. That is, steps 2 and 3 are repeated until final paths have been assigned to all nodes in the network:

1. **[Initialization]**

   $T = \{s\}$ i.e., the set of nodes so far incorporated consists of only the source node

   $L(n) = w(s, n)$ for $n \neq s$ i.e., the initial path costs to neighboring nodes are simply the link costs

2. **[Get Next Node]** Find the neighboring node not in T that has the least-cost path from node s and incorporate that node into T. Also incorporate the edge that is incident on that node and a node in T that contributes to the path. This can be expressed as

   $$\text{Find } x \notin T \text{ such that } L(x) = \min_{j \notin T} L(j)$$

Add x to T; add to T the edge that is incident on x and that contributes the least-cost component to $L(x)$, that is, the last hop in the path.

3. **[Update Least-Cost Paths]**

$$L(n) = \min[L(n), L(x) + w(x, n)] \qquad \text{for all } n \notin T$$

If the latter term is the minimum, the path from s to n is now the path from s to x concatenated with the edge from x to n.

The algorithm terminates when all nodes have been added to T. At termination, the value $L(x)$ associated with each node x is the cost (length) of the least-cost path from s to x. In addition, T defines the least-cost path from s to each other node.

One iteration of steps 2 and 3 adds one new node to T and defines the least-cost path from s to that node. That path passes only through nodes that are in T. To see this, consider the following line of reasoning: After k iterations, there are k nodes in T, and the least-cost path from s to each of these nodes has been defined. Now consider all possible paths from s to nodes not in T. Among those paths, there is one of least cost that passes exclusively through nodes in T (see Problem 11.4), ending with a direct link from some node in T to a node not in T. This node is added to T and the associated path is defined as the least-cost path for that node.

Let us consider the example configuration of Figure 11.5. In this figure, each node represents a network. The two arrowed lines between a pair of nodes represent a router connecting the pair of networks, and the corresponding numbers represent the current cost in each direction.

Table 11.1a and Figure 11.6 show the result of applying this algorithm to the configuration of Figure 11.5, using $s = 1$. The shaded edges define the spanning tree for the graph. The values in each circle are the current estimates of $L(x)$ for each node x. A node is shaded when it is added to T. Note that at each step the path to each node plus the total cost of that path is generated. After the final iteration, the least-cost path to each node and the cost of that path have been developed. The same procedure can be used with node 2 as source node, and so on.

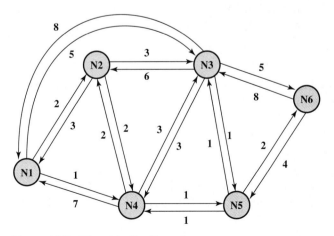

Figure 11.5   Example Configuration

Table 11.1 Example of Least-Cost Routing Algorithms (using Figure 11.1)

(a) Dijkstra'a Algorithm ($s = 1$)

Iteration	T	$L(2)$	Path	$L(3)$	Path	$L(4)$	Path	$L(5)$	Path	$L(6)$	Path
1	{1}	2	1–2	5	1–3	1	1–4	∞	—	∞	—
2	{1, 4}	2	1–2	4	1–4–3	1	1–4	2	1–4–5	∞	—
3	{1, 2, 4}	2	1–2	4	1–4–3	1	1–4	2	1–4–5	∞	—
4	{1, 2, 4, 5}	2	1–2	3	1–4–5–3	1	1–4	2	1–4–5	4	1–4–5–6
5	{1, 2, 3, 4, 5}	2	1–2	3	1–4–5–3	1	1–4	2	1–4–5	4	1–4–5–6
6	{1, 2, 3, 4, 5, 6}	2	1–2	3	1–4–5–3	1	1–4	2	1–4–5	4	1–4–5–6

(b) Bellman-Ford Algorithm ($s = 1$)

h	$L_h(2)$	Path	$L_h(3)$	Path	$L_h(4)$	Path	$L_h(5)$	Path	$L_h(6)$	Path
0	∞	—	∞	—	∞	—	∞	—	∞	—
1	2	1–2	5	1–3	1	1–4	∞	—	∞	—
2	2	1–2	4	1–4–3	1	1–4	2	1–4–5	10	1–3–6
3	2	1–2	3	1–4–5–3	1	1–4	2	1–4–5	4	1–4–5–6
4	2	1–2	3	1–4–5–3	1	1–4	2	1–4–5	4	1–4–5–6

Bellman–Ford Algorithm

The Bellman-Ford algorithm [FORD62] can be stated as follows: Find the shortest paths from a given source node subject to the constraint that the paths contain at most one link, then find the shortest paths with a constraint of paths of at most two links, and so on. This algorithm also proceeds in stages. The algorithm can be formally described as follows. Define:

s = source node

$w(i, j)$ = link cost from node i to node j; $w(i, i) = 0$; $w(i, j) = \infty$ if the two nodes are not directly connected; $w(i, j) \geq 0$ if the two nodes are directly connected

h = maximum number of links in a path at the current stage of the algorithm

$L_h(n)$ = cost of the least-cost path from node s to node n under the constraint of no more than h links

1. **[Initialization]**

$$L_0(n) = \infty, \quad \text{for all } n \neq s$$
$$L_h(s) = 0, \quad \text{for all } h$$

2. **[Update]**

For each successive $h \geq 0$:

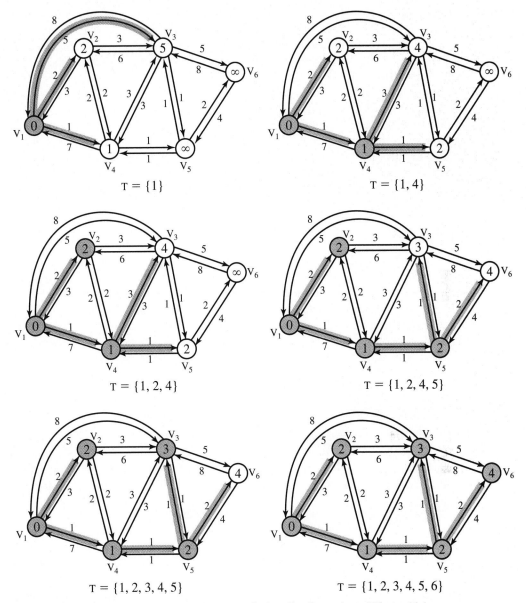

Figure 11.6   Dijkstra's Algorithm Applied to Configuration of Figure 11.1

For each $n \neq s$, compute

$$L_{h+1}(n) = \min_{j} \left[L_h(j) + w(j, n) \right]$$

Connect n with the predecessor node j that achieves the minimum, and eliminates any connection of n with a different predecessor node formed during an earlier iteration. The path from s to n terminates with the link from j to n.

For the iteration of step 2 with $h = K$, and for each destination node n, the algorithm compares potential paths from s to n of length $K + 1$ with the path that existed at the end of the previous iteration. If the previous, shorter, path has less cost, then that path is retained. Otherwise a new path with length $K + 1$ is defined from s to n; this path consists of a path of length K from s to some node j, plus a direct hop from node j to node n. In this case, the path from s to j that is used is the K-hop path for j defined in the previous iteration (see Problem 11.5).

Table 11.1b and Figure 11.7 show the result of applying this algorithm to the configuration of Figure 11.5, using $s = 1$. At each step, the least-cost paths with a maximum number of links equal to h are found. After the final iteration, the least-cost path to each node and the cost of that path have been developed. The same procedure can be used with node 2 as source node, and so on. Note that the results agree with those obtained using Dijkstra's algorithm.

Comparison

One interesting comparison can be made between these two algorithms, having to do with what information needs to be gathered. Consider first the Bellman-Ford algorithm. In step 2, the calculation for node n involves knowledge of the link cost to all neighboring nodes to node n [i.e., $w(j, n)$] plus the total path cost to each of those neighboring nodes from a particular source node s [i.e., $L_h(j)$]. Each node can maintain a set of costs and associated paths for every other node in the network and exchange this information with its direct neighbors from time to time. Each node can therefore use the expression in step 2 of the Bellman-Ford algorithm, based

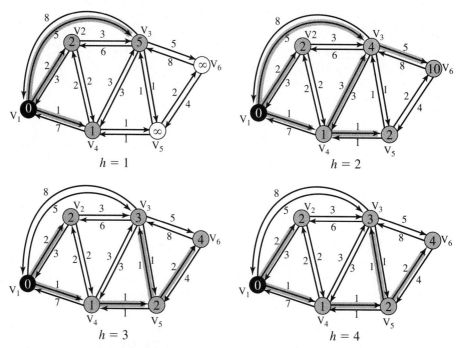

Figure 11.7 Bellman-Ford Algorithm Applied to Configuration of Figure 11.1

only on information from its neighbors and knowledge of its link costs, to update its costs and paths. On the other hand, consider Dijkstra's algorithm. Step 3 appears to require that each node must have complete topological information about the network. That is, each node must know the link costs of all links in the network. Thus, for this algorithm, information must be exchanged with all other nodes.

In general, evaluation of the relative merits of the two algorithms should consider the processing time of the algorithms and the amount of information that must be collected from other nodes in the network or internet. The evaluation will depend on the implementation approach and the specific implementation.

A final point: Both algorithms are known to converge under static conditions of topology, and link costs and will converge to the same solution. If the link costs change over time, the algorithm will attempt to catch up with these changes. However, if the link cost depends on traffic, which in turn depends on the routes chosen, then a feedback condition exists, and instabilities may result.

11.3 DISTANCE-VECTOR PROTOCOL: RIP

A relatively simple interior routing protocol is the Routing Information Protocol (RIP).[2] Despite its simplicity, it remains suitable for smaller internets and is one of the most widely used routing protocols.

A key feature of RIP is that it uses a technique known as distance-vector routing. We begin with a general description of this technique. Then we show how this technique is adapted for use in RIP. Finally, we define the RIP packet format and discuss RIP's limitations.

Distance-Vector Routing Approach

The Algorithm For purposes of the protocol, each node maintains three vectors. First, each node x maintains a link cost vector of the form:

$$\mathbf{W}_x = \begin{bmatrix} w(x, 1) \\ \cdot \\ \cdot \\ \cdot \\ w(x, M) \end{bmatrix}$$

where M is the number of networks to which node x directly attaches. A link cost $w(x, i)$ is associated with the output side of each node for each attached network i. For example, in the configuration of Figure 11.1, all of the link costs are indicated. Host X attaches to only one network and so has only one link cost, with a value of 1; router A attaches to networks 1 and 4 and has link costs of $w(A, 1) = 7$ and $w(A, 4) = 1$.

---

[2]Defined in RFC 1058. There is a newer version, known as RIP-2, but this was never widely deployed and is not covered in this chapter.

Two other vectors are maintained:

$$\mathbf{L}_x = \begin{bmatrix} L(x,1) \\ \cdot \\ \cdot \\ \cdot \\ L(x,N) \end{bmatrix} \qquad \mathbf{R}_x = \begin{bmatrix} R(x,1) \\ \cdot \\ \cdot \\ \cdot \\ R(x,N) \end{bmatrix}$$

where

$\mathbf{L}_x$ = distance vector for node x

$L(x,j)$ = current estimate of minimum delay from node x to network j

N = number of networks in the configuration

$\mathbf{R}_x$ = next-hop vector for node x

$R(x,j)$ = the next router in the current minimum-delay route from node x to network j

Periodically (every 30 seconds), each node exchanges its distance vector with all of its neighbors. On the basis of all incoming distance vectors, a node x updates both of its vectors as follows:

$$L(x,j) = \min_{y \in A} \left[L(y,j) + w(x, N_{xy}) \right] \tag{11.1}$$

$R(x,j) = y$ \qquad (using y that minimizes the preceding expression)

where

A = set of neighbor nodes for node x

N_{xy} = network that connects node x and router y

Figure 11.8 illustrates the operation of the algorithm, using the network of Figure 11.1. Figure 11.8a shows the routing table for host X at an instant in time that reflects the link costs of Figure 11.1. For each destination network, a path delay is specified, and the next router on the route that produces that delay. At some point, suppose the link costs change (i.e., the observed link delays change) as follows: Both link costs from E become 1, and both link costs from F become 1. Assume that X's neighbors (routers A, B, and C) learn of the change. Each of these nodes updates its distance vector and sends a copy to all of its neighbors, including X (Figure 11.8b). X replaces its current routing table with a new one, based solely on the incoming distance vector and its own estimate of link delay to each of its neighbors. In this case, the link delay to all three neighbors is the same, because all three routers are reached via network 1. The result is shown in Figure 11.8c.

Distributed Bellman-Ford Algorithm In the example just shown, the algorithm appears to work. To understand why, compare Equation (11.1) with the update step in the Bellman-Ford algorithm defined in Section 11.2. The equation is essentially the same. In essence, the routing algorithm used in RIP is a distributed version of the Bellman-Ford algorithm. This algorithm was used as the original routing algorithm in the ARPANET packet-switching network.

Destination Network	Next Router R(X,j)	Metric L(X,j)	B	C	A
1	—	1	3	8	6
2	B	2	1	8	3
3	B	5	4	5	2
4	A	2	3	6	1
5	A	6	4	6	2

(a) Routing table of host X before update   (b) Distance vectors send to host X from neighbor routers

Destination Network	Next Router R(X, j)	Metric L(X, j)
1	—	1
2	B	2
3	A	3
4	A	2
5	A	3

(c) Routing table of host X after update

Figure 11.8 Distance-Vector Algorithm Applied to Figure 11.1

It may help to clarify the nature of the distributed Bellman-Ford algorithm to consider a synchronous version of the algorithm. Suppose that each router x begins with the following assignment:

$$L(x, j) = \begin{cases} w(x, j) & \text{(if } x \text{ is directly connected to network } j) \\ \infty & \text{(otherwise)} \end{cases} \quad (11.2)$$

Then all routers simultaneously exchange their distance vectors and compute Equation (11.1). After computation is complete, all routers again simultaneously exchange their distance vectors and compute Equation (11.1). Each iteration is equivalent to one iteration of step 2 of the Bellman-Ford algorithm (incrementing h by 1) executed in parallel at each node of the graph. Consider a single node s. After the first iteration, it is aware of all shortest-length paths with a distance of at most one hop. After the second iteration, it is aware of all shortest-length paths with a distance of at most two hops, and so on, until all true shortest-length paths from s are found.

It would be difficult to coordinate the activities of all routers so that the algorithm could be executed synchronously. Instead, RIP and all other routing protocols based on distance-vector routing use an asynchronous method. When a node is started up, it initializes itself according to Equation (11.2) and performs an update according to Equation (11.1) after new distance vectors are received from all its neighbors. Every 30 seconds, by its own timer, each router transmits its distance vector to its neighbors. It can be shown that this algorithm is valid; that is, it produces the correct results for each node. If one or more changes occur in link costs in the configuration, then the new shortest-path calculations will converge to the correct answer within a finite time proportional to the number of routers. The derivation is lengthy and can be found in [BERT92].

RIP Details

The preceding general description of a distance-vector routing algorithm ignores some practical details in the distributed operation of the algorithm among a number of cooperating nodes. In this subsection, we look at the details of the algorithm as actually implemented in RIP.

Incremental Update Equation (11.1) assumes that a node receives distance vector updates from all of its neighbors within a short window of time and then does a total update based on all of the incoming vectors. This requirement is not practical for several reasons. Because the algorithm operates asynchronously, there is no guarantee that all updates will be received within any given window. Further, RIP packets are sent using UDP, which is an unreliable transport protocol, so that some RIP packets may not arrive.

Therefore, RIP is designed to operate incrementally by updating its routing table after receipt of any individual distance vector. The following rules are obeyed:

1. If the incoming distance vector includes a new destination network, this information is added to the routing table.

2. If the node receives a route with a smaller delay metric to a destination, it replaces the existing route. For example, suppose we have the configuration of Figure 11.1 and the routing table for host X of Figure 11.8a. Now suppose that X receives only one update, namely, the update from B shown in Figure 11.8b. In that case, the only change that is made to X's routing table is to set $L(X, 5) = 5$ and $R(X, 5) = $ B. If the distance vector from A, shown in Figure 11.8b, subsequently arrives, then X's routing table is updated to that of Figure 11.8c.

3. If the node receives an update vector from router R and the node currently has one or more entries in its routing table for which R is the next hop, then all of these entries are updated to reflect the new information from R.

To see the need for the third rule, suppose that Figure 11.8c is the current routing table for X, reflecting the configuration of Figure 11.1, except that the link costs from E are both 1 and the link costs from F are both 1. Now suppose that router F goes down and this is detected by A. Soon, A will send a distance vector to X that reports a path distance to network 5 of 3. In this case, it is necessary for X to increase the value of $L(X, 5)$ from 3 to 4.

Topology Changes In the preceding paragraph we supposed that A became aware that F had failed. How is this possible? The mechanism used in RIP is the following: Every router is supposed to send an update vector to its neighbors every 30 seconds. If a node K has an entry in its routing table for network i with the next hop to router N, and if K receives no updates from N within 180 seconds, it marks the route as invalid. The assumption is made that either router N has crashed or that the network connecting K to N has become unstable. When K hears from any neighbor that has a valid route to i, the valid route replaces the invalid one.

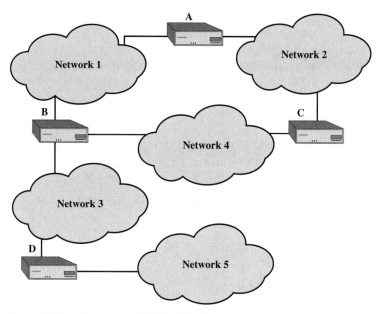

Figure 11.9 Counting to Infinity Problem

The way in which a route is marked invalid is to set the value of the distance to the route to infinity. In practice, RIP uses a value of 16 to equal infinity, for reasons explained subsequently.

Counting to Infinity Problem One of the more significant problems with RIP is its slow convergence to a change in topology. Consider the configuration of Figure 11.9, with all link costs equal to one. B maintains a distance to network 5 of 2, with a next hop of D, while A and C both maintain a distance to network 5 of 3, with a next hop to B. Now suppose that router D fails. Then the following scenario could occur:

1. B determines that network 5 is no longer reachable via D and sets its distance count to 4, based on a report from A or C. This happens because B has recently received a report from both A and C that D is reachable with a distance of 3. At the next reporting interval, B advertises this information in distance vectors to A and C.

2. A and C receive this increased distance information from D and increment their reachability information to network 5 to a distance of 5 (4 from B plus 1 to reach B).

3. B receives the distance count of 5 and assumes that network 5 is now a distance 6 away.

This pattern continues until the distance value reaches infinity, which is only 16 in RIP. Once this value is obtained, a node determines that the target network is no longer reachable. With a reporting interval of 30 seconds, this type of condition can take from 8 to 16 minutes to resolve itself.

Split Horizon with Poisoned Reverse The counting-to-infinity problem is caused by a mutual misunderstanding between B and A (and between B and C). Each thinks that it can reach network 5 via the other. The **split horizon rule** in RIP states that it is never useful to send information about a route back in the direction from which it came, as the router sending you the information is nearer to the destination than you are. The split horizon rule does speed things up; an erroneous route will be eliminated within the interval of the 180-second timeout.

At a small increase in message size, RIP provides even faster response by using **poisoned reverse**. This rule differs from simple split horizon by sending updates to neighbors with a hop count of 16 for routes learned from those neighbors. If two routers have routes pointing at each other, advertising reverse routes with a metric of 16 breaks the loop immediately.

RIP Packet Format

Figure 11.10 shows the format of a RIP packet. Each packet includes a header with the following fields:

- **Command:** 1 for a request, 2 for a reply. Routing updates are sent as replies whether requested or not. When a node initializes RIP, it broadcasts a RIP request; each router receiving the request immediately sends out a reply.
- **Version:** 1 for the original RIP, 2 for RIP-2.

This header is followed by one or more blocks, each of which gives the path distance to a particular target network. The relevant fields are as follows:

- **Address Family:** Always 2 for IP addresses.
- **IP Address:** An IP address that has a nonzero network portion and a zero host portion. This uniquely defines a particular network.
- **Metric:** The path distance from this router to the identified network.

Typically, a link cost of 1 is used, so that the metric is a simple hop count. If larger values of link cost are allowed, then the number of hops that can be measured is correspondingly smaller.

RIP Limitations

RIP continues to be a popular routing protocol because it is simple and because it is well suited to small internets, of which there are many. However, it does have a number of limitations, including the following:

1. As internets grow, destinations that require a metric of more than 15 become unreachable, making RIP unsuitable for large configurations. On the other hand, if larger metrics were allowed, the convergence of the protocol upon initialization or after topology changes can be lengthy.
2. The overly simplistic metric leads to suboptimal routing tables, resulting in packets being sent over slow (or otherwise costly) links when better paths are available.
3. RIP-enabled devices will accept RIP updates from any device. This enables a misconfigured device to easily disrupt an entire configuration.

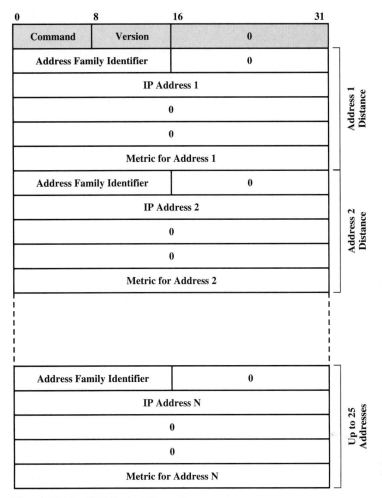

Figure 11.10   RIP Packet Format

11.4 LINK-STATE PROTOCOL: OSPF

As the size and speed of the Internet and other internets have increased, the limitations of RIP have eroded its popularity. Although RIP is still widely used, the Open Shortest Path First protocol (OSPF) is now considered the preferred interior routing protocol for TCP/IP-based internets.

Central to the operation of OSPF is the use of link-state routing. We begin with a general description of this technique. Then we show how this technique is adapted for use in OSPF.

Link-State Routing Approach

General Description   When a router is initialized, it determines the link cost on each of its network interfaces. The router then advertises this set of link costs to all other routers in the internet topology, not just neighboring routers. From then on,

Table 11.2 A Comparison of Routing Philosophies

Distance-Vector Routing	Link-State Routing
Each router sends routing information to its neighbors.	Each router sends routing information to all other routers.
The information sent is an estimate of its path cost to all networks.	The information sent is the exact value of its link cost to adjacent networks.
Information is sent on a regular periodic basis.	Information is sent when changes occur.
A router determines next-hop information by using the distributed Bellman-Ford algorithm on the received estimated path costs.	A router first builds up a description of the topology of the internet and then may use any routing algorithm to determine next-hop information.

the router monitors its link costs. Whenever there is a significant change (a link cost increases or decreases substantially, a new link is created, an existing link becomes unavailable), the router again advertises its set of link costs to all other routers in the configuration.

Because each router receives the link costs of all routers in the configuration, each router can construct the topology of the entire configuration and then calculate the shortest path to each destination network. Having done this, the router can construct its routing table, listing the first hop to each destination. Because the router has a representation of the entire network, it does not use a distributed version of a routing algorithm, as is done in distance-vector routing. Rather, the router can use any routing algorithm to determine the shortest paths. In practice, Dijkstra's algorithm is used.

Table 11.2 compares distance-vector and link-state routing.

Flooding Link-state routing uses a simple technique known as flooding. This technique requires no network topology information and works as follows. A packet is sent by a source router to every one of its neighbors. At each router, an incoming packet is retransmitted on all outgoing links except for the link on which it arrived. The use of flooding in the configuration of Figure 11.1 is shown in Figure 11.11. After

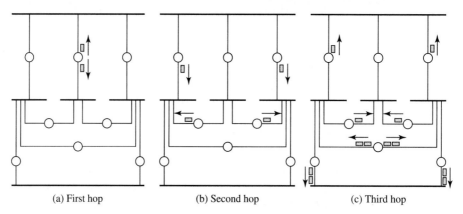

| (a) First hop | (b) Second hop | (c) Third hop |

Figure 11.11 Flooding Example

the first transmission, all routers within one hop of the source have received the packet. After the second transmission, all routers within two hops of the source have received the packet, and so on.

Unless something is done to stop the incessant retransmission of packets, the number of packets in circulation just from a single source packet grows without bound. In our example, two packets are generated for the first hop, four packets for the second hop, and twelve packets for the third hop, which in this case is unnecessary. One way to prevent this is for each node to remember the identity of those packets it has already retransmitted. When duplicate copies of the packet arrive, they are discarded. This is the method used in OSPF.

The flooding technique has three remarkable properties:

- All possible routes between source and destination are tried. Thus, no matter what link or node outages have occurred, a packet will always get through if at least one path between source and destination exists.

- Because all routes are tried, at least one copy of the packet to arrive at the destination will have used a minimum-delay route.

- All nodes that are directly or indirectly connected to the source node are visited.

Because of the first property, the flooding technique is highly robust. Because of the second property, flooded information reaches all routers quickly. Because of the third property, all routers receive the information needed to create a routing table.

The principal disadvantage of flooding is the high traffic load that it generates, which is directly proportional to the connectivity of the network.

OSPF Overview

Each router maintains descriptions of the state of its local links to subnetworks and from time to time transmits updated state information to all of the routers of which it is aware. Every router receiving an update packet must acknowledge it to the sender. Such updates produce a fair amount of routing traffic because the link descriptions, though small, often need to be sent.

Each router maintains a database that reflects the known topology of the configuration. The topology is expressed as a directed graph. The graph consists of the following:

- Vertices, or nodes, of two types:
  —Router
  —Network, which is, in turn, of two types:
    - Transit if it can carry data that neither originates nor terminates on an end system attached to this network
    - Stub if it is not a transit network
- Edges of two types:
  —Graph edges that connect two router vertices when the corresponding routers are connected to each other by a direct point-to-point link
  —Graph edges that connect a router vertex to a network vertex when the router is directly connected to the network

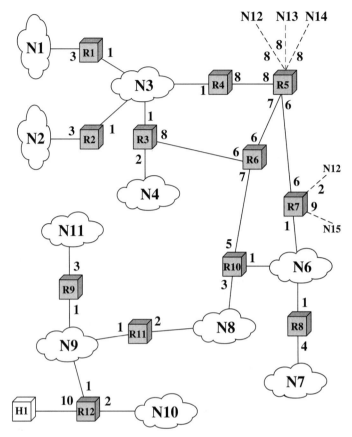

Figure 11.12 A Sample Autonomous System

Figure 11.12, based on one in RFC 2328, shows an example of a configuration, and Figure 11.13 is the resulting directed graph. The mapping is straightforward:

- Two routers joined by a point-to-point link are represented in the graph as being directly connected by a pair of edges, one in each direction (e.g., routers 6 and 10).

- When multiple routers are attached to a network (such as a LAN or packet-switching network), the directed graph shows all routers bidirectionally connected to the network vertex (e.g., routers 1, 2, 3, and 4 all connect to network 3).

- If a single router is attached to a network, the network will appear in the graph as a stub connection (e.g., network 7).

- An end system, called a host, can be directly connected to a router, in which case it is depicted in the corresponding graph (e.g., host 1).

- If a router is connected to other autonomous systems, then the path cost to each network in the other system must be obtained by some exterior routing protocol (ERP). Each such network is represented on the graph by a stub and an edge to the router with the known path cost (e.g., networks 12 through 15).

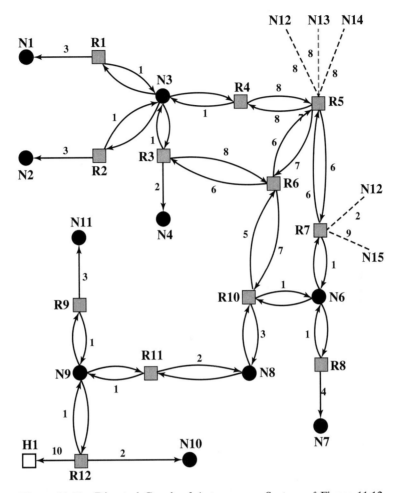

Figure 11.13   Directed Graph of Autonomous System of Figure 11.12

A cost is associated with the output side of each router interface. This cost is configurable by the system administrator. Arcs on the graph are labeled with the cost of the corresponding router output interface. Arcs having no labeled cost have a cost of 0. Note that arcs leading from networks to routers always have a cost of 0.

A database corresponding to the directed graph is maintained by each router. It is pieced together from link-state messages from other routers in the internet. Using Dijkstra's algorithm (see Section 11.2), a router calculates the least-cost path to all destination networks. The result for router 6 of Figure 11.12 is shown as a spanning tree in Figure 11.14, with R6 as the root of the tree. The tree gives the entire route to any destination network or host. However, only the next hop to the destination is used in the forwarding process. The resulting routing table for router 6 is shown in Table 11.3. The table includes entries for routers advertising external routes (routers 5 and 7). For external networks whose identity is known, entries are also provided.

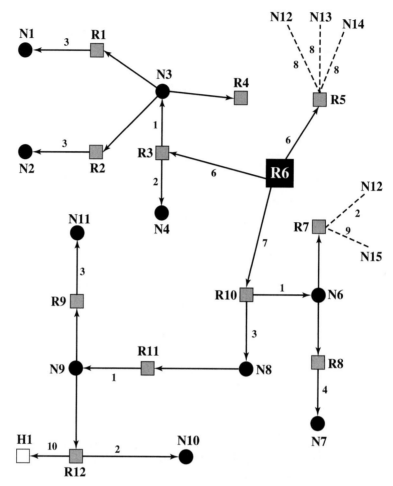

Figure 11.14 The SPF Tree for Router R6

Link Costs

The costs associated with each hop, in each direction, are referred to as routing metrics. OSPF provides a flexible routing metric scheme based on the concept of type of service (TOS). These categories are used:

- **Normal (TOS 0):** This is the default routing metric and is assigned by routing administrators to satisfy any administrative policies. The default metric is understood by every router. The values may be assigned arbitrarily. The simplest technique would be to assign a constant value of 1 to every hop, resulting in a minimum-hop calculation. More typically, the metric will be assigned to reflect performance in some way.
- **Minimize Monetary Cost (TOS 2):** This metric can be used if actual monetary costs can be assigned to network use.
- **Maximize Reliability (TOS 4):** This metric could be preconfigured or could be based on a recent history of outages or on measured packet error rates.

Table 11.3 Routing Table for R6

Destination	Next Hop	Distance
N1	R3	10
N2	R3	10
N3	R3	7
N4	R3	8
N6	R10	8
N7	R10	12
N8	R10	10
N9	R10	11
N10	R10	13
N11	R10	14
H1	R10	21
R5	R5	6
R7	R10	8
N12	R10	10
N13	R5	14
N14	R5	14
N15	R10	17

- **Maximize Throughput (TOS 8):** This metric is preconfigured based on the data rate of the interface. Typically, the metric is the duration of a bit in 10-nanosecond units. Thus, a 10-Mbps Ethernet is assigned a value 10, and a 56-kbps link is assigned 1785.
- **Minimize Delay (TOS 16):** This is a measure of the transit time or delay through a particular hop. Typically, this consists of propagation delay plus queuing delay at the router and is measured dynamically by each router for each of its network interfaces.

These are the same categories used in the IPv4 TOS field.[3] When a router advertises, it provides a link cost for each TOS that is implemented by that router. If a metric for some TOS is not specified, its cost usually defaults to the cost for TOS 0.

Each router may therefore construct up to five distinct routing tables, one for each TOS. In effect, each router generates five spanning trees for the configuration. IP datagrams are then routed on the basis of TOS. Each IP datagram may include a requested TOS. If no request is included in the datagram header, then the default TOS 0 is used for routing.

---

[3]This field has been replaced by the DS and ECN fields (Figure 8.4).

Areas

To make the complexity of large internets more manageable, OSPF incorporates the concept of area. Any internet can be configured to consist of a backbone and multiple areas, defined as follows:

- **Area:** A collection of contiguous networks and hosts, together with routers having interfaces to any one of the included networks
- **Backbone:** A contiguous collection of networks not contained in any area, their attached routers, and those routers that belong to multiple areas

Each area runs a separate copy of the basic link-state routing algorithm and thus maintains a topological database and corresponding graph that reflects the topology of just that area. Link-state information is broadcast only to other routers in the same area. This reduces the amount of OSPF traffic considerably in a large internet. If the source and destination of an IP datagram are within the same area, then only intra-area routing is required. In this case, the routing relies solely on the link-state information generated within the area.

If the source and destination of an IP datagram are within different areas, then the routing involves a path consisting of three legs. The first leg of the path is within the source area, and the third leg is within the destination area; these two legs use intra-area routing. The second leg of the path requires that the datagram be routed through the backbone from the source area to the destination area. The backbone itself has all of the properties of an area and uses the link-state routing algorithm to perform inter-area routing.

At a top level, OSPF views the internet as having a star configuration. The root or hub is the backbone, and each of the areas is attached to the backbone.

OSPF Packet Format

Whereas RIP packets are sent using UDP over IP, OSPF functions directly over IP. Thus, an OSPF packet is sent as the payload of an IP packet. On a point-to-point network or a broadcast network (e.g., a LAN), the IP packet containing an OSPF packet contains a standard multicast IP address of 224.0.0.5, which refers to OSPF routers. On nonbroadcast networks, specific destination IP addresses are used, with the addresses configured into the router ahead of time.

All OSPF packets use the same 24-byte header (Figure 11.15) consisting of the following fields:

- **Version Number:** Number 2 is the current version.
- **Type:** Specifies one of five packet types, as discussed subsequently.
- **Packet Length:** Length of this OSPF packet in octets, including the OSPF header.
- **Router ID:** Identifies this packet's source. Each router in an area is assigned a unique 32-bit identifier.
- **Area ID:** Identifies the area to which the source router belongs. All OSPF packets are associated with a single area.

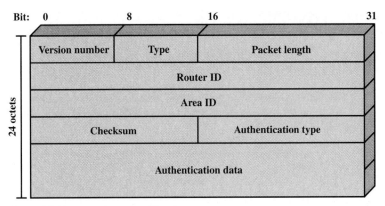

Figure 11.15   OSPF Packet Header

- **Checksum:** The standard IP checksum of the entire contents of the packet, starting with the OSPF packet header but excluding the 64-bit authentication field. This checksum is calculated as the 16-bit ones complement of the ones complement sum of all the 16-bit words in the packet.

- **Authentication Type:** Identifies the authentication procedure to be used for this packet. The approved procedures are null (no authentication), simple password, or cryptographic.

- **Authentication Data:** A 64-bit field for use by the authentication procedure.

Following the OSPF packet header is the packet body, whose contents depends on the type of packet. OSPF uses five packet types:

- **Hello:** Used in neighbor discovery. Each router periodically sends out hello packets on all router interfaces. The packet contains the identities of neighbor routers whose hello packets have already been received over a specific interface.

- **Database description:** Used in the database exchange process. The exchange defines the set of link-state information present in the database of each router; what is conveyed is the structure, rather than the contents of the database. In essence, this allows routers to synchronize their network topologies, so that both routers have the same understanding of that topology.

- **Link-state request:** Used to request specific portions of a neighboring router's link-state database.

- **Link-state update:** Used to transport link-state advertisements to neighboring nodes.

- **Link-state acknowledgment:** Acknowledges a link-state update, providing for a reliable distribution of link-state information.

11.5 RECOMMENDED READING AND WEB SITES

A number of worthwhile books provide detailed coverage of various routing algorithms: [HUIT00], [BLAC00], [PERL00], and [SPOR99]. [MOY98] provides a thorough treatment of OSPF.

[KESH98] provides an instructive look at present and future router functionality. [NARV00] analyzes a variety of dynamic versions of the Dijkstra and Bellman-Ford algorithms that optimize router efficiency.

BLAC00   Black, U. *IP Routing Protocols: RIP, OSPF, BGP, PNNI & Cisco Routing Protocols.* Upper Saddle River, NJ: Prentice Hall, 2000.

HUIT00   Huitema, C. *Routing in the Internet.* Upper Saddle River, NJ: Prentice Hall, 2000.

KESH98   Keshav, S., and Sharma, R. "Issues and Trends in Router Design." *IEEE Communications Magazine*, May 1998.

MOY98   Moy, J. *OSPF: Anatomy of an Internet Routing Protocol.* Reading, MA: Addison-Wesley, 1998.

NARV00   Narvaez, P.; Siu, K.; and Tzeng, H. "New Dynamic Algorithms for Shortest Path Tree Computation." *IEEE/ACM Transactions on Networking*, December 2000.

PERL00   Perlman, R. *Interconnections: Bridges, Routers, Switches, and Internetworking Protocols.* Reading, MA: Addison-Wesley, 2000.

SPOR99   Sportack, M. *IP Routing Fundamentals.* Indianapolis, IN: Cisco Press, 1999.

Recommended Web Site:

- **OSPF working group:** Chartered by IETF to develop OSPF and related standards. The web site includes all relevant RFCs and Internet drafts.

11.6 KEY TERMS, REVIEW QUESTIONS, AND PROBLEMS

Key Terms

adaptive routing	fixed routing	Open Shortest Path First
autonomous system	fluttering	(OSPF)
Bellman-Ford algorithm	interior routing protocol	path-vector routing
Dijkstra's algorithm	least-cost algorithms	Routing Information
distance-vector routing	link-state routing	Protocol (RIP)
exterior routing protocol	looping	

Review Questions

11.1   What is an autonomous system?

11.2   What is the difference between an interior router protocol and an exterior router protocol?

11.3   Compare the three main approaches to routing.

11.4   What is flooding?

11.5   What are the advantages and disadvantages of adaptive routing?

11.6   What is a least-cost algorithm?

11.7   What is the essential difference between Dijkstra's algorithm and the Bellman-Ford algorithm?

11.8   Which routing algorithm is used by RIP?

11.9   What is meant by incremental update in RIP?

11.10   Describe the counting to infinity problem in RIP.

11.11   Explain the split horizon strategy in RIP.

11.12   Explain the poisoned reverse strategy in RIP.

11.13   List the principal limitations of RIP.

11.14   What properties of flooding make it useful as a strategy for OSPF?

11.15   In what way are directed graphs used in OSPF?

11.16   What categories of link costs are used in OSPF?

11.17   Which routing algorithm is used by RIP?

Problems

11.1   One would expect the loss of some segments during network link failures for TCP connections. If a link fails and segments are lost, TCP cuts down its window size after detecting the loss. Unicast routing adapts to the failed link (that was on the shortest path) by routing through another path (longer than the failed path). Describe the behavior of the TCP connection when the old route becomes available again. (Consider the case where TCP window size is such that the communication pipe between the sender and receiver on the longer path is filled with segments. Assume the same data rate on all links.)

11.2   Draw a directed graph corresponding to Figure 11.1.

11.3   Dijkstra's algorithm, for finding the least-cost path from a specified vertex s to a specified vertex t, can be expressed in the following program:

```
for n := 1 to N do
  begin
      L[n] := ∞; final[n] :=  false; {all vertices are temporarily labeled with ∞}
      pred[n] :=  1
  end;
L[s] := 0; final[s] := true;  {vertex s is permanently labeled with 0}
recent := s; {the most recent vertex to be permanently labeled is s}
path :=  true;
{initialization over }

while final[t] = false do
begin
  for n := 1 to N do    {find new label}
      if (w[recent, n] < ∞) AND (NOT final[n]) then
      {for every immediate successor of recent that is not permanently labeled, do }
          begin {update temporary labels}
              newlabel := L[recent] + w[recent,n];
              if newlabel <L[n] then
                  begin L[n] :=  newlabel; pred[n] := recent end
                  {re-label n if there is a shorter path via vertex recent and make
                      recent the predecessor of n on the shortest path from s}
          end;
  temp := ∞;
  for x := 1 to N do {find vertex with smallest temporary label}
      if (NOT final[x]) AND (L[x] < temp) then
              begin y := x; temp :=L[x] end;
  if temp < ∞ then {there is a path} then
```

```
      begin final[y] := true; recent := y end
   {y, the next closest vertex to s gets permanently labeled}
  else begin path := false; final[t] := true end
end
```

In this program, each vertex is assigned a temporary label initially. As a final path to a vertex is determined, it is assigned a permanent label equal to the cost of the path from s. Write a similar program for the Bellman-Ford algorithm. *Hint:* The Bellman-Ford algorithm is often called a label-correcting method, in contrast to Dijkstra's label-setting method.

11.4 In the discussion of Dijkstra's algorithm, it is asserted that at each iteration, a new vertex is added to T and that the least-cost path for that new vertex passes only through vertices already in T. Demonstrate that this is true. *Hint:* Begin at the beginning. Show that the first vertex added to T must have a direct link to the source vertex. Then show that the second vertex to T must either have a direct link to the source vertex or a direct link to the first vertex added to T, and so on. Remember that all link costs are assumed nonnegative.

11.5 In the discussion of the Bellman-Ford algorithm, it is asserted that at the iteration for which $h = K$, if any path of length $K + 1$ is defined, the first K hops of that path form a path defined in the previous iteration. Demonstrate that this is true.

11.6 In step 3 of Dijkstra's algorithm, the least-cost path values are only updated for vertices not yet in T. Is it possible that a lower-cost path could be found to a vertex already in T? If so, demonstrate by example. If not, provide reasoning as to why not.

11.7 Using Dijkstra's algorithm, generate a least-cost route to all other vertices for vertices 2 through 6 of Figure 11.5. Display the results as in Table 11.1a.

11.8 Repeat Problem 11.7 using the Bellman-Ford algorithm.

11.9 Apply Dijkstra's routing algorithm to the graphs in Figure 11.16. In the figure, the weights between two adjacent vertices are the same in both directions. Provide a table similar to Table 11.1a and a figure similar to Figure 11.6.

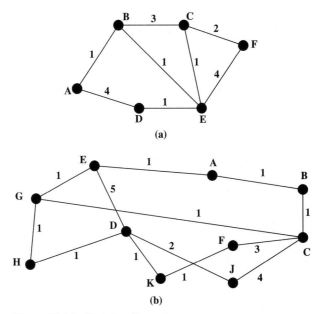

Figure 11.16 Two Configurations

11.10 Repeat Problem 11.9 using the Bellman-Ford algorithm.

11.11 Will Dijkstra's algorithm and the Bellman-Ford algorithm always yield the same solutions? Why or why not?

11.12 Both Dijkstra's algorithm and the Bellman-Ford algorithm find the least-cost paths from one vertex to all other vertices. The Floyd-Warshall algorithm finds the least-cost paths between all pairs of vertices together. Define:

N = set of vertices in the network

$w(i, j)$ = link cost from vertex i to vertex j; $w(i, i) = 0$; $w(i, j) = \infty$ if the two vertices are not directly connected

$L_n(i, j)$ = cost of the least-cost path from vertex i to vertex j with the constraint that only vertices $1, 2, \ldots, n$ can be used as intermediate vertices on paths

The algorithm has the following steps:

1. Initialize:

$$L_0(i, j) = w(i, j), \qquad \text{for all } i, j, i \neq j$$

2. For $n = 0, 1, \ldots, N - 1$

$$L_{n+1}(i, j) = \min[L_n(i, j), L_n(i, n + 1) + L_n(n + 1, j)] \qquad \text{for all } i, j$$

Explain the algorithm in words. Use induction to demonstrate that the algorithm works.

11.13 For each of the entries in each of the vectors of Figure 11.8b, show the path that produces the path cost.

11.14 Show the routing table for router A for Figure 11.1. Now assume that within a 30-second period, both link costs from E become 1, and both link costs from F become 1 and that the updated distance vectors from E and F arrive at A. Further assume that updated distance vectors have not yet arrived from any other router. Show the result after A has updated its routing table on the basis of the new information from E and F.

11.15 In discussing the distance-vector routing algorithm used in RIP, it was stated that "It would be difficult to coordinate the activities of all routers so that the algorithm could be executed synchronously." State two problems that create the difficulty.

11.16 The counting-to-infinity problem discussed with reference to Figure 11.9 can occur without a network becoming unreachable. Add a WAN to Figure 11.9 that connects C and D, with a link cost of 10 in each direction.

  a. Show the distance, $L(x, 5)$, and next hop, $R(x, 5)$, to network 5 for each router.

  b. Now assume that network 3 fails. The routes should now adjust to use the link from C to D. The routing changes start when B notices that the route to D is no longer usable. Show the values of $L(x, 5)$ and $R(x, 5)$ for each router over time until stable new values are reached.

11.17 In RIP, the split horizon with poisoned reverse rule clearly works for a point-to-point link between two routers. But on a broadcast network, such as Ethernet, RIP messages are broadcast to all other nodes implementing RIP; they are not addressed to a specific node. Suppose that A, B, and C are routers on the same Ethernet, and that A sends a poisoned reverse message to C because A has a route that goes through C. The same message will also go to B. Will this cause a problem? If not, why not?

11.18 Assume a router has 30 routes to advertise using RIP, requiring one datagram with 25 routes and another with the remaining 5. What happens if once an hour the first datagram with 25 routes is lost?

11.19 Why is there a checksum field in the OSPF packet format but not in the RIP packet format?

11.20 When multiple equal-cost routes to a destination exist, OSPF may distribute traffic equally among the routes. This is called *load balancing*. What effect does such load balancing have on a transport layer protocol, such as TCP?

CHAPTER 12

EXTERIOR ROUTING PROTOCOLS AND MULTICAST

Prior to the recent explosion of sophisticated research, scientists believed that birds required no special awareness or intelligence to perform their migrations and their navigational and homing feats. Accumulated research shows that in addition to performing the difficult tasks of correcting for displacement (by storms, winds, mountains, and other hindrances), birds integrate an astonishing variety of celestial, atmospheric, and geological information to travel between their winter and summer homes. In brief, avian navigation is characterized by the ability to gather a variety of informational cues and to interpret and coordinate them so as to move closer toward a goal.

—The Human Nature of Birds,
Theodore Barber

KEY POINTS

- The Border Gateway Protocol (BGP) is the preferred exterior routing protocol for the Internet.

- BGP employs path-vector routing and provides three key functions: neighbor acquisition, neighbor reachability, and network reachability.

- The act of sending a packet from a source to multiple destinations is referred to as multicasting. Multicasting raises design issues in the areas of addressing and routing.

- The Internet Group Management Protocol (IGMP) is used by hosts and routers to exchange multicast group membership information over a LAN.

- Multicast Extensions to Open Shortest Path First (MOSPF) is an enhancement to OSPF that enables the routing of IP multicast datagrams.

- Protocol Independent Multicast (PIM) is a routing protocol that is independent of any existing unicast routing protocol. PIM is designed to extract needed routing information from any unicast routing protocol and may work across multiple ASs with a number of different unicast routing protocols.

In this chapter, we continue our study of routing protocols. First, we examine two path-vector routing protocols: BGP and IDRP. This chapter concludes with a discussion of internet multicasting and examines the routing protocols needed to support multicasting.

12.1 PATH-VECTOR PROTOCOLS: BGP AND IDRP

The Border Gateway Protocol (BGP) is an exterior routing protocol developed for use in conjunction with internets that employ the TCP/IP protocol suite, although the concepts are applicable to any internet. BGP is the preferred exterior routing protocol for the Internet.

Table 12.1 BGP-4 Messages

Open	Used to open a neighbor relationship with another router.
Update	Used to (1) transmit information about a single route and/or (2) list multiple routes to be withdrawn.
Keepalive	Used to (1) acknowledge an Open message and (2) periodically confirm the neighbor relationship.
Notification	Send when an error condition is detected.

A key feature of BGP is that it uses a technique known as path-vector routing, described in general terms in Chapter 11. In this section we look at some of the details of BGP, and then introduce IDRP, which is a follow-on protocol intended for use with IPv6.

Border Gateway Protocol

Functions BGP was designed to allow routers (called gateways in the standard) in different autonomous systems (ASs) to cooperate in the exchange of routing information. The protocol uses messages, which are sent over TCP connections. The repertoire of messages is summarized in Table 12.1. The current version of BGP is known as BGP-4 (RFC 1771).

Three functional procedures are involved in BGP:

- Neighbor acquisition
- Neighbor reachability
- Network reachability

Two routers are considered to be **neighbors** if they are attached to the same subnetwork. If the two routers are in different autonomous systems, they may wish to exchange routing information. For this purpose, it is necessary to first perform **neighbor acquisition**. In essence, neighbor acquisition occurs when two neighboring routers in different autonomous systems agree to exchange routing information regularly. A formal acquisition procedure is needed because one of the routers may not wish to participate. For example, the router may be overburdened and does not want to be responsible for traffic coming in from outside the system. In the neighbor acquisition process, one router sends a request message to the other, which may either accept or refuse the offer. The protocol does not address the issue of how one router knows the address or even the existence of another router, nor how it decides that it needs to exchange routing information with that particular router. These issues must be dealt with at configuration time or by active intervention of a network manager.

To perform neighbor acquisition, two routers send Open messages to each other after a TCP connection is established. If each router accepts the request, it returns a Keepalive message in response.

Once a neighbor relationship is established, the **neighbor reachability** procedure is used to maintain the relationship. Each partner needs to be assured that the other partner still exists and is still engaged in the neighbor relationship. For this purpose, the two routers periodically issue Keepalive messages to each other.

The final procedure specified by BGP is **network reachability**. Each router maintains a database of the subnetworks that it can reach and the preferred route for reaching that network. When a change is made to this database, the router issues an Update message that is broadcast to all other routers that implement BGP. Because the Update message is broadcast, all BGP routers can build up and maintain their routing information.

BGP Messages Figure 12.1 illustrates the formats of all of the BGP messages. Each message begins with a 19-octet header containing three fields, as indicated by the shaded portion of each message in the figure:

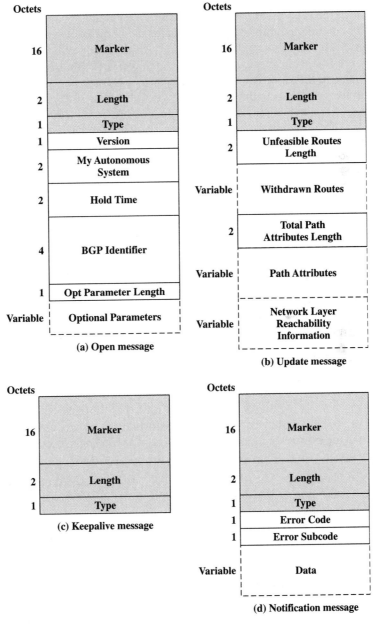

Figure 12.1 BGP Message Formats

- **Marker:** Reserved for authentication. The sender may insert a value in this field that would be used as part of an authentication mechanism to enable the recipient to verify the identity of the sender.
- **Length:** Length of message in octets.
- **Type:** Type of message: Open, Update, Keepalive, Notification.

To acquire a neighbor, a router first opens a TCP connection to the neighbor router of interest. It then sends an Open message. This message identifies the AS to which the sender belongs and provides the IP address of the router. It also includes a Hold Time parameter, which indicates the number of seconds that the sender proposes for the value of the Hold Timer. If the recipient is prepared to open a neighbor relationship, it calculates a value of Hold Timer that is the minimum of its Hold Time and the Hold Time in the Open message. This calculated value is the maximum number of seconds that may elapse between the receipt of successive Keepalive and/or Update messages by the sender.

The Keepalive message consists simply of the header. Each router issues these messages to each of its peers often enough to prevent the Hold Time from expiring.

The Update message communicates two types of information:

1. Information about a single route through the Internet. This information is available to be added to the database of any recipient router.
2. A list of routes previously advertised by this router that are being withdrawn.

An Update message may contain one or both types of information. Let us consider the first type of information first. Information about a single route through the network involves three fields: the Network Layer Reachability Information (NLRI) field, the Total Path Attributes Length field, and the Path Attributes field. The NLRI field consists of a list of identifiers of subnetworks that can be reached by this route. Each subnetwork is identified by its IP address, which is actually a portion of a full IP address. Recall that an IPv4 address (Figure 8.5) is a 32-bit quantity of the form {network, end system}. The left-hand or prefix portion of this quantity identifies a particular subnetwork.

The Path Attributes field contains a list of attributes that apply to this particular route. The following are the defined attributes:

- **Origin:** Indicates whether this information was generated by an interior routing protocol (e.g., OSPF) or an exterior routing protocol (in particular, BGP).
- **AS_Path:** A list of the ASs that are traversed for this route.
- **Next_Hop:** The IP address of the border router that should be used as the next hop to the destinations listed in the NLRI field. A border router is one that attaches to multiple areas.
- **Multi_Exit_Disc:** Used to communicate some information about routes internal to an AS. This is described later in this section.
- **Local_Pref:** Used by a router to inform other routers within the same AS of its degree of preference for a particular route. It has no significance to routers in other ASs.
- **Atomic_Aggregate, Aggregator:** These two fields implement the concept of route aggregation. In essence, an internet and its corresponding address space

can be organized hierarchically (i.e., as a tree). In this case, network addresses are structured in two or more parts. All of the subnetworks of a given subtree share a common partial internet address. Using this common partial address, the amount of information that must be communicated in NLRI can be significantly reduced.

The AS_Path attribute actually serves two purposes. Because it lists the ASs that a datagram must traverse if it follows this route, the AS_Path information enables a router to implement routing policies. That is, a router may decide to avoid a particular path to avoid transiting a particular AS. For example, information that is confidential may be limited to certain kinds of ASs. Or a router may have information about the performance or quality of the portion of the Internet that is included in an AS that leads the router to avoid that AS. Examples of performance or quality metrics include link speed, capacity, tendency to become congested, and overall quality of operation. Another criterion that could be used is minimizing the number of transit ASs.

The reader may wonder about the purpose of the Next_Hop attribute. The requesting router will necessarily want to know which networks are reachable via the responding router, but why provide information about other routers? This is best explained with reference to Figure 11.4. In this example, router R1 in autonomous system 1 and router R5 in autonomous system 2 implement BGP and acquire a neighbor relationship. R1 issues Update messages to R5, indicating which networks it could reach and the distances (network hops) involved. R1 also provides the same information on behalf of R2. That is, R1 tells R5 what networks are reachable via R2. In this example, R2 does not implement BGP. Typically, most of the routers in an autonomous system will not implement BGP. Only a few routers will be assigned responsibility for communicating with routers in other autonomous systems. A final point: R1 is in possession of the necessary information about R2, because R1 and R2 share an interior routing protocol (IRP).

The second type of update information is the withdrawal of one or more routes. In this case, the route is identified by the IP address of the destination subnetwork.

Finally, the Notification Message is sent when an error condition is detected. The following errors may be reported:

- **Message header error:** Includes authentication and syntax errors.
- **Open message error:** Includes syntax errors and options not recognized in an Open message. This message can also be used to indicate that a proposed Hold Time in an Open message is unacceptable.
- **Update message error:** Includes syntax and validity errors in an Update message.
- **Hold timer expired:** If the sending router has not received successive Keepalive and/or Update and/or Notification messages within the Hold Time period, then this error is communicated and the connection is closed.
- **Finite state machine error:** Includes any procedural error.
- **Cease:** Used by a router to close a connection with another router in the absence of any other error.

BGP Routing Information Exchange The essence of BGP is the exchange of routing information among participating routers in multiple ASs. This process can be quite complex. In what follows, we provide a simplified overview.

Let us consider router R1 in autonomous system 1 (AS1) in Figure 11.4. To begin, a router that implements BGP will also implement an internal routing protocol such as OSPF. Using OSPF, R1 can exchange routing information with other routers within AS1, build up a picture of the topology of the subnetworks and routers in AS1, and construct a routing table. Next, R1 can issue an Update message to R5 in AS2. The Update message could include the following:

- **AS_Path:** The identity of AS1
- **Next_Hop:** The IP address of R1
- **NLRI:** A list of all of the networks in AS1

This message informs R5 that all of the subnetworks listed in NLRI are reachable via R1 and that the only autonomous system traversed is AS1.

Suppose now that R5 also has a neighbor relationship with another router in another autonomous system, say R9 in AS3. R5 will forward the information just received from R1 to R9 in a new Update message. This message includes the following:

- **AS_Path:** The list of identifiers {AS2, AS1}
- **Next_Hop:** The IP address of R5
- **NLRI:** A list of all of the networks in AS1

This message informs R9 that all of the subnetworks listed in NLRI are reachable via R5 and that the autonomous systems traversed are AS2 and AS1. R9 must now decide if this is its preferred route to the subnetworks listed. It may have knowledge of an alternate route to some or all of these subnetworks that it prefers for reasons of performance or some other policy metric. If R9 decides that the route provided in R5's Update message is preferable, then R9 incorporates that routing information into its routing database and forwards this new routing information to other neighbors. This new message will include an AS_Path field of {AS1, AS2, AS3}.

In this fashion, routing update information is propagated through the larger Internet consisting of a number of interconnected autonomous systems. The AS_Path field is used to assure that such messages do not circulate indefinitely: If an Update message is received by a router in an AS that is included in the AS_Path field, that router will not forward the update information to other routers, preventing looping of messages.

Routers within the same AS, called internal neighbors, may exchange BGP information. In this case, the sending router does not add the identifier of the common AS to the AS_Path field. When a router has selected a preferred route to an external destination, it transmits this route to all of its internal neighbors. Each of these routers then decides if the new route is preferred, in which case the new route is added to its database and a new Update message goes out.

When there are multiple entry points into an AS that are available to a border router in another AS, the Multi_Exit_Disc attribute may be used to choose among them. This attribute contains a number that reflects some internal metric for reaching destinations within an AS. For example, suppose in Figure 11.4 that both R1 and R2 implemented BGP and both had a neighbor relationship with R5. Each provides an Update message to R5 for subnetwork 1.3 that includes a routing metric used internal to AS1, such as a routing metric associated with the OSPF internal router protocol. R5 could then use these two metrics as the basis for choosing between the two routes.

Inter-Domain Routing Protocol

The Inter-Domain Routing Protocol (IDRP)[1] is an exterior routing protocol that has been designated for use with IPv6. IDRP is an ISO standard defined within the OSI family of protocols. However, it is not dependent on OSI networking or the use of the OSI internet protocol. Instead, IDRP can be used with any other internet protocol and in an internet with a mixture of internet protocols.

Like BGP, IDRP is based on path-vector routing and represents a superset of BGP's functions. The key differences are as follows:

- BGP operates over TCP, whereas IDRP operates over the internet protocol used in the configuration. IDRP includes its own handshaking exchanges to guarantee delivery of messages.
- BGP uses 16-bit autonomous system numbers. IDRP uses variable-length identifiers.
- IDRP can deal with multiple internet protocols and multiple internet address schemes. Indeed, in a single route advisory, an IDRP message can carry different network address formats.
- BGP communicates a path by specifying the complete list of autonomous systems that a path visits. IDRP is able to aggregate this information using the concept of routing domain confederations.

The last point is perhaps the most important difference between BGP-4 and IDRP. In IDRP, a set of connected autonomous systems may be grouped together to form a confederation. A system administrator may configure autonomous systems into a confederation so that they appear to the outside world as a single autonomous system. Therefore, any path that terminates in or passes through the confederation is identified by a single entry in the path vector, rather than one entry for each autonomous system that is visited. This process is recursive, so that groups of connected confederations can be aggregated into a single confederation. The result is a routing strategy that scales effectively with increasing size and complexity of the internet environment.

12.2 MULTICASTING

Typically, an IP address refers to an individual host on a particular network. IP also accommodates addresses that refer to a group of hosts on one or more networks. Such addresses are referred to as **multicast addresses**, and the act of sending a packet from a source to the members of a multicast group is referred to as **multicasting**.

---

[1]ISO 10747, *Protocol for Exchange of Inter-Domain Routing Information among Intermediate Systems to Support Forwarding of ISO 8473 PDUs.*

Multicasting has a number of practical applications. For example,

- **Multimedia:** A number of users "tune in" to a video or audio transmission from a multimedia source station.
- **Teleconferencing:** A group of workstations form a multicast group such that a transmission from any member is received by all other group members.
- **Database:** All copies of a replicated file or database are updated at the same time.
- **Distributed computation:** Intermediate results are sent to all participants.
- **Real-time workgroup:** Files, graphics, and messages are exchanged among active group members in real time.

Multicasting done within the scope of a single LAN segment is simplicity itself. IEEE 802 and other LAN protocols include provision for MAC-level multicast addresses. A packet with a multicast address is transmitted on a LAN segment. Those stations that are members of the corresponding multicast group recognize the multicast address and accept the packet. In this case, only a single copy of the packet is ever transmitted. This technique works because of the broadcast nature of a LAN: A transmission from any one station is received by all other stations on the LAN.

In an internet environment, multicasting is a far more difficult undertaking. To see this, consider the configuration of Figure 12.2; a number of LANs are interconnected by routers. Routers connect to each other either over high-speed links or across a wide area network (network N4). A cost is associated with each link or network in each direction, indicated by the value shown leaving the router for that link or network. Suppose that the multicast server on network N1 is transmitting packets to a multicast address that represents the workstations indicated on networks N3, N5, N6. Suppose that the server does not know the location of the members of the multicast group. Then one way to assure that the packet is received by all members of the group is to **broadcast** a copy of each packet to each network in the configuration, over the least-cost route for each network. For example, one packet would be addressed to N3 and would traverse N1, link L3, and N3. Router B is responsible for translating the IP-level multicast address to a MAC-level multicast address before transmitting the MAC frame onto N3. Table 12.2 summarizes the number of packets generated on the various links and networks in order to transmit one packet to a multicast group by this method. In this table, the source is the multicast server on network N1 in Figure 12.2; the multicast address includes the group members on N3, N5, and N6. Each column in the table refers to the path taken from the source host to a destination router attached to a particular destination network. Each row of the table refers to a network or link in the configuration of Figure 12.2. Each entry in the table gives the number of packets that traverse a given network or link for a given path. A total of 13 copies of the packet are required for the broadcast technique.

Now suppose the source system knows the location of each member of the multicast group. That is, the source has a table that maps a multicast address into a list of networks that contain members of that multicast group. In that case, the source need only send packets to those networks that contain members of the group. We could refer to this as the **multiple unicast** strategy. Table 12.2 shows that in this case, 11 packets are required.

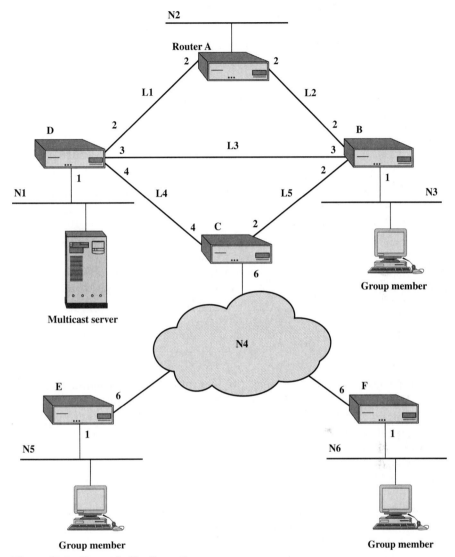

Figure 12.2 Example Configuration

Both the broadcast and multiple unicast strategies are inefficient because they generate unnecessary copies of the source packet. In a true **multicast** strategy, the following method is used:

1. The least-cost path from the source to each network that includes members of the multicast group is determined. This results in a spanning tree of the configuration. Note that this is not a full spanning tree of the configuration. Rather, it is a spanning tree that includes only those networks containing group members.

2. The source transmits a single packet along the spanning tree.

3. The packet is replicated by routers only at branch points of the spanning tree.

Table 12.2 Traffic Generated by Various Multicasting Strategies

	(a) Broadcast					(b) Multiple Unicast				(c) Multicast
	S→N2	S→N3	S→N5	S→N6	Total	S→N3	S→N5	S→N6	Total	
N1	1	1	1	1	4	1	1	1	3	1
N2										
N3		1			1	1			1	1
N4			1	1	2		1	1	2	2
N5			1		1		1		1	1
N6				1	1			1	1	1
L1	1				1					
L2										
L3		1			1	1			1	1
L4			1	1	2		1	1	2	1
L5										
Total	2	3	4	4	13	3	4	4	11	8

Figure 12.3a shows the spanning tree for transmissions from the source to the multicast group, and Figure 12.3b shows this method in action. The source transmits a single packet over N1 to router D. D makes two copies of the packet, to transmit over links L3 and L4. B receives the packet from L3 and transmits it on N3, where it is read by members of the multicast group on the network. Meanwhile, C receives the packet sent on L4. It must now deliver that packet to both E and F. If network

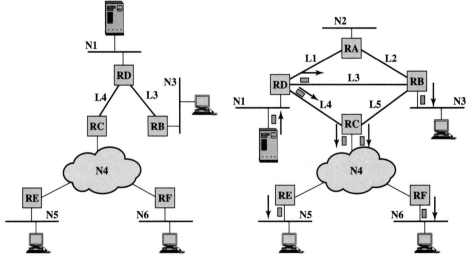

(a) Spanning tree from source to multicast group   (b) Packets generated for multicast transmission

Figure 12.3 Multicast Transmission Example

N4 were a broadcast network (e.g., an Ethernet LAN), then C would only need to transmit one instance of the packet for both routers to read. If N4 is a packet-switching WAN, then C must make two copies of the packet and address one to E and one to F. Each of these routers, in turn, retransmits the received packet on N5 and N6, respectively. As Table 12.2c shows, the multicast technique requires only eight copies of the packet.

Requirements for Multicasting

In ordinary unicast transmission over an internet, in which each datagram has a unique destination network, the task of each router is to forward the datagram along the shortest path from that router to the destination network. With multicast transmission, the router may be required to forward two or more copies of an incoming datagram. In our example, routers D and C both must forward two copies of a single incoming datagram.

Thus, we might expect that the overall functionality of multicast routing is more complex than unicast routing. The following is a list of required functions:

1. A convention is needed for identifying a multicast address. In IPv4, Class D addresses are reserved for this purpose (Figure 8.5). These are 32-bit addresses with 1110 as their high-order 4 bits, followed by a 28-bit group identifier. In IPv6, a 128-bit multicast address consists of an 8-bit prefix of all ones, a 4-bit flags field, a 4-bit scope field, and a 112-bit group identifier. Currently, the flags field only indicates whether this address is permanently assigned or not. The scope field indicates the scope of applicability of the address, ranging from a single subnetwork to global.

2. Each node (router or source node participating in the routing algorithm) must translate between an IP multicast address and a list of networks that contain members of this group. This information allows the node to construct a shortest-path spanning tree to all of the networks containing group members.

3. A router must translate between an IP multicast address and a network multicast address in order to deliver a multicast IP datagram on the destination network. For example, in IEEE 802 networks, including Ethernet, a MAC-level address is 48 bits long. If the highest-order bit is 1, then it is a multicast address. For multicast delivery, a router attached to an IEEE 802 network must translate a 32-bit IPv4 or a 128-bit IPv6 multicast address into a 48-bit IEEE 802 MAC-level multicast address.

4. Although some multicast addresses may be assigned permanently, the more usual case is that multicast addresses are generated dynamically and that individual hosts may join and leave multicast groups dynamically. Thus, a mechanism is needed by which an individual host informs routers attached to the same network as itself of its inclusion in and exclusion from a multicast group. IGMP, described subsequently, provides this mechanism.

5. Routers must exchange two sorts of information. First, routers need to know which networks include members of a given multicast group. Second, routers need sufficient information to calculate the shortest path to each network containing group members. These requirements imply the need for a routing protocol.

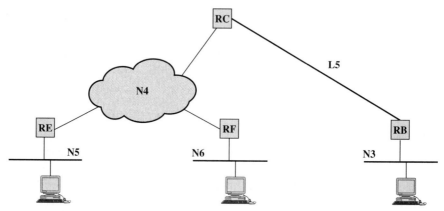

Figure 12.4 Spanning Tree from Router C to Multicast Group

6. A routing algorithm is needed to calculate shortest paths to all group members.
7. Each router must determine multicast routing paths on the basis of both source and destination addresses.

The last point is a subtle consequence of the use of multicast addresses. To illustrate the point, consider again Figure 12.2. If the multicast server transmits a unicast packet addressed to a host on network N5, the packet is forwarded by router D to C, which then forwards the packet to E. Similarly, a packet addressed to a host on network N3 is forwarded by D to B. But now suppose that the server transmits a packet with a multicast address that includes hosts on N3, N5, and N6. As we have discussed, D makes two copies of the packet and sends one to B and one to C. So far, so good. But what will C do when it receives a packet with such a multicast address? C knows that this packet is intended for networks N3, N5, and N6. A simple-minded approach would be for C to calculate the shortest path to each of these three networks. This produces the shortest-path spanning tree shown in Figure 12.4. As a result, C sends two copies of the packet out over N4, one intended for N5 and one intended for N6. But it also sends a copy of the packet to B for delivery on N3. Thus B will receive two copies of the packet, one from D and one from C. This is clearly not what was intended by the host on N1 when it launched the packet.

To avoid unnecessary duplication of packets, each router must route packets on the basis of both source and multicast destination. When C receives a packet intended for the multicast group from a source on N1, it must calculate the spanning tree with N1 as the root (shown in Figure 12.3a) and route on the basis of that spanning tree.

The remainder of this section examines three important protocols related to multicast routing. First, we look at IGMP, which is a protocol that enables hosts to join and leave multicast groups. Next, MOSPF is examined; this is an extension to the OSPF protocol discussed in Chapter 11 that enables multicast routing within an autonomous system. Finally, PIM is a protocol for interdomain multicast routing.

Internet Group Management Protocol (IGMP)

IGMP, defined in RFC 3376, is used by hosts and routers to exchange multicast group membership information over a LAN. IGMP takes advantage of the broadcast nature of a LAN to provide an efficient technique for the exchange of information among multiple hosts and routers. In general, IGMP supports two principal operations:

1. Hosts send messages to routers to subscribe to and unsubscribe from a multicast group defined by a given multicast address.
2. Routers periodically check which multicast groups are of interest to which hosts.

IGMP is currently at version 3. In IGMPv1, hosts could join a multicast group and routers used a timer to unsubscribe group members. IGMPv2 enabled a host to specifically unsubscribe from a group. The first two versions used essentially the following operational model:

- Receivers have to subscribe to multicast groups.
- Sources do not have to subscribe to multicast groups.
- Any host can send traffic to any multicast group.

This paradigm is very general, but it also has some weaknesses:

1. Spamming of multicast groups is easy. Even if there are application-level filters to drop unwanted packets, still these packets consume valuable resources in the network and in the receiver that has to process them.
2. Establishment of the multicast distribution trees is problematic. This is mainly because the location of sources is not known.
3. Finding globally unique multicast addresses is difficult. It is always possible that another multicast group uses the same multicast address.

IGMPv3 addresses these weaknesses by

1. Allowing hosts to specify the list of hosts from which they want to receive traffic. Traffic from other hosts is blocked at routers.
2. Allowing hosts to block packets that come from sources that send unwanted traffic.[2]

The remainder of this section discusses IGMPv3.

IGMP Message Format All IGMP messages are transmitted in IP datagrams. The current version defines two message types: Membership Query and Membership Report.

A **Membership Query** message is sent by a multicast router. There are three subtypes: a **general query**, used to learn which groups have members on an attached network; a **group-specific query**, used to learn if a particular group has any members on an attached network; and a **group-and-source specific query**, used to learn if any attached device desires reception of packets sent to a specified multicast address, from any of a specified list of sources. Figure 12.5a shows the message format, which consists of the following fields:

- **Type:** Defines this message type.

---

[2]The preceding overview of IGMP is based on one by Christo Gkantsidis (cc.gatech.edu/~gantsich/ igmpv3.htm).

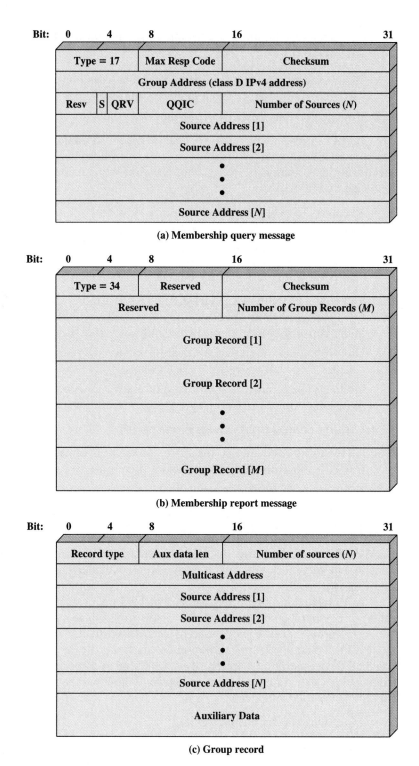

Bit: 0   4   8   16   31

| Type = 17 | Max Resp Code | Checksum |
| Group Address (class D IPv4 address) | | |

| Resv | S | QRV | QQIC | Number of Sources (*N*) |

Source Address [1]

Source Address [2]

•
•
•

Source Address [*N*]

(a) Membership query message

Bit: 0   4   8   16   31

| Type = 34 | Reserved | Checksum |
| Reserved | | Number of Group Records (*M*) |

Group Record [1]

Group Record [2]

•
•
•

Group Record [*M*]

(b) Membership report message

Bit: 0   4   8   16   31

| Record type | Aux data len | Number of sources (*N*) |
| Multicast Address | | |

Source Address [1]

Source Address [2]

•
•
•

Source Address [*N*]

Auxiliary Data

(c) Group record

Figure 12.5   IGMPv3 Message Formats

432

- **Max Response Code:** Indicates the maximum allowed time before sending a responding report in units of 1/10 second.
- **Checksum:** An error-detecting code, calculated as the 16-bit ones complement addition of all the 16-bit words in the message. For purposes of computation, the Checksum field is itself initialized to a value of zero. This is the same checksum algorithm used in IPv4.
- **Group Address:** Zero for a general query message; a valid IP multicast group address when sending a group-specific query or group-and-source specific query.
- **S Flag:** When set to one, indicates to any receiving multicast routers that they are to suppress the normal timer updates they perform upon hearing a query.
- **QRV (querier's robustness variable):** If nonzero, the QRV field contains the RV value used by the querier (i.e., the sender of the query). Routers adopt the RV value from the most recently received query as their own RV value, unless that most recently received RV was zero, in which case the receivers use the default value or a statically configured value. The RV dictates how many times a host will retransmit a report to assure that it is not missed by any attached multicast routers.
- **QQIC (querier's querier interval code):** Specifies the QI value used by the querier, which is a timer for sending multiple queries. Multicast routers that are not the current querier adopt the QI value from the most recently received query as their own QI value, unless that most recently received QI was zero, in which case the receiving routers use the default QI value.
- **Number of Sources:** Specifies how many source addresses are present in this query. This value is nonzero only for a group-and-source specific query.
- **Source Addresses:** If the number of sources is N, then there are N 32-bit unicast addresses appended to the message.

A **Membership Report** message consists of the following fields:

- **Type:** Defines this message type.
- **Checksum:** An error-detecting code, calculated as the 16-bit ones complement addition of all the 16-bit words in the message.
- **Number of Group Records:** Specifies how many group records are present in this report.
- **Group Records:** If the number of group records is M, then there are M group records appended to the message.

A group record includes the following fields:

- **Record Type:** Defines this record type, as described subsequently.
- **Aux Data Length:** Length of the auxiliary data field, in 32-bit words.
- **Number of Sources:** Specifies how many source addresses are present in this record.
- **Multicast Address:** The IP multicast address to which this record pertains.

- **Source Addresses:** If the number of sources is N, then there are N 32-bit unicast addresses appended to the message.
- **Auxiliary Data:** Additional information pertaining to this record. Currently, no auxiliary data values are defined.

IGMP Operation   The objective of each host in using IGMP is to make itself known as a member of a group with a given multicast address to other hosts on the LAN and to all routers on the LAN. IGMPv3 introduces the ability for hosts to signal group membership with filtering capabilities with respect to sources. A host can either signal that it wants to receive traffic from all sources sending to a group except for some specific sources (called EXCLUDE mode) or that it wants to receive traffic only from some specific sources sending to the group (called INCLUDE mode). To join a group, a host sends an IGMP membership report message to neighboring routers, in which the group address field is the multicast address of the group.

To maintain a valid current list of active group addresses, a multicast router periodically issues an IGMP general query message, sent in an IP datagram with an *all-hosts* multicast address. Each host that still wishes to remain a member of one or more multicast groups must read datagrams with the all-hosts address. When such a host receives the query, it must respond with a Group Record for each group to which it claims membership.

When a host leaves a group, it sends a leave group message to the all-routers static multicast address. This is accomplished by sending a membership report message with the INCLUDE option and a null list of source addresses; that is, no sources are to be included, effectively leaving the group. When a router receives such a message for a group that has group members on the reception interface, it needs to determine if there are any remaining group members. For this purpose, the router uses the group-specific query message.

Group Membership with IPv6   IGMP was defined for operation with IPv4 and makes use of 32-bit addresses. IPv6 internets need this same functionality. Rather than to define a separate version of IGMP for IPv6, its functions have been incorporated into the new version of the Internet Control Message Protocol (ICMPv6). ICMPv6 includes all of the functionality of ICMPv4 and IGMP. For multicast support, ICMPv6 includes both a group-membership query and a group-membership report message, which are used in the same fashion as in IGMP.

Multicast Extensions to Open Shortest Path First (MOSPF)

MOSPF (RFC 1584) is an enhancement to OSPF (described in Chapter 11) that enables the routing of IP multicast datagrams. MOSPF is designed to operate within a single autonomous system.

MOSPF follows the strategy outlined in the preceding general discussion of internet multicasting. Each router attached to a LAN uses IGMP to maintain a current picture of local group membership. Periodically, each router floods information about local group membership to all other routers in its area. The result is that all routers in an area are able to build up a complete picture of the location of all group members for each multicast group. Using Dijkstra's algorithm, each router constructs the shortest-path spanning tree from a source network to all networks containing members of a multicast group. Because this source-destination calculation is time-consuming, it is done only on demand. That is, a router does not construct a source-destination spanning tree for a given source and a given multicast destination until it receives a multicast IP datagram with that source and that multicast destination address.

When a router receives a multicast packet for forwarding or delivery, it will perform the following actions:

1. If the multicast address is not recognized, the datagram is discarded.

2. If the router attaches to a network containing at least one member of this group, it transmits a copy of the datagram on that network.

3. The router consults the spanning tree that it has calculated for this source-destination pair to determine if one or more copies of the datagram should be forwarded to other routers and performs the necessary transmission.

For any hop that is across a broadcast network such as a LAN, an IP multicast datagram is transmitted inside a MAC-level multicast frame addressed to all routers on the LAN.

MOSPF must deal with a number of special circumstances that complicate the algorithm just described. We examine each of these in turn.

Equal-Cost Multipath Ambiguities It may be that there are multiple paths between a given source and a given destination network of equal cost. Dijkstra's algorithm will generate a spanning tree that includes one of these paths. Which path is included depends on the order in which nodes are processed. In the case of unicast routing, it is not important that each router perform Dijkstra's algorithm in the same way to generate the same spanning tree, because each node is determining the shortest paths to all networks from itself. However, for multicast routing, each node determines the shortest paths to all destination networks that are covered by a multicast address from some other source network. Accordingly, it is important that all routers agree on a unique spanning tree for a given source node. To enforce this, MOSPF includes a tiebreaker rule that is deterministic so that all routers will agree.

Interarea Multicasting Recall from Chapter 11 that OSPF incorporates the concept of area. An internet can be organized as a two-level hierarchy. At a top level is a backbone, and subordinate to the backbone are a number of areas. Each area is a contiguous set of networks and hosts, plus routers attached to any of those networks. The backbone is a contiguous set of networks and routers not contained in any area, plus routers that belong to multiple areas. The OSPF link-state algorithm is performed within each area. That is, the routers within an area have a detailed picture of the topology of their area and can perform Dijkstra's algorithm within the area. To reach a host outside the area, packets are routed to a border router, which forwards the datagrams through the backbone to the target area.

Multicasting complicates the use of areas, because a multicast group may contain members in more than one area. To minimize the size of the database that must be maintained by each router within an area, each such router only knows about the multicast groups that have members in its area. To achieve full connectivity, a subset of an area's border routers, called **interarea multicast forwarders**, forward group membership information and multicast datagrams between areas. The key functions are as follows:

1. Because each interarea multicast forwarder is attached to an area, it receives the multicast link status reports from that area and therefore knows all of the multicast groups in that area. Conversely, because each area includes at least one interarea multicast forwarder, its multicast group information is known to at least one router in the backbone.

2. Backbone routers exchange information about multicast groups so that all routers in the backbone know which areas contain members of each group.

3. Each interarea multicast forwarder also functions as a **wildcard multicast receiver**. Such routers automatically receive all multicast datagrams generated in an area, regardless of the destination multicast group. A wildcard multicast router will forward a multicast datagram if necessary and discard it otherwise. The wildcard multicast receiver guarantees that all multicast traffic originating in an area is delivered to its interarea multicast forwarder and then, if necessary, into the backbone.

Figures 12.6a and b illustrate the key concepts for interarea multicast routing. If the source of a multicast datagram resides in the same area as the router performing the spanning-tree calculation, that router must be sure that the spanning tree includes branches to subnetworks in the area with group members plus branches to each wildcard multicast receiver in the area. The local router does not know if there are group members residing in other areas and so must retain the wildcard multicast receivers.

If the source of a multicast datagram resides in a different area than the router performing the spanning-tree calculation, then the datagram has entered the area through an interarea multicast forwarder; this entry point is used as the base of the spanning tree by routers in the area in calculating the spanning tree.

Inter-AS Multicasting OSPF and its extension, MOSPF, function within an autonomous system (AS), or domain, of an internet. No detailed routing information is sent outside of the AS. In the case of unicast routing, we saw that some sort of interdomain routing protocol, such as BGP, is needed to route datagrams across multiple ASs. We would like to extend this capability to multicasting and, in the next subsection, show an example of an interdomain routing protocol that supports multicasting, namely PIM.

Although MOSPF has no responsibility for multicasting beyond its AS, it is responsible for providing multicast group information to outside entities and for

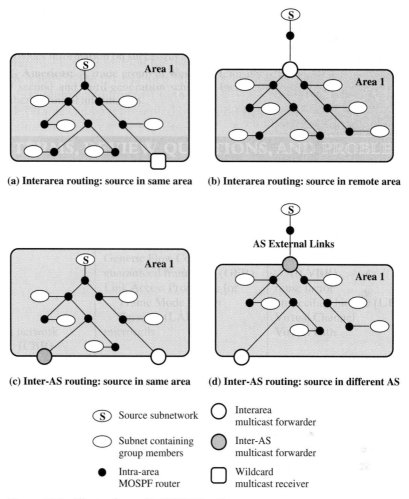

(a) Interarea routing: source in same area (b) Interarea routing: source in remote area

(c) Inter-AS routing: source in same area (d) Inter-AS routing: source in different AS

(S) Source subnetwork	◯	Interarea multicast forwarder
◯ Subnet containing group members	◉	Inter-AS multicast forwarder
● Intra-area MOSPF router	▢	Wildcard multicast receiver

Figure 12.6 Illustrations of MOSPF Routing

accepting multicast datagrams for groups contained within its AS. MOSPF support inter-AS multicasting in the following ways:

1. Certain boundary routers (routers within this AS that are also a neighbor to a non-AS router; a boundary router may be an internal router or a border router) will be configured as **inter-AS multicast forwarders**. In addition to running MOSPF and OSPF, these routers also run an inter-AS multicast routing protocol.

2. MOSPF guarantees that the inter-AS multicast forwarders receive all multicast datagrams from within the AS; in other words, each inter-AS multicast forwarder functions as a wildcard multicast receiver. Each such router determines whether the datagram should be forwarded to other ASs, based on the inter-AS routing protocol. Figure 12.6c illustrates this feature.

3. Recall that internal multicast routing requires knowledge of the source of a datagram. For this purpose, MOSPF uses a technique known as reverse-path routing. This technique assumes that a multicast datagram originating at source X (outside the AS) will enter the MOSPF AS at the point that is advertising (into OSPF) the best route back to X. MOSPF calculates that path of the datagram through the MOSPF AS based on this assumption. In other words, suppose that a router internal to the MOSPF AS receives a multicast datagram for forwarding whose source IP address is X, which is external to the AS. The router first determines what route it would use to send a unicast datagram to X; this involves sending that unicast datagram to a boundary router within the AS. The router then assumes that this multicast datagram entered the AS at that particular boundary router and does its source-destination routing on that basis. Figure 12.6d illustrates this situation.

Protocol Independent Multicast (PIM)

Most multicast routing protocols have two characteristics:

1. The multicast protocol is an extension to an existing unicast routing protocol and requires that routers implement the unicast routing protocol. MOSPF as an extension to OSPF is an example.
2. In most cases, the multicast routing protocol is designed to be efficient when there is a relatively high concentration of multicast group members.

The use of a multicast extension to a unicast routing protocol is appropriate within a single autonomous system, where it is typical that a single unicast routing protocol is implemented. The assumption of a high concentration of multicast group members is often valid within a single autonomous system and for applications such as groupware. However, a different approach is needed to deal with a large internet of multiple autonomous systems and to deal with applications such as multimedia, in which the size of a given multicast group may be relatively small and widely scattered.

To provide a more general solution to multicast routing, a new protocol has been developed, known as Protocol Independent Multicast (PIM). As the name suggests, PIM is a separate routing protocol, independent of any existing unicast routing protocol. PIM is designed to extract needed routing information from any unicast routing protocol and may work across multiple ASs with a number of different unicast routing protocols.

PIM Strategy The design of PIM recognizes that a different approach may be needed to multicast routing depending on the concentration of multicast group members. When there are many multicast members and many subnetworks within a configuration have members of a given multicast group, then the frequent exchange of group membership information is justified. In such an environment, it is desirable to build shared spanning trees, such as we saw in Figure 12.3b, so that packet duplication occurs as infrequently as possible. However, when there are a few widely scattered members to a given multicast group, different considerations apply. First, flooding of multicast group information to all routers is inefficient, be-cause most routers will not be along the path of any members of a given multicast group. Second, there will be relatively little opportunity for using shared spanning trees, and therefore the focus should be on providing multiple shortest-path uni-cast routes.

To accommodate these differing requirements, PIM defines two modes of op-eration: dense-mode and sparse-mode operation. These are, in fact, two separate protocols. The dense-mode protocol is appropriate for intra-AS multicast routing and may be viewed as a potential alternative to MOSPF. The sparse-mode protocol is suited for inter-AS multicast routing. The remainder of this discussion concerns sparse-mode PIM (RFC 2362).

Sparse-Mode PIM   The PIM specification defines a sparse group as one in which

- The number of networks/domains with group members present is significantly smaller than the number of networks/domains in the internet.
- The internet spanned by the group is not sufficiently resource rich to ignore the overhead of current multicast routing schemes.

Before proceeding, let us define a group destination router to be a router with local group members (members attached to a subnetwork interfaced by that router). A router becomes a destination router for a given group when at least one local host joins that group using IGMP or a similar protocol. A group source router is a router that attaches to a network with at least one host that is transmitting packets on the multicast group address via that router. For some groups, a given router will be both a source and a destination router. However, for broadcast types of applications, such as video distribution, there may be one or a small number of source routers with many destination routers.

The approach taken for sparse-mode PIM has the following elements:

1. For a multicast group, one router is designated as a *rendezvous point* (RP).

2. A group destination router sends a Join message toward the RP requesting that its members be added to the group. The requesting router uses a unicast shortest-path route to transmit the message toward the RP. The reverse of this path becomes part of the distribution tree from this RP to listeners in this group.

3. Any node that wishes to send to a multicast group sends packets toward the RP, using a shortest-path unicast route.

A transmission by this scheme, as defined so far, can be summarized as fol-lows: A single packet follows the shortest unicast path from the sending node to the RP. From the RP, transmission occurs down the tree to the listeners, with each packet replicated at each split in the tree. This scheme minimizes the exchange of routing information, because routing information goes only from each router that supports group members to the RP. The scheme also provides reasonable efficiency. In particular, from the RP to the multicast receivers, a shared tree is used, minimiz-ing the number of packets duplicated.

In a widely dispersed group, any RP will, of necessity, be remote from many of the group members, and paths for many group members will be much longer than the least-cost path. To help alleviate these drawbacks while maintaining the benefits of the PIM scheme, PIM allows a destination router to replace the group-shared tree with a shortest-path tree to any source. Once a destination router receives a multicast packet, it may elect to send a Join message back to the source router of that packet along a unicast shortest path. From then on, multicast packets between that source and all group members that are neighbors to that destination router follow the unicast shortest path.

Figure 12.7 illustrates the sequence of events. Once the destination begins to receive packets from the source by the shortest-path router, it sends a Prune message to the RP. This Prune message instructs the RP not to send any multicast packets from that source to this destination. The destination will continue to receive multicast packets from other sources via the RP-based tree, unless and until it prunes those sources. Any source router must continue to send multicast packets to the RP router for delivery to other multicast members.

The selection of an RP for a given multicast group is a dynamic process. The initiator of a multicast group selects a primary RP and a small ordered set of alternative

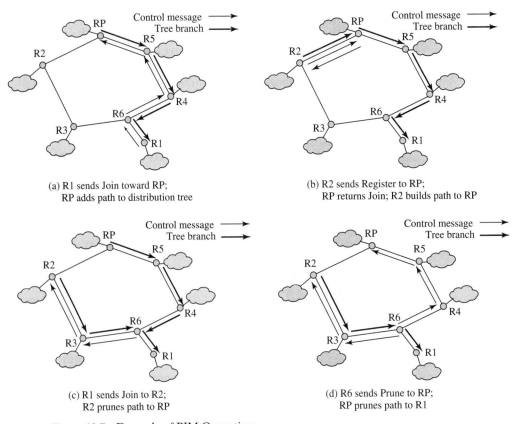

(a) R1 sends Join toward RP;
    RP adds path to distribution tree

(b) R2 sends Register to RP;
    RP returns Join; R2 builds path to RP

(c) R1 sends Join to R2;
    R2 prunes path to RP

(d) R6 sends Prune to RP;
    RP prunes path to R1

Figure 12.7 Example of PIM Operation

RPs. In general, RP placement is not a critical issue because the RP-based tree will not be used for most receivers after shortest-path routers are followed.

12.3 RECOMMENDED READING AND WEB SITES

[DEER90] is a seminal paper that describes the general approach and most of the mechanisms now in use for internet multicasting. [SAHA00] is a comprehensive discussion of multicast routing algorithms plus a survey of multicast routing protocols. [ALME00] provides an account of the development of multicasting protocols and looks at future directions. [RAMA00] is a detailed and exhaustive survey of multicast routing protocols. [LI02] is a comprehensive survey of network and transport layer issues related to Internet multicasting.

The general references cited in Chapter 11 are also relevant to BGP and IDRP. For more information on IDRP, see [REKH93].

[MOY94] describes the philosophy and general approach of MOSPF. [HUIT00] provides an overview of both dense- and sparse-mode PIM. [DEER96] is a detailed account of sparse-mode PIM.

ALME00   Almeroth, K. "The Evolution of Multicast: From the Mbone to Interdomain Multicast to Internet2 Deployment." *IEEE Network*, January/February 2000.

DEER90   Deering, S., and Cheriton, D. "Multicast Routing in Datagram Internetworks and Extended LANs." *ACM Transactions on Computer Systems*, May 1990.

DEER96   Deering, S., et al., " The PIM Architecture for Wide-Area Multicast Routing." *IEEE/ACM Transactions on Networking*, April 1996.

HUIT00   Huitema, C. *Routing in the Internet.* Upper Saddle River, NJ: Prentice Hall, 2000.

LI02   Li, V., and Zhang, Z. "Internet Multicast Routing and Transport Control Protocols." *Proceedings of the IEEE*, March 2002.

MOY94   Moy, J. "Multicast Routing Extensions for OSPF." *Communications of the ACM*, August 1994.

RAMA00   Ramalho, M. "Intra- and Inter-Domain Multicast Routing Protocols: A Survey and Taxonomy." *IEEE Communications Surveys and Tutorial*, First Quarter 2000. www.comsoc.org/livepubs/surveys.

REKH93   Rekhter, Y. "Inter-Domain Routing Protocol (IDRP)." *Internetworking: Research and Experience*, June 1993.

SAHA00   Sahasrabuddhe, L., and Mukherjee, B. "Multicast Routing Algorithms and Protocols: A Tutorial." *IEEE Network*, January/February 2000.

 Recommended Web Sites:

- **PIM Working Group:** Chartered by IETF to develop standards related to PIM. The Web site includes all relevant RFCs and Internet drafts.
- **MOSPF Working Group:** Chartered by IETF to develop standards related to MOSPF. The Web site includes all relevant RFCs and Internet drafts.
- **Reliable Multicast Links:** List of reliable multicast and fault-tolerant project/paper/ page/etc. references.

12.4 KEY TERMS, REVIEW QUESTIONS, AND PROBLEMS

Key Terms

Border Gateway Protocol (BGP)	multicast address	neighbor reachability
broadcast	multicasting	network reachability
Inter-Domain Routing Protocol (IDRP)	Multicast Extensions to Open Shortest Path First (MOSPF)	path-vector routing Protocol Independent Multicast (PIM)
Internet Group Management Protocol (IGMP)	neighbor neighbor acquisition	Sparse-Mode PIM

Review Questions

12.1 In BGP, what is a neighbor?

12.2 Briefly describe the three functional procedures of BGP.

12.3 What are the key differences between BGP and IDRP?

12.4 What are the essential steps in a true multicast strategy?

12.5 What operations are provided by IGMP?

12.6 Explain the problem with equal-cost multipath ambiguity in MOSPF.

12.7 How does MOSPF deal with equal-cost multipath ambiguity?

12.8 What is the difference, in terms of applicability, between dense-mode and sparse-mode PIM?

Problems

12.1 Besides its use for authentication, the Marker field of a BGP message can be used for synchronization. Why is synchronization necessary? What would change if a datagram-oriented transport protocol were used instead of TCP?

12.2 BGP's AS_PATH attribute identifies the autonomous systems through which routing information has passed. How can the AS_PATH attribute be used to detect routing information loops?

12.3 BGP provides a list of autonomous systems on the path to the destination. However, this information cannot be considered a distance metric. Why?

12.4 We've seen that BGP uses TCP as its transport protocol. However, in order to test network connectivity, BGP defines a keepalive message at the application layer instead of using TCP's keepalive feature. Why?

12.5 IGMP specifies that query messages be sent in IP datagrams that have the Time to Live field set to 1. Why?

12.6 In IGMPv1 and IGMPv2, a host will cancel sending a pending membership report if it hears another host claiming membership in that group, in order to control the generation of IGMP traffic. However, IGMPv3 removes this suppression of host membership reports. Analyze the reasons behind this design decision.

12.7 IGMP Membership Queries include a "Max Resp Code" field that specifies the maximum time allowed before sending a responding report. The actual time allowed, called the Max Resp Time, is represented in units of $1/10$ second and is derived from the Max Resp Code as follows:

If MaxRespCode $<$ 128, MaxRespTime = Max Resp Code

If MaxRespCode $\geq$ 128, MaxRespTime is a floating-point value as follows:

0	1	2	3	4	5	6	7
1		exp			mant		

MaxRespTime $=$ (mant$|$0 $\times$ 10) $\ll$ (exp $+$ 3)   in C notation

MaxRespTime $=$ (mant $+$ 16) $\times$ $2^{(exp+3)}$

Explain the motivation for the smaller values and the larger values.

12.8 Multicast applications call an API function on their sockets in order to ask the IP layer to enable or disable reception of packets sent from some specific IP address(es) to a specific multicast address.

For each of these sockets, the system records the desired multicast reception state. In addition to these per-socket multicast reception states, the system must maintain a multicast reception state for each of its interfaces, which is derived from the per-socket reception states.

Suppose four multicast applications run on the same host, and participate in the same multicast group, M1. The first application uses an EXCLUDE {A1, A2, A3} filter. The second one uses an EXCLUDE {A1, A3, A4} filter. The third one uses an INCLUDE {A3, A4} filter. And the fourth one uses an INCLUDE {A3} filter. What's the resulting multicast state (multicast-address, filter-mode, source-list) for the network interface?

12.9 We've talked about multicast applications that use UDP or RTP as their transport protocol. However, we have not mentioned any multicast application using TCP as its transport protocol. What's the problem with TCP?

12.10 With multicasting, packets are delivered to multiple destinations. Thus, in case of errors (such as routing failures), one IP packet might trigger multiple ICMP error packets, leading to a packet storm. How is this potential problem avoided?

12.11 In the discussion of Figure 12.2, three alternatives for transmitting a packet to a multicast address were discussed: broadcast, multiple unicast, and true multicast. Yet another alternative is flooding. The source transmits one packet to each neighboring router. Each router, when it receives a packet, retransmits the packet on all outgoing interfaces except the one on which the packet is received. Each packet is labeled with a unique identifier so that a router does not flood the same packet more than once. Fill out a matrix similar to those of Table 12.2 and comment on the results.

12.12 In a manner similar to Figure 12.4, show the spanning tree from router B to the multicast group.

12.13 Most multicast routing protocols, such as MOSPF, minimize the path cost to each group member, but they do not necessarily optimize the use of the Internet as a whole. This problem demonstrates this fact.

a. Sum the hop costs incurred by each packet involved in a multicast transmission of a source packet using the spanning tree of Figure 12.3a.

b. Design an alternative spanning tree that minimizes the total cost. Show the tree and the total cost.

12.14 Explain why MOSPF would be inefficient in a sparse multicast environment.

12.15 "In sparse-mode PIM, for the route between a given source and a given destination, the RP-based tree may be replaced with a path that is the shortest unicast path from source to destination." This is not quite accurate. What is wrong with the statement?

12.16 Some researchers argue that the optimal placement of the center of the shared tree (i.e., the rendezvous point in PIM) is crucial for achieving good delay characteristics for the multicast traffic. Argue for or against this statement.

PART SIX

Network and Link Layers

CHAPTER 13

WIDE AREA NETWORKS

He got into a District Line train at Wimbledon Park, changed on to the Victoria Line at Victoria and on to the Jubilee Line at Green Park for West Hampstead. It was a long and awkward journey but he enjoyed it.
                                             —King Solomon's Carpet,
                                               Barbara Vine (Ruth Rendell)

KEY POINTS

- Frame relay is a form of packet switching that provides a streamlined interface compared to X.25, with improved performance.

- ATM is a streamlined packet transfer interface. ATM makes use of fixed-size packets, called cells. The use of a fixed size and fixed format results in an efficient scheme for transmission over high-speed networks.

- ATM provides both real-time and non-real-time services. An ATM-based network can support a wide range of traffic, including synchronous TDM streams such as T-1 using the constant bit rate (CBR) service; compressed voice and video using the real-time variable bit rate (rt-VBR) service; traffic with specific quality-of-service requirements using the non-real-time VBR (nrt-VBR) service; and IP-based traffic using the available bit rate (ABR), unspecified bit rate (UBR), and guaranteed frame rate (GFR) services.

- The essence of a cellular wireless network is the use of multiple low-power transmitters. The area to be covered is divided into cells in a hexagonal tile pattern that provides full coverage of the area.

Wide area networks (WANs) generally cover a large geographical area, require the crossing of public right-of-ways, and rely at least in part on circuits provided by a common carrier. Typically, a WAN consists of a number of interconnected switching nodes. A transmission from any one device is routed through these internal nodes to the specified destination device. These nodes (including the boundary nodes) are not concerned with the content of the data; rather, their purpose is to provide a switching facility that will move the data from node to node until they reach their destination.

Traditionally, WANs have been implemented using one of two technologies: circuit switching and packet switching. More recently, frame relay, ATM, and wireless networks have assumed major roles. We look at each of these three types of WANs in this chapter.

13.1 FRAME RELAY

Frame relay is designed to provide a more efficient transmission scheme than packet switching. The standards for frame relay matured earlier than those for ATM, and commercial products also arrived earlier. Accordingly, there is a large installed base of frame relay products. Interest has since shifted to ATM for high-speed data networking, but because of the remaining popularity of frame relay, we provide a survey in this section.

Background

The traditional approach to packet switching makes use of a protocol between the user and the network known as X.25. X.25 not only determines the user-network interface but also influences the internal design of the network. Several key features of the X.25 approach are as follows:

- Call control packets, used for setting up and clearing virtual circuits, are carried on the same channel and same virtual circuit as data packets. In effect, inband signaling is used.
- Multiplexing of virtual circuits takes place at layer 3.
- Both layer 2 and layer 3 include flow control and error control mechanisms.

The X.25 approach results in considerable overhead. At each hop through the network, the data link control protocol involves the exchange of a data frame and an acknowledgment frame. Furthermore, at each intermediate node, state tables must be maintained for each virtual circuit to deal with the call management and flow control/error control aspects of the X.25 protocol. All of this overhead may be justified when there is a significant probability of error on any of the links in the network. This approach may not be the most appropriate for modern digital communication facilities. Today's networks employ reliable digital transmission technology over high-quality, reliable transmission links, many of which are optical fiber. In addition, with the use of optical fiber and digital transmission, high data rates can be achieved. In this environment, the overhead of X.25 is not only unnecessary but degrades the effective utilization of the available high data rates.

Frame relaying is designed to eliminate much of the overhead that X.25 imposes on end user systems and on the packet-switching network. The key differences between frame relaying and a conventional X.25 packet-switching service are as follows:

- Call control signaling is carried on a separate logical connection from user data. Thus, intermediate nodes need not maintain state tables or process messages relating to call control on an individual per-connection basis.
- Multiplexing and switching of logical connections takes place at layer 2 instead of layer 3, eliminating one entire layer of processing.
- There is no hop-by-hop flow control and error control. End-to-end flow control and error control are the responsibility of a higher layer, if they are employed at all.

Thus, with frame relay, a single user data frame is sent from source to destination, and an acknowledgment, generated at a higher layer, is carried back in a frame. There are no hop-by-hop exchanges of data frames and acknowledgments.

Let us consider the advantages and disadvantages of this approach. The principal potential disadvantage of frame relaying, compared to X.25, is that we have lost the ability to do link-by-link flow and error control. (Although frame relay does not provide end-to-end flow and error control, this is easily provided at a higher layer.) In X.25, multiple virtual circuits are carried on a single physical link, and the link level protocol provides reliable transmission from the source to the packet-switching network and from the packet-switching network to the destination. In addition, at each hop through the network, the link control protocol can be used for reliability. With the use of frame relaying, this hop-by-hop link control is lost. However, with the increasing reliability of transmission and switching facilities, this is not a major disadvantage.

The advantage of frame relaying is that we have streamlined the communications process. The protocol functionality required at the user-network interface is reduced, as is the internal network processing. As a result, lower delay and higher throughput can be expected. Studies indicate an improvement in throughput using frame relay, compared to X.25, of an order of magnitude or more [HARB92]. The ITU-T Recommendation I.233 indicates that frame relay is to be used at access speeds up to 2 Mbps. However, frame relay service at even higher data rates is now available.

Frame Relay Protocol Architecture

Figure 13.1 depicts the protocol architecture to support the frame mode bearer service. We need to consider two separate planes of operation: a control (C) plane, which is involved in the establishment and termination of logical connections, and a user (U) plane, which is responsible for the transfer of user data between subscribers. Thus, C-plane protocols are between a subscriber and the network, while U-plane protocols provide end-to-end functionality.

Control Plane The control plane for frame mode bearer services is similar to that for common channel signaling for circuit-switching services, in that a separate logical channel is used for control information. At the data link layer, LAPD (Q.921) is used to provide a reliable data link control service, with error control and flow control, between user (TE) and network (NT). This data link service is used for the exchange of Q.933 control signaling messages.

User Plane For the actual transfer of information between end users, the user-plane protocol is LAPF (Link Access Procedure for Frame Mode Bearer Services), which is defined in Q.922. Only the core functions of LAPF are used for frame relay:

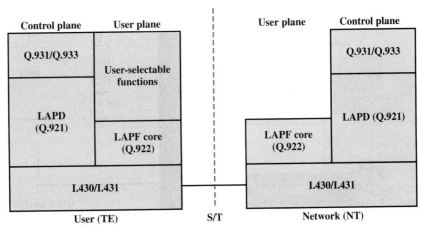

Figure 13.1   Frame Relay User-Network Interface Protocol Architecture

- Frame delimiting, alignment, and transparency
- Frame multiplexing/demultiplexing using the address field
- Inspection of the frame to ensure that it consists of an integral number of octets prior to zero bit insertion or following zero bit extraction
- Inspection of the frame to ensure that it is neither too long nor too short
- Detection of transmission errors
- Congestion control functions

The last function listed is new to LAPF. The remaining functions listed are also functions of LAPD.

The core functions of LAPF in the user plane constitute a sublayer of the data link layer. This provides the bare service of transferring data link frames from one subscriber to another, with no flow control or error control. Above this, the user may choose to select additional data link or network-layer end-to-end functions. These are not part of the frame relay service. Based on the core functions, a network offers frame relaying as a connection-oriented link layer service with the following properties:

- Preservation of the order of frame transfer from one edge of the network to the other
- A small probability of frame loss

User Data Transfer

The operation of frame relay for user data transfer is best explained by considering the frame format, illustrated in Figure 13.2a. This is the format defined for the minimum-function LAPF protocol (known as LAPF core protocol). The format is

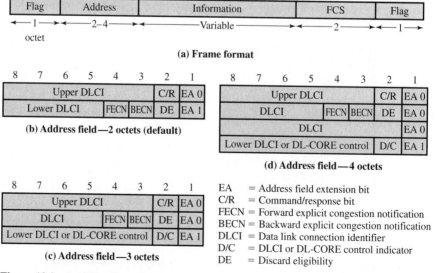

Figure 13.2 LAPF—Core Formats

similar to that of LAPD and other link control protocols with one obvious omission: There is no Control field. This has the following implications:

- There is only one frame type, used for carrying user data. There are no control frames.
- It is not possible to use inband signaling; a logical connection can only carry user data.
- It is not possible to perform flow control and error control, because there are no sequence numbers.

The Flag and Frame Check Sequence (FCS) fields function as in HDLC, described in Chapter 14. The information field carries higher-layer data. If the user selects to implement additional data link control functions end-to-end, then a data link frame can be carried in this field. Specifically, a common selection will be to use the full LAPF protocol (known as LAPF control protocol), to perform functions above the LAPF core functions. Note that the protocol implemented in this fashion is strictly between the end subscribers and is transparent to the frame relay network.

The address field has a default length of 2 octets and may be extended to 3 or 4 octets. It carries a data link connection identifier (DLCI) of 10, 16, or 23 bits. The DLCI allows multiple logical frame relay connections to be multiplexed over a single channel. The connection identifier has only local significance: Each end of the logical connection assigns its own DLCI from the pool of locally unused numbers, and the network must map from one to the other. The alternative, using the same DLCI on both ends, would require some sort of global management of DLCI values.

The length of the Address field, and hence of the DLCI, is determined by the Address field extension (EA) bits. The C/R bit is application specific and not used by the standard frame relay protocol. The remaining bits in the address field have to do with congestion control.

13.2 ASYNCHRONOUS TRANSFER MODE (ATM)

Frame relay is designed to support access speeds up to 2 Mbps. But now, even the streamlined design of frame relay is faltering in the face of a requirement for wide area access speeds in the tens and hundreds of megabits per second. To accommodate these gargantuan requirements, a new technology has emerged: **asynchronous transfer mode** (ATM), also known as **cell relay**.

Cell relay is similar in concept to frame relay. Both frame relay and cell relay take advantage of the reliability and fidelity of modern digital facilities to provide faster packet switching than X.25. Cell relay is even more streamlined than frame relay in its functionality and can support data rates several orders of magnitude greater than frame relay.

Virtual Channels and Virtual Paths

ATM is a packet-oriented transfer mode. Like frame relay and X.25, it allows multiple logical connections to be multiplexed over a single physical interface. The information flow on each logical connection is organized into fixed-size packets, called **cells**. As with frame relay, there is no link-by-link error control or flow control.

Logical connections in ATM are referred to as **virtual channels**. A virtual channel is analogous to a virtual circuit in X.25 or a frame relay logical connection. It is the basic unit of switching in an ATM network. A virtual channel is set up between two end users through the network and a variable-rate, full-duplex flow of fixed-size cells is exchanged over the connection. Virtual channels are also used for user-network exchange (control signaling) and network-network exchange (network management and routing).

For ATM, a second sublayer of processing has been introduced that deals with the concept of **virtual path** (Figure 13.3). A virtual path is a bundle of virtual channels that have the same endpoints. Thus, all of the cells flowing over all of the virtual channels in a single virtual path are switched together.

Several advantages can be listed for the use of virtual paths:

- **Simplified network architecture:** Network transport functions can be separated into those related to an individual logical connection (virtual channel) and those related to a group of logical connections (virtual path).

- **Increased network performance and reliability:** The network deals with fewer, aggregated entities.

- **Reduced processing and short connection setup time:** Much of the work is done when the virtual path is set up. The addition of new virtual channels to an existing virtual path involves minimal processing.

- **Enhanced network services:** The virtual path is used internal to the network but is also visible to the end user. Thus, the user may define closed user groups or closed networks of virtual-channel bundles.

Virtual-Path/Virtual-Channel Characteristics ITU-T Recommendation I.150 lists the following as characteristics of virtual channel connections:

- **Quality of service:** A user of a virtual channel is provided with a quality of service specified by parameters such as cell loss ratio (ratio of cells lost to cells transmitted) and cell delay variation.

- **Switched and semipermanent virtual-channel connections:** Both switched connections, which require call-control signaling, and dedicated channels can be provided.

- **Cell sequence integrity:** The sequence of transmitted cells within a virtual channel is preserved.

- **Traffic parameter negotiation and usage monitoring:** Traffic parameters can be negotiated between a user and the network for each virtual channel. The

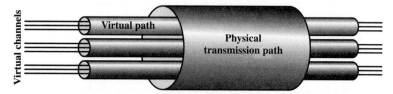

Figure 13.3   ATM Connection Relationships

input of cells to the virtual channel is monitored by the network to ensure that the negotiated parameters are not violated.

The types of traffic parameters that can be negotiated include average rate, peak rate, burstiness, and peak duration. The network may need a number of strategies to deal with congestion and to manage existing and requested virtual channels. At the crudest level, the network may simply deny new requests for virtual channels to prevent congestion. Additionally, cells may be discarded if negotiated parameters are violated or if congestion becomes severe. In an extreme situation, existing connections might be terminated.

I.150 also lists characteristics of virtual paths. The first four characteristics listed are identical to those for virtual channels. That is, quality of service, switched and semipermanent virtual paths, cell sequence integrity, and traffic parameter negotiation and usage monitoring are all also characteristics of a virtual path. There are a number of reasons for this duplication. First, this provides some flexibility in how the network manages the requirements placed upon it. Second, the network must be concerned with the overall requirements for a virtual path, and within a virtual path may negotiate the establishment of virtual circuits with given characteristics. Finally, once a virtual path is set up, it is possible for the end users to negotiate the creation of new virtual channels. The virtual path characteristics impose a discipline on the choices that the end users may make.

In addition, a fifth characteristic is listed for virtual paths:

- **Virtual channel identifier restriction within a virtual path:** One or more virtual channel identifiers, or numbers, may not be available to the user of the virtual path but may be reserved for network use. Examples would be virtual channels used for network management.

Control Signaling In ATM, a mechanism is needed for the establishment and release of virtual paths and virtual channels. The exchange of information involved in this process is referred to as control signaling and takes place on separate connections from those that are being managed.

For virtual channels, I.150 specifies four methods for providing an establishment/release facility. One or a combination of these methods will be used in any particular network:

1. **Semipermanent virtual channels** may be used for user-to-user exchange. In this case, no control signaling is required.

2. If there is no preestablished call control signaling channel, one must be set up. For that purpose, a control signaling exchange must take place between the user and the network on some channel. Hence we need a permanent channel, probably of low data rate, that can be used to set up a virtual channel that can be used for call control. Such a channel is called a **meta-signaling channel**, because the channel is used to set up signaling channels.

3. The meta-signaling channel can be used to set up a virtual channel between the user and the network for call control signaling. This user-to-network signaling virtual channel can then be used to set up virtual channels to carry user data.

4. The meta-signaling channel can also be used to set up a user-to-user signaling virtual channel. Such a channel must be set up within a preestablished virtual

path. It can then be used to allow the two end users, without network intervention, to establish and release user-to-user virtual channels to carry user data.

For virtual paths, three methods are defined in I.150:

1. A virtual path can be established on a **semipermanent** basis by prior agreement. In this case, no control signaling is required.

2. Virtual path establishment/release may be **customer controlled**. In this case, the customer uses a signaling virtual channel to request the virtual path from the network.

3. Virtual path establishment/release may be **network controlled**. In this case, the network establishes a virtual path for its own convenience. The path may be network-to-network, user-to-network, or user-to-user.

ATM Cells

The asynchronous transfer mode makes use of fixed-size cells, consisting of a 5-octet header and a 48-octet information field. There are several advantages to the use of small, fixed-size cells. First, the use of small cells may reduce queuing delay for a high-priority cell, because it waits less if it arrives slightly behind a lower-priority cell that has gained access to a resource (e.g., the transmitter). Second, it appears that fixed-size cells can be switched more efficiently, which is important for the very high data rates of ATM [PARE88]. With fixed-size cells, it is easier to implement the switching mechanism in hardware.

Figure 13.4a shows the header format at the user-network interface. Figure 13.4b shows the cell header format internal to the network.

The **Generic Flow Control** (GFC) field does not appear in the cell header internal to the network, but only at the user-network interface. Hence, it can be used for control of cell flow only at the local user-network interface. The field could be used to assist the customer in controlling the flow of traffic for different qualities of service. In any case, the GFC mechanism is used to alleviate short-term overload conditions in the network.

I.150 lists as a requirement for the GFC mechanism that all terminals be able to get access to their assured capacities. This includes all constant-bit-rate (CBR) terminals as well as the variable-bit-rate (VBR) terminals that have an element of guaranteed capacity (CBR and VBR are explained subsequently). The current GFC mechanism is described in a subsequent subsection.

The **Virtual Path Identifier** (VPI) field constitutes a routing field for the network. It is 8 bits at the user-network interface and 12 bits at the network-network interface, allowing for more virtual paths to be supported within the network. The **Virtual Channel Identifier** (VCI) field is used for routing to and from the end user. Thus, it functions much as a service access point.

The **Payload Type** (PT) field indicates the type of information in the information field. Table 13.1 shows the interpretation of the PT bits. A value of 0 in the first bit indicates user information (that is, information from the next higher layer). In this case, the second bit indicates whether congestion has been experienced; the

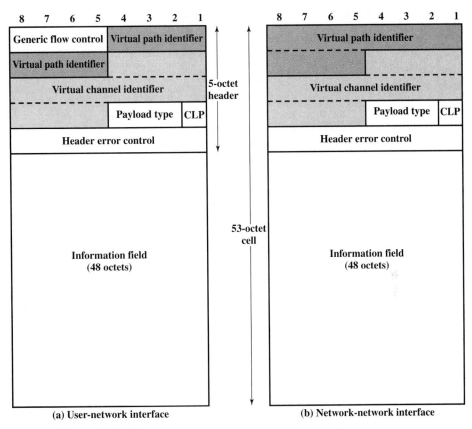

Figure 13.4 ATM Cell Format

Table 13.1 Payload Type (PT) Field Coding

PT Coding	Interpretation		
0 0 0	User data cell,	congestion not experienced,	SDU type = 0
0 0 1	User data cell,	congestion not experienced,	SDU type = 1
0 1 0	User data cell,	congestion experienced,	SDU type = 0
0 1 1	User data cell,	congestion experienced,	SDU type = 1
1 0 0	OAM segment associated cell		
1 0 1	OAM end-to-end associated cell		
1 1 0	Resource management cell		
1 1 1	Reserved for future function		

SDU = Service Data Unit
OAM = Operations, Administration, and Maintenance

third bit, known as the service data unit (SDU)[1] type bit, is a one-bit field that can be used to discriminate two types of ATM SDUs associated with a connection. The term *SDU* refers to the 48-octet payload of the cell. A value of 1 in the first bit of the payload type field indicates that this cell carries network management or maintenance information. This indication allows the insertion of network-management cells onto a user's virtual channel without impacting the user's data. Thus, the PT field can provide inband control information.

The **cell loss priority** (CLP) bit is used to provide guidance to the network in the event of congestion. A value of 0 indicates a cell of relatively higher priority, which should not be discarded unless no other alternative is available. A value of 1 indicates that this cell is subject to discard within the network. The user might employ this field so that extra cells (beyond the negotiated rate) may be inserted into the network, with a CLP of 1, and delivered to the destination if the network is not congested. The network may set this field to 1 for any data cell that is in violation of an agreement concerning traffic parameters between the user and the network. In this case, the switch that does the setting realizes that the cell exceeds the agreed traffic parameters but that the switch is capable of handling the cell. At a later point in the network, if congestion is encountered, this cell has been marked for discard in preference to cells that fall within agreed traffic limits.

The **Header Error Control** (HEC) field is an 8-bit error code that can be used to correct single-bit errors in the header and to detect double-bit errors. In the case of most existing protocols, such as LAPD and HDLC, the data field that serves as input to the error code calculation is in general much longer than the size of the resulting error code. This allows for error detection. In the case of ATM, the input to the calculation is only 32 bits, compared to 8 bits for the code. The fact that the input is relatively short allows the code to be used not only for error detection but also, in some cases, for actual error correction. This is because there is sufficient redundancy in the code to recover from certain error patterns.

The error protection function provides both recovery from single-bit header errors and a low probability of the delivery of cells with errored headers under bursty error conditions. The error characteristics of fiber-based transmission systems appear to be a mix of single-bit errors and relatively large burst errors. For some transmission systems, the error correction capability, which is more time-consuming, might not be invoked.

Generic Flow Control I.150 specifies the use of the GFC field to control traffic flow at the user-network interface (UNI) in order to alleviate short-term overload conditions. The actual flow control mechanism is defined in I.361. GFC flow control is part of a proposed controlled cell transfer (CCT) capability intended to meet the requirements of non-ATM LANs connected to a wide area ATM network [LUIN97]. In particular, CCT is intended to provide good service for high-volume bursty traffic with variable-length messages. In the remainder of this subsection, we examine the GFC mechanism, as so far standardized.

---

[1]This is the term used in ATM Forum documents. In ITU-T documents, this bit is referred to as the ATM-user-to-ATM-user (AAU) indication bit. The meaning is the same.

When the equipment at the UNI is configured to support the GFC mechanism, two sets of procedures are used: uncontrolled transmission and controlled transmission. In essence, every connection is identified as either subject to flow control or not. Of those subject to flow control, there may be one group of controlled connections (Group A) that is the default, or controlled traffic may be classified into two groups of controlled connections (Group A and Group B); these are known, respectively, as the 1-queue and 2-queue models. Flow control is exercised in the direction from the subscriber to the network by the network side.

First, we consider the operation of the GFC mechanism when there is only one group of controlled connections. The controlled equipment, called terminal equipment (TE), initializes two variables: TRANSMIT is a flag initialized to SET (1), and GO_CNTR, which is a credit counter, is initialized to 0. A third variable, GO_VALUE, is either initialized to 1 or set to some larger value at configuration time. The rules for transmission by the controlled device are as follows:

1. If TRANSMIT = 1, cells on uncontrolled connections may be sent at any time. If TRANSMIT = 0, no cells may be sent on either controlled or uncontrolled connections.

2. If a HALT signal is received from the controlling equipment, TRANSMIT is set to 0 and remains at zero until a NO_HALT signal is received, at which time TRANSMIT is set to 1.

3. If TRANSMIT = 1 and there is no cell to transmit on any uncontrolled connections, then
   —If GO CNTR > 0, then the TE may send a cell on a controlled connection. The TE marks that cell as a cell on a controlled connection and decrements GO_CNTR.
   —If GO CNTR = 0, then the TE may not send a cell on a controlled connection.

4. The TE sets GO_CNTR to GO_VALUE upon receiving a SET signal; a null signal has no effect on GO_CNTR.

The HALT signal is used logically to limit the effective ATM data rate and should be cyclic. For example, to reduce the data rate over a link by half, the HALT command is issued by the controlling equipment so as to be in effect 50% of the time. This is done in a predictable, regular pattern over the lifetime of the physical connection.

For the 2-queue model, there are two counters, each with a current counter value and an initialization value: GO_CNTR_A, GO_VALUE_A, GO_CNTR_B, and GO_VALUE_B. This enables the network to control two separate groups of connections.

Table 13.2 summarizes the rules for setting GFC bits.

ATM Service Categories

An ATM network is designed to be able to transfer many different types of traffic simultaneously, including real-time flows such as voice, video, and bursty TCP flows. Although each such traffic flow is handled as a stream of 53-octet cells traveling through a virtual channel, the way in which each data flow is handled within

Table 13.2 Generic Flow Control (GFC) Field Coding

	Uncontrolled	Controlling → controlled		Controlled → controlling	
		1-queue model	2-queue model	1-queue model	2-queue model
First bit	0	HALT(0)/ NO_HALT(1)	HALT(0)/ NO_HALT(1)	0	0
Second bit	0	SET(1)/NULL(0)	SET(1)/NULL(0) for Group A	cell belongs to controlled(1)/ uncontrolled(0)	cell belongs to Group A(1)/ or not (0)
Third bit	0	0	SET(1)/NULL(0) for Group B	0	cell belongs to Group B(1)/ or not (0)
Fourth bit	0	0	0	equipment is uncontrolled(0)/ controlled(1)	equipment is uncontrolled(0)/ controlled(1)

the network depends on the characteristics of the traffic flow and the requirements of the application. For example, real-time video traffic must be delivered within minimum variation in delay.

In this subsection, we summarize ATM service categories, which are used by an end system to identify the type of service required. The following service categories have been defined by the ATM Forum:

- **Real-Time Service**
  - Constant bit rate (CBR)
  - Real-time variable bit rate (rt-VBR)

- **Non-Real-Time Service**
  - Non-real-time variable bit rate (nrt-VBR)
  - Available bit rate (ABR)
  - Unspecified bit rate (UBR)
  - Guaranteed frame rate (GFR)

Real-Time Services The most important distinction among applications concerns the amount of delay and the variability of delay, referred to as jitter, that the application can tolerate. Real-time applications typically involve a flow of information to a user that is intended to reproduce that flow at a source. For example, a user expects a flow of audio or video information to be presented in a continuous, smooth fashion. A lack of continuity or excessive loss results in significant loss of quality. Applications that involve interaction between people have tight constraints on delay. Typically, any delay above a few hundred milliseconds becomes noticeable and annoying. Accordingly, the demands in the ATM network for switching and delivery of real-time data are high.

The **Constant Bit Rate (CBR)** service is perhaps the simplest service to define. It is used by applications that require a fixed data rate that is continuously available during the connection lifetime and a relatively tight upper bound on transfer delay.

CBR is commonly used for uncompressed audio and video information. Example of CBR applications include the following:

- Videoconferencing
- Interactive audio (e.g., telephony)
- Audio/video distribution (e.g., television, distance learning, pay-per-view)
- Audio/video retrieval (e.g., video-on-demand, audio library)

The **Real-Time Variable Bit Rate (rt-VBR)** category is intended for time-sensitive applications; that is, those requiring tightly constrained delay and delay variation. The principal difference between applications appropriate for rt-VBR and those appropriate for CBR is that rt-VBR applications transmit at a rate that varies with time. Equivalently, an rt-VBR source can be characterized as somewhat bursty. For example, the standard approach to video compression results in a sequence of image frames of varying sizes. Because real-time video requires a uniform frame transmission rate, the actual data rate varies.

The rt-VBR service allows the network more flexibility than CBR. The network is able to statistically multiplex a number of connections over the same dedicated capacity and still provide the required service to each connection.

Non–Real-Time Services Non-real-time services are intended for applications that have bursty traffic characteristics and do not have tight constraints on delay and delay variation. Accordingly, the network has greater flexibility in handling such traffic flows and can make greater use of statistical multiplexing to increase network efficiency.

For some non-real-time applications, it is possible to characterize the expected traffic flow so that the network can provide substantially improved quality of service (QoS) in the areas of loss and delay. Such applications can use the **Non-Real-Time Variable Bit Rate (nrt-VBR)** service. With this service, the end system specifies a peak cell rate, a sustainable or average cell rate, and a measure of how bursty or clumped the cells may be. With this information, the network can allocate resources to provide relatively low delay and minimal cell loss.

The nrt-VBR service can be used for data transfers that have critical response-time requirements. Examples include airline reservations, banking transactions, and process monitoring.

At any given time, a certain amount of the capacity of an ATM network is consumed in carrying CBR and the two types of VBR traffic. Additional capacity is available for one or both of the following reasons: (1) Not all of the total resources have been committed to CBR and VBR traffic, and (2) the bursty nature of VBR traffic means that at some times less than the committed capacity is being used. All of this unused capacity could be made available for the **Unspecified Bit Rate (UBR)** service. This service is suitable for applications that can tolerate variable delays and some cell losses, which is typically true of TCP-based traffic. With UBR, cells are forwarded on a first-in, first-out (FIFO) basis using the capacity not consumed by other services; both delays and variable losses are possible. No initial commitment is made to a UBR source and no feedback concerning congestion is provided; this is referred to as a **best-effort service**. Examples of UBR applications include

- Text/data/image transfer, messaging, distribution, retrieval
- Remote terminal (e.g., telecommuting)

Bursty applications that use a reliable end-to-end protocol such as TCP can detect congestion in a network by means of increased round-trip delays and packet discarding, as discussed in Chapter 7. However, TCP has no mechanism for causing the resources within the network to be shared fairly among many TCP connections. Further, TCP does not minimize congestion as efficiently as is possible using explicit information from congested nodes within the network.

To improve the service provided to bursty sources that would otherwise use UBR, the **Available Bit Rate (ABR)** service has been defined. An application using ABR specifies a peak cell rate (PCR) that it will use and a minimum cell rate (MCR) that it requires. The network allocates resources so that all ABR applications receive at least their MCR capacity. Any unused capacity is then shared in a fair and controlled fashion among all ABR sources. The ABR mechanism uses explicit feedback to sources to assure that capacity is fairly allocated. Any capacity not used by ABR sources remains available for UBR traffic.

An example of an application using ABR is LAN interconnection. In this case, the end systems attached to the ATM network are routers.

The most recent addition to the set of ATM service categories is **Guaranteed Frame Rate (GFR)**, which is designed specifically to support IP backbone subnetworks. GFR provides better service than UBR for frame-based traffic, including IP and Ethernet. A major goal of GFR is to optimize the handling of frame-based traffic that passes from a LAN through a router onto an ATM backbone network. Such ATM networks are increasingly being used in large enterprise, carrier, and Internet service provider networks to consolidate and extend IP services over the wide area. While ABR is also an ATM service meant to provide a greater measure of guaranteed packet performance over ATM backbones, ABR is relatively difficult to implement between routers over an ATM network. With the increased emphasis on using ATM to support IP-based traffic, especially traffic that originates on Ethernet LANs, GFR may offer the most attractive alternative for providing ATM service.

One of the techniques used by GFR to provide improved performance compared to UBR is to require that network elements be aware of frame or packet boundaries. Thus, when congestion requires the discard of cells, network elements must discard all of the cells that comprise a single frame. GFR also allows a user to reserve capacity for each GFR VC. The user is guaranteed that this minimum capacity will be supported. Additional frames may be transmitted if the network is not congested.

13.3 CELLULAR WIRELESS NETWORKS

Of all the tremendous advances in data communications and telecommunications, perhaps the most revolutionary is the development of cellular networks. Cellular technology is the foundation of mobile wireless communications and supports users in locations that are not easily served by wired networks. Cellular technology is the underlying technology for mobile telephones, personal communications systems, wireless Internet and wireless Web applications, and much more.

Cellular radio is a technique that was developed to increase the capacity available for mobile radio telephone service. Prior to the introduction of cellular radio, mobile radio telephone service was only provided by a high-power transmitter/ receiver. A typical system would support about 25 channels with an effective radius of about 80 km. The way to increase the capacity of the system is to use lower-power systems with shorter radius and to use numerous transmitters/receivers.

Cellular Network Organization

The essence of a cellular network is the use of multiple low-power transmitters, on the order of 100 W or less. Because the range of such a transmitter is small, an area can be divided into cells, each one served by its own antenna. Each cell is allocated a band of frequencies and is served by a **base station**, consisting of transmitter, receiver, and control unit. Adjacent cells are assigned different frequencies to avoid interference or crosstalk. However, cells sufficiently distant from each other can use the same frequency band.

The first design decision to make is the shape of cells to cover an area. A matrix of square cells would be the simplest layout to define (Figure 13.5a). However, this geometry is not ideal. If the width of a square cell is d, then a cell has four neighbors at a distance d and four neighbors at a distance $\sqrt{2}d$. As a mobile user within a cell moves toward the cell's boundaries, it is best if all of the adjacent antennas are equidistant. This simplifies the task of determining when to switch the user to an adjacent antenna and which antenna to choose. A hexagonal pattern provides for equidistant antennas (Figure 13.5b). The radius of a hexagon is defined to be the radius of the circle that circumscribes it (equivalently, the distance from the center to each vertex; also equal to the length of a side of a hexagon). For a cell radius R, the distance between the cell center and each adjacent cell center is $d = \sqrt{3}R$.

In practice, a precise hexagonal pattern is not used. Variations from the ideal are due to topographical limitations, local signal propagation conditions, and practical limitation on siting antennas.

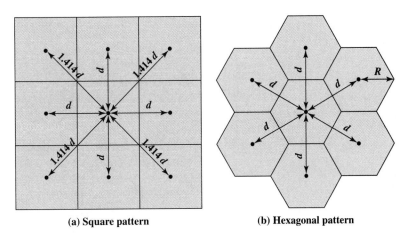

(a) Square pattern   (b) Hexagonal pattern

Figure 13.5 Cellular Geometries

With a wireless cellular system, you are limited in how often you can use the same frequency for different communications because the signals, not being constrained, can interfere with one another even if geographically separated. Systems supporting a large number of communications simultaneously need mechanisms to conserve spectrum.

Frequency Reuse In a cellular system, each cell has a base transceiver. The transmission power is carefully controlled (to the extent that it is possible in the highly variable mobile communication environment) to allow communication within the cell using a given frequency while limiting the power at that frequency that escapes the cell into adjacent ones. The objective is to use the same frequency in other nearby cells, thus allowing the frequency to be used for multiple simultaneous conversations. Generally, 10 to 50 frequencies are assigned to each cell, depending on the traffic expected.

The essential issue is to determine how many cells must intervene between two cells using the same frequency so that the two cells do not interfere with each other. Various patterns of frequency reuse are possible. Figure 13.6 shows some

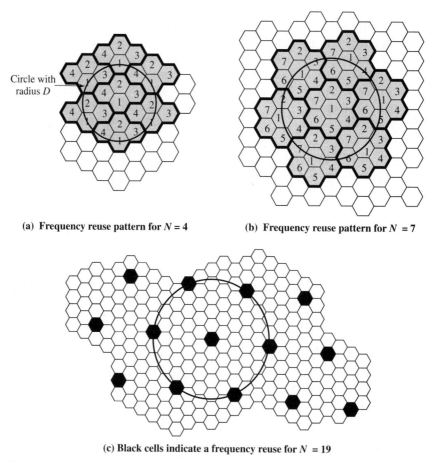

(a) Frequency reuse pattern for $N = 4$ (b) Frequency reuse pattern for $N = 7$

(c) Black cells indicate a frequency reuse for $N = 19$

Figure 13.6 Frequency Reuse Patterns

examples. If the pattern consists of N cells and each cell is assigned the same number of frequencies, each cell can have K/N frequencies, where K is the total number of frequencies allotted to the system. For AMPS (Advanced Mobile Phone Service, a widely used first-generation cellular scheme), $K = 395$, and $N = 7$ is the smallest pattern that can provide sufficient isolation between two uses of the same frequency. This implies that there can be at most 57 frequencies per cell on average.

In characterizing frequency reuse, the following parameters are commonly used:

D = minimum distance between centers of cells that use the same band of frequencies (called cochannels)

R = radius of a cell

d = distance between centers of adjacent cells ($d = \sqrt{3}R$)

N = number of cells in a repetitious pattern (each cell in the pattern uses a unique band of frequencies), termed the **reuse factor**

In a hexagonal cell pattern, only the following values of N are possible:

$$N = I^2 + J^2 + (I \times J), \qquad I, J = 0, 1, 2, 3, \ldots$$

Hence, possible values of N are 1, 3, 4, 7, 9, 12, 13, 16, 19, 21, and so on. The following relationship holds:

$$\frac{D}{R} = \sqrt{3N}$$

This can also be expressed as $D/d = \sqrt{N}$.

Increasing Capacity In time, as more customers use the system, traffic may build up so that there are not enough frequencies assigned to a cell to handle its calls. A number of approaches have been used to cope with this situation, including the following:

- **Adding new channels:** Typically, when a system is set up in a region, not all of the channels are used, and growth and expansion can be managed in an orderly fashion by adding new channels.

- **Frequency borrowing:** In the simplest case, frequencies are taken from adjacent cells by congested cells. The frequencies can also be assigned to cells dynamically.

- **Cell splitting:** In practice, the distribution of traffic and topographic features is not uniform, and this presents opportunities for capacity increase. Cells in areas of high usage can be split into smaller cells. Generally, the original cells are about 6.5 to 13 km in size. The smaller cells can themselves be split; however, 1.5-km cells are close to the practical minimum size as a general solution (but see the subsequent discussion of microcells). To use a smaller cell, the power level used must be reduced to keep the signal within the cell. Also, as the mobile units move, they pass from cell to cell, which requires transferring of the call from one base transceiver to another. This process is called a *handoff*. As the cells get smaller, these handoffs become much more frequent.

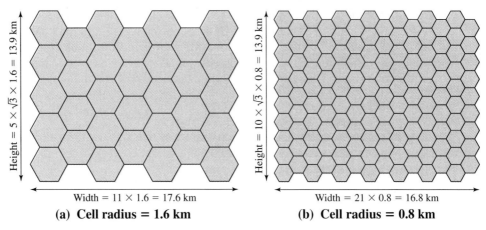

(a) **Cell radius = 1.6 km**

(b) **Cell radius = 0.8 km**

Figure 13.7 Frequency Reuse Example

A radius reduction by a factor of F reduces the coverage area and increases the required number of base stations by a factor of F^2.

- **Cell sectoring:** With cell sectoring, a cell is divided into a number of wedge-shaped sectors, each with its own set of channels, typically 3 or 6 sectors per cell. Each sector is assigned a separate subset of the cell's channels, and directional antennas at the base station are used to focus on each sector.

- **Microcells:** As cells become smaller, antennas move from the tops of tall buildings or hills, to the tops of small buildings or the sides of large buildings, and finally to lamp posts, where they form microcells. Each decrease in cell size is accompanied by a reduction in the radiated power levels from the base stations and the mobile units. Microcells are useful in city streets, in congested areas, along highways, and inside large public buildings.

Table 13.3 suggests typical parameters for traditional cells, called macrocells, and microcells with current technology. The average delay spread refers to multipath delay spread (i.e., the same signal follows different paths and there is a time delay between the earliest and latest arrival of the signal at the receiver). As indicated, the use of smaller cells enables the use of lower power and provides superior propagation conditions.

Table 13.3 Typical Parameters for Macrocells and Microcells [ANDE95]

	Macrocell	**Microcell**
Cell radius	1 to 20 km	0.1 to 1 km
Transmission power	1 to 10 W	0.1 to 1 W
Average delay spread	0.1 to 10 μs	10 to 100 ns
Maximum bit rate	0.3 Mbps	1 Mbps

EXAMPLE 13.1 [HAAS00]. Assume a system of 32 cells with a cell radius of 1.6 km, a total of 32 cells, a total frequency bandwidth that supports 336 traffic channels, and a reuse factor of $N = 7$. If there are 32 total cells, what geographic area is covered, how many channels are there per cell, and what is the total number of concurrent calls that can be handled? Repeat for a cell radius of 0.8 km and 128 cells.

Figure 13.7a shows an approximately square pattern. The area of a hexagon of radius R is $1.5R^2\sqrt{3}$. A hexagon of radius 1.6 km has an area of 6.65 km², and the total area covered is $6.65 \times 32 = 213$ km². For $N = 7$, the number of channels per cell is $336/7 = 48$, for a total channel capacity of $48 \times 32 = 1536$ channels. For the layout of Figure 13.7b, the area covered is $1.66 \times 128 = 213$ km². The number of channels per cell is $336/7 = 48$, for a total channel capacity of $48 \times 128 = 6144$ channels.

Operation of Cellular Systems

Figure 13.8 shows the principal elements of a cellular system. In the approximate center of each cell is a base station (BS). The BS includes an antenna, a controller, and a number of transceivers, for communicating on the channels assigned to that cell. The controller is used to handle the call process between the mobile unit and the rest of the network. At any time, a number of mobile user units may be active and moving about within a cell, communicating with the BS. Each BS is connected to a mobile telecommunications switching office (MTSO), with one MTSO serving multiple BSs. Typically, the link between an MTSO and a BS is by a wire line, although a wireless link is also possible. The MTSO connects calls between mobile units. The MTSO is also connected to the public telephone or telecommunications network and can make a connection between a fixed subscriber to the public network and a mobile subscriber to the cellular network. The MTSO assigns the voice channel to each call, performs handoffs, and monitors the call for billing information.

The use of a cellular system is fully automated and requires no action on the part of the user other than placing or answering a call. Two types of channels are

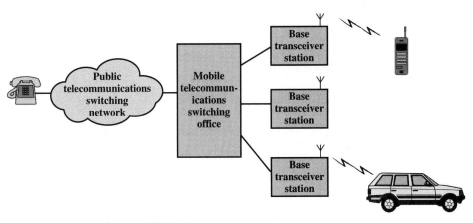

Figure 13.8 Overview of Cellular System

available between the mobile unit and the base station (BS): control channels and traffic channels. **Control channels** are used to exchange information having to do with setting up and maintaining calls and with establishing a relationship between a mobile unit and the nearest BS. **Traffic channels** carry a voice or data connection between users. Figure 13.9 illustrates the steps in a typical call between two mobile users within an area controlled by a single MTSO:

- **Mobile unit initialization:** When the mobile unit is turned on, it scans and selects the strongest setup control channel used for this system (Figure 13.9a). Cells with different frequency bands repetitively broadcast on different setup channels. The receiver selects the strongest setup channel and monitors that

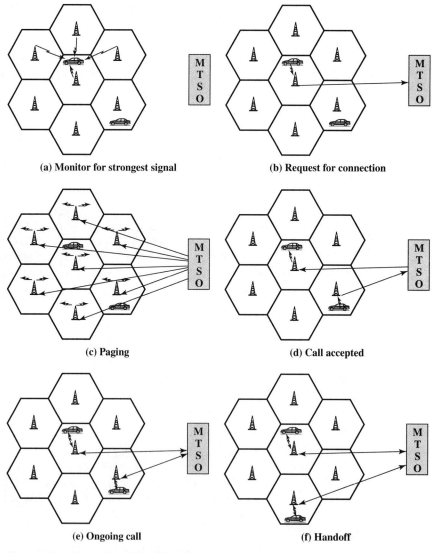

(a) Monitor for strongest signal

(b) Request for connection

(c) Paging

(d) Call accepted

(e) Ongoing call

(f) Handoff

Figure 13.9 Example of Mobile Cellular Call

channel. The effect of this procedure is that the mobile unit has automatically selected the BS antenna of the cell within which it will operate.[2] Then a handshake takes place between the mobile unit and the MTSO controlling this cell, through the BS in this cell. The handshake is used to identify the user and register its location. As long as the mobile unit is on, this scanning procedure is repeated periodically to account for the motion of the unit. If the unit enters a new cell, then a new BS is selected. In addition, the mobile unit is monitoring for pages, discussed subsequently.

- **Mobile-originated call:** A mobile unit originates a call by sending the number of the called unit on the preselected setup channel (Figure 13.9b). The receiver at the mobile unit first checks that the setup channel is idle by examining information in the forward (from the BS) channel. When an idle channel is detected, the mobile may transmit on the corresponding reverse (to BS) channel. The BS sends the request to the MTSO.

- **Paging:** The MTSO then attempts to complete the connection to the called unit. The MTSO sends a paging message to certain BSs depending on the called mobile number (Figure 13.9c). Each BS transmits the paging signal on its own assigned setup channel.

- **Call accepted:** The called mobile unit recognizes its number on the setup channel being monitored and responds to that BS, which sends the response to the MTSO. The MTSO sets up a circuit between the calling and called BSs. At the same time, the MTSO selects an available traffic channel within each BS's cell and notifies each BS, which in turn notifies its mobile unit (Figure 13.9d). The two mobile units tune to their respective assigned channels.

- **Ongoing call:** While the connection is maintained, the two mobile units exchange voice or data signals, going through their respective BSs and the MTSO (Figure 13.9e).

- **Handoff:** If a mobile unit moves out of range of one cell and into the range of another during a connection, the traffic channel has to change to one assigned to the BS in the new cell (Figure 13.9f). The system makes this change without either interrupting the call or alerting the user.

Other functions performed by the system but not illustrated in Figure 13.9 include the following:

- **Call blocking:** During the mobile-initiated call stage, if all the traffic channels assigned to the nearest BS are busy, then the mobile unit makes a preconfigured number of repeated attempts. After a certain number of failed tries, a busy tone is returned to the user.

- **Call termination:** When one of the two users hangs up, the MTSO is informed and the traffic channels at the two BSs are released.

- **Call drop:** During a connection, because of interference or weak signal spots in certain areas, if the BS cannot maintain the minimum required signal strength for a certain period of time, the traffic channel to the user is dropped and the MTSO is informed.

---

[2]Usually, but not always, the antenna and therefore the base station selected is the closest one to the mobile unit. However, because of propagation anomalies, this is not always the case.

- **Calls to/from fixed and remote mobile subscriber:** The MTSO connects to the public switched telephone network. Thus, the MTSO can set up a connection between a mobile user in its area and a fixed subscriber via the telephone network. Further, the MTSO can connect to a remote MTSO via the telephone network or via dedicated lines and set up a connection between a mobile user in its area and a remote mobile user.

13.4 RECOMMENDED READING AND WEB SITES

A more in-depth treatment of frame relay can be found in [STAL99]. An excellent book-length treatment is [BUCK00].

[MCDY99] and [BLAC99] provide good coverage of ATM. The virtual path/virtual channel approach of ATM is examined in [SATO90], [SATO91], and [BURG91]. [GARR96] provides a rationale for the ATM service categories and discusses the traffic management implications of each.

BLAC99   Black, U. *ATM Volume I: Foundation for Broadband Networks.* Upper Saddle River, NJ: Prentice Hall, 1992.

BUCK00   Buckwalter, J. *Frame Relay: Technology and Practice.* Reading, MA: Addison-Wesley, 2000.

BURG91   Burg, J., and Dorman, D. "Broadband ISDN Resource Management: The Role of Virtual Paths." *IEEE Communications Magazine*, September 1991.

GARR96   Garrett, M. "A Service Architecture for ATM: From Applications to Scheduling." *IEEE Network*, May/June 1996.

MCDY99   McDysan, D., and Spohn, D. *ATM: Theory and Application.* New York: McGraw-Hill, 1999.

SATO90   Sato, K.; Ohta, S.; and Tokizawa, I. "Broadband ATM Network Architecture Based on Virtual Paths." *IEEE Transactions on Communications*, August 1990.

SATO91   Sato, K.; Ueda, H.; and Yoshikai, M. "The Role of Virtual Path Crossconnection." *IEEE LTS*, August 1991.

STAL99   Stallings, W. *ISDN and Broadband ISDN, with Frame Relay and ATM.* Upper Saddle River, NJ: Prentice Hall, 1999.

Recommended Web Sites:

- **Frame Relay Forum:** An association of corporate members comprised of vendors, carriers, users, and consultants committed to the implementation of frame relay in accordance with national and international standards. Site includes list of technical and implementation documents for sale.
- **Frame Relay Resource Center:** Good source of information on frame relay.
- **ATM Hot Links:** Excellent collection of white papers and links maintained by the University of Minnesota.
- **ATM Forum:** Contains technical specifications and white papers.

- **Cell Relay Retreat:** Contains archives of the cell-relay mailing list, links to numerous ATM-related documents, and links to many ATM-related Web sites.
- **Cellular Telecommunications and Internet Association:** An industry consortium that provides information on successful applications of wireless technology.
- **3G Americas:** A trade group of Western Hemisphere companies supporting a variety of second and third-generation schemes. Includes industry news, white papers, and other technical information.

13.5 KEY TERMS, REVIEW QUESTIONS, AND PROBLEMS

Key Terms

asynchronous transfer mode (ATM)	frame relay	non-real-time variable bit rate (nrt-VBR)
available bit rate (ABR)	frequency borrowing	paging
base station	frequency reuse	real-time variable bit rate
cell	Generic Flow Control	(rt-VBR)
cell relay	guaranteed frame rate (GFR)	reuse factor
cell sectoring	Link Access Procedure for	unspecified bit rate (UBR)
cell splitting	Frame Mode Bearer	Virtual Channel
cellular wireless network	Services (LAPF)	Virtual Path
constant bit rate (CBR)	microcells	

Review Questions

13.1 How does frame relay differ from X.25?

13.2 What are the relative advantages and disadvantages of frame relay compared to X.25?

13.3 How does ATM differ from frame relay?

13.4 What are the relative advantages and disadvantages of ATM compared to frame relay?

13.5 What is the difference between a virtual channel and a virtual path?

13.6 What are the advantages of the use of virtual paths?

13.7 What are the characteristics of a virtual channel?

13.8 What are the characteristics of a virtual path?

13.9 List and briefly explain the fields in an ATM cell.

13.10 List and briefly define the ATM service categories.

13.11 What geometric shape is used in cellular system design?

13.12 What is the principle of frequency reuse in the context of a cellular network?

13.13 List five ways of increasing the capacity of a cellular system.

13.14 Explain the paging function of a cellular system.

Problems

13.1 Q.933 recommends a procedure for negotiating the sliding-window flow control window, which may take on a value from 1 to 127. The negotiation makes use of a variable k that is calculated from the following parameters:

L_d = data frame size in octets

R_u = throughput bits/sec

T_{td} = end-to-end transit delay in sec

k = window size (maximum number of outstanding data frames)

The procedure is described as follows:

> The window size should be negotiated as follows. The originating user should calculate k using the above formula substituting maximum end-to-end transit delay and outgoing maximum frame size for T_{td} and L_d, respectively. The SETUP message shall include the link layer protocol parameters, the link layer core parameters, and the end-to-end transit delay information elements. The destination user should calculate its own k using the above formula substituting cumulative end-to-end transit delay and its own outgoing maximum frame size for T_{td} and L_d, respectively. The CONNECT message shall include the link layer core parameters and the end-to-end transit delay information element so that the originating user can adjust its k based on the information conveyed in these information elements. The originating user should calculate k using the above formula, substituting cumulative end-to-end transit delay and incoming maximum frame size for T_{td} and L_d, respectively.

SETUP and CONNECT are messages exchanged on a control channel during the setup of a frame relay connection. Suggest a formula for calculating k from the other variables and justify the formula.

13.2 List all 16 possible values of the GFC field and the interpretation of each value (some values are illegal).

13.3 One key design decision for ATM was whether to use fixed or variable length cells. Let us consider this decision from the point of view of efficiency. We can define transmission efficiency as follows:

$$N = \frac{\text{Number of information octets}}{\text{Number of information octets} + \text{Number of overhead octets}}$$

  a. Consider the use of fixed-length packets. In this case the overhead consists of the header octets. Define

  L = Data field size of the cell in octets
  H = Header size of the cell in octets
  X = Number of information octets to be transmitted as a single message

  Derive an expression for N. *Hint:* The expression will need to use the operator $\lceil \cdot \rceil$, where $\lceil Y \rceil$ = the smallest integer greater than or equal to Y.

  b. If cells have variable length, then overhead is determined by the header, plus the flags to delimit the cells or an additional length field in the header. Let Hv = additional overhead octets required to enable the use of variable-length cells. Derive an expression for N in terms of X, H, and Hv.

  c. Let $L = 48$, $H = 5$, and $Hv = 2$. Plot N versus message size for fixed- and variable-length cells. Comment on the results.

13.4 Another key design decision for ATM is the size of the data field for fixed-size cells. Let us consider this decision from the point of view of efficiency and delay.

  a. Assume that an extended transmission takes place, so that all cells are completely filled. Derive an expression for the efficiency N as a function of H and L.

  b. Packetization delay is the delay introduced into a transmission stream by the need to buffer bits until an entire packet is filled before transmission. Derive an expression for this delay as a function of L and the data rate R of the source.

  c. Common data rates for voice coding are 32 kbps and 64 kbps. Plot packetization delay as a function of L for these two data rates; use a left-hand y-axis with a maximum value of 2 ms. On the same graph, plot transmission efficiency as a function of L; use a right-hand y-axis with a maximum value of 100%. Comment on the results.

13.5   Consider compressed video transmission in an ATM network. Suppose standard ATM cells must be transmitted through 5 switches. The data rate is 43 Mbps.

   a.   What is the transmission time for one cell through one switch?

   b.   Each switch may be transmitting a cell from other traffic all of which we assume to have lower (non-preemptive for the cell) priority. If the switch is busy transmitting a cell, our cell has to wait until the other cell completes transmission. If the switch is free, our cell is transmitted immediately. What is the maximum time from when a typical video cell arrives at the first switch (and possibly waits) until it is finished being transmitted by the fifth and last one? Assume that you can ignore propagation time, switching time, and everything else but the transmission time and the time spent waiting for another cell to clear a switch.

   c.   Now suppose we know that each switch is utilized 60% of the time with the other low priority traffic. By this we mean that with probability 0.6 when we look at a switch it is busy. Suppose that if there is a cell being transmitted by a switch, the average delay spent waiting for a cell to finish transmission is one-half a cell transmission time. What is the average time from the input of the first switch to clearing the fifth?

   d.   The measure of most interest is not delay but jitter, which is the variability in the delay. Use parts (b) and (c) to calculate the maximum and average variability, respectively, in the delay.

   In all cases assume that the various random events are independent of one another; for example, we ignore the burstiness typical of such traffic.

13.6   Consider four different cellular systems that share the following characteristics. The frequency bands are 825 to 845 MHz for mobile unit transmission and 870 to 890 MHz for base station transmission. A duplex circuit consists of one 30-kHz channel in each direction. The systems are distinguished by reuse factor, which is 4, 7, 12, and 19, respectively.

   a.   Suppose that in each of the systems, the cluster of cells (4, 7, 12, 19) is duplicated 16 times. Find the number of simultaneous communications that can be supported by each system.

   b.   Find the number of simultaneous communications that can be supported by a single cell in each system.

   c.   What is the area covered, in cells, by each system?

   d.   Suppose the cell size is the same in all four systems and a fixed area of 100 cells is covered by each system. Find the number of simultaneous communications that can be supported by each system.

13.7   Describe a sequence of events similar to that of Figure 13.9 for

   a.   a call from a mobile unit to a fixed subscriber

   b.   a call from a fixed subscriber to a mobile unit

13.8   An analog cellular system has a total of 33 MHz of bandwidth and uses two 25-kHz simplex (one-way) channels to provide full duplex voice and control channels.

   a.   What is the number of channels available per cell for a frequency reuse factor of (1) 4 cells, (2) 7 cells, and (3) 12 cells?

   b.   Assume that 1 MHz is dedicated to control channels but that only one control channel is needed per cell. Determine a reasonable distribution of control channels and voice channels in each cell for the three frequency reuse factors of part (a).

DATA LINK CONTROL

I had throughout the greatest misgivings of an impulsive offensive by the French that was not based on calm calculations of numbers, distances, and times.

—The World Crisis,
Winston Churchill

KEY POINTS

- Because of the possibility of transmission errors, and because the receiver of data may need to regulate the rate at which data arrive, synchronization and interfacing techniques are insufficient by themselves. It is necessary to impose a layer of control in each communicating device that provides functions such as flow control, error detection, and error control. This layer of control is known as a **data link control protocol**.

- **Flow control** enables a receiver to regulate the flow of data from a sender so that the receiver's buffers do not overflow.

- **Error detection** is performed by calculating an error-detecting code that is a function of the bits being transmitted. The code is appended to the transmitted bits. The receiver calculates the code based on the incoming bits and compares it to the incoming code to check for errors.

- In a data link control protocol, **error control** is achieved by retransmission of damaged frames that have not been acknowledged or for which the other side requests a retransmission.

In this chapter, we look at a set of techniques that, collectively, is embodied in a control mechanism known as a data link control protocol. Such a protocol includes techniques for coordinating the presence of more than two devices on a line, as well as techniques for regulating the flow of data and for compensating for transmission errors. Once all of these techniques have been introduced, we turn to a discussion of a specific data link control protocol, HDLC. This protocol is one of the most commonly used ones, and it illustrates the techniques used in such protocols.

14.1 FLOW CONTROL

Flow control is a technique for assuring that a transmitting entity does not overwhelm a receiving entity with data. The receiving entity typically allocates a data buffer of some maximum length for a transfer. When data are received, the receiver must do a certain amount of processing before passing the data to the higher-level software. In the absence of flow control, the receiver's buffer may fill up and overflow while it is processing old data.

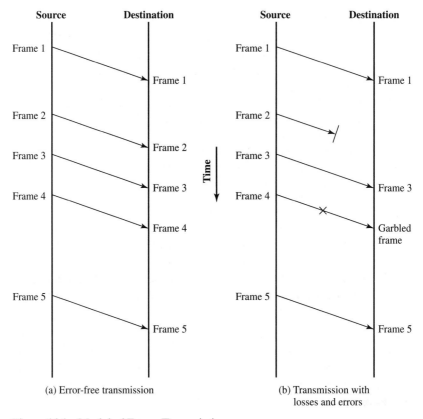

Figure 14.1 Model of Frame Transmission

To begin, we examine mechanisms for flow control in the absence of errors. The model we will use is depicted in Figure 14.1a, which is a vertical-time sequence diagram. It has the advantages of showing time dependencies and illustrating the correct send-receive relationship. Each arrow represents a single frame transiting a data link between two stations. The data are sent in a sequence of frames, with each frame containing a portion of the data and some control information. The time it takes for a station to emit all of the bits of a frame onto the medium is the transmission time; this is proportional to the length of the frame. The propagation time is the time it takes for a bit to traverse the link between source and destination. For this section, we assume that all frames that are transmitted are successfully received; no frames are lost and none arrive with errors. Furthermore, frames arrive in the same order in which they are sent. However, each transmitted frame suffers an arbitrary and variable amount of delay before reception.[1]

---

[1]On a direct point-to-point link, the amount of delay is fixed rather than variable. However, a data link control protocol can be used over a network connection, such as a circuit-switched or ATM network, in which case the delay may be variable.

Stop-and-Wait Flow Control

The simplest form of flow control, known as stop-and-wait flow control, works as follows. A source entity transmits a frame. After the destination entity receives the frame, it indicates its willingness to accept another frame by sending back an acknowledgment to the frame just received. The source must wait until it receives the acknowledgment before sending the next frame. The destination can thus stop the flow of data simply by withholding acknowledgment. This procedure works fine and, indeed, can hardly be improved upon when a message is sent in a few large frames. However, it is often the case that a source will break up a large block of data into smaller blocks and transmit the data in many frames. This is done for the following reasons:

- The buffer size of the receiver may be limited.
- The longer the transmission, the more likely that there will be an error, necessitating retransmission of the entire frame. With smaller frames, errors are detected sooner, and a smaller amount of data needs to be retransmitted.
- On a shared medium, such as a LAN, it is usually desirable not to permit one station to occupy the medium for an extended period, thus causing long delays at the other sending stations.

With the use of multiple frames for a single message, the stop-and-wait procedure may be inadequate. The essence of the problem is that only one frame at a time can be in transit. Recall, from our discussion of Section 5.3, that if the bit length of the link is greater than the frame length ($a > 1$), serious inefficiencies result.

To explain we first define the bit length of a link as follows:

$$B = R \times \frac{d}{V} \tag{14.1}$$

where

B = length of the link in bits; this is the number of bits present on the link when a stream of bits fully occupies the link

R = data rate of the link, in bps

d = length, or distance, of the link in meters

V = velocity of propagation, in m/s

In situations where the bit length of the link is greater than the frame length, serious inefficiencies result. This is illustrated in Figure 5.6. In the figure, the transmission time (the time it takes for a station to transmit a frame) is normalized to one, and the propagation delay (the time it takes for a bit to travel from sender to receiver) is expressed as the variable a. Thus, we can express a as

$$a = \frac{B}{L} \tag{14.2}$$

where L is the number of bits in the frame (length of the frame in bits).

EXAMPLE 14.1 Consider a 200-m optical fiber link operating at 1 Gbps. The velocity of propagation of optical fiber is typically about 2×10^8 m/s. We can express the length of the data length in bits as the parameter B, as follows: $B = (10^9 \times 200)/(2 \times 10^8) = 1000$. Assume a frame of 1000 octets, or 8000 bits, is transmitted. Using Equation (14.2), $a = (1000/8000) = 0.125$. Using Figure 5.6b as a guide, assume transmission starts at time $t = 0$. After 1 μs (a normalized time of 0.125 frame times), the leading edge (first bit) of the frame has reached R, and the first 1000 bits of the frame are spread out across the link. At time $t = 8$ μs, the trailing edge (final bit) of the frame has just been emitted by T, and the final 1000 bits of the frame are spread out across the link. At $t = 9$ μs, the final bit of the frame arrives at R. R now sends back an ACK frame. If we assume the frame transmission time is negligible (very small ACK frame) and that the ACK is sent immediately, the ACK arrives at T at $t = 10$ μs. At this point, T can begin transmitting a new frame. The actual transmission time for the frame was 8 μs, but the total time to transmit the first frame and receive and ACK is 10 μs.

Now consider a 1-Mbps link between two ground stations that communicate via a satellite relay. A geosynchronous satellite has an altitude of roughly 36,000 km. Then $B = (10^6 \times 2 \times 36,000,000)/(3 \times 10^8) = 240,000$. For a frame length of 8000 bits, $a = (240,000/8000) = 30$. Using Figure 5.6a as a guide, we can work through the same steps as before. In this case, it takes 240 ms for the leading edge of the frame to arrive and an additional 8 ms for the entire frame to arrive. The ACK arrives back at T at $t = 488$ ms. The actual transmission time for the first frame was 8 ms, but the total time to transmit the first frame and receive and ACK is 488 ms.

Sliding-Window Flow Control

The essence of the problem described so far is that only one frame at a time can be in transit. Efficiency can be greatly improved by allowing multiple frames to be in transit at the same time.

Let us examine how this might work for two stations, A and B, connected via a full-duplex link. Station B allocates buffer space for W frames. B can accept W frames, and A is allowed to send W frames without waiting for any acknowledgments. To keep track of which frames have been acknowledged, each is labeled with a sequence number. B acknowledges a frame by sending an acknowledgment that includes the sequence number of the next frame expected. This acknowledgment also implicitly announces that B is prepared to receive the next W frames, beginning with the number specified. This scheme can also be used to acknowledge multiple frames. For example, B could receive frames 2, 3, and 4, but withhold acknowledgment until frame 4 has arrived. By then returning an acknowledgment with sequence number 5, B acknowledges frames 2, 3, and 4 at one time. A maintains a list of sequence numbers that it is allowed to send, and B maintains a list of sequence numbers that it is prepared to receive. Each of these lists can be thought of as a *window* of frames. The operation is referred to as **sliding-window flow control**.

Several additional comments need to be made. Because the sequence number to be used occupies a field in the frame, it is clearly of bounded size. For example, for a 3-bit field, the sequence number can range from 0 to 7. In this case, frames are numbered modulo 8; that is, after sequence number 7, the next number is 0. In general, for a k-bit field the range of sequence numbers is 0 through $2^k - 1$, and frames are numbered modulo 2^k. As will be shown subsequently, the maximum window size is $2^k - 1$.

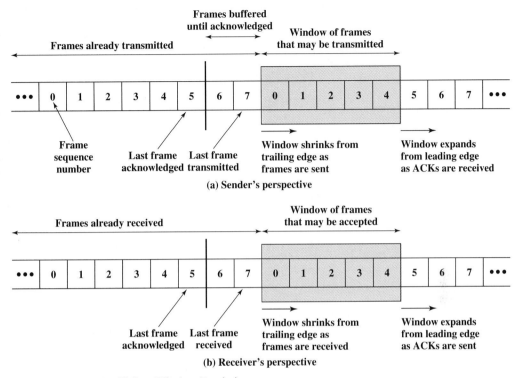

Figure 14.2 Sliding-Window Depiction

Figure 14.2 is a useful way of depicting the sliding-window process (compare Figure 6.2). It assumes the use of a 3-bit sequence number, so that frames are numbered sequentially from 0 through 7, and then the same numbers are reused for subsequent frames. The shaded rectangle indicates the frames that may be sent; in this figure, the sender may transmit five frames, beginning with frame 0. Each time a frame is sent, the shaded window shrinks; each time an acknowledgment is received, the shaded window grows. Frames between the vertical bar and the shaded window have been sent but not yet acknowledged. As we shall see, the sender must buffer these frames in case they need to be retransmitted.

The window size need not be the maximum possible size for a given sequence number length. For example, using a 3-bit sequence number, a window size of 4 could be configured for the stations using the sliding-window flow control protocol.

An example is shown in Figure 14.3 (compare Figure 6.1). The example assumes a 3-bit sequence number field and a maximum window size of seven frames. Initially, A and B have windows indicating that A may transmit seven frames, beginning with frame 0 (F0). After transmitting three frames (F0, F1, F2) without acknowledgment, A has shrunk its window to four frames and maintains a copy of the three transmitted frames. The window indicates that A may transmit four frames, beginning with frame number 3. B then transmits an RR (receive ready) 3, which means "I have received all frames up through frame number 2 and am ready to receive frame number 3; in fact, I am prepared to receive seven frames, beginning with frame number 3." With this acknowledgment, A is back up to permission to transmit

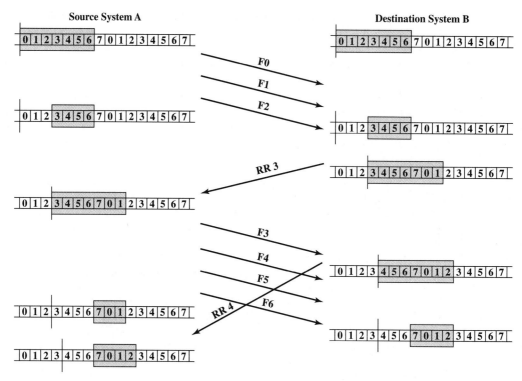

Figure 14.3 Example of a Sliding-Window Protocol

seven frames, still beginning with frame 3. A may discard the buffered frames that have now been acknowledged. A proceeds to transmit frames 3, 4, 5, and 6. B returns RR 4, which acknowledges F3, and allows transmission of F4 through the next instance of F2. By the time this RR reaches A, it has already transmitted F4, F5, and F6, and therefore A may only open its window to permit sending four frames beginning with F7.

The mechanism so far described does indeed provide a form of flow control: The receiver must only be able to accommodate seven frames beyond the one it has last acknowledged. Most protocols also allow a station to cut off the flow of frames from the other side by sending a Receive Not Ready (RNR) message, which acknowledges former frames but forbids transfer of future frames. Thus, RNR 5 means "I have received all frames up through number 4 but am unable to accept any more." At some subsequent point, the station must send a normal acknowledgment to reopen the window.

So far, we have discussed transmission in one direction only. If two stations exchange data, each needs to maintain two windows, one for transmit and one for receive, and each side needs to send the data and acknowledgments to the other. To provide efficient support for this requirement, a feature known as **piggybacking** is typically provided. Each **data frame** includes a field that holds the sequence number of that frame plus a field that holds the sequence number used for acknowledgment. Thus, if a station has data to send and an acknowledgment to send, it sends both together in one frame, saving communication capacity. Of course, if a station has an acknowledgment but no data to send, it sends a separate **acknowledgment frame,** such as RR or RNR. If a station has data to send but no new acknowledgment to send, it must repeat the last acknowledgment sequence number that it sent. This is because the data frame includes a field for the acknowledgment number, and some value must be put into that field. When a station receives a duplicate acknowledgment, it simply ignores it.

Sliding-window flow control is potentially much more efficient than stop-and-wait flow control. The reason is that, with sliding-window flow control, the transmission link is treated as a pipeline that may be filled with frames in transit. In contrast, with stop-and-wait flow control, only one frame may be in the pipe at a time. Appendix 14B quantifies the improvement in efficiency.

> **EXAMPLE 14.2**   Let us consider the use of sliding-window flow control for the two configurations of Example 14.1. As was calculated in Example 14.1, it takes 10 μs for an ACK to the first frame to be received. It takes 8 μs to transmit one frame, so the sender can transmit one frame and part of a second frame by the time the ACK to the first frame is received. Thus, a window size of 2 is adequate to enable the sender to transmit frames continuously, or a rate of one frame every 8 μs. With stop-and-wait, a rate of only one frame per 10 μs is possible.
>
> For the satellite configuration, it takes 488 ms for an ACK to the first frame to be received. It takes 8 ms to transmit one frame, so the sender can transmit 61 frames by the time the ACK to the first frame is received. With a window size of 6 bits or more, the sender can transmit continuously, or a rate of one frame every 8 ms. If the window size is 7, using a 3-bit window field, then the sender can only send 7 frames and then must wait for an ACK before sending more. In this case, the sender can transmit at a rate of 7 frames per 488 ms, or about one frame every 70 ms. With stop-and-wait, a rate of only one frame per 488 ms is possible.

14.2 ERROR DETECTION

Any transmission facility has the potential of introducing errors. The ability to control those errors is an increasingly important task of a data communications system. This is partly because the issue of data integrity is becoming increasingly important. There is downward pressure on the allowable error rates for communication and mass storage systems as bandwidths and volumes of data increase. Certain data cannot be wrong; for example, no one can be complacent about the effect of an undetected data error on an electronic funds transfer. More generally, in any system that handles large amounts of data, uncorrected and undetected errors can degrade performance, response time, and possibly increase the need for intervention by human operators.

The process of **error control** involves two elements:

- **Error detection:** Redundancy is introduced into the data stream so that the occurrence of an error will be detected.
- **Error correction:** Once an error is detected by the receiver, the receiver and the transmitter cooperate to cause the frames in error to be retransmitted.

In this section, we look at the error detection process. We examine error correction in the next section.

Types of Errors

In digital transmission systems, an error occurs when a bit is altered between transmission and reception; that is, a binary 1 is transmitted and a binary 0 is received, or a binary 0 is transmitted and a binary 1 is received. Two general types of errors can occur: single-bit errors and burst errors. A single-bit error is an isolated error condition that alters one bit but does not affect nearby bits. A burst error of length B is a contiguous sequence of B bits in which the first and last bits and any number of intermediate bits are received in error. More precisely, IEEE Std 100 defines an error burst as follows:

> **Error burst:** A group of bits in which two successive erroneous bits are always separated by less than a given number x of correct bits. The last erroneous bit in the burst and the first erroneous bit in the following burst are accordingly separated by x correct bits or more.

Thus, in an error burst, there is a cluster of bits in which a number of errors occur, although not necessarily all of the bits in the cluster suffer an error.

A single-bit error can occur in the presence of white noise, when a slight random deterioration of the signal-to-noise ratio is sufficient to confuse the receiver's decision of a single bit. Burst errors are more common and more difficult to deal with. Burst errors can be caused by impulse noise, which is a high-amplitude, short-duration noise pulse. Another cause is fading in a mobile wireless environment; fading is a variation of received signal power caused by changes in the transmission medium or path(s).

Note that the effects of burst errors are greater at higher data rates.

> **EXAMPLE 14.3**   An impulse noise event or a fading event of 1 μs occurs. At a data rate of 10 Mbps, there is a resulting error burst of 10 bits. At a data rate of 100 Mbps, there is an error burst of 100 bits.

Parity Check

The simplest error-detection scheme is to append a parity bit to the end of a block of data. A typical example is character transmission, in which a parity bit is attached to each 7-bit IRA character. The value of this bit is selected so that the character has an even number of 1s (even parity) or an odd number of 1s (odd parity).

> **EXAMPLE 14.4**   If the transmitter is transmitting an IRA G (1110001) and using odd parity, it will append a 1 and transmit 11110001.[2] The receiver examines the received character and, if the total number of 1s is odd, assumes that no error has occurred. If one bit (or any odd number of bits) is erroneously inverted during transmission (for example, 11100001), then the receiver will detect an error.

---

[2]The least significant bit of a character is transmitted first, and the parity bit is the most significant bit.

Note, however, that if two (or any even number) of bits are inverted due to error, an undetected error occurs. Typically, even parity is used for synchronous transmission and odd parity for asynchronous transmission.

The use of the parity bit is not foolproof, as noise impulses are often long enough to destroy more than one bit, particularly at high data rates.

Cyclic Redundancy Check

When synchronous transmission is used, it is possible to employ an error-detection technique that is both more efficient (lower percentage of overhead bits) and more powerful (more errors detected) than the simple parity bit. This technique requires the addition of a **frame check sequence (FCS)**, or **error-detecting code**, to each synchronous frame. The use of an FCS is illustrated in Figure 14.4. On transmission, a calculation is performed on the bits of the frame to be transmitted; the result is inserted as an additional field in the frame. On reception, the same calculation is performed on the received bits and the calculated result is compared to the value stored in the incoming frame. If there is a discrepancy, the receiver assumes that an error has occurred.

One of the most common, and one of the most powerful, of the error-detecting codes is the **cyclic redundancy check (CRC)**. For this technique, the message to be transmitted is treated as one long binary number. This number is divided by a unique

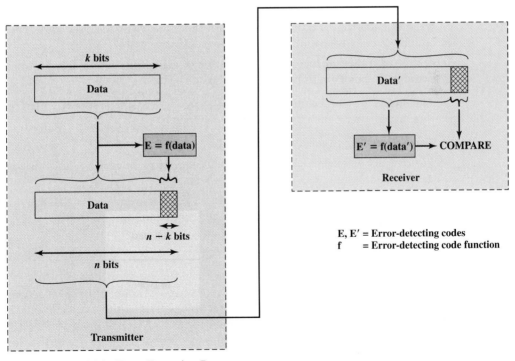

Figure 14.4 Error Detection Process

prime binary number (a number divisible only by itself and 1), and the remainder is attached to the frame to be transmitted. When the frame is received, the receiver performs the same division, using the same divisor, and compares the calculated remainder with the remainder received in the frame. The most commonly used divisors are a 17-bit divisor, which produces a 16-bit remainder, and a 33-bit divisor, which produces a 32-bit remainder.

The measure of effectiveness of any error-detecting code is what percentage of errors it detects. For a CRC of length N, the rate of undetected errors is on the order of 2^{-N} (see [STAL03] for details). In summary, the CRC is a very powerful means of error detection and requires very little overhead. As an example, if a 16-bit FCS is used with frames of 1000 bits, then the overhead is only 1.6%. With a 32-bit FCS, the overhead is 3.2%.

Appendix 14A provides a brief description of the CRC algorithm.

14.3 ERROR CONTROL

Error control refers to mechanisms to detect and correct errors that occur in the transmission of frames. The model that we will use, which covers the typical case, is illustrated in Figure 14.1b. As before, data are sent as a sequence of frames; frames arrive in the same order in which they are sent; and each transmitted frame suffers an arbitrary and potentially variable amount of delay before reception. In addition, we consider two types of errors:

- **Lost frame:** A frame fails to arrive at the other side. For example, a noise burst may damage a frame to the extent that the receiver is not aware that a frame has been transmitted.
- **Damaged frame:** A recognizable frame does arrive, but some of the bits are in error (have been altered during transmission).

The most common techniques for error control are based on some or all of the following ingredients:

- **Error detection:** As discussed in Section 14.2.
- **Positive acknowledgment:** The destination returns a positive acknowledgment to successfully received, error-free frames.
- **Retransmission after timeout:** The source retransmits a frame that has not been acknowledged after a predetermined amount of time.
- **Negative acknowledgment and retransmission:** The destination returns a negative acknowledgment to frames in which an error is detected. The source retransmits such frames.

Collectively, these mechanisms are all referred to as **automatic repeat request** (ARQ); the effect of ARQ is to turn an unreliable data link into a reliable one. In this section, we look at the two most common forms of ARQ: Stop-and-wait ARQ and Go-back-N ARQ. Both of these mechanisms are based on the use of the flow control techniques discussed in Section 14.1.

Stop-and-Wait ARQ

Stop-and-wait ARQ is based on the stop-and-wait flow control technique outlined previously. The source station transmits a single frame and then must await an acknowledgment (ACK). No other data frames can be sent until the destination station's reply arrives at the source station.

Two sorts of errors could occur. First, the frame that arrives at the destination could be damaged. The receiver detects this by using the error-detection technique referred to earlier and simply discards the frame. To account for this possibility, the source station is equipped with a timer. After a frame is transmitted, the source station waits for an acknowledgment. If no acknowledgment is received by the time that the timer expires, then the same frame is sent again. Note that this method requires that the transmitter maintain a copy of a transmitted frame until an acknowledgment is received for that frame.

The second sort of error is a damaged acknowledgment. Consider the following situation. Station A sends a frame. The frame is received correctly by station B, which responds with an acknowledgment (ACK). The ACK is damaged in transit and is not recognizable by A, which will therefore time out and resend the same frame. This duplicate frame arrives and is accepted by B. B has therefore accepted two copies of the same frame as if they were separate. To avoid this problem, frames are alternately labeled with 0 or 1, and positive acknowledgments are of the form ACK0 and ACK1. In keeping with the sliding-window convention, an ACK0 acknowledges receipt of a frame numbered 1 and indicates that the receiver is ready for a frame numbered 0.

Figure 14.5 gives an example of the use of stop-and-wait ARQ, showing the transmission of a sequence of frames from source A to destination B. The figure shows the two types of errors just described. The third frame transmitted by A is lost or damaged, and therefore no ACK is returned by B. A times out and retransmits the frame. Later, A transmits a frame labeled 1 but the ACK0 for that frame is lost. A times out and retransmits the same frame. When B receives two frames in a row with the same label, it discards the second frame but sends back an ACK0 to each.

The principal advantage of stop-and-wait ARQ is its simplicity. Its principal disadvantage, as discussed in Section 14.1, is that stop-and-wait is an inefficient mechanism. The sliding-window flow control technique can be adapted to provide more efficient line use; in this context, it is sometimes referred to as **continuous ARQ**.

Go-Back-N ARQ

The form of error control based on sliding-window flow control that is most commonly used is called go-back-N ARQ. In this method, a station may send a series of frames sequentially numbered modulo some maximum value. The number of unacknowledged frames outstanding is determined by window size, using the sliding-window flow control technique. While no errors occur, the destination will acknowledge incoming frames as usual (RR = receive ready, or piggybacked acknowledgement). If the destination station detects an error in a frame, it may send a negative acknowledgment (REJ = reject) for that frame, as explained in the following rules.

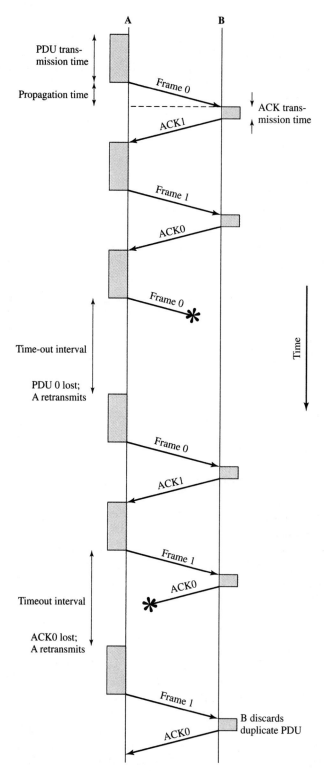

Figure 14.5 Stop-and-Wait ARQ

The destination station will discard that frame and all future incoming frames until the frame in error is correctly received. Thus, the source station, when it receives a REJ, must retransmit the frame in error plus all succeeding frames that were transmitted in the interim.

Suppose that station A is sending frames to station B. After each transmission, A sets an acknowledgment timer for the frame just transmitted. Suppose that B has previously successfully received frame $(i - 1)$ and A has just transmitted frame i. The go-back-N technique takes into account the following contingencies:

1. **Damaged frame.** If the received frame is invalid (i.e., B detects an error, or the frame is so damaged that B does not even perceive that it has received a frame), B discards the frame and takes no further action as the result of that frame. There are two subcases:

   a. Within a reasonable period of time, A subsequently sends frame $(i + 1)$. B receives frame $(i + 1)$ out of order and sends a REJ i. A must retransmit frame i and all subsequent frames.

   b. A does not soon send additional frames. B receives nothing and returns neither an RR nor a REJ. When A's timer expires, it transmits an RR frame that includes a bit known as the P bit, which is set to 1. B interprets the RR frame with a P bit of 1 as a command that must be acknowledged by sending an RR indicating the next frame that it expects, which is frame i. When A receives the RR, it retransmits frame i. Alternatively, A could just retransmit frame i when its timer expires.

2. **Damaged RR.** There are two subcases:

   a. B receives frame i and sends RR $(i + 1)$, which suffers an error in transit. Because acknowledgments are cumulative (e.g., RR 6 means that all frames through 5 are acknowledged), it may be that A will receive a subsequent RR to a subsequent frame and that it will arrive before the timer associated with frame i expires.

   b. If A's timer expires, it transmits an RR command as in Case 1b. It sets another timer, called the P-bit timer. If B fails to respond to the RR command, or if its response suffers an error in transit, then A's P-bit timer will expire. At this point, A will try again by issuing a new RR command and restarting the P-bit timer. This procedure is tried for a number of iterations. If A fails to obtain an acknowledgment after some maximum number of attempts, it initiates a reset procedure.

3. **Damaged REJ.** If a REJ is lost, this is equivalent to Case 1b.

Figure 14.6 is an example of the frame flow for go-back-N ARQ. Because of the propagation delay on the line, by the time that an acknowledgment (positive or negative) arrives back at the sending station, it has already sent at least one additional frame beyond the one being acknowledged. In this example, frame 4 is damaged. Frames 5 and 6 are received out of order and are discarded by B. When frame 5 arrives, B immediately sends a REJ 4. When the REJ to frame 4 is received, not only frame 4 but frames 5 and 6 must be retransmitted. Note that the transmitter must keep a copy of all unacknowledged frames.

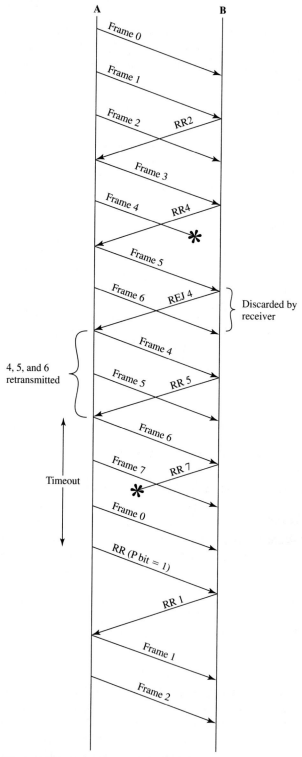

Figure 14.6   Go-Back-N ARQ Protocol

In Section 14.1, we mentioned that for a k-bit sequence number field, which provides a sequence number range of 2^k, the maximum window size is limited to $2^k - 1$. This has to do with the interaction between error control and acknowledgment. Consider that if data are being exchanged in both directions, station B must send piggybacked acknowledgments to station A's frames in the data frames being transmitted by B, even if the acknowledgment has already been sent. As we have mentioned, this is because B must put some number in the acknowledgment field of its data frame. As an example, assume a 3-bit sequence number (sequence number space = 8). Suppose a station sends frame 0 and gets back an RR 1, and then sends frames 1, 2, 3, 4, 5, 6, 7, 0 and gets another RR 1. This could mean that all eight frames were received correctly and the RR 1 is a cumulative acknowledgment. It could also mean that all eight frames were damaged or lost in transit, and the receiving station is repeating its previous RR 1. The problem is avoided if the maximum window size is limited to $7(2^3 - 1)$.

14.4 HIGH-LEVEL DATA LINK CONTROL (HDLC)

The most important data link control protocol is HDLC. Not only is HDLC widely used, but it is the basis for many other important data link control protocols, which use the same or similar formats and the same mechanisms as employed in HDLC.

Basic Characteristics

To satisfy a variety of applications, HDLC defines three types of stations, two link configurations, and three data transfer modes of operation. The three station types are as follows:

- **Primary station:** Responsible for controlling the operation of the link. Frames issued by the primary are called commands.
- **Secondary station:** Operates under the control of the primary station. Frames issued by a secondary are called responses. The primary maintains a separate logical link with each secondary station on the line.
- **Combined station:** Combines the features of primary and secondary. A combined station may issue both commands and responses.

The two link configurations are as follows:

- **Unbalanced configuration:** Consists of one primary and one or more secondary stations and supports both full-duplex and half-duplex transmission.
- **Balanced configuration:** Consists of two combined stations and supports both full-duplex and half-duplex transmission.

The three data transfer modes are as follows:

- **Normal response mode (NRM):** Used with an unbalanced configuration. The primary may initiate data transfer to a secondary, but a secondary may only transmit data in response to a command from the primary.
- **Asynchronous balanced mode (ABM):** Used with a balanced configuration. Either combined station may initiate transmission without receiving permission from the other combined station.

- **Asynchronous response mode (ARM):** Used with an unbalanced configuration. The secondary may initiate transmission without explicit permission of the primary. The primary still retains responsibility for the line, including initialization, error recovery, and logical disconnection.

NRM is used on multidrop lines, in which a number of terminals are connected to a host computer. The computer polls each terminal for input. NRM is also sometimes used on point-to-point links, particularly if the link connects a terminal or other peripheral to a computer. ABM is the most widely used of the three modes; it makes more efficient use of a full-duplex point-to-point link because there is no polling overhead. ARM is rarely used; it is applicable to some special situations in which a secondary may need to initiate transmission.

Frame Structure

HDLC uses synchronous transmission. All transmissions are in the form of frames, and a single frame format suffices for all types of data and control exchanges.

Figure 14.7 depicts the structure of the HDLC frame. The Flag, Address, and Control fields that precede the information field are known as a **header**. The FCS and Flag fields following the data field are referred to as a **trailer**.

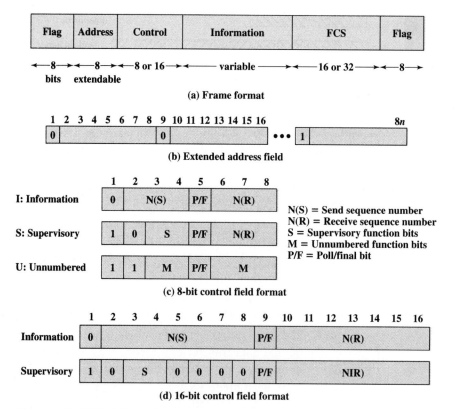

Figure 14.7 HDLC Frame Structure

Flag Fields Flag fields delimit the frame at both ends with the unique pattern 01111110. A single flag may be used as the closing flag for one frame and the opening flag for the next. On both sides of the user-network interface, receivers are continuously hunting for the flag sequence to synchronize on the start of a frame. While receiving a frame, a station continues to hunt for that sequence to determine the end of the frame. Because the protocol allows the presence of arbitrary bit patterns (i.e., there are no restrictions on the content of the various fields imposed by the link protocol), there is no assurance that the pattern 01111110 will not appear somewhere inside the frame, thus destroying synchronization. To avoid this problem, a procedure known as *bit stuffing* is used. For all bits between the starting and ending flags, the transmitter inserts an extra 0 bit after each occurrence of five 1s in the frame. After detecting a starting flag, the receiver monitors the bit stream. When a pattern of five 1s appears, the sixth bit is examined. If this bit is 0, it is deleted. If the sixth bit is a 1 and the seventh bit is a 0, the combination is accepted as a flag. If the sixth and seventh bits are both 1, the sender is indicating an abort condition.

With the use of bit stuffing, arbitrary bit patterns can be inserted into the data field of the frame. This property is known as **data transparency**.

Figure 14.8a shows an example of bit stuffing. Note that in the first two cases, the extra 0 is not strictly necessary for avoiding a flag pattern but is necessary for the operation of the algorithm. Figures 14.8b and c illustrate the pitfalls of bit stuffing. When a flag is used as both an ending and a starting flag, a 1-bit error merges two frames into one. Conversely, a 1-bit error inside the frame could split one frame in two.

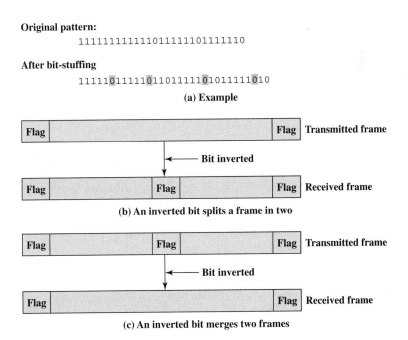

Original pattern:
```
111111111111011111101111110
```

After bit-stuffing
```
11111011111011011111010111110 10
```
(a) Example

(b) An inverted bit splits a frame in two

(c) An inverted bit merges two frames

Figure 14.8   Bit Stuffing

Address Field The Address field identifies the secondary station that transmitted or is to receive the frame. This field is not needed for point-to-point links but is always included for the sake of uniformity. The address field is usually 8 bits long but, by prior agreement, an extended format may be used in which the actual address length is a multiple of 7 bits. The leftmost bit of each octet is 1 or 0 according as it is or is not the last octet of the address field. The remaining 7 bits of each octet form part of the address. The single-octet address of 11111111 is interpreted as the all-stations address in both basic and extended formats. It is used to allow the primary to broadcast a frame for reception by all secondaries.

Control Field HDLC defines three types of frames, each with a different control field format. **Information frames** (I-frames) carry the data to be transmitted for the user (the logic above HDLC that is using HDLC). Additionally, flow and error control data, using the ARQ mechanism, are piggybacked on an information frame. **Supervisory frames** (S-frames) provide the ARQ mechanism when piggybacking is not used. **Unnumbered frames** (U-frames) provide supplemental link control functions. The first one or two bits of the control field serve to identify the frame type. The remaining bit positions are organized into subfields, as indicated in Figures 14.7c and d. Their use is explained in the discussion of HDLC operation later in this chapter.

All of the control field formats contain the poll/final (P/F) bit. Its use depends on context. Typically, in command frames, it is referred to as the P bit and is set to 1 to solicit (poll) a response frame from the peer HDLC entity. In response frames, it is referred to as the F bit and is set to 1 to indicate the response frame transmitted as a result of a soliciting command.

Note that the basic control field for S- and I-frames uses 3-bit sequence numbers. With the appropriate set-mode command, an extended control field can be used for S- and I-frames that employ 7-bit sequence numbers. U-frames always contain an 8-bit control field.

Information Field The Information field is present only in I-frames and some U-frames. The field can contain any sequence of bits but must consist of an integral number of octets. The length of the information field is variable up to some system-defined maximum.

Frame Check Sequence Field The frame check sequence (FCS) is an error-detecting code calculated from the remaining bits of the frame, exclusive of flags. The normal code is the 16-bit CRC-CCITT, defined in Appendix 14A. An optional 32-bit FCS, using CRC-32, may be employed if the frame length or the line reliability dictates this choice.

Operation

HDLC operation consists of the exchange of I-frames, S-frames, and U-frames between two stations. The various commands and responses defined for these frame types are listed in Table 14.1. In describing HDLC operation, we will discuss these three types of frames.

Table 14.1   HDLC Commands and Responses

Name	Command/ Response	Description
Information (I)	C/R	Exchange user data
Supervisory (S)		
Receive ready (RR)	C/R	Positive acknowledgment; ready to receive I-frame
Receive not ready (RNR)	C/R	Positive acknowledgment; not ready to receive
Reject (REJ)	C/R	Negative acknowledgment; go back N
Selective reject (SREJ)	C/R	Negative acknowledgment; selective reject
Unnumbered (U)		
Set normal response/extended mode (SNRM/SNRME)	C	Set mode; extended = 7-bit sequence numbers
Set asynchronous response/extended mode (SARM/SARME)	C	Set mode; extended = 7-bit sequence numbers
Set asynchronous balanced/extended mode (SABM, SABME)	C	Set mode; extended = 7-bit sequence numbers
Set initialization mode (SIM)	C	Initialize link control functions in addressed station
Disconnect (DISC)	C	Terminate logical link connection
Unnumbered acknowledgment (UA)	R	Acknowledge acceptance of one of the set-mode commands
Disconnected mode (DM)	R	Responder is in disconnected mode
Request disconnect (RD)	R	Request for DISC command
Request initialization mode (RIM)	R	Initialization needed; request for SIM command
Unnumbered information (UI)	C/R	Used to exchange control information
Unnumbered poll (UP)	C	Used to solicit control information
Reset (RSET)	C	Used for recovery; resets N(R), N(S)
Exchange identification (XID)	C/R	Used to request/report status
Test (TEST)	C/R	Exchange identical information fields for testing
Frame reject (FRMR)	R	Report receipt of unacceptable frame

The operation of HDLC involves three phases. First, one side or another initializes the data link so that frames may be exchanged in an orderly fashion. During this phase, the options that are to be used are agreed upon. After initialization, the two sides exchange user data and the control information to exercise flow and error control. Finally, one of the two sides signals the termination of the operation.

Initialization Initialization may be requested by either side by issuing one of the six set-mode commands. This command serves three purposes:

1. It signals the other side that initialization is requested.
2. It specifies which of the three modes (NRM, ABM, ARM) is requested.
3. It specifies whether 3- or 7-bit sequence numbers are to be used.

If the other side accepts this request, then the HDLC module on the accepting side transmits an unnumbered acknowledged (UA) frame back to the initiating side. If the request is rejected, then a disconnected mode (DM) frame is sent.

Data Transfer When initialization has been requested and accepted, then a logical connection is established. Both sides may send user data in I-frames, starting with sequence number 0. The N(S) and N(R) fields of the I-frame are sequence numbers that support flow control and error control. An HDLC module sending a sequence of I-frames will number them sequentially, modulo 8 or 128, depending on whether 3- or 7-bit sequence numbers are used, and place the sequence number in N(S). N(R) is the acknowledgment for I-frames received; it enables the HDLC module to indicate which number I-frame it expects to receive next.

S-frames are also used for flow control and error control. The receive ready (RR) frame acknowledges the last I-frame received by indicating the next I-frame expected. The RR is used when there is no reverse user data traffic (I-frames) to carry an acknowledgment. Receive not ready (RNR) acknowledges an I-frame, as with RR, but also asks the peer entity to suspend transmission of I-frames. When the entity that issued RNR is again ready, it sends an RR. REJ initiates the go-back-N ARQ. It indicates that the last I-frame received has been rejected and that retransmission of all I-frames beginning with number N(R) is required. Selective reject (SREJ) is used to request retransmission of just a single frame.

Disconnect Either HDLC module can initiate a disconnect, either on its own initiative if there is some sort of fault, or at the request of its higher-layer user. HDLC issues a disconnect by sending a disconnect (DISC) frame. The remote entity must accept the disconnect by replying with a UA and informing its layer 3 user that the connection has been terminated. Any outstanding unacknowledged I-frames may be lost, and their recovery is the responsibility of higher layers.

Examples of Operation To better understand HDLC operation, several examples are presented in Figure 14.9. In the example diagrams, each arrow includes a legend that specifies the frame name, the setting of the P/F bit, and, where appropriate, the values of N(R) and N(S). The setting of the P or F bit is 1 if the designation is present and 0 if absent.

Figure 14.9a shows the frames involved in link setup and disconnect. The HDLC protocol entity for one side issues an SABM command to the other side and starts a timer. The other side, upon receiving the SABM, returns a UA response and sets local variables and counters to their initial values. The initiating entity receives the UA response, sets its variables and counters, and stops the timer. The logical connection is now active, and both sides may begin transmitting frames. Should the timer expire without a response to an SABM, the originator will repeat the SABM,

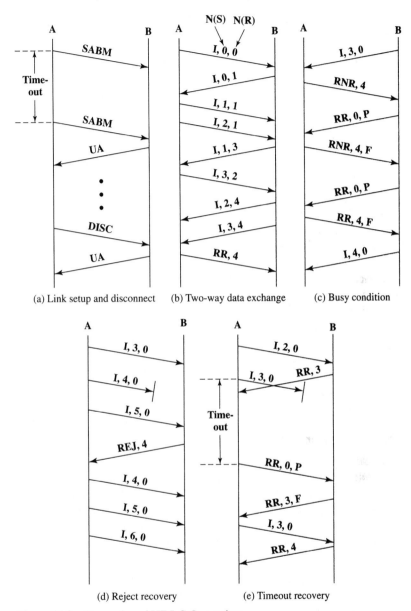

Figure 14.9   Examples of HDLC Operation

as illustrated. This would be repeated until a UA or DM is received or until, after a given number of tries, the entity attempting initiation gives up and reports failure to a management entity. In such a case, higher-layer intervention is necessary. The same figure (Figure 14.9a) shows the disconnect procedure. One side issues a DISC command, and the other responds with a UA response.

Figure 14.9b illustrates the full-duplex exchange of I-frames. When an entity sends a number of I-frames in a row with no incoming data, then the receive sequence number is simply repeated (e.g., I,1,1; I,2,1 in the A-to-B direction). When an entity receives a number of I-frames in a row with no outgoing frames, then the receive sequence number in the next outgoing frame must reflect the cumulative activity (e.g., I,1,3 in the B-to-A direction). Note that, in addition to I-frames, data exchange may involve supervisory frames.

Figure 14.9c shows an operation involving a busy condition. Such a condition may arise because an HDLC entity is not able to process I-frames as fast as they are arriving, or the intended user is not able to accept data as fast as they arrive in I-frames. In either case, the entity's receive buffer fills up and it must halt the incoming flow of I-frames, using an RNR command. In this example, A issues an RNR, which requires B to halt transmission of I-frames. The station receiving the RNR will usually poll the busy station at some periodic interval by sending an RR with the P bit set. This requires the other side to respond with either an RR or an RNR. When the busy condition has cleared, A returns an RR, and I-frame transmission from B can resume.

An example of error recovery using the REJ command is shown in Figure 14.9d. In this example, A transmits I-frames numbered 3, 4, and 5. Number 4 suffers an error and is lost. When B receives I-frame number 5, it discards this frame because it is out of order and sends an REJ with an N(R) of 4. This causes A to initiate retransmission of I-frames previously sent, beginning with frame 4. A may continue to send additional frames after the retransmitted frames.

An example of error recovery using a timeout is shown in Figure 14.9e. In this example, A transmits I-frame number 3 as the last in a sequence of I-frames. The frame suffers an error. B detects the error and discards it. However, B cannot send an REJ, because there is no way to know if this was an I-frame. If an error is detected in a frame, all of the bits of that frame are suspect, and the receiver has no way to act upon it. A, however, would have started a timer as the frame was transmitted. This timer has a duration long enough to span the expected response time. When the timer expires, A initiates recovery action. This is usually done by polling the other side with an RR command with the P bit set, to determine the status of the other side. Because the poll demands a response, the entity will receive a frame containing an N(R) field and be able to proceed. In this case, the response indicates that frame 3 was lost, which A retransmits.

These examples are not exhaustive. However, they should give the reader a good feel for the behavior of HDLC.

14.5 RECOMMENDED READING

An excellent and very detailed treatment of flow control and error control is to be found in [BERT92]. A good survey of data link control protocols is [BLAC93]. [FIOR95] points out some of the real-world reliability problems with HDLC.

The classic treatment of error detecting codes and CRC is [PETE61]. [RAMA88] is an excellent tutorial on CRC.

There is a large body of literature on the performance of ARQ link control protocols. Three classic papers, well worth reading, are [BENE64], [KONH80], and [BUX80]. A readable survey with simplified performance results is [LIN84]. A more recent analysis is [ZORZ96]. Two books with good coverage of link level performance are [SPRA91] and [WALR98].

BENE64 Benice, R. "An Analysis of Retransmission Systems." *IEEE Transactions on Communication Technology*, December 1964.

BERT92 Bertsekas, D., and Gallager, R. *Data Networks.* Englewood Cliffs, NJ: Prentice Hall, 1992.

BLAC93 Black, U. *Data Link Protocols.* Englewood Cliffs, NJ: Prentice Hall, 1993.

BUX80 Bux, W.; Kummerle, K.; and Truong, H. "Balanced HDLC Procedures: A Performance Analysis." *IEEE Transactions on Communications*, November 1980.

FIOR95 Fiorini, D.; Chiani, M.; Tralli, V.; and Salati, C. "Can We Trust HDLC?" *Computer Communications Review*, October 1995.

KONH80 Konheim, A. "A Queuing Analysis of Two ARQ Protocols." *IEEE Transactions on Communications*, July 1980.

LIN84 Lin, S.; Costello, D.; and Miller, M. "Automatic-Repeat-Request Error-Control Schemes." *IEEE Communications Magazine*, December 1984.

PETE61 Peterson, W., and Brown, D. "Cyclic Codes for Error Detection." *Proceedings of the IEEE*, January 1961.

RAMA88 Ramabadran, T., and Gaitonde, S. "A Tutorial on CRC Computations." *IEEE Micro*, August 1988.

SPRA91 Spragins, J.; Hammond, J.; and Pawlikowski, K. *Telecommunications: Protocols and Design.* Reading, MA: Addison-Wesley, 1991.

WALR98 Walrand, J. *Communication Networks: A First Course.* New York: McGraw-Hill, 1998.

ZORZ96 Zorzi, M., and Rao, R. "On the Use of Renewal Theory in the Analysis of ARQ Protocols." *IEEE Transactions on Communications*, September 1996.

14.6 KEY TERMS, REVIEW QUESTIONS, AND PROBLEMS

Key Terms

cyclic redundancy check (CRC)	flow control	parity check
data frame	frame	piggybacking
data link	frame synchronization	sliding-window flow control
data link control protocol	frame check sequence (FCS)	stop-and-wait ARQ
data transparency	go-back-N ARQ	stop-and-wait flow control
error control	header	trailer
error detection	high-level data link	
error-detection code	control (HDLC)	
flag field	parity bit	

Review Questions

14.1 List and briefly define some of the requirements for effective communications over a data link.

14.2 Define *flow control.*

14.3 Describe stop-and-wait flow control.

14.4 What are reasons for breaking a long data transmission up into a number of frames?

14.5 Describe sliding-window flow control.

14.6 What is the advantage of sliding-window flow control compared to stop-and-wait flow control?

14.7 What is piggybacking?

14.8 What is a parity bit?

14.9 What is the CRC?

14.10 Why would you expect a CRC to detect more errors than a parity bit?

14.11 List two different ways in which the CRC algorithm can be described.

14.12 Define *error control*.

14.13 List common ingredients for error control for a link control protocol.

14.14 Describe automatic repeat request (ARQ).

14.15 List and briefly define two versions of ARQ.

14.16 What are the station types supported by HDLC? Describe each.

14.17 What are the transfer modes supported by HDLC? Describe each.

14.18 What is the purpose of the Flag field?

14.19 Define *data transparency*.

14.20 What are the three frame types supported by HDLC? Describe each.

Problems

14.1 Consider a half-duplex point-to-point link using a stop-and-wait scheme, in which a series of messages is sent, with each message segmented into a number of frames. Ignore errors and frame overhead.

a. What is the effect on line utilization of increasing the message size so that fewer messages will be required? Other factors remain constant.

b. What is the effect on line utilization of increasing the number of frames for a constant message size?

c. What is the effect on line utilization of increasing frame size?

14.2 A channel has a data rate of 4 kbps and a propagation delay of 20 ms. For what range of frame sizes does stop-and-wait give an efficiency of at least 50%?

14.3 Consider the use of 1000-bit frames on a 1-Mbps satellite channel with a 270-ms delay. What is the maximum link utilization for

a. Stop-and-wait flow control?

b. Continuous flow control with a window size of 7?

c. Continuous flow control with a window size of 127?

d. Continuous flow control with a window size of 255?

14.4 In Figure 14.10 frames are generated at node A and sent to node C through node B. Determine the minimum data rate required between nodes B and C so that the buffers of node B are not flooded, based on the following:

The data rate between A and B is 100 kbps.

The propagation delay is 5 μs/km for both lines.

There are full duplex lines between the nodes.

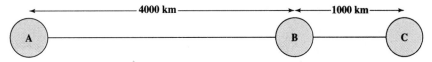

Figure 14.10 Configuration for Problem 14.4

All data frames are 1000 bits long; ACK frames are separate frames of negligible length.

Between A and B, a sliding-window protocol with a window size of 3 is used.

Between B and C, stop-and-wait is used.

There are no errors.

Hint: In order not to flood the buffers of B, the average number of frames entering and leaving B must be the same over a long interval.

14.5 A channel has a data rate of R bps and a propagation delay of t s/km. The distance between the sending and receiving nodes is L kilometers. Nodes exchange fixed-size frames of B bits. Find a formula that gives the minimum sequence field size of the frame as a function of R, t, B, and L (considering maximum utilization). Assume that ACK frames are negligible in size and the processing at the nodes is instantaneous.

14.6 No mention was made of reject (REJ) frames in the stop-and-wait ARQ discussion. Why is it not necessary to have REJ0 and REJ1 for stop-and-wait ARQ?

14.7 Would you expect that the inclusion of a parity bit with each character would change the probability of receiving a correct message?

14.8 What is the purpose of using modulo 2 arithmetic rather than binary arithmetic in computing an FCS?

14.9 Consider a frame consisting of two characters of four bits each. Assume that the probability of bit error is 10^{-3} and that it is independent for each bit.
   a. What is the probability that the received frame contains at least one error?
   b. Now add a parity bit to each character. What is the probability?

14.10 Using the CRC-CCITT polynomial, generate the 16-bit CRC code for a message consisting of a 1 followed by 15 0s.

14.11 For $P = 110011$ and $M = 11100011$, find the CRC.

14.12 **a.** In a CRC error-detection scheme, choose $P(x) = x^4 + x + 1$. Encode the bits 10010011011.
   b. Suppose the channel introduces an error pattern 100010000000000 (i.e., a flip from 1 to 0 or from 0 to 1 in position 1 and 5). What is received? Can the error be detected?
   c. Repeat part (b) with error pattern 100110000000000.

14.13 A modified CRC procedure is commonly used in communications standards. It is defined as follows:

$$\frac{X^{16}M(X) + X^k L(X)}{P(X)} = Q + \frac{R(X)}{P(X)}$$

$$FCS = L(X) + R(X)$$

where

$$L(X) = X^{15} + X^{14} + X^{13} + \ldots + X + 1$$

and k is the number of bits being checked (Address, Control, and Information fields).

a. Describe in words the effect of this procedure.

b. Explain the potential benefits.

14.14 Using the same assumptions that are used for Figure 14.14 in Appendix 14B, plot line utilization as a function of P, the probability that a single frame is in error for the following error-control techniques:

a. Stop-and-wait

b. Go-back-N with $W = 7$

c. Go-back-N with $W = 127$

Do all of the preceding for the following values of a: 0.1, 1, 10, 100. Draw conclusions about which technique is appropriate for various ranges of a.

14.15 Two neighboring nodes (A and B) use a sliding-window protocol with a 3-bit sequence number. As the ARQ mechanism, go-back-N is used with a window size of 4. Assuming that A is transmitting and B is receiving, show the window positions for the following succession of events:

a. Before A sends any frames

b. After A sends frames 0, 1, 2 and receives acknowledgment from B for 0 and 1

c. After A sends frames 3, 4, and 5 and B acknowledges 4 and the ACK is received by A

14.16 Two stations communicate via a 1-Mbps satellite link with a propagation delay of 270 ms. The satellite serves merely to retransmit data received from one station to another, with negligible switching delay. Using HDLC frames of 1024 bits with 3-bit sequence numbers, what is the maximum possible data throughput; that is, what is the throughput of data bits carried in HDLC frames?

14.17 It is clear that bit stuffing is needed for the address, data, and FCS fields of an HDLC frame. Is it needed for the control field?

14.18 Suggest improvements to the bit stuffing-algorithm to overcome the problems of single-bit errors.

14.19 Assume that the primary HDLC station in NRM has sent six I-frames to a secondary. The primary's N(S) count was three (011 binary) prior to sending the six frames. If the poll bit is on in the sixth frame, what will be the N(R) count back from the secondary after the last frame? Assume error-free operation.

14.20 Consider that several physical links connect two stations. We would like to use a "multilink HDLC" that makes efficient use of these links by sending frames on a FIFO basis on the next available link. What enhancements to HDLC are needed?

APPENDIX 14A CYCLIC REDUNDANCY CHECK

One of the most common, and one of the most powerful, error-detecting codes is the cyclic redundancy check (CRC), which can be described as follows. Given a k-bit block of bits, or message, the transmitter generates an $(n - k)$-bit sequence, known as a frame check sequence (FCS), such that the resulting frame, consisting of n bits, is exactly divisible by some predetermined number. The receiver then divides the incoming frame by that number and, if there is no remainder, assumes there was no error.

To clarify this, we present the procedure in two equivalent ways: modulo 2 arithmetic and polynomials.

Modulo 2 Arithmetic

Modulo 2 arithmetic uses binary addition with no carries, which is just the exclusive-OR (XOR) operation. Binary subtraction with no carries is also interpreted as the XOR operation: For example,

$$
\begin{array}{r}
1111 \\
+\ 1010 \\
\hline
0101
\end{array}
\qquad
\begin{array}{r}
1111 \\
-\ 0101 \\
\hline
1010
\end{array}
\qquad
\begin{array}{r}
11001 \\
\times\ \ 11 \\
\hline
11001 \\
11001 \\
\hline
101011
\end{array}
$$

Now define

$T = n$-bit frame to be transmitted

$D = k$-bit block of data, or message, the first k bits of T

$F = (n - k)$-bit FCS, the last $(n - k)$ bits of T

P = pattern of $n - k + 1$ bits; this is the predetermined divisor

We would like T/P to have no remainder. It should be clear that

$$T = 2^{n-k}D + F$$

That is, by multiplying D by 2^{n-k}, we have in effect shifted it to the left by $n - k$ bits and padded out the result with zeroes. Adding F yields the concatenation of D and F, which is T. We want T to be exactly divisible by P. Suppose that we divide $2^{n-k}D$ by P:

$$\frac{2^{n-k}D}{P} = Q + \frac{R}{P} \tag{14.3}$$

There is a quotient and a remainder. Because division is modulo 2, the remainder is always at least one bit shorter than the divisor. We will use this remainder as our FCS. Then

$$T = 2^{n-k}D + R \tag{14.4}$$

Does this R satisfy our condition that T/P have no remainder? To see that it does, consider the following:

$$\frac{T}{P} = \frac{2^{n-k}D + R}{P} = \frac{2^{n-k}D}{P} + \frac{R}{P}$$

Substituting Equation (14.3), we have

$$\frac{T}{P} = Q + \frac{R}{P} + \frac{R}{P}$$

However, any binary number added to itself modulo 2 yields zero. Thus

$$\frac{T}{P} = Q + \frac{R + R}{P} = Q$$

There is no remainder, and therefore T is exactly divisible by P. Thus, the FCS is easily generated: Simply divide $2^{n-k}D$ by P and use the $(n - k)$-bit remainder as the FCS. On reception, the receiver will divide T by P and will get no remainder if there have been no errors.

EXAMPLE 14.5

1. Given

$$\text{Message } D = 1010001101 \ (10 \text{ bits})$$
$$\text{Pattern } P = 110101 \ (6 \text{ bits})$$
$$\text{FCS } R = \text{to be calculated} \ (5 \text{ bits})$$

   Thus, $n = 15$, $k = 10$, and $(n - k) = 5$.

2. The message is multiplied by 2^5, yielding 101000110100000.

3. This product is divided by P:

```
                              1101010110  ← Q
 P → 110101 ⟌ 101000110100000            ← 2ⁿ⁻ᵏD
              110101
              111011
              110101
                111010
                110101
                  111110
                  110101
                    101100
                    110101
                      110010
                      110101
                       01110  ← R
```

4. The remainder is added to 2^5D to give $T = 101000110101110$, which is transmitted.

5. If there are no errors, the receiver receives T intact. The received frame is divided by P:

```
                              1101010110  ← Q
 P → 110101 ⟌ 101000110101110            ← T
              110101
              111011
              110101
                111010
                110101
                  111110
                  110101
                    101111
                    110101
                      110101
                      110101
                          0  ← R
```

Because there is no remainder, it is assumed that there have been no errors.

The pattern P is chosen to be one bit longer than the desired FCS, and the exact bit pattern chosen depends on the type of errors expected. At minimum, both the high- and low-order bits of P must be 1.

There is a concise method for specifying the occurrence of one or more errors. An error results in the reversal of a bit. This is equivalent to taking the XOR of the bit and 1 (modulo 2 addition of 1 to the bit): $0 + 1 = 1; 1 + 1 = 0$. Thus, the errors in an n-bit frame can be represented by an n-bit field with 1s in each error position. The resulting frame T_r can be expressed as

$$T_r = T \oplus E$$

where

T = transmitted frame

E = error pattern with 1s in positions where errors occur

T_r = received frame

If there is an error ($E \neq 0$), the receiver will fail to detect the error if and only if T_r is divisible by P, which is equivalent to E divisible by P. Intuitively, this seems an unlikely occurrence.

Polynomials A second way of viewing the CRC process is to express all values as polynomials in a dummy variable X, with binary coefficients. The coefficients correspond to the bits in the binary number. Thus, for $D = 110011$, we have $D(X) = X^5 + X^4 + X + 1$, and for $P = 11001$, we have $P(X) = X^4 + X^3 + 1$. Arithmetic operations are again modulo 2. The CRC process can now be described as follows:

$$\frac{X^{n-k}D(X)}{P(X)} = Q(X) + \frac{R(X)}{P(X)}$$

$$T(X) = X^{n-k}D(X) + R(X)$$

Compare these equations with Equations (14.3) and (14.4).

EXAMPLE 14.6 Using the preceding example, for $D = 1010001101$, we have $D(X) = X^9 + X^7 + X^3 + X^2 + 1$, and for $P = 110101$, we have $P(X) = X^5 + X^4 + X^2 + 1$. We should end up with $R = 01110$, which corresponds to $R(X) = X^3 + X^2 + X$. Figure 14.11 shows the polynomial division that corresponds to the binary division in the preceding example.

An error $E(X)$ will only be undetectable if it is divisible by $P(X)$. It can be shown [PETE 61, RAMA88] that all of the following errors are not divisible by a suitably chosen $P(X)$ and hence are detectable:

- All single-bit errors, if $P(X)$ has more than one nonzero term
- All double-bit errors, as long as $P(X)$ has a factor with three terms
- Any odd number of errors, as long as $P(X)$ contains a factor $(X + 1)$
- Any burst error for which the length of the burst is less than or equal to $n - k$; that is, less than or equal to the length of the FCS

$$
\begin{array}{r}
X^9 + X^8 + X^6 + X^4 + X^2 + X \quad \leftarrow Q(X) \\
\hline
\end{array}
$$

$$P(X) \rightarrow X^5 + X^4 + X^2 + 1 \,\big/\, X^{14} \qquad X^{12} \qquad\qquad X^8 + X^7 + \quad X^5 \quad \leftarrow X^5 D(X)$$

$$
\begin{array}{l}
\underline{X^{14} + X^{13} + \quad X^{11} + \quad X^9} \\
\quad X^{13} + X^{12} + X^{11} + \quad X^9 + X^8 \\
\quad \underline{X^{13} + X^{12} + \quad X^{10} + \quad X^8} \\
\qquad\qquad X^{11} + X^{10} + X^9 + \quad X^7 \\
\qquad\qquad \underline{X^{11} + X^{10} + \quad X^8 + \quad X^6} \\
\qquad\qquad\qquad X^9 + X^8 + X^7 + X^6 + X^5 \\
\qquad\qquad\qquad \underline{X^9 + X^8 + \quad X^6 + \quad X^4} \\
\qquad\qquad\qquad\qquad X^7 + \quad X^5 + X^4 \\
\qquad\qquad\qquad\qquad \underline{X^7 + X^6 + \quad X^4 + \quad X^2} \\
\qquad\qquad\qquad\qquad\qquad X^6 + X^5 + \qquad X^2 \\
\qquad\qquad\qquad\qquad\qquad \underline{X^6 + X^5 + \quad X^3 + \quad X} \\
\qquad\qquad\qquad\qquad\qquad\qquad X^3 + X^2 + X \quad \leftarrow R(X)
\end{array}
$$

Figure 14.11 Example of Polynomial Division

- A fraction of error bursts of length $n - k + 1$; the fraction equals $1 - 2^{-(n-k-1)}$
- A fraction of error bursts of length greater than $n - k + 1$; the fraction equals $1 - 2^{-(n-k)}$

In addition, it can be shown that if all error patterns are considered equally likely, then for a burst error of length $r + 1$, the probability of an undetected error ($E(X)$ is divisible by $P(X)$) is $1/2^{r-1}$, and for a longer burst, the probability is $1/2^r$, where r is the length of the FCS.

Four versions of $P(X)$ are widely used:

CRC-12 $= X^{12} + X^{11} + X^3 + X^2 + X + 1$

CRC-16 $= X^{16} + X^{15} + X^2 + 1$

CRC-CCITT $= X^{16} + X^{12} + X^5 + 1$

CRC-32 $= X^{32} + X^{26} + X^{23} + X^{22} + X^{16} + X^{12} + X^{11}$

$+ X^{10} + X^8 + X^7 + X^5 + X^4 + X^2 + X + 1$

The CRC-12 system is used for transmission of streams of 6-bit characters and generates a 12-bit FCS. Both CRC-16 and CRC-CCITT are popular for streams of 8-bit characters, in the United States and Europe, respectively, and both result in a 16-bit FCS. This would seem adequate for most applications, although CRC-32 is specified as an option in some point-to-point synchronous transmission standards and is used in IEEE 802 LAN standards.

APPENDIX 14B PERFORMANCE ISSUES

In this appendix, we examine some of the performance issues related to the use of sliding-window flow control.

The Parameter a

In Section 5.3, we introduced the parameter a, defined as

$$a = \frac{\text{propagation delay}}{\text{transmission delay}} = \frac{d/v}{L/R} = \frac{R \times D}{L} \tag{14.5}$$

where

R = data rate, or capacity, of the link

L = number of bits in a packet

d = distance between source and destination

v = velocity of propagation of the signal

D = propagation delay

Looking at the final fraction in Equation (14.5), we see that a can also be expressed as

$$a = \frac{\text{length of the transmission channel in bits}}{\text{length of the packet in bits}}$$

Stop-and-Wait Flow Control

Let us determine the maximum potential efficiency of a half-duplex point-to-point line using the stop-and-wait scheme described in Section 14.3. Recall that for the stop-and-wait protocol, the sources sends a sequence of packets to the destination and, for each packet, waits for an acknowledgement before sending the next packet.

Figure 5.6 illustrates Equation (14.5). In this figure, transmission time is normalized to 1 and hence the propagation time, by Equation (14.5), is a. For the case of $a < 1$, the link's bit length is less than that of the frame. The station T begins transmitting a frame at time t_0. At $t_0 + a$, the leading edge of the frame reaches the receiving station R, while T is still in the process of transmitting the frame. At $t_0 + 1$, T completes transmission. At $t_0 + 1 + a$, R has received the entire frame and immediately transmits a small acknowledgment frame. This acknowledgment arrives back at T at $t_0 + 1 + 2a$. Total elapsed time: $1 + 2a$. Total transmission time: 1. Hence utilization is

$$U = \frac{1}{1 + 2a} \tag{14.6}$$

The same result is achieved with $a > 1$, as illustrated in Figure 5.6.

EXAMPLE 14.7 First, consider a wide area network (WAN) using ATM (asynchronous transfer mode, described in Part Three), with the two stations a thousand kilometers apart. The standard ATM frame size (called a cell) is 424 bits and one of the standardized data rates is 155.52 Mbps. Thus, transmission time equals $424/(155.52 \times 10^6) = 2.7 \times 10^{-6}$ seconds. If we assume an optical fiber link, then the propagation time is $(10^6 \text{ meters})/(2 \times 10^8 \text{ m/s}) = 0.5 \times 10^{-2}$ seconds. Thus, $a = (0.5 \times 10^{-2})/(2.7 \times 10^{-6}) \approx 1850$, and efficiency is only $1/3701 = 0.00027$.

At the other extreme, in terms of distance, is the local area network (LAN). Distances range from 0.1 to 10 km, with data rates of 10 Mbps to 1 Gbps; higher data rates tend to be associated with shorter distances. Using a value of $V = 2 \times 10^8$ m/s, a frame size of 1000 bits, and a data rate of 10 Mbps, the value of a is in the range of 0.005 to 0.5. This yields a utilization in the range of 0.5 to 0.99. For a 100-Mbps LAN, given the shorter distances, comparable utilizations are possible.

We can see that LANs are typically quite efficient, whereas high-speed WANs are not. As a final example, let us consider digital data transmission via modem over a voice-grade line. A typical data rate is 56 kbps. Again, let us consider a 1000-bit frame. The link distance can be anywhere from a few tens of meters to thousands of kilometers. If we pick, say, as a short distance $d = 1000$ m, then $a = (56{,}000 \text{ bps} \times 1000 \text{ m})/(2 \times 10^8 \text{ m/s} \times 1000 \text{ bits}) = 2.8 \times 10^{-4}$, and utilization is effectively 1.0. Even in a long-distance case, such as $d = 5000$ km, we have $a = (56{,}000 \times 5 \times 10^6)/(2 \times 10^8 \times 1000 \text{ bits}) = 1.4$ and efficiency equals 0.26.

Error-Free Sliding-Window Flow Control

For sliding-window flow control, the throughput on the line depends on both the window size W and the value of a. For convenience, let us again normalize frame transmission time to a value of 1; thus, the propagation time is a. Figure 14.12 illustrates the efficiency of a full duplex point-to-point line.[3] Station A begins to emit a sequence of frames at time $t = 0$. The leading edge of the first frame reaches station B at $t = a$. The first frame is entirely absorbed by $t = a + 1$. Assuming negligible processing time, B can immediately acknowledge the first frame (ACK). Let us also assume that the acknowledgment frame is so small that transmission time is negligible. Then the ACK reaches A at $t = 2a + 1$. To evaluate performance, we need to consider two cases:

- **Case 1:** $W \geq 2a + 1$. The acknowledgment for frame 1 reaches A before A has exhausted its window. Thus, A can transmit continuously with no pause and normalized throughput is 1.0.

- **Case 2:** $W < 2a + 1$. A exhausts its window at $t = W$ and cannot send additional frames until $t = 2a + 1$. Thus, normalized throughput is W time units out of a period of $(2a + 1)$ time units.

Therefore, we can express the utilization as follows:

$$U = \begin{cases} 1 & W \geq 2a + 1 \\ \dfrac{W}{2a + 1} & W < 2a + 1 \end{cases} \quad (14.7)$$

---

[3]For simplicity, we assume that a is an integer, so that an integer number of frames exactly fills the line. The argument does not change for noninteger values of a.

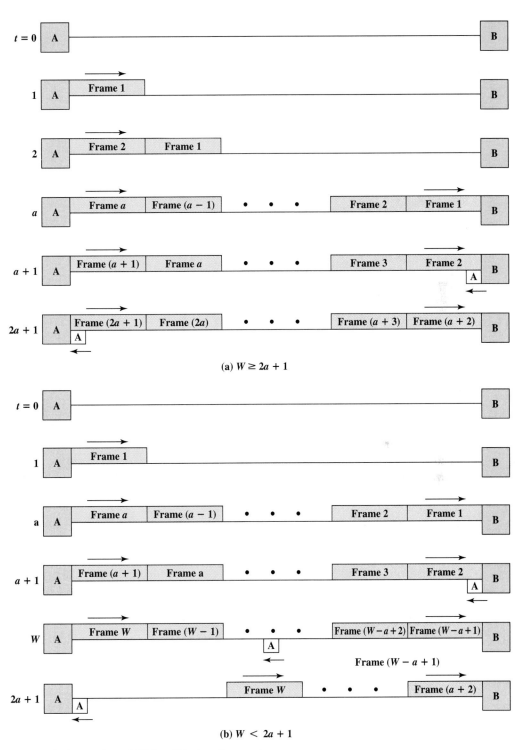

Figure 14.12 Timing of Sliding-Window Protocol

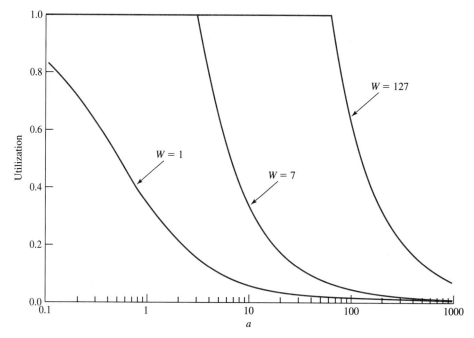

Figure 14.13 Sliding-Window Utilization as a Function of a

Typically, the sequence number is provided for in an n-bit field and the maximum window size is $W = 2^n - 1$ (not 2^n; this is explained in Section 14.3). Figure 14.13 shows the maximum utilization achievable for window sizes of 1, 7, and 127 as a function of a. A window size of 1 corresponds to stop and wait. A window size of 7 (3 bits) is adequate for many applications. A window size of 127 (7 bits) is adequate for larger values of a, such as may be found in high-speed WANs.

ARQ

We have seen that sliding-window flow control is more efficient than stop-and-wait flow control. We would expect that when error control functions are added that this would still be true: that is, that go-back-N ARQ is more efficient than stop-and-wait ARQ. Let us develop some approximations to determine the degree of improvement to be expected.

First, consider stop-and-wait ARQ. With no errors, the maximum utilization is $1/(1 + 2a)$ as shown in Equation (7.4). We want to account for the possibility that some frames are repeated because of bit errors. To start, note that the utilization U can be defined as

$$U = \frac{T_f}{T_t} \tag{14.8}$$

where

T_f = time for transmitter to emit a single frame

T_t = total time that line is engaged in the transmission of a single frame

For error-free operation using stop-and-wait ARQ,

$$U = \frac{T_f}{T_f + 2T_p}$$

where T_p is the propagation time. Dividing by T_f and remembering that $a = T_p/T_f$, we again have Equation (14.6). If errors occur, we must modify Equation (14.8) to

$$U = \frac{T_f}{N_r T_t}$$

where N_r is the expected number of transmissions of a frame. Thus, for stop-and-wait ARQ, we have

$$U = \frac{1}{N_r(1 + 2a)}$$

A simple expression for N_r can be derived by considering the probability P that a single frame is in error. If we assume that ACKs and NAKs are never in error, the probability that it will take exactly k attempts to transmit a frame successfully is $P^{k-1}(1 - P)$. That is, we have $(k - 1)$ unsuccessful attempts followed by one successful attempt; the probability of this occurring is just the product of the probability of the individual events occurring. Then[4]

$$N_r = E[\text{transmissions}] = \sum_{i=1}^{\infty} (i \times \Pr[i \text{ transmissions}])$$

$$= \sum_{i=1}^{\infty} (iP^{i-1}(1 - P)) = \frac{1}{1 - P}$$

So we have

Stop-and-Wait:	$U = \dfrac{1 - P}{1 + 2a}$

For the sliding-window protocol, Equation (14.7) applies for error-free operation. For go-back-N ARQ, we can use the same reasoning as applied to stop-and-wait

---

[4]This derivation uses the equality $\sum_{i=1}^{\infty} (iX^{i-1}) = \frac{1}{(1 - X)^2}$ for $(-1 < X < 1)$.

ARQ. That is, the error-free equations must be divided by N_r. Each error generates a requirement to retransmit K frames rather than just one frame. Thus

$$N_r = \text{E}[\text{number of transmitted frames to successfully transmit one frame}]$$

$$= \sum_{i=1}^{\infty} f(i) P^{i-1}(1 - P)$$

where $f(i)$ is the total number of frames transmitted if the original frame must be transmitted i times. This can be expressed as

$$f(i) = 1 + (i - 1)K$$
$$= (1 - K) + Ki$$

Substituting yields[5]

$$N_r = (1 - K) \sum_{i=1}^{\infty} P^{i-1}(1 - P) + K \sum_{i=1}^{\infty} i P^{i-1}(1 - P)$$

$$= 1 - K + \frac{K}{1 - P}$$

$$= \frac{1 - P + KP}{1 - P}$$

By studying Figure 14.12, the reader should conclude that K is approximately equal to $(2a + 1)$ for $W \geq (2a + 1)$, and $K = W$ for $W < (2a + 1)$. Thus

Go-back-N:	$U = $	$\begin{cases} \dfrac{1 - P}{1 + 2aP} & W \geq 2a + 1 \\[2ex] \dfrac{W(1 - P)}{(2a + 1)(1 - P + WP)} & W < 2a + 1 \end{cases}$

Note that for $W = 1$, go-back-N ARQ reduces to stop and wait. Figure 14.14 compares these two error control techniques for a value of $P = 10^{-3}$. This figure and the equations are only approximations. For example, we have ignored errors in acknowledgment frames and, in the case of go-back-N, errors in retransmitted frames other than the frame initially in error. However, the results do give an indication of the relative performance of the three techniques.

---

[5]This derivation uses the equality $\sum_{i=1}^{\infty} X^{i-1} = \dfrac{1}{1 - X}$ for $(-1 < X < 1)$.

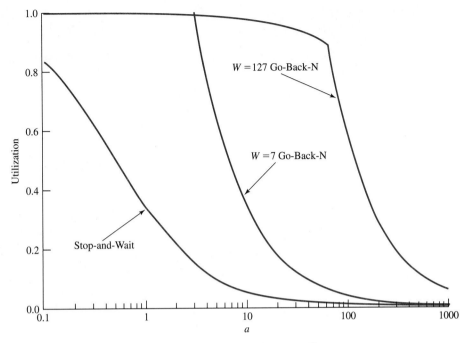

Figure 14.14 ARQ Utilization as a Function of a ($P = 10^{-3}$)

CHAPTER 15

LOCAL AREA NETWORKS

The reader who has persevered thus far in this account will realize the difficulties that were coped with, the hazards that were encountered, the mistakes that were made, and the work that was done.

—*The World Crisis,*
Winston Churchill

KEY POINTS

- A LAN protocol architecture has been specified by the IEEE 802 standards committee. This architecture consists of three layers: physical, medium access control (MAC), and logical link control (LLC).

- The IEEE 802.3 standard, known as Ethernet, now encompasses data rates of 10 Mbps, 100 Mbps, 1 Gbps, and 10 Gbps. For the lower data rates, the CSMA/CD MAC protocol is used. For the 1 Gbps and 10 Gbps options, a switched technique is used.

- The IEEE 802.11 standard defines a set of services and physical layer options for wireless LANs.

- The IEEE 802.11 services include managing associations, delivering data, and security.

- The IEEE 802.11 physical layer includes infrared and spread spectrum and covers a range of data rates.

Recent years have seen rapid changes in the technology, design, and commercial applications for local area networks (LANs). A major feature of this evolution is the introduction of a variety of new schemes for high-speed local networking.

To keep pace with the changing local networking needs of business, a number of approaches to high-speed LAN design have become commercial products. The most important of these are as follows:

- **Fast Ethernet and Gigabit Ethernet:** The extension of 10-Mbps CSMA/CD (carrier sense multiple access with collision detection) to higher speeds is a logical strategy, because it tends to preserve the investment in existing systems.
- **High-speed wireless LANs:** Wireless LAN technology and standards have at last come of age, and high-speed standards and products are being introduced.

15.1 THE EMERGENCE OF HIGH-SPEED LANS

Personal computers and microcomputer workstations began to achieve widespread acceptance in business computing in the early 1980s and have now achieved virtually the status of the telephone: an essential tool for office workers.

511

Until relatively recently, office LANs provided basic connectivity services—connecting personal computers and terminals to mainframes and midrange systems that ran corporate applications, and providing workgroup connectivity at the departmental or divisional level. In both cases, traffic patterns were relatively light, with an emphasis on file transfer and electronic mail. The LANs that were available for this type of workload, primarily Ethernet and token ring, are well suited to this environment.

In recent years, two significant trends have altered the role of the personal computer and therefore the requirements on the LAN:

- The speed and computing power of personal computers has continued to enjoy explosive growth. Today's more powerful platforms support graphics-intensive applications and ever more elaborate graphical user interfaces to the operating system.

- MIS organizations have recognized the LAN as a viable and indeed essential computing platform, resulting in the focus on network computing. This trend began with client/server computing, which has become a dominant architecture in the business environment and the more recent intranetwork trend. Both of these approaches involve the frequent transfer of potentially large volumes of data in a transaction-oriented environment.

The effect of these trends has been to increase the volume of data to be handled over LANs and, because applications are more interactive, to reduce the acceptable delay on data transfers. The earlier generation of 10-Mbps Ethernets and 16-Mbps token rings are simply not up to the job of supporting these requirements.

The following are examples of requirements that call for higher-speed LANs:

- **Centralized server farms:** In many applications, there is a need for user, or client, systems to be able to draw huge amounts of data from multiple centralized servers, called server farms. An example is a color publishing operation, in which servers typically contain tens of gigabytes of image data that must be downloaded to imaging workstations. As the performance of the servers themselves has increased, the bottleneck has shifted to the network. Switched Ethernet alone would not solve this problem because of the limit of 10 Mbps on a single link to the client.

- **Power workgroups:** These groups typically consist of a small number of cooperating users who need to draw massive data files across the network. Examples are a software development group that runs tests on a new software version, or a computer-aided design (CAD) company that regularly runs simulations of new designs. In such cases, large amounts of data are distributed to several workstations, processed, and updated at very high speed for multiple iterations.

- **High-speed local backbone:** As processing demand grows, LANs proliferate at a site, and high-speed interconnection is necessary.

15.2 LAN PROTOCOL ARCHITECTURE

The architecture of a LAN is best described in terms of a layering of protocols that organize the basic functions of a LAN. This section opens with a description of the standardized protocol architecture for LANs, which encompasses physical, medium access control (MAC), and logical link control (LLC) layers. This section then provides an overview of the MAC and LLC layers.

IEEE 802 Reference Model

Protocols defined specifically for LAN and MAN transmission address issues relating to the transmission of blocks of data over the network. In OSI terms, higher-layer protocols (layer 3 or 4 and above) are independent of network architecture and are applicable to LANs, MANs, and WANs. Thus, a discussion of LAN protocols is concerned principally with lower layers of the OSI model.

Figure 15.1 relates the LAN protocols to the OSI architecture (Figure 2.6). This architecture was developed by the IEEE 802 committee and has been adopted by all organizations working on the specification of LAN standards. It is generally referred to as the IEEE 802 reference model.

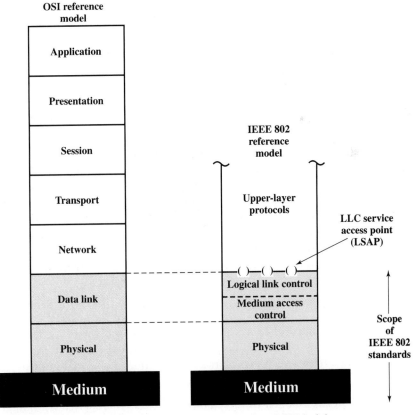

Figure 15.1   IEEE 802 Protocol Layers Compared to OSI Model

Working from the bottom up, the lowest layer of the IEEE 802 reference model corresponds to the **physical layer** of the OSI model and includes such functions as

- Encoding/decoding of signals
- Preamble generation/removal (for synchronization)
- Bit transmission/reception

In addition, the physical layer of the 802 model includes a specification of the transmission medium and the topology. Generally, this is considered "below" the lowest layer of the OSI model. However, the choice of transmission medium and topology is critical in LAN design, and so a specification of the medium is included.

Above the physical layer are the functions associated with providing service to LAN users. These include the following:

- On transmission, assemble data into a frame with address and error-detection fields.
- On reception, disassemble frame, and perform address recognition and error detection.
- Govern access to the LAN transmission medium.
- Provide an interface to higher layers and perform flow and error control.

These are functions typically associated with OSI layer 2. The functions in the last bullet item are grouped into a **logical link control (LLC)** layer. The functions in the first three bullet items are treated as a separate layer, called **medium access control (MAC)**. The separation is done for the following reasons:

- The logic required to manage access to a shared-access medium is not found in traditional layer 2 data link control.
- For the same LLC, several MAC options may be provided.

Figure 15.2 illustrates the relationship between the levels of the architecture (compare Figure 2.15). Higher-level data are passed down to LLC, which appends control information as a header, creating an **LLC protocol data unit (PDU)**. This control information is used in the operation of the LLC protocol. The entire LLC PDU is then passed down to the MAC layer, which appends control information at the front and back of the packet, forming a **MAC frame**. Again, the control information in the frame is needed for the operation of the MAC protocol. For context, the figure also shows the use of TCP/IP and an application layer above the LAN protocols.

Logical Link Control

Logical link control (LLC) is a common link protocol for all the LANs. LLC specifies the mechanisms for addressing stations across the medium and for controlling the exchange of data between two users. The operation and format of this standard is based on HDLC. Three services are provided as alternatives for attached devices using LLC:

- **Unacknowledged connectionless service:** This service is a datagram-style service. It is a very simple service that does not involve any of the flow control and error control mechanisms. Thus, the delivery of data is not guaranteed.

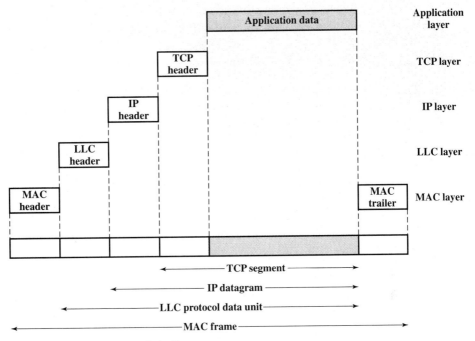

Figure 15.2 LAN Protocols in Context

However, in most devices there will be some higher layer of software that deals with reliability issues.

- **Connection-mode service:** This service is similar to that offered by HDLC. A logical connection is set up between two users exchanging data, and flow control and error control are provided.

- **Acknowledged connectionless service:** This is a cross between the previous two services. It provides that datagrams are to be acknowledged, but no prior logical connection is set up.

Typically, a vendor will provide these services as options that the customer can select when purchasing the equipment. Alternatively, the customer can purchase equipment that provides two or all three services and select a specific service based on application.

The **unacknowledged connectionless service** requires minimum logic and is useful in two contexts. First, it will often be the case that higher layers of software will provide the necessary reliability and flow control mechanism, and it is efficient to avoid duplicating them. For example, TCP provides the mechanisms needed to ensure that data are delivered reliably. Second, there are instances in which the overhead of connection establishment and maintenance is unjustified or even counterproductive (for example, data collection activities that involve the periodic sampling of data sources, such as sensors and automatic self-test reports from security equipment or network components). In a monitoring application, the loss of an occasional data unit would not cause distress, as the next report should arrive shortly. Thus, in most cases, the unacknowledged connectionless service is the preferred option.

The **connection-mode service** could be used in very simple devices, such as terminal controllers, that have little software operating above this level. In these cases, it would provide the flow control and reliability mechanisms normally implemented at higher layers of the communications software.

The **acknowledged connectionless service** is useful in several contexts. With connection-mode service, the logical link control software must maintain some sort of table for each active connection, to keep track of the status of that connection. If the user needs guaranteed delivery, but there are a large number of destinations for data, connection-mode service may be impractical because of the large number of tables required. An example is a process control or automated factory environment, where a central site may need to communicate with a large number of processors and programmable controllers. Another use of this is the handling of important and time-critical alarm or emergency control signals in a factory. Because of their importance, an acknowledgment is needed so that the sender can be assured that the signal got through. Because of the urgency of the signal, the user might not want to take the time to first establish a logical connection and then send the data.

Medium Access Control

All LANs and MANs (metropolitan area networks) consist of collections of devices that must share the network's transmission capacity. Some means of controlling access to the transmission medium is needed to provide an orderly and efficient use of that capacity. This is the function of a **medium access control** (MAC) protocol.

The relationship between LLC and the MAC protocol can be seen by considering the transmission formats involved. User data are passed down to the LLC layer, which prepares a link level frame, known as an LLC protocol data unit (PDU). This PDU is then passed down to the MAC layer, where it is enclosed in a MAC frame.

The exact format of the MAC frame differs somewhat for the various MAC protocols in use. In general, all of the MAC frames have a format similar to that of Figure 15.3. The fields of this frame are as follows:

- **MAC Control:** This field contains any protocol control information needed for the functioning of the MAC protocol. For example, a priority level could be indicated here.

- **Destination MAC Address:** The destination physical attachment point on the LAN for this frame.

- **Source MAC Address:** The source physical attachment point on the LAN for this frame.

- **LLC PDU:** The LLC data from the next higher layer. This includes the user data plus the source and destination service access point (SAPs), which indicate the user of LLC.

- **CRC:** The cyclic redundancy check field (also known as the Frame Check Sequence, FCS, field). This is an error-detecting code, as we have seen in HDLC and other data link control protocols (Chapter 14).

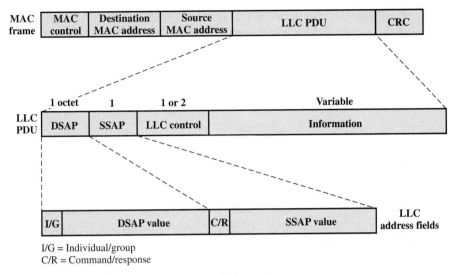

I/G = Individual/group
C/R = Command/response

Figure 15.3 LLC PDU in a Generic MAC Frame Format

In most data link control protocols, the data link protocol entity is responsible not only for detecting errors using the CRC, but for recovering from those errors by retransmitting damaged frames. In the LAN protocol architecture, these two functions are split between the MAC and LLC layers. The MAC layer is responsible for detecting errors and discarding any frames that are in error. The LLC layer optionally keeps track of which frames have been successfully received and retransmits unsuccessful frames.

15.3 ETHERNET

The most widely used high-speed LANs today are based on Ethernet and were developed by the IEEE 802.3 standards committee. A family of 100-Mbps LANs known as Fast Ethernet currently dominates the high-speed LAN market. More recent entries are Gigabit Ethernet and 10-Gbps Ethernet. Before looking at these high-speed LANs, we provide a brief overview of the original 10-Mbps Ethernet and introduce the concept of switched LANs.

Classical Ethernet

Ethernet was originally developed by Xerox and subsequently used as the basis for a family of LAN standards by the IEEE 802.3 committee. Classical Ethernet operates at 10 Mbps over a bus topology LAN using the CSMA/CD (carrier sense multiple access with collision detection) medium access control protocol. In this subsection, we introduce the concepts of bus LANs and CSMA/CD operation.

Bus Topology LAN In a bus topology LAN, all stations attach, through appropriate hardware interfacing known as a tap, directly to a linear transmission medium, or bus. Full-duplex operation between the station and the tap allows data to be transmitted onto the bus and received from the bus. A transmission from any station propagates the length of the medium in both directions and can be received by all other stations. At each end of the bus is a terminator, which absorbs any signal, removing it from the bus.

Two problems present themselves in this arrangement. First, because a transmission from any one station can be received by all other stations, there needs to be some way of indicating for whom the transmission is intended. Second, a mechanism is needed to regulate transmission. To see the reason for this, consider that if two stations on the bus attempt to transmit at the same time, their signals will overlap and become garbled. Or consider that one station decides to transmit continuously for a long period of time, blocking the access of other users.

To solve these problems, stations transmit data in small blocks, known as frames. Each frame consists of a portion of the data that a station wishes to transmit, plus a frame header that contains control information. Each station on the bus is assigned a unique address, or identifier, and the destination address for a frame is included in its header.

Figure 15.4 illustrates the scheme. In this example, station C wishes to transmit a frame of data to A. The frame header includes A's address. As the frame propagates along the bus, it passes B. B observes the address and ignores the frame. A, on the other hand, sees that the frame is addressed to itself and therefore copies the data from the frame as it goes by.

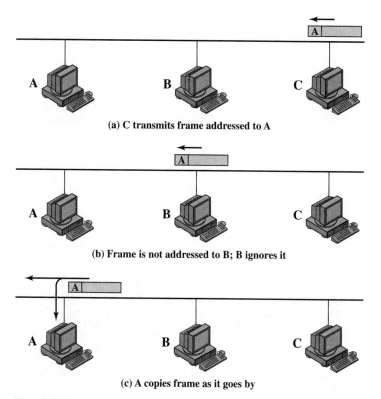

Figure 15.4   Frame Transmission on a Bus LAN

So the frame structure solves the first problem mentioned previously: It provides a mechanism for indicating the intended recipient of data. It also provides the basic tool for solving the second problem, the regulation of access. In particular, the stations take turns sending frames in some cooperative fashion, as explained in the next subsection.

CSMA/CD With CSMA/CD, a station wishing to transmit first listens to the medium to determine if another transmission is in progress (carrier sense). If the medium is idle, the station may transmit. It may happen that two or more stations attempt to transmit at about the same time. If this happens, there will be a **collision**; the data from both transmissions will be garbled and not received successfully. Thus, a procedure is needed that specifies what a station should do if the medium is found busy and what it should do if a collision occurs:

1. If the medium is idle, transmit; otherwise, go to step 2.
2. If the medium is busy, continue to listen until the channel is idle; then transmit immediately.
3. If a collision is detected during transmission, transmit a brief jamming signal to assure that all stations know that there has been a collision and then cease transmission.
4. After transmitting the jamming signal, wait a random amount of time, referred to as the **backoff**; then attempt to transmit again (repeat from step 1).

Figure 15.5 illustrates the technique. The upper part of the figure shows a bus LAN layout. The remainder of the figure depicts activity on the bus at four successive instants in time. At time t_0, station A begins transmitting a packet addressed to D. At t_1, both B and C are ready to transmit. B senses a transmission and so defers. C, however, is still unaware of A's transmission and begins its own transmission. When A's transmission reaches C, at t_2, C detects the collision and ceases transmission. The effect of the collision propagates back to A, where it is detected some time later, t_3, at which time A ceases transmission.

To maintain stability, the amount of delay employed in step 4 is determined by a technique known as **binary exponential backoff**. A station will attempt to transmit repeatedly in the face of repeated collisions. For the first 10 retransmission attempts, the mean value of the random delay is doubled. This mean value then remains the same for 6 additional attempts. After 16 unsuccessful attempts, the station gives up and reports an error. Thus, as congestion increases, stations back off by larger and larger amounts to reduce the probability of collision.

The advantage of CSMA/CD is its simplicity. It is easy to implement the logic required for this protocol. Furthermore, there is little to go wrong in the execution of the protocol. For example, if for some reason a station fails to detect a collision, the worst that can happen is that it continues to transmit its frame, wasting some time on the medium. Once the transmission is over, the algorithm continues to function as before.

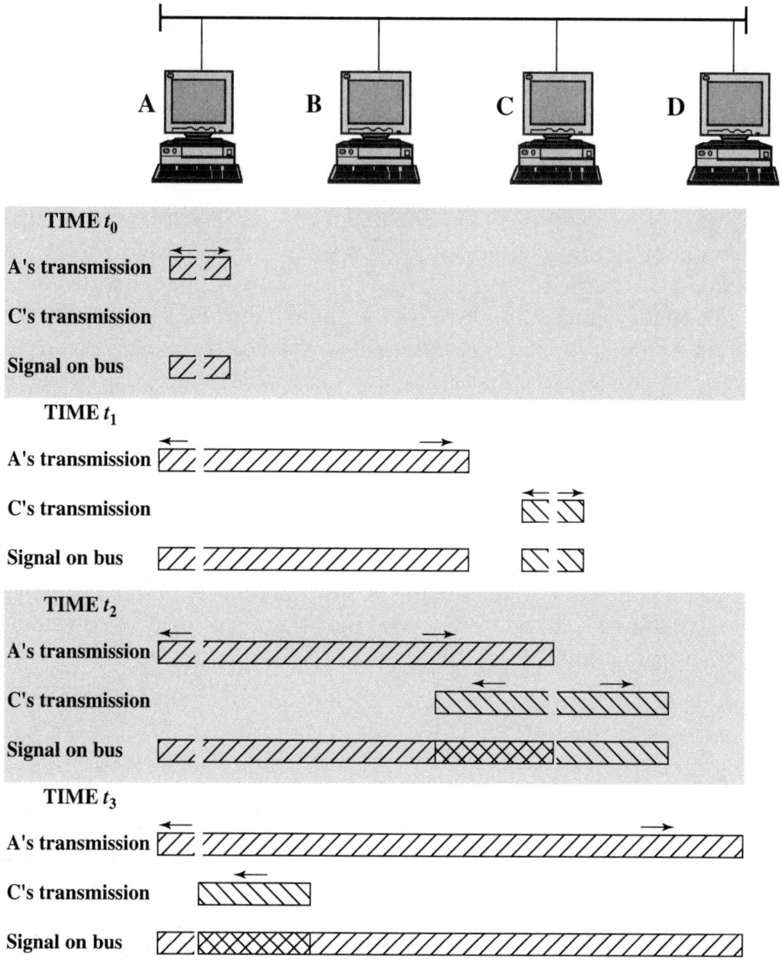

Figure 15.5 CSMA/CD Operation

MAC Frame Figure 15.6 depicts the frame format for the 802.3 protocol. It consists of the following fields:

- **Preamble:** A 7-octet pattern of alternating 0s and 1s used by the receiver to establish bit synchronization.

- **Start Frame Delimiter (SFD):** The sequence 10101011, which indicates the actual start of the frame and enables the receiver to locate the first bit of the rest of the frame.

- **Destination Address (DA):** Specifies the station(s) for which the frame is intended. It may be a unique physical address, a group address, or a global address.

- **Source Address (SA):** Specifies the station that sent the frame.

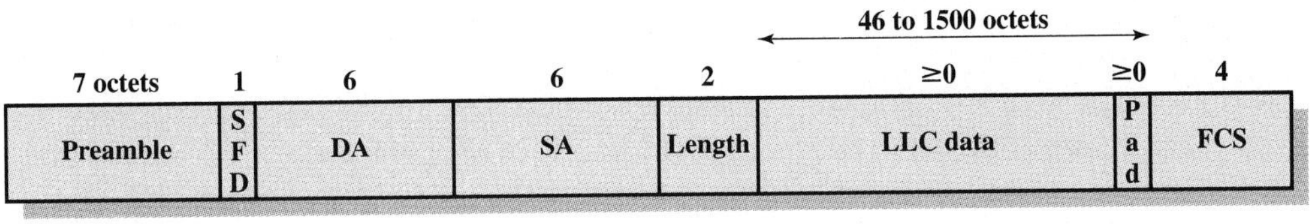

SFD = Start of frame delimiter
DA = Destination address
SA = Source address
FCS = Frame check sequence

Figure 15.6   IEEE 802.3 Frame Format

- **Length/Type:** Length of LLC data field in octets, or Ethernet Type field, depending on whether the frame conforms to the IEEE 802.3 standard or the earlier Ethernet specification. In either case, the maximum frame size, excluding the Preamble and SFD, is 1518 octets.

- **LLC Data:** Data unit supplied by LLC.

- **Pad:** Octets added to ensure that the frame is long enough for proper CD operation.

- **Frame Check Sequence (FCS):** A 32-bit cyclic redundancy check, based on all fields except preamble, SFD, and FCS.

IEEE 802.3 Medium Options at 10 Mbps

The IEEE 802.3 committee has defined a number of alternative physical configurations. This is both good and bad. On the good side, the standard has been responsive to evolving technology. On the bad side, the customer, not to mention the potential vendor, is faced with a bewildering array of options. However, the committee has been at pains to ensure that the various options can be easily integrated into a configuration that satisfies a variety of needs. Thus, the user who has a complex set of requirements may find the flexibility and variety of the 802.3 standard to be an asset.

To distinguish the various implementations that are available, the committee has developed a concise notation:

<data rate in Mbps> <signaling method>
<maximum segment length in hundreds of meters>

In this subsection, we consider the two most important options that operate at 10 Mbps, the rate of the original commercial Ethernet; higher-speed options are discussed in later subsections. The alternatives are as follows:

- 10BASE5
- 10BASE-T

Note that 10BASE-T does not quite follow the notation: "T" stands for twisted pair.

10BASE5 Medium Specification 10BASE5 is the original 802.3 medium specification and is based directly on Ethernet. 10BASE5 specifies the use of 50-ohm coaxial cable bus and uses Manchester digital signaling.[1] The maximum length of a cable segment is set at 500 meters. The length of the network can be extended by the use of repeaters. A repeater is transparent to the link level; as it does no buffering, it does not isolate one segment from another. So, for example, if two stations on different segments attempt to transmit at the same time, their transmissions will collide. To avoid looping, only one path of segments and repeaters is allowed between any two stations. The standard allows a maximum of four repeaters in the path between any two stations, extending the effective length of the medium to 2.5 km.

10BASE-T Medium Specification By sacrificing some distance, it is possible to develop a 10-Mbps LAN using the unshielded twisted pair medium. Such wire is often found prewired in office buildings as excess telephone cable and can be used for LANs. Such an approach is specified in the 10BASE-T specification. The 10BASE-T specification defines a star-shaped topology. A simple system consists of a number of stations connected to a central point, referred to as a multiport repeater, via two twisted pairs. The central point accepts input on any one line and repeats it on all of the other lines.

Stations attach to the multiport repeater via a point-to-point link. Ordinarily, the link consists of two unshielded twisted pairs. Because of the high data rate and the poor transmission qualities of unshielded twisted pairs, the length of a link is limited to 100 m. As an alternative, an optical fiber link may be used. In this case, the maximum length is 500 m.

In the simplest 10BASE-T arrangement, the central element of the star is an active element, referred to as the **hub**. Each station is connected to the hub by two twisted pairs (transmit and receive). The hub acts as a repeater: When a single station transmits, the hub repeats the signal on the outgoing line to each station. Note that although this scheme is physically a star, it is logically a bus: A transmission from any one station is received by all other stations, and if two stations transmit at the same time there will be a collision.

Multiple levels of hubs can be cascaded in a hierarchical configuration. Figure 15.7 illustrates a two-level configuration. There is one **header hub** (HHUB) and one or more **intermediate hubs** (IHUB). Each hub may have a mixture of stations and other hubs attached to it from below. This layout fits well with building wiring practices. Typically, there is a wiring closet on each floor of an office building, and a hub can be placed in each one. Each hub could service the stations on its floor.

15.4 BRIDGES, HUBS, AND SWITCHES

Before continuing our discussion of Ethernet, we need to take a detour and examine the concepts of bridges, hubs, and switches.

---

[1]This is a form of digital signaling that guarantees at least one signal transition (change of voltage level) during each bit time.

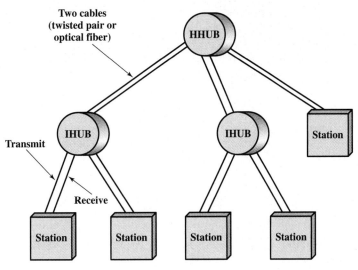

Figure 15.7 Two-Level Star Topology

Bridges

In virtually all cases, there is a need to expand beyond the confines of a single LAN, to provide interconnection to other LANs and to wide area networks. Two general approaches are used for this purpose: bridges and routers. The **bridge** is the simpler of the two devices and provides a means of interconnecting similar LANs. The router is a more general-purpose device, capable of interconnecting a variety of LANs and WANs.

The bridge is designed for use between local area networks (LANs) that use identical protocols for the physical and link layers (e.g., all conforming to IEEE 802.3). Because the devices all use the same protocols, the amount of processing required at the bridge is minimal. More sophisticated bridges are capable of mapping from one MAC format to another (e.g., to interconnect an Ethernet and a token ring LAN).

Because the bridge is used in a situation in which all the LANs have the same characteristics, the reader may ask, why not simply have one large LAN? Depending on circumstance, there are several reasons for the use of multiple LANs connected by bridges:

- **Reliability:** The danger in connecting all data processing devices in an organization to one network is that a fault on the network may disable communication for all devices. By using bridges, the network can be partitioned into self-contained units.

- **Performance:** In general, performance on a LAN declines with an increase in the number of devices or the length of the wire. A number of smaller LANs will often give improved performance if devices can be clustered so that intranetwork traffic significantly exceeds internetwork traffic.

- **Security:** The establishment of multiple LANs may improve security of communications. It is desirable to keep different types of traffic (e.g., accounting, personnel, strategic planning) that have different security needs on physically separate media. At the same time, the different types of users with different levels of security need to communicate through controlled and monitored mechanisms.

• **Geography:** Clearly, two separate LANs are needed to support devices clustered in two geographically distant locations. Even in the case of two buildings separated by a highway, it may be far easier to use a microwave bridge link than to attempt to string coaxial cable between the two buildings.

Figure 15.8 illustrates the action of a bridge connecting two LANs, A and B, using the same MAC protocol. In this example, a single bridge attaches to both LANs; frequently, the bridge function is performed by two "half-bridges," one on each LAN. The functions of the bridge are few and simple:

• Read all frames transmitted on A and accept those addressed to any station on B.
• Using the medium access control protocol for B, retransmit each frame on B.
• Do the same for B-to-A traffic.

Several design aspects of a bridge are worth highlighting:

• The bridge makes no modification to the content or format of the frames it receives, nor does it encapsulate them with an additional header. Each frame to be transferred is simply copied from one LAN and repeated with exactly the same bit pattern as the other LAN. Because the two LANs use the same LAN protocols, it is permissible to do this.
• The bridge should contain enough buffer space to meet peak demands. Over a short period of time, frames may arrive faster than they can be retransmitted.

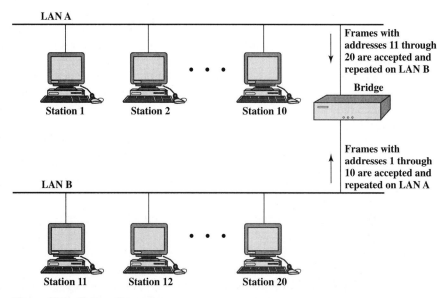

Figure 15.8 Bridge Operation

- The bridge must contain addressing and routing intelligence. At a minimum, the bridge must know which addresses are on each network to know which frames to pass. Further, there may be more than two LANs interconnected by a number of bridges. In that case, a frame may have to be routed through several bridges in its journey from source to destination.
- A bridge may connect more than two LANs.

In summary, the bridge provides an extension to the LAN that requires no modification to the communications software in the stations attached to the LANs. It appears to all stations on the two (or more) LANs that there is a single LAN on which each station has a unique address. The station uses that unique address and need not explicitly discriminate between stations on the same LAN and stations on other LANs; the bridge takes care of that.

Hubs and Switches

We have used the term *hub* in the context of the 10BASE-T standard, but this term is used to refer to a number of different types of devices. The most important distinction is between the shared-medium hub and the switched LAN hub, the latter usually referred to as a layer 2 switch.

To clarify the distinction between hubs and switches, Figure 15.9a shows a typical bus layout of a traditional 10-Mbps Ethernet. A bus is installed that is laid out so that all the devices to be attached are in reasonable proximity to a point on the bus. A transmission from any one station is propagated along the length of the bus and may be received by all other stations. In the figure, station B is transmitting. This transmission goes from B, across the lead from B to the bus, along the bus in both directions, and along the access lines of each of the other attached stations. In this configuration, all the stations must share the total capacity of the bus, which is 10 Mbps.

A shared-medium hub, such as specified by 10BASE-T, has a central hub, often in a building wiring closet. A star wiring arrangement is used to attach the stations to the hub. In this arrangement, a transmission from any one station is received by the hub and retransmitted on all of the outgoing lines. Therefore, to avoid collision, only one station can transmit at a time. Again, the total capacity of the LAN is the same as that of the access lines from each station, namely 10 Mbps. The shared-medium hub has several advantages over the simple bus arrangement. It exploits standard building wiring practices in the layout of cable. In addition, the hub can be configured to recognize a malfunctioning station that is jamming the network, and to cut that station out of the network. Figure 15.9b illustrates the operation of a shared-medium hub. Here again, station B is transmitting. This transmission goes from B, across the transmit line from B to the hub, and from the hub along the receive lines of each of the other attached stations.

We can achieve greater performance with a layer 2 switch. In this case, the central hub acts as a switch, similar to a packet switch. An incoming frame from a particular station is switched to the appropriate output line to be delivered to the intended destination. At the same time, other unused lines can be used for switching other traffic. Figure 15.9c shows an example in which B is transmitting a frame to A and at the same time C is transmitting a frame to D. So, in this example, the current

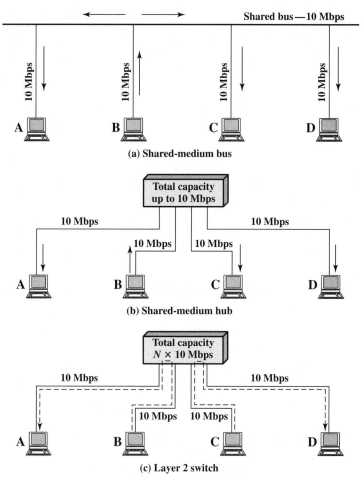

Figure 15.9 LAN Hubs and Switches

throughput on the LAN is 20 Mbps, although each individual device is limited to 10 Mbps. The switching hub has several attractive features:

1. No change is required to the software or hardware of the attached devices to convert a bus LAN or a hub LAN to a switched LAN. In the case of an Ethernet LAN, each attached device continues to use the Ethernet medium access control protocol to access the LAN. From the point of view of the attached devices, nothing has changed in the access logic.

2. Each attached device has a dedicated capacity equal to that of the entire original LAN, assuming that the layer 2 switch has sufficient capacity to keep up with all attached devices. For example, in Figure 15.9c, if the layer 2 switch can sustain a throughput of 20 Mbps, each attached device appears to have a dedicated capacity for either input or output of 10 Mbps.

3. The layer 2 switch scales easily. Additional devices can be attached to the layer 2 switch by increasing the capacity of the layer 2 switch correspondingly.

Two types of layer 2 switches are available as commercial products:

- **Store-and-forward switch:** The layer 2 switch accepts a frame on an input line, buffers it briefly, and then routes it to the appropriate output line.

- **Cut-through switch:** The layer 2 switch takes advantage of the fact that the destination address appears at the beginning of the MAC (medium access control) frame. The layer 2 switch begins repeating the incoming frame onto the appropriate output line as soon as the layer 2 switch recognizes the destination address.

The cut-through switch yields the highest possible throughput but at some risk of propagating bad frames, because the switch is not able to check the CRC prior to retransmission. The store-and-forward switch involves a delay between sender and receiver but boosts the overall integrity of the network.

A layer 2 switch can be viewed as a full-duplex version of the hub. It can also incorporate logic that allows it to function as a multiport bridge. [BREY99] lists the following differences between layer 2 switches and bridges:

- Bridge frame handling is done in software. A layer 2 switch performs the address recognition and frame forwarding functions in hardware.

- A bridge can typically only analyze and forward one frame at a time, whereas a layer 2 switch has multiple parallel data paths and can handle multiple frames at a time.

- A bridge uses store-and-forward operation. With a layer 2 switch, it is possible to have cut-through instead of store-and-forward operation.

Because a layer 2 switch has higher performance and can incorporate the functions of a bridge, the bridge has suffered commercially. New installations typically include layer 2 switches with bridge functionality rather than bridges.

Layer 3 Switches

Layer 2 switches provide increased performance to meet the needs of high-volume traffic generated by personal computers, workstations, and servers. However, as the number of devices in a building or complex of buildings grows, layer 2 switches reveal some inadequacies. Two problems in particular present themselves: broadcast overload and the lack of multiple links.

A set of devices and LANs connected by layer 2 switches is considered to have a flat address space. The term *flat* means that all users share a common MAC broadcast address. Thus, if any device issues a MAC frame with a broadcast address, that frame is to be delivered to all devices attached to the overall network connected by layer 2 switches and/or bridges. In a large network, frequent transmission of broadcast frames can create tremendous overhead. Worse, a malfunctioning device can create a *broadcast storm*, in which numerous broadcast frame clog the network and crowd out legitimate traffic.

A second performance-related problem with the use of bridges and/or layer 2 switches is that the current standards for bridge protocols dictate that there be no closed loops in the network. That is, there can only be one path between any two devices. Thus, it is impossible, in a standards-based implementation, to provide multiple paths through multiple switches between devices. This restriction limits both performance and reliability.

To overcome these problems, it seems logical to break up a large local network into a number of **subnetworks** connected by routers. A MAC broadcast frame is then limited to only the devices and switches contained in a single subnetwork. Furthermore, IP-based routers employ sophisticated routing algorithms that allow the use of multiple paths between subnetworks going through different routers.

However, the problem with using routers to overcome some of the inadequacies of bridges and layer 2 switches is that routers typically do all of the IP-level processing involved in the forwarding of IP traffic in software. High-speed LANs and high-performance layer 2 switches may pump millions of packets per second whereas a software-based router may only be able to handle well under a million packets per second. To accommodate such a load, a number of vendors have developed layer 3 switches, which implement the packet-forwarding logic of the router in hardware.

There are various layer 3 schemes on the market, but fundamentally they fall into two categories: packet by packet and flow based. The packet-by-packet switch operates in the identical fashion as a traditional router. Because the forwarding logic is in hardware, the packet-by-packet switch can achieve an order of magnitude increase in performance compared to the software-based router. A flow-based switch tries to enhance performance by identifying flows of IP packets that have the same source and destination. This can be done by observing ongoing traffic or by using a special flow label in the packet header (allowed in IPv6 but not IPv4; see Figure 2.13). Once a flow is identified, a predefined route can be established through the network to speed up the forwarding process. Again, huge performance increases over a pure software-based router are achieved.

Figure 15.10 is a typical example of the approach taken to local networking in an organization with a large number of PCs and workstations (thousands to tens of thousands). Desktop systems have links of 10 Mbps to 100 Mbps into a LAN controlled by a layer 2 switch. Wireless LAN connectivity is also likely to be available for mobile users. Layer 3 switches are at the local network's core, forming a local backbone. Typically, these switches are interconnected at 1 Gbps and connect to layer 2 switches at from 100 Mbps to 1 Gbps. Servers connect directly to layer 2 or layer 3 switches at 1 Gbps or possible 100 Mbps. A lower-cost software-based router provides WAN connection. The circles in the figure identify separate LAN subnetworks; a MAC broadcast frame is limited to its own subnetwork.

15.5 HIGH-SPEED ETHERNET

Fast Ethernet

Fast Ethernet refers to a set of specifications developed by the IEEE 802.3 committee to provide a low-cost, Ethernet-compatible LAN operating at 100 Mbps. The blanket designation for these standards is 100BASE-T. The committee defined a number of alternatives to be used with different transmission media.

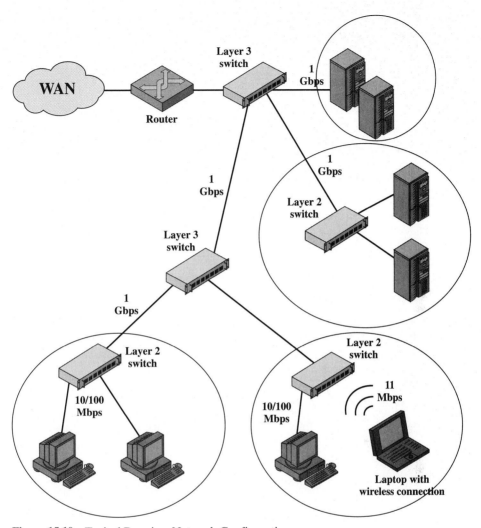

Figure 15.10   Typical Premises Network Configuration

Figure 15.11 shows the terminology used in labeling the specifications and indicates the media used. All of the 100BASE-T options use the IEEE 802.3 MAC protocol and frame format. 100BASE-X refers to a set of options that use two physical links between nodes; one for transmission and one for reception. 100BASE-TX makes use of shielded twisted pair (STP) or high-quality (Category 5) unshielded twisted pair (UTP). 100BASE-FX uses optical fiber. For all of these schemes the distance involved between hubs and stations is on the order of a maximum of 100 to 200 m.

In many buildings, any of the 100BASE-X options requires the installation of new cable. To minimize costs for buildings that do not have the required cable in place, 100BASE-T4 defines a lower-cost alternative that can use Category-3, voice

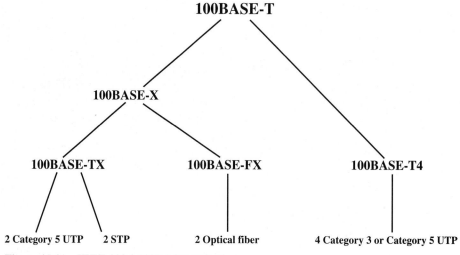

Figure 15.11   IEEE 802.3 100BASE-T Options

grade UTP in addition to the higher-quality Category 5 UTP.[2] To achieve the 100-Mbps data rate over lower-quality cable, 100BASE-T4 dictates the use of four twisted pair lines between nodes, with the data transmission making use of three pairs in one direction at a time.

For all the 100BASE-T options, the topology is similar to that of 10BASE-T, namely a star-wire topology.

100BASE-X For all of the transmission media specified under 100BASE-X, a unidirectional data rate of 100 Mbps is achieved by transmitting over a single link (single twisted pair, single optical fiber). For all these media, an efficient and effective signal encoding scheme is required. The one chosen is referred to as 4B/5B-NRZI. This encoding technique is more efficient than the Manchester technique used for 10-Mbps Ethernet and is therefore desirable at the higher data rate.

The 100BASE-X designation includes two physical medium specifications: one for twisted pair known as 100BASE-TX, and one for optical fiber, known as 100-BASE-FX. 100BASE-TX makes use of two pairs of twisted-pair cable, one pair used for transmission and one for reception. Both STP and Category 5 UTP are allowed. 100BASE-FX makes use of two optical fiber cables, one for transmission and one for reception.

100BASE-T4 100BASE-T4 is designed to produce a 100-Mbps data rate over lower-quality Category 3 cable, thus taking advantage of the large installed base of

---

[2]Category 3 twisted pair is standard telephone wire, which has limited data rate capability. Category 5 is intended to operate at much higher data rates. A key difference between Category 3 and Category 5 cable is the number of twists in the cable per unit distance. Category 5 is much more tightly twisted, typically 3 to 4 twists per inch compared to 3 to 4 twists per foot for Category 3. The tighter twisting is more expensive but provides much better performance than Category 3.

Category 3 cable in office buildings. The specification also indicates that the use of Category 5 cable is optional.

For 100BASE-T4 using voice-grade Category 3 cable, it is not reasonable to expect to achieve 100 Mbps on a single twisted pair. Instead, 100BASE-T4 specifies that the data stream to be transmitted is split up into three separate data streams, each with an effective data rate of $33\frac{1}{3}$ Mbps. Four twisted pairs are used. Data are transmitted using three pairs and received using three pairs. Thus, two of the pairs must be configured for bidirectional transmission.

Full-Duplex Operation A traditional Ethernet is half duplex: A station can either transmit or receive a frame, but it cannot do both simultaneously. With full-duplex operation, a station can transmit and receive simultaneously. If a 100-Mbps Ethernet ran in full-duplex mode, the theoretical transfer rate becomes 200 Mbps.

Several changes are needed to operate in full-duplex mode. The attached stations must have full-duplex rather than half-duplex adapter cards. The central point in the star wire cannot be a simple multiport repeater but rather must be a switching hub. In this case each station constitutes a separate collision domain. In fact, there are no collisions, and the CSMA/CD algorithm is no longer needed. However, the same 802.3 MAC frame format is used and the attached stations can continue to execute the CSMA/CD algorithm, even though no collisions can ever be detected.

Gigabit Ethernet

In late 1995, the IEEE 802.3 committee formed a High-Speed Study Group to investigate means for conveying packets in Ethernet format at speeds in the gigabit-per-second range. A set of 1000-Mbps standards have now been issued.

The strategy for Gigabit Ethernet is the same as that for Fast Ethernet. While defining a new medium and transmission specification, Gigabit Ethernet retains the CSMA/CD protocol and frame format of its 10-Mbps and 100-Mbps predecessors. It is compatible with 100BASE-T and 10BASE-T, preserving a smooth migration path. As more organizations move to 100BASE-T, putting huge traffic loads on backbone networks, demand for Gigabit Ethernet has intensified.

Figure 15.12 shows a typical application of Gigabit Ethernet. A 1-Gbps LAN switch provides backbone connectivity for central servers and high-speed workgroup switches. Each workgroup LAN switch supports both 1-Gbps links, to connect to the backbone LAN switch and to support high-performance workgroup servers, and 100-Mbps links, to support high-performance workstations, servers, and 100-Mbps LAN switches.

The current 1-Gbps specification for IEEE 802.3 includes the following physical layer alternatives (Figure 15.13):

- **1000BASE-LX:** This long-wavelength option supports duplex links of up to 550 m of 62.5-μm or 50-μm multimode fiber or up to 5 km of 10-μm single-mode fiber. Wavelengths are in the range of 1270 to 1355 nm.

- **1000BASE-SX:** This short-wavelength option supports duplex links of up to 275 m using 62.5-μm multimode or up to 550 m using 50-μm multimode fiber. Wavelengths are in the range of 770 to 860 nm.

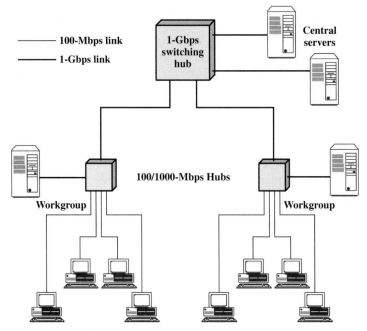

Figure 15.12   Example Gigabit Ethernet Configuration

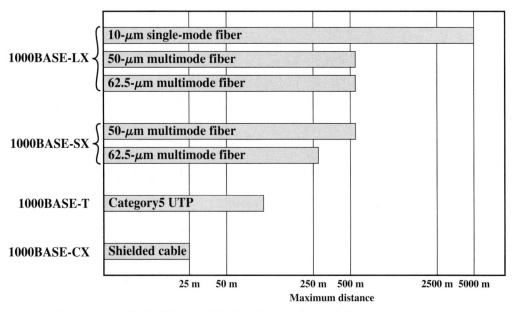

Figure 15.13   Gigabit Ethernet Medium Options (log scale)

- **1000BASE-CX:** This option supports 1-Gbps links among devices located within a single room or equipment rack, using copper jumpers (specialized shielded twisted pair cable that spans no more than 25 m). Each link is composed of a separate shielded twisted pair running in each direction.
- **1000BASE-T:** This option makes use of four pairs of Category 5 unshielded twisted pair to support devices over a range of up to 100 m.

10–Gbps Ethernet

With gigabit products still fairly new, attention has turned in the past several years to a 10-Gbps Ethernet capability. The principle driving requirement for 10 Gigabit Ethernet is the increase in Internet and intranet traffic. A number of factors contribute to the explosive growth in both Internet and intranet traffic:

- An increase in the number of network connections
- An increase in the connection speed of each end-station (e.g., 10 Mbps users moving to 100 Mbps, analog 56k users moving to DSL and cable modems)
- An increase in the deployment of bandwidth-intensive applications such as high-quality video
- An increase in Web hosting and application hosting traffic

Initially network managers will use 10-Gbps Ethernet to provide high-speed, local backbone interconnection between large-capacity switches. As the demand for bandwidth increases, 10-Gbps Ethernet will be deployed throughout the entire network and will include server farm, backbone, and campuswide connectivity. This technology enables Internet service providers (ISPs) and network service providers (NSPs) to create very high-speed links at a very low cost, between co-located, carrier-class switches and routers.

The technology also allows the construction of metropolitan area networks (MANs) and WANs that connect geographically dispersed LANs between campuses or points of presence (PoPs). Thus, Ethernet begins to compete with ATM and other wide area transmission/networking technologies. In most cases where the customer requirement is data and TCP/IP transport, 10-Gbps Ethernet provides substantial value over ATM transport for both network end users and service providers:

- No expensive, bandwidth-consuming conversion between Ethernet packets and ATM cells is required; the network is Ethernet, end to end.
- The combination of IP and Ethernet offers quality of service and traffic policing capabilities that approach those provided by ATM, so that advanced traffic engineering technologies are available to users and providers.
- A wide variety of standard optical interfaces (wavelengths and link distances) have been specified for 10 Gigabit Ethernet, optimizing its operation and cost for LAN, MAN, or WAN applications.

The goal for maximum link distances cover a range of applications: from 300 m to 40 km. The links operate in full-duplex mode only, using a variety of optical fiber physical media.

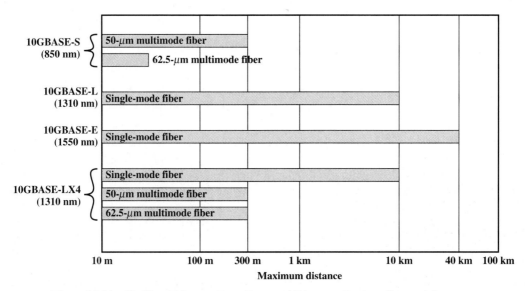

Figure 15.14   10-Gbps Ethernet Data Rate and Distance Options (log scale)

Four physical layer options are defined for 10-Gbps Ethernet (Figure 15.14):

- **10GBASE-S (short):** Designed for 850-nm transmission on multimode fiber. This medium can achieve distances up to 300 m.

- **10GBASE-L (long):** Designed for 1310-nm transmission on single-mode fiber. This medium can achieve distances up to 10 km.

- **10GBASE-E (extended):** Designed for 1550-nm transmission on single-mode fiber. This medium can achieve distances up to 40 km.

- **10GBASE-LX4:** Designed for 1310-nm transmission on single-mode or multimode fiber. This medium can achieve distances up to 10 km. This medium uses wavelength-division multiplexing (WDM) to multiplex the bit stream across four light waves.

15.6 WIRELESS LANS

Wireless LANs have come to occupy a significant niche in the local area network market. Increasingly, organizations are finding that wireless LANs are an indispensable adjunct to traditional wired LANs, to satisfy requirements for mobility, relocation, ad hoc networking, and coverage of locations difficult to wire.

As the name suggests, a wireless LAN is one that makes use of a wireless transmission medium. Until relatively recently, wireless LANs were little used. The reasons for this included high prices, low data rates, occupational safety concerns, and licensing requirements. As these problems have been addressed, the popularity of wireless LANs has grown rapidly.

Wireless LAN Applications

Early wireless LAN products, introduced in the late 1980s, were marketed as substi-
tutes for traditional wired LANs. A wireless LAN saves the cost of the installation
of LAN cabling and eases the task of relocation and other modifications to network
structure. However, this motivation for wireless LANs was overtaken by events.
First, as awareness of the need for LANs became greater, architects designed new
buildings to include extensive prewiring for data applications. Second, with advances in data transmission technology, there is an increasing reliance on twisted
pair cabling for LANs and, in particular, Category 3 and Category 5 unshielded
twisted pair. Most older buildings are already wired with an abundance of Category 3 cable, and many newer buildings are prewired with Category 5. Thus, the use of
a wireless LAN to replace wired LANs has not happened to any great extent.

However, in a number of environments, there is a role for the wireless LAN as
an alternative to a wired LAN. Examples include buildings with large open areas,
such as manufacturing plants, stock exchange trading floors, and warehouses; histor-
ical buildings with insufficient twisted pair and where drilling holes for new wiring is
prohibited; and small offices where installation and maintenance of wired LANs is
not economical. In all of these cases, a wireless LAN provides an effective and more
attractive alternative. In most of these cases, an organization will also have a wired
LAN to support servers and some stationary workstations. For example, a manufacturing facility typically has an office area that is separate from the factory floor but
that must be linked to it for networking purposes. Therefore, typically, a wireless
LAN will be linked into a wired LAN on the same premises. Thus, this application
area is referred to as LAN extension.

Figure 15.15 indicates a simple wireless LAN configuration that is typical of
many environments. There is a backbone wired LAN, such as Ethernet, that supports servers, workstations, and one or more bridges or routers to link with other
networks. In addition, there is a control module (CM) that acts as an interface to a
wireless LAN. The control module includes either bridge or router functionality to
link the wireless LAN to the backbone. It includes some sort of access control logic,
such as a polling or token-passing scheme, to regulate the access from the end systems. Note that some of the end systems are standalone devices, such as a workstation or a server. Hubs or other user modules (UMs) that control a number of
stations off a wired LAN may also be part of the wireless LAN configuration.

The configuration of Figure 15.15 can be referred to as a single-cell wireless
LAN; all of the wireless end systems are within range of a single control module.
Another common configuration is a multiple-cell wireless LAN. In this case, there
are multiple control modules interconnected by a wired LAN. Each control module
supports a number of wireless end systems within its transmission range. For example, with an infrared LAN, transmission is limited to a single room; therefore, one
cell is needed for each room in an office building that requires wireless support.

Another use of wireless LAN technology is to support nomadic access by providing a wireless link between a LAN hub and a mobile data terminal equipped with
an antenna, such as a laptop computer or notepad computer. One example of the
utility of such a connection is to enable an employee returning from a trip to transfer data from a personal portable computer to a server in the office. Nomadic access
is also useful in an extended environment such as a campus or a business operating

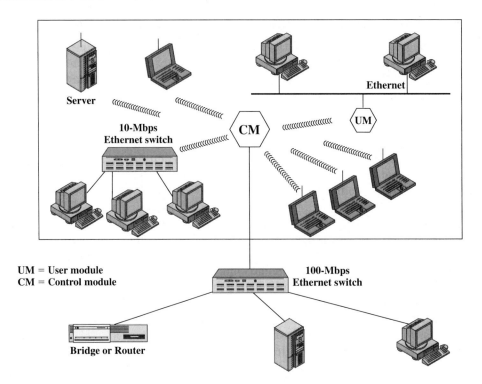

Figure 15.15 Example Single-Cell Wireless LAN Configuration

out of a cluster of buildings. In both of these cases, users may move around with their portable computers and may wish access to the servers on a wired LAN from various locations.

Another example of a wireless LAN application is an ad hoc network, which is a peer-to-peer network (no centralized server) set up temporarily to meet some immediate need. For example, a group of employees, each with a laptop or palmtop computer, may convene in a conference room for a business or classroom meeting. The employees link their computers in a temporary network just for the duration of the meeting.

Wireless LAN Requirements

A wireless LAN must meet the same sort of requirements typical of any LAN, including high capacity, ability to cover short distances, full connectivity among attached stations, and broadcast capability. In addition, there are a number of requirements specific to the wireless LAN environment. The following are among the most important requirements for wireless LANs:

- **Throughput:** The medium access control protocol should make as efficient use as possible of the wireless medium to maximize capacity.

- **Number of nodes:** Wireless LANs may need to support hundreds of nodes across multiple cells.

- **Connection to backbone LAN:** In most cases, interconnection with stations on a wired backbone LAN is required. For infrastructure wireless LANs, this is easily accomplished through the use of control modules that connect to both types of LANs. There may also need to be accommodation for mobile users and ad hoc wireless networks.

- **Service area:** A typical coverage area for a wireless LAN has a diameter of 100 to 300 m.

- **Battery power consumption:** Mobile workers use battery-powered workstations that need to have a long battery life when used with wireless adapters. This suggests that a MAC protocol that requires mobile nodes to monitor access points constantly or engage in frequent handshakes with a base station is inappropriate. Typical wireless LAN implementations have features to reduce power consumption while not using the network, such as a sleep mode.

- **Transmission robustness and security:** Unless properly designed, a wireless LAN may be interference prone and easily eavesdropped. The design of a wireless LAN must permit reliable transmission even in a noisy environment and should provide some level of security from eavesdropping.

- **Collocated network operation:** As wireless LANs become more popular, it is quite likely for two or more wireless LANs to operate in the same area or in some area where interference between the LANs is possible. Such interference may thwart the normal operation of a MAC algorithm and may allow unauthorized access to a particular LAN.

- **License-free operation:** Users would prefer to buy and operate wireless LAN products without having to secure a license for the frequency band used by the LAN.

- **Handoff/roaming:** The MAC protocol used in the wireless LAN should enable mobile stations to move from one cell to another.

- **Dynamic configuration:** The MAC addressing and network management aspects of the LAN should permit dynamic and automated addition, deletion, and relocation of end systems without disruption to other users.

A set of wireless LAN standards has been developed by the IEEE 802.11 committee. The remainder of this section provides an overview.

IEEE 802.11 Architecture

Figure 15.16 illustrates the model developed by the 802.11 working group. The smallest building block of a wireless LAN is a basic service set (BSS), which consists of some number of stations executing the same MAC protocol and competing for access to the same shared wireless medium. A BSS may be isolated or it may connect to a backbone distribution system (DS) through an access point (AP). The access point functions as a bridge. The MAC protocol may be fully distributed or controlled by a central coordination function housed in the access point. The BSS generally corresponds to what is referred to as a cell in the literature. The DS can be a switch, a wired network, or a wireless network.

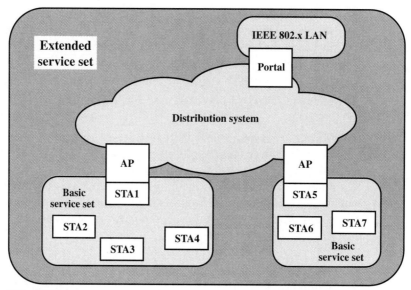

STA = Station
AP = Access point

Figure 15.16 IEEE 802.11 Architecture

The simplest configuration is shown in Figure 15.16, in which each station belongs to a single BSS; that is, each station is within wireless range only of other stations within the same BSS. It is also possible for two BSSs to overlap geographically, so that a single station could participate in more than one BSS. Further, the association between a station and a BSS is dynamic. Stations may turn off, come within range, and go out of range.

An extended service set (ESS) consists of two or more basic service sets interconnected by a distribution system. Typically, the distribution system is a wired backbone LAN, but can be any communications network. The extended service set appears as a single logical LAN to the logical link control (LLC) level.

Figure 15.16 indicates that an access point (AP) is implemented as part of a station; the AP is the logic within a station that provides access to the DS by providing DS services in addition to acting as a station. To integrate the IEEE 802.11 architecture with a traditional wired LAN, a portal is used. The portal logic is implemented in a device, such as a bridge or router, that is part of the wired LAN and that is attached to the DS.

IEEE 802.11 Services

IEEE 802.11 defines a number of services that need to be provided by the wireless LAN to provide functionality equivalent to that which is inherent to wired LANs. The most important services are as follows:

- **Association:** Establishes an initial association between a station and an access point. Before a station can transmit or receive frames on a wireless LAN, its identity and address must be known. For this purpose, a station must establish an association with an access point. The access point can then communicate this information to other access points to facilitate routing and delivery of addressed frames.

- **Reassociation:** Enables an established association to be transferred from one access point to another, allowing a mobile station to move.

- **Disassociation:** A notification from either a station or an access point that an existing association is terminated. A station should give this notification before leaving an area or shutting down. However, the MAC management facility protects itself against stations that disappear without notification.

- **Authentication:** Used to establish the identity of stations to each other. In a wired LAN, it is generally assumed that access to a physical connection conveys authority to connect to the LAN. This is not a valid assumption for a wireless LAN, in which connectivity is achieved simply by having an attached antenna that is properly tuned. The authentication service is used by stations to establish their identity with stations they wish to communicate with. The standard does not mandate any particular authentication scheme, which could range from relatively unsecure handshaking to public-key encryption schemes.

- **Privacy:** Used to prevent the contents of messages from being read by other than the intended recipient. The standard provides for the optional use of encryption to assure privacy.

IEEE 802.11 Medium Access Control

The IEEE 802.11 MAC layer covers three functional areas: reliable data delivery, access control, and security. In this section we examine reliable data delivery and access control; the security area is beyond our scope.

Reliable Data Delivery As with any wireless network, a wireless LAN using the IEEE 802.11 physical and MAC layers is subject to considerable unreliability. Noise, interference, and other propagation effects result in the loss of a significant number of frames. Even with error-correction codes, a number of MAC frames may not successfully be received. This situation can be dealt with by reliability mechanisms at a higher layer, such as TCP. However, timers used for retransmission at higher layers are typically on the order of seconds. It is therefore more efficient to deal with errors at the MAC level. For this purpose, IEEE 802.11 includes a frame exchange protocol. When a station receives a data frame from another station, it returns an acknowledgment (ACK) frame to the source station. This exchange is treated as an atomic unit, not to be interrupted by a transmission from any other station. If the source does not receive an ACK within a short period of time, either because its data frame was damaged or because the returning ACK was damaged, the source retransmits the frame.

Thus, the basic data transfer mechanism in IEEE 802.11 involves an exchange of two frames. To further enhance reliability, a four-frame exchange may be used. In this scheme, a source first issues a Request to Send (RTS) frame to the destination. The destination then responds with a Clear to Send (CTS). After receiving the CTS, the source transmits the data frame, and the destination responds with an ACK. The RTS alerts all stations that are within reception range of the source that an exchange is under way; these stations refrain from transmission in order to avoid a collision between two frames transmitted at the same time. Similarly, the CTS alerts all stations that are within reception range of the destination that an exchange is under way. The RTS/CTS portion of the exchange is a required function of the MAC but may be disabled.

Access Control The 802.11 working group considered two types of proposals for a MAC algorithm: distributed access protocols, which, like Ethernet, distribute the decision to transmit over all the nodes using a carrier-sense mechanism; and centralized access protocols, which involve regulation of transmission by a centralized decision maker. A distributed access protocol makes sense for an ad hoc network of peer workstations and may also be attractive in other wireless LAN configurations that consist primarily of bursty traffic. A centralized access protocol is natural for configurations in which a number of wireless stations are interconnected with each other and some sort of base station that attaches to a backbone wired LAN; it is especially useful if some of the data are time sensitive or high priority.

The end result for 802.11 is a MAC algorithm called DFWMAC (distributed foundation wireless MAC) that provides a distributed access control mechanism with an optional centralized control built on top of that. Figure 15.17 illustrates the architecture. The lower sublayer of the MAC layer is the distributed coordination function (DCF). DCF uses a Ethernet-style contention algorithm to provide access to all

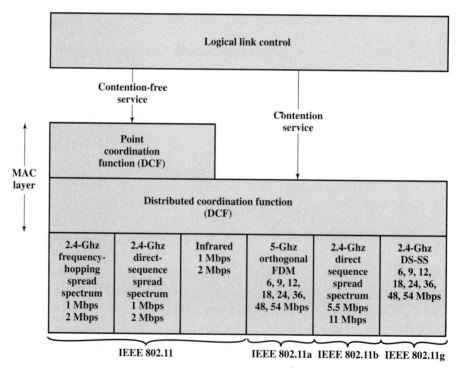

Figure 15.17 IEEE 802.11 Protocol Architecture

traffic. Ordinary asynchronous traffic directly uses DCF. The point coordination function (PCF) is a centralized MAC algorithm used to provide contention-free service; this is done by polling stations in turn. Higher-priority traffic, or traffic with greater timing requirements, makes use of the PCF. PCF is built on top of DCF and exploits features of DCF to assure access for its users. Finally, the logical link control (LLC) layer provides an interface to higher layers and performs basic link layer functions such as error control.

IEEE 802.11 Physical Layer

The physical layer for IEEE 802.11 has been issued in four stages; the first part was issued in 1997, two additional parts in 1999, and the most recent in 2002. The first part, simply called IEEE 802.11, includes the MAC layer and three physical layer specifications, two in the 2.4-GHz band and one in the infrared, all operating at 1 and 2 Mbps. IEEE 802.11a operates in the 5-GHz band at data rates up to 54 Mbps. IEEE 802.11b operates in the 2.4-Ghz band at 5.5 and 11 Mbps. IEEE 802.g extends IEEE 802.11b to higher data rates. We look at each of these in turn.

Three physical media are defined in the original 802.11 standard:

- Direct-sequence spread spectrum (DSSS) operating in the 2.4 GHz ISM band, at data rates of 1 Mbps and 2 Mbps
- Frequency-hopping spread spectrum (FHSS) operating in the 2.4 GHz ISM band, at data rates of 1 Mbps and 2 Mbps
- Infrared at 1 Mbps and 2 Mbps operating at a wavelength between 850 and 950 nm

The infrared option never gained market support. The other two schemes use spread spectrum approaches. In essence, spread spectrum involves the use of a much wider bandwidth than is actually necessary to support a given data rate. The result of using the wider bandwidth is to minimize interference and drastically reduce the error rate. In the case of FHSS, spread spectrum is achieved by frequently jumping from one carrier frequency to another; thus, if there is interference or performance degradation at a given frequency, it only affects a small fraction of the transmission. DSSS effectively increases the data rate of a signal by mapping each data bit into a string of bits, with one string used for binary 1 and another used for binary 0. The higher data rate uses a greater bandwidth. The effect is to spread each bit out over time, which minimizes the effects of interference and degradation. FHSS, which is simpler, was employed in most early 802.11 networks. Products using DSSS, which is more effective in the 802.11 scheme, followed. However, all of the original 802.11 products were of limited utility because of the low data rates.

IEEE 802.11b is an extension of the IEEE 802.11 DSSS scheme, providing data rates of 5.5 and 11 Mbps. A higher data rate is achieved by using a more complex modulation technique. The 802.11b specification quickly led to product offerings, including chipsets, PC cards, access points, and systems. Apple Computer was the first company to offer 802.11b products, with its iBook portable computer using the AirPort wireless network option. Other companies, including Cisco, 3Com, and Dell, have followed. Although these new products are all based on the same standard, there is always a concern whether products from different vendors will successfully interoperate. To meet this concern, the Wireless Ethernet Compatibility Alliance (WECA) created a test suite to certify interoperability for 802.11b products. Interoperability tests have been going on since last year, and a number of products have achieved certification.

One other concern for both the original 802.11 and the 802.11b products is interference with other systems that operate in the 2.4-GHz band, such as Bluetooth, HomeRF, and many other devices that use the same portion of the spectrum (including baby monitors and garage door openers). A coexistence study group (IEEE 802.15) is examining this issue, and so far the prospects are encouraging.

Although 802.11b is achieving a certain level of success, its limited data rate results in limited appeal. To meet the needs for a truly high-speed LAN, IEEE 802.11a has been developed. The IEEE 802.11a specification makes use of the 5-GHz band. Unlike the 2.4-GHz specifications, IEEE 802.11 does not use a spread spectrum scheme but rather uses orthogonal frequency division multiplexing (OFDM). OFDM, also called multicarrier modulation, uses multiple carrier signals (up to 52) at different frequencies, sending some of the bits on each channel. The possible data rates for IEEE 802.11a are 6, 9, 12, 18, 24, 36, 48, and 54 Mbps. First-generation 802.11b products should appear this year, with WECA interoperability and compliance testing also beginning this year.

IEEE 802.11g is a higher-speed extension to IEEE 802.11b. This scheme combines a variety of physical layer encoding techniques used in 802.11a and 802.11b to provide service at a variety of data rates.

15.7 RECOMMENDED READING AND WEB SITES

[STAL00] covers in greater detail all of the LAN systems discussed in this chapter.

[SPUR00] provides a concise but thorough overview of all of the 10-Mbps through 1-Gbps 802.3 systems, including configuration guidelines for a single segment of each media type, as well as guidelines for building multisegment Ethernets using a variety of media types. Two excellent treatments of both 100-Mbps and Gigabit Ethernet are [SEIF98] and [KADA98]. A good survey article on Gigabit Ethernet is [FRAZ99]. [10GE02] is a white paper providing a useful introduction to 10-Gbps Ethernet.

[OHAR99] is an excellent technical treatment of IEEE 802.11. Another good treatment is [LARO02]. [GEIE99] also provides detailed coverage of the IEEE 802.11 standards, and numerous case studies. [CROW97] is a good survey article on the 802.11 standards. Neither of the last two references covers IEEE 802.11a and IEEE 802.11b. [GEIE01] has a good discussion of IEEE 802.11a. [SHOE02] provides an overview of IEEE 802.11b.

10GE02 10 Gigabit Ethernet Alliance. *10 Gigabit Ethernet Technology Overview.* White paper, May 2002.

CROW97 Crow, B., et al., "IEEE 802.11 Wireless Local Area Networks." *IEEE Communications Magazine*, September 1997.

FRAZ99 Frazier, H., and Johnson, H. "Gigabit Ethernet: From 100 to 1,000 Mbps." *IEEE Internet Computing*, January/February 1999.

GEIE99 Geier, J. *Wireless LANs*. New York: Macmillan Technical Publishing, 1999.

GEIE01 Geier, J. "Enabling Fast Wireless Networks with OFDM." *Communications System Design*, February 2001. (www.csdmag.com)

KADA98 Kadambi, J.; Crayford, I.; and Kalkunte, M. *Gigabit Ethernet*. Upper Saddle River, NJ: Prentice Hall, 1998.

LARO02 LaRocca, J., and LaRocca, R. *802.11 Demystified*. New York: McGraw-Hill, 2002.

OHAR99 Ohara, B., and Petrick, A. *IEEE 802.11 Handbook: A Designer's Companion*. New York: IEEE Press, 1999.

SEIF98 Seifert, R. *Gigabit Ethernet*. Reading, MA: Addison-Wesley, 1998.

SHOE02 Shoemake, M. "IEEE 802.11g Jells as Applications Mount." *Communications System Design*, April 2002. www.commsdesign.com.

SPUR00 Spurgeon, C. *Ethernet: The Definitive Guide*. Cambridge, MA: O'Reilly and Associates, 2000.

STAL00 Stallings, W. *Local and Metropolitan Area Networks, 6th ed.* Upper Saddle River, NJ: Prentice Hall, 2000.

Useful Web Sites:

- **IEEE 802 LAN/MAN Standards Committee:** Status and documents for all of the working groups.
- **Interoperability Lab:** University of New Hampshire site for equipment testing for high-speed LANs.
- **Charles Spurgeon's Ethernet Web Site:** Provides extensive information about Ethernet, including links and documents.
- **10 Gigabit Ethernet Alliance:** This group promotes the 10-Gbps Ethernet standard.
- **Wireless LAN Alliance:** Gives an introduction to the technology, including a discussion of implementation considerations and case studies from users. Links to related sites.
- **The IEEE 802.11 Wireless LAN Working Group:** Contains working group documents plus discussion archives.
- **Wi-Fi Alliance:** An industry group promoting the interoperabiltiy of 802.11 products with each other and with Ethernet.

15.8 KEY TERMS, REVIEW QUESTIONS, AND PROBLEMS

Key Terms

backoff	Ethernet	logical link control (LLC)
binary exponential backoff	frame	medium access control
bridge	hub	(MAC)
bus topology	layer 2 switch	store-and-forward switch
collision	layer 3 switch	switch
cut-through switch	local area network (LAN)	wireless LAN

Review Questions

15.1 List and briefly define the services provided by LLC.

15.2 List and briefly define the types of operation provided by the LLC protocol.

15.3 List some basic functions performed at the MAC layer.

15.4 What is CSMA/CD?

15.5 Explain binary exponential backoff.

15.6 What are the transmission medium options for Fast Ethernet?

15.7 How does Fast Ethernet differ from 10BASE-T, other than the data rate?

15.8 List and briefly define four application areas for wireless LANs.

15.9 List and briefly define key requirements for wireless LANs.

15.10 What is the difference between a single-cell and a multiple-cell wireless LAN?

15.11 List and briefly define IEEE 802.11 services.

Problems

15.1 Consider a bus LAN with a number of equally spaced stations with a data rate of 10 Mbps and a bus length of 1 km.

    a. What is the mean time to send a frame of 1000 bits to another station, measured from the beginning of transmission to the end of reception? Assume a propagation speed of 200 m/μs.

    b. If two stations begin to transmit at exactly the same time, their packets will interfere with each other. If each transmitting station monitors the bus during transmission, how long before it notices an interference, in second? In bit times?

15.2 Repeat Problem 15.1 for a data rate of 100 Mbps.

15.3 A disadvantage of the contention approach for LANs is the capacity wasted due to multiple stations attempting to access the channel at the same time. Suppose that time is divided into discrete slots, with each of N stations attempting to transmit with probability p during each slot. What fraction of slots are wasted due to multiple simultaneous transmission attempts?

15.4 A simple medium access control protocol would be to use a fixed assignment time division multiplexing (TDM) scheme. Each station is assigned one time slot per cycle for transmission. For a bus LAN, assume that the length of each slot is the time to transmit 100 bits plus the end-to-end propagation delay. Stations monitor all time slots for reception. Assume a propagation time of 2×10^8 m/s. What are the limitations, in terms of number of stations and throughput per station, for a 1-km, 10-Mbps LAN bus?

15.5 The binary exponential backoff algorithm is defined by IEEE 802 as follows:

> The delay is an integral multiple of slot time. The number of slot times to delay before the nth retransmission attempt is chosen as a uniformly distributed random integer r in the range $0 \le r < 2^K$, where $K = \min(n, 10)$.

Slot time is, roughly, twice the round-trip propagation delay. Assume that two stations always have a frame to send. After a collision, what is the mean number of retransmission attempts before one station successfully retransmits? What is the answer if three stations always have frames to send?

PART SEVEN

Management Topics

As the networks used in an organization and the distributed applications they support grow in scale and complexity, management issues become increasingly difficult and important. In this final part, we look at the issues involved in including the Internet in the corporate computing environment and the operational management of computer networks.

ROAD MAP FOR PART SEVEN

Chapter 16 Network Security

Network security has become increasingly important with the growth in the number and importance of networks. Chapter 16 provides a survey of security techniques and services. The chapter begins with a look at encryption techniques for ensuring confidentiality, which include the use of conventional and public-key encryption. Then the area of authentication and digital signatures is explored. The two most important encryption algorithms, AES and RSA, are examined, as well as SHA-1, a one-way hash function important in a number of security applications. Chapter 16 also discusses SSL and the set of IP security standards.

Chapter 17 Network Management

A vital element for any business network is network management. Chapter 17 lays out the requirements for network management and then looks at the key elements of network management systems. The important Simple Network Management Protocol (SNMP) is examined in detail.

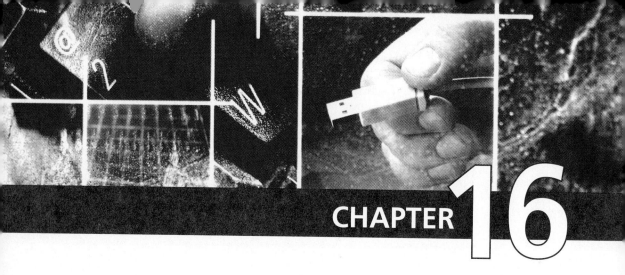

NETWORK SECURITY

To guard against the baneful influence exerted by strangers is therefore an elementary dictate of savage prudence. Hence before strangers are allowed to enter a district, or at least before they are permitted to mingle freely with the inhabitants, certain ceremonies are often performed by the natives of the country for the purpose of disarming the strangers of their magical powers, or of disinfecting, so to speak, the tainted atmosphere by which they are supposed to be surrounded.

            —*The Golden Bough*,
            Sir James George Frazer

KEY POINTS

- Network security threats fall into two categories. **Passive threats**, sometimes referred to as eavesdropping, involve attempts by an attacker to obtain information relating to a communication. **Active threats** involve some modification of the transmitted data or the creation of false transmissions.

- By far the most important automated tool for network and communications security is **encryption**. With **symmetric encryption**, two parties share a single encryption/decryption key. The principal challenge with symmetric encryption is the distribution and protection of the keys. A **public-key encryption** scheme involves two keys, one for encryption and a paired key for decryption. The party that generated the key pair keeps one of the keys private and makes the other key public.

- Symmetric encryption and public-key encryption are often combined in secure networking applications. Symmetric encryption is used to encrypt transmitted data, using a one-time or short-term session key. The session key can be distributed by a trusted key distribution center or transmitted in encrypted form using public-key encryption. Public-key encryption is also used to create digital signatures, which can authenticate the source of transmitted messages.

547

- The Secure Sockets Layer (SSL) and the follow-on Internet standard known as Transport Layer Security (TLS) provide security services for Web transactions.
- A security enhancement used with both IPv4 and IPv6, called IPSec, provides both confidentiality and authentication mechanisms.

The requirements of **information security** within an organization have undergone two major changes in the last several decades. Before the widespread use of data processing equipment, the security of information felt to be valuable to an organization was provided primarily by physical and administrative means. An example of the former is the use of rugged filing cabinets with a combination lock for storing sensitive documents. An example of the latter is personnel screening procedures used during the hiring process.

With the introduction of the computer, the need for automated tools for protecting files and other information stored on the computer became evident. This is especially the case for a shared system, such as a time-sharing system, and the need is even more acute for systems that can be accessed over a public telephone or data network. The generic name for the collection of tools designed to protect data and to thwart hackers is **computer security**. Although this is an important topic, it is beyond the scope of this chapter.

The second major change that affected security is the introduction of distributed systems and the use of networks and communications facilities for carrying data between terminal user and computer and between computer and computer. **Network security** measures are needed to protect data during their transmission and to guarantee that data transmissions are authentic.

The essential technology underlying virtually all automated network and computer security applications is encryption. Two fundamental approaches are in use: symmetric encryption and public-key encryption, also known as asymmetric encryption. As we look at the various approaches to network security, these two types of encryption will be explored.

This chapter begins with an overview of the requirements for network security. Next, we look at symmetric encryption and its use to provide confidentiality. This is followed by a discussion of message authentication. We then look at the use of public-key encryption and digital signatures. The chapter closes with an examination of security features in SSL and IPSec.

16.1 SECURITY REQUIREMENTS AND ATTACKS

To understand the types of threats to security that exist, we need to have a definition of security requirements. Computer and network security address four requirements:

- **Confidentiality:** Requires that data only be accessible by authorized parties. This type of access includes printing, displaying, and other forms of disclosure, including simply revealing the existence of an object.

- **Integrity:** Requires that data can be modified only by authorized parties. Modification includes writing, changing, changing status, deleting, and creating.
- **Availability:** Requires that data are available to authorized parties.
- **Authenticity:** Requires that a host or service be able to verify the identity of a user.

A useful means of classifying security attacks (RFC 2828) is in terms of *passive attacks* and *active attacks*. A passive attack attempts to learn or make use of information from the system but does not affect system resources. An active attack attempts to alter system resources or affect their operation.

Passive Attacks

Passive attacks are in the nature of eavesdropping on, or monitoring of, transmissions. The goal of the opponent is to obtain information that is being transmitted. Two types of passive attacks are release of message contents and traffic analysis.

The **release of message contents** is easily understood. A telephone conversation, an electronic mail message, or a transferred file may contain sensitive or confidential information. We would like to prevent an opponent from learning the contents of these transmissions.

A second type of passive attack, **traffic analysis**, is subtler. Suppose that we had a way of masking the contents of messages or other information traffic so that opponents, even if they captured the message, could not extract the information from the message. The common technique for masking contents is encryption. Even with encryption protection in place, an opponent might still be able to observe the pattern of these messages. The opponent could determine the location and identity of communicating hosts and could observe the frequency and length of messages being exchanged. This information might be useful in guessing the nature of the communication that was taking place.

Passive attacks are very difficult to detect because they do not involve any alteration of the data. Typically, the message traffic is sent and received in an apparently normal fashion and neither the sender nor receiver is aware that a third party has read the messages or observed the traffic pattern. However, it is feasible to prevent the success of these attacks, usually by means of encryption. Thus, the emphasis in dealing with passive attacks is on prevention rather than detection.

Active Attacks

Active attacks involve some modification of the data stream or the creation of a false stream and can be subdivided into four categories: masquerade, replay, modification of messages, and denial of service.

A **masquerade** takes place when one entity pretends to be a different entity. A masquerade attack usually includes one of the other forms of active attack. For example, authentication sequences can be captured and replayed after a valid authentication sequence has taken place, thus enabling an authorized entity with few privileges to obtain extra privileges by impersonating an entity that has those privileges.

Replay involves the passive capture of a data unit and its subsequent retransmission to produce an unauthorized effect.

Modification of messages simply means that some portion of a legitimate message is altered, or that messages are delayed or reordered, to produce an unauthorized effect. For example, a message meaning "Allow John Smith to read confidential file *accounts*" is modified to mean "Allow Fred Brown to read confidential file *accounts.*"

The **denial of service** prevents or inhibits the normal use or management of communications facilities. This attack may have a specific target; for example, an entity may suppress all messages directed to a particular destination (e.g., the security audit service). Another form of service denial is the disruption of an entire network or a server, either by disabling the network server, or by overloading it with messages so as to degrade performance.

Active attacks present the opposite characteristics of passive attacks. Whereas passive attacks are difficult to detect, measures are available to prevent their success. On the other hand, it is quite difficult to prevent active attacks absolutely, because to do so would require physical protection of all communications facilities and paths at all times. Instead, the goal is to detect them and to recover from any disruption or delays caused by them. Because the detection has a deterrent effect, it may also contribute to prevention.

16.2 CONFIDENTIALITY WITH SYMMETRIC ENCRYPTION

The universal technique for providing confidentiality for transmitted data is symmetric encryption. This section looks first at the basic concept of symmetric encryption, followed by a discussion of the two most important symmetric encryption algorithms: the Data Encryption Standard (DES) and the Advanced Encryption Standard (AES). We then examine the application of symmetric encryption to achieve confidentiality.

Symmetric Encryption

Symmetric encryption, also referred to as conventional encryption or single-key encryption, was the only type of encryption in use prior to the introduction of public-key encryption in the late 1970s. Countless individuals and groups, from Julius Caesar to the German U-boat force to present-day diplomatic, military, and commercial users, have used symmetric encryption for secret communication. It remains by far the more widely used of the two types of encryption.

A symmetric encryption scheme has five ingredients (Figure 16.1):

- **Plaintext:** This is the original message or data that is fed into the algorithm as input.

- **Encryption algorithm:** The encryption algorithm performs various substitutions and transformations on the plaintext.

- **Secret key:** The secret key is also input to the encryption algorithm. The exact substitutions and transformations performed by the algorithm depend on the key.

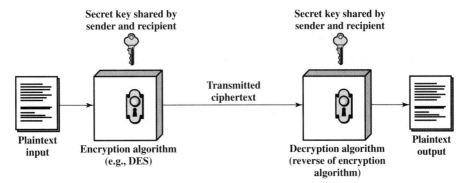

Figure 16.1 Simplified Model of Symmetric Encryption

- **Ciphertext:** This is the scrambled message produced as output. It depends on the plaintext and the secret key. For a given message, two different keys will produce two different ciphertexts.

- **Decryption algorithm:** This is essentially the encryption algorithm run in reverse. It takes the ciphertext and the secret key and produces the original plaintext.

There are two requirements for secure use of symmetric encryption:

1. We need a strong encryption algorithm. At a minimum, we would like the algorithm to be such that an opponent who knows the algorithm and has access to one or more ciphertexts would be unable to decipher the ciphertext or figure out the key. This requirement is usually stated in a stronger form: The opponent should be unable to decrypt ciphertext or discover the key even if he or she is in possession of a number of ciphertexts together with the plaintext that produced each ciphertext.

2. Sender and receiver must have obtained copies of the secret key in a secure fashion and must keep the key secure. If someone can discover the key and knows the algorithm, all communication using this key is readable.

There are two general approaches to attacking a symmetric encryption scheme. The first attack is known as **cryptanalysis**. Cryptanalytic attacks rely on the nature of the algorithm plus perhaps some knowledge of the general characteristics of the plaintext or even some sample plaintext-ciphertext pairs. This type of attack exploits the characteristics of the algorithm to attempt to deduce a specific plaintext or to deduce the key being used. If the attack succeeds in deducing the key, the effect is catastrophic: All future and past messages encrypted with that key are compromised.

The second method, known as the **brute-force** attack, is to try every possible key on a piece of ciphertext until an intelligible translation into plaintext is obtained. On average, half of all possible keys must be tried to achieve success. Table 16.1 shows how much time is involved for various key sizes. The table shows results for each key size, assuming that it takes 1 μs to perform a single decryption, a reasonable order of magnitude for today's computers. With the use of massively parallel organizations of microprocessors, it may be possible to achieve processing rates many

Table 16.1   Average Time Required for Exhaustive Key Search

Key Size (bits)	Number of Alternative Keys	Time Required at 1 Encryption/μs	Time Required at 10^6 Encryptions/μs
32	$2^{32} = 4.3 \times 10^9$	$2^{31}\ \mu s = 35.8$ minutes	2.15 milliseconds
56	$2^{56} = 7.2 \times 10^{16}$	$2^{55}\ \mu s = 1142$ years	10.01 hours
128	$2^{128} = 3.4 \times 10^{38}$	$2^{127}\ \mu s = 5.4 \times 10^{24}$ years	5.4×10^{18} years
168	$2^{168} = 3.7 \times 10^{50}$	$2^{167}\ \mu s = 5.9 \times 10^{36}$ years	5.9×10^{30} years

orders of magnitude greater. The final column of the table considers the results for a system that can process 1 million keys per microsecond. As one can see, at this performance level, a 56-bit key can no longer be considered computationally secure.

Encryption Algorithms

The most commonly used symmetric encryption algorithms are block ciphers. A block cipher processes the plaintext input in fixed-size blocks and produces a block of ciphertext of equal size for each plaintext block. The two most important symmetric algorithms, both of which are block ciphers, are the Data Encryption Standard (DES) and the Advanced Encryption Standard (AES).

Data Encryption Standard   DES has been the dominant encryption algorithm since its introduction in 1977. However, because DES uses only a 56-bit key, it was only a matter of time before computer processing speed made DES obsolete. In 1998, the Electronic Frontier Foundation (EFF) announced that it had broken a DES challenge using a special-purpose "DES cracker" machine that was built for less than $250,000. The attack took less than three days. The EFF has published a detailed description of the machine, enabling others to build their own cracker [EFF98]. And, of course, hardware prices will continue to drop as speeds increase, making DES worthless.

The life of DES was extended by the use of triple DES (3DES), which involves repeating the basic DES algorithm three times, using either two or three unique keys, for a key size of 112 or 168 bits.

The principal drawback of 3DES is that the algorithm is relatively sluggish in software. A secondary drawback is that both DES and 3DES use a 64-bit block size. For reasons of both efficiency and security, a larger block size is desirable.

Advanced Encryption Standard   Because of these drawbacks, 3DES is not a reasonable candidate for long-term use. As a replacement, the National Institute of Standards and Technology (NIST) in 1997 issued a call for proposals for a new Advanced Encryption Standard (AES), which should have a security strength equal to or better than 3DES and significantly improved efficiency. In addition to these general requirements, NIST specified that AES must be a symmetric block cipher with a block length of 128 bits and support for key lengths of 128, 192, and 256 bits. Evaluation criteria include security, computational efficiency, memory requirements, hardware and software suitability, and flexibility. In 2001, AES was issued as a federal information processing standard (FIPS 197).

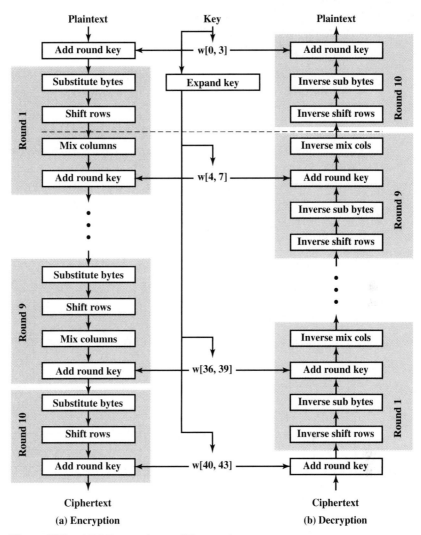

Figure 16.2 AES Encryption and Decryption

In the description of this section, we assume a key length of 128 bits, which is likely to be the one most commonly implemented.

Figure 16.2 shows the overall structure of AES. The input to the encryption and decryption algorithms is a single 128-bit block. In FIPS 197, this block is depicted as a square matrix of bytes. This block is copied into the **State** array, which is modified at each stage of encryption or decryption. After the final stage, **State** is copied to an output matrix. Similarly, the 128-bit key is depicted as a square matrix of bytes. This key is then expanded into an array of key schedule words; each word is four bytes and the total key schedule is 44 words for the 128-bit key. The ordering of bytes within a matrix is by column. So, for example, the first four bytes of a 128-bit plaintext input to the encryption cipher occupy the first column of the **in** matrix, the second four bytes occupy the second column, and so on. Similarly, the first four bytes of the expanded key, which form a word, occupy the first column of the **w** matrix.

The following comments give some insight into AES:

1. The key that is provided as input is expanded into an array of forty-four 32-bit words, $\mathbf{w}[i]$. Four distinct words (128 bits) serve as a round key for each round.
2. Four different stages are used, one of permutation and three of substitution:
    *   **Substitute bytes:** Uses a table, referred to as an S-box,[1] to perform a byte-by-byte substitution of the block
    *   **Shift rows:** A simple permutation that is performed row by row
    *   **Mix columns:** A substitution that alters each byte in a column as a function of all of the bytes in the column
    *   **Add round key:** A simple bitwise XOR of the current block with a portion of the expanded key
3. The structure is quite simple. For both encryption and decryption, the cipher begins with an Add Round Key stage, followed by nine rounds that each include all four stages, followed by a tenth round of three stages. Figure 16.3 depicts the structure of a full encryption round.

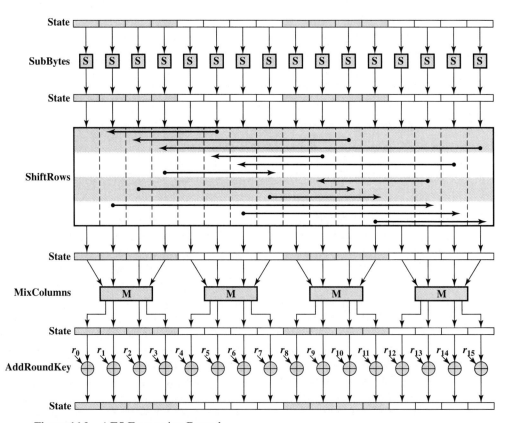

Figure 16.3 AES Encryption Round

---

[1]The term *S-box*, or substitution box, is commonly used in the description of symmetric ciphers to refer to a table used for a table-lookup type of substitution mechanism.

4. Only the Add Round Key stage makes use of the key. For this reason, the cipher begins and ends with an Add Round Key stage. Any other stage, applied at the beginning or end, is reversible without knowledge of the key and so would add no security.

5. The Add Round Key stage by itself would not be formidable. The other three stages together scramble the bits, but by themselves would provide no security because they do not use the key. We can view the cipher as alternating operations of XOR encryption (Add Round Key) of a block, followed by scrambling of the block (the other three stages), followed by XOR encryption, and so on. This scheme is both efficient and highly secure.

6. Each stage is easily reversible. For the Substitute Byte, Shift Row, and Mix Columns stages, an inverse function is used in the decryption algorithm. For the Add Round Key stage, the inverse is achieved by XORing the same round key to the block, using the result that $A \oplus A \oplus B = B$.

7. As with most block ciphers, the decryption algorithm makes use of the expanded key in reverse order. However, the decryption algorithm is not identical to the encryption algorithm. This is a consequence of the particular structure of AES.

8. Once it is established that all four stages are reversible, it is easy to verify that decryption does recover the plaintext. Figure 16.2 lays out encryption and decryption going in opposite vertical directions. At each horizontal point (e.g., the dashed line in the figure), **State** is the same for both encryption and decryption.

9. The final round of both encryption and decryption consists of only three stages. Again, this is a consequence of the particular structure of AES and is required to make the cipher reversible.

Location of Encryption Devices

The most powerful, and most common, approach to countering the threats to network security is encryption. In using encryption, we need to decide what to encrypt and where the encryption gear should be located. As Figure 16.4 indicates, there are two fundamental alternatives: link encryption and end-to-end encryption.

With link encryption, each vulnerable communications link is equipped on both ends with an encryption device. Thus, all traffic over all communication links is secured. Although this requires a lot of encryption devices in a large network, it provides a high level of security. One disadvantage of this approach is that the message must be decrypted each time it enters a packet switch; this is necessary because the switch must read the address (virtual circuit number) in the packet header to route the packet. Thus, the message is vulnerable at each switch. If this is a public packet-switching network, the user has no control over the security of the nodes.

With end-to-end encryption, the encryption process is carried out at the two end systems. The source host or terminal encrypts the data. The data, in encrypted form, are then transmitted unaltered across the network to the destination terminal or host. The destination shares a key with the source and so is able to decrypt the data. This approach would seem to secure the transmission against attacks on the network links or switches. There is, however, still a weak spot.

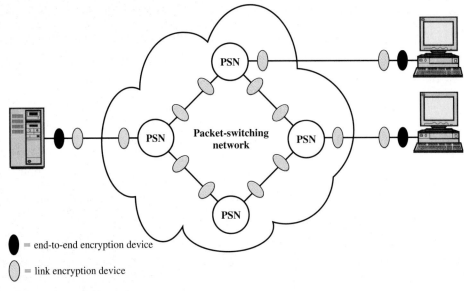

= end-to-end encryption device

= link encryption device

PSN = packet-switching node

Figure 16.4 Encryption across a Packet-Switching Network

Consider the following situation. A host connects to an X.25 packet-switching network, sets up a virtual circuit to another host, and is prepared to transfer data to that other host using end-to-end encryption. Data are transmitted over such a network in the form of packets, consisting of a header and some user data. What part of each packet will the host encrypt? Suppose that the host encrypts the entire packet, including the header. This will not work because, remember, only the other host can perform the decryption. The packet-switching node will receive an encrypted packet and be unable to read the header. Therefore, it will not be able to route the packet. It follows that the host may only encrypt the user data portion of the packet and must leave the header in the clear, so that the network can read it.

Thus, with end-to-end encryption, the user data are secure. However, the traffic pattern is not, because packet headers are transmitted in the clear. To achieve greater security, both link and end-to-end encryption are needed, as is shown in Figure 16.4.

To summarize, when both forms are employed, the host encrypts the user data portion of a packet using an end-to-end encryption key. The entire packet is then encrypted using a link encryption key. As the packet traverses the network, each switch decrypts the packet using a link encryption key to read the header and then encrypts the entire packet again for sending it out on the next link. Now the entire packet is secure except for the time that the packet is actually in the memory of a packet switch, at which time the packet header is in the clear.

Key Distribution

For symmetric encryption to work, the two parties to a secure exchange must have the same key, and that key must be protected from access by others. Furthermore, frequent key changes are usually desirable to limit the amount of data compromised if an attacker learns the key. Therefore, the strength of any cryptographic system rests with the key distribution technique, a term that refers to the means of delivering a key to two parties that wish to exchange data, without allowing others to see the key. Key distribution can be achieved in a number of ways. For two parties A and B,

1. A key could be selected by A and physically delivered to B.
2. A third party could select the key and physically deliver it to A and B.
3. If A and B have previously and recently used a key, one party could transmit the new key to the other, encrypted using the old key.
4. If A and B each have an encrypted connection to a third party C, C could deliver a key on the encrypted links to A and B.

Options 1 and 2 call for manual delivery of a key. For link encryption, this is a reasonable requirement, because each link encryption device is only going to be exchanging data with its partner on the other end of the link. However, for end-to-end encryption, manual delivery is awkward. In a distributed system, any given host or terminal may need to engage in exchanges with many other hosts and terminals over time. Thus, each device needs a number of keys, supplied dynamically. The problem is especially difficult in a wide area distributed system.

Option 3 is a possibility for either link encryption or end-to-end encryption, but if an attacker ever succeeds in gaining access to one key, then all subsequent keys are revealed. Even if frequent changes are made to the link encryption keys, these should be done manually. To provide keys for end-to-end encryption, option 4 is preferable.

Figure 16.5 illustrates an implementation of option 4 for end-to-end encryption. In the figure, link encryption is ignored. This can be added, or not, as required. For this scheme, two kinds of keys are identified:

- **Session key:** When two end systems (hosts, terminals, etc.) wish to communicate, they establish a logical connection (e.g., virtual circuit). For the duration of that logical connection, all user data are encrypted with a one-time session key. At the conclusion of the session, or connection, the session key is destroyed.

- **Permanent key:** A permanent key is a key used between entities for the purpose of distributing session keys.

The configuration consists of the following elements:

- **Key distribution center:** The key distribution center determines which systems are allowed to communicate with each other. When permission is granted for two systems to establish a connection, the key distribution center provides a one-time session key for that connection.

- **Security service module (SSM):** This module, which may consist of functionality at one protocol layer, performs end-to-end encryption and obtains session keys on behalf of users.

The steps involved in establishing a connection are shown in the figure. When one host wishes to set up a connection to another host, it transmits a connection-request packet (step 1). The SSM saves that packet and applies to the KDC for permission to establish the connection (step 2). The communication between the SSM

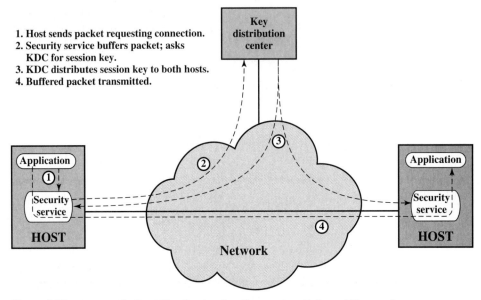

1. Host sends packet requesting connection.
2. Security service buffers packet; asks KDC for session key.
3. KDC distributes session key to both hosts.
4. Buffered packet transmitted.

Figure 16.5   Automatic Key Distribution for Connection-Oriented Protocol

and the KDC is encrypted using a master key shared only by this SSM and the KDC. If the KDC approves the connection request, it generates the session key and delivers it to the two appropriate SSMs, using a unique permanent key for each SSM (step 3). The requesting SSM can now release the connection request packet, and a connection is set up between the two end systems (step 4). All user data exchanged between the two end systems are encrypted by their respective SSMs using the one-time session key.

The automated key distribution approach provides the flexibility and dynamic characteristics needed to allow a number of terminal users to access a number of hosts and for the hosts to exchange data with each other.

Another approach to key distribution uses public-key encryption, which is discussed in Section 16.4.

Traffic Padding

We mentioned that, in some cases, users are concerned about security from traffic analysis. With the use of link encryption, packet headers are encrypted, reducing the opportunity for traffic analysis. However, it is still possible in those circumstances for an attacker to assess the amount of traffic on a network and to observe the amount of traffic entering and leaving each end system. An effective countermeasure to this attack is traffic padding.

Traffic padding is a function that produces ciphertext output continuously, even in the absence of plaintext. A continuous random data stream is generated. When plaintext is available, it is encrypted and transmitted. When input plaintext is not present, the random data are encrypted and transmitted. This makes it impossible for an attacker to distinguish between true data flow and noise and therefore impossible to deduce the amount of traffic.

16.3 MESSAGE AUTHENTICATION AND HASH FUNCTIONS

Encryption protects against passive attack (eavesdropping). A different requirement is to protect against active attack (falsification of data and transactions). Protection against such attacks is known as message authentication.

Approaches to Message Authentication

A message, file, document, or other collection of data is said to be authentic when it is genuine and came from its alleged source. Message authentication is a procedure that allows communicating parties to verify that received messages are authentic. The two important aspects are to verify that the contents of the message have not been altered and that the source is authentic. We may also wish to verify a message's timeliness (it has not been artificially delayed and replayed) and sequence relative to other messages flowing between two parties.

Authentication Using Symmetric Encryption It is possible to perform authentication simply by the use of symmetric encryption. If we assume that only the sender and receiver share a key (which is as it should be), then only the genuine sender would be able successfully to encrypt a message for the other participant. Furthermore, if the message includes an error-detection code and a sequence number, the receiver is assured that no alterations have been made and that sequencing is proper. If the message also includes a timestamp, the receiver is assured that the message has not been delayed beyond that normally expected for network transit.

Message Authentication without Message Encryption In this section, we examine several approaches to message authentication that do not rely on message encryption. In all of these approaches, an authentication tag is generated and appended to each message for transmission. The message itself is not encrypted and can be read at the destination independent of the authentication function at the destination.

Because the approaches discussed in this section do not encrypt the message, message confidentiality is not provided. Because symmetric encryption will provide authentication, and because it is widely used with readily available products, why not simply use such an approach, which provides both confidentiality and authentication? [DAVI89] suggests three situations in which message authentication without confidentiality is preferable:

1. There are a number of applications in which the same message is broadcast to a number of destinations. For example, notification to users that the network is now unavailable or an alarm signal in a control center. It is cheaper and more reliable to have only one destination responsible for monitoring authenticity. Thus, the message must be broadcast in plaintext with an associated message authentication tag. The responsible system performs authentication. If a violation occurs, the other destination systems are alerted by a general alarm.

2. Another possible scenario is an exchange in which one side has a heavy load and cannot afford the time to decrypt all incoming messages. Authentication is carried out on a selective basis, with messages chosen at random for checking.

3. Authentication of a computer program in plaintext is an attractive service. The computer program can be executed without having to decrypt it every time, which would be wasteful of processor resources. However, if a message authentication tag were attached to the program, it could be checked whenever assurance is required of the integrity of the program.

Thus, there is a place for both authentication and encryption in meeting security requirements.

Message Authentication Code One authentication technique involves the use of a secret key to generate a small block of data, known as a message authentication code, that is appended to the message. This technique assumes that two communicating parties, say A and B, share a common secret key K_{AB}. When A has a message M to send to B, it calculates the message authentication code as a function of the message and the key: $\text{MAC}_M = F(K_{AB}, M)$. The message plus code are transmitted to the intended recipient. The recipient performs the same calculation on the received message, using the same secret key, to generate a new message authentication code. The received code is compared to the calculated code (Figure 16.6). If we assume that only the receiver and the sender know the identity of the secret key, and if the received code matches the calculated code, then

1. The receiver is assured that the message has not been altered. If an attacker alters the message but does not alter the code, then the receiver's calculation of the code will differ from the received code. Because the attacker is assumed not to know the secret key, the attacker cannot alter the code to correspond to the alterations in the message.

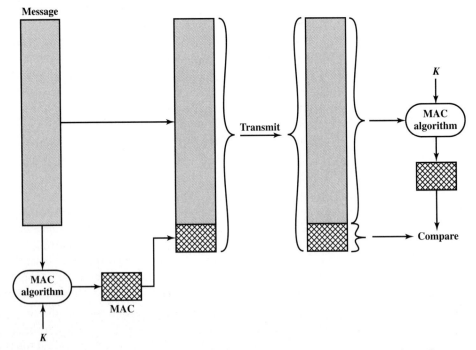

Figure 16.6   Message Authentication Using a Message Authentication Code (MAC)

2. The receiver is assured that the message is from the alleged sender. Because no one else knows the secret key, no one else could prepare a message with a proper code.

3. If the message includes a sequence number (such as is used with X.25, HDLC, and TCP), then the receiver can be assured of the proper sequence, because an attacker cannot successfully alter the sequence number.

A number of algorithms could be used to generate the code. The National Bureau of Standards, in its publication *DES Modes of Operation*, recommends the use of DES. DES is used to generate an encrypted version of the message, and the last number of bits of ciphertext are used as the code. A 16- or 32-bit code is typical.

The process just described is similar to encryption. One difference is that the authentication algorithm need not be reversible, as it must for decryption. It turns out that because of the mathematical properties of the authentication function, it is less vulnerable to being broken than encryption.

One-Way Hash Function A variation on the message authentication code that has received much attention recently is the one-way hash function. As with the message authentication code, a hash function accepts a variable-size message M as input and produces a fixed-size message digest $H(M)$ as output. Unlike the MAC, a hash function does not also take a secret key as input. To authenticate a message, the message digest is sent with the message in such a way that the message digest is authentic.

Figure 16.7 illustrates three ways in which the message can be authenticated. The message digest can be encrypted using symmetric encryption (part a); if it is assumed that only the sender and receiver share the encryption key, then authenticity is assured. The message digest can also be encrypted using public-key encryption (part b); this is explained in Section 16.4. The public-key approach has two advantages: it provides a digital signature as well as message authentication, and it does not require the distribution of keys to communicating parties.

These two approaches have an advantage over approaches that encrypt the entire message in that less computation is required. Nevertheless, there has been interest in developing a technique that avoids encryption altogether. Several reasons for this interest are pointed out in [TSUD92]:

- Encryption software is somewhat slow. Even though the amount of data to be encrypted per message is small, there may be a steady stream of messages into and out of a system.

- Encryption hardware costs are nonnegligible. Low-cost chip implementations of DES are available, but the cost adds up if all nodes in a network must have this capability.

- Encryption hardware is optimized toward large data sizes. For small blocks of data, a high proportion of the time is spent in initialization/invocation overhead.

- Encryption algorithms may be covered by patents and must be licensed, adding a cost.

- Encryption algorithms may be subject to export control.

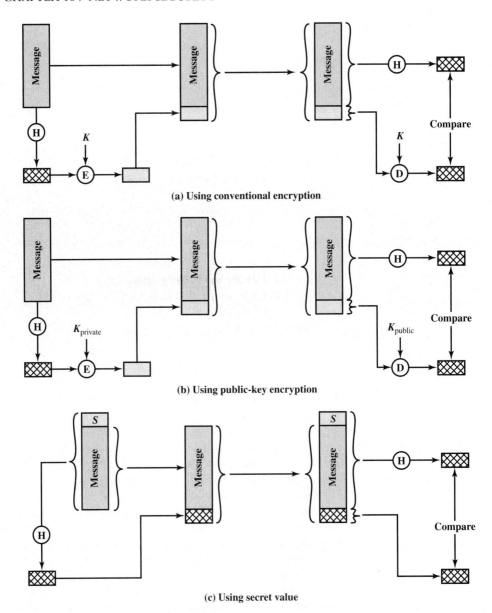

(a) Using conventional encryption

(b) Using public-key encryption

(c) Using secret value

Figure 16.7 Message Authentication Using a One-Way Hash Function

Figure 16.7c shows a technique that uses a hash function but no encryption for message authentication. This technique assumes that two communicating parties, say A and B, share a common secret value S_{AB}. When A has a message to send to B, it calculates the hash function over the concatenation of the secret value and the message: $MD_M = H(S_{AB} \| M)$.[2] It then sends $[M \| MD_M]$ to B. Because B possesses S_{AB}, it can

---
[2] $\|$ denotes concatenation.

recompute $H(S_{AB}\|M)$ and verify MD_M. Because the secret value itself is not sent, it is not possible for an attacker to modify an intercepted message. As long as the secret value remains secret, it is also not possible for an attacker to generate a false message.

This third technique, using a shared secret value, is the one adopted for IP security; it has also been specified for SNMPv3, discussed in Chapter 17.

Secure Hash Functions

The one-way hash function, or secure hash function, is important not only in message authentication but in digital signatures. In this section, we begin with a discussion of requirements for a secure hash function. Then we look at one of the most important hash functions, SHA-1.

Hash Function Requirements The purpose of a hash function is to produce a "fingerprint" of a file, message, or other block of data. To be useful for message authentication, a hash function H must have the following properties:

1. H can be applied to a block of data of any size.
2. H produces a fixed-length output.
3. $H(x)$ is relatively easy to compute for any given x, making both hardware and software implementations practical.
4. For any given code h, it is computationally infeasible to find x such that $H(x) = h$.
5. For any given block x, it is computationally infeasible to find $y \neq x$ with $H(y) = H(x)$.
6. It is computationally infeasible to find any pair (x, y) such that $H(x) = H(y)$.

The first three properties are requirements for the practical application of a hash function to message authentication.

The fourth property is the one-way property: It is easy to generate a code given a message, but virtually impossible to generate a message given a code. This property is important if the authentication technique involves the use of a secret value (Figure 16.7c). The secret value itself is not sent; however, if the hash function is not one way, an attacker can easily discover the secret value: If the attacker can observe or intercept a transmission, the attacker obtains the message M and the hash code $MD_M = H(S_{AB}\|M)$. The attacker then inverts the hash function to obtain $S_{AB}\|M = H^{-1}(MD_M)$. Because the attacker now has both M and $S_{AB}\|M$, it is a trivial matter to recover S_{AB}.

The fifth property guarantees that it is impossible to find an alternative message with the same hash value as a given message. This prevents forgery when an encrypted hash code is used (Figures 16.7a and b). If this property were not true, an attacker would be capable of the following sequence: First, observe or intercept a message plus its encrypted hash code; second, generate an unencrypted hash code from the message; third, generate an alternate message with the same hash code.

A hash function that satisfies the first five properties in the preceding list is referred to as a weak hash function. If the sixth property is also satisfied, then it is referred to as a strong hash function. The sixth property protects against a sophisticated class of attack known as the birthday attack.[3]

---

[3] See [STAL03] for a discussion of birthday attacks.

In addition to providing authentication, a message digest also provides data integrity. It performs the same function as a frame check sequence: If any bits in the message are accidentally altered in transit, the message digest will be in error.

The SHA-1 Secure Hash Function

The Secure Hash Algorithm (SHA) was developed by NIST and published as a federal information processing standard (FIPS 180) in 1993; a revised version was issued as FIPS 180-1 in 1995 and is generally referred to as SHA-1.

The algorithm takes as input a message with a maximum length of less than 2^{64} bits and produces as output a 160-bit message digest. The input is processed in 512-bit blocks. Figure 16.8 depicts the overall processing of a message to produce a digest. The processing consists of the following steps:

- **Step 1: Append padding bits.** The message is padded so that its length is congruent to 448 modulo 512 (length = 448 mod 512). That is, the length of the padded message is 64 bits less than a multiple of 512 bits. Padding is always added, even if the message is already of the desired length. Thus, the number of padding bits is in the range of 1 to 512. The padding consists of a single 1-bit followed by the necessary number of 0-bits.

- **Step 2: Append length.** A block of 64 bits is appended to the message. This block is treated as an unsigned 64-bit integer (most significant byte first) and contains the length of the original message (before the padding). The inclusion of a length value makes more difficult a kind of attack known as a padding attack [TSUD92].

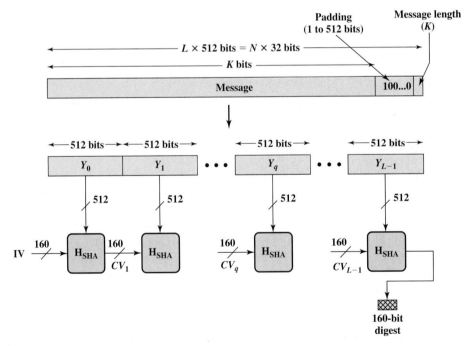

Figure 16.8 Message Digest Generation Using SHA-1

The outcome of the first two steps yields a message that is an integer multiple of 512 bits in length. In Figure 16.8, the expanded message is represented as the sequence of 512-bit blocks $Y_0, Y_1, \ldots, Y_{L-1}$, so that the total length of the expanded message is $L \times 512$ bits. Equivalently, the result is a multiple of 16 32-bit words.

- **Step 3: Initialize MD buffer.** A 160-bit buffer is used to hold intermediate and final results of the hash function.

- **Step 4: Process message in 512-bit (16-word) blocks.** The heart of the algorithm is a module that consists of four rounds of processing of 20 steps each. The four rounds have a similar structure, but each uses a different primitive logical function. Each round takes as input the current 512-bit block being processed (Y_q) and the 160-bit buffer value and updates the contents of the buffer.

- **Step 5: Output.** After all L 512-bit blocks have been processed, the output from the Lth stage is the 160-bit message digest.

The SHA-1 algorithm has the property that every bit of the hash code is a function of every bit in the input. The algorithm produces results that are well mixed; that is, it is unlikely that two messages chosen at random, even if they exhibit similar regularities, will have the same hash code. Unless there is some hidden weakness in SHA-1, which has not so far been published, the difficulty of coming up with two messages having the same message digest is on the order of 2^{80} operations, while the difficulty of finding a message with a given digest is on the order of 2^{160} operations.

16.4 PUBLIC-KEY ENCRYPTION AND DIGITAL SIGNATURES

Of equal importance to symmetric encryption is public-key encryption, which finds use in message authentication and key distribution. This section looks first at the basic concept of public-key encryption, followed by a discussion of digital signatures. Then we discuss the most widely-used public-key algorithm: RSA. We then look at the problem of key distribution.

Public-Key Encryption

Public-key encryption, first publicly proposed by Diffie and Hellman in 1976 [DIFF76], is the first truly revolutionary advance in encryption in literally thousands of years. For one thing, public-key algorithms are based on mathematical functions rather than on simple operations on bit patterns. More important, public-key cryptography is asymmetric, involving the use of two separate keys, in contrast to symmetric encryption, which uses only one key. The use of two keys has profound consequences in the areas of confidentiality, key distribution, and authentication.

Before proceeding, we should first mention several common misconceptions concerning public-key encryption. One is that public-key encryption is more secure from cryptanalysis than symmetric encryption. In fact, the security of any encryption scheme depends on (1) the length of the key and (2) the computational work involved in breaking a cipher. There is nothing in principle about either symmetric or public-key encryption that makes one superior to another from the viewpoint of resisting cryptanalysis. A second misconception is that public-key encryption is a general-purpose technique that has made symmetric encryption obsolete. On the contrary, because of the computational overhead of current public-key encryption schemes, there seems no foreseeable likelihood that symmetric encryption will be abandoned. Finally, there is a feeling that key distribution is trivial when using public-key encryption, compared to the rather cumbersome handshaking involved with key distribution centers for symmetric encryption. In fact, some form of protocol is needed, often involving a central agent, and the procedures involved are no simpler or any more efficient than those required for symmetric encryption.

A public-key encryption scheme has six ingredients (Figure 16.9):

- **Plaintext:** This is the readable message or data that is fed into the algorithm as input.

- **Encryption algorithm:** The encryption algorithm performs various transformations on the plaintext.

- **Public and private key:** This is a pair of keys that has been selected so that if one is used for encryption the other is used for decryption. The exact transformations performed by the encryption algorithm depend on the public or private key that is provided as input.

- **Ciphertext:** This is the scrambled message produced as output. It depends on the plaintext and the key. For a given message, two different keys will produce two different ciphertexts.

- **Decryption algorithm:** This algorithm accepts the ciphertext and the matching key and produces the original plaintext.

As the names suggest, the public key of the pair is made public for others to use, while the private key is known only to its owner. A general-purpose public-key cryptographic algorithm relies on one key for encryption and a different but related key for decryption. Furthermore, these algorithms have the following important characteristics:

- It is computationally infeasible to determine the decryption key given only knowledge of the cryptographic algorithm and the encryption key.

- For most public-key schemes, either of the two related keys can be used for encryption, with the other used for decryption.

The essential steps are the following:

1. Each user generates a pair of keys to be used for the encryption and decryption of messages.

2. Each user places one of the two keys in a public register or other accessible file. This is the public key. The companion key is kept private. As Figure 16.9 suggests, each user maintains a collection of public keys obtained from others.

3. If Bob wishes to send a private message to Alice, Bob encrypts the message using Alice's public key.

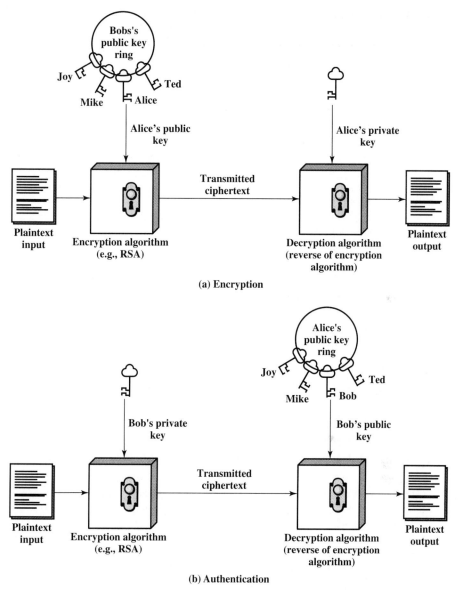

(a) Encryption

(b) Authentication

Figure 16.9   Public-Key Cryptography

4. When Alice receives the message, she decrypts it using her private key. No other recipient can decrypt the message because only Alice knows Alice's private key.

With this approach, all participants have access to public keys, and private keys are generated locally by each participant and therefore need never be distributed. As long as a user protects his or her private key, incoming communication is secure. At any time, a user can change the private key and publish the companion public key to replace the old public key.

Digital Signature

Public-key encryption can be used in another way, as illustrated in Figure 16.9b. Suppose that Bob wants to send a message to Alice and, although it is not important that the message be kept secret, he wants Alice to be certain that the message is indeed from him. In this case Bob uses his own private key to encrypt the message. When Alice receives the ciphertext, she finds that she can decrypt it with Bob's public key, thus proving that the message must have been encrypted by Bob. No one else has Bob's private key and therefore no one else could have created a ciphertext that could be decrypted with Bob's public key. Therefore, the entire encrypted message serves as a **digital signature**. In addition, it is impossible to alter the message without access to Bob's private key, so the message is authenticated both in terms of source and in terms of data integrity.

In the preceding scheme, the entire message is encrypted, which, although validating both author and contents, requires a great deal of storage. Each document must be kept in plaintext to be used for practical purposes. A copy also must be stored in ciphertext so that the origin and contents can be verified in case of a dispute. A more efficient way of achieving the same results is to encrypt a small block of bits that is a function of the document. Such a block, called an authenticator, must have the property that it is infeasible to change the document without changing the authenticator. If the authenticator is encrypted with the sender's private key, it serves as a signature that verifies origin, content, and sequencing. A secure hash code such as SHA-1 can serve this function.

It is important to emphasize that the digital signature does not provide confidentiality. That is, the message being sent is safe from alteration but not safe from eavesdropping. This is obvious in the case of a signature based on a portion of the message, because the rest of the message is transmitted in the clear. Even in the case of complete encryption, there is no protection of confidentiality because any observer can decrypt the message by using the sender's public key.

The RSA Public-Key Encryption Algorithm

One of the first public-key schemes was developed in 1977 by Ron Rivest, Adi Shamir, and Len Adleman at MIT and first published in 1978 [RIVE78]. The RSA scheme has since that time reigned supreme as the only widely accepted and implemented approach to public-key encryption. RSA is a block cipher in which the plaintext and ciphertext are integers between 0 and $n - 1$ for some n.

Encryption and decryption are of the following form, for some plaintext block M and ciphertext block C:

$$C = M^e \bmod n$$
$$M = C^d \bmod n = (M^e)^d \bmod n = M^{ed} \bmod n$$

Both sender and receiver must know the values of n and e, and only the receiver knows the value of d. This is a public-key encryption algorithm with a public key of $KU = \{e, n\}$ and a private key of $KR = \{d, n\}$. For this algorithm to be satisfactory for public-key encryption, the following requirements must be met:

1. It is possible to find values of e, d, n such that $M^{ed} = M \bmod n$ for all $M < n$.

Key Generation	
Select p, q	p and q both prime, $p \neq q$
Calculate $n = p \times q$	
Calculate $\phi(n) = (p - 1)(q - 1)$	
Select integer e	$\gcd(\phi(n), e) = 1; 1 < e < \phi(n)$
Calculate d	$de \bmod \phi(n) = 1$
Public key	$KU = \{e, n\}$
Private key	$KR = \{d, n\}$

Encryption	
Plaintext:	$M < n$
Ciphertext:	$C = M^e \pmod{n}$

Decryption	
Ciphertext:	C
Plaintext:	$M = C^d \pmod{n}$

Figure 16.10   The RSA Algorithm

2. It is relatively easy to calculate M^e and C^d for all values of $M < n$.

3. It is infeasible to determine d given e and n.

The first two requirements are easily met. The third requirement can be met for large values of e and n.

Figure 16.10 summarizes the RSA algorithm. Begin by selecting two prime numbers, p and q and calculating their product n, which is the modulus for encryption and decryption. Next, we need the quantity $\phi(n)$, referred to as the Euler totient of n, which is the number of positive integers less than n and relatively prime to n.[4] Then select an integer e that is relatively prime to $\phi(n)$ [i.e., the greatest common divisor of e and $\phi(n)$ is 1]. Finally, calculate d such that $de \bmod \phi(n) = 1$. It can be shown that d and e have the desired properties.

Suppose that user A has published its public key and that user B wishes to send the message M to A. Then B calculates $C = M^e \pmod{n}$ and transmits C. On receipt of this ciphertext, user A decrypts by calculating $M = C^d \pmod{n}$.

An example, from [SING99], is shown in Figure 16.11. For this example, the keys were generated as follows:

1. Select two prime numbers, $p = 17$ and $q = 11$.

2. Calculate $n = pq = 17 \times 11 = 187$.

3. Calculate $\phi(n) = (p - 1)(q - 1) = 16 \times 10 = 160$.

---

[4]It can be shown that when n is a product of two primes, pq, then $\phi(n) = (p - 1)(q - 1)$.

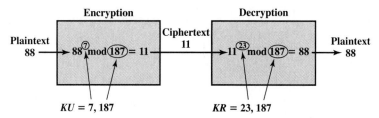

Figure 16.11 Example of RSA Algorithm

4. Select e such that e is relatively prime to $\phi(n) = 160$ and less than $\phi(n)$; we choose $e = 7$.
5. Determine d such that $de \bmod 160 = 1$ and $d < 160$. The correct value is $d = 23$, because $23 \times 7 = 161 = 10 \times 160 + 1$.

The resulting keys are public key $KU = \{7, 187\}$ and private key $KR = \{23, 187\}$. The example shows the use of these keys for a plaintext input of $M = 88$. For encryption, we need to calculate $C = 88^7 \bmod 187$. Exploiting the properties of modular arithmetic, we can do this as follows:

$$88^7 \bmod 187 = [(88^4 \bmod 187) \times (88^2 \bmod 187) \times (88^1 \bmod 187)] \bmod 187$$

$$88^1 \bmod 187 = 88$$

$$88^2 \bmod 187 = 7744 \bmod 187 = 77$$

$$88^4 \bmod 187 = 59{,}969{,}536 \bmod 187 = 132$$

$$88^7 \bmod 187 = (88 \times 77 \times 132) \bmod 187 = 894{,}432 \bmod 187 = 11$$

For decryption, we calculate $M = 11^{23} \bmod 187$:

$$11^{23} \bmod 187 = [(11^1 \bmod 187) \times (11^2 \bmod 187) \times (11^4 \bmod 187)$$

$$\times (11^8 \bmod 187) \times (11^8 \bmod 187)] \bmod 187$$

$$11^1 \bmod 187 = 11$$

$$11^2 \bmod 187 = 121$$

$$11^4 \bmod 187 = 14{,}641 \bmod 187 = 55$$

$$11^8 \bmod 187 = 214{,}358{,}881 \bmod 187 = 33$$

$$11^{23} \bmod 187 = (11 \times 121 \times 55 \times 33 \times 33) \bmod 187$$

$$= 79{,}720{,}245 \bmod 187 = 88$$

There are two possible approaches to defeating the RSA algorithm. The first is the brute force approach: try all possible private keys. Thus, the larger the number of bits in e and d, the more secure the algorithm. However, because the calculations involved, both in key generation and in encryption/decryption, are complex, the larger the size of the key, the slower the system will run.

Most discussions of the cryptanalysis of RSA have focused on the task of factoring n into its two prime factors. For a large n with large prime factors, factoring is a hard problem, but not as hard as it used to be. A striking illustration of this is the following. In 1977, the three inventors of RSA dared *Scientific American* readers to decode a cipher they printed in Martin Gardner's "Mathematical Games" column. They offered a $100 reward for the return of a plaintext sentence, an event they predicted might not occur for some 40 quadrillion years. In April of 1994, a group working over the Internet and using over 1600 computers claimed the prize after only eight months of work [LEUT94]. This challenge used a public-key size (length of n) of 129 decimal digits, or around 428 bits. This result does not invalidate the use of RSA; it simply means that larger key sizes must be used. Currently, a 1024-bit key size (about 300 decimal digits) is considered strong enough for virtually all applications.

Key Management

With symmetric encryption, a fundamental requirement for two parties to communicate securely is that they share a secret key. Suppose Bob wants to create a messaging application that will enable him to exchange e-mail securely with anyone who has access to the Internet or to some other network that the two of them share. Suppose Bob wants to do this using only symmetric encryption. With symmetric encryption, Bob and his correspondent, say, Alice, must come up with a way to share a unique secret key that no one else knows. How are they going to do that? If Alice is in the next room from Bob, Bob could generate a key and write it down on a piece of paper or store it on a diskette and hand it to Alice. But if Alice is on the other side of the continent or the world, what can Bob do? Well, he could encrypt this key using symmetric encryption and e-mail it to Alice, but this means that Bob and Alice must share a secret key to encrypt this new secret key. Furthermore, Bob and everyone else who uses this new e-mail package faces the same problem with every potential correspondent: Each pair of correspondents must share a unique secret key.

How to distribute secret keys securely is the most difficult problem for symmetric encryption. This problem is wiped away with public-key encryption by the simple fact that the private key is never distributed. If Bob wants to correspond with Alice and other people, he generates a single pair of keys, one private and one public. He keeps the private key secure and broadcasts the public key to all and sundry. If Alice does the same, then Bob has Alice's public key, Alice has Bob's public key, and they can now communicate securely. When Bob wishes to communicate with Alice, Bob can do the following:

1. Prepare a message.
2. Encrypt that message using symmetric encryption with a one-time symmetric session key.
3. Encrypt the session key using public-key encryption with Alice's public key.
4. Attach the encrypted session key to the message and send it to Alice.

Only Alice is capable of decrypting the session key and therefore of recovering the original message.

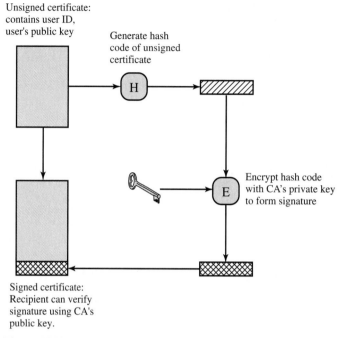

Unsigned certificate:
contains user ID,
user's public key

Generate hash
code of unsigned
certificate

Encrypt hash code
with CA's private key
to form signature

Signed certificate:
Recipient can verify
signature using CA's
public key.

Figure 16.12   Public-Key Certificate Use

It is only fair to point out, however, that we have replaced one problem with another. Alice's private key is secure because she need never reveal it; however, Bob must be sure that the public key with Alice's name written all over it is in fact Alice's public key. Someone else could have broadcast a public key and said it was Alice's.

The solution to this problem is the **public-key certificate**. In essence, a certificate consists of a public key plus a User ID of the key owner, with the whole block signed by a trusted third party. Typically, the third party is a certificate authority (CA) that is trusted by the user community, such as a government agency or a financial institution. A user can present his or her public key to the authority in a secure manner and obtain a certificate. The user can then publish the certificate. Anyone needing this user's public key can obtain the certificate and verify that it is valid by way of the attached trusted signature. Figure 16.12 illustrates the process.

16.5 SECURE SOCKET LAYER AND TRANSPORT LAYER SECURITY

One of the most widely used security services is the Secure Sockets Layer (SSL) and the follow-on Internet standard known as Transport Layer Security (TLS), the latter defined in RFC 2246. SSL is a general-purpose service implemented as a set of protocols that rely on TCP. At this level, there are two implementation choices. For full generality, SSL (or TLS) could be provided as part of the underlying protocol suite and therefore be transparent to applications. Alternatively, SSL can be embedded in specific packages. For example, Netscape and Microsoft Explorer browsers come equipped with SSL, and most Web servers have implemented the protocol.

This section discusses SSLv3. Only minor changes are found in TLS.

SSL Architecture

SSL is designed to make use of TCP to provide a reliable end-to-end secure service. SSL is not a single protocol but rather two layers of protocols, as illustrated in Figure 16.13.

The SSL Record Protocol provides basic security services to various higher-layer protocols. In particular, the Hypertext Transfer Protocol (HTTP), which provides the transfer service for Web client/server interaction, can operate on top of SSL. Three higher-layer protocols are defined as part of SSL: the Handshake Protocol, The Change Cipher Spec Protocol, and the Alert Protocol. These SSL-specific protocols are used in the management of SSL exchanges and are examined later in this section.

Two important SSL concepts are the SSL session and the SSL connection, which are defined in the specification as follows:

- **Connection:** A connection is a transport (in the OSI layering model definition) that provides a suitable type of service. For SSL, such connections are peer-to-peer relationships. The connections are transient. Every connection is associated with one session.

- **Session:** An SSL session is an association between a client and a server. Sessions are created by the Handshake Protocol. Sessions define a set of cryptographic security parameters, which can be shared among multiple connections. Sessions are used to avoid the expensive negotiation of new security parameters for each connection.

Between any pair of parties (applications such as HTTP on client and server), there may be multiple secure connections. In theory, there may also be multiple simultaneous sessions between parties, but this feature is not used in practice.

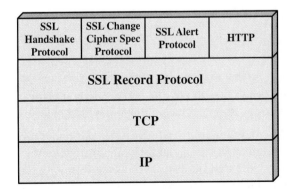

Figure 16.13 SSL Protocol Stack

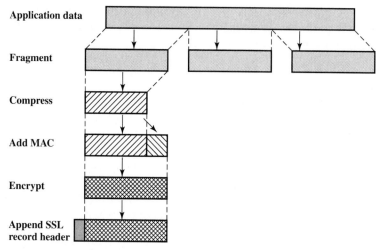

Figure 16.14   SSL Record Protocol Operation

SSL Record Protocol

The SSL Record Protocol provides two services for SSL connections:

- **Confidentiality:** The Handshake Protocol defines a shared secret key that is used for symmetric encryption of SSL payloads.

- **Message Integrity:** The Handshake Protocol also defines a shared secret key that is used to form a message authentication code (MAC).

Figure 16.14 indicates the overall operation of the SSL Record Protocol. The first step is **fragmentation**. Each upper-layer message is fragmented into blocks of 2^{14} bytes (16384 bytes) or less. Next, **compression** is optionally applied. The next step in processing is to compute a **message authentication code** over the compressed data. Next, the compressed message plus the MAC are **encrypted** using symmetric encryption.

The final step of SSL Record Protocol processing is to prepend a header, consisting of the following fields:

- **Content Type (8 bits):** The higher-layer protocol used to process the enclosed fragment.

- **Major Version (8 bits):** Indicates major version of SSL in use. For SSLv3, the value is 3.

- **Minor Version (8 bits):** Indicates minor version in use. For SSLv3, the value is 0.

- **Compressed Length (16 bits):** The length in bytes of the plaintext fragment (or compressed fragment if compression is used). The maximum value is $2^{14} + 2048$.

The content types that have been defined are change_cipher_spec, alert, handshake, and application_data. The first three are the SSL-specific protocols, discussed next. Note that no distinction is made among the various applications (e.g., HTTP) that might use SSL; the content of the data created by such applications is opaque to SSL.

The Record Protocol then transmits the resulting unit in a TCP segment. Received data are decrypted, verified, decompressed, and reassembled and then delivered to higher-level users.

Change Cipher Spec Protocol

The Change Cipher Spec Protocol is one of the three SSL-specific protocols that use the SSL Record Protocol, and it is the simplest. This protocol consists of a single message, which consists of a single byte with the value 1. The sole purpose of this message is to cause the pending state to be copied into the current state, which updates the cipher suite to be used on this connection.

Alert Protocol

The Alert Protocol is used to convey SSL-related alerts to the peer entity. As with other applications that use SSL, alert messages are compressed and encrypted, as specified by the current state.

Each message in this protocol consists of two bytes. The first byte takes the value warning(1) or fatal(2) to convey the severity of the message. If the level is fatal, SSL immediately terminates the connection. Other connections on the same session may continue, but no new connections on this session may be established. The second byte contains a code that indicates the specific alert. An example of a fatal alert is an incorrect MAC. An example of a nonfatal alert is a close_notify message, which notifies the recipient that the sender will not send any more messages on this connection.

Handshake Protocol

The most complex part of SSL is the Handshake Protocol. This protocol allows the server and client to authenticate each other and to negotiate an encryption and MAC algorithm and cryptographic keys to be used to protect data sent in an SSL record. The Handshake Protocol is used before any application data is transmitted.

The Handshake Protocol consists of a series of messages exchanged by client and server. Figure 16.15 shows the initial exchange needed to establish a logical connection between client and server. The exchange can be viewed as having four phases.

Phase 1 is used to initiate a logical connection and to establish the security capabilities that will be associated with it. The exchange is initiated by the client, which sends a client_hello message with the following parameters:

- **Version:** The highest SSL version understood by the client.

- **Random:** A client-generated random structure, consisting of a 32-bit timestamp and 28 bytes generated by a secure random number generator. These values are used during key exchange to prevent replay attacks.

- **Session ID:** A variable-length session identifier. A nonzero value indicates that the client wishes to update the parameters of an existing connection or create a new connection on this session. A zero value indicates that the client wishes to establish a new connection on a new session.

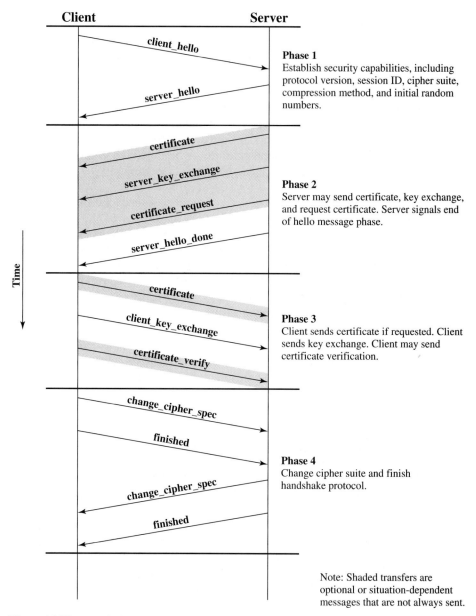

Figure 16.15 Handshake Protocol Action

- **CipherSuite:** This is a list that contains the combinations of cryptographic algorithms supported by the client, in decreasing order of preference. Each element of the list (each cipher suite) defines both a key exchange algorithm and a CipherSpec.

- **Compression Method:** This is a list of the compression methods the client supports.

After sending the client_hello message, the client waits for the server_hello message, which contains the same parameters as the client_hello message.

The details of **Phase 2** depend on the underlying public-key encryption scheme that is used. In some cases, the server passes a certificate to the client, possibly additional key information, and a request for a certificate from the client.

The final message in Phase 2, and one that is always required, is the server_done message, which is sent by the server to indicate the end of the server hello and associated messages. After sending this message, the server will wait for a client response.

In **Phase 3**, upon receipt of the server_done message, the client should verify that the server provided a valid certificate if required and check that the server_hello parameters are acceptable. If all is satisfactory, the client sends one or more messages back to the server, depending on the underlying public-key scheme.

Phase 4 completes the setting up of a secure connection. The client sends a change_cipher_spec message and copies the pending CipherSpec into the current CipherSpec. Note that this message is not considered part of the Handshake Protocol but is sent using the Change Cipher Spec Protocol. The client then immediately sends the finished message under the new algorithms, keys, and secrets. The finished message verifies that the key exchange and authentication processes were successful.

In response to these two messages, the server sends its own change_cipher_spec message, transfers the pending to the current CipherSpec, and sends its finished message. At this point the handshake is complete and the client and server may begin to exchange application layer data.

16.6 IPV4 AND IPV6 SECURITY

In 1994, the Internet Architecture Board (IAB) issued a report entitled *Security in the Internet Architecture* (RFC 1636). The report stated the general consensus that the Internet needs more and better security, and it identified key areas for security mechanisms. Among these were the need to secure the network infrastructure from unauthorized monitoring and control of network traffic and the need to secure end-user-to-end-user traffic using authentication and encryption mechanisms.

These concerns are fully justified. As confirmation, the 2002 annual report from the Computer Emergency Response Team (CERT) lists over 82,000 reported security incidents [CERT03]. The most serious types of attacks included IP spoofing, in which intruders create packets with false IP addresses and exploit applications that use authentication based on IP; and various forms of eavesdropping and packet sniffing, in which attackers read transmitted information, including logon information and database contents.

In response to these issues, the IAB included authentication and encryption as necessary security features in the next-generation IP, which has been issued as IPv6. Fortunately, these security capabilities were designed to be usable both with IPv4 and IPv6. This means that vendors can begin offering these features now, and many vendors do now have some IPSec capability in their products.

Applications of IPSec

IPSec provides the capability to secure communications across a LAN, across private and public WANs, and across the Internet. Examples of its use include the following:

- **Secure branch office connectivity over the Internet:** A company can build a secure virtual private network over the Internet or over a public WAN. This enables a business to rely heavily on the Internet and reduce its need for private networks, saving costs and network management overhead.

- **Secure remote access over the Internet:** An end user whose system is equipped with IP security protocols can make a local call to an Internet service provider (ISP) and gain secure access to a company network. This reduces the cost of toll charges for traveling employees and telecommuters.

- **Establishing extranet and intranet connectivity with partners:** IPSec can be used to secure communication with other organizations, ensuring authentication and confidentiality and providing a key exchange mechanism.

- **Enhancing electronic commerce security:** Even though some Web and electronic commerce applications have built-in security protocols, the use of IPSec enhances that security.

The principal feature of IPSec that enables it to support these varied applications is that it can encrypt and/or authenticate *all* traffic at the IP level. Thus, all distributed applications, including remote logon, client/server, e-mail, file transfer, Web access, and so on, can be secured.

The Scope of IPSec

IPSec provides three main facilities: an authentication-only function referred to as Authentication Header (AH), a combined authentication/encryption function called Encapsulating Security Payload (ESP), and a key exchange function. For virtual private networks, both authentication and encryption are generally desired, because it is important both to (1) assure that unauthorized users do not penetrate the virtual private network and (2) assure that eavesdroppers on the Internet cannot read messages sent over the virtual private network. Because both features are generally desirable, most implementations are likely to use ESP rather than AH. The key exchange function allows for manual exchange of keys as well as an automated scheme.

The IPSec specification is quite complex and covers numerous documents. The most important of these, issued in November of 1998, are RFCs 2401, 2402, 2406, and 2408. In this section, we provide an overview of some of the most important elements of IPSec.

Security Associations

A key concept that appears in both the authentication and confidentiality mechanisms for IP is the security association (SA). An association is a one-way relationship between a sender and a receiver that affords security services to the traffic carried on it. If a peer relationship is needed, for two-way secure exchange, then two security associations are required. Security services are afforded to an SA for the use of AH or ESP, but not both.

A security association is uniquely identified by three parameters:

- **Security parameters index (SPI):** A bit string assigned to this SA and having local significance only. The SPI is carried in AH and ESP headers to enable the receiving system to select the SA under which a received packet will be processed.

- **IP destination address:** Currently, only unicast addresses are allowed; this is the address of the destination endpoint of the SA, which may be an end user system or a network system such as a firewall or router.

- **Security protocol identifier:** This indicates whether the association is an AH or ESP security association.

Hence, in any IP packet, the security association is uniquely identified by the Destination Address in the IPv4 or IPv6 header and the SPI in the enclosed extension header (AH or ESP).

An IPSec implementation includes a security association data base that defines the parameters associated with each SA. A security association is defined by the following parameters:

- **Sequence number counter:** A 32-bit value used to generate the sequence number field in AH or ESP headers.

- **Sequence counter overflow:** A flag indicating whether overflow of the sequence number counter should generate an auditable event and prevent further transmission of packets on this SA.

- **Antireplay window:** Used to determine whether an inbound AH or ESP packet is a replay, by defining a sliding window within which the sequence number must fall.

- **AH information:** Authentication algorithm, keys, key lifetimes, and related parameters being used with AH.

- **ESP information:** Encryption and authentication algorithm, keys, initialization values, key lifetimes, and related parameters being used with ESP.

- **Lifetime of this security association:** A time interval or byte count after which an SA must be replaced with a new SA (and new SPI) or terminated, plus an indication of which of these actions should occur.

- **IPSec protocol mode:** Tunnel, transport, or wildcard (required for all implementations). These modes are discussed later in this section.

- **Path MTU:** Any observed path maximum transmission unit (maximum size of a packet that can be transmitted without fragmentation) and aging variables (required for all implementations).

The key management mechanism that is used to distribute keys is coupled to the authentication and privacy mechanisms only by way of the security parameters index. Hence, authentication and privacy have been specified independent of any specific key management mechanism.

Authentication Header

The authentication header provides support for data integrity and authentication of IP packets. The data integrity feature ensures that undetected modification to a packet's content in transit is not possible. The authentication feature enables an end system or network device to authenticate the user or application and filter traffic accordingly; it also prevents the address spoofing attacks observed in today's Internet. The AH also guards against the replay attack described later in this section.

Authentication is based on the use of a message authentication code (MAC), as described in Section 16.3; hence the two parties must share a secret key.

The authentication header consists of the following fields (Figure 16.16):

- **Next Header (8 bits):** Identifies the type of header immediately following this header.

- **Payload Length (8 bits):** Length of authentication header in 32-bit words, minus 2. For example, the default length of the authentication data field is 96 bits, or three 32-bit words. With a three-word fixed header, there are a total of six words in the header, and the Payload Length field has a value of 4.

- **Reserved (16 bits):** For future use.

- **Security Parameters Index (32 bits):** Identifies a security association.

- **Sequence Number (32 bits):** A monotonically increasing counter value.

- **Authentication Data (variable):** A variable-length field (must be an integral number of 32-bit words) that contains the integrity check value (ICV), or MAC, for this packet.

The authentication data field is calculated over the following:

- IP header fields that either do not change in transit (immutable) or that are predictable in value upon arrival at the endpoint for the AH SA. Fields that may change in transit and whose values on arrival are unpredictable are set to zero for purposes of calculation at both source and destination.

- The AH header other than the Authentication Data field. The Authentication Data field is set to zero for purposes of calculation at both source and destination.

- The entire upper-level protocol data, which is assumed to be immutable in transit.

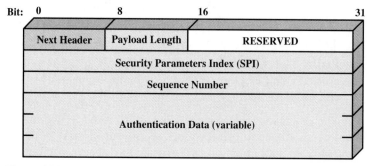

Figure 16.16   IPSec Authentication Header

For IPv4, examples of immutable fields are Internet Header Length and Source Address. An example of a mutable but predictable field is the Destination Address (with loose or strict source routing). Examples of mutable fields that are zeroed prior to ICV calculation are the Time to Live and Header Checksum fields. Note that both source and destination address fields are protected, so that address spoofing is prevented.

For IPv6, examples in the base header are Version (immutable), Destination Address (mutable but predictable), and Flow Label (mutable and zeroed for calculation).

Encapsulating Security Payload

The encapsulating security payload provides confidentiality services, including confidentiality of message contents and limited traffic flow confidentiality. As an optional feature, ESP can also provide an authentication service.

Figure 16.17 shows the format of an ESP packet. It contains the following fields:

- **Security Parameters Index (32 bits):** Identifies a security association.
- **Sequence Number (32 bits):** A monotonically increasing counter value.
- **Payload Data (variable):** This is an upper-level segment protected by encryption.
- **Padding (0–255 bytes):** May be required if the encryption algorithm requires the plaintext to be a multiple of some number of octets.
- **Pad Length (8 bits):** Indicates the number of pad bytes immediately preceding this field.
- **Next Header (8 bits):** Identifies the type of data contained in the payload data field by identifying the first header in that payload (for example, an extension header in IPv6, or an upper-layer protocol such as TCP).

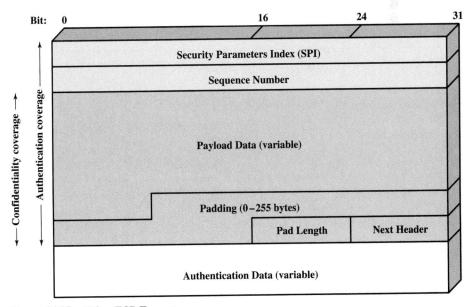

Figure 16.17 IPSec ESP Format

- **Authentication Data (variable):** A variable-length field (must be an integral number of 32-bit words) that contains the integrity check value computed over the ESP packet minus the Authentication Data field.

16.7 RECOMMENDED READING AND WEB SITES

The topics in this chapter are covered in greater detail in [STAL03]. For coverage of cryptographic algorithms, [SCHN96] is an essential reference work; it contains descriptions of numerous cryptographic algorithms and protocols.

SCHN96 Schneier, B. *Applied Cryptography.* New York: Wiley, 1996.
STAL03 Stallings, W. *Cryptography and Network Security: Principles and Practice, Third Edition.* Upper Saddle River, NJ: Prentice Hall, 2003.

Recommended Web Sites:

- **COAST:** Comprehensive set of links related to cryptography and network security.
- **IETF Security Area:** Provides up-to-date information on Internet security standardization efforts.
- **IEEE Technical Committee on Security and Privacy:** Provides copies of IEEE's newsletter and information on IEEE-related activities.

16.8 KEY TERMS, REVIEW QUESTIONS, AND PROBLEMS

Key Terms

active attack	hash function	public-key certificate
authenticity	integrity	public-key encryption
availability	IP Security (IPSec)	replay
Advanced Encryption Standard (AES)	key distribution	RSA
brute-force attack	key distribution center	secret key
ciphertext	key management	secure hash function
confidentiality	masquerade	Secure Socket Layer (SSL)
cryptanalysis	message authentication	session key
Data Encryption Standard (DES)	message authentication code (MAC)	SHA-1
decryption algorithm	one-way hash function	symmetric encryption
denial of service	passive attack	traffic analysis
digital signature	plaintext	traffic padding
encryption algorithm	private key	Transport Layer Security (TLS)
	public key	

Review Questions

16.1 What is the difference between passive and active security threats?

16.2 List and briefly define categories of passive and active security threats.

16.3 What are DES and triple DES?

16.4 How is the AES expected to be an improvement over triple DES?

16.5 Explain traffic padding.

16.6 List and briefly define various approaches to message authentication.

16.7 What is a secure hash function?

16.8 Explain the difference between symmetric encryption and public-key encryption.

16.9 What are the distinctions among the terms *public key, private key, secret key*?

16.10 What is a digital signature?

16.11 What is a public-key certificate?

16.12 What protocols comprise SSL?

16.13 What is the difference between and SSL connection and an SSL session?

16.14 What services are provided by the SSL Record Protocol?

16.15 What services are provided by IPSec?

Problems

16.1 Give some examples where traffic analysis could jeopardize security. Describe situations where end-to-end encryption combined with link encryption would still allow enough traffic analysis to be dangerous.

16.2 Key distribution schemes using an access control center and/or a key distribution center have central points vulnerable to attack. Discuss the security implications of such centralization.

16.3 Suppose that someone suggests the following way to confirm that the two of you are both in possession of the same secret key. You create a random bit string the length of the key, XOR it with the key, and send the result over the channel. Your partner XORs the incoming block with the key (which should be the same as your key) and sends it back. You check and if what you receive is your original random string, you have verified that your partner has the same secret key, yet neither of you has ever transmitted the key. Is there a flaw in this scheme?

16.4 Prior to the discovery of any specific public-key schemes, such as RSA, an existence proof was developed whose purpose was to demonstrate that public-key encryption is possible in theory. Consider the functions $f_1(x_1) = z_1; f_2(x_2, y_2) = z_2; f_3(x_3, y_3) = z_3$, where all values are integers with $1 \le x_i, y_i, z_i \le N$. Function f_1 can be represented by a vector M1 of length N, in which the kth entry is the value of $f_1(k)$. Similarly, f_2 and f_3 can be represented by $N \times N$ matrices M2 and M3. The intent is to represent the encryption/decryption process by table look-ups for tables with very large values of N. Such tables would be impractically huge but could, in principle, be constructed. The scheme works as follows: construct M1 with a random permutation of all integers between 1 and N; that is, each integer appears exactly once in M1. Construct M2 so that each row contains a random permutation of the first N integers. Finally, fill in M3 to satisfy the following condition:

$$f_3(f_2(f_1(k), p), k) = p \quad \text{for all } k, p \text{ with } 1 \le k, p \le N$$

In words,

1. M1 takes an input k and produces an output x.
2. M2 takes inputs x and p giving output z.
3. M3 takes inputs z and k and produces p.

The three tables, once constructed, are made public.

a. It should be clear that it is possible to construct M3 to satisfy the preceding condition. As an example, fill in M3 for the following simple case:

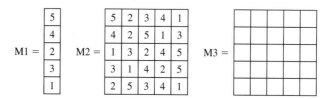

Convention: The ith element of M1 corresponds to $k = i$. The ith row of M2 corresponds to $x = i$; the jth column of M2 corresponds to $p = j$. The ith row of M3 corresponds to $z = i$; the jth column of M3 corresponds to $k = j$.

b. Describe the use of this set of tables to perform encryption and decryption between two users.

c. Argue that this is a secure scheme.

16.5 Perform encryption and decryption using the RSA algorithm, as in Figure 16.11, for the following:

a. $p = 3$; $q = 11$, $d = 7$; $M = 5$
b. $p = 5$; $q = 11$, $e = 3$; $M = 9$
c. $p = 7$; $q = 11$, $e = 17$; $M = 8$
d. $p = 11$; $q = 13$, $e = 11$; $M = 7$
e. $p = 17$; $q = 31$, $e = 7$; $M = 2$.
    Hint: Decryption is not as hard as you think; use some finesse.

16.6 In a public-key system using RSA, you intercept the ciphertext $C = 10$ sent to a user whose public key is $e = 5, n = 35$. What is the plaintext M?

16.7 In an RSA system, the public key of a given user is $e = 31, n = 3599$. What is the private key of this user?

16.8 Suppose we have a set of blocks encoded with the RSA algorithm and we don't have the private key. Assume $n = pq, e$ is the public key. Suppose also someone tells us they know one of the plaintext blocks has a common factor with n. Does this help us in any way?

16.9 Show how RSA can be represented by matrices M1, M2, and M3 of Problem 16.4.

16.10 Consider the following scheme:

1. Pick an odd number, E.
2. Pick two prime numbers, P and Q, where $(P - 1)(Q - 1) - 1$ is evenly divisible by E.
3. Multiply P and Q to get N.
4. Calculate $D = \dfrac{(P - 1)(Q - 1)(E - 1) + 1}{E}$.

Is this scheme equivalent to RSA? Show why or why not.

16.11 Consider using RSA with a known key to construct a one-way hash function. Then process a message consisting of a sequence of blocks as follows: Encrypt the first block, XOR the result with the second block and encrypt again, and so on. Show that this scheme is not secure by solving the following problem. Given a two-block message B1, B2, and its hash

$$RSAH(B1, B2) = RSA(RSA(B1) \oplus B2)$$

Given an arbitrary block C1, choose C2 so that RSAH(C1, C2) = RSAH(B1, B2).

16.12 In SSL and TLS, why is there a separate Change Cipher Spec Protocol rather than including a change_cipher_spec message in the Handshake Protocol?

16.13 In discussing AH processing, it was mentioned that not all of the fields in an IP header are included in MAC calculation.

   a. For each of the fields in the IPv4 header, indicate whether the field is immutable, mutable but predictable, or mutable (zeroed prior to ICV calculation).

   b. Do the same for the IPv6 header.

   c. Do the same for the IPv6 extension headers.

   In each case, justify your decision for each field.

NETWORK MANAGEMENT

The control of a large force is the same in principle as the control of a few men; it is merely a question of instituting signs and signals.

—The Art of War,
Sun Tzu

KEY POINTS

- The key areas that comprise network management are fault management, accounting management, configuration and name management, performance management, and security management.

- A **network management system** is a collection of tools for network monitoring and control.

- The most important standardized scheme for supporting network management applications is the Simple Network Management Protocol (SNMP). The original version of SNMP is available on a wide array of products and is widely used. SNMPv2 contains a number of functional enhancements to SNMP and is supplanting it. SNMPv3 provides security features that are added on to SNMPv2.

Networks and distributed processing systems are of critical and growing importance in enterprises of all sorts. The trend is toward larger, more complex networks supporting more applications and more users. As these networks grow in scale, two facts become painfully evident:

- The network and its associated resources and distributed applications become indispensable to the organization.

- More things can go wrong, disabling the network or a portion of the network or degrading performance to an unacceptable level.

A large network cannot be put together and managed by human effort alone. The complexity of such a system dictates the use of automated network management tools. The urgency of the need for such tools is increased, and the difficulty of supplying such tools is also increased, if the network includes equipment from multiple vendors. Moreover, the increasing decentralization of network services as exemplified by the increasing importance of workstations and client/server computing makes coherent and coordinated network management increasingly difficult. In such complex information systems, many significant network assets are dispersed far from network management personnel.

This chapter provides an overview of network management. We begin by looking at the requirements for network management. This should give some idea of the scope of the task to be accomplished. To manage a network, it is fundamental to know something about the current status and behavior of that network.

For either LAN management alone, or for a combined LAN/WAN environment, what is needed is a network management system that includes a comprehensive set of data gathering and control tools and that is integrated with the network hardware and software. We look at the general architecture of a network management system and then examine the most widely used standardized software package for supporting network management: SNMP.

17.1 NETWORK MANAGEMENT REQUIREMENTS

Table 17.1 lists key areas of network management as suggested by the International Organization for Standardization (ISO). These categories provide a useful way of organizing our discussion of requirements.

Fault Management

Overview To maintain proper operation of a complex network, care must be taken that systems as a whole, and each essential component individually, are in proper working order. When a fault occurs, it is important, as rapidly as possible, to

- Determine exactly where the fault is.
- Isolate the rest of the network from the failure so that it can continue to function without interference.
- Reconfigure or modify the network in such a way as to minimize the impact of operation without the failed component or components.
- Repair or replace the failed components to restore the network to its initial state.

Central to the definition of fault management is the fundamental concept of a fault. Faults are to be distinguished from errors. A **fault** is an abnormal condition that requires management attention (or action) to repair. A fault is usually indicated by failure to operate correctly or by excessive errors. For example, if a communications

Table 17.1   ISO Management Functional Areas

Fault Management

> The facilities that enable the detection, isolation, and correction of abnormal operation of the OSI environment.

Accounting Management

> The facilities that enable charges to be established for the use of managed objects and costs to be identified for the use of those managed objects.

Configuration and Name Management

> The facilities that exercise control over, identify, collect data from, and provide data to managed objects for the purpose of assisting in providing for continuous operation of interconnection services.

Performance Management

> The facilities needed to evaluate the behavior of managed objects and the effectiveness of communication activities.

Security Management

> Those aspects of OSI security essential to operate OSI network management correctly and to protect managed objects.

line is physically cut, no signals can get through. Or a crimp in the cable may cause wild distortions so that there is a persistently high bit error rate. Certain errors (e.g., a single bit error on a communication line) may occur occasionally and are not normally considered to be faults. It is usually possible to compensate for errors using the error control mechanisms of the various protocols.

User Requirements Users expect fast and reliable problem resolution. Most end users will tolerate occasional outages. When these infrequent outages do occur, however, the user generally expects to receive immediate notification and expects that the problem will be corrected almost immediately. To provide this level of fault resolution requires very rapid and reliable fault detection and diagnostic management functions. The impact and duration of faults can also be minimized by the use of redundant components and alternate communication routes, to give the network a degree of fault tolerance. The fault management capability itself should be redundant to increase network reliability.

Users expect to be kept informed of the network status, including both scheduled and unscheduled disruptive maintenance. Users expect reassurance of correct network operation through mechanisms that use confidence tests or analyze dumps, logs, alerts, or statistics. After correcting a fault and restoring a system to its full operational state, the fault management service must ensure that the problem is truly resolved and that no new problems are introduced. This requirement is called problem tracking and control.

As with other areas of network management, fault management should have minimal effect on network performance.

Accounting Management

Overview In many enterprise networks, individual divisions or cost centers, or even individual project accounts, are charged for the use of network services. These are internal accounting procedures rather than actual cash transfers, but they are important to the participating users nevertheless. Furthermore, even if no such internal charging is employed, the network manager needs to be able to track the use of network resources by user or user class for a number of reasons, including the following:

- A user or group of users may be abusing their access privileges and burdening the network at the expense of other users.
- Users may be making inefficient use of the network, and the network manager can assist in changing procedures to improve performance.
- The network manager is in a better position to plan for network growth if user activity is known in sufficient detail.

User Requirements The network manager needs to be able to specify the kinds of accounting information to be recorded at various nodes, the desired interval between successive sendings of the recorded information to higher-level management nodes, and the algorithms to be used in calculating the charging. Accounting reports should be generated under network manager control.

To limit access to accounting information, the accounting facility must provide the capability to verify users' authorization to access and manipulate that information.

Configuration and Name Management

Overview Modern data communication networks are composed of individual components and logical subsystems (e.g., the device driver in an operating system) that can be configured to perform many different applications. The same device, for example, can be configured to act either as a router or as an end system node or both. Once it is decided how a device is to be used, the configuration manager can choose the appropriate software and set of attributes and values (e.g., a transport layer retransmission timer) for that device.

Configuration management is concerned with initializing a network and gracefully shutting down part or all of the network. It is also concerned with maintaining, adding, and updating the relationships among components and the status of components themselves during network operation.

User Requirements Startup and shutdown operations on a network are the specific responsibilities of configuration management. It is often desirable for these operations on certain components to be performed unattended (e.g., starting or shutting down a network interface unit). The network manager needs the capability to identify initially the components that comprise the network and to define the desired connectivity of these components. Those who regularly configure a network with the same or a similar set of resource attributes need ways to define and modify default attributes and to load these predefined sets of attributes into the specified network components. The network manager needs the capability to change the connectivity of network components when users' needs change. Reconfiguration of a network is often desired in response to performance evaluation or in support of network upgrade, fault recovery, or security checks.

Users often need to, or want to, be informed of the status of network resources and components. Therefore, when changes in configuration occur, users should be notified of these changes. Configuration reports can be generated either on some routine periodic basis or in response to a request for such a report. Before reconfiguration, users often want to inquire about the upcoming status of resources and their attributes.

Network managers usually want only authorized users (operators) to manage and control network operation (e.g., software distribution and updating).

Performance Management

Overview Modern data communications networks are composed of many and varied components, which must intercommunicate and share data and resources. In some cases, it is critical to the effectiveness of an application that the communication over the network be within certain performance limits. Performance management of a computer network comprises two broad functional categories— monitoring and controlling. Monitoring is the function that tracks activities on the network. The controlling function enables performance management to make adjustments to improve network performance. Some of the performance issues of concern to the network manager are as follows:

- What is the level of capacity utilization?
- Is there excessive traffic?

- Has throughput been reduced to unacceptable levels?
- Are there bottlenecks?
- Is response time increasing?

To deal with these concerns, the network manager must focus on some initial set of resources to be monitored to assess performance levels. This includes associating appropriate metrics and values with relevant network resources as indicators of different levels of performance. For example, what count of retransmissions on a transport connection is considered to be a performance problem requiring attention? Performance management, therefore, must monitor many resources to provide information in determining network operating level. By collecting this information, analyzing it, and then using the resultant analysis as feedback to the prescribed set of values, the network manger can become more and more adept at recognizing situations indicative of present or impending performance degradation.

User Requirements Before using a network for a particular application, a user may want to know such things as the average and worst case response times and the reliability of network services. Thus performance must be known in sufficient detail to assess specific user queries. End users expect network services to be managed in such a way as to afford their applications consistently good response time.

Network managers need performance statistics to help them plan, manage, and maintain large networks. Performance statistics can be used to recognize potential bottlenecks before they cause problems to end users. Appropriate corrective action can then be taken. This action can take the form of changing routing tables to balance or redistribute traffic load during times of peak use or when a bottleneck is identified by a rapidly growing load in one area. Over the long term, capacity planning based on such performance information can indicate the proper decisions to make, for example, with regard to expansion of lines in that area.

Security Management

Overview Security management is concerned with generating, distributing, and storing encryption keys. Passwords and other authorization or access control information must be maintained and distributed. Security management is also concerned with monitoring and controlling access to computer networks and access to all or part of the network management information obtained from the network nodes. Logs are an important security tool, and therefore security management is very much involved with the collection, storage, and examination of audit records and security logs, as well as with the enabling and disabling of these logging facilities.

User Requirements Security management provides facilities for protection of network resources and user information. Network security facilities should be available for authorized users only. Users want to know that the proper security policies are in force and effective and that the management of security facilities is itself secure.

17.2 NETWORK MANAGEMENT SYSTEMS

Architecture of a Network Management System

A **network management system** is a collection of tools for network monitoring and control that is integrated in the following senses:

- A single operator interface with a powerful but user-friendly set of commands for performing most or all network management tasks.
- A minimal amount of separate equipment. That is, most of the hardware and software required for network management is incorporated into the existing user equipment.

A network management system consists of incremental hardware and software additions implemented among existing network components. The software used in accomplishing the network management tasks resides in the host computers and communications processors (e.g., front-end processors, terminal cluster controllers, bridges, routers). A network management system is designed to view the entire network as a unified architecture, with addresses and labels assigned to each point and the specific attributes of each element and link known to the system. The active elements of the network provide regular feedback of status information to the network control center.

Figure 17.1 suggests the architecture of a network management system. Each network node contains a collection of software devoted to the network management

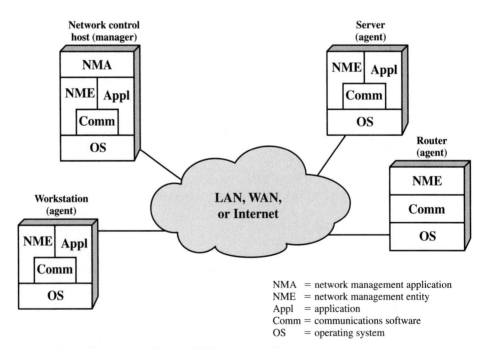

NMA = network management application
NME = network management entity
Appl = application
Comm = communications software
OS   = operating system

Figure 17.1   Elements of a Network Management System

task, referred to in the diagram as a network management entity (NME). Each NME performs the following tasks:

- Collect statistics on communications and network-related activities.
- Store statistics locally.
- Respond to commands from the network control center, including commands to

  1. Transmit collected statistics to network control center.
  2. Change a parameter (e.g., a timer used in a transport protocol).
  3. Provide status information (e.g., parameter values, active links).
  4. Generate artificial traffic to perform a test.

- Send messages to the NCC when local conditions undergo a significant change.

At least one host in the network is designated as the network control host, or **manager**. In addition to the NME software, the network control host includes a collection of software called the network management application (NMA). The NMA includes an operator interface to allow an authorized user to manage the network. The NMA responds to user commands by displaying information and/or by issuing commands to NMEs throughout the network. This communication is carried out using an application-level network management protocol that employs the communications architecture in the same fashion as any other distributed application.

Each other node in the network that is part of the network management system includes a NME and, for purposes of network management, is referred to as an **agent**. Agents include end systems that support user applications as well as nodes that provide a communications service, such as front-end processors, cluster controllers, bridges, and routers.

As depicted in Figure 17.1, the network control host communicates with and controls the NMEs in other systems. For maintaining high availability of the network management function, two or more network control hosts are used. In normal operation, one of the centers is idle or simply collecting statistics, while the other is used for control. If the primary network control host fails, the backup system can be used.

17.3 SIMPLE NETWORK MANAGEMENT PROTOCOL (SNMP)

Simple Network Management Protocol Version 1 (SNMPv1)

SNMP was developed for use as a network management tool for networks and internetworks operating TCP/IP. It has since been expanded for use in all types of networking environments. The term *simple network management protocol (SNMP)* is actually used to refer to a collection of specifications for network management that include the protocol itself, the definition of a database, and associated concepts.

Basic Concepts The model of network management that is used for SNMP includes the following key elements:

- Management station, or manager
- Agent

- Management information base
- Network management protocol

The **management station** is typically a standalone device, but may be a capability implemented on a shared system. In either case, the management station serves as the interface for the human network manager into the network management system. The management station will have, at minimum, the following:

- A set of management applications for data analysis, fault recovery, and so on
- An interface by which the network manager may monitor and control the network
- The capability of translating the network manager's requirements into the actual monitoring and control of remote elements in the network
- A database of network management information extracted from the databases of all the managed entities in the network

Only the last two elements are the subject of SNMP standardization.

The other active element in the network management system is the **management agent**. Key platforms, such as hosts, bridges, routers, and hubs, may be equipped with agent software so that they may be managed from a management station. The agent responds to requests for information from a management station, responds to requests for actions from the management station, and may asynchronously provide the management station with important but unsolicited information.

To manage resources in the network, each resource is represented as an object. An object is, essentially, a data variable that represents one aspect of the managed agent. The collection of objects is referred to as a **management information base** (MIB). The MIB functions as a collection of access points at the agent for the management station. These objects are standardized across systems of a particular class (e.g., bridges all support the same management objects). A management station performs the monitoring function by retrieving the value of MIB objects. A management station can cause an action to take place at an agent or can change the configuration settings of an agent by modifying the value of specific variables.

The management station and agents are linked by a **network management protocol**. The protocol used for the management of TCP/IP networks is the Simple Network Management Protocol (SNMP). An enhanced version of SNMP, known as SNMPv2, is intended for both TCP/IP- and OSI-based networks. Each of these protocols includes the following key capabilities:

- **Get:** Enables the management station to retrieve the value of objects at the agent
- **Set:** Enables the management station to set the value of objects at the agent
- **Notify:** Enables an agent to send unsolicited notifications to the management station of significant events

In a traditional centralized network management scheme, one host in the configuration has the role of a network management station; there may be one or two other management stations in a backup role. The remainder of the devices on the network contain agent software and a MIB, to allow monitoring and control from

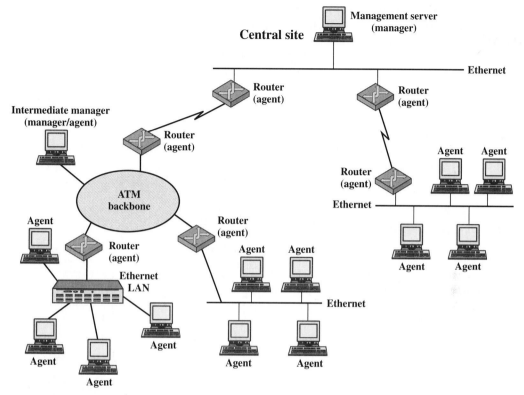

Figure 17.2 Example of a Distributed Network Management Configuration

the management station. As networks grow in size and traffic load, such a centralized system is unworkable. Too much burden is placed on the management station, and there is too much traffic, with reports from every single agent having to wend their way across the entire network to headquarters. In such circumstances, a decentralized, distributed approach works best (e.g., Figure 17.2). In a decentralized network management scheme, there may be multiple top-level management stations, which might be referred to as management servers. Each such server might directly manage a portion of the total pool of agents. However, for many of the agents, the management server delegates responsibility to an intermediate manager. The intermediate manager plays the role of manager to monitor and control the agents under its responsibility. It also plays an agent role to provide information and accept control from a higher-level management server. This type of architecture spreads the processing burden and reduces total network traffic.

Network Management Protocol Architecture SNMP is an application-level protocol that is part of the TCP/IP protocol suite. It is intended to operate over the user datagram protocol (UDP). Figure 17.3 suggests the typical configuration of protocols for SNMPv1. For a standalone management station, a manager process controls access to a central MIB at the management station and provides an interface to the network manager. The manager process achieves network management by using SNMP, which is implemented on top of UDP, IP, and the relevant network-dependent protocols (e.g., Ethernet, ATM, frame relay).

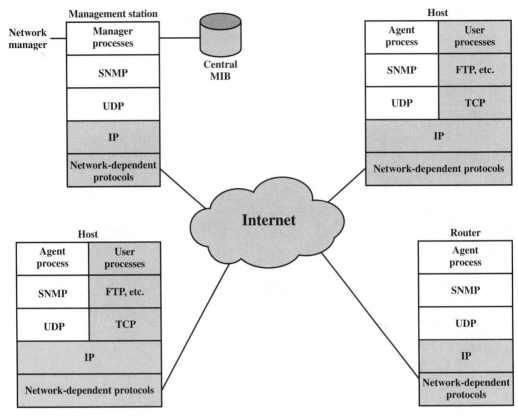

Figure 17.3   SNMPv1 Configuration

Each agent must also implement SNMP, UDP, and IP. In addition, there is an agent process that interprets the SNMP messages and controls the agent's MIB. For an agent device that supports other applications, such as FTP, TCP as well as UDP is required. In Figure 17.3, the shaded portions depict the operational environment: that which is to be managed. The unshaded portions provide support to the network management function.

Figure 17.4 provides a somewhat closer look at the protocol context of SNMP. From a management station, three types of SNMP messages are issued on behalf of a management application: GetRequest, GetNextRequest, and SetRequest. The first two are two variations of the get function. All three messages are acknowledged by the agent in the form of a GetResponse message, which is passed up to the management application. In addition, an agent may issue a trap message in response to an event that affects the MIB and the underlying managed resources. Management requests are sent to UDP port 161, while the agent sends traps to UDP port 162.

Because SNMP relies on UDP, which is a connectionless protocol, SNMP is itself connectionless. No ongoing connections are maintained between a management station and its agents. Instead, each exchange is a separate transaction between a management station and an agent.

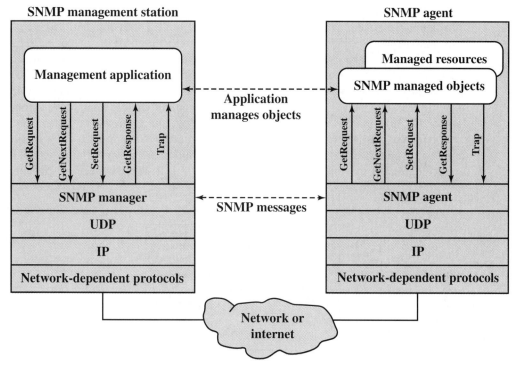

Figure 17.4 The Role of SNMPv1

Simple Network Management Protocol Version 2 (SNMPv2)

In August of 1988, the specification for SNMP was issued and rapidly became the dominant network management standard. A number of vendors offer standalone network management workstations based on SNMP, and most vendors of bridges, routers, workstations, and PCs offer SNMP agent packages that allow their products to be managed by an SNMP management station.

As the name suggests, SNMP is a simple tool for network management. It defines a limited, easily implemented management information base (MIB) of scalar variables and two-dimensional tables, and it defines a streamlined protocol to enable a manager to get and set MIB variables and to enable an agent to issue unsolicited notifications, called *traps*. This simplicity is the strength of SNMP. SNMP is easily implemented and consumes modest processor and network resources. Also, the structure of the protocol and the MIB are sufficiently straightforward that it is not difficult to achieve interoperability among management stations and agent software from a mix of vendors.

With its widespread use, the deficiencies of SNMP became increasingly apparent; these include both functional deficiencies and a lack of a security facility. As a result, an enhanced version, known as SNMPv2, was issued (RFCs 1901, 1905 through 1909, and 2578 through 2580). SNMPv2 has quickly gained support, and a number of vendors announced products within months of the issuance of the standard.

The Elements of SNMPv2 As with SNMPv1, SNMPv2 provides a framework on which network management applications can be built. Those applications, such as fault management, performance monitoring, accounting, and so on, are outside the scope of the standard. SNMPv2 provides the infrastructure for network management. Figure 17.5 is an example of a configuration that illustrates that infrastructure.

The essence of SNMPv2 is a protocol that is used to exchange management information. Each "player" in the network management system maintains a local database of information relevant to network management, known as the management information base (MIB). The SNMPv2 standard defines the structure of this information and the allowable data types; this definition is known as the structure of management information (SMI). We can think of this as the language for defining

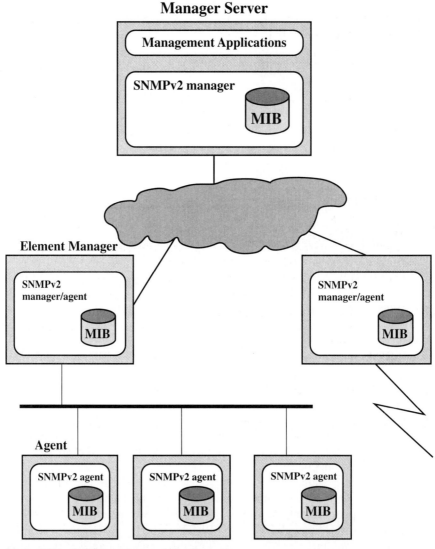

Figure 17.5   SNMPv2-Managed Configuration

management information. The standard also supplies a number of MIBs that are generally useful for network management.[1] In addition, new MIBs may be defined by vendors and user groups.

At least one system in the configuration must be responsible for network management. It is here that any network management applications are hosted. There may be more than one of these management stations, to provide redundancy or simply to split up the duties in a large network. Most other systems act the role of agent. An agent collects information locally and stores it for later access by a manager. The information includes data about the system itself and may also include traffic information for the network or networks to which the agent attaches.

SNMPv2 supports either a highly centralized network management strategy or a distributed one. In the latter case, some systems operate both in the role of manager and of agent. In its agent role, such a system will accept commands from a superior management system. Some of those commands relate to the local MIB at the agent. Other commands require the agent to act as a proxy for remote devices. In this case, the proxy agent assumes the role of manager to access information at a remote agent, and then assumes the role of an agent to pass that information on to a superior manager.

All of these exchanges take place using the SNMPv2 protocol, which is a simple request/response type of protocol. Typically, SNMPv2 is implemented on top of the user datagram protocol (UDP), which is part of the TCP/IP suite. Because SNMPv2 exchanges are in the nature of discrete request-response pairs, an ongoing reliable connection is not required.

Structure of Management Information The structure of management information (SMI) defines the general framework within which a MIB can be defined and constructed. The SMI identifies the data types that can be used in the MIB, and how resources within the MIB are represented and named. The philosophy behind SMI is to encourage simplicity and extensibility within the MIB. Thus, the MIB can store only simple data types: scalars and two-dimensional arrays of scalars, called tables. The SMI does not support the creation or retrieval of complex data structures. This philosophy is in contrast to that used with OSI systems management, which provides for complex data structures and retrieval modes to support greater functionality. SMI avoids complex data types and structures to simplify the task of implementation and to enhance interoperability. MIBs will inevitably contain vendor-created data types and, unless tight restrictions are placed on the definition of such data types, interoperability will suffer.

There are three key elements in the SMI specification. At the lowest level, the SMI specifies the data types that may be stored. Then the SMI specifies a formal technique for defining objects and tables of objects. Finally, the SMI provides a scheme for associating a unique identifier with each actual object in a system, so that data at an agent can be referenced by a manager.

---

[1]There is a slight fuzziness about the term *MIB*. In its singular form, the term *MIB* can be used to refer to the entire database of management information at a manager or an agent. It can also be used in singular or plural form to refer to a specific defined collection of management information that is part of an overall MIB. Thus, the SNMPv2 standard includes the definition of several MIBs and incorporates, by reference, MIBs defined in SNMPv1.

Table 17.2 Allowable Data Types in SNMPv2

Data Type	Description
INTEGER	Integers in the range of -2^{31} to $2^{31} - 1$,
UInteger32	Integers in the range of 0 to $2^{32} - 1$,
Counter32	A nonnegative integer that may be incremented modulo 2^{32}.
Counter64	A nonnegative integer that may be incremented modulo 2^{64}.
Gauge32	A nonnegative integer that may increase or decrease, but shall not exceed a maximum value. The maximum value can not be greater than $2^{32} - 1$.
TimeTicks	A nonnegative integer that represents the time, modulo 2^{32}, in hundredths of a second.
OCTET STRING	Octet strings for arbitrary binary or textual data; may be limited to 255 octets.
IPAddress	A 32-bit internet address.
Opaque	An arbitrary bit field.
BIT STRING	An enumeration of named bits.
OBJECT IDENTIFIER	Administratively assigned name to object or other standardized element. Value is a sequence of up to 128 nonnegative integers.

Table 17.2 shows the data types that are allowed by the SMI. This is a fairly restricted set of types. For example, real numbers are not supported. However, it is rich enough to support most network management requirements.

Protocol Operation The heart of the SNMPv2 framework is the protocol itself. The protocol provides a straightforward, basic mechanism for the exchange of management information between manager and agent.

The basic unit of exchange is the message, which consists of an outer message wrapper and an inner protocol data unit (PDU). The outer message header deals with security and is discussed later in this section.

Seven types of PDUs may be carried in an SNMP message. The general formats for these are illustrated informally in Figure 17.6. Several fields are common to a number of PDUs. The request-id field is an integer assigned such that each outstanding request can be uniquely identified. This enables a manager to correlate incoming responses with outstanding requests. It also enables an agent to cope with duplicate PDUs generated by an unreliable transport service. The variable-bindings field contains a list of object identifiers; depending on the PDU, the list may also include a value for each object.

The GetRequest-PDU, issued by a manager, includes a list of one or more object names for which values are requested. If the get operation is successful, then the responding agent will send a Response-PDU. The variable-bindings list will contain the identifier and value of all retrieved objects. For any variables that are not in the relevant MIB view, its identifier and an error code are returned in the variable-bindings list. Thus, SNMPv2 permits partial responses to a GetRequest, which is a significant improvement over SNMP. In SNMP, if one or more of the variables in a

t

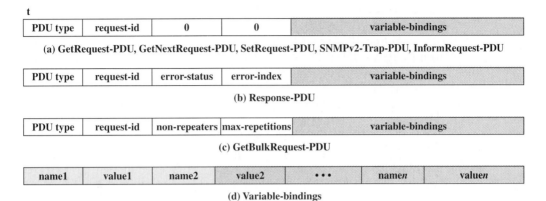

PDU type	request-id	0	0	variable-bindings

(a) GetRequest-PDU, GetNextRequest-PDU, SetRequest-PDU, SNMPv2-Trap-PDU, InformRequest-PDU

PDU type	request-id	error-status	error-index	variable-bindings

(b) Response-PDU

PDU type	request-id	non-repeaters	max-repetitions	variable-bindings

(c) GetBulkRequest-PDU

name1	value1	name2	value2	• • •	name$n$	value$n$

(d) Variable-bindings

Figure 17.6 SNMPv2 PDU Format

GetRequest is not supported, the agent returns an error message with a status of noSuchName. To cope with such an error, the SNMP manager must either return no values to the requesting application, or it must include an algorithm that responds to an error by removing the missing variables, resending the request, and then sending a partial result to the application.

The GetNextRequest-PDU also is issued by a manager and includes a list of one or more objects. In this case, for each object named in the variable-bindings field, a value is to be returned for the object that is next in lexicographic order, which is equivalent to saying next in the MIB in terms of its position in the tree structure of object identifiers. As with the GetRequest-PDU, the agent will return values for as many variables as possible. One of the strengths of the GetNext-Request-PDU is that it enables a manager entity to discover the structure of a MIB view dynamically. This is useful if the manager does not know a priori the set of objects that is supported by an agent or that is in a particular MIB view.

One of the major enhancements provided in SNMPv2 is the GetBulkRequest-PDU. The purpose of this PDU is to minimize the number of protocol exchanges required to retrieve a large amount of management information. The GetBulk-Request-PDU allows an SNMPv2 manager to request that the response be as large as possible given the constraints on message size.

The SetRequest-PDU is issued by a manager to request that the values of one or more objects be altered. The receiving SNMPv2 entity responds with a Response-PDU containing the same request-id. The SetRequest operation is atomic: Either all of the variables are updated or none are. If the responding entity is able to set values for all of the variables listed in the incoming variable-bindings list, then the Response-PDU includes the variable-bindings field, with a value supplied for each variable. If at least one of the variable values cannot be supplied, then no values are returned, and no values are updated. In the latter case, the error-status code indicates the reason for the failure, and the error-index field indicates the variable in the variable-bindings list that caused the failure.

The SNMPv2-Trap-PDU is generated and transmitted by an SNMPv2 entity acting in an agent role when an unusual event occurs. It is used to provide the management station with an asynchronous notification of some significant event. The variable-bindings list is used to contain the information associated with the trap message. Unlike the GetRequest, GetNextRequest, GetBulkRequest, SetRequest, and InformRequest-PDUs, the SNMPv2-Trap-PDU does not elicit a response from the receiving entity; it is an unconfirmed message.

The InformRequest-PDU is sent by an SNMPv2 entity acting in a manager role, on behalf of an application, to another SNMPv2 entity acting in a manager role, to provide management information to an application using the latter entity. As with the SNMPv2-Trap-PDU, the variable-bindings field is used to convey the associated information. The manager receiving an InformRequest acknowledges receipt with a Response-PDU.

For both the SNMPv2-Trap and the InformRequest, various conditions can be defined that indicate when the notification is generated; the information to be sent is also specified.

Simple Network Management Protocol Version 3 (SNMPv3)

Many of the functional deficiencies of SNMP were addressed in SNMPv2. To correct the security deficiencies of SNMPv1/v2, SNMPv3 was issued as a set of Proposed Standards in January 1998 (currently RFCs 2570 through 2575). This set of documents does not provide a complete SNMP capability but rather defines an overall SNMP architecture and a set of security capabilities. These are intended to be used with the existing SNMPv2.

SNMPv3 provides three important services: authentication, privacy, and access control. The first two are part of the User-Based Security (USM) model, and the last is defined in the View-Based Access Control Model (VACM). Security services are governed by the identity of the user requesting the service; this identity is expressed as a principal, which may be an individual or an application or a group of individuals or applications.

The authentication mechanism in USM assures that a received message was transmitted by the principal whose identifier appears as the source in the message header. This mechanism also assures that the message has not been altered in transit and has not been artificially delayed or replayed. The sending principal provides authentication by including a message authentication code with the SNMP message it is sending. This code is a function of the contents of the message, the identity of the sending and receiving parties, the time of transmission, and a secret key that should be known only to sender and receiver. The secret key must be set up outside of USM as a configuration function. That is, the configuration manager or network manager is responsible for distributing secret keys to be loaded into the databases of the various SNMP managers and agents. This can be done manually or using some form of secure data transfer outside of USM. When the receiving principal gets the message, it uses the same secret key to calculate the message authentication code once again. If the receiver's version of the code matches the value appended to the incoming message, then the receiver knows that the message can only have originated from the authorized manager and that the message was not altered in transit. The shared secret key between sending and receiving parties must be preconfigured. The actual authentication code used is known as HMAC, which is an Internet-standard authentication mechanism.

The privacy facility of USM enables managers and agents to encrypt messages. Again, manager principal and agent principal must share a secret key. In this case, if the two are configured to use the privacy facility, all traffic between them is encrypted using the Data Encryption Standard (DES). The sending principal encrypts the message using the DES algorithm and its secret key, and sends the message to the receiving principal, which decrypts it using the DES algorithm and the same secret key.

The access control facility makes it possible to configure agents to provide different levels of access to the agent's management information base (MIB) to different managers. An agent principal can restrict access to its MIB for a particular manager principal in two ways. First, it can restrict access to a certain portion of its MIB. For example, an agent may restrict most manager parties to viewing performance-related statistics and only allow a single designated manager principal to view and update configuration parameters. Second, the agent can limit the operations that a manager can use on that portion of the MIB. For example, a particular manager principal could be limited to read-only access to a portion of an agent's MIB. The access control policy to be used by an agent for each manager must be preconfigured and essentially consists of a table that detail the access privileges of the various authorized managers.

17.4 RECOMMENDED READING AND WEB SITES

[STAL99] provides a comprehensive and detailed examination of SNMP, SNMPv2, and SNMPv3; the book also provides an overview of network management technology. One of the few textbooks on the subject of network management is [SUBR00].

STAL99 Stallings, W. *SNMP, SNMPv2, SNMPv3, and RMON 1 and 2.* Reading, MA: Addison-Wesley, 1999.

SUBR00 Subranamian, M. *Network Management: Principles and Practice.* Reading, MA: Addison-Wesley, 2000.

 Recommended Web Site:

- **Simple Web Site:** Maintained by the University of Twente. It is a good source of information on SNMP, including pointers to many public-domain implementations and lists of books and articles.

17.5 KEY TERMS, REVIEW QUESTIONS, AND PROBLEMS

Key Terms

accounting management	management station	security management
agent	manager	Simple Network
configuration and name	network management	Management Protocol
management	network management	(SNMP)
fault	protocol	Structure of Management
fault management	network management	Information (SMI)
management information base	system	
(MIB)	performance management	

Review Questions

17.1 List and briefly define the key areas that comprise network management.

17.2 List two ways in which a network management system may be characterized as integrated.

17.3 List and briefly define the key elements of SNMP.

17.4 What functions are provided by SNMP?

17.5 Describe two different interpretations of the term *MIB*.

17.6 What are the differences among SNMPv1, SNMPv2, and SNMPv3?

Problems

17.1 Because SNMP uses two different port numbers (UDP ports 161 and 162), a single system can easily run both a manager and an agent. What would happen if the same port number were used for both?

17.2 The original (version 1) specification of SNMP has the following definition of a new type:

```
Gauge ::= [APPLICATION 2] IMPLICIT INTEGER (0..4294967295)
```

The standard includes the following explanation of the semantics of this type:

> This application-wide type represents a non-negative integer, which may increase or decrease, but which latches at a maximum value. This standard specifies a maximum value of $2^{32} - 1$ (4294967295 decimal) for gauges.

Unfortunately, the word *latch* is not defined, and this has resulted in two different interpretations. The SNMPv2 standard cleared up the ambiguity with the following definition:

> The value of a Gauge has its maximum value whenever the information being modeled is greater than or equal to that maximum value; if the information being modeled subsequently decreases below the maximum value, the Gauge also decreases.

a. What is the alternative interpretation?

b. Discuss the pros and cons of the two interpretations.

APPENDIX A

RFCS CITED IN THIS BOOK

There are some dogs who wouldn't debase what are to them sacred forms. A very fine, very serious German Shepherd I worked with, for instance, grumbled noisily at other dogs when they didn't obey. When training him to retrieve, at one point I set the dumbbell on its end for the fun of it. He glared disapprovingly at the dumbbell and at me, then pushed it carefully back into its proper position before picking it up and returning with it, rather sullenly.

—Adams Task: Calling Animals by Name, Vicki Hearne

Number	Title	Date
768	User Datagram Protocol (UDP)	1980
791	Internet Protocol (IP)	1981
792	Internet Control Message Protocol (ICMP)	1981
793	Transmission Control Protocol (TCP)	1981
821	Simple Mail Transfer Protocol (SMTP)	1982
822	Standard for the Format of ARPA Internet Text Messages	1982
854	Telnet Protocol Specification	1983
855	Telnet Option Specification	1983
959	File Transfer Protocol	1985
1034	Domain Names—Concepts and Facilities	1987
1035	Domain Names—Implementation and Specification	1987
1058	Routing Information Protocol	1988
1122	Requirements for Internet Hosts—Communication Layers	1989
1123	Requirements for Internet Hosts—Application and Supoprt	1989
1323	TCP Extensions for High Performance	1992
1350	Trivial File Transfer Protocol (Revision 2)	1992
1584	Multicast Extensions to OSPF	1994
1633	Integrated Service in the Internet Architecture: An Overview	1994
1636	Security in the Internet Architecture	1994
1752	The Recommendation for the IP Next Generation Protocol	1995
1771	A Border Gateway Protocol 4 (BGP-4)	1995
1812	Requirements for IP Version 4 Routers	1995
1889	RTP: A Transport Protocol For Real-Time Applications	1996

Number	Title	Date
1890	RTP Profile for Audio and Video Conferences with Minimal Control	1996
1901	Introduction to Community-Based SNMPv2	1996
1905	Protocol Operations for SNMPv2	1996
1906	Transport Mappings for SNMPv2	1996
1907	Management Information Base for SNMPv2	1996
1908	Coexistence Between Version 1 and Version 2 of the Internet-Standard Network Management Framework	1996
1909	An Administrative Infrastructure for SNMPv2	1996
1935	What is the Internet, Anyway?	1996
2018	TCP Selective Acknowledgement Options	1996
2026	The Internet Standards Process—Revision 3	1996
2045	Multipurpose Internet Mail Extensions (MIME) Part One: Format of Internet Message Bodies	1996
2046	Multipurpose Internet Mail Extensions (MIME) Part Two: Media Types	1996
2047	MIME (Multipurpose Internet Mail Extensions) Part Three: Message Header Extensions for Non-ASCII Text	1996
2048	Multipurpose Internet Mail Extensions (MIME) Part Four: Registration Procedures	1996
2049	Multipurpose Internet Mail Extensions (MIME) Part Five: Conformance Criteria and Examples	1996
2205	Resource ReSerVation Protocol (RSVP)—Version 1 Functional Specification	1997
2327	SDP: Session Description Protocol	1998
2328	Open Shortest Path First (OSPF) Version 2	1998
2246	The TLS Protocol	1999
2352	Protocol Independent Multicast—Sparse Mode	1998
2373	IP Version 6 Addressing Architecture	1998
2396	Uniform Resource Identifiers (URI): Generic Syntax	1998
2401	Security Architecture for the Internet Protocol	1998
2402	IP Authentication Header	1998
2406	IP Encapsulating Security Payload (ESP)	1998
2408	Internet Security Association and Key Management Protocol	1998
2460	Internet Protocol, Version 6 Specification	1998
2474	Definition of the Differentiated Services Field in the IPv4 and IPv6 Headers	1998

Number	Title	Date
2475	An Architecture for Differentiated Services	1998
2570	Introduction to Version 3 of the Internet-Standard Network Management Framework	1999
2571	An Architecture for Describing SNMP Management Frameworks	1999
2572	Message Processing and Dispatching for SNMP	1999
2573	SNMP Applications	1999
2574	User-Based Security Model for SNMPv3	1999
2575	View-Based Access Control Model (VACM) for SNMP	1999
2578	Structure of Management Information Version 2 (SMIv2)	1999
2579	Textual Conventions for SMIv2	1999
2580	Conformance Statements for SMIv2	1999
2597	Assured Forwarding PHB Group	1999
2581	TCP Congestion Control	1999
2616	Hypertext Transfer Protocol—HTTP/1.1	1999
2676	QoS Routing Mechanisms and OSPF Extensions	1999
2702	MPLS Traffic Engineering	1999
2782	A DNS RR for Specifying the Location of Services	2000
2828	Internet Security Glossary	2000
2848	The PINT Service Protocol: Extensions to SIP and SDP for IP Access to Telephone Call Services	2000
2953	Telnet Encryption	2000
2988	Computing TCP's Retransmission Timer	2000
3031	Multiprotocol Label Switching Architecture	2001
3032	MPLS Label Stack Encoding	2001
3042	Enhancing TCP's Loss Recovery Using Limited Transmit	2001
3168	The Addition of Explicit Congestion Notification (ECN) to IP	2001
3246	An Expedited Forwarding (PHB Per-Hop Behavior)	2002
3247	Supplemental Information for the New Definition of the EF PHB	2002
3260	New Terminology and Clarifications for DiffServ	2002
3261	SIP: Session Initiation Protocol	2002
3376	Internet Group Management Protocol, Version 3	2002

APPENDIX B

PROJECTS FOR TEACHING COMPUTER NETWORKS

Analysis and observation, theory and experience must never disdain or exclude each other; on the contrary, they support each other.

—*On War,* Carl von Clausewitz

Many instructors believe that research or implementation projects are crucial to the clear understanding of the concepts of computer networks. Without projects, it may be difficult for students to grasp some of the basic concepts and interactions among components. Projects reinforce the concepts introduced in the book, give the student a greater appreciation of the how protocols and transmission schemes work, and can motivate students and give them confidence that they have mastered the material.

In this text, I have tried to present the concepts as clearly as possible and have provided nearly 200 homework problems to reinforce those concepts. Many instructors will wish to supplement this material with projects. This appendix provides some guidance in that regard and describes support material available in the instructor's manual. The support material covers five types of projects:

- Sockets programming projects
- Simulation projects
- Performance modeling projects
- Research projects
- Reading/report assignments

B.1 SOCKETS PROGRAMMING PROJECTS

The concept of sockets and sockets programming was developed in the 1980s in the Unix environment as the Berkeley Sockets Interface. In essence, a socket enables communications between a client and server process and may be either connection-oriented or connectionless. A socket can be considered an endpoint in a communication. A client socket in one computer uses an address to call a server socket on another computer. Once the appropriate sockets are engaged, the two computers can exchange data.

Typically, computers with server sockets keep a TCP or UDP port open, ready for unscheduled incoming calls. The client typically determines the socket identification of the desired server by finding it in a Domain Name System (DNS) database. Once a connection is made, the server switches the dialogue to a different port number to free up the main port number for additional incoming calls.

Internet applications, such as TELNET and remote login (rlogin) make use of sockets, with the details hidden from the user. However, sockets can be constructed from within a program (in a language such as C or Java), enabling the programmer to easily support networking functions and applications. The sockets programming mechanism includes sufficient semantics to permit unrelated processes on different hosts to communicate.

608

The Berkeley Sockets Interface is the de facto standard application programming interface (API) for developing networking applications, spanning a wide range of operating systems. The sockets API provides generic access to interprocess communications services. Thus, the sockets capability is ideally suited for students to learn the principles of protocols and distributed applications by hands-on program development.

The Web site for this course includes an overview of sockets programming prepared especially for this book plus links to sites with more information on the subject. In addition, the instructor's manual includes a set of programming projects.

B.2 SIMULATION PROJECTS

An excellent way to obtain a grasp of the operation of communication protocols and network configurations, and to study and appreciate some of the design tradeoffs and performance implications, is by simulating key elements. A tool that is useful for this purpose is *cnet*.

Compared to actual hardware/software implementation, simulation provides several advantages for both research and educational use:

- With simulation, it is easy to modify various elements of a network configuration or various features of a protocol, to vary the performance characteristics of various components, and then to analyze the effects of such modifications.
- Simulation provides for detailed performance statistics collection, which can be used to understand performance tradeoffs.

The *cnet* network simulator [MCDO91] enables experimentation with various data link layer, network layer, routing and transport layer protocols, and with various network configurations. It has been specifically designed for undergraduate computer networking courses and used worldwide by thousands of students since 1991.

The *cnet* simulator was developed by Professor Chris McDonald at the University of Western Australia. Professor McDonald has developed a Student User's Manual and a set of project assignments specifically for use with this book and are available to professors on request.

The *cnet* simulator runs under a variety of UNIX and LINUX platforms. The software can be downloaded from the *cnet* Web site. It is available at no cost for noncommercial use.

B.3 PERFORMANCE MODELING

An alternative to simulation for assessing the performance of a communications system or networking protocol is analytic modeling. As used here, analytic modeling refers to tools for doing queuing analysis, as well as tools for doing simple statistical tests on network traffic data and tools for generating time series for analysis.

A powerful and easy-to-use set of tools has been developed by Professor Kenneth Christensen at the University of South Florida. His *tools page* contains downloadable tools primarily related to performance evaluation of computer networks and to TCP/IP sockets programming. Each tool is written in ANSI C. The format for each tool is the same, with the program header describing tool purpose, general notes, sample input, sample output, build instructions, execution instructions, and author/contact information. The code is documented with extensive inline comments and header blocks for all functions. The goal for each tool is that it can serve as a teaching tool for the concept implemented by the tool (and as a model for good programming practices). Thus, the emphasis is on simplicity and clarity. It is assumed that the student will have access to a C compiler and have at least moderate experience in C programming.

Professor Christensen has developed a Student User's Manual and a set of project assignments specifically for use with this book and are available to professors on request. The software can be downloaded from the *tools* Web site. It is available at no cost for noncommercial use.

B.4 RESEARCH PROJECTS

An effective way of reinforcing basic concepts from the course and for teaching students research skills is to assign a research project. Such a project could involve a literature search as well as a Web search of vendor products, research lab activities, and standardization efforts. Projects could be assigned to teams or, for smaller projects, to individuals. In any case, it is best to require some sort of project proposal early in the term, giving the instructor time to evaluate the proposal for appropriate topic and appropriate level of effort. Student handouts for research projects should include the following:

- A format for the proposal
- A format for the final report
- A schedule with intermediate and final deadlines
- A list of possible project topics

The students can select one of the listed topics or devise their own comparable project. The instructor's manual includes a suggested format for the proposal and final report plus a list of possible research topics.

B.5 READING/REPORT ASSIGNMENTS

Another excellent way to reinforce concepts from the course and to give students research experience is to assign papers from the literature to be read and analyzed. The instructor's manual includes a suggested list of papers to be assigned. All of the papers are readily available either via the Internet or in any good college technical library. The manual also includes a suggested assignment wording.

GLOSSARY

In studying the Imperium, Arrakis, and the whole culture which produced Maud'Dib, many unfamiliar terms occur. To increase understanding is a laudable goal, hence the definitions and explanations given below.

—*Dune,* Frank Herbert

Some of the definitions in this glossary are from the *American National Standard Dictionary of Information Technology*, ANSI Standard X3.172, 1995. These are marked with an asterisk.

Abstract Syntax Notation One (ASN.1)   A formal language used to define syntax. In the case of SNMP, ASN.1 notation is used to defined the format of SNMP protocol data units and of objects.

Application layer   Layer 7 of the OSI model. This layer determines the interface of the system with the user.

Asymmetric encryption   A form of cryptosystem in which encryption and decryption are performed using two different keys, one of which is referred to as the public key and one of which is referred to as the private key. Also known as public-key encryption.

Asynchronous transmission   Transmission in which each information character is individually synchronized (usually by the use of start elements and stop elements).

Authentication*   A process used to verify the integrity of transmitted data, especially a message.

Automatic repeat request   A feature that automatically initiates a request for retransmission when an error in transmission is detected.

Bandwidth*   The difference between the limiting (upper and lower) frequencies of a continuous frequency spectrum.

Bit error rate   The probability that a transmitted bit is received in error.

Bit stuffing   The insertion of extra bits into a data stream to avoid the appearance of unintended control sequences.

Bridge*   A functional unit that interconnects two local area networks (LANs) that use the same logical link control protocol but may use different medium access control protocols.

Broadcast   The simultaneous transmission of data to a number of stations.

Broadcast address   An address that designates all entities within a domain (e.g., network, internet).

Broadcast communication network   A communication network in which a transmission from one station is broadcast to and received by all other stations.

Byte   A group of bits, usually eight, used to represent a character of other data.

Checksum An error-detecting code based on a summation operation performed on the bits to be checked.

Ciphertext The output of an encryption algorithm; the encrypted form of a message or data.

Circuit switching A method of communicating in which a dedicated communications path is established between two devices through one or more intermediate switching nodes. Unlike packet switching, digital data are sent as a continuous stream of bits. Bandwidth is guaranteed, and delay is essentially limited to propagation time. The telephone system uses circuit switching.

Common carrier In the United States, companies that furnish communication services to the public. The usual connotation is for long-distance telecommunications services. Common carriers are subject to regulation by federal and state regulatory commissions.

Communications architecture The hardware and software structure that implements the communications function.

Communication network A collection of interconnected functional units that provides a data communications service among stations attached to the network.

Connectionless data transfer A protocol for exchanging data in an unplanned fashion and without prior coordination (e.g., datagram).

Connection-oriented data transfer A protocol for exchanging data in which a logical connection is established between the endpoints (e.g., virtual circuit).

Contention The condition when two or more stations attempt to use the same channel at the same time.

Conventional encryption Symmetric encryption.

Cyclic redundancy check An error-detecting code in which the code is the remainder resulting from dividing the bits to be checked by a predetermined binary number.

Datagram* In packet switching, a packet, independent of other packets, that carries information sufficient for routing from the originating data terminal equipment (DTE) to the destination DTE without the necessity of establishing a connection between the DTEs and the network.

Data Link Layer* In OSI, the layer that provides service to transfer data between network layer entities, usually in adjacent nodes. The data link layer detects and possibly corrects errors that may occur in the physical layer.

Data terminal equipment (DTE)* Equipment consisting of digital end instruments that convert the user information into data signals for transmission, or reconvert the received data signals into user information.

Decryption The translation of encrypted text or data (called ciphertext) into original text or data (called plaintext). Also called deciphering.

Digital signature   An authentication mechanism that enables the creator of a message to attach a code that acts as a signature. The signature guarantees the source and integrity of the message.

Digital transmission   The transmission of digital data, using either an analog or digital signal, in which the digital data are recovered and repeated at intermediate points to reduce the effects of noise.

Digitize*   To convert an analog signal to a digital signal.

Encapsulation   The addition of control information by a protocol entity to data obtained from a protocol user.

Encrypt*   To convert plaintext or data into unintelligible form by the use of a code in such a manner that reconversion to the original form is possible.

Error-detecting code*   A code in which each expression conforms to specific rules of construction, so that if certain errors occur in an expression, the resulting expression will not conform to the rules of construction and thus the presence of the errors is detected.

Error rate*   The ratio of the number of data units in error to the total number of data units.

Flow control   The function performed by a receiving entity to limit the amount or rate of data that is sent by a transmitting entity.

Frame   A group of bits that includes data plus one or more addresses and other protocol control information. Generally refers to a link layer (OSI layer 2) protocol data unit.

Frame check sequence   An error-detecting code inserted as a field in a block of data to be transmitted. The code serves to check for errors upon reception of the data.

Frequency   Rate of signal oscillation in hertz.

Full-duplex transmission   Data transmission in both directions at the same time.

Half-duplex transmission   Data transmission in either direction, one direction at a time.

Hash function   A function that maps a variable length data block or message into a fixed-length value called a hash code. The function is designed in such a way that, when protected, it provides an authenticator to the data or message. Also referred to as a message digest.

HDLC (high-level data link control)   A very common bit-oriented data link protocol (OSI layer 2) issued by ISO. Similar protocols are LAPB, LAPD, and LLC.

Header   System-defined control information that precedes user data.

Hop count   The number of hops along a path from a given source to a given destination is the number of network nodes (packet-switching nodes, ATM switches, routers, etc.) that a packet encounters along that path.

Intermediate system (IS)   A device attached to two or more networks in an internet and that performs routing and relaying of data between end systems. Examples of intermediate systems are bridges and routers.

Internet   An interconnected collection of networks based on the use of the TCP/IP protocol suite.

Internetwork   A collection of packet-switching and broadcast networks that are connected via routers.

Internet protocol   An internetworking protocol that provides connectionless service across multiple packet-switching networks.

Internetworking   Communication among devices across multiple networks.

Layer*   A group of services, functions, and protocols that is complete from a conceptual point of view, that is one out of a set of hierarchically arranged groups, and that extends across all systems that conform to the network architecture.

Local area network   A communication network that provides interconnection of a variety of data communicating devices within a small area.

Longitudinal redundancy check   The use of a set of parity bits for a block of characters such that there is a parity bit for each bit position in the characters.

Medium access control (MAC)   For broadcast networks, the method of determining which device has access to the transmission medium at any time. CSMA/CD and token are common access methods.

Modem (modulator/demodulator)   Transforms a digital bit stream into an analog signal (modulator), and vice versa (demodulator).

Modulation*   The process, or result of the process, of varying certain characteristics of a signal, called a carrier, in accordance with a message signal.

Multicast address   An address that designates a group of entities within a domain (e.g., network, internet).

Multiplexing   In data transmission, a function that permits two or more data sources to share a common transmission medium such that each data source has its own channel.

Network layer   Layer 3 of the OSI model. Responsible for routing data through a communication network.

Noise   Unwanted signals that combine with and hence distort the signal intended for transmission and reception.

Octet   A group of 8 bits, usually operated upon as an entity.

Open Systems Interconnection (OSI) Reference Model   A model of communications between cooperating devices. It defines a seven-layer architecture of communication functions.

Packet   A group of bits that includes data plus control information. Generally refers to a network layer (OSI layer 3) protocol data unit.

Packet switching   A method of transmitting messages through a communication network, in which long messages are subdivided into short packets. The packets are then transmitted as in message switching.

Parity bit*   A check bit appended to an array of binary digits to make the sum of all the binary digits, including the check bit, always odd (odd parity) or always even (even parity).

Peer layer   Two protocol layers in different systems are peer layers if they are at the same level of the protocol hierarchy (e.g., both layer 3) and if they share a common protocol.

Physical layer   Layer 1 of the OSI model. Concerned with the electrical, mechanical, and timing aspects of signal transmission over a medium.

Piggybacking   The inclusion of an acknowledgment to a previously received packet in an outgoing data packet.

Plaintext   The input to an encryption function or the output of a decryption function.

Port   A transport-layer address that identifies a user of a transport-layer protocol.

Presentation layer*   Layer 6 of the OSI model. Provides for the selection of a common syntax for representing data and for transformation of application data into and from the common syntax.

Private key   One of the two keys used in an asymmetric encryption system. For secure communication, the private key should only be known to its creator.

Propagation delay   The delay between the time a signal enters a channel and the time it is received.

Protocol   A set of rules that govern the operation of functional units to achieve communication.

Protocol architecture   The layered structure of hardware and software that supports the exchange of data between systems and supports distributed applications, such as electronic mail and file transfer.

Protocol control information*   Information exchanged between entities of a given layer, via the service provided by the next lower layer, to coordinate their joint operation.

Protocol data unit (PDU)*   A set of data specified in a protocol of a given layer and consisting of protocol control information of that layer, and possibly user data of that layer.

Public key   One of the two keys used in an asymmetric encryption system. The public key is made public, to be used in conjunction with a corresponding private key.

Public-key encryption   Asymmetric encryption.

Residual error rate   The error rate remaining after attempts at correction are made.

Repeater   A device that receives data on one communication link and transmits it, bit by bit, on another link as fast as the data are received, without buffering.

Router   An internetworking device that connects two computer networks. It makes use of an internet protocol and assumes that all of the attached devices on the networks use the same communications architecture and protocols. A router operates at OSI layer 3.

Routing   The determination of a path that a data unit (frame, packet, message) will traverse from source to destination.

Service access point   A means of identifying a user of the services of a protocol entity. A protocol entity provides one or more SAPs for use by higher-level entities.

Session layer   Layer 5 of the OSI model. Manages a logical connection (session) between two communicating processes or applications.

Signaling   The exchange of information specifically concerned with the establishment and control of connections, and with management, in a telecommunication network.

Sliding-window technique   A method of flow control in which a transmitting station may send numbered packets within a window of numbers. The window changes dynamically to allow additional packets to be sent.

Stop and wait   A flow control protocol in which the sender transmits a block of data and then awaits an acknowledgment before transmitting the next block.

Subnetwork   Refers to a constituent network of an internet. This avoids ambiguity because the entire internet, from a user's point of view, is a single network.

Symmetric encryption   A form of cryptosystem in which encryption and decryption are performed using the same key. Also known as conventional encryption.

Synchronous transmission   Data transmission in which the time of occurrence of each signal representing a bit is related to a fixed time frame.

Time-division multiplexing   The division of a transmission facility into two or more channels by allotting the facility to several different information channels, one at a time.

Transmission medium   The physical path between transmitters and receivers in a communications system.

Transport layer   Layer 4 of the OSI model. Provides reliable, transparent transfer of data between endpoints.

Virtual circuit   A packet-switching service in which a connection (virtual circuit) is established between two stations at the start of transmission. All packets follow the same route, need not carry a complete address, and arrive in sequence.

ACRONYMS

AAL	ATM Adaptation Layer
ADSL	Asymmetric Digital Subscriber Line
AES	Advanced Encryption Standard
AM	Amplitude Modulation
AMI	Alternate Mark Inversion
ANS	American National Standard
ANSI	American National Standard Institute
ARQ	Automatic Repeat Request
ASCII	American Standard Code for Information Interchange
ASK	Amplitude-Shift Keying
ATM	Asynchronous Transfer Mode
BER	Bit Error Rate
B-ISDN	Broadband ISDN
BGP	Border Gateway Protocol
BOC	Bell Operating Company
CBR	Constant Bit Rate
CCITT	International Consultative Committee on Telegraphy and Telephony
CIR	Committed Information Rate
CMI	Coded Mark Inversion
CRC	Cyclic Redundancy Check
CSMA/CD	Carrier Sense Multiple Access with Collision Detection
DCE	Data Circuit-Terminating Equipment
DEA	Data Encryption Algorithm
DES	Data Encryption Standard
DS	Differentiated Services
DTE	Data Terminal Equipment
FCC	Federal Communications Commission
FCS	Frame Check Sequence
FDM	Frequency-Division Multiplexing
FSK	Frequency-Shift Keying
FTP	File Transfer Protocol
FM	Frequency Modulation
GFR	Guaranteed Frame Rate
HDLC	High-Level Data Link Control
HTML	Hypertext Markup Language
HTTP	Hypertext Transfer Protocol
IAB	Internet Architecture Board
ICMP	Internet Control Message Protocol
IDN	Integrated Digital Network
IEEE	Institute of Electrical and Electronics Engineers
IETF	Internet Engineering Task Force
IGMP	Internet Group Management Protocol
IP	Internet Protocol
IPng	Internet Protocol - Next Generation
IRA	International Reference Alphabet
ISA	Integrated Services Architecture
ISDN	Integrated Services Digital Network

ISO	International Organization for Standardization
ITU	International Telecommunication Union
ITU-T	ITU Telecommunication Standardization Sector
LAN	Local Area Network
LAPB	Link Access Procedure - Balanced
LAPD	Link Access Procedure on the D Channel
LAPF	Link Access Procedure for Frame Mode Bearer Services
LLC	Logical Link Control
MAC	Medium Access Control
MAN	Metropolitan Area Network
MIME	Multi-Purpose Internet Mail Extension
NRZI	Nonreturn to Zero, Inverted
NRZL	Nonreturn to Zero, Level
NT	Network Termination
OSI	Open Systems Interconnection
OSPF	Open Shortest Path First
PBX	Private Branch Exchange
PCM	Pulse-Code Modulation
PDU	Protocol Data Unit
PSK	Phase-Shift Keying
PTT	Postal, Telegraph, and Telephone
PM	Phase Modulation
QAM	Quadrature Amplitude Modulation
QoS	Quality of Service
QPSK	Quadrature Phase Shift Keying
RBOC	Regional Bell Operating Company
RF	Radio Frequency
RSA	Rivest, Shamir, Adleman Algorithm
RSVP	Resource ReSerVation Protocol
SAP	Service Access Point
SDH	Synchronous Digital Hierarchy
SDU	Service Data Unit
SMTP	Simple Mail Transfer Protocol
SNMP	Simple Network Management Protocol
SONET	Synchronous Optical Network
SS7	Signaling System Number 7
STP	Shielded Twisted Pair
TCP	Transmission Control Protocol
TDM	Time-Division Multiplexing
TE	Terminal Equipment
UBR	Unspecified Bit Rate
UDP	User Datagram Protocol
UNI	User-Network Interface
UTP	Unshielded Twisted Pair
VAN	Value-Added Network
VBR	Variable Bit Rate
VCC	Virtual Channel Connection
VPC	Virtual Path Connection
WDM	Wavelength Division Multiplexing
WWW	World Wide Web

REFERENCES

In matters of this kind everyone feels he is justified in writing and publishing the first thing that comse into his head when he picks up a pen, and thinks his own idea as axiomatic as the fact that two and two make four. If critics would go to the trouble of thinking about the subject for years on end and testing each conclusion against the actual history of war, as I have done, they would undoubtedly be more careful of what they wrote.

—*On War,* Carl von Clausewitz

ABBREVIATIONS

ACM   Association for Computing Machinery
IEEE   Institute of Electrical and Electronics Engineers

10GE02   10 Gigabit Ethernet Alliance. *10 Gigabit Ethernet Technology Overview.* White paper, May 2002.

ALLM99   Allman, M., and Falk, A. "On the Effective Evaluation of TCP." *Computer Communication Review,* October 1999.

ALME00   Almeroth, K. "The Evolution of Multicast: From the Mbone to Interdomain Multicast to Internet2 Deployment." *IEEE Network,* January/February 2000.

ANDE95   Anderson, J.; Rappaport, T.; and Yoshida, S. "Propagation Measurements and Models for Wireless Communications Channels." *IEEE Communications Magazine,* January 1995.

ARAS94   Aras, C.; Kurose, J.; Reeves, D.; and Schulzrinne, H. "Real-Time Communication in Packet-Switched Networks." *Proceedings of the IEEE,* January 1994.

ARMI00   Armitage, G. *Quality of Service in IP Networks.* Indianapolis, IN: Macmillan Technical Publishing, 2000.

BALA98   Balakrishnan, H., et al. "TCP Behavior of a Busy Web Server." *Proceedings, IEEE INFOCOM,* March 1998.

BENE64   Benice, R. "An Analysis of Retransmission Systems." *IEEE Transactions on Communication Technology,* December 1964.

BENN99   Bennett, J.; Partridge, C.; and Shectman, N. "Packet Reordering is Not Pathological Network Behavior." *IEEE/ACM Transactions on Networking,* December 1999.

BERN00   Bernet, Y. "The Complementary Roles of RSVP and Differentiated Services in the Full-Service QoS Network." *IEEE Communications Magazine,* February 2000.

BERT92   Bertsekas, D., and Gallager, R. *Data Networks.* Englewood Cliffs, NJ: Prentice Hall, 1992.

BLAC93   Black, U. *Data Link Protocols.* Englewood Cliffs, NJ: Prentice Hall, 1993.

BLAC99   Black, U. *ATM Volume I: Foundation for Broadband Networks.* Upper Saddle River, NJ: Prentice Hall, 1992.

BLAC00   Black, U. *IP Routing Protocols: RIP, OSPF, BGP, PNNI & Cisco Routing Protocols.* Upper Saddle River, NJ: Prentice Hall, 2000.

BORT01   Borthick, S. "Today's Internet Can't Scale." *Business Communications Review*, May 2001.

BREY99   Breyer, R., and Riley, S. *Switched, Fast, and Gigabit Ethernet*. Net York: Macmillan Technical Publishing, 1999.

BRUN96   Bruna, C. "Internet Health Report: Condition Serious." *Network World*, September 1996.

BUCK00   Buckwalter, J. *Frame Relay: Technology and Practice*. Reading, MA: Addison-Wesley, 2000.

BURG91   Burg, J., and Dorman, D. "Broadband ISDN Resource Management: The Role of Virtual Paths." *IEEE Communications Magazine*, September 1991.

BUX80   Bux, W.; Kummerle, K.; and Truong, H. "Balanced HDLC Procedures: A Performance Analysis." *IEEE Transactions on Communications*, November 1980.

CARP02   Carpenter, B., and Nichols, K. "Differentiated Services in the Internet." *Proceedings of the IEEE*, September 2002.

CERT03   CERT Coordination Center. *CERT Coordination Center 2002 Annual Report*. Carnegie-Mellon University, 2003. http://www.cert.org/annual_rpts/cert_rpt_01.html.

CLAR88   Clark, D. "The Design Philosophy of the DARPA Internet Protocols." *Proceedings, SIGCOMM '88, Computer Communication Review*, August 1988; reprinted in *Computer Communication Review*, January 1995.

CLAR90   Clark, D., and Tennenhouse, D. "Architectural Considerations for a New Generation of Protocols." *Proceedings, SIGCOMM '90, Computer Communication Review*, September 1990.

CLAR92   Clark, D.; Shenker, S.; and Zhang, L. "Supporting Real-Time Applications in an Integrated Services Packet Network: Architecture and Mechanism" *Proceedings, SIGCOMM '92*, August 1992.

CLAR95   Clark, D. *Adding Service Discrimination to the Internet*. MIT Laboratory for Computer Science Technical Report, September 1995. Available at http://ana-www.lcs.mit.edu/anaWeb/papers.html.

CLAR98   Clark, D., and Fang, W. "Explicit Allocation of Best-Effort Packet Delivery Service." *IEEE/ACM Transactions on Networking*, August 1998.

COHE96   Cohen, J. "Rule Reversal: Old 80/20 LAN Traffic Model is Getting Turned on its Head." *Network World*, December 16, 1996.

COME99   Comer, D., and Stevens, D. *Internetworking with TCP/IP, Volume II: Design Implementation, and Internals*. Upper Saddle River, NJ: Prentice Hall, 1999.

COME00   Comer, D. *Internetworking with TCP/IP, Volume I: Principles, Protocols, and Architecture*. Upper Saddle River, NJ: Prentice Hall, 2000.

COME01   Comer, D., and Stevens, D. *Internetworking with TCP/IP, Volume III: Client-Server Programming and Applications*. Upper Saddle River, NJ: Prentice Hall, 2001.

CROL00   Croll, A., and Packman, E. *Managing Bandwidth: Deploying QoS in Enterprise Networks*. Upper Saddle River, NJ: Prentice Hall, 2000.

CROW92   Crowcroft, J.; Wakeman, I.; Wang, Z.; and Sirovica, D. "Is Layering Harmful?" *IEEE Network Magazine*, January 1992.

CROW97   Crow, B., et al. "IEEE 802.11 Wireless Local Area Networks." *IEEE Communications Magazine*, September 1997.

DAVI89   Davies, D., and Price, W. *Security for Computer Networks*. New York: Wiley, 1989.

DEER90   Deering, S., and Cheriton, D. "Multicast Routing in Datagram Internetworks and Extended LANs." *ACM Transactions on Computer Systems*, May 1990.

DEER96   Deering, S., et al. "The PIM Architecture for Wide-Area Multicast Routing." *IEEE/ACM Transactions on Networking*, April 1996.

DEME90   Demers, A.; Keshav, S.; and Shenker, S. "Analysis and Simulation of a Fair Queueing Algorithm." *Internetworking: Research and Experience*, September 1990.

DIAN02   Dianda, J.; Gurbani, V.; and Jones, M. "Session Initiation Protocol Services Architecture." *Bell Labs Technical Journal*, Volume 7, Number 1, 2002.

DIFF76   Diffie, W., and Hellman, M. "Multiuser Cryptographic Techniques." *IEEE Transactions on Information Theory*, November 1976.

DIJK59   Dijkstra, E. "A Note on Two Problems in Connection with Graphs." *Numerical Mathematics*, October 1959.

DONA01   Donahoo, M., and Clavert, K. *The Pocket Guide to TCP/IP Sockets*. San Francisco, CA: Morgan Kaufmann, 2001.

ECON01   *The Economist*. "Upgrading the Internet." March 24, 2001.

EFF98   Electronic Frontier Foundation. *Cracking DES: Secrets of Encryption Research, Wiretap Politics, and Chip Design*. Sebastopol, CA: O'Reilly, 1998.

FIOR95   Fiorini, D.; Chiani, M.; Tralli, V.; and Salati, C. "Can We Trust HDLC?" *Computer Communications Review*, October 1995.

FLOY93   Floyd, S., and Jacobson, V. "Random Early Detection Gateways for Congestion Avoidance." *IEEE/ACM Transactions on Networking*, August 1993.

FLOY94   Floyd, S. "TCP and Explicit Congestion Notification." *ACM Computer Communications Review*, October 1994.

FLOY97   Floyd, S., and Fall, K. "Router Mechanisms to Support End-to-End Congestion Control." *Proceedings, SIGCOMM '97*, 1997.

FLOY01   Floyd, S. "A Report on Some Recent Developments in TCP Congestion Control." *IEEE Communications Magazine*, April 2001.

FORD62   Ford, L., and Fulkerson, D. *Flows in Networks*. Princeton, NJ: Princeton University Press, 1962.

FRAZ99   Frazier, H., and Johnson, H. "Gigabit Ethernet: From 100 to 1,000 Mbps." *IEEE Internet Computing*, January/February 1999.

GARR96   Garrett, M. "A Service Architecture for ATM: From Applications to Scheduling." *IEEE Network*, May/June 1996.

GEIE99   Geier, J. *Wireless LANs*. New York: Macmillan Technical Publishing, 1999.

GEIE01   Geier, J. "Enabling Fast Wireless Networks with OFDM." *Communications System Design*, February 2001. (www.csdmag.com)

GERL80   Gerla, M., and Kleinrock, L. "Flow Control: A Comparative Survey." *IEEE Transactions on Communications*, April 1980.

GOOD02   Goode, B. "Voice Over Internet Protocol (VoIP)." *Proceedings of the IEEE*, September 2002.

GOUR02   Gourley, D., et al. *HTTP: The Definitive Guide*. Sebastopol, CA: O'Reilly, 2002.

GREE92   Greenberg, A., and Madras, N. "How Fair is Fair Queuing?" *Journal of the ACM*, July 1992.

GUNT00   Gunther, N. *The Practical Performance Analyst*. New York: Authors Choice Press, 2000.

GUYN88   Guynes, J. 1988. "Impact of System Response Time on State Anxiety." *Communications of the ACM*, March, 1988.

HAAS00   Haas, Z. "Wireless and Mobile Networks." In [TERP00].

HALL01   Hall, B. *Beej's Guide to Network Programming Using Internet Sockets*. 2001. http://www.ecst.csuchico.edu/~beej/guide/net/html/

HARB92   Harbison, R. "Frame Relay: Technology for Our Time." *LAN Technology*, December 1992.

HARJ00   Harju, J., and Kivimaki, P. "Cooperation and Comparison of DiffServ and IntServ: Performance Measurements." *Proceedings, 23rd Annual IEEE Conference on Local Computer Networks*, November 2000.

HARN02   Harnedy, S. *The MPLS Primer: An Introduction to Multiprotocol Label Switching*. Upper Saddle River, NJ: Prentice Hall, 2002.

HIND83   Hinden, R., Haverty, J. and Sheltzer, A. "The DARPA Internet: Interconnecting Heterogeneous Computer Networks with Gateways." *Computer*, September 1983.

HIND95   Hinden, R. "IP Next Generation Overview." *Connexions*, March 1995.

HOE96   Hoe, J. "Improving the Start-up Behavior of a Congestion Control Scheme for TCP." *Proceedings, SIGCOMM '96*, August 1996.

HOFF00   Hoffman, P. "Overview of Internet Mail Standards." *The Internet Protocol Journal*, June 2000 (www.cisco.com/warp/public/759)

HUIT98   Huitema, C. *IPv6: The New Internet Protocol*. Upper Saddle River, NJ: Prentice Hall, 1998.

HUIT00   Huitema, C. *Routing in the Internet*. Upper Saddle River, NJ: Prentice Hall, 2000.

HUST00   Huston, G. "TCP Performance." *The Internet Protocol Journal*, June 2000. http://www.cisco.com/warp/public/759.

IREN99   Iren, S.; Amer, P.; and Conrad, P. "The Transport Layer: Tutorial and Survey." *ACM Computing Surveys*, December 1999.

JACO88   Jacobson, V. "Congestion Avoidance and Control." *Proceedings, SIGCOMM '88, Computer Communication Review*, August 1988; reprinted in *Computer Communication Review*, January 1995; a slightly revised version is available at ftp.ee.lbl.gov/papers/congavoid.ps.Z.

JACO90a   Jacobson, V. "Berkeley TCP Evolution from 4.3 Tahoe to 4.3-Reno." *Proceedings of the Eighteenth Internet Engineering Task Force*, September 1990.

JACO90b   Jacobson, V. "Modified TCP Congestion Avoidance Algorithm." *end2end-interest mailing list*, 20, April 1990. Available at ftp://ftp.ee.lbl.gov/email/vanj.90apr30.txt.

JAIN90   Jain, R. "Congestion Control in Computer Networks: Issues and Trends." *IEEE Network Magazine*, May 1990.

JAIN92   Jain, R. "Myths About Congestion Management in High-Speed Networks." *Internetworking: Research and Experience*, Volume 3, 1992.

KADA98   Kadambi, J.; Crayford, I.; and Kalkunte, M. *Gigabit Ethernet*. Upper Saddle River, NJ: Prentice Hall, 1998.

KANE98   Kanel, J.; Givler, J.; Leiba, B.; and Segmuller, W. "Internet Messaging Frameworks." *IBM Systems Journal*, No. 1, 1998.

KARN91   Karn, P., and Partridge, C. "Improving Round-Trip Estimates in Reliable Transport Protocols." *ACM Transactions on Computer Systems*, November 1991.

KESH98   Keshav, S., and Sharma, R. "Issues and Trends in Router Design." *IEEE Communications Magazine*, May 1998.

KHAR98a   Khare, R. "Telnet: The Mother of All (Application) Protocols." *IEEE Internet Computing*, May/June 1998.

KHAR98b   Khare, R. "I Want My FTP: Bits on Demand." *IEEE Internet Computing*, July/August 1998.

KHAR98c   Khare, R. "The Spec's in the Mail." *IEEE Internet Computing*, September/October 1998.

KILK99   Kilkki, K. *Differentiated Services for the Internet*. Indianapolis, IN: Macmillan Technical Publishing, 1999.

KONH80   Konheim, A. "A Queuing Analysis of Two ARQ Protocols." *IEEE Transactions on Communications*, July 1980.

KLEI92   Kleinrock, L. "The Latency/Bandwidth Tradeoff in Gigabit Networks." *IEEE Communications Magazine*, April 1992.

KLEI93   Kleinrock, L. "On the Modeling and Analysis of Computer Networks." *Proceedings of the IEEE*, August 1993.

KRIS01   Krishnamurthy, B., and Rexford, J. *Web Protocols and Practice: HTTP/1.1, Networking Protocols, Caching, and Traffic Measurement*. Upper Saddle River, NJ: Prentice Hall, 2001.

KUMA98   Kumar, V.; Lakshman, T.; and Stiliadis, D. "Beyond Best Effort: Router Architectures for the Differentiated Services of Tomorrow's Internet." *IEEE Communications Magazine*, May 1998.

LARO02   LaRocca, J., and LaRocca, R. *802.11 Demystified*. New York: McGraw-Hill, 2002.

LAWR01   Lawrence, J. "Designing Multiprotocol Label Switching Networks." *IEEE Communications Magazine*, July 2001.

LELA94   Leland, W.; Taqqu, M.; Willinger, W.; and Wilson, D. "On the Self-Similar Nature of Ethernet Traffic (Extended Version)." *IEEE/ACM Transactions on Networking*, February 1994.

LEUT94   Leutwyler, K. "Superhack." *Scientific American*, July 1994.

LI02   Li, V., and Zhang, Z. "Internet Multicast Routing and Transport Control Protocols." *Proceedings of the IEEE*, March 2002.

LIN84   Lin, S.; Costello, D.; and Miller, M. "Automatic-Repeat-Request Error-Control Schemes." *IEEE Communications Magazine*, December 1984.

LIN98   Lin, D., and Kung, H. "TCP Fast Recovery Strategies." *Proceedings, IEEE INFOCOM*, March 1998.

LUIN97   Luinen, S., Budrikis, Z.; and Cantoni, A. "The Controlled Cell Transfer Capability." *Computer Communications Review*, January 1997.

MART88   Martin, J, and Leban, J. *Principles of Data Communication*. Englewood Cliffs, NJ: Prentice Hall, 1988.

MCDO91   McDonald, C. "A Network Specification Language and Execution Environment for Undergraduate Teaching." *Proceedings of the ACM Computer Science Educational Technical Symposium*, March 1991.

MCDY99   McDysan, D., and Spohn, D. *ATM: Theory and Application*. New York: McGraw-Hill, 1999.

MCKU96   McKusick, M.; Bostic, K.; Karels, M.; and Quartermain, J. *The Design and Implementation of the 4.4BSD UNIX Operating System.* Reading, MA: Addison-Wesley, 1996.

METZ02   Metz C. "IP Anycast." *IEEE Internet Computing*, March 2002.

MORR97   Morris, R. "TCP Behavior with Many Flows." *Proceedings of the Fifth IEEE International Conference on Network Protocols*, October 1997.

MOY94   Moy, J. "Multicast Routing Extensions for OSPF." *Communications of the ACM*, August 1994.

MOY98   Moy, J. *OSPF: Anatomy of an Internet Routing Protocol.* Reading, MA: Addison-Wesley, 1998.

NAGL87   Nagle, J. "On Packet Switches with Infinite Storage." *IEEE Transactions on Communications*, April 1987.

NARV00   Narvaez, P.; Siu, K.; and Tzeng, H. "New Dynamic Algorithms for Shortest Path Tree Computation." *IEEE/ACM Transactions on Networking*, December 2000.

OHAR99   Ohara, B., and Petrick, A. *IEEE 802.11 Handbook: A Designer's Companion.* New York: IEEE Press, 1999.

PARE88   Parekh, S., and Sohraby, K. "Some Performance Trade-Offs Associated with ATM Fixed-Length Vs. Variable-Length Cell Formats." *Proceedings, Globe-Com*, November 1988.

PARE94   Parekh, A., and Gallager, G. "A Generalized Processor Sharing Approach to Flow Control in Integrated Services Networks: The Multiple Node Case." *IEEE/ACM Transactions on Networking*, April 1994.

PAXS95   Paxson, V., and Floyd, S. "Wide Area Traffic: The Failure of Poisson Modeling." *IEEE/ACM Transactions on Networking*, June 1995.

PAXS97   Paxson, V. "End-to-End Routing Behavior in the Internet." *IEEE/ACM Transactions on Networking*, October 1997.

PERL00   Perlman, R. *Interconnections: Bridges, Routers, Switches, and Internetworking Protocols.* Reading, MA: Addison-Wesley, 2000.

PETE61   Peterson, W., and Brown, D. "Cyclic Codes for Error Detection." *Proceedings of the IEEE*, January 1961.

RAMA88   Ramabadran, T., and Gaitonde, S. "A Tutorial on CRC Computations." *IEEE Micro*, August 1988.

RAMA00   Ramalho, M. "Intra- and Inter-Domain Multicast Routing Protocols: A Survey and Taxonomy." *IEEE Communications Surveys and Tutorial*, First Quarter 2000. www.comsoc.org/livepubs/surveys.

RAMJ94   Ramjee, R., et al. "Adaptive Playout Mechanisms for Packetized Audio Applications in Wide-Area Networks." *Proceedings, IEEE INFOCOM*, June 1994.

REDF00   Redford, R. "Enabling Business IP Services with Multiprotocol Label Switching." *Cisco White Paper*, July 2000 (www.cisco.com).

REKH93   Rekhter, Y. "Inter-Domain Routing Protocol (IDRP)." *Internetworking: Research and Experience*, June 1993.

RIVE78   Rivest, R.; Shamir, A.; and Adleman, L. "A Method for Obtaining Digital Signatures and Public Key Cryptosystems." *Communications of the ACM*, February 1978.

RODR02   Rodriguez, A., et al. *TCP/IP Tutorial and Technical Overview.* Upper Saddle River: NJ: Prentice Hall, 2002.

ROSE98 Rose, M., and Strom, D. *Internet Messaging: From the Desktop to the Enterprise*. Upper Saddle River, NJ: Prentice Hall, 1998.

SAHA00 Sahasrabuddhe, L., and Mukherjee, B. "Multicast Routing Algorithms and Protocols: A Tutorial." *IEEE Network*, January/February 2000.

SATO90 Sato, K.; Ohta, S.; and Tokizawa, I. "Broad-band ATM Network Architecture Based on Virtual Paths." *IEEE Transactions on Communications*, August 1990.

SATO91 Sato, K.; Ueda, H.; and Yoshikai, M. "The Role of Virtual Path Crossconnection." *IEEE LTS*, August 1991.

SAVA99 Savage, S.; Cardwell, N.; Witherall, D.; and Anderson, T. "TCP Congestion Control with Misbehaving Receiver." *ACM Computer Communications Review*, October 1999.

SCHN96 Schneier, B. *Applied Cryptography*. New York: Wiley, 1996.

SCHU98 Schulzrinne, H. and Rosenberg, J. "The Session Initiation Protocol: Providing Advanced Telephony Access Across the Internet." *Bell Labs Technical Journal*, October-December 1998.

SCHU99 Schulzrinne, H. and Rosenberg, J. "The IETF Internet Telephony Architecture and Protocols." IEEE Network, May/June 1999.

SEIF98 Seifert, R. *Gigabit Ethernet*. Reading, MA: Addison-Wesley, 1998.

SEVC96 Sevcik, P. "Designing a High-Performance Web Site." Business Communications Review, March 1996.

SHEN95 Shenker, S. "Fundamental Design Issues for the Future Internet." *IEEE Journal on Selected Areas in Communications*, September 1995.

SHNE84 Shneiderman, B. "Response Time and Display Rate in Human Performance with Computers." *ACM Computing Surveys*, September 1984.

SHOE02 Shoemake, M. "IEEE 802.11g Jells as Applications Mount." *Communications System Design*, April 2002. www.commsdesign.com.

SIKE00 Siket, J., and Proch, D. "MPLS—Bring IP Networks and Connection-Oriented Networks Together." *Business Communications Review*, April 2000.

SING99 Singh, S. *The Code Book: The Science of Secrecy from Ancient Egypt to Quantum Cryptography*. New York: Anchor Books, 1999.

SMIT88 Smith, M. "A Model of Human Communication." *IEEE Communications Magazine*, February 1988.

SPOH97 Spohn, D. *Data Network Design*. New York: McGraw-Hill, 1997.

SPOR99 Sportack, M. *IP Routing Fundamentals*. Indianapolis, IN: Cisco Press, 1999.

SPRA91 Spragins, J.; Hammond, J.; and Pawlikowski, K. *Telecommunications Protocols and Design*. Reading, MA: Addison-Wesley, 1991.

SPUR00 Spurgeon, C. *Ethernet: The Definitive Guide*. Cambridge, MA: O'Reilly and Associates, 2000.

STAL99 Stallings, W. *ISDN and Broadband ISDN, with Frame Relay and ATM*. Upper Saddle River, NJ: Prentice Hall, 1999.

STAL00 Stallings, W. *Local and Metropolitan Area Networks, Sixth Edition*. Upper Saddle River, NJ: Prentice Hall, 2000.

STAL02 Stallings, W. *High-Speed Networks and Internets: Performance and Quality of Service, Second Edition*. Upper Saddle River, NJ: Prentice Hall, 2002.

STAL03a Stallings, W. *Data and Computer Communications, Seventh Edition*. Upper Saddle River, NJ: Prentice Hall, 2003.

STAL03b   Stallings, W. *Cryptography and Network Security: Principles and Practice, Third Edition*. Upper Saddle River, NJ: Prentice Hall, 2003.

STEI95   Steinke, S. "IP Addresses and Subnet Masks." *LAN Magazine*, October 1995.

STEV94   Stevens, W. *TCP/IP Illustrated, Volume 1: The Protocols*. Reading, MA: Addison-Wesley, 1994.

STEV96   Stevens, W. *TCP/IP Illustrated, Volume 3: TCP for Transactions, HTTP, NNTP, and the UNIX(R) Domain Protocol*. Reading, MA: Addison-Wesley, 1996.

TANN95   Tanner, M. *Practical Queueing Analysis*. New York: McGraw-Hill, 1995.

TEGE95   Teger, S. "Multimedia: From Vision to Reality." *AT&T Technical Journal*, September/October 1995.

TERP00   Terplan, K., and Morreale, P. eds. *The Telecommunications Handbook*. Boca Raton, FL: CRC Press, 2000.

THAD81   Thadhani, A. "Interactive User Productivity." *IBM Systems Journal*, No. 1, 1981.

THOM96   Thomas, S. *IPng and the TCP/IP Protocols: Implementing the Next Generation Internet*. New York: Wiley, 1996.

TIER01   Tierney, B. "TCP Tuning Guide for Distributed Applications on Wide Area Networks." *;login:*, February 2001. http://www-didc.lbl.gov/TCP-tuning.

TSUD92   Tsudik, G. "Message Authentication with One-Way Hash Functions." *Proceedings, INFOCOM '92*, May 1992.

VISW98   Viswanathan, A., et al. "Evolution of Multiprotocol Label Switching." *IEEE Communications Magazine*, May 1998.

WALR98   Walrand, J. *Communication Networks: A First Course*. New York: McGraw-Hill, 1998.

WANG01   Wang, Z. *Internet QoS: Architectures and Mechanisms for Quality of Service*. San Francisco, CA: Morgan Kaufmann, 2001.

WEIS98   Weiss, W. "QoS with Differentiated Services." *Bell Labs Technical Journal*, October-December 1998.

WHIT97   White, P., and Crowcroft, J. "The Integrated Services in the Internet: State of the Art." *Proceedings of the IEEE*, December 1997.

WRIG95   Wright, G., and Stevens, W. *TCP/IP Illustrated, Volume 2: The Implementation*. Reading, MA: Addison-Wesley, 1995.

XIAO99   Xiao, X., and Ni, L. "Internet QoS: A Big Picture." *IEEE Network*, March/April 1999.

YANG95   Yang, C., and Reddy, A. "A Taxonomy for Congestion Control Algorithms in Packet Switching Networks." *IEEE Network*, July/August 1995.

ZHAN86   Zhang, L. "Why TCP Timers Don't Work Well." *Proceedings, SIGCOMM '86 Symposium*, August 1986.

ZHAN93   Zhang, L.; Deering, S.; Estrin, D.; Shenker, S.; and Zappala, D. "RSVP: A New Resource ReSerVation Protocol." *IEEE Network*, September 1993.

ZHAN95   Zhang, H. "Service Disciplines for Guaranteed Performance Service in Packet-Switching Networks." *Proceedings of the IEEE*, October 1995.

ZORZ96   Zorzi, M., and Rao, R. "On the Use of Renewal Theory in the Analysis of ARQ Protocols." *IEEE Transactions on Communications*, September 1996.

INDEX

A

ABORT primitive, 231
About RTP (Web site), 379
Accept field, 124
Acceptable use policies, 27
Accept-Encoding field, 124
Accept-Language field, 124
Accounting management, 589
  user requirements, 589
ACK method, SIP, 143
Acknowledged connectionless service, logical link control (LLC), 515–516
Acknowledgment frame, 478
Acknowledgment Number field, TCP header, 229
ACM Special Interest Group on Communications (SIGCOMM), 6
Active attacks, 549–550
  denial of service, 550
  masquerade, 549
  modification of messages, 550
  replay, 549
Active threats, 547
Adaptive routing, 22, 387–390
Address Family field, RIP packet, 404
Address mask reply message, 290
Address mask request message, 290
Addresses, 284–287
  network classes, 284–285
  subnets/subnet masks, 285–287
Addressing, 280–281
  level, 280
  modes, 281
  reliable sequencing network service, 204–206
  schemes, and routers, 63
  scope, 281
Admission control, 309
Adobe Pagemill, 32
ADSL, 29
Advance Research Projects Agency (ARPA), 24
Advanced Encryption Standard (AES), 552–555
.aero, 130
AFS value, Content-type field, 106
AH information, and security association, 579
Algorithms:
  Bellman-Ford, 396–398
  constraint-based routing, 367
  decryption, 551, 566
  Dijkstra's, 394–396
  distributed Bellman-Ford, 400–402
  encryption, 550, 552–555, 566
  general-purpose, 566–568
  Jacobson's, 250–253
  Karn's, 253–254
  least-cost, 393–399
  RED, 323–327
  routing, 309

RSA, 568–571
Secure Hash Algorithm (SHA-1), 564–565, 568
Allow field, 127
America Online, 28–29
ANcount field, 130
Andreasson, Mark, 31
Anon-FTP value, Content-type field, 106
Antireplay window, and security association, 579
Anycast, 297
Applicability statement (AS), 9
Application layer, 42
Application type, MIME, 106–107
Application/octet-stream subtype, MIME, 106–107
Application/Postscript subtype, MIME, 107
ARcount field, 130
Area field, OSPF packets, 412
.arpa, 130
ARPANET, 24–26, 29, 54, 78–79
ASCII, 71
ASPath attribute, Path Attributes field, 422–423
Assured forwarding (AF) PHB, 335–336
Asynchronous balanced mode (ABM), 487
Asynchronous response mode (ARM), 488
Asynchronous transfer mode (ATM), 14, 15, 23, 31, 167, 447, 451–460
  cells, 454–457
    cell loss priority (CLP), 456
    Generic Flow Control (GFC), 456–457
    Generic Flow Control (GFC) field, 454
    Header Error Control (HEC) field, 456
  logical connections in, 452
  meta-signaling channel, 453
  Payload Type (PT) field, 454–456
  semipermanent virtual channels, 453
  service categories, 457–460
    Available Bit Rate (ABR) service, 460
    Constant Bit Rate (CBR) service, 458–459
    Guaranteed Frame Rate (GFR) service, 460
    Non-Real-Time Service, 458, 459–460
    Non-Real-Time Variable Bit Rate (nrt-VBR), 459
    Real-Time Service, 458–459
    Real-Time Variable Bit Rate (rt-VBR), 459
    Unspecified Bit Rate (UBR), 459–460
  Virtual Channel, 451–454
    characteristics 452–453
    control signaling 453–454

    Identifier (VCI) field, 454
  Virtual Path, 451–454
    characteristics, 452–453
    control signaling, 453–454
    Identifier (VPI) field, 454
AT&T Center for Internet Research, 267
ATM, *See* Asynchronous transfer mode (ATM)
ATM Forum, 468
ATM Hot Links, 468
AtomicAggregate, Aggregator attribute, Path Attributes field, 422–423
Attacks:
  active, 549–550
  brute-force, 551–552
  denial of service, 550
  masquerade, 549
  modification of messages, 550
  passive, 549
  replay, 549
Audio/Video Transport Working Group, 379
Authentication Data field:
  Authentication header, 580
  ESP packet, 581
  OSPF packets, 413
Authentication header, IPv6, 292
Authentication Type field, OSPF packets, 413
Authenticator, 568
Authenticity, 549
Authoritative Answer field, 135
Authorization field, 124
Automatic repeat request (ARQ), 482–487
Autonomous system (AS), 390–392, 436
Aux Data Length field, group record, 433
Auxiliary Data field, group record, 433
Available Bit Rate (ABR) service, 460
Availability, 549

B

Backoff, 253, 519
  binary exponential, 253, 519
  exponential RTO, 253
Backpressure, 184–185
Backward explicit congestion notification (BECN), 269
Barber, Theodore, 115, 419
Base station, 461, 465
Base64 transfer encoding, 108
Basic e-mail operation, SMTP, 95–97
Batch retransmission strategy, 233
Bellman-Ford algorithm, 396–398
Berners-Lee, Tim, 27–28
Best Current Practice (BCP), 9
Best-effort service, 167, 459
BGP, *See* Border Gateway Protocol (BGP)

627

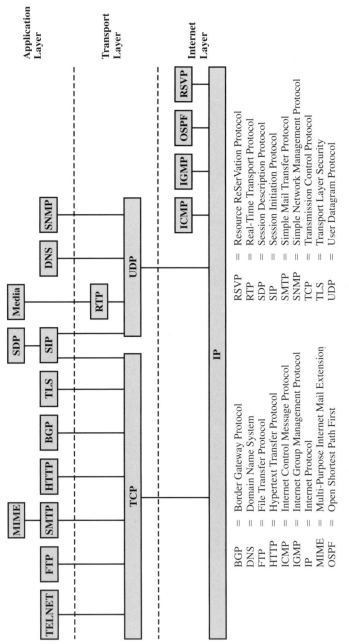

Application Layer

Transport Layer

Internet Layer

Some Protocols in the TCP/IP Protocol Suite

BGP	=	Border Gateway Protocol	RSVP	=	Resource ReSerVation Protocol
DNS	=	Domain Name System	RTP	=	Real-Time Transport Protocol
FTP	=	File Transfer Protocol	SDP	=	Session Description Protocol
HTTP	=	Hypertext Transfer Protocol	SIP	=	Session Initiation Protocol
ICMP	=	Internet Control Message Protocol	SMTP	=	Simple Mail Transfer Protocol
IGMP	=	Internet Group Management Protocol	SNMP	=	Simple Network Management Protocol
IP	=	Internet Protocol	TCP	=	Transmission Control Protocol
MIME	=	Multi-Purpose Internet Mail Extension	TLS	=	Transport Layer Security
OSPF	=	Open Shortest Path First	UDP	=	User Datagram Protocol